ORGANIZATION
Text, cases, and readings
on the management of
organizational design and change

The Irwin Series in Management and The Behavioral Sciences

L. L. Cummings *and* E. Kirby Warren   *Consulting Editors*
John F. Mee   *Advisory Editor*

ORGANIZATION

Text, cases, and readings on the management of organizational design and change

JOHN P. KOTTER
Associate Professor

LEONARD A. SCHLESINGER
Assistant Professor

VIJAY SATHE
Assistant Professor

all of the
Graduate School of Business Administration
Harvard University

1979

RICHARD D. IRWIN, INC.
Homewood, Illinois   60430

Irwin-Dorsey Limited
Georgetown, Ontario   L7G 4B3

ISBN 0-256-02226-7
Library of Congress Catalog Card No. 78–61194

Printed in the United States of America

1 2 3 4 5 6 7 8 9 0 K 6 5 4 3 2 1 0 9

Preface

The existing literature on organizational design and organizational change falls into two major categories. On the one hand, most of the research and theorizing is being done by social scientists (psychologists, sociologists, anthropologists, social psychologists, and, most recently, organizational behaviorists) who write primarily for others in their profession. Few managers read this literature. On the other hand, what the practitioners do read is frequently based only on personal experience and observation or "armchair theorizing."

This book represents an attempt to bridge the widening gap between these two bodies of literature. We have written it for both students of management and practicing managers. It is based on the best social science research available, with the emphasis being on practical application. We hope this effort will stimulate and help those who are engaged in designing and managing today's organizations as well as those who will bear this responsibility in the future.

As the citations in the text, cases, and readings of the book will indicate, we have drawn on the research and systematic thinking of many people. What is less obvious is the substantial contribution made on a more informal basis by numerous individuals who were involved in developing and teaching the first-year Harvard MBA course titled Organizational Problems, on which this book is based. Without the benefit of this groundwork, which was laid over the past ten years, this book could not have been written.

We also owe special thanks to our students in that course, who provided us with useful feedback, to Connie Bourke, who helped us manage the development of the first and second drafts of this manuscript, and to Irwin consulting editors Larry Cummings and Kirby Warren, who provided useful suggestions regarding the shaping of those drafts.

But most of all, we owe thanks to two of our colleagues, Paul Lawrence and Jay Lorsch, on whose work we have attempted to build. It is to them that we dedicate this book.

December 1978

John P. Kotter
Leonard A. Schlesinger
Vijay Sathe

91424

Contents

viii

Tactics for dealing with resistance: *Education/communication. Participation Facilitation and support. Negotiation. Co-optation. Manipulation. Coercion. Using change tactics.* Change strategies. Implications for managing organizational change.

Chapter 8.   Developing an organization that contributes to long-run effectiveness   479

The long run: A case of organizational decline. The characteristics of an effective organization—from a long-range point of view. Bureaucratic dry rot. Organizing for the future: *Organizational development (OD). OD change efforts.*

Chapter 9.   Organizational analysis and action planning: A summary   605

Chapter 1

Introduction

The real secret of the greatness of the Romans was their genius for organization.

James Mooney, *Vice President*
General Motors, 1931

It was on the strength of their extensive organization that the peasants went into action and within four months (in 1926) brought about a great revolution in the countryside, a revolution without parallel in history.

Mao Tse-tung, 1927

Organizing human resources

An important aspect of managerial work in any setting involves organizing human resources—that is, ensuring that the right people are focusing on the right tasks, that they have the proper information, tools, incentives, and controls to perform these tasks effectively and efficiently,[1] and that their efforts are coordinated such that the organization's overall objectives are accomplished. Generally, the higher one goes in an organization, the more responsibility managers have for large numbers of human resources, and the more time and effort they spend on this aspect of managerial work.

In a very small group of people, a manager can create and maintain an appropriate organization through face-to-face interaction with his or her employees. The manager can verbally assign tasks, watch that they are carried out, coordinate activities personally, compensate people fairly,

---

[1] Effectiveness is measured by the degree to which an organization meets its goals. Efficiency is measured by the amount of resources expended in achieving results.

Figure 1–1
The human organization

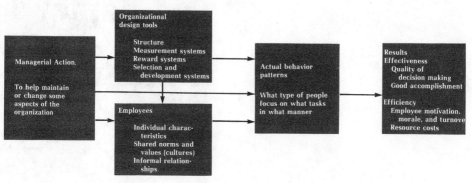

and so on. If the organization begins to break down, the manager can spot this immediately and deal with it. The only real "tool" such a manager needs is interpersonal skills.

As the number of people a manager is responsible for grows, interpersonal skills soon prove to be insufficient to maintain an appropriate organization. A single manager can no longer deal with everyone face to face, coordinate everything personally, and always be around to deal with breakdowns. Many entrepreneurs have learned this lesson the hard way.

To organize large numbers of people, or people who are often spatially separated from one another, managers use a number of different organization design tools. These tools include, for example, job design, compensation systems, performance appraisal systems, and training programs. Considerable evidence today suggests that the design and implementation of these tools can have a major impact on an organization's financial performance as well as the quality of work life of its employees (see Figure 1–1). Furthermore, research indicates that improper design can undermine an organization's performance and generate a variety of disruptive problems.

Organizational problems

Inappropriate organizational designs often lead to the following types of recurring problems:

Ineffective decision making (e.g., production personnel in one company continuously made poor decisions about inventory levels, which created a variety of problems).

High employee turnover (e.g., one firm's management turnover was 30 percent per year, compared with less than 5 percent for other companies in its industry).

Low morale (e.g., nearly 50 percent of the employees in one company complained that they didn't like their jobs and felt the company was a poor place to work).

Expensive conflict among individuals and groups (e.g., the production and sales personnel within one company literally plotted against one another).

A lack of employee motivation (e.g., the sales employees in one firm worked, on average, a five-hour day).

Wasted employee energy (e.g., using the same equipment, and working just as hard, the production employees in one firm produced only 60 percent of the daily output of another similar firm).

A general lack of goal accomplishment (e.g., the sales department in one company missed its sales objectives for ten consecutive quarters).

An important characteristic of these "organizational problems" and one that differentiates them from other types of problems, is that they *recur*. They do so because they are not caused by an idiosyncratic individual, group, or environmental event, but by the organizational design itself.

In addition, inappropriate attempts to introduce changes in organizational design can also be very costly. They can disrupt a company's operations, generate resistance and hostility among employees, and lead to any of the organizational problems previously listed. Such improper strategies can simply fail to produce a needed change, or they can generate a change at an unnecessarily burdensome cost to an organization.

The purpose and organization of this book

The basic purpose of this book is to increase the reader's understanding of how to avoid potential organizational problems through organizational planning and of how to solve existing organizational problems through organizational analysis and action planning. Specifically, our objectives are:

1. To provide the reader with examples that illustrate a wide variety of real situations in which managers are trying to deal with organizational issues.

2. To provide the reader with the best available research-based conceptual maps that can help in the analysis of organizational design and change issues.

3. To provide the reader with a sequence of material that will allow for the efficient development of new awarenesses, ideas, and skills related to organizational design and change.

To achieve these objectives, the book contains text, cases, and readings. The text provides an integrated analytical framework based on recent organizational research. The readings explore questions and issues identified in the text, but in greater detail and from more diverse viewpoints. The cases, most of which have been written in the past five years, focus on the most common organizational problems and questions that managers face today.

The book is organized into six parts, each of which builds on the previous one. It begins by looking at organizational design questions within the basic building block of modern organizations—the specialized department. Primary issues in this section relate to turnover and morale, personnel selection and development, performance appraisal, employee motivation, job design, career paths, compensation, equity, and management by objectives. In the second section the focus moves up one level in complexity, and the material deals with multiple, interdependent departments within single business companies. Major issues in this section relate to coordination, interdepartmental conflict, management control systems, and organizational structure. In section three the focus once again moves up one level to large multidivisional and multinational organizations, each of which is made up of numerous single business units. Primary issues at this point relate to coordination and control, the management of extreme diversity, crosscultural conflict, group structures, and the misuse of power. Section four focuses on organizational change processes that are initiated to correct the types of organizational design problems dealt with in the first three sections. Important issues here relate to resistance to change, planning change processes, questions of timing and speed, and power and influence. In section five the focus shifts to a longer time horizon and to questions relating to developing an organization for long-run survival and effectiveness. The key issue here concerns the systematic development of adaptability while coping with short-run realities. The book concludes with a brief summary of the analytical and action planning frameworks developed and presented in previous sections.

ORGANIZATION DESIGN

Chapter 2

Organization design tools

There are many ways one can conceptualize the formal elements of organizational design. In this book, we will do so in terms of structure, measurement systems, reward systems, and selection and development systems.

Structure

The elements of formal structure include: individual jobs, subunits (departments/divisions), a management hierarchy, rules and plans, and committees and task forces. These design tools are generally used to influence behavior by clearly specifying what individuals are responsible for, where in the organization they should work and with whom, what authority they have and to whom they are responsible, and how they should go about performing their tasks.

A job is simply a set of tasks assigned to an individual. These tasks can be very clearly defined, perhaps in a detailed job description, or left very vague. Most organizations, except for those which are very small, are made up of many different kinds of jobs. Some of these jobs contain very similar tasks which can either be relatively difficult (staff specialists) or simple (many clerical and assembly line jobs), while others require a more varied set of tasks (many managerial jobs).

Organizational structure generally groups jobs into subunits such as departments, and subunits into large subunits such as divisions. This grouping is usually based on functional similarity (all marketing jobs or subunits are grouped into a marketing department); product or service similarity (all jobs or subunits dealing with consulting are grouped into the consulting service department); or geographical area (all jobs or subunits dealing with Europe are grouped into the European division). While most organizations place a single job into just one subunit, so-called matrix organizations group individual jobs into two or even more subunits (e.g., a job may be in both the marketing department and the consulting services department). See Figure 2–1.

Closely related to such groupings is a management hierarchy which specifies reporting relationships and distributes formal authority for people and decisions to managers throughout the organization. Typically, the head of an organization is given the most formal authority. The people who report to him or her, some or all of whom are in charge of the organization's largest subunits, are given somewhat less formal authority. And so on down into the organization. Organizations are commonly called centralized if the formal authority is heavily concentrated in the hands of a few top people. If authority is widely distributed throughout the organization, the organization is often called decentralized. Hierarchies are sometimes described as "tall" and "flat," depending on the number of people reporting to each manager. A small span of control (few people reporting to each manager) creates relatively tall structures, and vice versa.

A fourth part of the structure of organizations includes rules, procedures, goals, and plans. Rules and procedures simply inform employees of how to perform their jobs. An organization with many rules and procedures is often called very bureaucratic. Plans and goals may be thought of as temporary rules and procedures; they also more clearly define what people are to do, although for a limited period of time.

A final part of structure consists of committees and task forces. These devices formalize team, as opposed to individual, efforts to work on some

Figure 2–1
Examples of some basic types of structural groupings

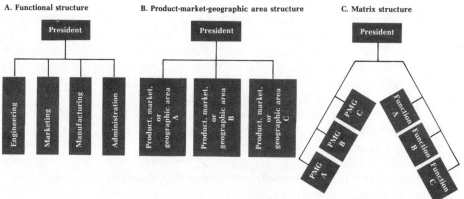

A. Functional structure   B. Product-market-geographic area structure   C. Matrix structure

task. The only significant difference between the two devices is that task forces tend to be more temporary in nature. Both sometimes contain as few as 3 or as many as 20 members, who often come from different subunits within the organization.

Measurement systems

Measurement systems attempt to influence human behavior by gathering, aggregating, disseminating, and evaluating information on the activities of individuals and groups within the organization. Measurement helps managers ask and answer such questions as: Are our managers achieving the organization's objectives? Do our employees perform according to the organization's expectations?

Measurement systems are either focused on the monitoring of ongoing activities or are designed primarily to appraise past performance. Either type can be based on financial, quantitative (other than financial), and/or qualitative data. The two most common types of measurement systems are management control systems and performance appraisal systems.

Management control systems are generally aimed at ensuring that the organization's (or its subunits') resources are being used in ways that are consistent with its goals and objectives. These systems focus on financial data and are usually referred to by the way in which information is collected and assessed: standard cost centers, revenue centers, discretionary expense centers, profit centers, or investment centers.

Performance appraisal systems attempt to measure factors associated with individual employees. These systems commonly ask a supervisor or a group of managers to rate individuals periodically on some scale regarding general characteristics of their work or personal traits. Other types of performance appraisal systems include those in which managers must rank all their employees from best to worst performers, those which are closely tied to Management by Objectives systems (MBO) or Assessment Centers, and those in which managers periodically write essays about their employees' performance.

Reward systems

Reward systems are generally designed to induce people to join the organization, to work as its structure directs, and to work toward certain measured objectives. The two main characteristics of a reward system are: the criteria used to allocate rewards, and the nature of the rewards themselves.

Reward systems are sometimes closely tied to measurement systems, so that rewards are allocated primarily on the basis of measured results.

Other common criteria for the allocation of rewards include past (as opposed to current) achievements, seniority, loyalty, and other factors such as the cost of living in the local area, family size, and education.

The most common rewards used by organizations include: money; fringe benefits, both monetary and nonmonetary; promotions; job assignments which are intrinsically satisfying; and job security.

Organizations typically offer money as either a base salary or as a base plus incentives. Incentive plans can be based on individual performance, group performance, or organization-wide performance. Fringe benefits typically include an allowance for overtime work; holidays, vacations, and sick days off with pay; various types of insurance; and special employee services (e.g., inexpensive lunches at the cafeteria). Additional fringes for managers include bigger and better offices, a company-owned or leased car, first-class travel on business trips, stock options, etc. Promotions reward an individual with more status, more power, and more responsibility. A job assignment that the individual likes can give him or her any number of different kinds of rewards—challenge, agreeable social relations, a comfortable work pace, excitement, and so on. Job security provides a stable flow of income as well as other types of rewards over time.

Selection and development systems

Selection and development are separate but interrelated formal organizational systems. They have an indirect effect on behavior patterns by influencing the knowledge, skills, values, and personalities of those people who work on the organization's tasks.

Selection systems range from very simple to very elaborate, and the selection process can even vary within an organization, depending on the job requirements and experience of the candidates. At one extreme, new employees may be selected on the basis of a relatively simple form that they are asked to fill out. At the other extreme, an applicant's past work experience may be carefully examined, and he or she may be asked to take a series of tests and undergo a large number of interviews with various managers. In either case, data on the person, once compiled, are sometimes compared to clear selection criteria, but more often are given to one or more individuals who then make a judgment.

Development systems also range from the simple to the elaborate. Some organizations provide only informal on-the-job training and development, which is based entirely on the skills and interests of individual managers. At the other extreme, some organizations offer formal internal training courses or send their employees to university programs. Some also systematically keep track of skill levels and work experience of certain employees with manpower planning systems and periodically make development decisions (transfer, rotation, promotion, training) based on that data. These organizations might also systematically encourage managers, through their measurement and reward systems, to develop their subordinates' skills.

Choices

In designing the overall structure, as well as the measurement, reward, and selection and development systems of an organization, managers face many choices. Should they use a functional structure, for example, or a product structure? How many people should report to each manager? What type of people should be hired for each subunit? What is the best way to measure the performance of individuals? Should people be paid for performance, or for their seniority, or for their potential for the future?

In some cases making these choices is relatively easy. For example, a small company that produces only one product for a limited geographical area will probably not have to think very long before adopting a functional structure. But in many cases the best choice is not so obvious. For example, how much of a salesmen's income should depend on his current sales performance—0 percent (a flat salary), 25 percent, 50 percent, 75 percent, or 100 percent (all commission)? Or how much money should an organization spend on management training programs—none, 1 percent of net income, or 10 percent of net? Or how many people should be assigned to a multibusiness company's corporate staff?

The basic purpose of the first three sections of this book is to help you develop the ability to analyze the available design alternatives and make these difficult choices.

PART I

The first section of this book focuses on the most basic of organizational building blocks—the specialized subunit that performs a limited functional task. Examples of such subunits which are included as cases in this section are a corporate finance department (Megalith/Hay Associates), a sales organization (Alcon Laboratories), and service operations branches (First Federal Savings).

Managers of specialized subunits, as the cases illustrate, often face a variety of human resource problems associated with high turnover, inadequate individual performance, and low morale. The text provides a research-based framework for analyzing these problems and for deciding how to successfully address them through the use of organization design tools. The readings focus in greater detail on those four tools which tend to be particularly important at the subunit level— job design, reward systems, performance appraisal systems, and Management by Objectives (MBO).

Chapter 3

Organizing human resources within specialized subunits

In the late 18th century, Adam Smith convincingly demonstrated the significant economic advantages of applying the concept of specialization in organizations. Through specialization, he argued, people develop expertise in performing a limited set of activities and thus become highly effective at accomplishing those activities. In addition, Smith noted, specialization often produces significant economies of scale, thus helping an organization to be more efficient in its use of resources.

Virtually all of today's organizations consist of parts based on the Smithian notion of specialization. If we are to understand the organizational issues that confront modern corporations, we must begin by focusing on the most basic organizational building block—the subunit which performs a limited, specialized function.

CONCEPTUALIZING ORGANIZATION DESIGN WITHIN SPECIALIZED SUBUNITS

The logical objective of the organizational design of a specialized subunit is to select, develop, direct, motivate, and control a group of human resources in order to accomplish a limited set of assigned tasks efficiently and effectively, and in the short and long run. Recent research suggests that a useful way of conceptualizing how the organization design of a subunit achieves this objective is in terms of the three-way "fit" shown in Figure 3–1.[1] It indicates that an organization design that fits both the

[1] Jay Lorsch and John Morse, *Organizations and Their Members* (New York: Harper & Row, 1974).

15

Figure 3–1
A conceptualization of the function of organization design within a
specialized subunit

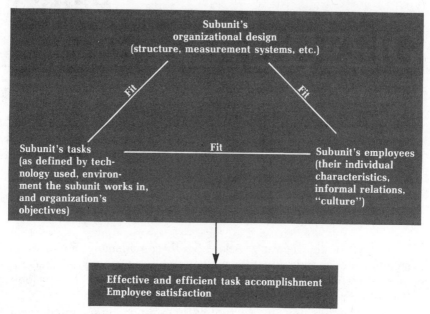

subunit's tasks and its employees, will lead toward efficient and effective
task accomplishment as well as satisfied employees.

Organizational designs that do not exhibit the type of three-way fit
presented in Figure 3–1 typically generate a number of problems. If either
the design or the employees do not fit the tasks, the subunit tasks will
usually not be accomplished effectively. If either the design or the tasks
do not fit the employees, the subunit's employees will become dissatisfied
and may exhibit the corresponding negative organizational outcomes—
turnover, absenteeism, lateness, etc.

When conceptualized as in Figure 3–1, the task of organizing a specialized subunit may appear to be quite simple. In reality it seldom is. Achieving an appropriate three-way fit in a specific situation is generally difficult
because of the large number of relevant task, human, and organizational
design variables. (Figure 3–2 presents a list of such variables.) It is possible
to have a situation where task, human, and organizational design variables
all *fit* on dozens of dimensions, and yet organizational problems will
result because of a misfit on one or two additional dimensions. And since
the people as well as the tasks in a subunit can change, even in the

Figure 3-2
Some examples of relevant task, people, and design variables

Task	Organizational Design
Amount of diversity within the task	Number of rules and procedures
Task complexity	Diversity of the activities in each job
Routineness of task	Span of control of first-line supervision
Time span of task completion	Amount of detail on job descriptions
Amount of personal contact involved	Dimensions measured in performance
Magnitude of task	evaluation system
Relevant dimensions on which task ac-	Frequency of appraisal reviews
complishment can be measured	Criteria under which people receive
	rewards
People	Percent of compensation that is fixed
Age	or variable (due to incentive, bonus,
Education	etc.)
Expectations (re: work)	Selection criteria
Native ability	Amount of money allocated to formal
Nature of special skills	training programs
Needs/drives/motives	
Values	
Adaptability	

short run, misfits on a dimension or two, and the resultant organizational problems, can easily develop.

Because there are so many potentially relevant variables and relationships implied in Figure 3-1, it is impossible to provide an exhaustive listing. It is possible, however, to examine some of the more important relationships and the more common mismatches that cause organizational problems.

THE ORGANIZATION-DESIGN-PEOPLE RELATIONSHIP

A fit between a specialized subunit's organizational design and its employees implies that the subunit's structure, measurement, reward, and selection and development systems are congruent with its employees' needs, abilities, personalities, and expectations.

Structure

Perhaps the most obvious and important aspect of this relationship is the link between job design and employee skills and abilities. All jobs require some type of cognitive and interpersonal skills on the part of their incumbents. A mismatch between job requirements and employee abilities obviously creates problems.

A variety of techniques has been developed in the past 30–40 years to assist in matching job requirements with employee skills and abilities, such as systems for job content measurements, psychological tests, and assessment centers.[2] While these techniques can help eliminate job-design–people mismatches and are widely used today, they have their drawbacks. The more complex techniques, such as assessment centers, can be very expensive to develop and use. The simpler methods, such as tests, can be relatively ineffective in dealing with complex jobs or with jobs where requirements tend to change over time. As a result, managers still tend to rely heavily on their own judgments in trying to match job design and employees. Successful managers seem to be generally effective in making these kinds of judgments.

Job–people mismatches are typically the result of insufficient analysis of a job's requirements or of inappropriate measurement of people's abilities and skills. The underlying problem in both cases is usually that managers make assumptions (which are usually a function of *past* events) about what a job demands or what certain people can provide without testing those assumptions in a serious analysis of the current situation.

Many factory jobs, for example, have been designed in extremely narrow, routine, and predictable ways. Such jobs may well have fit the needs and abilities of a poor, uneducated, largely immigrant work force, but they are becoming increasingly inconsistent with the characteristics of today's worker who is better educated, more affluent, and holds considerably higher expectations for job variety and challenge. The most widely used solutions to this type of organizational problem are called "job enlargement" and "job enrichment," both of which involve changing job designs to correct the misfit. With job enlargement, elements of several routine jobs are combined to increase the variety of the work. With job enrichment, job designs are altered to allow for more challenge, responsibility, and autonomy.[3] Though both of these techniques have been used successfully in a large number of situations, both have also failed in numerous situations.[4]

The common theme in these failures is that job designs were altered without a clear objective of matching the current tasks involved or the current employee groups. In some cases the "enlarged" or "enriched" jobs simply did not fit the existing set of technologically determined tasks,

[2] Edgar Schein, *Organizational Psychology* (Englewood Cliffs, N.J.: Prentice Hall, 1965), pp. 19–26.

[3] John J. Morse, "A Contingency Look at Job Design," *California Management Review* Fall, 1973, p. 68.

[4] Ibid., p. 69.

and costs went up considerably. In other situations they provided employees with more variety, ambiguity, and challenge than they wanted or could handle and so led to poor performance and angry employees.[5]

Job-design–people mismatches are also often created by changes in the subunit's task environment. These changes lead management to redesign jobs, which then do not fit the skills of current employees. Management subsequently is faced with the choice of either training its employees to fit the new job demands or replacing them.

In growing organizations, for example, the nature of managerial jobs at the subunit level tends to change continuously. The job of an advertising manager in a company with sales of $5 million a year and an advertising department with only 2 people, for instance, is very different from the job of advertising manager in a $100 million company that has an advertising department with 20 people in it. Constantly replacing managers because their jobs outgrow them can be a very expensive and demoralizing solution to this problem. But getting managers to grow or change with their jobs can also be difficult, especially if the changes occur regularly.[6]

Changes in an organization's size, usually due to growth, can produce a variety of other structure-people mismatches. For example, research shows that as organizations add more and more people, subunit structure usually changes by adding more levels in the hierarchy, increasing the amount of specialization in jobs, increasing the number of formal rules and procedures, and decentralizing decision-making authority.[7]

Many other aspects of subunit structure can also, upon occasion, be found to be mismatched with the current employees. The structure, for example, might include many commitees and meetings, while the employees are highly independent and not group-oriented. The management hierarchy might have a very wide span of control (many people reporting to one supervisor), while many of the employees are new and unskilled and need fairly close supervision. A large and old corporation might have many rules and procedures, while its newer college-educated managers and professionals might be used to a more informal and permissive environment. In all of these cases, the subunits involved will experience a continuing series of problems unless the mismatch is identified and corrected.

---

[5] For a good discussion of the problems job enrichment programs have encountered, see J. Richard Hackman, "Is Job Enrichment Just a Fad?" *Harvard Business Review*, September–October 1975.

[6] See, for example, Peter Drucker, *The Practice of Management* (New York: Harper & Row, 1975), pp. 246–62.

[7] See Chapters 2 and 3 in John Child, *Organization* (New York: Harper & Row, 1977). For a good discussion of the decentralization question, see Howard Carlisle, "A Contingency Approach to Decentralization," *Advanced Management Journal*, July 1974.

Measurement systems

Another significant aspect of the organization-design–people relationship that often creates problems is related to the type and frequency of feedback that performance appraisal and other measurement systems provide. It is possible for measurement systems to provide too little, too much, or the wrong kind of information to fit the needs and expectations of employees.

It is not uncommon, for example, to find a mismatch between relatively new, college-educated employees and the almost nonexistent performance appraisal systems in some organizations. A person with a bachelor's degree has typically received concrete, often quantitative performance feedback within short and predictable intervals for most of his or her life. When such a person begins to work in an organization that provides nothing equivalent to what he or she has come to expect, one predictably finds problems.

In contrast, where elaborate appraisal systems do exist, they sometimes ignore the social psychological research that identifies types of feedback which cause people to become defensive and angry, thus creating a different kind of mismatch. Ideal feedback, this research suggests, should be: descriptive rather than evaluative; directed at something the person can control; timely; specific rather than general, with clear and preferably recent examples; and not given in overly large amounts at any one particular time.[9] Some performance appraisal systems, on the other hand, are designed to provide a large amount of evaluative feedback about a person's traits (e.g., one's aggressiveness, good humor, leadership potential, etc.) in very general terms on an annual basis.

Performance appraisal systems often are inconsistent with the objectives or skills of the people who must implement them—the subunit's managers. For example, the systems sometimes require providing feedback at appraisal interviews—a skill that many managers do not possess. They sometimes generate strains in a manager's relationships with either subordinates (if the ratings seem low) or with peers (if the ratings seem high).[10] They also sometimes put supervisors in the uncomfortable and conflicting roles of both evaluators and coaches/helpers.[11] As a result

---

[9] See John Anderson's "Giving and Receiving Feedback," in *Organizational Change and Development* by Gene Dalton, Paul Lawrence, and Larry Greiner (Homewood, Ill.: Richard D. Irwin, 1970).

[10] Alan Patz, "Performance Appraisal: Useful but Still Resisted," *Harvard Business Review*, May–June 1975.

[11] See "Split Roles in Performance Appraisal," by Herbert Meyer, Emanuel Kay, and John French, Jr., *Harvard Business Review*, January–February 1965, pp. 123–29.

of one or more of these mismatches, many managers resist using performance appraisal systems altogether.[12]

Virtually any aspect of a measurement system can, in certain situations, be out of phase with the employees involved. An information/control system, for example, might provide data on a subunit's results only once every three months, completely frustrating a group of employees whose high achievement motivation leads them to seek more frequent feedback.[13] Or a performance appraisal system could force supervisors and employees to interact in appraisal interviews in ways that are completely inconsistent with their normal interaction preferences, e.g., scientists in a research laboratory who work as colleagues and view one another accordingly.

Reward systems

Possibly the most important aspect of the organization-design–people relationship deals with the fit between reward systems and people's needs and perceptions of what they deserve from the organization. Reward systems can create severe problems for a company if they do not provide both the type and the amount of rewards that employees perceive as appropriate and fair.

The *types* of rewards that an individual or group of people will find attractive are affected by many factors, including their cultural backgrounds, education, age, career aspirations, off-the-job life-styles, and work experiences to date.[14] Effective reward systems take these factors into account and attempt to offer different types of individuals and groups different reward possibilities. Pay may be stressed in some cases, while in others promotion opportunities, job security, challenging assignments, or fringe benefits may be emphasized.[15]

A second related group of factors affects the *amount* of rewards that an employee group will perceive as fair. These include general economic conditions, the nature of the jobs people have, people's perception of their performance on those jobs, seniority, and the rewards employees in other companies receive.[16] To help match pay levels and employees'

---

[12] For a good discussion of the underlying problem and some ideas for solutions, see L. L. Cummings and Donald P. Schwab, "Designing Appraisal Systems for Different Purposes and Performance Histories," *California Management Review*, in press.

[13] See David McClelland's "That Urge to Achieve," *Think Magazine*, 1966.

[14] See Chapter 5 in *People and Productivity*, ed. Robert Suttermeister (New York: McGraw-Hill, 1976).

[15] Edward E. Lawler III, "Reward Systems," in *Improving Life at Work*, by J. Richard Hackman and J. Lloyd Suttle (Santa Monica, Calif.: Goodyear Publishing, 1977), p. 167.

[16] Ibid.

feelings of equity, many large organizations have developed elaborate personnel systems that:

a. Periodically measure the skills required for all jobs, often assigning each a specific numerical score to represent its "content."
b. Assign a pay range to all jobs. The higher the content score, the higher the pay range.
c. Periodically compare the company's compensation with other companies—those in the same locale, and/or in the same industry.
d. Devise detailed formulas to determine a person's compensation within his or her job's pay range (usually a function of performance and/or seniority).[17]

Selection and development systems

The selection and development systems in a company's subunits can be inappropriate for its employees if they do not provide the training people expect or need for their jobs, or if they bring in people who are unable to get along with fellow employees.

In one study, for example, recently graduated MBAs reported that the largest discrepancy between their expectations of what they would receive in their first jobs and what their companies expected to offer them related to personal and professional development opportunities. The MBAs expected more than they received.[18] Where this was an important expectation from the MBA's standpoint, the person quit and moved on to another employer.

Another problem many organizations face is related to environmental change and its impact on the nature of the subunit tasks. For example, one company's customers began to change, subsequently causing the selling task to also change in important ways. The sales management responded by beginning to hire a different type of salesperson. When the older employees realized what was happening, many began to actively oppose the new selection criteria. Because these criteria represented a clear signal that their skills and abilities were no longer valued as much, some fought long and hard against the new standards. The disruptive fighting continued for nearly two years.

---

[17] For a further discussion of these types of systems, see *Handbook of Wage and Salary Administration,* ed. Milton Rock (New York: McGraw-Hill, 1972).

[18] John P. Kotter, "The Psychological Contract: Managing the Joining-Up Process," *California Management Review,* Spring 1973, p. 91.

THE ORGANIZATION-DESIGN–TASK RELATIONSHIP

A fit between a specialized subunit's organization design and its tasks implies a fit between the various organization design tools and the attributes of the subunit's activities.

Structure

A subunit structure that fits its assigned tasks is one that directs employees to work on those tasks in effective and efficient ways. One of the more important aspects of the fit between a subunit's structure and its tasks is the relationship between task certainty/uncertainty and structural formality/informality. Extensive research suggests that subunits that deal with very certain, predictable tasks are most effective when they are structured very formally, with clear job descriptions, rules, and procedures, while subunits that deal with very uncertain, unpredictable tasks are best structured informally.[19] The logic behind this relationship is simple. If a subunit's tasks are routine and predictable, careful study can determine the most efficient ways to perform them. These conclusions can then be programmed into job descriptions and rules. If, on the other hand, a subunit's tasks are highly uncertain, nonroutine, and unpredictable, such an analysis would be extremely difficult and would not identify a single best way to perform the tasks. In this kind of situation, detailed job descriptions and rules would be generally impossible and inappropriate. More informality and flexibility are required.

The relationship between the degree of predictability of tasks and formality of structure can be seen by comparing a factory with a research laboratory. Most manufacturing plants are technologically designed to contain fairly routine and predictable tasks; such plants are typically structured very formally. Research laboratories, on the other hand, engage in highly uncertain and nonroutine tasks, and are usually structured very loosely and informally. These differences in structure are not random or accidental; rather, they are created by managers who explicitly or intuitively recognize this structure-task relationship.

A second important aspect of the subunit structure–task relationship concerns job design. In general, job designs that fit task requirements tend to be those that facilitate the completion of tasks effectively at a minimum cost.

For example, the vice-president of sales in a clothing manufacturing firm was presented with two primary options for the design of his sales

---

[19] Paul Lawrence and Jay Lorsch, *Organization and Environment* (Boston: Harvard Business School, 1967).

force. In Option One, each salesperson would carry one of the firm's three lines of clothing (men's, women's, and junior's), and sell to about 60 customers in a geographical area. In Option Two, each salesperson would carry all three lines and sell to about 20 customers in a smaller area. In making his choice, the manager focused on three critical questions: (1) Is product knowledge or customer relations the more important factor in successful selling in our business? (2) How difficult and costly is it for a salesperson to learn a product line versus building a relationship with a customer? (3) How much more will the product-line specialization option cost in travel expenses and in the costs of coordinating the three salespeople that work together in a sales area? Based on an analysis of the situation, the vice president of sales decided that the customer relationship was more important than product knowledge. While training a salesperson in all three lines was expensive, it was not as expensive as the travel and coordination costs associated with Option One. Therefore, he chose the second option and designed sales jobs to carry all three lines for about 20 customers.

Still another aspect of the structure-task relationship that can cause problems for managers relates to span of control. Research shows that the number of people who can effectively report to a single manager can vary a great deal—literally from only one or two to two or three dozen—depending on a number of different task characteristics. For example, the more complex the tasks, the more time it will take a manager to hire, train, and evaluate a single subordinate, and thus the smaller the span of control needed. Likewise, the more interdependent the tasks performed by different employees, the more time it will take the manager to manage that interdependence, and thus the smaller the span of control required.[20]

Measurement systems

To fit a set of subunit tasks, measurement systems need to focus on the more important task-related variables and provide feedback on these variables to people who can control them. When measurement systems focus on the wrong variables, feed information to the wrong people, or provide untimely information, they can cause serious problems.[21]

A rather extreme example of a measurement system that did not fit task requirements was once created by the new director of a corporation's

---

[20] For a further discussion of this issue, see H. Stieglitz, "Optimizing Span of Control," *Management Record*, 24, 1962.

[21] Edward E. Lawler III and John Grant Rhode, *Information and Control in Organizations* (Santa Monica, Calif.: Goodyear Publishing, 1976), chap. 8.

research laboratory. Under this system, all professional personnel received a monthly report that indicated the total number of patents the laboratory had filed that month and the year to date, as well as the number of patents attributable to the individuals receiving the report. This system, intended to help motivate the scientists to work on the laboratory's tasks, created some serious problems for a number of reasons. First, the research projects the division worked on that led to profitable ventures for the corporation tended, in many cases to take five to ten years to complete, while the measurement system focused on monthly accomplishments. Second, the successful research projects were accomplished by teams, not individuals, yet the measurement system focused on individual accomplishment. Finally, while successful research projects did usually lead to patents, the patent itself was only a by-product. The result of the company's focus on patents as an end product was an increase in the number of patents filed, and a decrease in the number of successful research projects.

Probably the most common problem that organizational subunits encounter in the measurement-system–task linkage is a result of utilizing "off the shelf" performance appraisal systems. These systems, designed to be used by anybody, anywhere, sometimes measure people's personal characteristics, sometimes their behavior, and sometimes the results of their efforts. But they provide these measurements without consideration of the subunit's specific tasks. These systems are designed without serious attention to questions such as:

What type of behavior and results are needed to effectively and efficiently achieve the subunit's tasks?

How can these be measured?

In light of an analysis of the tasks, how often should they be measured?

The fact that performance appraisal systems so often ignore these questions is a major contributor to their ineffectiveness.[22]

Reward systems

For a reward system to fit a set of subunit tasks it must motivate the type of behavior that is necessary, and it must do so at a cost that is reasonable in light of the importance of those tasks.[23] The most common

---

[22] A 1974 Bureau of National Affairs survey revealed that while 93 percent of the firms polled had performance appraisal programs, only 10 percent of these firms' personnel executives felt that their appraisal programs were effective.

[23] Lyman W. Porter and Edward E. Lawler III, "What Job Attitudes Tell About Motivation," *Harvard Business Review,* January–February 1968, pp. 118–26.

reward-system–task misfits occur when relatively unimportant behavior is rewarded while more important task-related behavior is not rewarded, or when uncontrolled task outcomes are rewarded while outcomes under a person's control are not rewarded.

For example, the president of one organization decided to change the compensation system for marketing managers to one in which (a) the variable component in the average salary was higher and the fixed component was lower than before; and (b) the variable was calculated in a way that was based 25 percent on individual performance and 75 percent on corporate earnings. Three years later he abandoned this scheme after his managers bitterly protested its unfairness. They argued that they had very little control over corporate profits and that it just did not make sense to reward (or punish) them so heavily based on corporate profits.

In another situation, the compensation plan for the managers of a manufacturing plant was revised to provide up to a 50 percent bonus if they kept their costs within a fixed annual budget. This change was made when the company's sales were flat but its costs were rising. The plan worked well until the company's business changed three years later. As a result of introducing new products, its sales started to increase dramatically beyond forecasts. But the sales increase soon died out because the company could not make timely delivery on its orders. Regardless of how much the sales department pleaded with the plant to quickly increase its output, the plant managers refused to budge until the company's president granted them a change in their expense budget.

Reward-system–task mismatches sometimes occur, as in the previous example, because the subunit's tasks change. They occur even more often because some managers have a "pet" compensation, bonus, or commission system that they think fits all situations. Sometimes a manager has learned about such a system from friends, books, or a consultant, but most often it is one that the manager has observed working very effectively somewhere else. He or she simply does not recognize that the tasks in that environment are different from those in his or her own subunit.

Selection and development systems

Selection and development systems that fit task demands are those that help staff a subunit with the quantity and quality of people needed to perform the tasks effectively. The creation of good selection and development systems is central to facilitating a dynamic fit between a subunit's tasks and its employees.

As is the case with many of the organizational problems one finds in specialized subunits, mismatches between selection and development systems and subunit tasks are often caused by changes in the subunit's tasks. Alterations in an organizations's technologies, its external environment, or its mission are inevitable over long periods of time, and these changes will often cause the subunit's tasks to change. A selection and development system that is consistent with a given set of tasks can become completely inappropriate if there is a significant change in those tasks.[24]

For example, over a period of 15 years, one small, predominantly industrial products, manufacturing company developed a large number of consumer products. As a part of a general audit of the company's human resources, a consulting firm found that its sales force had abnormally high turnover and a low morale. Further investigation found that the selection process for a salesperson had changed very little over the preceding 15 years, despite the shift in the company's business and despite other organizational changes such as the addition of product managers. The company was still hiring salespeople whose skills and expectations were better suited to the old industrial products, which accounted for only about 25 percent of their total sales.

In another case, a technological change in a plant modified the nature of a number of tasks, including routine supervisory ones. Job descriptions were changed, and employees were given special training to help them adjust to the new jobs. But no one changed the routine training and development activities that the plant had used for years. Three years later, plant management determined that many new employees and newly promoted employees were not performing well. An investigation finally identified the mismatch between the old training activities and the new tasks.

MANAGING THE RELATIONSHIPS AMONG ORGANIZATION DESIGN, PEOPLE, AND TASKS

One of the major responsibilities of any subunit manager is to manage the relationships among organization design, employee, and task variables. While in some situations this responsibility is relatively simple, often it is not. A subunit's tasks can sometimes be so complex that they are difficult to comprehend completely. But without a clear understanding, it is extremely difficult for a manager to keep task variables aligned with the subunit's organizational design and employees. When a subunit has a large number of employees with diverse backgrounds, it can be equally difficult to accurately comprehend the people. And if either the tasks or the employees change very frequently, the potential problems are even greater.

---

[24] Leonard Schlesinger and Richard Walton, "Supervisory Roles in Participative Work Systems," *Academy of Management Proceedings*, August 1978.

Over the last few decades a variety of techniques have been developed to help managers better manage the relationships among organization design, people, and task variables. One of the most widely used is called Management by Objectives, or simply, MBO.

MBO

Championed by Peter Drucker,[25] Douglas McGregor,[26] and George Odiorne,[27] MBO has taken many specific forms in actual practice, but usually involves five basic steps:

1. A job description is developed for every job.
2. A list of objectives is developed for each employee in light of the job description. The objectives typically focus on both task accomplishment and employee development. These objectives cover some specific period of time, typically one year.
3. The employee and supervisor determine how and when they will be able to tell how well the objectives have been achieved. This step involves deciding how to measure the achievement of objectives and when to review the results.
4. In accordance with the plan determined in step 3, employee and supervisor review the employee's results against the plan.
5. At the end of the period for which objectives have been established, the employee and supervisor repeat the cycle starting either at step one or two.

Within this basic framework, MBO is practiced in many different ways.[28] For example, sometimes the employee is responsible for writing the first draft of the job description, the objectives, and the appraisals; sometimes the supervisor is. Regardless of these details, however, the underlying logic for the approach remains the same. That is, by emphasizing the five steps, one can systematically get people throughout the organization to:

Design jobs, plans, goals, and measurement systems to fit task requirements.

Create employee expectations and develop employee abilities that are consistent with job designs, plans, goals, and potential rewards.

---

[25] *Management* (New York: Harper & Row, 1974), chap. 34.

[26] *The Human Side of Enterprise* (New York: McGraw-Hill, 1960), chap. 5.

[27] *Management by Objectives* (New York: Pitman, 1965).

[28] Stephen Singular, "Has MBO Failed?" *MBA*, October 1975, pp. 47–50.

Under the right circumstances, MBO can be extremely helpful in managing the fit among organization design, task, and people variables. Nevertheless, despite MBO's popularity, it often ironically creates more organizational problems than it solves.[29]

Many managers have adopted specific MBO systems from consultants or books and have tried to implement them in all of their subunits without carefully considering how appropriate they are, given the subunit's tasks, employee groups, and organizational designs. Predictably, misfits have caused problems, leading a significant number of organizations to abandon their MBO systems.[30]

The most common problems companies have encountered with MBO systems are:

1. MBO-employee misfit: MBO systems are sometimes implemented without training employees adequately to use them. Setting appropriate, measurable objectives, for example, does not come naturally or easily for most people. In fact, some people, even if taught, cannot use such a system effectively because it is so much at odds with their natural styles.
2. MBO-task misfits: MBO systems must be used in an environment where task results are at least somewhat measurable, and where goal setting is a meaningful activity. If, for example, tasks are so predictable that goal setting is unnecessary, or if tasks are so unpredictable that goal setting is impossible, MBO will not work.
3. MBO-organization design misfits: MBO systems are sometimes simply added onto an organization, not integrated into its existing design. Inconsistencies between an MBO system and the prevailing measurement systems, job designs, and so on, can create serious problems.

No panaceas exist for managing the relationships among a subunit's organization design, task, and people. Ultimately, only careful attention and monitoring by managers equipped with skills in organizational analysis will do the job.

ORGANIZATIONAL ANALYSIS

Within the context of the specialized subunit (see Figure 3–3), an organizational analysis consists of the following steps:

1. Clearly identify and understand the subunit's tasks. To do this, one needs to consider:

---

[29] Dallas T. DeFee, "Management by Objectives: When and How Does it Work?" *Personnel Journal*, January 1977, pp. 37–42.

[30] Singular, "Has MBO Failed?"

The organization's and subunit's environment in terms of general characteristics and key success factors.

The organization's overall strategy and its relationship to the subunit.

The subunit's technology (especially if it is a manufacturing subunit).

2. Clearly identify and understand the most relevant characteristics of a subunit's current employees, such as their:
   Number.
   Background.
   Skills and abilities.
   Values and norms.
   Expectations, especially regarding their work and the organization.

3. Clearly identify the elements of the current organizational design:
   Structure.
   Measurement systems.
   Reward systems.
   Selection and development systems.

Figure 3–3
Organizational analysis at the subunit level

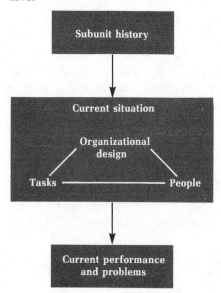

4. Identify the current performance of the subunit, as well as any problems or symptoms of problems.

5. Trace the history of the subunit with special attention to important changes that have occurred in its tasks, people, or organization design. Has the subunit grown in the recent past? Have its tasks changed, as the result of a change in technology, business strategy, size, or the organization's environment? How has the organization design changed during this period?

6. Identify the relationships between the subunit's history, its current tasks/people/organization design, and its current performance. A good analysis is characterized by intelligent inferences about these relationships.

Competent organizational analysis not only provides one with a basis for designing viable action alternatives to correct organization design/ people/task misfits, but it also helps one decide if there really is a problem, and if so, how important it is. Unlike some types of managerial problems, significant organizational problems may sometimes be invisible to most people, while conspicuous problems may be unimportant. Under such circumstances, doing what seems obvious is not a very effective way to manage, and skillful organizational analysis becomes particularly important.

Case 3–1
Megalith, Inc.—Hay Associates (A)
John P. Kotter, John A. Seeger, Anne Harlan

*Frank, there's no question about it. We're out of line. Way out of line. The
situation is real. It's hurting us, and I have two resignations here to prove it.*

John C. Boyd, senior vice president of Finance for Megalith, Inc., paced
across his office in agitation. Near the door stood Frank C. Nicodemus,
Megalith's vice president for Human Resources. The two men, long-time
colleagues in the successful multinational firm, were continuing a debate
begun much earlier, when Boyd had attempted to raise the salaries of
his key managers by 25 percent.

*You told me last June that these people were too young and inexperienced
to be worth the money,* Boyd continued. *And I told you we'd have to pay based
on their competence, not their seniority. Now it's October and two of them have
given notice in the past month. You know both of them—Lonny Jackson and
George Arnold are two of the best managers in the company. They're half of
the team I brought in here to bring the Finance Group out of the stone age, and
they've been absolutely vital to the development of the group. And now they're
both leaving—to get salaries I wanted to pay them months ago.*

Boyd turned and shook his head. *Frank, I know that what's done is done,
and we're not going to get Lonny and George back. But what if my other key
people take off, too? Where would that leave us? I've got to have more room in
the salary schedule to take care of the exceptional people who've made this
group click!*

Boyd paused, and Frank Nicodemus responded. *John, you'll remember I showed
you that all four of your key people were right at the top of our scale. Megalith's
compensation system isn't something we've arbitrarily picked out of the air; every
year we check the schedule against trade associations' published data, and we
adjust it to make sure we're above average—that we're competitive with the
best in the labor market. To make exceptions to a well-grounded scale would
be both hasty and rash. It would raise hell around here, throwing everything
out of balance.*

*So I held the line. But since then I've been checking to see just how sound
our schedules are. We found a consulting firm that has a very good reputation
in comparative compensation, and for the past month I've been working with
one of their partners. His name is Ed Rogers, and the firm is Hay Associates.
You know them: they're the people conducting the Climate Study right now, and
reviewing all our corporate-level job descriptions. Would you like to talk to
Rogers?*

Frank, I've got the comparisons I need, right here, John Boyd waved a file folder at his friend. *Lonny Jackson will start with an extra twelve thousand a year in direct salary, and will make a bonanza if he does well as Executive Vice President of R. G. Miller, and I'm sure he'll succeed. Megalith will have to pay at least twelve thousand to find and break in a replacement Vice President for Information Systems. What are we saving by putting our budget into search instead of salary?*

And the same thing goes for George Arnold, my Treasurer. He's going to take over a new leasing division for Rockwell, and his chance for profit incentive payments there puts anything we can offer to shame.

I just can't compete, Frank. You've got us locked in with a pay schedule that looks competitive on the surface, but when the chips are down, it's a loser. John Boyd hesitated, then continued slowly, *We've never before failed to reach agreement, Frank, but I'm afraid I'll have to fight you on this one. If we haven't solved the problem by the time Allen Whitfield* [Megalith's president] *gets back from Europe, I intend to ask him to call the Board's Compensation Committee in, to review the whole damn system.*

A silence of several seconds was finally broken by the Human Resources Vice President. *John, what could the Com-Com really* do? *They'd have to call in professional help, and they'd probably rely on our CPAs or a firm of specialists, like the ones I've already brought in. Wouldn't it make sense to hear what Rogers has to say, before we admit defeat? Won't you talk to him?*

Megalith, Inc.

In its 50 years of operations, Megalith, Inc., had grown to international prominence as a manufacturer of printing equipment, as a publisher, as a supplier of office equipment and supplies, and more recently as a builder of computer-related printers, plotters, and data recorders. From its beginnings, the firm had led the field in development of lithography and photo-offset printing techniques; basic patents in both printing and plate-making equipment had allowed Megalith to penetrate international markets early in its history. Megalith trademarks were found in virtually every job shop printing house in the world.

Shortly after World War II the company diversified into publishing; by 1975 it operated large-scale printing plants in seven countries. In the late 1950s Megalith attacked the office equipment industry; primarily through acquisitions it had achieved significant shares of markets in copying equipment, dictating systems, and typewriters—although it had failed to threaten the dominance of Xerox or IBM in these fields. Megalith's newest diversification strategy recognized that computers had come of age as sources of the written word; the firm began acquiring technology-based companies making high-speed line printers, plotters, microfilm output printers, and data recorders. By 1975, Megalith was a leading producer

Exhibit 1
Corporate organization chart, 1975

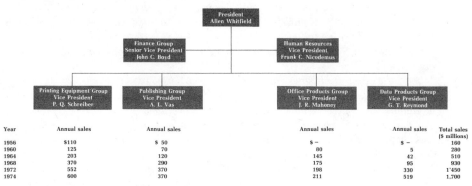

Year	Annual sales	Annual sales	Annual sales	Annual sales	Total sales ($ millions)
1956	$110	$ 50	$ –	$ –	160
1960	125	70	80	5	280
1964	203	120	145	42	510
1968	370	290	175	95	930
1972	552	370	198	330	1'450
1974	600	370	211	519	1,700

of computer peripheral equipment under its own name, as well as a leading supplier to the computer industry itself. Worldwide sales volume reached $1.7 billion in 1974, and profitability remained at traditionally high levels, in spite of generally poor economic conditions. (Exhibit 1 shows Megalith's corporate-level organization chart, with annual sales by product group since 1956).

Megalith executives credited the company's success to well-chosen strategy (dominance in printed communication), to technological leadership, and to strength in financial control. They were quick to admit that the company's only failure to reach market dominance—in the office equipment field—was due to the relative unimportance there of financial controls and engineering leadership; marketing genius was required to displace the leaders there. Still, the Megalith Office Products Group contributed significantly to profits and was considered a good investment.

Behind the desk of Megalith President Allen G. Whitfield hung a large, ornately framed poster, loudly proclaiming, "WE PRINT MONEY." The poster had been commissioned when the company had closed the order to equip the United States Mint; it had become an informal slogan of the firm, and smaller reproductions of the poster were common in executive offices and factory washrooms. Megalith people were proud of their "blue chip" reputation.

Hay Associates

In its own, much different market, Hay Associates was also proud of its leadership position. Founded in Philadelphia in 1943, the firm originally offered consulting services in the field of management compensation. By 1975 its specialties included comprehensive services in integrated planning systems, performance management, and reward management; it employed 275 professional people, operating from 29 offices in 14 countries. Hay's 1975 billings reached $21 million, and had grown at an annual rate of 30 percent since 1964.

Hay Associates brought an approach to compensation problems that organized known management judgments into a systematic measurement process. It separated the requirements and descriptions of the jobs from the performance of the job-holders, considering each separately in determining appropriate pay levels. Jobs themselves were analyzed according to know-how and problem-solving requirements, and according to the end results for which the position was accountable. The Hay system assigned "content points" for each criterion and gave the firm a basis for measuring the relative importance of different jobs and for ensuring an equitable internal balance of salary scales.

A key part of the process recognized that management positions were based on an organization's need for certain end results, but that each incumbent also had an impact on his job's content. Interviews with job-holders were used to develop descriptions acceptable to both the organization and the incumbent.

A comprehensive data base, collected annually from hundreds of client firms (1500 participated in 1975) permitted clients to compare their base salary practice and total remuneration, including benefits, with those of a broad industrial group. Since all contributors to the data base used the same measurement process, comparisons were always made on the basis of uniform content values for any position.

Hay's service allowed a company to compare its own salary practices, benefit programs, or even its "working climate" with others in its own industry or with the economy as a whole. The analysis identified jobs where a client company was overpaying or underpaying its people, compared to the policy or the actual practice reflected in the continually updated data base.

*   *   *   *   *

John Boyd sat comfortably in a leather-upholstered chair beside the window of his Manhattan office. Across a low coffee table, Edmund Law Rogers, partner in the firm of Hay Associates, leaned forward intently, listening.

So there's my situation, Ed. With this team of four really outstanding managers, we've built the Finance Group from a skeleton crew of budget-assemblers into one of the finest, most professional teams in industry. Now I'm losing the people responsible for breathing life into this outfit, because our bureaucratic salary system doesn't recognize the difference between talent and mediocrity. Can your system tell the difference?"

John, that's a judgment no formal system can make. Only the responsible executive—the man in your own shoes—can tell how well his people are performing, or how high they can go. But a formal system can say something about the jobs themselves. We can compare the jobs in the Finance Group to each other, based on their contents, to give you a measure of internal equity—of how fairly you're paying your people relative to each other. Then we can compare your salaries to those paid for similar-content jobs by a broad spectrum of industry. We can help define what end results each position is accountable for, and those definitions can sharpen your measurement of performance. That can help you decide what "outstanding" means, and how much you're willing to pay for it.

I'd like to know more about these key positions. Do you have a group organization chart handy?

The Megalith Finance Group

In early 1969, Allen Whitfield had asked John Boyd to move from the group vice presidency for office products to the new position as senior vice president for Finance. The corporation, with advice from a major American consulting firm, had decided to increase the size of its central financial staff, to bring together in the New York headquarters the analytic and control talents which were then scattered rather unevenly between the operating companies. Whitfield wanted a proven leader to build a coherent finance group, and Boyd was his first choice.

The Finance Group, Whitfield and Boyd decided, should be responsible for end results in the areas of strategy, planning, policy, and control. Exhibit 2 details the specifics of the Finance Group mandate.

Exhibit 2
Expected outcomes for the Finance Group's activities

1. Financial strategy which significantly contributes to corporate profit and growth objectives.
2. Financial policies, processes, and controls to provide timely and accurate information, comply with accepted practices and regulatory authorities, and protect assets.
3. Corporate planning and measurement process which provides an effective means to integrate group operations, evaluate achievement, and assure top management awareness of problems and opportunities.
4. Continuity of a corporate financial management team organized and competent to achieve functional objectives and a significant contribution to group financial management continuity and competence.
5. Effective asset and liability management which contribute to corporate short-term profit objective and long-term growth and stability.
6. Significant contribution to acquisition strategy and effective implementation through development of objectives, evaluations and analysis.
7. Systems and control capability to provide effective management information services.
8. An informed top management and Board of Directors aware of financial results and projections.

Under Boyd's direction, the Finance Group had grown since 1969 from 110 to 630 employees. (The 1975 organization chart for the department is included as Exhibit 3. Exhibit 3A shows growth in employment from 1969 to 1975.) The expansion had required new personnel, and Boyd had consciously decided to seek out energetic, competent, young people who could respond to the challenge, and to bring his new recruits up through the ranks of the group as fast as possible. This "fast track" policy had helped attract the four key people who, Boyd said, had made the concept work. All four of the "young stars" had performed beyond all expectations,

Exhibit 3
Organization Chart, Finance Group: July 1, 1975

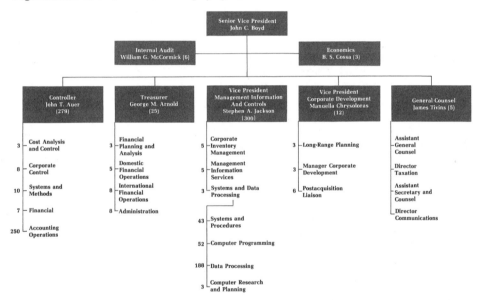

Exhibit 3A
Growth in employment

Year	Number of employees
1969	110
1970	165
1971	260
1972	390
1973	510
1974	600
1975	630

impressing the entire senior management group with their imagination, forcefulness, and effectiveness. All four had received every possible commendation, promotion, salary increase, and incentive bonus. (Exhibit 4 shows annual salaries and brief personal data on the key group personnel.)

John Boyd stated to Ed Rogers, *It was in June's performance planning meetings with people, I began to feel uneasy. There had been more and more complaints coming from people, about money. Most of them could be handled all right, but*

Exhibit 4
Excerpts from Personnel Resources Reference, July 1, 1975

Senior Vice President, Finance: John Covert Boyd, age 47. MBA, Harvard, 1958. Founded Duplicopy, Inc., and served as its president until its acquisition by Megalith in 1963. Became Group Vice President, Office Products, in 1967, and SVP in 1970.
1975 salary: $90,000 plus $25,132 incentive.*

Controller: John T. Auer, age 38. MBA, Wharton, 1960. Financial analyst, then Assistant Controller of Itek International until 1964, when he joined a small consulting firm as an Associate. Recruited by Boyd in 1970 to head the Controller's Systems and Methods group. Promoted to Director of Accounting Operations in 1972, and to Controller in 1974.
1975 salary: $59,000 plus $21,500 incentive.

Treasurer: George Miles Arnold, age 42. MS, London School of Economics, 1959. Lecturer in Finance, University of Bologna, then joined a major international oil company as coordinator of financial planning for Europe and the Middle East. Joined Barclay International in 1965 to form a new consulting services group in international money management. Recruited in 1969 by Boyd, to head Megalith International Financial Operations department; set up the Domestic Financial Operations office in 1970, and reorganized the Accounting Operations department in 1971. Promoted to Treasurer in 1973.
1975 salary: $54,000 plus $18,160 incentive (plus car).

Vice President, Management Information Systems: Stephen Alonzo Jackson, age 35. BS, MIT, 1962. Partner in a small, Boston-based software consulting firm for three years, then head of systems analysis for McGraw-Hill West Coast operations. MBA, Stanford, 1970. Joined Megalith as Director of Systems and Procedures; became Director of Management Information Services in early 1972; Director of Systems and Data Processing in 1973; and VP for MIS in 1974.
1975 salary: $55,000 plus $18,700 (plus car).

Vice President, Corporate Development: Manuella Chrysoloras, age 39. MBA, Darden, 1963. Joined an investment banking firm, and three years later set up her own brokerage in mergers and acquisitions. Retained by Megalith to assist in acquisition of four small computer peripheral manufacturers, and became executive vice president of the largest one. Drafted into finance group by Allen Whitfield in early 1971.
1975 salary: $48,000 plus $14,760 incentive.

General Counsel: James Tivins, age 61. LLB, University of Virginia, 1940. Joined legal staff of one of Megalith's printing equipment companies in 1949. Extensive work in anti-trust, finance, and tax law. Appointed Corporate Secretary in 1960, and General Counsel in 1966.
1975 salary: $65,000 plus $12,600 incentive.

---

*Incentive plan payments are based on results for fiscal year ended June 30, 1975; they were approved by the Compensation Committee of the Board of Directors on September 1, and paid the following week.

with my key people, we were up against the ceilings in both direct salaries and Management Incentive Opportunity. I couldn't offer them enough, and I couldn't get Frank Nicodemus to relax the constraints. You know those personnel people, they always seem to stand in your way. [See Exhibit 5 for a summary of the Megalith compensation system.] *It's clear now: I should have fought harder. Lonny and George both gave notice in September. Now I'm waiting for the other shoe to drop; if John Auer and Manuella should also leave, it would be like starting over from scratch, to build a new team.*

Exhibit 5
Summary: Compensation Policy, Revised July 1, 1971

Compensation Objective: To attract and motivate professional management people, enhancing their positive identification with corporate strategy and goals. Total compensation practice shall be competitive with an appropriate market mix of similar high-growth companies.

Compensation Components: Cash compensation shall consist of base salary (determined by comparison with appropriate markets); and Management Incentive Opportunity (determined by formula and approved in each case by the Compensation Committee of the Board).

Noncash compensation includes Pension Plan; Deferred Savings Plan; Group Life Insurance; Medical Plan; Short-Term Disability and Long-Term Disability Plans. These combined benefits approximate 35 percent of base salary expenditures for the Company; details of all plans are available from the Vice President, Human Resources.

Compensation Procedures: All positions shall be described in writing whenever changed or filled following a vacancy; all descriptions shall be audited annually by the Human Resources staff. Changed or added descriptions shall be evaluated by the appropriate HR Review Committee to maintain internal consistency and equity.

Management Incentive Opportunity Plan: MIO payments apply to all positions specifically determined°by the Compensation Committee of the Board to have both a direct impact on corporate earnings and a distinct requirement for individual discretion in their performance.

   Corporate Threshold: Before any MIO awards are paid, Megalith must earn a targeted Earnings Per Share as set by the Executive Committee. The EPS goal must equal or exceed the average EPS of the latest three years' operations. The Executive Committee may make an exception to the threshold for a division or group which achieves exceptional results.

   Performance Planning: Each MIO participant shall agree with his supervisor, before the beginning of each year, on his own performance goals and implementation plans. Group and Functional heads are responsible for coordination of these goals within the framework of corporate strategy, and shall inform each participant of his own potential MIO earnings for the forthcoming year, at different levels of performance.

Performance Growth Plan: Participants will be eligible for annual awards, determined by the Compensation Committee and calculated as a percentage of the MIO payments received during the immediately preceding four years.

   Participants may accept awards wholly in Megalith stock (with a 20 percent inducement premium for doing so), or half in stock and half in cash. PGP awards may be deferred until after retirement, and taken over a period not to exceed ten years, at the participant's option. Cash deferred awards will accrue interest at the prime rate; stock deferred options shall re-invest dividends in additional stock.

Was there any connection between the two resignations?

No, Ed. Neither man knew the other was going to quit, and they both feel bad that the Group here will suffer. But the money was too much for them to resist.

Are you sure it's the money that made them go?

That's what they both said, and I'm sure they're leveling with me. If we'd been competitive, neither one of them would have given the time of day to the recruiters who contacted them. Besides, it all fits in with other comments I've heard—that the pay is inadequate.

But let me get back to the question: would your compensation system allow for the exceptional managers? Can we get Frank to give in on those damn ceilings? I need a fast answer, because I'm starting to recruit replacements, and I have to tell them what they can look forward to.

Boyd and Rogers spent the next half hour discussing the Hay evaluation system, which focuses on the content of the job, rather than the talents of the individual. Rogers briefly described the evaluation process (see Exhibit 6). Responding to Boyd's questions, he detailed how a specific job might be evaluated:

1. Know-how, in the Hay system, is scored according to three different aspects of the job's requirements—technical or practical knowledge, however acquired; managerial knowledge, in terms of degree of integration and coordination with other functions or activities required by the position; and human relations skills needed to perform the job, classified as basic, important, or critical.

(A sample section of the guide chart, used by Rogers to demonstrate the rating of three typical jobs, is included in Exhibit 7. A similar, but more comprehensive guide chart had been developed for Megalith's own job evaluations, Rogers said.)

2. Problem-solving requirements of a job are rated according to two dimensions—the thinking environment, ranging from strictly routine to abstractly defined; and the thinking challenge of the job, ranging from repetitive choice-making to creative concept-formation.

3. Accountability, the last major area for rating, is measured on three dimensions—the position's freedom to act, ranging from totally prescribed to unconstrained-except-for-broad-policy; its impact on end results, ranging from indirect-remote to direct-primary; and the dollar magnitude of the area most clearly affected by the job.

Given a large number of jobs, consistently described and rated, we can compare the salaries and incentives paid for job contents, rather than job titles, Rogers summed up. *You can't compare on the basis of title, because incumbents, organizations' needs, and/or organizations' styles make the jobs different.*

Exhibit 6

IN A NUTSHELL

HAY JOB DESCRIPTION — JOB CONTENT IN TERMS OF: • KNOW-HOW • PROBLEM SOLVING • ACCOUNTABILITY

EVALUATION FOR INTERNAL CONSISTENCY

ACCOUNTABILITY AC — PROBLEM SOLVING PS — KNOW-HOW KH

BASED ON HAY GUIDE CHARTS TO ASSURE CONSISTENT MEASUREMENTS, JOB CONTENT IS EVALUATED AND CURRENT SALARY PRACTICE IS SHOWN ON A SCATTERGRAM:

LOCAL SURVEYS — COMPOSITE

SCATTERGRAM   CHART 1 — SALARY — ACTUAL — JOB CONTENT

EXTERNAL COMPARISONS ARE MADE AT BOTH ◄——LOCAL AND NATIONAL——► LEVELS,

INDUSTRY GROUPS — HAY ANNUAL CHARTS

A POLICY MIDPOINT LINE IS ESTABLISHED,

CHART 2 — RECOMMENDED — ACTUAL

AND ADMINISTRATIVE GUIDES ARE FIXED.

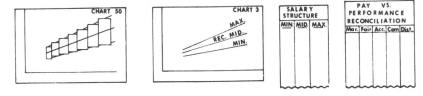

CHART 50

CHART 3 — MAX. — REC. MID. — MIN.

SALARY STRUCTURE — MIN. MID. MAX.

PAY VS. PERFORMANCE RECONCILIATION — Mar. Fair Acc. Com Dist.

Exhibit 7

Sample Evaluation

KNOW-HOW

Technical/practical know-how required

		I LIMITED			II RELATED			III DIVERSE			IV COMPREHENSIVE		
		Performance or supervision within a single function with operational regard for relevant activities.			Primarily within a single function with some internal or external integration with related fields.			Integration and coordination of diversified activities in an operating unit, or in a corporate-wide function.			Comprehensive integration and coordination in a major management complex, or of a corporate-wide activity.		
		1.	2.	3.	1.	2.	3.	1.	2.	3.	1.	2.	3.
A. PRIMARY: Elementary plus some secondary (or equivalent) education, plus work indoctrination.		50	57	66	66	76	87						152	A
		57	66	76	76	87	100						175	
		66	76	87	87	100	115	Human relations skills					200	
B. ELEMENTARY VOCATIONAL: Uninvolved, standardized work routines and/or use of simple equipment and machines.		66	76	87	87	100	115	required by the position:					200	B
		76	87	100	100	115	132						230	
		87	100	115	115	132	152	1 = basic (courtesy)					264	
C. VOCATIONAL: Procedural or systematic proficiency, which may involve the use of specialized equipment.		87	100	115	115	132	152	2 = intermediate (get along well)					264	C
		100	115	132	132	152	175	3 = critical (motivate people)					304	
		115	132	152	152	175	200	200	230	264	264	304	350	
D. ADVANCED VOCATIONAL: Some specialized (generally nontechnical) skills, however acquired, giving additional depth to a generally single function.		115	132	(152)	152	175	200	200	230	264	264	304	350	D
		132	152	175	175	200	230	230	264	304	304	350	400	
		152	175	200	200	230	264	264	304	350	350	400	460	
E. BASIC TECHNICAL-SPECIALIZED: Sufficiency in a technique requiring a grasp either of involved practices and precedents, or of scientific theory and principles, or both.		152	175	200	200	230	264	264	304	350	350	400	460	E
		175	200	230	230	264	304	304	350	400	400	460	528	
		200	230	264	264	304	350	350	400	460	460	528	608	
F. SEASONED TECHNICAL-SPECIALIZED: Proficiency, gained through wide experiences in a specialized or technical field.		200	230	264	264	304	350	350	400	460	460	528	608	F
		230	264	304	304	350	400	400	460	528	528	608	700	
		264	304	350	350	400	460	460	528	608	608	700	800	
G. TECHNICAL-SPECIALIZED MASTERY: Determinative mastery of techniques, practices and theories gained through wide seasoning and/or special development.		264	304	350	350	400	460	460	528	608	608	700	800	G
		304	350	400	400	460	528	528	608	700	700	800	920	
		350	400	460	460	528	608	608	700	800	800	920	1056	
H. PROFESSIONAL MASTERY: Exceptional competence and unique mastery in scientific or other learned discipline.		350	400	460	460	528	608	608	700	800	800	920	1056	H
		400	460	528	528	608	700	700	800	920	920	1056	1216	
		460	528	608	608	700	800	800	920	1056	1056	1216	1400	

KH	PS	AC	TOTAL	KH	PS	AC	TOTAL	KH	PS	AC	TOTAL
152				**304**				**700**			

SUPERVISOR KEY PUNCH   ACTUARIAL SPECIALIST RESEARCH ASSOCIATE   AREA MANAGER

Here in Megalith, we've finished with the updating of job descriptions [see Exhibit 8 for a sample description], *and I expect to submit our final report to Frank Nicodemus in two weeks. He's said you'll be the first one he sends a copy to.*

John Boyd thought for a moment as he lit a cigarette. *O.K.,* he said. *You'll tell us how our pay scale stacks up in terms of the jobs we pay for. But you're not going to evaluate the individuals involved, or the problem of identifying exceptional talent and holding it. Is that right?*

John, that's got to be your job. We can help, by giving you information, and an analysis of your own system's strengths and weaknesses, and our suggestions for changing the system.

Our numbers data will *show Megalith's current salary practice, compared with the practice of a broad industrial spectrum. We* will *include an analysis showing what your current salaries would be, if they were fully consistent with the measured content of the jobs. But Frank Nicodemus hasn't asked us to go beyond that in this report.*

In addition to the numbers, you'll see the results of the Climate Study we've just finished here. About 50 of your finance people have filled out our survey

Exhibit 8
Position Description, November 1, 1975

Position: Treasurer	Organization Unit: Financial
Incumbent: George M. Arnold	Location: New York

Accountability objective:

This position is accountable for planning of debt/equity financing and the direction and coordination of cash mobilization, short-term investment, insurance, and benefit plan services.

Dimensions:

Department Operating Expenses:	$1.0M
Short-Term Investment Earnings:	$2–5MM
Department Employees:	24

Nature and scope:

Megalith, Inc., is a major, multinational corporation with financing requirements and cash management operations throughout the world. Major outlays of cash are anticipated to continue an upward trend during the next 8–10 years. Possible changes in accounting for, and reporting of, off-book financing, the need to generate increased amounts of capital overseas for use in overseas operations, and the uncertainties created by new international monetary arrangements pose formidable challenges to the corporation's financial capability and plans for growth. The Treasurer's function has been recently reorganized to concentrate on these problems.

Reporting to the Treasurer are four Directors. Their areas of concentration are:

1. *Financial planning and analysis* (3 employees)—This unit conducts overall analysis of debt/equity financing and performs similar analyses in developed plans for financing foreign operations from foreign financing sources; develops plans for the management of foreign exchange; makes buy/lease analyses of property from the financial point of view; and generates, regularly, total forecasts of cash requirements worldwide for short- and mid-term periods of time, and updates forecasts periodically during the year.
2. *Domestic financial operations* (5 employees)—This unit makes short-term investments in the money market including treasury notes, CDs and banker's acceptances; gathers and deposits cash through the operation and collection of 500 bank accounts throughout the United States, and monitors compensating balances in relation to lines of credit.
3. *International financial operations* (8 employees)—This unit coordinates overseas project financing; manages more than 40 bank accounts in approximately 12 different foreign countries, including the transfer of funds between accounts; deals with a variety of currencies; borrows money from other than offshore finance companies; and provides advice and counsel to management on the implications of the cash management and financing support for their operations.
4. *Administration* (8 employees)—This unit develops working company policies, including those having to do with credit and collection, for the guidance of all operating groups; buys insurance (premiums amounting to $2–3MM per year) for the corporation in the form of blanket policies covering worldwide risks (a $3MM deductible provision is a feature of all covered risks). In addition, this unit performs cost/benefit analyses of group benefit plans and participates in negotiating and placing benefits with carriers.

Principal end results:

1. Financial plans, and forecasts which reliably project the financing needs of the company.
2. Optimum cash availability for current needs through effective use of cash mobilization systems and policies, and efficient financial operations.

Exhibit 8 (*continued*)

3. Maximum return on short-term investments consistent with the company needs for liquidity.
4. A worldwide system of banking relationships that facilitates the management of funds, the availability of cash, short-term investments, and assures required borrowings.
5. Risk and benefits plan placement which effectively meets company objectives.
6. Knowledgeable advice and counsel to management concerning proposed capital expenditures and investments for domestic expansions, acquisitions, mergers, and other business ventures.
7. Continuity and development of a professionally competent staff of financial managers and specialists.

---

forms, and we'll digest that information for you, relating it to the answers given by several thousand other respondents.

Boyd stubbed out his cigarette and stood. *I'll look forward to seeing that report. And I assume we'll meet again to talk about what it means—probably with Frank.* Boyd smiled. *I've tried a couple of times to pin you down on an answer to this, but you've dodged me. Before you go, I'd like to ask you directly . . . do you have any opinion yet on raising these ceilings of ours?*

No way, John, Rogers smiled in return. *But I'll look forward to seeing you again after the report is finished.*

Case 3–2
Alcon Laboratories, Inc.
Paul H. Thompson

condensed by
Joseph Seher and John P. Kotter

In the summer of 1966, Mr. George Leone, National Sales Manager of Alcon Laboratories, initiated an appraisal of the organization and morale of his 70-man sales force. Mr. Leone expressed particular concern over the high turnover in the sales force (28 percent in the fiscal year 1965–1966). He had considered a number of changes which might reduce the turnover but was unsure as to just what action he should take. While he was willing to make any changes that might improve the situation, he felt that it would be better to do nothing than to attempt changes that were inappropriate to the needs of his organization.

The company history

In 1947 in Fort Worth, Texas, two pharmacists founded Alcon Laboratories on the principle that more accurate, sterile, and stable pharmaceutical compounds could be manufactured by Alcon on a large-scale basis than was possible in retail drug stores, where most prescribed drugs were being compounded at that time.

In early years Alcon management decided to achieve growth by concentrating their marketing efforts in specialty fields. The field in which Alcon first specialized was ophthalmological drugs (drugs used in the treatment of defects and diseases of the eye). In 1947, 85 percent of all eye-care drugs were being compounded in drug stores.

As doctors became familiar with the company's products and their quality, they prescribed them more and more, and Alcon prospered. By 1957 a sales force of 30 men was promoting the company's eye-care product nationally, and sales had grown to nearly $1 million.

Alcon Laboratories continued to grow both domestically and internationally. In fiscal 1966, total sales were $9.1 million. Domestic sales of 33 products were about $6 million and were promoted by a 70-man sales force. In addition, by purchasing another small specialized pharmaceutical firm, Alcon had entered a second specialty field. Furthermore, they had achieved some backward integration by purchasing a manufacturer of plastic containers for pharmaceutical products. Internationally, Alcon manufactured and sold its product line through foreign subsidiaries and joint agreements.

Exhibit 1 shows selected historical operating and financial information for the period 1958 to 1966. Exhibit 2 gives the consolidated income statement for 1966.

Alcon's eye care products: Their use and distribution

Alcon manufactured products for a wide array of eye problems, ranging from treatments for serious eye diseases to less serious infections and cleansing agents. Similarly, Alcon sold products used in diagnostics and for surgical assists. These products were available either directly or through wholesalers both to hospitals and to retail drug stores. Ninety percent of total sales were prescribed by one of the 6,000 ophthalmologists (medical doctors specializing in the treatment of eye diseases and defects)

Exhibit 1
Highlights of operating and financial data

	1966	1965	1964	1963	1962	1961	1960	1959	1958
Earnings per share	1.30	1.05	1.20	0.86	0.66	0.50	0.40	0.30	0.13
Current ratio	3.24	3.06	2.39	1.96	1.87	1.31	2.25	2.03	2.02
					(In $,000)				
Net sales	9,114	8,749	8,697	7,718	6,392	3,057	3,094	2,035	1,347
Net income	821	663	750	534	404	268	215	163	69
Working capital	3,262	2,448	1,846	1,065	734	186	532	381	169
Total Assets	7,016	6,007	5,426	4,413	3,648	2,606	1,810	1,478	545

Exhibit 2
Income Statement

	Year Ended *April 30, 1966* *(in $,000)*
Net sales	9,114
Costs and expenses	
Costs of goods sold	3,129
Selling, general, and administrative expenses*	4,411
Total Costs and Expenses	7,450
Income before provision for federal taxes	1,574
Provision for federal income taxes	753
Net Income	821

* Research and development represented a significant portion of general and administrative expenses.

or by one of 2,000 eye-ear-nose-throat doctors who practiced in the United States. Alcon salesmen regularly visited these doctors.

The market and competition

In 1965, total retail sales of ophthalmological drugs in the United States were $30 million.

Alcon Laboratories' shares of the total domestic ophthalmological drug market was nearly 20 percent. Small, specialized manufacturers like Alcon, which attempted to find a niche in the total market by catering specifically to the ophthalmic market, competed directly with Alcon. Also, Alcon competed with large, diversified drug manufacturers for whom certain segments of the ophthalmic market were large and lucrative enough to warrant attention. Alcon management stated that in 1966 two large drug manufacturing firms controlled about 30 percent of the domestic ophthalmic market.

The active chemical compounds used in various ophthalmological preparations were essentially the same, regardless of manufacturer. Competing products were differentiated primarily on the basis of their form[1] and vehicle.[2] Competing manufacturers were constantly looking for new preparations which would have performance superior to existing ones. While Alcon was interested in developing new compounds of active ingredients,

---

[1] Form referred to whether the compounds came in solution, ointment, cream, pill, etc.

[2] The vehicle comprised the inactive ingredients which were important in determining such product qualities as the stability of the product, how well the product stayed in the eyes (instead of "sweating out"), the irritation and/or side effects of the product.

the major thrust of their research was to improve the performance of existing compounds by developing better or new forms and vehicles.

The marketing department

Organization. The Marketing Department of Alcon Laboratories was under the direction of the marketing director, who was also a vice president of Alcon and a member of the company's executive management group. Ed Schollmaier, who currently held this position, was 32 years old and had risen rapidly at Alcon. After receiving his MBA at the Harvard Business School in 1958, he had started as a salesman with Alcon and in a short time he had been promoted to district sales manager. After less than two years with Alcon he had been called into the home office to assist in directing the sales effort. In 1963 he had been appointed director of marketing. Reporting to Mr. Schollmaier were the national sales manager, product managers (marketing responsibility other than direct sales), and the director of market research.

The primary responsibility of the Marketing Department was to assure the success of the sales effort. The home office was responsible for the design of the sales program, while the field sales organization was responsible for the program's execution. Great time and effort were typically expended in both areas. According to a 1965 study, drug and pharmaceutical firms' selling costs were twice those of U.S. industry as a whole. The survey showed that in 1964 the cost of selling pharmaceuticals amounted to 30.5 percent of gross sales revenue. The study presented the following breakdown of total selling costs:[3]

	Drug industry	Average (all industries)
Salesmen's compensation	37.3%	45.2%
Salesmen's travel and other expenses	13.6	12.8
Sales management costs	14.0	16.2
Advertising, merchandising, and promotion	29.9	14.2
Servicing	3.0	7.4
All other costs	2.2	4.2
Total	100.0	100.0

---

[3] This study included as selling costs such items as seminars held for doctors to acquaint them with new drugs, and samples sent out as part of a product's introductory stage. Other industries did not have such expenses to the degree that the drug industry had, and some companies included similar costs in research and development, for accounting purposes. Another factor to consider in comparing drug industry costs with those of other industries is that most consumer goods manufacturers shared costs of advertising with retailers; drug companies, on the other hand, bore most of these costs alone. In addition, allowances for returned merchandise were higher in the drug industry, since companies regularly took back unopened stock that was out of date.

Between 1961 and 1966, Alcon's total annual expenses for advertising, merchandising, and promotion increased from $90,000 to $750,000.

The central activity of the Marketing Department was the planning of promotion programs, a joint responsibility of the product managers and the national sales manager. Prior to the beginning of each fiscal year, the product managers would meet with Mr. Leone, the National Sales Manager. On the basis of the size of the total promotion budget, the length of time since a product had been actively promoted, Mr. Leone's estimate of market potential, the current share of market held by the products involved, and competitive activity, this group would draw up a list of the particular products to be promoted in the coming year. Products on the list were then assigned specific dates for promotion. This promotion schedule was then approved by the marketing director.

The promotional campaign was developed by the product managers, who first consulted with the national sales manager for his ideas on market positioning. After the campaign had been designed, the national sales manager and his subordinates taught the sales force how to carry it out.

To provide salesmen with the information that was desired by doctors, the Marketing Department needed the aid of the Medical Department and the Research Department.

The Medical Department was responsible for professional contact with members of the medical profession. Through a "Clinical Liaison Group" the Medical Department engaged physicians doing clinical research to conduct studies to test the uses or find new uses for Alcon's products. The findings were frequently used, in the form of professional articles or in technical bulletins, in promotional campaigns. It was not uncommon for a member of the Marketing Department to ask the Medical Department to help in developing some technical data to support particular claims for a product.

Alcon's R&D Department was also important to the marketing effort. The development of new chemical compounds, new uses of existing compounds, and improvements in existing compounds, were all considered to be of prime importance. Introducing new and improved drug preparations was considered to be one of the most effective ways to increase sales and enhance the company's reputation in the medical community. Sales of various ophthalmological preparations tended to be more stable than the sales of pharmaceutical preparations in general, which were characterized by extreme volatility due to the frequent introduction of new chemical compounds which made existing compounds, in all types of forms and vehicles, obsolete. Alcon management stated, however, that "the impact of new products (i.e., new formulations of existing ophthalmological compounds) since 1960, accounted for more than half of Alcon's growth, and half of that growth was attributable to innovations in the steroid product category in particular."

The mutual interests of the Marketing, Medical, and R&D Departments were coordinated through meetings of the product committee whose members included Mr. Ed Schollmaier, Marketing Vice President; Dr. Earl Maxwell, Medical Director and Director of R&D; Mr. Frank Buhler, Director of International Operations; and Mr. William Conner, who was Chairman of the Board and President. For example, through the product committee the time and resources of the R&D Department might be allocated to fill gaps in the product line, as determined by sales management and product managers. The need for and provision of technical data by the Medical Department was also coordinated through the product committee.

The national sales manager

Mr. George Leone headed the 70-man sales force in 1966. He had been with Alcon since 1950, when there were only six salesmen in the company. After doing an outstanding job as a salesman he was made a district sales manager in 1955, a regional sales manager in 1961, and national sales manager in 1963.

As National Sales Manager, Mr. Leone was responsible for the overall administration and performance of the sales force and for coordinating the activities of the sales force with other groups in the Marketing Department. In his administrative capacity, Mr. Leone was primarily concerned with the establishment of company programs in the areas of recruitment and selection, training and development, supervision, standards of per-

Exhibit 3
Organization chart of the sales group

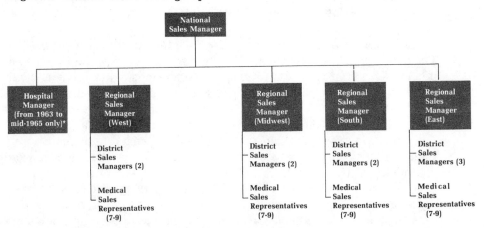

* Dropped in 1965 because of the overlap between calls on doctors when they were at the hospital and when they were at their private office.

formance appraisal, and compensation and benefits. He was also responsible for identifying and developing field sales managers.

Mr. Leone directed three groups of men: regional sales managers, district sales managers, and medical sales representatives. The latter were more commonly known within the industry as salesmen, and were frequently identified by physicians as "detail men." (Exhibit 3 is an organization chart of the sales organization.)

The regional sales managers

Alcon divided the United States into four large sales regions, each supervised by a regional sales manager. The job description in the company's supervisory reference manual listed five major functions for the regional sales manager (RSM):

1. Recruitment and selection of candidates for field sales work (medical service representatives) with special emphasis on applicants with management potential.
2. Training and developing the district managers.
3. Supervising, directing, and controlling the activities of the district sales managers.
4. Maintaining communications with the home office through weekly reports and with the sales force through quarterly regional sales meetings.
5. Planning and organizing to help set the objectives for the region and to help the district sales managers set their goals.

The job description stated that RSMs should spend a minimum of 35 percent of his time in personal field visits with his district sales managers. He had no direct customer responsibilities.

Three of the four regional sales managers worked in the home office and spent a good deal of their time working with Mr. Leone in planning the national sales effort. They were involved in sales promotion, planning, meetings, and developing company policies and procedures for recruiting, selection, training, and supervision of the sales force. The fourth RSM was in the process of moving from Chicago to the home office.

The district sales manager

Reporting to each of the four regional sales managers were two to three district sales managers (DSMs). An Alcon district was a subdivision of a region (for example, the New England states comprised one district of Alcon's eastern region). The district sales manager's job description listed five major duties:

1. Recruiting, selecting, and with approval from RSM, hiring salesmen to become medical sales representatives.
2. Training and developing the field sales force.
3. Supervising, directing, and controlling the activities of the field sales force.
4. Maintaining communications with home office and with the RSM, and conducting quarterly district sales meetings.
5. Planning and organizing operation of districts through setting objectives for field salesmen.

The job description further stated that the DSM should allocate his time as follows:

A minimum of 75 percent of his time in personal field visits with the medical sales representatives, and the remainder (25 percent) at medical meetings, sales meetings, and visits with regional sales manager.

The DSMs, like the RSMs, had no direct customer responsibilities.

The salesmen

Reporting to each of the nine district sales managers were seven to nine medical sales representatives (MSRs), or salesmen. These 70 salesmen were responsible for Alcon's direct customer contacts. Each MSR covered one Alcon "territory." The medical sales representatives' job description listed six major duties:

1. Call on each of the following:
   a. All eye physicians within his territory.
   b. All pharmacies on his call list.
   c. All hospitals on his call list.
   d. All wholesalers on his call list.
2. Follow the sales program, including using all sales tools outlined by the program.
3. All MSRs must fulfill their performance standards and objectives each month in the following areas:
   a. Doctor-call standards (item "a" above).
   b. Retail-call standards (item "b" above).
   c. Wholesale-call standards (item "d" above).
   d. Increased sales objective (the DSM and MSR together set a specific objective as to how much sales will increase in the current year over the previous year).
   e. Ratio of increased sales to sales cost. For example:

	1966		*1965*	
Total territory sales	$100,000	8.3	$120,000	6
Total territory costs	12,000 = 1		20,000 = 1	

    f. Featured product (the one being promoted or detailed) objective.
    g. Turnover order[4] objective.
4. Planning and organizing territory coverage by maintaining territory coverage plan and territory records.
5. Maintaining communications with supervisor and the home office by submitting the required daily, weekly, and monthly reports.
6. Meeting standards of self-development by attaining an adequate product knowledge, and knowing and complying with company policies on appearance, conduct, and maintaining company property.

Top management described the salesmen's activities as falling into two distinct categories: *creating demand* (when the MSR is in the doctor's office, trying to get him to prescribe Alcon's products) and *distribution* (supporting demand by getting the product to the wholesaler and retailer).

Selling in the drug industry

Salesmen in the drug industry as a whole made an average of 48 calls per week. A typical day for an Alcon salesman started by driving 50 miles to a city to make calls. He waited a considerable time, up to 30 minutes, to see a doctor, actually saw only five of the nine doctors he called on, and was able to spend only about five minutes with each doctor because of their busy schedules. The salesman also called on, in a normal day, one drug wholesaler and three drug retailers, spending only about 15 minutes with each.

An Alcon salesman typically saw his DSM only once a month, but maintained contact with him weekly by telephone. Alcon salesmen generally saw each other at their bimonthly sales meetings. Although they had infrequent contact with other Alcon salesmen, the typical MSR had the opportunity for more frequent contact with other companies' salesmen who were detailing the same area as himself.

The doctor call

Alcon, as well as other drug companies, considered that "detailing" the doctor was one of the best ways to create demand for both new and existing products. Alcon called on eye doctors once a month. On a

---

[4] Turnover orders were those which the drug salesman wrote for the drug retailer, and hand-carried or mailed to the drug wholesaler to be filled.

typical visit to an eye specialist, the Alcon salesman was expected to detail one primary product, one secondary product, and one "door handle" product (one that was just mentioned on the way out). Any one product was usually detailed for three consecutive months, though some were detailed for only one month and others were detailed for as long as seven consecutive months.

The MSR was supposed to discuss with the doctor whether he or she now used the product being detailed, or would use it in the near future. Because doctors were so busy, the salesmen had only a brief period to make their presentations. One doctor commented:

> The detail men have to see you at your office. I'm very busy there so it is hard to find time to see them. I can only give them five to ten minutes and that is time away from seeing my patients.

It was hoped that the salesman's brief presentation would make a lasting impression on the doctor. Journal advertising and direct mail promotions from Alcon were timed to support the salesman's message to the doctor.

The retailer call

The Alcon salesman also called on the retail druggist. There were 55,000 drugstores in the United States, but according to Alcon management, the Alcon sales force called only on the 10 percent which did the most business in ophthalmological drugs.

In the course of his call on the retail druggist the salesman would make it known which product(s) were being detailed in the area and thus which drug(s) doctors would probably be prescribing. If Alcon had any promotional deals on over-the-counter items (usually an offer of free goods with each purchase, e.g., one free item with each 12 purchased) the MSR would bring these to the druggist's attention. During the call, the MSR checked the druggist's stock of Alcon products and indicated which areas the druggist should replenish. The MSR attempted to persuade the druggist to stock at least one bottle of all Alcon products and several bottles of the fast-moving items. The MSR would write up the order and mail it or take it to the wholesaler of the druggist's choosing.

The wholesaler call

To obtain adequate distribution of a product it was also important to call on drug wholesalers. The average Alcon territory contained six drug wholesalers who served as intermediaries between drug manufacturers and drug retailers. Wholesalers maintained sales staffs on their own by which they contacted many more retail druggists than Alcon was able to do. A wholesaler's salesmen would call on each retail druggist once a week, and would have daily contact with each druggist by telephone. Thus wholesalers, once sold on Alcon products, could shoulder a considerable part of the sales effort.

When a new product was being introduced, or when an existing product was being promoted, the Alcon salesman was expected to call on each wholesaler to gain his support of the product(s) in question. He was instructed to contact him on the product. The purpose of this effort was to persuade the wholesaler's sales manager to use his sales force to give special attention to Alcon's product. The Alcon salesman was supposed to show the sales manager the detail piece on the product, along with any literature he had. While at the wholesaler's he also attempted to see the buyer or purchasing agent to ensure that six to eight weeks' supply of Alcon's products was maintained.

The casewriter observed that few Alcon salesmen were able to execute promotion of new products. The buyer and sales manager of the wholesaler saw about 100 drug salesmen per week and were pressed for time.

The call mix

Alcon's management explained that one salesman called on the doctor, the retailer, and the wholesaler because the calls were highly related and needed careful coordination. For instance, since no order was written in the doctor's office, the salesman would not know if the doctor would actually prescribe the detailed product or not. One of the best ways to find out was to call on the pharmacist a few days after detailing the doctor and inquire whether Dr. X was prescribing the product in question. If the salesman had established a good relationship with the pharmacist, the pharmacist would, in all likelihood, tell him. In fact, the pharmacist often went so far as to let the salesman check through the pharmacy's prescription file to see what all of the doctors were prescribing. With this type of information, the salesman knew which products were selling well and which products he should discuss with a doctor on his next visit.

In addition, Alcon managers emphasized that distribution and demand creation had to be closely coordinated. By handling all three types of calls, the salesman could assure doctors that pharmacists had in stock the drugs prescribed, and he could assure pharmacists that doctors would prescribe the drugs they stocked.

Alcon managers observed that the retailer calls and the wholesaler calls were directly related. First, they were both distribution calls. Secondly, the turnover order took the salesman back to the wholesaler with a definite order from a retailer, thus giving the salesman an opportunity to urge further purchases of Alcon's products.

While Alcon's management had agreed that one salesman should handle both demand creation (doctor calls) and distribution (wholesaler and retailer calls), in the past there had been a difference of opinion in the Marketing Department as to which of the two areas should receive the greatest emphasis. As a result, emphasis had shifted from time to time.

In the past, when a new product was introduced, Alcon management had emphasized demand creation. Historically, this had resulted in a sales increase which was consistent with top management's commitment to rapid growth. As sales began to level off, however, an easy way to boost sales was to emphasize distribution by loading up the wholesaler and retailer with inventory. The distribution campaigns had included deals, the use of promotion money to the wholesaler's salesmen, and sales contests for Alcon's salesmen. In addition, "automatic" shipments (i.e., shipments of goods which Alcon estimated could be sold, but which had not been ordered by the wholesaler) would often be made to wholesalers during these periods.

There had been a number of "distribution campaigns" during periods of slow sales growth. The most recent one had been in May 1964, when a six-months' distribution campaign was launched and a sales contest was initiated, in which the winner from each of the four regions won a trip to Mexico. When the contest was over, however, some wholesalers shipped goods back to Alcon (all of Alcon's sales were guaranteed, i.e., Alcon agreed to take back products which were unsold after a specific time). In one winner's territory, returns exceeded sales for a month or two. During the nine months following the contest, three of the four winners left Alcon.

Such distribution campaigns caused wide fluctuations in sales and strained relations with wholesalers and retailers. Management recognized the undesirable consequences of such actions and concluded that enduring sales growth came only from demand creation. In October 1964, with this in mind, Mr. Leone shifted the emphasis of the sales effort to demand creation. He instructed salesmen to spend 75 percent of their time calling on doctors (compared with 40 percent during the distribution campaign). The salesmen told the casewriter they welcomed this shift in their call mix because they preferred doctor calls to distribution calls. Management believed that men who preferred distribution calls, such as the four contest winners, left the company when the shift in emphasis took place.

Alcon maintained this emphasis on demand creation, and managers stated that they did not intend to return to the practice of using distribution campaigns to boost sales in periods of slow growth.

Administration of salesmen

Alcon, like the rest of the industry, had found that it was difficult to find and keep a man who could perform all of the required functions of the medical sales representative. In the past six years the annual turnover of Alcon's sales force had averaged approximately 33 percent.

Recruiting and selection

The district sales manager was responsible for recruiting and selecting salesmen for his territory. He had an instruction manual to help him. One page was entitled "The Man You Want" and listed the following characteristics:

> Twenty-five to thirty-five years of age.
> Preferably married—stable domestic life.
> College degree.
> Scientific and business courses.
> Above average grades in school.
> Good work history, preferably in sales/marketing.
> Good grooming and physical appearance.
> Good health, past and present.
> Sound financial position.
> Good diction and use of grammar—articulate.
> Able to understand and project emotions and ideas.
> Has self-confidence and poise.
> Self-starter.
> Doesn't object to travel.
> Enjoys working with people.
> Ambitious with maturity.
> Honesty and integrity.
> Enthusiasm and capacity for work.

The district managers used several techniques to find men with these qualifications. When a vacancy occurred in an area, the district manager typically first contacted schools if the opening occurred around commencement time.

Mr. Leone said that Alcon recruited at business schools, in particular, because Alcon liked to hire MBAs. He felt that the training and ambition of MBAs made them compatible with Alcon's objectives and organization.[5] A brochure in the Harvard Business School Placement Office contained the following statement:

The company is small by usual standards, but it offers the opportunity for easy recognition of contribution and rapid promotion to greater management responsibilities. Initial assignments are in field sales. MBAs are expected to reach district manager level within 18–24 months.

If qualified applicants were unavailable at schools, the district sales manager next contacted an employment agency, where he would typically interview about 40 people. After the first round of interviews he would narrow his interests to 10–12 applicants, with whom he would have second interviews.

If he was unable to fill the vacant positions on his sales force using these sources, a district sales manager would then use a classified advertisement to recruit applicants. One district sales manager had used the following ad several times under such circumstances:

Careers in Sales

Leading to sales management for qualified men based on performance. Young dynamic pharmaceutical company, growth rate of 47 percent per year. Leader in its field has openings local and away. Creative ambitious men with drive and determination, college degree. Science background helpful. Unusual remuneration and incentive plan tops in the industry. Excellent training program, liberal benefits, insurance, pension, stock options, profit sharing. Rare opportunity for growth for self-motivators. Men with an outstanding record of success in selling considered. Call OL 3–4818, Sunday, 1 to 5 p.m.

Resumes to
Box X
[City, State]

---

[5] Mr. Leone believed that Alcon had hired approximately 20 MBAs within the last ten years. Four to eight had left the company. Mr. Leone identified those still with Alcon as listed below. He believed that there were two others whom he had not included on the list.

Salesman	School where received MBA	Present position
A	HBS '57	Financial Vice President
B*	HBS '58	Marketing Vice President
C	HBS '60	Comptroller's Department
D	HBS '59	Product Manager
E*	HBS '62	Product Manager
F*	HBS '64	Assistant Product Manager
G	Chicago	International Comptroller
H*	North Texas	Salesman
I*	Northwestern	District Manager
J	Wharton '65	District Manager

* Began by working as an MSR.

This district sales manager reported to the casewriter that the ad had brought him an average of 75 resumés each time he had used it in a large, East Coast city. Forty to 45 of these resumés he could discard immediately on the basis of age or educational background. After telephone interviews with the remaining 30 to 35 applicants, the sales manager would discard 10 to 15 more. He would then personally interview the remaining 10 to 15 applicants.

One district manager was quoted as saying, "My selection is generally made during the second interview as to my first, second, and third choices for a man to fill a vacancy. Then I have two or three more interviews with these men and their wives. The average interview time for a man who is hired is a total of approximately ten hours. By the time he is hired we really know one another and what we expect from one another. In rare instances, where there is competition for manpower for other industries in a given area, I may make a tentative offer on the spot during the first interview. In a case like this the first interview would run one and a half to two hours."

Selection was based primarily on the characteristics listed previously under "The Man You Want." The extent to which applicants fulfilled these characteristics was determined on the basis of information gathered through interviews, on application forms, and testing.

The district sales manager was required to spend a good deal of his time recruiting because of the high turnover in the sales force. In 1965–66, the region with the highest turnover had 6 men out of 19 leave. This region had the equivalent of four sales territories vacant for the year.

Training

After a new salesman was hired he entered a four-week training program, which was under the direction of the DSM and took place in the field. In the first week, the DSM worked with the new salesman and showed him how to call on the doctor, the wholesaler, and the retailer. In the evening the new MSR was expected to learn company policies and procedures and to gain an adequate product knowledge, including (a) basic anatomy, physiology, and pathology of the eye; (b) basic ocular therapy and medical concepts; (c) basic pharmacology; (d) Alcon product advantages; and (e) competitive products.

During the second and third weeks the new MSR went into the territory of a senior salesman in the district and made as many field calls with the senior salesman as possible, to perfect the first week's training. In addition, he was expected to spend his evenings expanding his product knowledge.

In the fourth week the new MSR was to work in his own area under the supervision of the DSM. At this point the MSR was to be making most of the calls while the DSM was observing. The DSM made sure that the new MSR was prepared to handle his own territory.

This concluded the formal training of the new MSR. After this initial training the DSM worked with the salesman only periodically to give him any additional training that was necessary. The new salesmen reported to the casewriter that while an effort was made to do this, the DSM was often too busy to carry out the training as planned.

In order to develop field sales managers, Alcon introduced, at the end of 1964, a program for training managers called the Advanced Development Program (ADP). Outstanding salesmen who were interested in advancement were included in this program (there were nine ADPs in the summer of 1966). The program consisted of each ADP doing a number of individual projects which were usually activities performed by field managers; for example, the ADP would recruit and train new salesmen. Mr. Leone said, "Four of our best field managers today came from this program."

Control and evaluation

In order to keep track of what each salesman was doing, Alcon required that two reports be submitted by each salesman to the DSM and the home office, including the following:

1. A daily report of all calls made, by type of call, and the number and amount of turnover orders. This report is cumulative on a monthly basis.
2. An expense voucher to be filled in daily and mailed to Fort Worth on Saturday morning.

In addition, the MSR was required to keep territory records, including a doctor call book with information such as the doctor's day off, the best time to see him, his specialty, etc.

Once a year the district sales manager conducted a performance appraisal of the MSR. The DSM then made a recommendation for a salary increase for the salesman based on this performance appraisal and the MSRs commission for the past year. Management maintained that the introduction of regular performance appraisals greatly improved the compensation of the sales force at Alcon, making it more equitable by relating salary increases more closely to performance. In addition the company made it a practice to terminate salesmen who did not meet the high standards set for salesmen.

Compensation

Compensation for salesmen was in the form of salary plus commission. Alcon's starting salaries ranged from $400–$700 per month, depending on the training and experience of the new man. In 1966 Alcon's salesmen's salaries ranged from $500–$916 per month, and averaged $580 per month. Each salesman was eligible for a salary increase each year, and the annual increase could be up to one half of the commission he received the preceding year. Exhibit 4 presents salesmen's salaries from 1962 to 1966.

Management expressed the opinion that although Alcon had been behind the industry in compensation a few years before, their significant salary increases in the last three years had made Alcon quite competitive

---

Exhibit 4
Salesmen's salaries at Alcon, Inc.*

Year ending	Average annual salary of all salesmen
April 30, 1962	$5,760
April 30, 1963	6,168
April 30, 1964	6,744
April 30, 1965	6,900
April 30, 1966	6,960

* Excludes commission.

Exhibit 5
Data for the pharmaceutical industry's salesmen's total compensation

(Salary and commission, 1964)

100th percentile	$25,000
75th percentile	9,000
50th percentile	8,000
25th percentile	7,000
1st percentile	5,000

A group of 28 companies manufacturing drugs, chemicals, and cosmetics reported the following data concerning the compensation (salary and commission) of their salesmen:

Compensation for:

Highest man		Top half of sales force	
Midpoint	Range	Midpoint	Range
$12,000	$8,000–$25,000	$9,000	$8,000–$10,000

Lowest man		Lowest half of sales force	
Midpoint	Range	Midpoint	Range
$6,000	$5,000–$7,000	$7,000	$6,000–$8,000

Source: *Sales Management,* January 21, 1966.

in the drug industry. Exhibit 5 presents data on the drug industry's compensation of salesmen in 1964.

Commissions were handled in the following manner: a new salesman was placed on commission after three months of employment with Alcon and following a performance review and approval by all levels of field supervision. Commissions were paid twice each fiscal year and were based on 10 percent of increased sales after total MSR expenses (including car expenses, motel, telephone, meals) had been deducted. The following is an illustration of the commission plan:

MSRs sales in 1965	$75,000
in 1964	50,000
Sales increase	$25,000
Salesman's expenses	−12,000
	$13,000
Commission (10 percent)	$ 1,300

The current commission plan had been introduced in 1960 when the company was having trouble controlling salesmen's expenses. Recently some Alcon managers had expressed the feeling that the current plan was not equitable because it penalized the salesmen with a large territory requiring overnight travel. Total commissions paid to the 70 salesmen in 1965–66 were $26,000, ranging from $0–$1,500 individually, but Mr. Leone observed that 80 percent of the commission payments went to 20 percent of the salesmen.

Thirty-eight salesmen had been hired and retained since 1964. Of these more than two thirds were between the ages of 25 to 30 and more than three fourths were married. Virtually all of them had earned a Bachelor's degree; these were in a wide range of fields. Prior to joining Alcon they had 31 collective years of sales experience and 52 years' experience in a variety of occupations.

Attitudes of managers, salesmen, and customers

In the course of gathering material for the case, the casewriter interviewed individuals at different organizational levels within Alcon. In addition, he interviewed a number of eye doctors, drug retailers, and drug wholesalers concerning their attitudes toward drug salesmen.

The two DSMs interviewed by the casewriter reported that other activities prevented them from spending 75 percent of their time with the MSR as their job description required. With a high turnover in the sales force, it was necessary for them to spend a great deal of time on recruiting and selection of new salesmen. One DSM had three vacancies to fill in a four-month period, and it was necessary for him to spend nearly all his time trying to fill those vacancies during that period. The DSM also reported that "the job has changed a lot in the past two to three years. Before, I just worked with the men, but now I am running an organization. I hire, fire, train, and evaluate men. I also run a good bit of the sales meetings. We have one about every two months."

Views of selected MSRs

Don Wade, an Alcon salesman for eight years, made the following comments, which seemed typical of Alcon's older salesmen:

The most important thing is to sell the doctor and create demand for your product. If you just get it into the retailer and then the doctor doesn't write it you have problems because the retailer will send it back. I provide information to the doctor. The doctors ask me about drugs, ours and our competition's; they ask me what they are and what they do, etc. If I don't know about a product I don't try to bluff it, so they trust me. If a competitor's product is good I tell the doctor it is. I've been with Alcon a long time, so I know the doctors and they write my products. When I come around with a new drug the doctors trust me, so they'll start right in and use it.

The doctor call is indirect selling; you don't write up an order and you don't know if you have sold him. That's what makes it such a challenge. I enjoy trying to match wits with the doctor and I can tell about 80 percent of the time whether I have sold him or not. But you have to know what he is saying. A doctor will promise you anything. They want to be nice to you like they are to their patients, so they will say they will use your drug and then they won't follow up and prescribe it.

You have to use finesse with the doctor—it's a soft sell. You have to know where he went to school, his likes and dislikes. The more you can get him to talk the better you can sell him. The doctor is more professional and more ethical.

A distribution call, on the other hand, is direct selling. The pharmacist is more interested in money so you have to show how your product will make him a profit. The pharmacist trusts me so I just check his inventory, decide what he needs, and write up the turnover order. Usually, he doesn't even see it. I just send it to the wholesaler. It's the same way with the wholesalers. I have a good relationship with them and they just let me write up the orders.

An interview with John Cook revealed the attitude of the younger, more ambitious salesmen. Cook had been with Alcon just one year and was described by the DSM as a good management prospect. He said:

It's a hard sell with the doctor. You're in there as a salesman to sell your product. You really have to know your doctors because you can really pin some of them down and get a commitment to write your product, but with others you can't do much. So you have to know which ones to push. You have to get to know the receptionist, too, because she guards the doctor and can prevent you from seeing him.

I would rather call on the doctor because he treats me like a professional man. It's just a chore to make retail calls. I spend 85 percent of my time calling on doctors because I'd rather call on them. Some of our wholesalers are upset because they say Alcon is high pressure as a result of the distribution campaign two years ago.

Bob Jensen, a salesman with three years' experience at Alcon commented:

I studied pre-med in college but I didn't have good enough grades to get into medical school. However, I still wanted some dealings with the medical profession, so after I got some sales experience I came with Alcon. Because the eye doctors know that Alcon only calls on eye doctors, they like to see the Alcon man. So I am accepted more by doctors than the detail men from other companies are.

I enjoy calling on the doctor because he is more professional—ethical. The only problem is that you don't know when you've sold the doctor. You get better feedback from the pharmacist because you write up an order there.

Ninety-nine percent of the doctors accept me very well; about 50 percent of them call me by my first name, but it's taken two years to get on a first-name basis. The doctor would rather discuss products with a friend, so if you have been calling on him a while and he knows you, he'll listen.

Comments from doctors

Doctor Jones was about 45, had a large practice, and also did some work with a well-respected eye clinic in the large eastern city where he practiced. His views were typical of the busy, successful ophthalmologist.

The detail man keeps the doctor informed. He makes the information available before it comes out in the journals (the journals are always months behind) and you can ask questions of him directly.

I like a detail man who is pleasant and sincere, and one who has a knowledge of his product or at least is honest enough to let you know when he doesn't. I also prefer one that makes no demands. Some of them will say, "I'll be back in 10 days to see how you've gotten along with my product," and it puts you on the spot.

When asked which companies were doing the best job of promoting their products, Dr. Jones replied:

The question really should be which ones see you most frequently. The answer is Alcon, Smith Miller Patch, and Upjohn, I guess. I tend to write more of their products when they call frequently and I have more knowledge of their products. I depend on the detail man to get information on things like products, sizes, availability, etc. They keep me up to date on new developments.

Dr. Barron was about 50 years old. Barron, less busy than some other eye doctors, commented that detail men could be quite helpful:

I am influenced by the detail man. I have an emotional affinity for him and he leaves a lot of samples. I feel an obligation to him and I'll write his drugs. But I don't like the overpowering salesman. I like a neat, well-dressed, polite man who just gives me information. I think all detail men are frustrated doctors— you wouldn't really want to be a detail man. Generally the salesmen are very nice people and very cooperative.

Pharmacist's view of the salesman

A pharmacist was asked about his feelings toward the salesman and the companies they represented. He expressed his views as follows:

The ethical drug salesman tells us about new products, price changes, and what's being detailed, because that's what sells. He comes in and writes up the order. Then we check it over and cut back if he's put in too much of any product.

All the major companies do a good job. Upjohn, Merck, etc. But the small companies have high turnover. They'll have a new man in here about every month. We sometimes have a problem with them.

The salesman expects us to keep his products in stock; he sells the products to the doctor. He also asks for information on what the doctors are writing. We have a prescription file and he's welcome to look through it.

Wholesaler's view of the salesman

The following interview with a buyer at a busy wholesaler's gives an indication of his attitude toward salesmen:

I like salesmen who take care of the details on their products, such as price changes, returns, checking inventory, and giving us information on new items.

Also, I don't like pressure. We are trying to sell merchandise and in order to sell we have to buy. We don't need anyone to pressure us. It's just the new man or the fly-by-night guy who gets this pitch from the home office and tries to shove it down our throat. But by and large they tend to be quite professional in their approach.

When asked specifically about Alcon, the buyer said:

They're a little pushy, a little bang-bang. But they are less so now than in the past. They tended to put up these deals at the home office and then put them off on us.

Sales force's view of the marketing effort

A number of managers and salesmen pointed out that the quality of the promotion developed by the product managers could greatly influence a salesman's success. With a high-quality program and the support of direct mail and journal advertising a salesman could significantly increase sales of featured products. The salesmen appeared to agree that the work of the product managers had improved a great deal in the past two to three years, and that they were doing an excellent job.

Many of the salesmen expressed concern, however, about the infrequency with which Alcon had introduced new products. One salesman said that in the past six years Alcon had introduced only "two big new products," and that it was only in those periods that the company had experienced rapid sales growth. One manager pointed out that Alcon had significantly expanded its R&D effort in the past two years and that "we now have in R&D more Ph.D.'s per sales dollar than anyone else in the industry, and we are currently spending 10 percent of sales for that purpose."

Salesmen's views of the company, compensation, and opportunity for advancement

The following is another part of the interview with Don Wade who has been with Alcon over eight years:

You can't make big money in the drug business, and if you compare Alcon with the others in the industry their salary is not the best, but they hit a happy medium. I've been offered more money by other drug companies, but Alcon has a great future and they have a good relationship with the doctors.

Alcon has the best opportunity for advancement in the industry, if you're looking for that. I'm not. I just want to be a salesman. The DSM has to travel too much and I don't want to be away from my family any more than I am now.

Our company has been weak in supervision compared with other drug companies. At least we've been weak in the past. But now they're doing a better job of training a man before they make him a DSM. Nobody can learn the drug business in two years so our managers just haven't had enough field experience.

When asked why so many salesmen had left Alcon, Wade replied:

Alcon promises you the sky in terms of advancement and then they just don't come through. So, when the boys have been here a while and they don't get a promotion as soon as they were told they would, they leave.

Nearly everyone the casewriter interviewed said that they believed that there were excellent opportunities for advancement with Alcon. Management indicated, however, that there were no plans to expand the sales force or the number of field managers in the immediate future. When the casewriter presented this apparent contradiction to Dave Colton, a salesman who had been with Alcon for five months, Colton replied that he expected to advance with Alcon because be believed that there would be an opportunity for him to be promoted into a management position in one of the companies that had been acquired or that would be acquired by Alcon.

Management concern

Management was aware that turnover was high among sales personnel throughout the drug industry (12.1 percent in 1964), but Alcon turnover was a great deal higher than that of other drug companies. In fact, it had been as high as 42 percent in 1964. (Exhibit 6 shows the turnover in Alcon's sales force from 1961 to 1966, and the length of service of the men leaving.)

Exhibit 6

Turnover of Alcon's sales force

Year ending April 30	Percent turnover
1961	35
1962	27
1963	35
1964	42
1965	34
1966	28

Length of service of salesmen terminating

Number of months employment	Number of personnel/percent	Cumulative number of personnel/percent
6 or less	4 (13.8)	4 (13.8)
12 or less	8 (27.6)	12 (41.4)
18 or less	4 (13.8)	16 (55.0)
24 or less	2 (6.9)	18 (62.0)
30 or less	5 (17.2)	23 (79.5)
36 or less	1 (3.5)	24 (82.7)
42 or less	1 (3.5)	25 (86.6)
48 or less	1 (3.5)	26 (89.6)
60 or less	3 (10.3)	29 (100.0)

Management was concerned about the high turnover for several reasons. First of all, it was costly. Although Alcon's figures were not available, one survey reported, "The cost of selecting, training, and supervising a new drug salesman averages $7,612, excluding salary." Just as important as cost was the fact that it took one to two years for a salesman to establish satisfactory relationships with the doctor, the wholesaler, and the retailer. Most of the men who left had been with Alcon less than two and one-half years. These salesmen just barely got to know the customers before leaving.

Mr. Leone was uncertain about why so many men had left Alcon. He indicated that almost all of them said they were leaving because they were not earning enough money, but he was not sure that was the whole reason. Alcon had raised salaries considerably in the past three years, but men were still leaving. Mr. Leone felt that part of the problem may have been the shift in emphasis from "demand" to "distribution" and then back to "demand." Mr. Leone noted that Alcon's higher turnover had occurred in the years when they had distribution campaigns.

Case 3–3
First Federal Savings
Stephen X. Doyle, Jay W. Lorsch

Late in the third quarter of 1974 the board of directors of First Federal Savings requested that their President, Gene Rice, submit a recommendation as to whether or not to grant branch managers a cash bonus that year. According to the company's Management by Objectives system, the granting of the yearly bonus was contingent upon the attainment of specific corporate profit objectives in addition to the individual managers' performance against pre-established MBO targets. Earnings in 1974 were targeted for a 15 percent increase over the 1973 profit of $7,800,000. This 15 percent growth objective was established late in 1973 when management fully expected that First Federal could continue compounding its growth at a rate of 15–20 percent per annum (see Exhibit 1). But the economic slowdown of 1974 hit the savings and loan industry particularly hard with depositors withdrawing their savings to meet living expenses and taking advantage of the higher interest rates offered on short-term treasury bills. This reduction in savings made it difficult to grant mortgages which, in turn, constrained corporate profits.

Gene Rice clearly knew that the 1974 MBO goals and profit objectives would not be met (see Exhibit 2). He commented:

We did a bad job of picking objectives for 1974. We had been lulled to sleep by a fantastic growth rate and a good economy. In 1974 the market went to

Exhibit 1

FIRST FEDERAL SAVINGS OF PHOENIX
Consolidated Five-Year Growth
(in $000 except growth statistics)

	1973	1972	1971	1970	1969
Deposits					
Passbooks	$156,270	$141,450	$106,066	$ 89,563	$ 84,153
Certificates	461,585	344,713	235,850	160,328	127,382
Total	$617,855	$486,163	$341,916	$249,891	$211,535
Loans					
First mortgage	$622,080	$488,111	$343,734	$241,035	$196,919
Property improvement	47,868	40,464	28,966	18,348	11,512
Mobile home	35,977	11,218	6,527	2,312	—
Other	12,614	9,029	8,687	8,395	8,310
Total	$718,539	$548,822	$387,914	$270,090	$216,741
Growth statistics					
Number savings accounts	137,703	109,415	92,867	82,610	80,019
Number first mortgage loans	26,072	22,540	17,998	16,099	15,409
Number property improvement loans	15,872	13,471	10,674	8,149	6,225
Number mobile home loans	2,046	1,128	578	177	—
Number full service offices	27	22	20	19	18
Operating results					
Total revenue	$ 57,092	$ 41,324	$ 26,979	$ 19,648	$ 15,404
Total expenses	46,414	32,810	22,493	17,548	13,885
Income before income taxes and extraordinary items	10,678	8,514	4,486	2,100	1,519
Income taxes	2,850	2,100	835	370	245
Income before extraordinary items	7,828	6,414	3,651	1,730	1,274
Extraordinary items	—	—	668	—	—
Net Income	$ 7,828	$ 6,414	$ 4,319	$ 1,730	$ 1,274

hell, and our targeted 15 percent increase in profit before tax was not realistic. You know we base our bonus on the company meeting its profit objectives. In the past years we have been able to give handsome bonuses, and in return, I expect a lot of our people. If our managers don't perform, then we are doing them a disservice by keeping them.

Rice considered the MBO system to be the cornerstone of management productivity and morale. He wondered if he should recommend a bonus to reward management for their exceptional efforts even though the desired results had not been achieved. If he did give the bonus, what impact would it have on the future credibility of the MBO system? (See Exhibit 3.)

Exhibit 2

FIRST FEDERAL SAVINGS AND WHOLLY OWNED SUBSIDIARIES
Consolidated Statement of Income
(for the six months ended June 30)

Revenues	1974	1973
Interest on loans	$29,291,641	$21,225,843
Loan fees and service charges	4,462,150	3,171,001
Investment income	2,260,391	1,290,610
Real estate operations—net	624,362	368,920
Other	799,976	818,433
	$37,438,520	$26,874,807
Expenses		
Interest on savings deposits	$21,435,918	$14,673,396
General and administrative expenses	8,007,838	5,083,259
Provision for loan losses	74,863	-0-
Other interest expense	3,480,144	1,326,407
	$32,998,763	$21,083,062
Income before income taxes	$ 4,439,757	$ 5,791,745
Provision for income taxes	1,240,344	1,542,180
Net Income	$ 3,199,413	$ 4,249,565

Exhibit 3

Carrot & Stick*

**More Concerns Tie
Bonuses to Meeting
Goals for Workers**

Programs Spur Employes
   To Do More, Firms Say;
   But Some Problems Seen

A Link to the Crime Rate

By Roger Ricklefs
Staff Reporter of The Wall Street Journal

Fourteen years ago, when Gene E. Rice was a branch manager of First Federal Savings & Loan Association of Phoenix, he received an annual bonus of exactly $580, and he didn't like it. "All the branch managers and all the vice presidents got the same thing. I thought I was working harder than the rest and I thought I should be paid more. So it was a negative incentive," he says.

Now Mr. Rice is president of the bank, and he has a bonus plan that he likes a lot better. Today payouts range up to 40 percent of salary—and down to nothing. The amount depends on the individual's performance against pre-established goals, ranging from the number of new savings accounts to the number of speeches delivered to real-estate groups.

The new bonus plan, which grew out of the "management-by-objectives" program the bank started in 1968, has "definitely encouraged people to work harder and has also helped us attract good people," Mr. Rice says.

Like First Federal, hundreds of companies have adopted management-by-objectives or similar plans in recent years, but they operated independently of bonus programs. The more jaded executives have often figured that they were just another management fad. But now companies are giving these programs the bite that counts: They're tying the plans to the size of paychecks.

Exhibit 3 (continued)

"A Growing Practice"

"Five years ago, setting the bonus on the basis of management by objectives was a rarity, but today it is a growing practice," says George A. Goddu, a principal and compensation specialist at Peat, Marwick, Mitchell & Co., the large accounting firm. Recently, International Business Machines Corp., Bendix Corp., CNA Financial Corp., PepsiCo Inc., and numerous others have all moved in one way or another to relate their bonuses more directly to the recipient's actual performance.

One result is that in companies where almost everybody with comparable rank could count on getting similar bonuses, executives now find their peers getting bonuses much smaller—or much bigger—than their own. Some of them are shocked by the discovery, especially when the difference may amount to thousands of dollars.

At First Texas Financial Corp., a Dallas savings-bank holding company, bonuses used to range up to 10 percent of salary. Starting last year, they ranged from zero to 30 percent of pay. Until last year, nobody at Norton Co., the large Worcester, Mass., abrasives maker, received any bonus. But in a new plan for 130 executives, some got a 30 percent bonus last year, and seven hapless managers again received nothing, the company says.

Bonuses of 100% of Salary

One Midwestern conglomerate started a new plan last year with specific performance goals and potential bonuses ranging up to 100 percent of salary. This replaced a program that left awards completely to management's discretion and paid 10 percent to 18 percent of salary, says Frederick A. Teague, vice president and compensation specialist at Booz, Allen & Hamilton Inc., management consultants.

Sometimes the new programs generate enormous sums for executives who rate highly. In a new performance-oriented plan at IBM, Frank T. Cary, chairman, earned a bonus of $246,000 last year, well over his salary of $200,000.

But sometimes, too, subordinates get awards while their bosses get nothing. At CNA Financial, the big insurance, finance and real-estate concern, where corporate earnings declined last year, the top officers didn't receive any bonuses. At subsidiaries, however, bonuses ranged up to $25,000, Frank Metzger, senior vice president, says.

Practically all of the new plans operate by setting fixed goals in advance, usually starting with profits. At First Texas Financial, for instance, the new bonus plan has a profit goal "that has to be met or nothing else happens," John L. Ingle, president, says. But in addition, the Dallas bank-holding company sets profit goals for individual units, then looks at other factors such as penetration of market in a given field, reduction of operating expenses and improvement of facilities.

What's a "Good Job"?

Of the nation's largest 100 companies, probably 30 to 40 now set bonuses by some sort of pre-agreed formula for what constitutes "a good job" and vary the awards from one profit center to another, says Graef S. Crystal, vice president of Towers, Perrin, Forster & Crosby Inc., compensation consultants. This figure compares with only five to 10 companies five years ago, he says. In addition, some companies, including PepsiCo, say they are constantly striving to make the goals more specific and detailed.

Companies find that the bonus plans can encourage the pursuit of all kinds of goals, not just increased profit. A plan started last year at Bendix includes routine financial goals but also adds objectives in "management development," minority and female employment and safety and health, says Kenneth L. Otto, vice president for personnel and organization development. Thus, a Bendix executive's bonus now depends in part on how well he conducts college recruiting, provides able executives to other units of the corporation, works with high schools to attract minority employes and meets goals for upward mobility of women and blacks, the official says.

J. C. Penney Co., which has paid cash bonuses based on annual results for many years, started a program in 1971 that awards bonuses in Penney stock based on results over a three-year period. "We wanted to get people interested in longer-range development." Ronald A. Johnson, compensation manager, says.

Outside of business, the incentive-bonus principle is being applied to crime fighting. The Orange, Calif., police department last year started a program that boosts police pay if

Exhibit 3 (concluded)

crime declines in four categories considered responsive to improved police prevention work: burglary, robbery, rape and auto theft. So far this year, crime in these categories has declined 17 percent from a year ago, and the police have received one raise of 2 percent. Police Chief Merrill Duncan says. As a check against fiddling with statistics, outsiders audit the program by monitoring reports of police calls, he adds.

Many companies say they are pleased with the performance-bonus approach. "You see results right away." says Samuel N. Hibbard, Norton Co.'s director of compensation and financial benefits. "An incentive plan focuses effort on what management wants effort to go into."

Knowing What Is Expected

By the same token, the new programs also help executives know exactly what management expects and why they are getting the money. Bendix Corp.'s Mr. Otto, who has pushed performance bonuses, says: "When I came here two years ago, I asked people. 'Do you know how you earned your bonus last year?' Most people didn't really know, and that is what got me on this kick."

In addition, companies say the specific goals and criteria of the new incentive programs force executives to reward the high performers and to squeeze the inept. "Our bonuses previously tended to be more or less the same for everybody." says Roland Beers, PepsiCo's personnel vice president. "Executives are reluctant to differentiate."

Mr. Crystal of Towers Perrin says that "if there isn't some sort of formula, everybody

tends to get the same thing because you can't blame the disparity of awards on an inanimate object. If you have an infinite amount of discretion, you don't use any." The consequent similarity of bonuses grates on the strong performers who feel they aren't being recognized, executives say.

Problems with the Plans

But performance-bonus plans take time to set up and can create problems of their own. "Nobody has ever designed a plan like this that worked right the first time." says Mr. Ingle of First Texas Financial. "Some of the goals we set had to be shifted around during the year due to things happening over which we had no control," he adds.

Mr. Crystal of Towers Perrin adds: "A lot of companies try basing the awards on meeting budgets. This gives the division manager a motive to set the budgeted profit too low. In some companies, people are always pleading to readjust the formula. It can get to be sort of like the chairman of the board holding night court."

Mr. Crystal says that one New York conglomerate that used to pay executives fairly similar bonuses switched in 1970 to bonuses based on divisional performance, but it went back to the old system last year. "The problem was that half the division heads got nothing, the others got up to $50,000 a year and the chairman wasn't sure that the right people were getting the $50,000. One big problem was a division president who got a huge award. But he had done well mostly because a key competitor was on strike for six months," Mr. Crystal says.

* Reprinted from *The Wall Street Journal,* © Dow Jones & Co., 1974. Reprinted with permission.

About First Federal Savings

First Federal Savings and Loan Association of Phoenix received its charter on November 1, 1934. In 1935 First Federal and the State Building and Loan Association initiated a merger. The merger was completed on February 2, 1938, and the surviving company, First Federal, recorded assets at the end of the year of $1,982,495.

Management, recognizing the growth potential in the Arizona economy, initiated a program of branch expansion. The criteria established for opening a new branch were the potential economic growth in the area and the marketing advantages of offering convenient services to local residents. By the late 1960s First Federal was serving ten cities located in four counties of Arizona. According to management, the development of these branches gave the company a unique competitive advantage, because in nearly every instance a branch opening was the forerunner of the development of a local shopping center.

This planned expansion continued through the late 1960s and early 1970s. In 1973, First Federal became the 25th largest savings and loan association in the nation. Combined assets stood at $778,000,000 (see Exhibit 4). By the end of 1974 First Federal planned to operate 27 branches

Exhibit 4
Recent financial trends

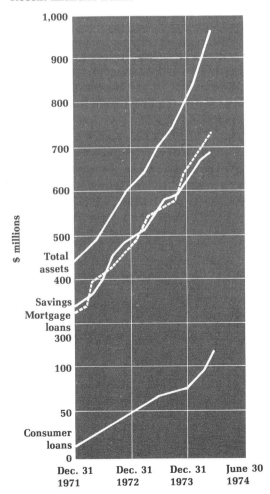

and five subsidiaries specializing in management services to the real estate industry and thrift institutions.

MBO and the bonus plan

In the eyes of top management superior employee performance would be the key to accelerated corporate growth and profits. Both George Leonard, chairman of the board and chief executive officer, and Gene Rice felt that if outstanding performance were to be expected, rewards of a sizable amount must be given at relatively frequent intervals. In 1968 a bonus program was introduced based on the amount of annual profits. The cost of the incentive plan was considered to be self-liquidating because the bonus pool came from funds which were generated above and beyond the expected profit levels.

Also, in 1968 a Management by Objectives system was introduced. MBO was considered to be a cornerstone of the bonus plan, because the MBO structure, with its clear and measurable goals, provided the opportunity to reward managers for results. Gene Rice commented on the MBO and bonus systems:

In the 1960s we were just an ordinary savings and loan association but we wanted to be something more. We were in need of an entrepreneurial climate, while ours was very much security and image conscious.

The MBO system was instituted as a planning tool for the future and the changes it would bring. The bonus was added as a sidelight to "help make things happen!" We viewed the bonus program as a vehicle which could be used to recruit the entrepreneurs which the bank's more aggressive stance would require.

The MBO process began late in the third quarter when the branch managers established financial and nonfinancial goals for the coming year. Each branch manager forwarded his/her goals to regional headquarters for approval. Often the regional manager and the branch manager renegotiated projections before the final results were forwarded to corporate headquarters in Phoenix where all the branch and divisional goals were combined into an annual profit plan. At the branch level, the following goals were typical:

MBO Targets—Branch Office

Financial goals

1. Produce a net savings increase of x dollars.
2. Produce a net increase in mortgage loans of x dollars.
3. Produce a net increase in consumer loans of x dollars.
4. Maintain sales, personnel, and office expenses within budgeted amounts.

Nonfinancial goals

1. Give one speech per month to community groups.
2. Complete one course at a local college per semester.
3. Serve on board of a community service agency.
4. Cross-train two employees per quarter.

Gene Rice expected each manager to be an outstanding example of First Federal in his area. He commented:

> *The company has a commitment to Arizona and I expect our managers not only to run the best savings and loan in regard to profit but also to become involved in community service. In fact this commitment is specified in our nonfinancial targets. We don't just want a good looking branch office. I expect every manager to be a statesman in his community, to offer services and leadership just as George Leonard does on a national basis. Sure it is expecting a lot, but our managers know that they will be rewarded for their performance.*

Each month the local manager received individual feedback in the form of a computer report on his office's performance against monthly financial objectives. In addition, regional management was expected to interact with local branch managers about performance variances and the local manager's progress on nonfinancial objectives. Participators in the bonus plan were as follows (see Exhibit 5):

I. *Upper Management Group*
   Chairman of the Board
   President
   Executive Vice President
   President First Service Mortgage Corporation
   Mortgage Loan Division Manager
   Savings and Branch Operations Division Manager
   Consumer Loan Division Manager
   Finance Division Manager
   Data Processing Division Manager
   Vice President, Personnel
   House Counsel
   Association Secretary
   Regional Managers (3)

II. *Department Heads and Specialist Group*
   Mortgage Loan Administration Manager
   P.I. Production Manager
   Accounting Department Manager
   Assistant Data Processing Manager
   Appraisal Department Manager
   Loan Officers (2)

Systems and Procedures Manager
Mobile Home Loan Manager
Treasurer

III.   *Branch Managers Group*
All branch managers

As previously stated, the amount of money available to the total bonus pool was based on profit generated above expected levels. The Executive Salary Committee, based on the Association's yearly forecasted profit plan, determined the profit levels that represented expected amounts and the levels that represented superior performance beyond what was expected, and that deserved to be rewarded. According to this policy a bonus would not be paid in 1974 unless 1974 profits exceeded 1973 profits by at least 15 percent.

The amount of the dollar reward to a manager was influenced by the individual's performance against his/her pre-agreed-to objectives set at the beginning of the year. The regional managers would review their subordinates and recommend a bonus amount. However, the actual deter-

Exhibit 5
Organization Chart—1974

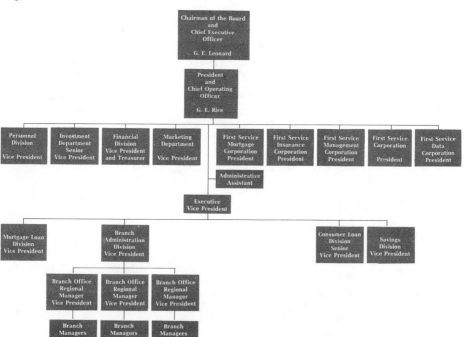

mination of the bonus was the prerogative of the Executive Salary Committee. Generally speaking, the committee used the following guidelines to approve individual rewards:

1. The first 50 percent of the bonus pool should be allocated to an eligible employee by the percent his/her salary is to the total salaries of all eligible employees in the incentive plan.
2. The second 50 percent of the bonus pool should be distributed with discretion by the committee.
3. No bonus should exceed 40 percent of an individual's base annual salary.

The branch managers

True to Gene Rice's expectations, the branch managers were perceived by the casewriter to be talented, highly motivated "statesmen" who actively sought to increase the influence of First Federal in their respective areas. Typical of the managers was Harry Turner, who was in charge of the Scottsdale branch. After graduating from Arizona State University in 1966, Harry entered the Air Force's flight training school. Harry remained in the Air Force for five years as a pilot. In 1971, Harry resigned his commission and joined First Federal as a management trainee. Harry commented about his experience at First Federal:

I was really impressed when I met Gene Rice. He told me that what was important was performance. If I performed, I would get paid for it . . . 1974 has been a hard year . . . I know that if the company does not hit a certain income level I will not get a bonus. It is hard to admit but I am programming myself for no bonus. What would bother me is if we hit 75 percent of our corporate profit objective and we get zero reward. The company is still making millions and we should get part of the pie. If the bonus is small or nonexistent, I would wonder what all the heartache, sweat and struggle is about. This year I think a $4,000 bonus would be fantastic, $2,500 acceptable, and anything under $2,000 very disappointing. Another important part of the bonus is that it has influenced my wife's attitude . . . branch managers tend to put in a lot of time. A $4,000 Christmas bonus can have a lot of meaning. From top management's point of view, the bonus could be a real problem because if Gene Rice pays this year, I might not be so concerned about meeting my financial objectives next year.

Another branch manager, Tom Walsh, provided more insight on the implications of Gene Rice's decision. Tom was middle-aged, a vice president and manager of the successful Tucson branch. Tom was recruited by Gene Rice to open up the new Tucson office. Previously he had been employed by Prudential Insurance as a district director of mortgage loans. Tom commented about MBO:

Before MBO we were all striving and working hard but not in a coordinated manner; MBO has made our goals more precise. We set targets for ourselves and we direct our efforts to meet these goals. The part that I like best about MBO is that it gives me an opportunity to see my own personal contribution to the company. You know, I guess I am a company man. The company has treated me very well and I feel proud about what First Federal is trying to accomplish. When I came on board I had a major hip operation. Both Gene and George Leonard knew about the operation and that I would be laid up for a couple of months. They told me not to worry, to go up to Tucson and just talk to customers. In regard to the bonus situation this year, I would love the extra dollars, but if it is not in the cards I don't think I would feel short-changed. The company and my job reward me in many ways. We have a chance to help others, generate new ideas, and see results from our efforts.

Ray Walker managed a medium-size branch in the southwest section of Phoenix. Ray's branch was situated at a busy intersection. Each corner of the intersection was occupied by a competing bank or savings and loan. Ray had two children and was a graduate of Arizona State University with a BA in Business Management. His present assignment was the third management position he had held since graduating from the company's management training program in 1969. Ray had a number of opinions about his work and 1974. He commented:

I was transferred into this office and I have had to accept someone else's goals. This is a growing problem because of expansion and the promotion-from-within policy. I am not sure that I agree with all the targets set by my predecessor, but the point is that I still am going to be judged on those targets. Right now I am beginning to think about my targets for next year. As a branch manager I set my own goals in key areas like savings deposit, mortgage loans, consumer loans, and expenses. I submit my forecasts to the regional headquarters, sometimes we disagree and then we negotiate. This forecasting is a very complex problem. I guess the only way to do it is to thoroughly know your area. But of course no one accurately predicted what happened recently. This year we changed our goals in midyear. We shifted our emphasis from generating new mortgages to developing more savings deposits. In order to meet my new savings objectives I hired six new tellers and the cost of these six tellers has placed me way above my expense budget. I know it and my boss knows it, but I do not expect to have my bonus penalized for being over budget. The bonus plan is one of the two reasons I am here today. The other reason is the opportunity for personal growth. If there is no bonus this year there will be a tremendous morale problem among managers. At my last branch assignment in Flagstaff I received a very mediocre bonus, and boy—was I discouraged! It wasn't the dollars that were important, it was my own feeling of self-worth. The bonus tells me how much the company appreciates my work. The severe winter storm hurt the Flagstaff tourist industry. We had over 200 inches of snow. Most businesses, instead of depositing, had to withdraw savings just to survive. I really put out and met four out of five goals, but as I mentioned, my bonus was small. I felt that the company did not appreciate my efforts and that they were inflexible. I was eventually promoted out of the office and I often wonder in my own mind if I did a poor job there. I hope I did okay but perhaps the company was disappointed in me.

Senior management

George Leonard, chairman and chief executive officer, was an acknowledged industry leader and spokesman. Leonard had recently returned from Washington where he was working with a number of congressmen on legislation that would affect the savings and loan industry. Leonard commented:

When I joined the Association, it was an autocratic institution. All decisions were made by the managing officer. Operationally, we were just not working together and there seemed to be little commitment or cooperation. I also think we tended to be short-sighted and were making decisions that would be beneficial on a short-term basis only.

I soon realized that, if we were to continue our growth and expansion, authority would have to be delegated down. With the delegation of authority and accompanying accountability, I believed that a reward system had to be set up that would motivate young and talented managers to grow with us. While a bonus had previously been paid, I know that there was a lot of discontent because the bonus was being given arbitrarily, with people at the top getting most of the dollars. One of the first things I did was to bring in some outside help, a consultant who started to make us think about our own corporate goals and industry position. These sessions led us to the conclusion that we wanted to be Number One in the savings and loan industry. To achieve this goal, we designed and implemented the MBO system and then later on tied the bonus in with achievement of MBO targets. The results have been outstanding. We have clear objectives, there is cooperation, and we have developed a group of talented and dedicated managers. This year we will not hit our target of 15 percent increase in profit before taxes. Our bonus is based on results, but I am concerned that we will ruin the spirit of the organization if we do not give a bonus.

Bill Blodgett was a vice president who had direct line responsibility for the 27 branch offices (Exhibit 5). Blodgett felt that MBO had made significant contributions, but that he had a problem on his hands in 1974. He commented:

In a bad economy the company may not meet its profit objectives but I could have a number of branches that are meeting or exceeding their office objectives. How do I tell them that there is no bonus this year? How do I motivate them next year?

Another vice president, Dave Braun, was in charge of the Financial Division. Braun graduated from Arizona State University in 1937 with a BA in accounting and returned to ASU in the late 1950s to earn an MBA. Braun commented about MBO:

We have the problem of matching numbers with behavior. When McSweeney and Associates, our management consultants, originally sold us the MBO approach, it was based on a rigid formula of profit attainment; 1973 was a good year with a $7,800,000 profit and we also had a good bonus. This year, the bonus situation has not been decided. We are accruing funds, but I don't know if they will be dispensed. I am not sure what my decision would be if I were Gene Rice . . . . On one side of the argument is the position that the goals in and of themselves are important. If we don't make our targets as a company, then there just is no dollar bonus that year. Also, how can we establish believable goals if we say one thing and then do another? On the other side of the argument is the fact that everyone has made a tremendous effort this year. We have achieved some of our objectives. If we do not give a bonus, then we are not acknowledging the hard work and flexibility of our staff. We asked our managers to shift gears right in the middle of the year. They shifted from an emphasis on new mortgages to an emphasis on generating new savings accounts . . . . We came up with a number of innovative marketing ideas, and our branch managers picked up the ball and started generating new accounts. I guess my main worry with the bonus this year is concern for motivation next year . . . . Would suspension of the 1974 bonus have serious negative impact on our managers?

Reading 3–1
Reward systems*
Edward E. Lawler III

Organizations distribute a large number of rewards to their members every day. Pay, promotions, fringe benefits, and status symbols are perhaps the most apparent but certainly not all of the important rewards. Because these rewards are important, the ways they are distributed have profound effects on the quality of work life that employees experience as well as on the effectiveness of organizations.

Despite the importance of rewards in organizations, most of the writings concerned with quality of work life have tended to ignore or play down their impact. This is a serious oversight and one that needs to be corrected if organizations are to be designed in ways that provide a high quality of work life. One reason for this oversight may be the often-made assumption that there is a very simple and direct relationship between the amount of reward received and the quality of work life. If this view is accepted, then improving the quality of work life is simply a matter of giving everyone more rewards. The research that has been done, however, shows that this is too simple a view. Some rewards have been found to contribute more to a high quality of work life than others and problems of equity cannot be solved simply by giving more rewards. These findings will be reviewed later in this chapter when we focus on the characteristics of different rewards and on some of the approaches to reward system design that promise to increase both the quality of work life and organizational effectiveness. But before specific rewards and reward practices are considered, it is necessary to review briefly what is known about the determinants of people's affective reactions to rewards, and about the impact of reward systems on organizational effectiveness.

REWARD SYSTEMS AND INDIVIDUAL SATISFACTION

A great deal of research has been done on what determines whether individuals will be satisfied with the rewards they receive from a situation. This research has shown that satisfaction is a complex reaction to a

* Reprinted by permission from chap. 3, "Reward Systems," in *Improving Life at Work: Behavioral Science Approaches to Organizational Change,* ed. J. R. Hackman and J. L. Suttle (Santa Monica, Calif.: Goodyear Publishing, 1977).

situation and is influenced by a number of factors. The research can be summarized in five conclusions:

1. *Satisfaction with a reward is a function of both how much is received and how much the individual feels should be received.* Most theories of satisfaction stress that people's feelings of satisfaction are determined by a comparison between what they receive and what they feel they should receive or would like to receive (Locke, 1969). When individuals receive less than they believe they should, they are dissatisfied; when they receive more than they believe they should, they tend to feel guilty and uncomfortable (Adams, 1965). Feelings of overreward seem to be easily reduced by individuals and therefore are very infrequent (surveys often show about five percent of an employee group feel overpaid). Feelings of overreward are usually reduced by individuals changing their perceptions of the situation. For example, they increase their perceptions of their worth, or their perceptions of the amount of pay deserved. Feelings of underreward are less easily reduced and often can be reduced only by an actual change in the objective situation—by higher pay or a new job.

2. *People's feelings of satisfaction are influenced by comparisons with what happens to others.* A great deal of research has shown that people's feelings are very much influenced by what happens to others like themselves (Patchen, 1961). People seem to compare what others do and what others receive with their own situations. These comparisons are made both inside and outside the organizations they work in, but are usually made with similar people. As a result of these comparisons, people reach conclusions about what rewards they should receive. When the overall comparison between their situations and those of others is favorable, people are satisfied. When the comparison is unfavorable, they are dissatisfied.

People consider such inputs as their education, training, seniority, job performance, and the nature of their jobs when they think about what their rewards should be. There are often substantial differences among people in which inputs they think should be most important in determining their rewards. Typically, people believe that the inputs that they excel in should be weighed most heavily (Lawler, 1966). This, of course, means that it is very difficult to have everyone satisfied with their rewards, because people tend to make their comparisons based on what is most favorable to them. Individuals also tend to rate their inputs higher than do others. It has often been noted, for example, that average employees rate their job performances at the 80th percentile (Meyer, 1975). Given this and the fact that the average person cannot be rewarded at the 80th percentile, it is not surprising that many individuals often are dissatisfied with their rewards. Still, it is possible to influence how satisfied employees are by altering the total amount of rewards that are given and by altering how those rewards are distributed. Some distribution patterns clearly are seen as more equitable and satisfying, because they are more closely related to the inputs of individuals and therefore to what people feel they should receive.

It is because individuals make comparisons that people who receive less of a given reward often are more satisfied with the amount of the reward they receive than are those who receive more (Lawler, 1971). For example, people who are highly paid in comparison to others doing the same job often are more satisfied than are individuals who receive more (for a different job) but are poorly paid in comparison to others doing the same kind of job.

3. *Overall job satisfaction is influenced by how satisfied employees are with both the intrinsic and extrinsic rewards they receive from their jobs.* A number of writers have debated the issue of whether extrinsic rewards are more important than intrinsic rewards in determining job satisfaction. No study has yet been done that definitely establishes one as more important than the other. Most studies show that both are very important and have a substantial impact on overall satisfaction (Vroom, 1964). It seems quite clear, also, that extrinsic and intrinsic rewards are not directly substitutable for each other, because they satisfy different needs. To have all their needs satisfied, most individuals must receive both the intrinsic and the extrinsic rewards they desire and feel they deserve. This means, for example, that money will not make up for a boring, repetitive job, just as an interesting job will not make up for low pay.

4. *People differ widely in the rewards they desire and in how important the different rewards are to them.* Probably the most frequently and hotly debated topic related to the quality of work life concerns how important different rewards are to employees. One group of writers says money is the most important, while another group says interesting work is (*Work in America, 1971*). Both groups, of course, are able to find examples to support their points of view, because for some people money is most important and for others job content is most important. People differ substantially and in meaningful ways in what is important to them. Some groups, because of their backgrounds and present situations, value extrinsic rewards more than do others. For example, one review gave the following description of a person who is likely to value pay highly: "The employee is a male, young (probably in his twenties); he has low self-assurance and high neuroticism; he comes from a small town or farm background; he belongs to few clubs and social groups, he owns his own home or aspires to own it and probably is a Republican and a Protestant" (Lawler, 1971). People with different personal and background characteristics, on the other hand, value an interesting job more highly.

The research on the importance of different rewards also quite clearly shows that the amount of reward a person has strongly influences the importance attached to it (Alderfer, 1969). In the case of extrinsic rewards, for example, those individuals who have a small amount of a reward typically value it the most. It also appears that the importance individuals attach to rewards shifts as they acquire and lose quantities of different rewards. Some evidence suggests that minimal amounts of the rewards that are required to maintain a person's physical well-being and security are needed before other rewards become very important (cf. Cofer and Appley, 1964).

Overall, reward systems seem to have a greater influence on individuals' satisfaction with rewards than on the importance attached to those rewards (Lawler, 1971). Both satisfaction and importance can be influenced by the amount of rewards that organizations provide. But satisfaction seems to be much more susceptible to influence, because it is directly affected by reward levels. The importance of rewards, on the other hand, is influenced by things that are beyond the control of organizations (such as family background and the economic climate), as well as by satisfaction.

5. *Many extrinsic rewards are important and satisfying only because they lead to other rewards.* There is nothing inherently valuable about many of the things that people seek in organizations. They are important only because they lead to other things or because of their symbolic value. A particular kind of desk or office, for example, often is seen as a reward because it is indicative of power and status. Money is important only because it leads to other things that are attractive, such as food, job security, and status. If money were to stop leading to some or all of these things, it would decrease in importance (Vroom, 1964). Because extrinsic rewards typically lead to other rewards, they can satisfy many needs and thus remain important even when conditions change.

Necessary reward system properties

On the basis of what has been said so far about rewards and satisfaction, we can identify four important properties that any organizational reward system must have if it is to produce a high quality of work life. First, the system must make enough rewards available so that individuals' basic needs are satisfied. If these needs are not met, employees will not be satisfied even if external comparisons are favorable. Fortunately in most work situations the employees' basic needs are satisfied, often because of the requirements of federal legislation and union contracts. It is often pointed out, however, that sometimes these needs are not met, particularly the need for security. When the need is not met, action to increase job security must be taken before a high quality of work life will be present. Just meeting basic needs is not enough.

Second, the reward levels in the organization must compare favorably with those in other organizations. Unless the reward levels compare favorably with what other organizations provide, individuals will not be satisfied with their rewards because they will inevitably note that they are not as well off as others.

Third, the rewards that are available must be distributed in a way that is seen as equitable by the people in the organization. People compare their own situations with those of others inside the organization. And they are likely to be dissatisfied if in their organization people they perceive as less deserving receive more rewards, even though they themselves are in a favorable position with respect to the outside market. People have a sense of equity, which involves considerations of how much they receive in comparison to what others around them receive, regardless of the absolute amount they receive or their position in the outside market. To construct a reward system that is high on internal (within organization) equity, it is necessary to base that system on the perceptions of the people in the organization. As will be emphasized later, the most direct way to take these perceptions into account is to have people in the organization make the decisions about how much different individuals will be rewarded.

Finally, the reward system must deal with organization members as individuals. This means recognizing their individuality by giving them the kinds of rewards they desire. This point is crucial because of the large differences among people in what rewards they want. Unless these differences are explicitly recognized, it is unlikely that a reward system will be broad enough and flexible enough to encompass the full range of individual differences.

In summary, because of the nature of people's reactions to reward systems, a reward system must be built in a way that allows it to provide four things: (1) enough rewards to fulfill basic needs, (2) equity with the external market, (3) equity within the organization, and (4) treatment of each member of the organization in terms of his or her individual needs.

REWARD SYSTEMS AND ORGANIZATIONAL EFFECTIVENESS

In looking at the role of rewards in organizations it is not enough to look only at their impact on the quality of work life. Consideration must also be given to the impact of rewards on organizational effectiveness. Indeed, the adoption of any reward system hinges partially on the impact it is expected to have on organizational effectiveness. A reward system that substantially reduces organizational effectiveness is not likely to be voluntarily adopted, no matter how much it contributes to a high quality of work life. Further, quality of work life and organizational effectiveness are closely tied together, because without some level of organizational effectiveness, there is no organization and no work life at all. Thus, the challenge is to find reward systems that contribute to both organizational effectiveness and a high quality of work life.

Organizations typically rely on reward systems to do four things that contribute to organizational effectiveness: (1) motivate employees to join the organization, (2) motivate employees to come to work, (3) motivate employees to perform effectively, and (4) reinforce the organizational structure by indicating the position of different individuals in the organization. The considerable amount of research that has been concerned with each of these functions of reward systems is summarized in the following four sections.

Reward systems and organizational membership

There is a great deal of evidence which shows that the rewards an organization offers directly influence the decisions people make about whether to join an organization, as well as their decisions about when and if to quit (see Lawler, 1971, and Yoder, 1956, for reviews). All other things being equal, individuals tend to gravitate toward and remain in those organizations that give the most desirable rewards. This behavior seems to be explainable because high reward levels lead to high satisfaction. Many studies have found that turnover is strongly related to job satisfaction and somewhat less strongly related to satisfaction with the extrinsic rewards a person receives (Porter and Steers, 1973). Apparently this is true because individuals who are presently satisfied with their jobs expect to continue to be satisfied and as a result want to stay with the same organization.

The relationship between turnover and organizational effectiveness is not so simple. It is often assumed that the lower the turnover rate the more effective the organization is likely to be. This probably is a valid generalization, because turnover is expensive. Studies that have actually costed it out have found that it often costs an organization five or more times an employee's monthly salary to replace him (Macy and Mirvis, 1974). However, not all turnover is harmful to organizational effectiveness. Clearly, organizations can afford to lose some individuals, and indeed may profit from losing them. Thus, turnover is a matter of both rate *and* who turns over.

The objective should be to design a reward system that is very effective at retaining the most valuable employees. To do this a reward system must distribute rewards in a way that will lead the better performers to feel satisfied when they compare their rewards with those received by individuals performing similar jobs in other organizations. The emphasis here is on *external* comparisons, because turnover means leaving an organization for a better situation elsewhere. One way to accomplish this, of course, is to reward everyone at a level that is above the reward levels in other organizations. However, this strategy has two drawbacks. In the case of some rewards (for example, money), it is very costly. And it can cause feelings of intraorganizational inequity, because the better performers are likely to feel inequitably treated when they are rewarded at the same level as poor performers in the same organization, even though they are fairly treated in terms of external comparisons. Faced with this situation the better performers may not quit, but they are likely to be dissatisfied, complain, look for internal transfers, and mistrust the organization.

What, then, is the best solution? It would seem to be to have competitive reward levels and to base rewards on performance. This should encourage the better performers to be satisfied and to stay with the organization. It is important to note, however, that not only must the better performers receive more rewards than the poor performers, but they also must receive *significantly* more rewards because they feel they deserve more (Porter and Lawler, 1968). Just rewarding them slightly more may do no more than make the better and poorer performers *equally* satisfied.

In summary, managing turnover means managing satisfaction. This depends on effectively relating rewards to performances, a task that is often difficult. When it cannot be done, about all an organization can do is to try to reward individuals at an above-average level. In situations where turnover is costly, this should be a cost-effective strategy even if it involves giving out expensive rewards.

Organizational effectiveness and absenteeism

Absenteeism, like turnover, is expensive. Like its twin, tardiness, it leads to overstaffing. Another result is that untrained and inexperienced individuals do the jobs of those who are absent. Thus, it makes sense for organizations to adopt reward policies that minimize absenteeism. What kind of reward policies will do this? A great deal of research has shown that absenteeism and satisfaction are related. When the workplace is pleasant and satisfying, individuals come regularly; when it isn't, they don't. Basically, therefore, reward policies that make work a satisfying place to be and that tie rewards to attendance will reduce absenteeism.

Several studies have shown that absenteeism can be reduced by tying pay bonuses and other rewards to attendance. This approach is costly, but sometimes it is less costly than absenteeism. It seems to be a particularly useful strategy in situations where both the work content and the working conditions are poor and do not lend themselves to meaningful improvements (see, for example, Hackman, 1977). In situations where work content or conditions can be improved, such improvements are often the most effective and cost-efficient way to deal with absenteeism. Thus, reward system policies are only one of several ways to influence absenteeism, but they are potentially effective if an organization is willing to tie important rewards to coming to work. In many ways this is easier to do than tying rewards to performance, because attendance is more measurable and visible.

Reward systems and motivation

When certain specifiable conditions exist, reward systems have been demonstrated to motivate performance (Lawler, 1971; Vroom, 1964; Whyte, 1955). What are those conditions? Important rewards must be perceived to be tied in a timely fashion to effective performance. Stated another way, research shows that organizations get the kind of behavior that is seen to lead to rewards employees value. In many ways this is a deceptively simple statement of the conditions that must exist if rewards are to motivate performance. It is deceptive in the sense that it suggests all an organization has to do is to actually relate pay and other frequently valued rewards to performance. Not only is this not the only thing an organization has to do, but it is very difficult to accomplish (Tosi, House, and Dunnette, 1972; Whyte, 1955). Tying rewards to performance requires a good measure of performance, the ability to identify which rewards are important to particular individuals, and the ability to control the amount of these rewards that an individual receives. None of these things are easy to accomplish in most organizational settings, a fact that has led some to conclude that it is not worth trying to relate rewards to performance (Meyer, 1975).

Organizations must not only tie important rewards to performance, but they must do so in a manner that will lead to employees' perceiving the relationship. This means that the connection between performance and rewards must be visible, and that a climate of trust and credibility must exist in the organization. The reason why visibility is necessary should be obvious; the importance of trust may be less so. The belief that performance will lead to rewards is essentially a prediction about the future. For individuals to make this kind of prediction they have to trust the system that is promising them the rewards. Unfortunately, it is not entirely clear how a climate of trust can be established. However, some research suggests that a high level of openness and the use of participation can contribute to trust.

Reward systems and organizational structure

In all complex organizations there is division of labor. Organizations differ, however, in the degree to which members have unique, highly specialized jobs, and in the degree of hierarchical differentiation that exists (Galbraith, 1973; Lawrence and Lorsch, 1967; Lorsch and Morse, 1974; Perrow, 1967). Some organizations, for example, are characterized by relatively flat structures and only a few levels of management; others have many levels—often as many as 20 in very large organizations. Some organizations are broken up into many departments, each of which has a function; others as a matter of policy try to discourage a high level of functional specialization.

In any organization, reward systems can be used to reinforce the existing or desired structure, and to help it operate effectively. The military is perhaps the clearest example of an organization that uses the reward system very effectively to differentiate between people in different positions. Each rank in the military has different privileges; there are even separate officer clubs and housing areas on bases. The argument in favor of such differentiation is that it helps make the organization more effective, because it clearly establishes who has authority and makes it easier for subordinates to take orders because they come from the position rather than from the person. Thus, the whole use of rewards in military organizations is designed to be congruent with the reliance on steep, strict hierarchies with decision making centered at the top.

At the other extreme are organizations that consciously try to give everyone the same fringe benefits, parking spaces, and offices, to diminish the distance between different organizational levels. The argument here is that the lack of differentiation among people in terms of rewards and symbols of office, when combined with a relatively flat organization structure, produces an organization that is highly participative, equalitarian, and flexible. The further argument is that large differences among people in a more participative organization are incongruent with this style of management and organization structure and would be counterproductive. This is an interesting argument but one lacking substantial research support. Nevertheless, as various reward system practices are considered, it is important to think about whether they lead to differential or similar treatment of organization members who are at different management levels.

REWARD SYSTEM REQUIREMENTS

Table 1 summarizes what has been said so far about what a reward system must do if it is to contribute to organizational effectiveness and the quality of work life. Although there is not perfect agreement between the reward system characteristics that lead to a high quality of work life and those that lead to organizational effectiveness, there is a high degree of overlap. Rewards that are seen to be fair in terms of both internal and external comparisons are functional for both, because they lead to high satisfaction, low absenteeism, and low turnover. Tailoring the rewards to the needs of the individual can also contribute to both a high quality of work life and organizational effectiveness. This approach leads to high satisfaction and can help make a performance motivation system more effective by assuring that valued or important rewards are tied to effective job performance.

Tying rewards to performance contributes to motivation. It can also contribute to satisfaction because people only feel equitably treated when rewards are based on their contributions, one of the most important of which is job performance. Satisfaction of basic needs and provision of high overall reward levels contribute primarily to a high quality of work life; congruence with organization structure seems to contribute primarily to organizational effectiveness. In order for reward systems to operate

---

Table 1
Overview of reward system requirements

Quality of work life

a.	Reward level	A reward level high enough to satisfy the basic needs of individuals
b.	External equity	Rewards equal to or greater than those in other organizations
c.	Internal equity	A distribution of rewards that is seen as fair by members
d.	Individuality	Provision of rewards that fit the needs of individuals

Organizational effectiveness

a.	Membership	High overall satisfaction, external equity, and higher reward level for better performers
b.	Absenteeism	Important rewards related to actually coming to work (high job satisfaction)
c.	Performance motivation	Important rewards perceived to be related to performance
d.	Organization structure	Reward distribution pattern that fits the management style and organization structure

in the manner that we have identified as optimally effective there are five identifiable characteristics that the rewards themselves should have. These include (1) importance, (2) flexibility, (3) frequency with respect to administration, (4) visibility, and (5) low cost.

A reward must be *important* to some individual or group of individuals if it is to influence organizational effectiveness and employee satisfaction. Thus, the first question that needs to be asked about any reward is whether it is valued by the particular individuals involved. Although it is possible to identify some rewards as more important than others *on the average,* there are large individual differences in how important rewards are.

A reward system that relies solely on generally important rewards inevitably is going to miss some employees, because even rewards that are important to most employees are not important to everyone. This creates the need for individualizing rewards (Lawler, 1971) so that employees will receive the rewards each specifically desires. In some situations, individualization can be accomplished—and the quality of work life improved—by giving people the choice of which extrinsic rewards they will receive. For example, one company allows workers who have finished their daily production quota the choice of going home or receiving extra pay. If rewards are to be tailored to individuals, those rewards must be flexible with respect to both the amount given and whether it is given to everyone in the organization. It is impossible to create individualized reward packages without flexibility. Further, unless there is flexibility in who receives rewards, it is impossible to vary rewards according to the performance of individuals; thus, equity is difficult to achieve. Overall then, *flexibility* is a desirable characteristic for a reward to have.

Related to the issue of flexibility is the issue of *frequency.* Giving rewards frequently is often helpful for sustaining extrinsic motivation and satisfaction. Thus, the best rewards are those that can be given frequently without losing their importance.

The *visibility* of rewards is important because it influences the ability of the reward to satisfy esteem and recognition needs. Low visibility rewards cannot satisfy these needs and therefore often are less valued by employees. Visibility is also important in clarifying the relationship between rewards and performance.

Finally, the *cost* of the reward is relevant because it is a constraint that the organization must consider. A high cost reward simply cannot be given as often, and when used reduces organizational effectiveness as a result of its cost.

Table 2 presents an evaluation of the common rewards that are used by organizations in terms of their average importance, flexibility, visibility, frequency, and cost. As can be seen from the table, none of the rewards rate high on all of the criteria. Interestingly, pay seems to possess all

Table 2
Evaluation of extrinsic rewards

	Average importance	Flexibility in amount	Visibility	Frequency	Dollar cost
Pay	High	High	Potentially high	High	High
Promotion	High	Low	High	Low	High
Dismissal	High	Low	High	Low	High
Job tenure	Moderate	Low	High	Low	High
Status symbols ...	Moderate	High	High	Low	Moderate
Special awards, certificates, and medals	Low	High	High	Low	Low
Fringe benefits	High	Moderate	Moderate	Low	High

the characteristics that are necessary to make it the perfect extrinsic reward except one—low cost. It is particularly expensive to use as an extrinsic reward, because individuals need to receive frequent pay increases or bonuses in order for sustained extrinsic motivation and satisfaction to be present.

Promotion, dismissal, and tenure are all low in flexibility. They cannot be easily varied in amount according to the situation. They also cannot be given very regularly. This makes it difficult to tie them closely to performance over a long period of time. Job tenure or a guarantee of permanent employment, for example, is a one-shot reward, and once it is given it loses all ability to motivate. These rewards also tend to be expensive. Their high cost is not as visible and obvious as is the cost of pay, but it is real. Special awards, certificates, and medals are examples of rewards with quite a different set of characteristics. They are high in flexibility and visibility. However, they can only be given a few times before they lose their value. And because many people do not value them at all, their average importance is relatively low.

In summary, there is no one reward or class of rewards that meets all the criteria for being a good extrinsic reward. Furthermore, organizations have little control over how important different outcomes are to individuals. However, organizations do control which outcomes they use. It is important that each organization carefully diagnose its situation and use the one or ones that are right for its particular situation. Failure to do this assures that the reward system will fail to contribute to a high quality of work life and organizational effectiveness.

Table 2 points out that promotion, fringe benefits, and pay are the extrinsic rewards that can have the greatest impact on the quality of work life as well as on organizational effectiveness, because they are important to most individuals. Each of these rewards also has other characteristics that make it potentially effective.

REFERENCES

Adams, J. S. "Injustice in Social Exchange." In *Advances in Experimental Social Psychology,* vol. 2, edited by L. Berkowitz. New York: Academic Press, 1965, pp. 267–99.

Alderfer, C. P. "An Empirical Test of a New Theory of Human Needs." *Organizational Behavior and Human Performance* 4 (1969), pp. 142–175.

Cofer, C., and Appley, M. *Motivation: Theory and Research.* New York: John Wiley & Sons, 1964.

Galbraith, Jay. *Designing Complex Organizations.* Reading, Mass.: Addison-Wesley, 1973.

Hackman, J. Richard. "Work Design." In *Improving Life at Work,* ed. J. Richard Hackman and J. Lloyd Suttle. Santa Monica, Calif.: Goodyear Publishing, 1977.

Lawler, E. E. III. "Managers' Attitudes Toward How Their Pay Is and Should Be Determined." *Journal of Applied Psychology* 50 (1966), pp. 273–79.

Lawler, E. E. III. *Pay and Organizational Effectiveness: A Psychological View.* New York: McGraw-Hill, 1971.

Lawrence, Paul R., and Lorsch, Jay W. *Organization and Environment.* Boston: Division of Research, Graduate School of Business Administration, Harvard University, 1967.

Locke, E. "What is Job Satisfaction?" *Organizational Behavior and Human Performance* 4 (1969), pp. 309–36.

Lorsch, Jay W., and Morse, John. *Organizations and Their Members: A Contingency Approach.* New York: Harper & Row, 1974.

Macy, B., and Mirvis, P. "Measuring Quality of Work and Organizational Effectiveness in Behavioral Economic Terms." Paper presented at American Psychological Association Convention, New Orleans, La., September 1974.

Meyer, H. "The Pay-for-Performance Dilemma." *Organizational Dynamics* (Winter 1975), pp. 39–50.

Patchen, M. *The Choice of Wage Comparisons.* Englewood Cliffs, N.J.: Prentice-Hall, 1961.

Perrow, C. "A Framework for the Comparative Analysis of Organizations." *American Sociological Review* 32 (1967), pp. 194–208.

Porter, L. W., and Lawler, E. E. *Managerial Attitudes and Performance.* Homewood, Ill.: Irwin-Dorsey, 1968.

Porter, L., and Steers, R. "Organizational, Work and Personal Factors in Employee Turnover and Absenteeism." *Psychological Bulletin* 80 (1973), pp. 151–76.

Tosi, H., House, R., and Dunnette, M., eds. *Managerial Motivation and Compensation.* East Lansing, Mich.: Michigan State University Business Studies, 1972.

Vroom, V. *Work and Motivation.* New York: John Wiley & Sons, 1964.

Whyte, W. F., ed. *Money and Motivation: An Analysis of Incentives for Industry.* New York: Harper & Row, 1955.

Work in America. Cambridge, Mass.: MIT Press, 1973.

Yoder, D. *Personnel Management and Industrial Relations.* Englewood Cliffs, N.J.: Prentice-Hall, 1956.

Reading 3–2
*Designing appraisal systems for different purposes and performance histories**

L. L. Cummings, Donald P. Schwab

The practice of performance appraisal suffers from a multitude of dilemmas. For example:

Shouldn't all employees be told where they stand?

Yes, but experience indicates that poor performers usually don't improve when told they are in trouble!

Shouldn't feedback about performance be given as frequently as possible?

Yes, but some routine jobs allow for little variation in performance and most experienced employees believe that they know how they are doing without being bugged by the boss!

Shouldn't appraisal techniques and feedback methods be tailored to fit each individual and each situation?

Yes, but that would cost most organizations a fortune in time and money!

The continued, but generally unsatisfactory, resolution of such stressful decisions has led to performance appraisals being both widely used and widely abused.

Much controversy surrounds their use. Concern continues to be ex-

* © by the Regents of the University of California. Reprinted from *California Management Review*, vol. 20, no. 4, pp. 18–25, by permission of The Regents.

pressed regarding their contribution to organizational and individual effec-tiveness and even their relevance.[1] Our purposes in this article are to:

1. Suggest that the typical dilemmas and problems in applying appraisals derive from conflicting goals and inadequate attention devoted to the context of appraisal.
2. Propose conditioning factors that should influence the diagnosis and specification of appropriate goals for appraisal.
3. Describe three systems of appraisal that are tailored to fit the differing purposes and contexts of effective performance evaluation.

Consider the following conversation between two second-level line managers of a major pharmaceutical manufacturer. Each has been re-minded recently by the divisional personnel manager that their appraisals of their subordinates are due within the week.

You know, Jimmy, these damn appraisals are a pain in the neck. Doing the damn things not only takes time away from the job but at least half of my people resent my talking with them about how they are doing. Take those gals working on the capsule machines. Most of them are over 40, married, and have been with the company for at least a dozen years. They want a steady job and friendly people to work with. They're not after promotions, status, development, and all that crap. They know damn well that the only reason for appraisals is to bug the gals who are not carrying their share of the load. Once in a while I can get a little bigger pay increase for one but I have to really build a big case for the old-man.

Jerry, you miss the point of why Personnel wants us to do these appraisals every year. The aim is to discover who has the track record and the capability of handling a bigger job. Without this appraisal process, some of our best people would be overlooked and forgotten when bigger, better jobs are open in the com-pany. Besides, it's important to emphasize to our people that their development on the job is an important thing around here. Without that, a helluva lot of people wouldn't find this place very attractive. What's more, with the company's promo-tion-from-within policy, it's part of our job to be on the lookout for comers. When we do that, people react favorably to opportunities for feedback and suggestions for improvement.

This incident illustrates the differences between an essentially *eval-uative* and a *developmental* use of appraisal systems and techniques. Evaluative uses of appraisal focus on providing information for making administrative decisions about employees. Examples of such decisions would be compensation changes, promotions, demotions, or transfers, and even termination decisions. As developmental tools, appraisals are

---

[1] David L. DeVries (chairman), "Performance Appraisal and Feedback: Flies in the Oint-ment," Symposium presented at the 84th Annual Convention of the American Psychological Association, Washington, D.C., 1976.

Figure 1
Appraisals for evaluation and development*

	Evaluative role of appraisal	Developmental role of appraisal
Focus	On past performance	On improvement in future performance
Objective	Improve performance by more effective personnel and reward administration	Improve performance through self-learning and growth
Method	Variety of rating and ranking procedures	Series of developmental steps as reflected, for example, in management by objectives.
Role of superior	To judge, to evaluate	To counsel, help, or guide
Role of subordinate	Passive or reactive, frequently to defend himself	Active involvement in learning

* Adapted from L. L. Cummings and Donald P. Schwab, *Performance in Organizations* (Glenview, Ill.: Scott, Foresman, 1973), p. 5.

aimed at improving both performance and the potential for performance by identifying areas for growth and personal development. The essential differences between these two approaches are depicted in Figure 1.

Historically, the predominant use of performance appraisals has been for evaluation of past and current performance of employees. This use of appraisal as an evaluative tool has been consistent with the use of the major techniques of the personnel profession. The responsibility for definition of organizational goals, the description and analysis of tasks to be completed, and the evaluation of employee performance rested on management's shoulders. The employee was viewed as largely constrained in his/her responsibility to carry out the activities contained within the job descriptions developed by managerial and staff personnel. This distinction between managerial and subordinate responsibilities became epitomized in the separation of the planning and controlling (appraising) versus the doing of work. Systems of work simplification, applied industrial engineering, and scientific management were developed to implement this distinction in the pursuit of employee efficiency.

TRENDS TOWARD DEVELOPMENT

Events and trends in managerial thinking during the past 15 years have transformed this predominantly evaluative philosophy. Several of these nudges toward a broader conception of appraisal are noteworthy.

First, there is increasing awareness that traditional performance appraisal techniques have failed to record the full variance or range of an individual's performance. This is partially because evaluators commit systematic errors when rating their subordinates. For example, tendencies toward unrealistically favorable (or unfavorable) evaluations are well documented. Appraisers also may tend to avoid spreading out their evaluations to the extent warranted by the actual performance differences among people. These, and other, errors in evaluating are well known and have generated considerable skepticism concerning traditional rating procedures and formats.[3]

Second, it has become increasingly apparent that most jobs are not solely and completely defined by the organization through the processes of job analysis and job description. Incumbents of jobs enact and change the nature of their jobs over time. The nuances and subtleties of performing, for many jobs, provide ample opportunities for individuals to express their preferences and skills in actually carrying out the formal requirements of the task. In addition, the requirements of a task change over time as the performer learns the fundamentals of a job and begins to see opportunities for innovation and constructive change. Typically, these differences among individual performers in their perceptions of a job and the dynamic nature of tasks are not captured in static appraisal systems and procedures.

Third, evaluative appraisal became a favorite straw man of a number of advocates of work and organization humanization. McGregor, Argyris, and Drucker[4] each attacked the traditional evaluative systems of appraisal as mechanical, hierarchically centered and controlled, and demotivating artifacts of the bureaucratic system. The pebble of truth in these assertions was just large enough to cause a ripple of popular attack and pessimism concerning appraisals for evaluative purposes. These largely philosophic and normative confrontations appeared to be supported by the early results of an empirical study of reactions to appraisals among General Electric employees.[5] It was observed that bosses typically resisted conducting appraisals and providing feedback and subordinates typically did not change their behavior as a consequence of receiving evaluations. At worst, employees were reported to react hostilely and defensively to attempts

[3] For a more sophisticated treatment of these issues, see L. L. Cummings and Donald P. Schwab, *Performance in Organizations: Determinants and Appraisal* (Glenview, Ill.: Scott, Foresman and Company, 1973), chap. 6 and 7.

[4] Douglas McGregor, *The Human Side of Enterprise* (New York: McGraw-Hill, 1960), chap. 6; Chris Argyris, *Personality and Organization: The Conflict Between The System and The Individual* (New York: Harper & Bros., 1957); and *Integrating the Individual and the Organization* (New York: John Wiley & Sons, 1964), chap. 12; Peter F. Drucker, *The Practice of Management* (New York: Harper & Bros.,), 1954.

[5] Herbert Meyer, Emanual Kay, and John R. F. French, Jr., "Split Roles in Performance Appraisal," *Harvard Business Review*, vol. 43 (1965), pp. 123 ff.

to improve their performance through evaluation and feedback. Thus, the essentially speculative arguments of the 1950s and 1960s and some empirical evidence suggested that appraisals for evaluation were of limited value. Despite the need to assess performance and make decisions based on those assessments, the hue and cry was heard for abandoning the evaluative tone and for focusing primarily on the developmental purpose and rationale of appraisal.

As a consequence of these types of events, specific strategies and techniques for implementing development-oriented performance assessment systems evolved during the 1960s. These systems have been variously labeled management by objectives (MBO), management by results, goal-oriented management, and purposive management. Labels and specific techniques aside, however, these programs shared an emphasis on performance improvement rather than on performance evaluation.

Yet systems aimed at improving performance do not vitiate the need for personnel decisions that, in turn, require evaluative appraisals. Thus it is now common for appraisal systems to have both development *and* evaluative objectives. Thus, the desires of the organizational humanists have not been completely fulfilled. The fundamental purpose of performance appraisal has not changed. Rather, a new objective has been added to the old. Organizations now expect managers to both evaluate performance for institutional reward and punishment purposes, and to use the appraisal process to improve employee performance levels. Herein lies one of the dilemmas perplexing appraisal systems. The techniques and modes of thinking appropriate for development of performance are different and may even be inconsistent with those appropriate for evaluating performance.

The potential problem has been rather widely recognized. Moreover, it is frequently recommended that the two objectives be procedurally separated insofar as possible. Recently, for example, Beer and Ruh described a three-stage appraisal system developed at Corning Glass Works.[6] A principal purpose of the three stages is the separation of developmental and evaluative aspects of the appraisal process. Nevertheless, it is surely naïve to suppose that employees completely compartmentalize the two objectives, no matter what the organization does in attempting to do so.

An alternative approach would involve a much more selective use of developmental appraisals than is recommended by the current conventional wisdom. Such selectivity is warranted primarily because of conditioning factors which limit the circumstances when the developmental use of appraisals is likely to be valuable. These conditioning factors have

---

[6] Michael Beer and Robert Ruh, "Employee Growth Through Performance Management," *Harvard Business Review,* vol. 54 (1976), pp. 59–66.

to do with assumptions about the behavioral processes underlying developmental appraisals and with assumptions about characteristics of organizations and individuals that are necessary for the successful utilization of appraisals for developmental purposes.

CONDITIONING FACTORS

Characteristics of goals

A critical behavioral assumption underlies most attempts to use developmental appraisals. It is assumed that *goal setting*, either by the manager and/or by the performer, will increase performance. Several characteristics of the goal-setting process and of the resulting goals are known to impact the effectiveness of attempts to use goals as developmental tools.[7] To exert maximum performance impact, the development process should produce goals which are:

1. Specifically stated, with magnitude of achievement and time frame for accomplishment clearly spelled out.
2. Perceived as attainable by the performer but yet difficult enough to stretch the performer incrementally beyond previous performance levels.
3. Accepted as meaningful and legitimate by the performer. Acceptance must be sought on two dimensions: the magnitude or level of the goal and the social or personal relevance of the goal.

Systems of performance improvement which do not include these components are not likely to yield positive results.[8] Additionally, there is a common problem associated with the implementation of the goal-setting process not specified above. This problem can be seen in the following example from a national distributor of industrial chemicals.

At the 1975 national sales meeting, each regional manager of sales was asked to set cost reduction goals for each of his regions. Goals were to be set in terms of percentage cost reductions for each quarter of the forthcoming year. The vice president for sales also emphasized that it was important for each manager to focus on improving the morale of his sales-persons to keep turnover to a minimum. One year later, at the 1976 national meeting, it was disclosed that 7 of 10 managers had met their cost reduction goals, but that no progress had been made on reducing salesperson turnover. Why?

---

[7] Richard M. Steers and Lyman W. Porter, "The Role of Task-Goal Attributes in Employee Performance," *Psychological Bulletin,* vol. 81 (1974), pp. 434–52.

[8] E. A. L̸   N. Cartledge, and C. S. Knerr, "Studies of the Relationship Between Satisfaction, Goal-Setting and Performance," *Organizational Behavior and Human Performance,* vol. 5 (1970), pp. 135–58.

One of the major reasons, recognized by the managers themselves, was that the specificity of the cost reduction goal (expressed in quantified terms) had focused their attention on that goal. The ambiguous, unspecified nature of the morale and turnover goals somehow communicated that these were less important and that performance was less likely to be measured against these general objectives.

While the problem of differential goal specificity can be resolved with planning, others are not so easily overcome. Indeed, a bit of reflection will suggest that the goal-setting requirements specified above are not applicable to some jobs and to some persons.

The nature of the job

A major problem for developmental appraisal and meaningful goal setting has to do with the *nature of the job performed*. Realistically, many jobs are designed so that it would be nearly impossible to provide developmental potential through the job. This frequently arises because of a technologically constrained or defined job definition coupled with a work specialization and standardization system. The control over the *quality of work,* at least above a minimally acceptable level, depends heavily on the quality of materials available to the performer and on the proper care and maintenance of the equipment (or other technology) available to the performer. On routine tasks these factors are often out of the employee's control. Essentially the same realities apply when examining the *pace* at which the performer operates. In many cases, the designs of jobs and work flows are such that the schedule and rapidity of work are essentially beyond the performer's control. The only opportunity to influence pace may well be in a negative direction.

In these circumstances, successful developmental efforts would be possible only if jobs were redesigned to provide individuals with greater performance discretion. Such redesign may be worth considering in some instances. Clearly, however, many jobs cannot be meaningfully altered, given the capital expenditures which would be required. Moreover, there is little evidence that job redesign consistently influences performance positively.[9]

Performer characteristics

Another problem with developmental appraisals has to do with the *characteristics of people performing on jobs.* There is a substantial body of literature identifying individual differences in ability to perform and

---

[9] Jon L. Pierce and Randall B. Dunham, "Task Design: A Literature Review," *Academy of Management Review,* vol. 1 (1976), pp. 83–97.

in actual performance. More recently it is becoming evident that persons differ substantially in their preferences for various types of work outcomes. Clearly, some seek task-related outcomes such as opportunity for growth and achievement, the type of outcomes successful developmental programs are built on. Others, however, seek more extrinsically oriented outcomes such as pay and pleasant working conditions. These people are less likely to be attracted to and motivated by a developmental orientation.

Also, it must be noted that peoples' behaviors and attitudes are more stable over time than change-focused managerial techniques typically assume. The best predictor of future behavior and preferences are the behaviors and preferences of the past. Someone with a record of poor performance in the past cannot reasonably be expected to evolve into a "hotshot" performer as a consequence of a developmental program. Indeed, it typically would be a waste of organizational resources to try to do so.

It is true that certain characteristics of developmental systems are attractive to employees. For example, there is reason to believe that it is satisfying to participate in the implementation of an appraisal system.[10] Moreover, opportunities to provide self-feedback in the form of appraising one's own performance also leads to satisfaction.[11]

At the same time, however, we know that self-feedback results in overstatements of performance relative to supervisory evaluations when rewards are attached to the results.[12] Thus, if a low performer is allowed to provide self-feedback, as is typical of developmental appraisal programs, the corrective features usually attributed to feedback are not likely to take place. Unfortunately, this undesirable consequence is most likely to occur among the persons who most need development, namely the low performers.

THREE SYSTEMS OF APPRAISAL

To review, the conditioning factors discussed above indicate that appraisals have developmental potential where meaningful and challenging goals can be established and accomplished. Characteristics of jobs, however, often prohibit significant performance variation, making the idea of goal setting and performance enhancement of limited value. Moreover,

---

[10] L. L. Cummings, "A Field Experimental Study of the Effects of Two Performance Appraisal Systems," *Personnel Psychology,* vol. 26 (1973), pp. 489–502.

[11] M. M. Greller and D. M. Herold, "Sources of Feedback: A Preliminary Investigation," *Organizational Behavior and Human Performance,* vol. 13 (1975), pp. 244–56.

[12] M. M. Greller, "Employee Reactions to Performance Feedback" (*working paper, Graduate School of Business,* New York University, New York, 1976).

Figure 2
Three appraisal systems

1. DAP = Development Action Program:
    Focused on proven high performer with upward potential.
2. MAP = Maintenance Action Program:
    Focused on acceptable performer with limited upward potential.
3. RAP = Remedial Action Program:
    Focused on substandard performer who requires close attention or who should be prepared for termination.

---

employees are associated with a history of abilities, needs, and performance. This history imposes greater constraints on change than the typical developmental appraisal system acknowledges.

While we have no hard data, it is reasonable to suppose that no more than half the jobs in a typical organization allow for the variability in performance and flexibility in goal setting required by developmental appraisal. In addition, given some reasonable assumptions about organizational staffing, training, and reward policies and practices, we can expect that relatively few very high and very low performers are employed. Eighty percent or more are likely to be average performers. These assumptions suggest the need to assume a *contingency* posture toward designing, implementing, and evaluating employee appraisals. The following three systems are presented as a movement in this direction and are outlined in Figure 2.[13]

Developmental action program

A developmental action program (DAP) is applicable for the relatively small number of employees with a history of high performance. Such employees are found on jobs where goal setting and performance enhancement can take place. They are, therefore, ideally suited to benefit from developmental appraisal systems. While specifics of such systems may vary, they will include:

1. Participation by the subordinate in the establishment of goals.
2. Subordinate and superior agreement on methods for measuring performance and/or additional skills and resources necessary to accomplish performance goals.
3. Participation in review sessions to assess goal progress.
4. Recycling through the goal-setting phase.

---

[13] These systems are developed in greater detail in Cummings and Schwab *Performance in Organizations.*

It can be reasonably assumed that individuals with a performance history justifying DAP can benefit from the implications of developmental appraisal. Participation in goal setting allows for the establishment of meaningful and challenging goals. Participation in review holds few of the dangers of distortion identified above because the individual is already a high performer. Finally, there is relatively little potential conflict between developmental and evaluative aspects in DAP since the manager can assure the performer that he/she will receive favorable organizational rewards. Indeed, a successfully implemented DAP will generally lead to promotion or increased responsibility through job enrichment.

Maintenance action program

For most employees an appraisal focused on a maintenance action program (MAP) will be appropriate. MAP is applicable for individuals (a) who are not likely to improve their performance because of ability or motivational constraints, and/or (b) on jobs that do not allow for meaningful goal setting and performance enhancement. The focus, therefore, of MAP is on maintaining performance at the currently acceptable levels.

Emphases, and therefore the processes, of MAP and DAP differ substantially. In a MAP the supervisor and the technology of the job will be primarily responsible for the establishment of work goals and objectives. Review of work performance is the supervisor's responsibility. While reviews should be scheduled in accordance with the completion time of the assigned tasks, frequently the timing of reviews is determined by the calendar, i.e., the employee's anniversary date with the organization.

We recognize that the premises of MAP (and remedial action programs to be discussed below) are contrary to the humanistic ideal of universal potential for growth and development. Certainly employees should not be relegated to a MAP until several appraisals point consistently in the same direction. Nevertheless, employees do reach growth limits and/or are placed on jobs which constrain further development. Attempts to develop such employees in their current roles is wasteful to the organization and potentially frustrating, if not threatening, to the employee.

If an individual on a MAP performs at a consistently high level he/she should be considered for a DAP. Such a possibility may require that the employee be assigned to a job allowing for greater performance variability. Regression from MAP is, of course, also possible. In that case the employee should be considered for a remedial action program.

Remedial action program

The most troubling employees for managers are those whose performance has been consistently marginal or unacceptable and are, therefore, candidates for a remedial action program (RAP). A RAP is aimed at performance improvement through close supervisory controls. Failing that, termination of the employee is the aim. Thus, a RAP must provide specific supervisory feedback on performance deficiencies. Frequent examples of behaviors reflecting acceptable and unacceptable behaviors are desirable. Clearly, self-appraisal is undesirable in a RAP, given the findings discussed above concerning the effects of self-feedback.

A RAP also should include specific programs for improved performance *imposed by the supervisor* which include the explicit identification of performance measures and time perspectives for review. Moreover, the review intervals should be of very short duration; at least until performance levels begin to improve.

If performance fails to improve or declines after the initiation of a RAP, the manager is obligated to initiate an explicit sequence resulting in a final step of termination. Ideally, the aim of such a sequence is either the return of performance to an acceptable level or the voluntary separation of the employee. Such a sequence must be explicit and formal in the sense that the employee understands that he/she has moved into this phase of the RAP. Such knowledge is not only an ethical requirement but will undoubtedly be necessary if the terminated employee takes legal action.

IMPLICATIONS

There are a number of important implications which follow from the three systems proposed. From a managerial point of view, the most important may well pertain to the nature, amount, and frequency of feedback suggested by each system. An attempt to summarize these is presented in Figure 3. The three appraisal programs are arrayed horizontally and the dimensions of feedback are displayed vertically.

In a DAP, the temporal orientation is toward the future with an explicit emphasis on what needs to be done to develop the performer to the limits of his/her present capabilities and/or to expand those capabilities. Feedback should imply goals or areas of performance within which goals are appropriate for expansion. At least initially, the feedback will be primarily self-generated, with the superior playing the role of organizational reality-tester. The essence of feedback in a DAP is the implication that the performer's task is always expandable and that the job is to be seen and designed as an arena for self-growth.

Feedback in a DAP should be task-specific. It should probably focus on the opportunities available for performer growth *and* on the constraints that the performer sees as inhibiting maximum performance. That is, feed-

Figure 3
Appraisal programs and dimensions of feedback

Feedback	Development action program	Maintenance action program	Remedial action program
Nature	Future-oriented Implied goals Self-generated Implies job scope expansion	Past-oriented General focus on exceptions System-generated Implies no change	Past- and future-oriented Detailed focus on method System (boss)-generated Implies punitive action
Amount and frequency	Task specific Intensive feedback Freqency highly influenced by performer	Time-paced Medium feedback	Nearly continuous monitoring Intensive feedback—decreasing frequency only if performance improves

back should include information concerning changes in technology and the nature of the work flow that would remove barriers to improved effectiveness as perceived by the performer. The feedback should be paced according to critical incidents, both positive and negative, in the performance pattern and should not be paced by the calendar. Finally, the frequency of feedback should be primarily under the control of the performer. Questions should be answered and opportunities explored when the performer sees the need.

In a MAP, feedback should be primarily past-oriented. The predominant emphasis is on maintaining the past pattern and level of performance. The essential theme is that "what *has been* is good enough for the future." Feedback should be used to focus on the exceptions or deviations from an established pattern of stable, acceptable performance. Feedback is generated from the managerial control system. This control may be provided by a superior or by a technology such as an accounting system or a quality control instrumentation. The performer in a MAP should not be expected to generate feedback about his/her performance as a part of the formal appraisal system. The essence of feedback in the MAP is that "no news is good news" to the performer, and the underlying managerial assumption is that change is unnecessary most of the time. The system should be designed to highlight exceptions but should not attempt to monitor the majority of employee behaviors or performances. Only when major deviations from standard behavior patterns occur and on the occasion of the time-paced reviews (e.g., one per year) is feedback likely to be an efficient strategy of control.

In a RAP the time orientation is toward both past and future. Emphasis is placed on the necessity for immediate improvements beyond past performance. In addition, the focus of the evaluation is on what, *in the eyes of the superior,* must be done to improve performance. The feedback should emphasize the exact, proper methods to be used to execute satisfactory performance. In addition, considerable detail needs to be provided concerning the specific deficiencies that exist. The feedback must be system-generated, usually by the immediate superior, with possible inputs from functional specialists in personnel or technical specialties directly related to the nature of the task. Clearly, the implication of a RAP is that punitive action lurks and that unless measurable, tangible performance improvements are quickly forthcoming, termination is the likely outcome.

Nearly continuous monitoring and feedback of performance is required in a RAP. Feedback must be intensive, certainly weekly, and possibly daily. Feedback is stretched only if performance improvements begin to appear and seem to be stabilized. Consideration can then be given to the advisability of shifting to a MAP. The desired goal of a RAP is performance improvement. Short of that attainment, an acceptable outcome would be the voluntary termination by the performer.

In summary, the three systems proposed here represent an improvement beyond typical performance appraisal systems as they operate in most organizations. They should encourage an efficient use of managerial time since the majority of employees in most jobs will best fit a MAP which requires the least managerial attention. MAP's operate essentially on a management by exception principle. In addition, the three systems serve to separate development and evaluation in the sense that DAP is primarily developmental in orientation while MAP is evaluative and RAP is clearly evaluative with some focus on immediate performance improvement.

Finally, implicit in the operation of the three systems is that every performer must be reviewed periodically. Without this systematic monitoring of performance, the three systems could lead to a performance "caste" system wherein employees become locked into a single appraisal categorization. Clearly, that is not the intent of an effective evaluation system.

Reading 3–3
Has MBO failed?*
Stephen Singular

Management by objectives—probably the most pervasive management idea of the last quarter-century, and certainly the most widely touted—is showing signs of failing. Recent surveys of the effectiveness of MBO have come up curiously—to some, astonishingly—empty-handed. This is all the more remarkable for the fact that MBO seems to have become almost as much a part of the corporate landscape as organization charts and annual reports.

Management by objectives made its first official appearance more than 20 years ago in Peter Drucker's book *Practice of Management.* (Later, as MBO grew in popularity, many companies were to claim that they were employing this technique or a similar one long before Drucker came along. "We never rejected Drucker's concept of MBO," says an executive at General Electric. "We just feel that we invented MBO first under a different name.") The claims for the technique were simple and compelling: Using a management-by-objectives approach would provide, in theory anyway, an opportunity for both more involvement in and more control over one's work for every subordinate in a corporation—and that usually included everyone except the chief executive officer. This would be done by having the subordinate participate in the establishment of objectives for his particular job. Periodically, thereafter, his performance would be measured against those objectives, and this process would help identify and reward good work and eliminate bad.

This description of MBO sounds, perhaps, like something every company does regardless of whether it has heard of MBO or not. As one corporation manager points out, "in any given job, it is necessary to know what objectives you are trying to accomplish." As basic as MBO is a concept, however, it took Drucker's book to lay the foundation for it as a formal system of management.

Today, there are as many varieties of MBO as there are types of corporate planning. These programs often have different names—"performance appraisal" or "managing for results"—but most fit under the generic umbrella of MBO. Interestingly, when questioned about their companies' MBO program, many younger managers look puzzled. Then, when the

* Reprinted with permission from the October 1975 *MBA*. Copyright © 1975 by MBA Communications, Inc.

program is described in terms of objectives setting and performance review, the managers immediately recognize what one is referring to. At the same time, they appear to be unschooled in the underlying philosophy of the technique.

To the proponents of MBO, the system promotes not only greater effectiveness among workers but also greater personal satisfaction. "Where an MBO program works as it can and should," reads one of the hundreds of articles lauding MBO, "a man becomes largely a master of his own fate. It is in this system that a man can experience one of the most powerful of all human drives, the desire to accomplish and do so largely on his own." All that and higher profits, too. It looks, as they say, good on paper.

With Drucker's imprimatur, plus the corporate rush—starting in the 1950s—for new management programs and techniques, MBO's popularity began to grow. Indeed, corporations were only too ready to try it. By the late 1960s MBO had become simply the thing to do. Management researchers tell of one personnel executive who, a few years ago, adamantly refused to let his company's management techniques be examined. Why? He feared the research would reveal the fact that the corporation wasn't using MBO and he didn't want anyone to think his company behind the times. In some ways MBO has become a canon of good management. "You just ain't modern," says one manager, a bit sardonically, "if you ain't got MBO."

But, today, the apostles of MBO are anything but evangelical. "While MBO is popular," writes W. J. Reddin in his book *Effective Management by Objectives,* "it also has more clear failures than successes. Some consulting firms spend more time taking MBO out than putting it in."

"It's still a spreading concept," says Harold Koontz, Mead Johnson Professor of Management at UCLA and coauthor of the classic management text *Principles of Management.* "But the important thing is not that it is spreading but that it is not being done well."

A survey, published last year in the University of Michigan's journal *Human Resource Management,* validates Koontz's opinion. Conducted by professors Fred Schuster of Florida Atlantic University and Alva Kindall of Harvard Business School, the survey revealed that considerably less than half of the *Fortune* list of the 500 largest industrial companies have management programs that can legitimately be called MBO-based. The professors defined those programs as having: "(1) initiation periodically by the employee of a set of written performance goals or targets for himself; (2) discussion of the goals between the employee and his superior, followed by mutual agreement on a set of goals to which the employee is committed; (3) periodic review (either formally or informally) by the employee and his superior to determine to what extent goals previously set have been met or exceeded."

Based on the researchers' estimate, less than 10 percent of those 500 corporations—somewhere between 36 and 50 companies—have MBO-based programs that are considered a success. And only 10 companies, or 2 percent, have programs that are considered "highly successful." "We did find," says Schuster, "a few organizations that *appeared* to be having spectacular success with MBO. But many corporations have widely publicized MBO programs that are clearly unsuccessful. A lot of them apply MBO only as a status symbol." (Another clue that perhaps MBO hasn't been working very well is that both Schuster and Kindall and most other researchers of MBO effectiveness are sworn to secrecy on how particular companies are faring with the technique.)

In a recent speech to Motorola managers at that company's Executive Institute in Phoenix, Harold Koontz called the results of the Schuster-Kindall survey "shocking." "If there is a low degree of effectiveness using MBO," Koontz told *MBA,* "people won't have a sense of commitment to it and it will die. It is too good an approach to let this happen."

The demise of MBO is more than shocking. It is genuinely disappointing, because MBO is not just another pretty face on the management scene. It is a technique based on real planning and thought and is, most agree, the best theoretical management program ever conceived. Why has MBO not been more effective?

Most students of management blame the users, not the system. "There are two primary reasons for the failure of MBO," says Dale McConkey, a professor at the University of Wisconsin's graduate business school. "The first is adoption in ignorance and the second is implementation in haste." "I have noticed," says Walter Wikstrom, director of organizational development and research for the Conference Board in New York, "that very few companies have even specified what their MBO programs are for when they implement them. And this is what MBO itself is all about."

Implementation of MBO involves a program aimed at restructuring communication and cooperation inside a corporation, a complex and time-consuming task. When top management has viewed it as anything less or started an MBO program simply "for show," the results have been predictable. "To many managers," says Wikstrom, who has done extensive research on MBO usage in corporations, "MBO is just a joke. In one instance, a manager thought the way to make MBO work was to set objectives so low that all his subordinates would get bonuses. The last I heard he was being transferred out of that division, which was known as the 'no-profit' section inside that company."

If MBO is sometimes a joke to managers, it's a cumbersome one. When one subordinate in a large corporation was asked what he thought of its MBO program, he just shrugged, obviously trying to avoid a question that bothered him. Finally, with a resigned smile, he started to answer. "Well, you know, it's very hard to set arbitrary goals when you are dependent on external forces. So, often, our MBO program is just so much paperwork. . . ." His voice trailed off as his superior came into the room.

The desire to please one's superiors, who themselves do not understand management by objectives, is often a critical reason for the failure of MBO. "In one electronics firm I studied," says Walter Wikstrom, "it was very obvious that MBO wasn't working. They had 5,500 managers in their program and the man in charge was saying what a success it was because all of the managers had their MBO forms in on time. To me, this meant that MBO wasn't working at all. The fact that they were all in promptly suggested to me that the people were filling our forms to get central management off their backs. These were, incidentally, the fanciest MBO forms I have ever seen. Their program has since ended."

In those few companies where MBO is considered successful, there is a definite reluctance to be bound by the trappings of the technique. "Kimberly-Clark," says Wikstrom, "has a good MBO program, and they have found that good ideas and their implementation are in inverse proportion to their use of MBO forms." Adds a manager at American Telephone & Telegraph, "You can't get bogged down in paperwork and expect MBO to do any good. The whole point of it is to manage better and not to make sure the forms are filled out just right."

If some corporations are guilty of "adoption of MBO in ignorance," as McConkey put it, others are equally guilty of "implementation in haste." According to some consultants, management has generally underestimated the time it takes to learn the basic techniques of MBO: first, how to set obtainable objectives and, second, how to assess whether those objectives have been achieved or not.

Harold Koontz claims that the MBO program at AT&T, for example, is less effective than it could be because of its difficulty in measuring achievement. "The company sets goals on a national basis, when it should be setting them on a regional basis," says Koontz. "Then, too, while most of AT&T's goals are quantifiable, they should also be verifiable. A verifiable objective is not measured in numbers. It is simply something you can look back on and say, yes, I accomplished it, or, no, I didn't."

(Determining whether or not an objective has been met is, perhaps, the thorniest element of MBO. One theorist, attempting to maintain a delicate balance in this matter, advises thus: strive to accomplish not all and not half of each objective you set but settle for about three-fourths. One is tempted to ask what is three-fourths of a standard objective like "being alert to customers' needs and qualified to serve them.")

In addition, there have been, thus far, very few companies willing to nurture their MBO programs through the faltering initial years. "You've got to take the long-range view," says Fred Schuster. "You can't just plug MBO in. Union Carbide, for example, admits that it took five years to get its MBO program operating and ten years to make it successful."

There are also misgivings about the use of MBO for individual performance appraisal. When connected to such appraisals, MBO has been seen by many employees as having a direct relationship to salary; in some cases, it has been used for just that purpose. "In some of the regional offices at AT&T," says Robert Varner, public relations director (planning) for the company, "This tie-in between salary and setting objectives has been stressed far too much. When this happens, employees see MBO as just one more way to tighten the screw and make them sweat. We have tried to avoid tying MBO to performance appraisal in our new program here in New York." Other companies, with experiences similar to AT&T's, are also moving away from MBO as a device for appraising subordinates.

All of this, so far, begs the question of whether there is anything inherently wrong with MBO. Bruce Kirchoff, an associate professor of management and organizational behavior at the University of Nebraska, attempted to tackle part of this question in a study of managers in 14 organizations using MBO. The managers tested had all been involved in formal goal setting and review for at least one year. Kirchoff concluded that MBO does make a difference in helping subordinates understand the importance of setting goals. But does it make for a more satisfied worker? No. Kirchoff writes: "These survey results suggest that there is no relationship between initiating structure [or how a subordinate helps initiate goals], consideration [which, Kirchoff explains, is closely related to subordinate involvement], and goal utilization within or across organizations. . . . The lack of correlation between consideration and goal utilization agrees with Carroll and Tosi's [two other MBO researchers] findings that involvement in the goal-setting process was not related to the use of the MBO program. . . . Perhaps goal formation and goal utilization are the significant variables, both of which bear striking resemblance to the functions of management proposed by [Henri] Fayol almost 60 years ago."

"MBO," says Kirchoff, "is usually sold as a democratic form of management and it is not necessarily that. It is primarily a control function. . . ."

"It is possible that MBO enters an organization and becomes an established part of the management system without affecting interpersonal relationships at all. MBO trainers and behavioral theorists will resist such a conclusion, but there is considerable evidence that even sensitivity training fails to have a lasting effect upon a manager's behavior."

Even this, say the defenders of MBO, is a consequence of poor implementation, not a weakness in MBO itself. Some feel that MBO programs
have not been well tailored to the specific needs of each corporation
that uses it. Others feel that, even after all these years, MBO just hasn't
had time to prove itself. "It's going to take a long time," says Wisconsin's
Dale McConkey. "We know where the bugs are now. The failure rate
has taught us a bitter lesson, damn it. MBO works, but it takes time
and competent implementation."

Fred Schuster contends that corporations are gradually developing
something like a state of consciousness that will prepare them for using
MBO successfully—both in terms of the corporation and of the individual.
"The future," says Schuster, "is in the direction of MBO because it fits
in so well with the other developments that are going on both inside
and outside the world of business. People are more educated now and
expect and demand more from their jobs than money. Managers will
want to have more impact on their own careers and on the goals of the
organization. Management by objectives hasn't worked where the organization hasn't evolved to a point where it is ready to accept it. But we
are 80 percent along in getting there, and by the 1980s all companies
will want to use MBO."

If MBO is to have more success in the future, it will probably have
to be designed to suit each corporation and its particular problems. Similar
to what is happening in the behavioral science field, MBO design and
implementation is gradually moving inside the corporation and away from
outside vendors. This movement inside, plus whatever can be learned
from two decades of experience with the technique, may help refine it.

It may be, as Schuster suggests, that MBO is just beginning to pick
up steam. Or it may be, as Koontz says, that MBO may have missed its
chance, at least in some companies: "If MBO comes to be regarded as
a gimmick, disenchantment . . . will surely follow," Koontz has written.
"When this happens, a program is discredited, and top management may
not be given a chance to reintroduce it for many years." Suffice it to
say that the big management idea of the past 25 years has still to prove
itself.

PART II

This section of the book expands our domain of analysis from the specialized subunit to the single business company, which consists of two or more specialized subunits. These organizations may be independent corporations or divisions of still larger organizations.

Managers of single business companies, as the cases illustrate, face a number of organizational issues that are most often associated with coordinating and controlling their interdependent subunits. The text suggests an analytical framework for thinking about those and other single business unit issues. The cases provide a range of situations, from relatively simple subunit interdependence (Continental Can of Canada) to relatively complex interdependence (TRW Systems), in which one can practice using that framework. Finally, the readings provide a more in-depth description of a number of the design tools used by single business unit managers to deal effectively with subunit interdependence.

Chapter 4

Organizing human resources in a single-business company

Designing the organization of human resources for a company operating in a single business area requires answers to three basic questions:

1. *Where do we draw the boundaries that define the company's major and minor specialized subunits? Exactly what tasks should we assign to each of these subunits?*

   For example, should the company be divided into three major parts, one of which focuses on marketing activities, another on manufacturing, and another on administration? Or should it be divided into two major parts, one of which focuses on all activities associated with product X, and a second of which focuses on all activities associated with product Y? Or would still another alternative be better? How should each major part be subdivided, if at all? If there is a manufacturing department, for example, should it be subdivided into two plants—one that produces product X and one that produces product Y? Or should it be subdivided into an East Coast plant and a West Coast plant, each manufacturing both X and Y? Or is there a still better alternative?

2. *How do we organize each of the major and minor specialized subunits we have created? That is, how do we structure each of these units, and what types of measurement, reward, selection and development systems are appropriate?*

   For example, suppose that a company is divided into three major parts—the product X group, the product Y group, and administration.

Further, suppose that the two product groups are each made up of a manufacturing department and a marketing department, and that the administrative unit is made up of a finance group, an EDP group, and personnel. This second design question then addresses the internal organization of each of these groups. That is, should the two engineering departments be organized in the same way? If not, how should they be different? Should a single performance appraisal system be used company-wide, or should different systems be used by each of the three major subunits? How should jobs be designed in the finance group? In the personnel group? What type of training is needed in the two marketing departments? And so on.

3. *How do we integrate these specialized subunits so that their individual contributions add up to achieve the company's overall objectives? How do we avoid a situation in which each part performs its role adequately and yet the whole doesn't accomplish its goals?*

For example, how should a company organize itself to ensure that its manufacturing and sales departments collaborate in the manner needed to achieve adequate levels of sales and profits? Would some type of company-wide incentive bonus system based on profits encourage the managers in manufacturing and sales to collaborate? Or should the company just work out a set of clearly understood ground rules concerning what each department is expected to do under different circumstances so that their contributions integrate into a whole? Or is still some other method needed?

We have discussed the second of these three questions in Chapter 3. In this chapter we will deal with the other two questions, starting with the third. After gaining a basic understanding of the factors involved in the second and third questions, it will be much easier to discuss the fundamental choices in the first question.

INTERDEPENDENCE: THE FACTOR CREATING A NEED FOR INTEGRATION

All organizations are composed of specialized parts that are to some degree interdependent. It is because of this interdependence that organizations must design ways to integrate their parts. If their parts were totally independent, this would not be necessary. Furthermore, if the nature of the interdependence among parts or organizations was always the same, or almost the same, then achieving integration would be relatively simple from a design point of view; there would exist some standard solution that could always be used. In reality, however, the nature of subunit interdependence varies significantly within and among organizations because of three important factors: (1) a company's external environment, (2) a company's technologies, and (3) a company's strategies and objectives. (See Figure 4–1).

Consider, for example, a small company (Company A) that makes and sells a standard product in a limited geographical area. The company's external environment is characterized by a stable and loyal customer base and little direct competition. The company develops no new products and relies on a relatively simple manufacturing technology. It is a family-owned business whose primary objective is to generate a stable income.

This company's sales and manufacturing activities are interdependent in a relatively simple way. The manufacturing people depend on the salespeople to give them orders in an accurate and timely manner. Without those orders the manufacturing people cannot accomplish their tasks effectively and efficiently. The salespeople, however, have no similar dependence on manufacturing. They can do their job for weeks at a time without ever even thinking about the plant. Only if something catastrophic happens at the plant, for example, something that stops shipments to customers, would the salespeople be affected.

Company B, which operates in the same geographic area as Company A, is in quite a different situation. Company B operates in a much more competitive environment and sells a nonstandard set of products that are almost always custom-made. Although also a family business, the family's business objectives are focused on profitable growth.

Sales and manufacturing in Company B are interdependent in very different ways than in A, due to differences in their environments, technologies, and business objectives. Sales at B depend on manufacturing for

Figure 4–1
Factors affecting the nature of the interdependence among a company's parts

Specialized
subunit A's ←――――――――― The nature of the interdependence ――――――――――→ Specialized
tasks   subunit B's
                                                                           tasks

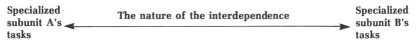

The company's external environment
Its technologies
Its objectives and strategies

Figure 4–2
Sales/manufacturing interdependence in two different companies

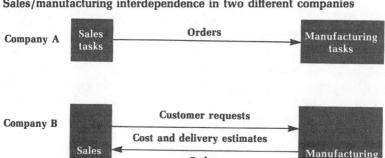

timely and accurate cost and delivery estimates because B's products do not have standard cost and delivery times like A's. If the plant doesn't respond quickly, or if it responds with cost and delivery times that are high, the salespeople will have great difficulty accomplishing their sales objectives. The salespeople also depend on the plant for supplying them with completed orders (salespeople deliver and install) that are on time and of the quality promised. Again, if the plant does not cooperate, sales will have difficulty doing its job. At the same time, manufacturing depends on sales for orders, as was the case in Company A, as well as for other types of customer data. Because the plant does not make standard products, it needs to know both what types of products customers want and what customers think about the products it makes. Without this information from sales, manufacturing cannot effectively accomplish its task.

The differences between the sales/manufacturing interdependence at Company A and Company B are summarized in Figure 4–2. These differences place dissimilar demands on the mechanisms that are needed to integrate sales and manufacturing. The key implication for organizational design is obvious: one would not use the same mechanisms to integrate manufacturing and sales in these two companies. One would use a different set of tools in each case—tools that are designed to fit the particular nature of the interdependence involved.[1]

To design mechanisms that can most appropriately integrate the parts of an organization requires that one understand how those parts are inter-

---

[1] For a further discussion of interdependence see chap. 5 in James Thompson, *Organizations in Action* (New York: McGraw-Hill, 1967), and chap. 13 in Pradip Khandwalla, *The Design of Organizations* (New York: Harcourt Brace Jovanovich, 1977).

dependent. But that alone, or even in conjunction with an understanding of the organization design tools that can be used to create integration, is not enough. One also needs an appreciation of those factors that make achieving integration economically difficult.

FACTORS THAT MAKE IT DIFFICULT TO COPE WITH INTERDEPENDENCE

In organizing an entire corporation, quite possibly the largest problem is related to the successful integration of its subunits. In talking to company presidents, it is not at all uncommon to have them report problems such as these:

Our line and staff departments just won't cooperate with each other, and it's costing us a lot of money.

The manufacturing-sales interface is a constant source of problems, and this is giving us a bad reputation among our customers.

We just can't seem to get the interdepartmental coordination we need to quickly bring out new products.

Complexity

A number of factors typically contribute to these kinds of integration problems, one of which has to do with the complexity and intensity of the interdependence itself.

Sometimes, because of the nature of a business's environment, technology, or strategy, its subunits will be interdependent in relatively simple ways. Such was the case of Company A in Figure 4–2. Other times, subunit interdependence can be moderate to very complex because of:

1. The volume of information (per unit of time) that must go from one unit to another.
2. The multidirectionality of that information (e.g., it is not just $A \rightarrow B$, but $A \rightleftharpoons B$).
3. The nonstandard nature of the information.

Consider, for example, a large, technologically complex manufacturer whose strategy is to achieve high profit margins by developing new products before any of its competitors. It has four major functional units: engineering, manufacturing, marketing, and administration (accounting, personnel, etc.). Bringing out complex new products that are successful in the marketplace requires hundreds of daily decisions, and often these decisions require expertise from many people in more than one functional unit. Consequently, a great deal of information needs to be transmitted among the functional units each day, and it would be difficult to predict, even a few days in advance, exactly what that information would be in any specific case. In situations like this, where the interdependence is intense and complex, achieving successful integration economically is obviously much more difficult than in situations where the interdependence is less complex.[2]

Differentiation

A second factor that contributes to integration problems is differentiation, that is, systematic differences in the values, attitudes, and behaviors of employees in different subunits. Social scientists have long established that communication and understanding usually are easiest to achieve among people who are very similar.[3] With similar goals, values, expectations, and world views, the potential for conflict or for simple misunderstandings is minimized. Through specialization, organizations purposely create differences among their subunits so that they can most effectively accomplish different kinds of tasks. But once created, these differences in objectives, personalities, education, time frames, and so on, can make the coordination of the subunits even more difficult.[4]

The following scene, for example, has probably been repeated, with slight variations, thousands of times.[5]

Factory Supervisor: *I'd like to get this work done as quickly as possible.*

Laboratory Group Leader: *Well, it will take us some time to understand the factors involved, and I also have to free up a person to work on it. . . .*

Factory Supervisor: *I understand that, but this work is critical to my operation. We've got a high spoilage rate now.*

Laboratory Group Leader: [To himself—*Hell, this isn't a challenging problem, none of my people will want to work on it.*] *I suspect we might make some progress in a month's time.*

Factory Supervisor: *A month? You've got to be kidding! That's a month of bad products and reduced output.* [To himself—*My boss will eat me alive if we don't get this solved before then.*] *I was hoping you could do it this week.*

Laboratory Group Leader: *No way . . .*

---

[2] For further discussion of how organizations cope with varying amounts and types of information processing among functional units see Jay Galbraith, *Designing Complex Organizations* (Reading, Mass.: Addison-Wesley, 1973), chap. 2.

[3] See Carl R. Rogers and F. J. Roethlisberger, "Barriers and Gateways to Communication," *Harvard Business Review,* July–August 1952, pp. 46–52.

[4] See Paul Lawrence and Jay Lorsch, *Organization and Environment* (Boston: Harvard Business School, 1967).

[5] From "Organization Design," by Jay Lorsch. (Intercollegiate Case Clearing House, Soldiers Field, Boston, Mass. 02163) 9–476–094, pp. 10–11.

In analyzing this type of situation, people often assume the problem is a function of the specific individuals involved, without realizing that the organization itself has systematically created the basis of their conflict. To do a good job at the research task, the company in the example staffed the laboratory with managers who enjoyed working on unstructured tasks and gave them a great deal of autonomy. They measured and rewarded these managers on their long-term effect on innovation and knowledge building. At the same time, however, to achieve its production goals the company organized the factory so that its managers thought in terms of costs, quality, and productivity in the short run, and liked a "no surprises," orderly operation. Under these circumstances, it is hardly surprising that a factory manager and a lab manager might find themselves arguing with one another.

Poor informal relationships

A third factor that leads to integration problems is poor informal relationships among subunits. For example, if an organization's history has created informal norms that encourage subunit independence, and informal relationships among people in subunits have been characterized by suspicion and distrust, then the potential for conflict and problems will certainly exist if the subunits become interdependent.

When the type of conflict characterized by the factory manager and the laboratory manager continues over a period of time, it is relatively easy for the subunits involved to grow resentful of each other. Once distrust has developed, it can perpetuate itself even without much direct group-to-group contact. For example, a new factory manager may seldom, if ever, interact with anyone from the lab, but may nevertheless be very distrustful of those "long haired crazies" simply because that attitude is pervasive in the factory.[6]

One of the most common types of integration problems found in organizations, line/staff conflict, is created by a combination of all three of the factors discussed so far. Line and staff organizations are usually designed so that they are highly interdependent. Specifically, the staff often depends on the line managers to take their advice, to act on it, and to give them proper recognition for their achievements. The line depends on the staff to give them helpful advice that does not interfere with their efforts either to achieve their job objectives or to relate to their superiors. In addition, staff and line units tend to be made up of different types of people, who are measured and rewarded differently. The staff are gener-

---

[6] Edgar Schein, *Organizational Psychology* (Englewood Cliffs, N.J.: Prentice-Hall, 1965), chap. 5.

ally more specialized and are not measured on bottom line results as are line executives. These built-in differences produce conflict which, over time, may lead to a deterioration in the relations between line and staff people. The complex interdependence, the different orientations, and the bad relationships then produce even more conflict. Under these circumstances it is hardly surprising that line managers often accuse the staff of being too specialized, of making unrealistic recommendations, of taking credit when things go well and hiding when they don't, and of acting as a spy for top management. Nor is it unusual that staff managers often complain that line people are resistant to change and are unwilling to provide the staff with proper recognition or adequate authority.[7]

Poor informal relationships among subunits can sometimes be traced to personality incompatibility. Although this factor is much less important than historical circumstances, occasionally one finds integration problems that are created by two subunit heads, or two key people in different subunits who would have difficulty relating to each other under any circumstance.

Size and physical distance

A fourth factor that can make integration difficult is size. As the number of employees in a firm increases, the number of potentially interdependent relationships among individuals in different subunits also increases. To take a simple example, in a firm with just one sales and one production employee, there is obviously just one interdependent human relationship between the sales unit and the production unit. In a firm with 100 sales and 100 production employees, each salesperson or sales manager easily might have an interdependent relationship with half a dozen production people—that is, people that he or she needs to communicate with regularly. Overall then, there could be hundreds of relevant interdependent relationships between the sales and production units. And as the number of relationships grows, the potential for creating integration problems also grows.[8]

A final factor that can contribute to integration problems is physical distance. It is much easier for people to manage their interdependence when they work in close proximity to one another. In large corporations, offices may be separated by as much as 10,000 miles. Although technological advances in communications and transportation make it much easier

---

[7] For an interesting description of line/staff conflict, see Melville Dalton, *Men Who Manage* (New York: John Wiley & Sons, 1969), chap. 4.

[8] William G. Ouchi and Reuben T. Harris, "The Dynamic Organization: Structure, Technology, and Environment," in *Organizational Behavior-Issues and Research,* ed. George Strauss et al. (Industrial Relations Research Association, 1974).

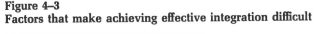

Figure 4–3
Factors that make achieving effective integration difficult

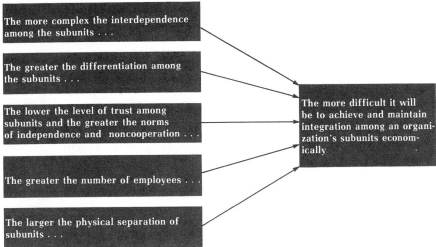

to integrate distant operations, physical separation can still create problems.[9]

A sensitivity to all of the factors that can contribute to integration problems is important. If several are involved in a specific situation, then achieving effective integration will probably require considerable effort. (Figure 4–3). Moreover, in designing solutions it is important to know exactly which factors are involved; just as was the case with different types of interdependence, different complicating factors tend to require different types of organizational design solutions.

COMMONLY USED INTEGRATING DEVICES

Virtually all organizational design tools can be used to solve certain types of integration problems. The key to using them efficiently and effectively is knowing exactly what each can accomplish and at what cost.

Management hierarchy

Perhaps the most common solution to solving an integration problem among two or more subunits has been to have them report to the same

---

[9] Harold J. Leavitt, *Managerial Psychology* (The University of Chicago Press, 1964), p. 236.

supervisor, who would then see to it that their activities were properly integrated by facilitating communications, resolving conflicts, and the like.[10] Furthermore, by having a continuous "chain of command" or set of management positions that link all the organization's major and minor subunits, one has a built-in mechanism for resolving conflict and coordinating activities throughout the organization. For example, if the head of the Eastern sales office and the supervisor for an assembly line cannot settle a conflict regarding delivery delays, the problem would be communicated up the chain from both departments until both messages came to the same person (perhaps the division manager), who would then resolve the problem.

If staffed with appropriate individuals, a management hierarchy can be very effective in fostering subunit integration. By itself, however, the hierarchy can easily become overloaded with conflicts to resolve, information to pass on, etc. In such cases, executives find themselves working long hours trying to coordinate activities personally while the backlog of conflicts and decisions to be made grows. Of course, one could reduce the overload by adding more positions in the hierarchy, thus reducing the span of control. Up to a point, this solution can help; but it can also become expensive and create a large number of levels in the hierarchy that can ultimately distort communication.[11]

Staff

The problem of hierarchy overload can also be alleviated to some degree through the use of staff. By giving a line manager assistants or functional specialists, one can increase the amount of information his or her position in the hierarchy can process, the number of decisions it can make, and the amount of conflict it can resolve. However, there are two drawbacks to using staff as an integrating device. The first is cost. It is not surprising that the smaller the company, the less staff its managers usually have. The second drawback, as already mentioned, is that a staff group can create integration problems as well as solve them—especially between themselves and line managers in the subunits.

Rules and procedures

Rules and procedures are another mechanism that can be used to keep the management hierarchy from becoming overloaded. When decision

---

[10] For example, "the most ancient, as well as the most important, device for achieving coordination is the supervisor." Harold Koontz and Cyril O'Donnell, *Principles of Management* (New York: McGraw-Hill, 1955), p. 38.

[11] Jay Galbraith, *Organization Design,* (Reading, Mass.: Addison-Wesley, 1977) pp. 48–49; and Richard H. Hall, *Organizations: Structure & Process* (Englewood Cliffs, N.J.: Prentice-Hall, 1972), chap. 9.

situations routinely arise that affect two or more parts of an organization, it is sometimes possible to establish rules or procedures regarding how they should be handled. For example: "Whenever a salesman receives an order over $5,000, he or she should inform the plant's production scheduler, by phone or in person, within four hours."

The biggest advantage of this mechanism is that it is a very economical way to achieve integration. Compare, for example, the one-time cost of developing and implementing a set of procedures with the ongoing cost of using an entire management hierarchy or a large staff. The problem with these integration devices, however, is that they only work when intelligent rules can be established and when the situation is stable enough that the company does not have to be constantly changing the rules. Furthermore, when organizations rely heavily on rules for integration or other purposes, there are a variety of dysfunctional consequences. For example, since rules have to be policed, they create stress between managers (policers) and workers. And since rules and procedures inevitably specify minimum acceptable behavior, they often cause behavior to settle at that minimum level.[12] Moreover, excessive reliance on rules and procedures can lead to "goal displacement," where the pursuance of those rules and procedures becomes an end in itself rather than a means toward the end of achieving the goals of the organization. That, in turn, can produce rigidity of behavior and an inability to respond to changing circumstances.[13]

Goals and plans

Goals and plans can serve a function similar to that of rules and procedures, but for a limited time. That is, once established, they allow two or more parts of an organization to operate relatively independently, and yet have their outputs integrated. For example, by setting exact specifications for modifying a product and by determining timetables for its production and introduction dates, the engineering, marketing, and manufacturing departments of a company can work independently on their part of the new product development task and at the same time be assured that it will still fit with the other parts. Coordination is thus achieved.

Except in circumstances where planning and goal setting are infeasible, perhaps because events are too unpredictable, these devices can be very useful in facilitating integration. The major drawback to using goals and plans is their cost. It takes time and energy to create realistic and intelligent goals and plans. In some circumstances, this cost simply precludes

[12] A. W. Gouldner, *Patterns of Industrial Bureaucracy* (The Free Press, 1954).

[13] R. K. Merton, "Bureaucratic Structure and Personality," *Social Forces*, vol. 18 (1970), pp. 560–68.

the use of these devices, particularly when compared with other devices (such as rules and procedures).[14]

Committees and task forces

Still another set of structural devices that can be used to facilitate integration consists of meetings, committees, task forces, and the like. To help coordinate sales and production, for example, the heads of the two units along with some of their staff might meet for a few hours each week.

Committees, task forces, and meetings are attractive in that they can solve integration problems that some other devices cannot. Unlike rules or plans, they can deal with nonroutine, spur-of-the-moment issues. Unlike a management hierarchy, they can process a lot of information and make many decisions in a relatively short period of time. The primary drawback of this device is cost. One committee of eight middle-level managers that meets once a week for two hours can easily cost an organization (in salary, benefits, and support services) over $15,000 a year. A second drawback is related to the need for small-group decision-making skills on the part of those participating in committees or task forces. Without these skills, the groups can become inefficient and ineffective, and employees can become frustrated and angry.[15]

Integrating roles

Under certain circumstances where coordination is particularly difficult to achieve and yet is particularly important, organizations can create special integrating roles or departments. A product manager position, for example, might be created to integrate the marketing and production subunits for a specific product or product line. Or a project manager position might be created to help integrate personnel from different subunits working on a project.

Typically, the integrator does not have direct authority over the personnel he or she coordinates. This prevents the integrator from "railroading" decisions against the better judgment of the specialists he or she coordinates. This lack of authority can be frustrating, because the coordinator is forced to rely on considerable initiative and personal skills (enthusiasm, energy, tact, judgment) to bring about the necessary integration. Accordingly, the selection of people with the appropriate background and skills

---

[14] Jay Galbraith, *Designing Complex Organizations* (Reading, Mass.: Addison-Wesley, 1973), pp. 12–14.

[15] For a good description of the types of skills that are needed and why, see Edgar Schein, *Process Consultation* (Reading, Mass.: Addison-Wesley, 1969), chaps. 3–7.

for the integration roles becomes crucial. To be effective, an integrator must be a good leader and have a somewhat "generalist" orientation—one that is different from that of the specialized subunits, yet allows him or her to understand each of them. Similarly, integrating departments seem to work best when they are structured in a way that is not identical to any of the subunits they must integrate but rather is in between them on important dimensions.[16]

Full-time integrators can be an expensive addition to an organization. The cost of just eight product managers can easily approach half a million dollars a year for salary and fringe benefits alone. A small company would have great difficulty justifying or affording such an expense.

Formal authority

Still another element of structure that can help or hinder effective integration is the distribution of formal authority in the organization, i.e., whether it is relatively centralized or decentralized, and whether subunits such as manufacturing and sales have equal power. To facilitate integration, authority should be distributed so that people or groups who have information relevant to making integrating decisions also have the power to make the decisions. For example, if a company depends on teams, meetings, and task forces to achieve integration, then power should be relatively decentralized. If a company relies almost exclusively on rules and a management hierarchy, then power should be relatively centralized.

The major problem with relying on formal authority to help achieve subunit integration is that once in place, it can be difficult to change when necessary. People seldom give up formal power without a fight.[17]

Measurement and reward systems

Measurement and reward systems are often used as integrating devices. In such cases, systems are set up to measure the variables related to the successful integration of certain subunits. This information is then sent to those decision makers who have the most control over the successful integration of these subunits, and their rewards are made partially contingent on their success at achieving it.[18]

---

[16] For a further discussion of integrating roles, see Paul R. Lawrence and Jay W. Lorsch, "New Management Job: The Integrator," *Harvard Business Review*, November–December 1967.

[17] Gene Dalton, Louis Barnes, and Abraham Zaleznik, *The Distribution of Authority in Formal Organizations* (Boston: Harvard Business School, 1968), chap. 3.

[18] J. Leslie Livingstone, "Managerial Accounting and Organizational Coordination," *The Accountant in a Changing Business Environment*, ed. Willard E. Stone (University of Florida Press, 1973), pp. 42–45.

For example, it is not uncommon for companies that utilize product managers to establish accounting systems which measure profitability, sales, and costs by individual product line. This information can be used by the product manager and is often tied in to his or her compensation.

While well-designed measurement and reward systems can motivate behavior that focuses on effective integration, they also have drawbacks. The first, again, is the direct cost of establishing and maintaining these systems. Other drawbacks relate to the indirect costs associated with the dysfunctional behavior these systems sometimes produce. To obtain the desired rewards these systems promise, people sometimes ignore important but unrewarded behaviors. Supervisors will, for example, stop helping others or investing time in their development unless their actions produce measured results. They will sometimes even focus on finding ways to fool the system into reporting invalid data that are favorable to them. In still other cases, they will simply stop working as hard or cooperating as much because of their resentment toward the "carrot and stick" system.[19]

Selection and development systems

Selection and development systems can serve as integration devices in two different ways. First, they can provide an organization with individuals who are capable of effectively playing key integrating roles. Second, they can help build better relationships between individuals or groups whose subunits require integration by providing formal training programs.

Selection systems provide organizations with people who can serve integrating roles by seeking and hiring people who have the characteristics of good integrators. Development systems can achieve similar results by taking existing personnel and, either with formal training programs or job rotation through specialist departments, develop them into effective integrators.

Selection systems can help improve relations between individuals or groups through occasional hiring and promotion decisions. For example, to help maintain good relations between sales and manufacturing personnel, some organizations periodically promote a few people across departmental lines.

Development systems also help provide integration among representatives of an organization's subparts through "team development" and "intergroup development" activities. Team development activities are usually focused on task forces, committees, or other groups that perform an inte-

---

[19] E. E. Lawler and J. G. Rhode, *Information and Control in Organizations* (Santa Monica, Calif.: Goodyear Publishing, 1976), chap. 6.

grating function. The objective of team development is to help these groups perform better. The method usually involves meeting in a nonwork setting for one to four days, with an agenda that focuses on group process and group problems. An expert in small-group process usually meets with the team to help the members identify and solve any communication, interpersonal, or leadership problems that impede their effectiveness.[20] Intergroup development activities focus on improving the relationships among the people in two or more subunits. They also usually involve an off-site meeting for one or two days with an expert facilitator. The activities typically focus on breaking down distorted beliefs on both sides, on helping each side understand the other better, and on building relationships and communication channels across the groups.[21] Both team and intergroup development activities are also used to encourage members to share norms in a company's culture that will facilitate effective integration. For example, there is considerable evidence that successful companies have norms that favor confronting conflicts and dealing with them through problem solving, rather than smoothing over conflict or avoiding it, or solving it by forcing one person's solution on another.[22] Team and intergroup development activities usually try to foster the development and maintenance of confronting and problem-solving norms.

Physical setting

Another element of organizational design that is sometimes used to facilitate integration is architecture. Because physical proximity makes communication easier, some organizations design their offices, conference areas, and open space with an eye toward meeting critical integration needs. For example, one money management firm felt that its 45-minute daily morning meeting was such an important device for facilitating coordination between the research and portfolio management departments that it spend over $100,000 to build a room that was specially designed for that meeting.[23]

Architecture has the same drawback as some of the other integrating devices. It can be expensive, and it can inadvertently reduce a company's needed specialization. For example, putting all the specialists that are

---

[20] For more information on team development see Shel Davis, "Building More Effective Teams," *Innovation,* vol. 15 (1970), pp. 32–41.

[21] For more information on intergroup development see Robert Blake and Jane Mouton, *Managing Intergroup Conflict for Industry* (Houston, Texas: Gulf, 1964).

[22] See, for example, Paul Lawrence and Jay Lorsch, *Organization and Environment* (Boston: Harvard Business School, 1967).

[23] For an in-depth look at physical settings as an integrating device, see Fritz Steele, *Physical Settings and Organizational Development* (Reading, Mass.: Addison-Wesley, 1973).

associated with product X in the same office area and providing them with team building activities will clearly help integration efforts concerning product X, but it might also lead to an erosion of the specialists' particular expertise. This can be threatening to specialists who view their career development contingent on continued specialization.

Departmentalization

A final way that managers can solve integration problems is to redesign subunit boundaries so as to include the required interdependence *within* the new subunit boundaries where it can be more easily managed.

One of the most common examples of the use of departmentalization as an integrating device is an organization that swithches from a functional to a product, market, or geographical structure. Small manufacturing firms typically use a functional structure; however, many switch to a product division structure after achieving a certain size. One of the key reasons they make this change is that integration across functions becomes increasingly difficult and expensive as they grow larger and larger. Increased size usually means a greater volume of information must flow between functions, thus increasing the complexity of the interdependence. With larger size come additional people and thus more interdependent relationships to be managed across functions. Specialization also tends to increase with size, and with it the differences among specialists in different functions are multiplied. The physical proximity of people in different functions tends to decrease with increases in size, and with it the possibility for easy face-to-face interaction. By shifting to product divisions, a company reduces the size of the functional units being integrated aroud each product, the amount of information flowing between the small functional units, and sometimes the physical distance between people in various functional units. These changes make functional integration around the designated products or product line easier.

Nevertheless, the switch from a functional to a product (or market or geographic) structure has some drawbacks. Achieving integration across the products can be more difficult. And often some functional specialization and/or economics of scale are sacrificed.[24]

Organizations that need both strong functional specialization and a high degree of integration across functions sometimes use a matrix structure. In bipolar matrix structures (the most common),[25] all jobs and minor

---

[24] For a further discussion of the trade-off between product and functional structures, see Jay Lorsch and Art Walker, "Organizational Choice: Product versus Function," *Harvard Business Review*, November–December 1968.

[25] Matrix structures can contain more than two dimensions. For an example of how a three-dimensional matrix is designed, see William C. Goggin, "How the Multidimensional Structure Works at Dow Corning," *Harvard Business Review*, January–February 1974.

departments are grouped into two major departments: usually one is associated with some function and the other is associated with some product or market. Everyone thus has two bosses.

In a sense, a matrix is an attempt to gain the benefits of *both* functional and product/market structures. It can do so, but not without its own costs. Because a matrix calls for two hierarchies, and because it requires time and effort to manage the ambiguity and tension which result from having multiple bosses for each person and subunit, a matrix can be expensive and difficult to maintain. In a matrix organization it is easy for unresovled conflicts between the two dimensions to slow down information flow and decisions. It is also possible for one side of the matrix to overpower the other, thus turning it back into a functional or a product/market organization for all practical purposes.[26]

Most organizations use some combination of functional, product, market, geographical, and matrix structures. For example, a manufacturing company might have five major subunits, four of which are functional departments (manufacturing, marketing, engineering, and administration) and one of which is a geographical department (international—all non-U.S. sales, manufacturing, etc.). The marketing department might be further divided into a number of market-oriented subunits. Manufacturing might be divided geographically, with plants in different regions of the country. Engineering might be structured as a matrix, where one side represents engineering functions (electrical, mechanical, etc.) while the other side represents new product development projects.

SELECTING A SET OF INTEGRATING MECHANISMS

In selecting a set of integrating mechanisms, an awareness of their individual strengths and weaknesses (Figure 4–4) is required. In addition, two generalizations may be made:

1. *The larger the number of factors that make achievement of integration difficult, the more costly the needed integration devices will be.*

    In an organization where there is little interdependence among the parts, where the parts are not highly specialized, and where informal relations among the parts are good, effective integration might well be achieved through a management hierarchy, along with some rules and procedures. In a large and geographically dispersed organization where there is intense interdependence among the parts, where the

---

[26] For more on matrix organizations, see Leonard Sayles, "Matrix Management," *Organizational Dynamics,* Autumn 1976, pp. 2–17; and Paul Lawrence, Harvey Kolodny, and Stanley Davis, "The Human Side of the Matrix," *Organizational Dynamics,* Summer 1977, pp. 43–61.

Figure 4–4
Costs and benefits of alternative integration methods

Integrating methods	Advantages	Drawbacks
The management hierarchy/span of control	Provides a network that links together all of an organization's major and minor functional units.	Can become overloaded and break down. A very narrow span can be expensive and cumbersome.
Staff	Can supplement the management hierarchy and help it perform a larger integration function.	Cost. Also can create its own integration problems (between staff and line).
Rules and procedures	Economical way to achieve integration around routine issues.	Limited to routine issues. Heavy use can create dysfunctional consequences.
Plans and goals	Can handle many nonroutine issues that rules and procedures cannot.	Cost, in time and effort.
Meetings, committees, task forces, etc.	Can deal with a large number of unpredictable problems and decisions.	Cost. People involved need skills at group decision making.
Integrating roles	Can deal with a large number of unpredictable problems and decisions	Cost. Can be difficult to find people with the right characteristics to fill the role.
Formal authority	No direct cost.	Can be abused; difficult to shift when shifts are needed.
Measurement and reward systems	Can motivate behavior directed at integration.	Cost. Activities or outcomes not measured and rewarded can be ignored or undermined. Can produce dysfunctional behavior.
Selection and development systems	Can solve certain types of problems more efficiently than other devices.	Can be expensive. Can erode specialized expertise.
Architecture	Under some circumstances, can be very inexpensive solution.	Can be expensive. Can erode specialized expertise.
Departmentalization: Functional structure Product/market geographic structure	Facilitates integration within functions. Promotes integration within and among functions associated with each product/market/geographical area.	Does not facilitate integration across functions. Does not promote integration between product/market/geographic area.
Matrix structure	Promotes integration between each side.	Expensive. Generates conflict and tension.

Figure 4–5
The relationship of integrating needs to integrating devices used*

	Industry		
	Container	Foods	Plastics
Integration needs	Low-	Moderate	High
Structural integration devices used	Hierarchy Procedures Some plans	Integrators Plans Hierarchy Procedures	Cross functional teams Integrators Departments of integrators Hierarchy, plans, and procedures

* Adapted from Paul R. Lawrence and Jay W. Lorsch, *Organization and Environment* (Boston: Harvard Business School, 1967).

parts are highly specialized, and where informal relations among the parts are poor, effective integration might require a hierarchy, rules, plans and goals, teams or task forces, integrating personnel, special measurement and reward systems, team building, and maybe more.

Lawrence and Lorsch, for example, in a study of companies in three different industries, found just this type of correlation between integration needs and integrating devices used[27] (see Figure 4–5).

2. *The effective solution to any integration problem is the one that costs the least and that does not seriously undermine the effectiveness of the specialized subunits.*

One of the most common problems managers encounter when trying to solve integration problems is related to cost. A second common problem is related to side effects. A good solution to any problem is one that does not create even more serious problems of a different kind. In solving integration problems managers sometimes seriously undermine the types of organization needed at the subunit level. More than one well-intentioned company president has managed to "get his people to start pulling together," but in the process, made them each less effective at their respective specialized tasks.

DRAWING SUBUNIT BOUNDARIES

In designing organizations, managers must make fundamental choices regarding not only how to organize subunits and how to integrate them,

[27] Paul Lawrence and Jay Lorsch, *Organization and Environment* (Boston: Harvard Business School, 1967).

but also regarding where to draw subunit boundaries in the first place. We have saved this issue until this point, because addressing it involves making trade-off judgments between:

1. The benefits to be gained from the development of specialized expertise and/or the economies of scale that are possible within subunit boundaries.
2. The cost of establishing, maintaining, and achieving effective integration across subunit boundaries.

An example will help clarify this issue:

A manufacturing company with 400 employees sold one product line to customers in three different industries. The firm was organized functionally, with marketing, engineering, manufacturing, and administrative departments reporting to the president (Figure 4–6A). In 1973, in response to an increasing number of recurring problems, the president decided to analyze the company's organization. A summary of his analysis follows:

a. *While we are currently serving customers in three industries, only eight years ago we were much smaller and were selling to customers in one industry only. This change is important because the demands that the customers in the three industries place on us are very different. The amount and type of special engineering that has to be done, the nature of selling and customer relations, and the way we can manufacture our products varies considerably between customers in different industries, but is very similar between customers in the same industry.*
b. *Our organization, which has grown in size but has not changed its structure in the past eight years, is just not able to effectively handle all three industries. We still do the best job and are most profitable in our original industry. That, I believe, is due to the fact that our engineering, sales, and manufacturing are still basically geared to that industry. I'm convinced that the key to increased sales and profitability is to better serve the different needs of customers in our two newer industries while retaining our ability to serve our older customers.*
c. *A number of people have suggested to me that we should reorganize into three industry-oriented groups (Figure 4–6B). I think that such a redefinition of our departmental boundaries would solve some problems but would create others. The industry-oriented structure would clearly allow us to develop expertise in serving customers in each of the three industries. But I think it is an impractical solution for a company of our size. It would require a number of additional managers. It would sacrifice a number of economies of scale we now have. It would be difficult to switch some slack engineering availability from one division to another, for example, which we can easily do with our current structure. And I'm not sure how we could keep from reinventing wheels within the three sales groups, the three engineering groups, etc., unless we had a lot of time-consuming meetings.*

Figure 4–6

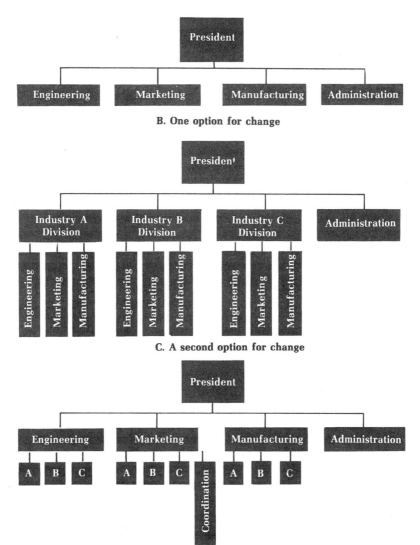

A. The 1973 organization

B. One option for change

C. A second option for change

d. *So I have tentatively decided on a modification of our current structure (Figure 4–6C), which essentially leaves the main department boundaries as they are, but creates a new set of groups within each department and adds three "industry coordinators" within marketing. This solution is economically feasible, and it will allow us to gain the expertise we need to serve all three industries.*

This solution was implemented during 1973, and after a period of adjustment, the company experienced large increases in sales and profits in 1975 and 1976.

Deciding where to draw major and minor subunit boundaries always involves an analytical and judgmental process similar to the one just described. The decision cannot be made according to any formula, and it must be made while considering the implications for organizing as well as integrating the subunits thus defined. The key to making this judgment, as well as to answering the other two major organizational questions raised at the beginning of this chapter, is a thorough analysis of the specific situation.

SUMMARY

Designing an organization or trying to solve an organizational problem from the point of view of an entire company requires a form of analysis that can be summarized in the following steps:

1. First one needs to identify the company's key activities, their diversity, and their interdependence. This business analysis can be accomplished only by thoroughly examining the company's external environment, its technology, and its strategy or goals. It is important here to be specific regarding exactly what the important characteristics of the activities are, how they are different, what the nature of the interdependence among them is, and what is really critical for success. If any of these factors have changed in the past five years or so, it is important to identify that as well as the reasons for the changes.

    Probably the biggest mistake that managers and consultants make in dealing with organizational issues is to begin defining problems and considering solutions without having completed a thorough examination of the business involved. Subunit boundary structure, integrating devices, and subunit organizational designs cannot be evaluated in the abstract. Rules, matrices, and profit centers are not "good" or "bad" by themselves. They are only appropriate or inappropriate in light of how well they fit a specific situation.

2. One must identify the company's current human resource organization in terms of staff characteristics, formal arrangements, and informal relationships. It is essential that one go beyond an analysis of the

Figure 4–7

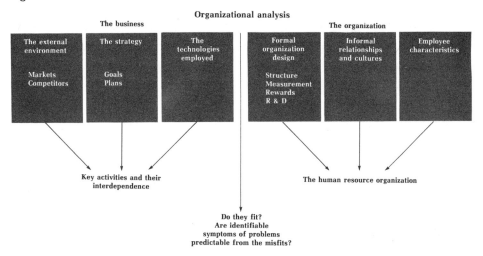

formal design. What is important is the actual human resource organization that has emerged in the situation. And that organization is very much a function of not only the formal design, but also of informal relations and employee characteristics.

Again, if any of these factors have changed recently, it is important to recognize that and the forces creating the change.

3. One should next make a judgment regarding how well the organization fits the company's business (see Figure 4–7).[28] This judgment can be compared with one's knowledge of the existence or absence of any recurring problems. If the analysis is sound, the logical consequences of the misfits should actually exist as problems in the organization.

4. Finally, one needs to identify alternative organizational designs that might solve the problems. That is, develop different solutions to the three basic questions raised at the beginning of this chapter. The answers can then be tested against the analysis, and a choice can be made.

There is no question that this mode of analysis involves making difficult judgments. No simple rule will dictate how a company should be organized. Nevertheless, the concepts and techniques outlined in this chapter provide analytical tools that can aid a manager in arriving at a decision that best fits the situation.

---

[28] For an example of this type of analysis as it pertains specifically to selecting management control systems, see Richard F. Vancil, "What Kind of Management Control Do You Need?" *Harvard Business Review*, March–April 1973.

Case 4–1
Continental Can Company
of Canada, Ltd.

Paul R. Lawrence

revised by John P. Kotter

By the fall of 1963, Continental Can Company of Canada had developed
a sophisticated control system for use in its plants. This control system,
begun in the years following World War II, stressed competition within
the company as well as against other companies in the industry. Within
its division at Continental, the can manufacturing plant at St. Laurent,
Quebec, had become a preferred site for production management trainees
as a result of its successful use of control systems. According to a division
training executive:

> *The St. Laurent people look at the controls as tools. They show trainees that
> they really work. The French-Canadian atmosphere is good too. In a French-
> Canadian family everything is open and above-board. There are no secrets. Train-
> ees can ask anyone anything and the friendliness and company parties give them
> a feel for good employee relations.*

PRODUCTS, TECHNOLOGY, AND MARKETS

Continental Can Company of Canada in 1963 operated a number of
plants in Canada. The principal products of the St. Laurent plant were
Open Top food cans, bottle caps and crowns, steel pails, and general
line containers. Of these Open Top cans constituted the largest group.
These were manufactured for the major packers of vegetable products—
peas, beans, corn, and tomatoes—and for the soup manufacturers. Beer
and soft drink cans were a growing commodity, and large quantities of
general line containers of many different configurations were produced
to hold solvents, paints, lighter fluids, waxes, antifreeze, and so on. Several
styles of steel pails of up to 5-gallon capacity were also produced to
hold many specialized products.

Most of the thousands of different products, varying in size, shape,
color, and decoration were produced to order. Typical lead times between
the customer's order and shipment from the plant were two to three weeks
in 1963, having been reduced from five and one half weeks in the early
1950s, according to St. Laurent plant executives.

Quality inspection in the can manufacturing operation was critical, as the can maker usually supplied the closing equipment and assisted in or recommended the process to be used in the final packing procedure. In producing Open Top food cans, for example, the can body was formed, soldered, and flanged at speeds exceeding 400 cans per minute. After the bottom or end unit was assembled to the body, each can was air tested to reject poor double seams or poor soldering or plate inclusions that could cause pin holes. Both side seams and double seams underwent periodic destruction testing to ensure that assembly specifications were met. Although a number of measuring devices were used in the process, much of the inspection was still visual, involving human inspection and monitoring. The quality of the can also affected the filling and processing procedure: it had to withstand internal pressures from expansion of the product as it was heated and then it had to sustain a vacuum without collapsing when it was cooled. Costly claims could result if the container failed in the field and the product had to be withdrawn from store shelves.

Almost all of the containers required protective coatings inside and out, and the majority were decorated. The coating and decorating equipment was sophisticated and required sizable investment. This part of the operation was unionized, and the lithographers or press men were among the highest paid of the various craftsmen in the plant.

Most of the key equipment was designed and developed by the parent organization over many years. The St. Laurent plant spend substantial sums each year to modernize and renovate its equipment. Modernization and the implementation of new techniques to increase speed, reduce material costs, and improve quality, were a necessity as volume increased. Over the years, many of the small run, handmade boxes and pails were discontinued and the equipment scrapped. Other lines were automated and personnel retrained to handle the higher mechanical skills and changeovers required. In spite of these changes, however, according to a general foreman, a production worker of the 1940s could return in 1963 and not feel entirely out of place. Many of the less skilled machine operators were required to handle several tasks on the higher speed equipment. In general, most of the jobs in the plant were relatively unskilled, highly repetitive, and gave the worker little control over method or pace. The die makers, who made and repaired the dies, and machine repairmen and those who made equipment set-up changes between different products were considered to possess the highest level of skill.

All production workers below the rank of assistant foreman were unionized; however, there had never been a strike at the plant. Wages were high compared to other similar industries in the Montreal area. The union was not part of the Master Agreement that governed all other plants in Canada and most of the plants in the United States, but management made every effort to apply equality to this plant. Output standards were established for all jobs, but no bonus was paid for exceeding standards.

The metal can industry was relatively stable with little product differentiation. The St. Laurent plant to some extent shipped its products throughout Canada although transportation costs limited its market primarily to Eastern Canada. While some of the customers were large and bought in huge quantities, (between 300–500 million cans) many were relatively small and purchased a more specialized product.

THE PLANT ORGANIZATION

Plant management

Andrew Fox, the plant manager at St. Laurent since 1961, had risen from an hourly worker through foreman up to plant manufacturing engineer in the maintenance end of the business. He had developed an intimate first-hand knowledge of operations and was frequently seen around the plant, a cigar clenched between his teeth.

As plant manager, Fox had no responsibility for sales or research and development activities. In fact, both Fox and the district sales manager in his area had separate executives to whom they reported in the division headquarters and it was in the superior of these executives that responsibility for both sales and production first came together.

Fox commented about the working relationships at the St. Laurent plant:

You will see that frequently two managers with different job titles are assigned responsibility for the same task. [He implied that it was up to them to work out their own pattern of mutual support and cooperation.] However, I don't have to adhere strictly to the description. I may end up asking a lot more of the man at certain times and under certain conditions than is ever put down on paper.

In effect, the staff[1] runs the plant. We delegate to the various staff department heads the authority to implement decisions within the framework of our budget planning. This method of handling responsibility means that staff members have to be prepared to sustantiate their decisions. At the same time, it gives them a greater sense of participation in and responsibility for plant income. We endeavor to carry this principle into the operating and service departments. The foreman is given responsibility and encouraged to act as though he were operating a business of his own. He is held responsible for all results generated in his department and is fully aware of how any decisions of his affect plant income.

Our division personnel counsel and assist the plant staff and the plant staff counsel and assist the department foreman. Regular visits are made to the plant

---

[1] The personnel reporting directly to Fox. The organization chart (see Exhibit 1) was prominently displayed on the wall of the lobby. See Exhibit 2 for other information on personnel.

Exhibit 1
St. Laurent Plant (March 1, 1963)

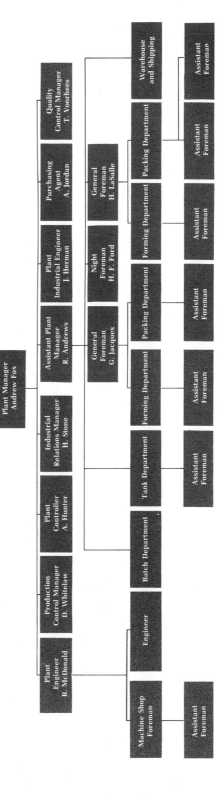

Exhibit 2
Information about certain personnel

| Name, Position | Approximate age | Approximate length of service | | College education |
		St. Laurent	CCC	
Andrew Fox,				
Plant Manager 40–45		8	18	None
Robert Andrews,				
Assistant Plant Manager 35		3	8	Agricultural Engineering
A. Hunter,				
Plant Controller 50		15	23	None
A. Whitelaw,				
Production Control Supervisor 45		18	18	None
Harold Stone,				
Personnel Supervisor 45–50		5	29	None
Joe Herman,				
Plant Industrial Engineer 30–35		1	10	Engineering
Tom Voorhees,				
Quality Control Supervisor 30		5	5	Engineering in Netherlands
G. E. Jacques,				
General Foreman 45–50		25	25	None
Henri LaSalle,				
General Foreman 50		18	18	None
L. G. Adams,				
District Sales Manager 45–50		18	18	None

by our division manager and members of his staff. The principal contact is through the division manager of manufacturing and his staff, the manager of industrial engineering, the manager of production engineering, and the manager of quality control. [There was no division staff officer in production control.]

However, the onus is on the plant to request help or assistance of any kind. We can contact the many resources of Continental Can Company, usually on an informal basis. That is, we deal with other plant managers directly for information when manufacturing problems exist, without going through the division office.

Each member of the staff understands that we, as a plant, have committed ourselves through the budget to provide a stated amount of income, and regardless of conditions which develop, this income figure must be maintained. If sales are off and a continuing trend is anticipated, we will reduce expenses wherever possible to retain income. Conversely, if we have a gain in sales volume we look for the complete conversion of the extra sales at the profit margin rate. However, this is not always possible, especially if the increase in sales comes at a peak time when facilities are already strained.

Fox was assisted by Robert Andrews, the assistant plant manager. Andrews, promoted from quality control manager in 1961, was responsible for all manufacturing operations within the plant. Andrews appeared more reserved than Fox, talked intently, and smiled easily while working with the persons that reported to him. Fifteen salaried supervisors reported to Andrews and helped him control the three-shift operation of the plant and its 500 hourly workers. (During peak periods during the summer, the plant employed as many as 800 people; most of the additional workers were the sons and daughters of plant employees).

Andrews: *Our foremen have full responsibility for running their departments; quality, conditions of equipment, employee relations, production according to schedule, control of inventory through accurate reporting of spoilage and production, and cost control. He is just as accountable for those in his department as the plant manager is for the entire plant.*

Andrews added that supervisory positions carried a good deal of status. Each supervisor had a personal parking spot and office and was expected to wear white shirts.[2] Andrews spoke of these symbols as an important aspect of the supervisor's position of authority. "He is no longer the best man with the wrench—he is the man with the best overall supervisory qualification."

Production control

Al Whitelaw, the production control manager, had worked all of his 18 years with Continental Can at the St. Laurent plant. He was responsible for planning and controlling plant inventories and production schedules to meet sales requirements consistent with efficient utilization of facilities, materials, and manpower. Whitelaw spoke quickly and chain-smoked cigarettes. According to him the main task of his job was ". . . to try to achieve the maximum length of run without affecting service or exceeding inventory budgets."

Whitelaw was assisted by a scheduler for each major operating department and clerks to service the schedulers. The schedulers worked closely with the department foreman in the plant and were in frequent telephone contact with the sales offices. Whitelaw commented: "We in production control are the buffer between sales and operating people."

To facilitate their work, Whitelaw and Andrews headed bi-weekly production control meetings, each lasting about one hour. Fox, the plant manager, was a frequent observer. These meetings were attended by the two general foremen. Each production foremen and the production control scheduler working for his department came into the meeting at

---

[2] The plant manager, management staff, foremen, and clerks in the office all wore white shirts and ties but no coat. The union president (a production worker) wore a white shirt but no tie. All other personnel wore colored sports shirts.

a prearranged time and when their turn came they reported on operations in their department and on problems they were encountering. Most of the questions, as well as instructions given in the meeting, came from Andrews. It was also he who usually dismissed one foreman/scheduler pair and called on the next. Questions from Andrews or Whitelaw were seldom clearly addressed to either the foreman or scheduler. They were answered more frequently by the scheduler than the foreman and often a scheduler would supplement comments made by the foreman. Generally the schedulers were younger but spoke with more self-assurance than the foreman.

In these meetings, there were frequent references to specific customers, their needs, complaints, and present attitudes toward Continental Can. Both Whitelaw and Andrews tended to put instructions and decisions in terms of what was required to satisfy some particular customer or group of customers.

A recent meeting involving a foreman, Maurice Pelletier, and the scheduler for his department, Dan Brown, is illustrative of the process. It was observed that while Dan presented the status report Maurice shook his head in disagreement without saying anything. Dan was discussing his plan to discontinue an order being processed on a certain line on Friday to shift to another order and then to return to the original order on Tuesday.

Andrews: *I don't think your plan makes much sense. You go off on Friday and then on again Tuesday.*

Maurice [*to Dan*]: *Is this all required before the end of the year?* [*This was asked with obvious negative emotional feeling and then followed by comments by both Andrews and Whitelaw.*]

Dan: *Mind you—I could call sales again.*

Whitelaw: *I can see the point, Dan. It is sort of nonsensical to change back after so short a run.*

Maurice: *This would mean our production would be reduced all week to around 300 instead of 350. You know it takes four hours to make the changeover.*

Dan: *But the order has been backed up.*

Andrews: *It is backed up only because their [sales] demands are unreasonable.*

Dan: *They only asked us to do the best we can.*

Andrews: *They always do this. We should never have put this order on in the first place.*

Maurice: *If you want to we could. . . . [Makes a suggestion about how to handle the problem.]*

Andrews: *Production-wise, this is the best deal. [Agreeing with Maurice's plan.]*

Dan: *Let me look at it again.*

Andrews: *Production-wise, this is best; make the changeover on the weekend.*

Whitelaw [*Summarizes; then to Dan*]: *The whole argument is the lost production you would have.*

Maurice: *It'll mean backing up the order only one day.*

Andrews [*After another matter in Maurice's department has been discussed and there is apparently nothing further, Andrews turns to Dan and smiles.*]: *It's been a pleasure, Dan.*

[*Dan then returned the smile weakly and got up to leave, somewhat nervously.*]

As Whitelaw left the conference room after the meeting he was heard to comment:

Danny got clobbered as you could see. I used to stand up for him but he just doesn't come up here prepared. He should have the plans worked out with his foreman before they come up.

When discussing his job Whitelaw frequently commented on how he thought a decision or problem would affect someone else in the plant:

If all you had to do was manage the nuts and bolts of production scheduling and not worry about the customer or how people were going to react, this would be the easiest job in the whole plant. You could just sit down with a paper and pencil and lay it out the best way. But because the customer is so important and because you've got to look ahead to how people are going to react to a given kind of schedule, it makes the whole job tremendously complicated. It isn't easy!

Other personnel and functions

Hunter, the plant accountant, reported directly to the plant manager, although he was functionally responsible to the division controller. The major tasks for Hunter's department were the development and application of many thousands of individual product costs and the coordination of the annual sales and income budget, developed by the responsible operating and staff groups. Explaining another of his duties Hunter noted:

We are the auditors who see that every other department is obeying rules and procedures. It is our responsibility to know all that is in the instruction manuals. There are 12 volumes of general instructions and lots of special manuals.

Joe Herman, the plant industrial engineer, explained the responsibilities of his department:

We're active in the fields of time study, budgetary control, job evaluation, and methods improvement. Our company is on a standard cost system—that is, all our product costs are based on engineered standards, accurately measuring all labor, direct and indirect, and material that is expended in the manufacture of each and every item we make in our plants. All the jobs in the St. Laurent plant, up to and including the foreman, have been measured and standards set. However, all our standards are forwarded to division which checks them against standards in use at other plants. There are company-wide benchmarks for most standards, since most of the machinery is the same in other Continental Can plants.

Herman noted that the budgeted savings from methods improvement was approximately $600,000 for the year, and he expected to exceed that by a substantial amount.

Harold Stone, the industrial relations manager, was proud that the St. Laurent plant had never experienced a strike and that formal written grievances were almost unheard of. Stone ran training programs and monitored safety, absenteeism, and turnover data. The St. Laurent plant had an outstanding record in these areas. Stone attributed this to the high wages and fringe benefits of the plant. He also maintained campaigns on housekeeping and posted slogans and comments, in both French and English, on job security and industrial competition. Also he was responsible for the display of a five-foot chart on an easel near the main entrance which showed the manufacturing efficiency rating (actual production cost versus standard cost) of the previous month for each of the Continental Can Company plants and their standing within the division.

On Continental Can's personnel policy, Stone stated:

We believe that it is important that the supervisor and the employee understand each other, that they know what the other person thinks about business, profit, importance of satisfying the customer, and any other aspect of business. We also believe that rapport between the supervisor and the employee can be improved in the social contacts which exist or can be organized. For this reason we sponsor dances, bowling leagues, golf days, fishing derbies, picnics, baseball leagues, supervision parties, management weekends, and many unofficial get-togethers. Over many years we have been convinced that these activities really improve management-labor relations. They also provide a means for union and management to work closely together in organizing and planning these events. These opportunities help provide a mutual respect for the other fellow's point of view.

It was Stone's responsibility to maintain the confidential file in connection with Continental's performance appraisal program for salaried employees. Procedures for handling the program were spelled out in one of the corporate manuals. Two forms were completed annually. One called for a rating of the employee by his supervisor, first on his performance of each of his responsibilities outlined in the Position Analysis Manual and then on each of 12 general characteristics such as cooperation, initiative, job knowledge and delegation. In another section the supervisor and the appraised employee were jointly required to indicate what experience, training, or self-development would improve performance or prepare for advancement by the employee prior to the next appraisal. The appraisal was to be discussed between the supervisor and the employee; the latter was required to sign the form and space was given for any comments he might want to make. The second form was not shown to the employee. It called for a rating on overall performance, an indication of promotability, and a listing of potential replacements. It was used for manpower planning, and after comments by the supervisor of the appraiser, it was forwarded to the division office.

MANAGERIAL PRACTICES

Managing with budgets

Management at the St. Laurent plant coordinated their activities through a number of informal, as well as scheduled, meetings. Impromptu meetings of two or more members of management were frequent, facilitated by the close proximity of their offices. Among the formal meetings, the most important was the monthly discussion of performance against the budget. This meeting was attended by all of the management staff as well as production supervisors. Other regularly scheduled meetings included the production control meeting (twice weekly) and the plant cost reduction committee meetings.

In discussing the budget, Fox explained that the manufacturing plant was organized as a profit center. Plant income was determined by actual sales, not a transfer price. Therefore income was adversely affected when, either, sales failed to come up to the forecast on which the budget was based or sales prices were reduced to meet competition. Fox also explained that sales managers also have their incentives based on making or exceeding the budget and that their forecasts had tended to be quite accurate. Over optimism of one group of products had usually been offset by underestimation of sales on other products. However, because no adjustment was permitted in budgeted profit when sales income was below forecast, the fact that sales were running 3 percent below the level budgeted for 1963 was forcing the plant to reduce expenses substantially in order to equal or exceed the profit budgeted for the year.

When asked whether the budget was a straightjacket or if there were some accounts which left slack for reducing expenses if sales fell below forecast, Fox replied:

We never put anything in the budget that is unknown or guessed at. We have to be able to back up every single figure in the budget. We have to budget our costs at standard assuming that we can operate at standard. We know we won't all the time. There will be errors and failures, but we are never allowed to budget for them.

Hunter agreed with Fox stating that "in this company there is very little opportunity to play footsy with the figures."

Fox conceded that there were some discretionary accounts like overtime and outside storage which involved arguments with the division. For example, "I might ask for $140,000 for overtime. The division manager will say $130,000, so we compromise at $135,000." As far as cost-reduction projects are concerned, Fox added that ". . . we budget for more than the expected savings. We might have $100,000 in specific projects and budget for $150,000."

Fox went on to note that equipment repairs and overhauls could be delayed to reduce expenses. But even the overhaul schedule was included as part of the budget, and any changes had to be approved at the division level.

Robert Andrews complained that the budget system didn't leave much room for imagination. He felt that overly optimistic sales estimates were caused by the sales people being fearful of sending a pessimistic estimate up to the division. These estimates, according to Andrews, were a major source of manufacturing inefficiency.

Andrews was asked whether he was concerned about increasing production volume, and he replied:

We have standards. So long as we are meeting the standards we are meeting our costs and we do not worry about increasing production. We don't tell the foreman that he needs to get more goods out the door. We tell him to get rid of the red in his budget. I'm content with a 100 percent performance. I'd like 105 percent but if we want more production it is up to industrial engineering to develop methods changes.

Andrews talked about the necessary skills for a foreman:

The foreman should be good at communications and the use of available control procedures. The foreman is expected to communicate effectively with all plant personnel, including staff heads. Our control procedures are easy to apply. In each department there is an engineered standard for each operation covering labor, materials, and spoilage. Without waiting for a formal statement from accounting, a foreman can analyze his performance in any area and take corrective action if necessary. Then he receives reports from accounting to assist him in maintaining tight cost control. One is a daily report which records labor and spoilage performance against standard. The monthly report provides a more detailed breakdown of labor costs, materials and supplies used, and spoilage. It also establishes the efficiency figure for the month. This report is discussed at a monthly meeting of all my supervisors. Generally the plant industrial engineer and a member of the accounting staff are present. Each foreman explains his variances from standard and submits a forecast for his next month's performance.

The bonus plan

Andrew Fox indicated that the budget was also used in rewarding employees of Continental Can. The incentive for managers was based on performance of the plant compared to budget. According to Fox:

The bonus is paid on the year's results. It is paid as a percentage of salary to all who are eligible—they are the ones on the organization chart (see Exhibit 1). There are three parts to it—one part is based on plant income, one on standards improvement or cost cutting, and the third on operating performance. We can make up to 20 percent by beating our plant income target and 25 percent on cost reduction and operating efficiency together. But we have to make 90 percent of our budgeted income figure to participate in any bonus at all.

I think we have the 25 percent on efficiency and cost reduction pretty well sewn up this year. If we go over our budgeted income, we can get almost 35 percent bonus.

In years past, St. Laurent managers had made about 10 percent of their salaries from the bonus. The improved performance was the result of a change in the design of the bonus plan. Hunter explained the effect of the change:

At one time the bonus plan was based on departmental results and efficiency. Under this there was a tendency for the departments to work at cross purposes, to compete rather than cooperate with each other. For the last seven or eight years, the emphasis has been on the plant, not the department. The latest plan is geared not only to the attainment of budgeted cost goals, but also the attainment of budgeted income. This is consistent with the attention we are placing on sales. I think the company was disturbed by what they sensed was a belief that those at the plant level can't do much about sales. Now we are trying to get the idea across that if we make better cans and give better service, we will sell more.

FOREMEN AND PRODUCTION WORKERS

General foremen

Guillaume Jacques and Henri LaSalle were the general foremen on two of the three shifts. They described their jobs as working closely with both the assistant plant manager and the production control manager, but more with the latter. Jacques and LaSalle were asked how they balanced employee satisfaction with the requirements of the budget. Jacques commented:

Management not only asks me to meet the budget but do better. So, you've got to make the worker understand the importance of keeping the budget. I get them in the office and explain that if we don't meet the budget we'll have to cut down somewhere else. It is mathematical. I explain all this to them; management has given me a budget to meet, I need them for this, they need me to give them work. We work like a team. I try to understand them. All supervisors work under tension. Myself, I ask the men to go out to have a beer with me, to go to a party. It relaxes them from our preoccupations. Right now, for example, there is this party with the foremen coming up. At these gatherings it is strictly against the rules to talk about work. These things are necessary.

LaSalle explained that while foremen have a copy of the budget for their department, the workers see only a machine operating standard. The standard was set so that if he works the machine at full capacity he achieves 110 percent of standard. LaSalle told of his way of handling workers.

Well, there is usually some needling when a man is down below standard. He's told, "Why don't you get to be part of the crew?" It doesn't hurt anything . . . you only get a good day's work out of people if they are happy. We strive to keep our people happy so they'll produce the standard and make the budget. We try to familiarize them with what is expected of them. We have targets set for us. The budget is reasonable, but it is not simple to attain. By explaining out problems to the workers we find it easier to reach the budget.

Foremen

Most of the foremen were aware of, and accepted, the necessity of keying their activities to the work standards and budgets. One young, and purportedly ambitious, foreman commented about his job:

What I like about this department is that I am in charge. I can do anything I like as long as I meet up with the budget. I can have that machine moved— send it over there—as long as I have a good reasons to justify it. The department, that's me. I do all the planning and I'm responsible for results. I'm perfectly free in the use of my time (gives examples of his different arrival time during the past week and the fact that he came in twice on Saturday and once on Sunday for short periods).

While other foremen expressed dislike for some of the pressures inherent in their jobs, there was general satisfaction. One notable exception was a foreman with many years' service who said:

We have a meeting once a month upstairs. They talk to us about budgets, quality, etc. That's all on the surface; that's b---s---. It looks good. It has to look good but it is all bull. For example, the other day a foreman had a meeting with the workers to talk about quality. After that an employee brought to his attention a defect in some products. He answered, "Send it out anyway." and they had just finished talking to us about quality.

Foremen tended to view the production worker as irresponsible and interested, insofar as his job is concerned, only in his pay check and quitting time. One foreman said, "We do all the work; they do nothing." Even an officer of the union, speaking about the workers, commented:

They don't give a damn about the standards. They work nonchalantly and they are very happy when their work slows up. If the foreman is obliged to stop the line for two minutes everyone goes to the toilet. There are some workers who do their work conscientiously, but this is not the case with the majority.

Comments from workers

Several of the production workers expressed feelings of pressure although others declared they were accustomed to their work and it did not bother them. One said:

Everyone is obsessed with meeting the standards—the machine adjuster, the foreman, the assistant foreman. They all get on my nerves.

One old-timer clearly differentiated the company, which he considered benevolent, from his foreman:

I can understand that these men are under tension as well as we are. They have meetings every week. I don't know what they talk about up there. The foremen have their standards to live up to. They're nervous. They don't even have a union like us. So if things go bad, well, that's all. They make us nervous with all this. But there's a way with people. We don't say to a man, "Do this, do that." If we said, "Would you do this?" it is not the same thing. You know a guy like myself who has been here for 35 years knows a few tricks. If I am mad at the foreman I could do a few little things to the machine to prevent it from keeping up with standards and no one would know.

While some workers stated they would work for less money if some of the tension were relieved, the majority were quite content with their jobs.[3]

ENFORCING THE BUDGET

By November 1963, sales for the year had fallen below expectations and the management bonus was in jeopardy as a result.

One day in early November there was an unusual amount of activity in the accounting section. Fox came into the area frequently and he and

---

[3] In a Harvard Business School research study of 12 plants in the United States and Canada, the St. Laurent plant workers ranked highest of the 12 plants in job satisfaction.

Hunter from time to time would huddle with one of the accountants over some figures. Hunter explained that the extra activity was in response to a report on the October results that had been issued about a week before.

Fox decided to schedule a joint meeting of the management staff and the line organization to go over the October results. This was a departure from the usual practice of having the groups in separate meetings. Prior to the meeting Fox outlined what he hoped to accomplish in the meeting:

Those figures we got last week showed that some of the accounts did what they were expected to do, some did more, and some did a good deal less. The thing we have to do now is to kick those accounts in the pants that are not making the savings they planned to make. What we've been doing is raising the expected savings as the time gets shorter. It may be easy to save 10 percent on your budget when you've got six months; but with only six weeks, it is an entirely different matter. The thing to do now is to get everybody together and excited about the possibility of doing it. We know how it can be done. Those decisions have already been made. It's not unattainable even though I realize we are asking an awful lot from these men. You see we are in a position now where just a few thousand dollars one way or the other can make as much as 10 percent difference in the amount of bonus the men get. There is some real money on the line. It can come either from a sales increase or an expense decrease, but the big chunk has to come out of an expense decrease.

Fox did not feel there would be a conflict in the meeting about who is right and who is wrong:

We never fight about the budget. It is simply a tool. All we want to know is what is going on. There are never any disagreements about the budget itself. Our purpose this afternoon is to pinpoint those areas where savings can be made, where there is a little bit of slack, and then get to work and pick up the slack.

Fox talked about his style in handling cost and people problems:

When budgeted sales expenses get out of line, management automatically takes in other accounts to make up the losses. We'll give the department that has been losing money a certain period of time to make it up. Also, anytime anybody has a gain, I tell them I expect them to maintain that gain.

The manager must make the final decisions and has to consider the overall relationships. But there are some things I can't delegate—relations with sales for example. The manager, and not production control, must make the final decisions.

Larry Adams, the sales manager in our district, feels that the budget gets in the way of the customer's needs. He thinks the budget dominates the thinking and actions around here. Maybe he's right. But I have to deal with the people and problems here.

The manager must be close to his people. I take a daily tour of the plant and talk to the people by name. My practice as a manager is to follow a head-

on approach. I don't write many memos. When I have something to say I go tell the person or persons right away. That's why I'm holding a meeting this afternoon.

Bob Andrews commented on the methods used to pick up the projected savings:

When you have lost money in one sector you have to look around for something else that you can "milk" to make up the difference. But we don't ask for volunteers, we do the "milking." Those guys just have to do what we say. How much we can save pretty much depends on how hard the man in the corner office wants to push on the thing. I mean if we really wanted to save money we probably could do it, but it would take a tremendous effort on everybody's part and Fox would really have to crack the whip.

Because of Fox's comments on relationships with sales, Larry Adams, the district sales manager, was asked about his feelings on working with the production people at the St. Laurent plant:

The budget comes to dominate people's thinking and influence all their actions. I'm afraid even my salesmen have swallowed the production line whole. They can understand the budget so well they can't understand their customers. And the St. Laurent plant boys are getting more and more local in their thinking with this budget. They're not thinking about what the customer needs today or may need tomorrow, they just think about their goddamned budget.

If the customer will not take account of your shortcomings, and if you can't take account of the customer's shortcomings, the two of you will eventually end up at each other's throats. That's what this budget system has built into it. Suppose, for example, you want to give a customer a break. Say he has originally planned for a two-week delivery date, but he phones you and says he really has problems and if you possibly could he would like about four days knocked off that delivery date. So I go trotting over to the plant, and I say, "Can we get it four days sooner?" Those guys go out of their minds, and they start hollering about the budget and how everything is planned just right and how I'm stirring them up. They get so steamed up I can't go running to them all the time but only when I really need something in the worst way. You can't let those plant guys see your strategy, you know. It is taking an awful lot out of a guy's life around here when he has to do everything by the numbers.

Special budget meeting

The meeting was held in the conference room at 4:00 P.M. Fox and Hunter sat at the far end of the table, facing the door, with an easel bearing a flip chart near them. The chart listed the projected savings in budgeted expenses for November and December, account by account. The group of about 30 arranged themselves at the table so that, with only a couple of exceptions, the management staff personnel and general foremen sat closest to Fox and Hunter and the foremen and assistant foremen sat toward the foot of the table.

Fox opened the meeting and declared that performance against the budget for October would first be reviewed, followed by discussion of the November and December projections. He stated rather emphatically that he was "disappointed" in the October performance. Although money had been saved, it represented good performance in some areas but rather poor performance in others. The gains made in the areas where performance had been good must be maintained and the weak areas brought up, Fox declared.

He then turned the meeting over to Hunter who reviewed the October results, reading from the report which everyone had in front of him. Where performance was not good, he called on the individual responsible for that area to explain. The typical explanation was that the original budgeted figure was unrealistic and that the actual amount expended was as low as it could possibly be under the circumstances. Fox frequently broke into the explanation with a comment like, "Well, that is not good enough" or, "Can you possibly do better for the rest of the year?" or, "I hope we have that straightened out now." When he sat down, the person giving the explanation was invariably thanked by Hunter.

Next, Hunter, followed by Whitelaw, commented on the sales outlook for the remainder of the year. They indicated that for two months as a whole sales were expected to be about on budget. After asking for questions and getting one from a foreman, Fox said:

Well now, are there any more questions? Ask them now if you have them. Everybody sees where we stand on the bonus, I assume. Right?

Fox then referred to the chart on plant expense savings and began to discuss it saying:

The problem now is time. We keep compressing the time and raising the gain (the projected savings for the year had been raised $32,000 above what had been projected in October). You can only do that so long. Time is running out, fellows. We've got to get on the stick.

Several times Fox demanded better upward communication on problems as they came up. Referring to a specific example, he said:

This sort of thing is absolutely inexcusable. We've got to know ahead of time when these mix-ups are going to occur so that we can allow for and correct them.

As Hunter was covering manufacturing efficiency projections for November, he addressed Andrews:

Now we have come to you, Bob. I see you're getting a little bit more optimistic on what you think you can do.

Andrews replied:

Yes, the boss keeps telling me I'm just an old pessimist and I don't have any faith in my people. I'm still a pessimist, but we are doing tremendously. I think it's terrific, fellows (pointing to a line graph). I don't know whether we can get off the top of this chart or not, but at the rate this actual performance line is climbing, we might make it. All I can say is, keep up the good work. . . . I guess I'm an optimistic pessimist.

During the discussion of projected savings for December in the equipment maintenance account, Hunter commented:

Where in the world are you fellows going to save $8,000 more than you originally said you would save?

Jones responded:

I'd just like to say at this point to the group that it would be a big help if you guys would take it easy on your machines. That's where we are going to save an extra $8,000—simply by only coming down to fix the stuff that won't run. You're really going to have to make it go as best you can. That's the only way we can possibly save the kind of money we have to save. You have been going along pretty well, but all I've got to say is I hope you can keep it up and not push those machines too hard.

Although Jones spoke with sincerity, a number of foremen sitting near the door exchanged sly smiles and pokes in the ribs.

Fox concluded the meeting at about 5:30, still chewing on his cigar:

There are just a couple of things I want to say before we break up. First, we've got to stop making stupid errors in shipping. Joe (foreman of shipping), you've absolutely got to get after those people to straighten them out. Second, I think it should be clear, fellows, that we can't break any more promises. Sales is our bread and butter. If we don't get those orders out in time we'll have no one but ourselves to blame for missing our budget. So I just hope it is clear that production control is running the show for the rest of the year. Third, the big push is on now! We sit around here expecting these problems to solve themselves, but they don't! It ought to be clear to all of you that no problem gets solved until it's spotted. Damn it, I just don't want any more dewy-eyed estimates about performance for the rest of the year. If something is going sour we want to hear about it. And there's no reason for not hearing about it! [Pounds the table, then voice falls and a smile begins to form.] It can mean a nice penny in your pocket if you can keep up the good work.

That's all I've got to say. Thank you very much.

The room cleared immediately, but Whitelaw lingered on. He reflected aloud on the just-ended meeting.

I'm afraid that little bit of advice there at the end won't make a great deal of difference in the way things work out. You have to play off sales against production. It's built into the job. When I attend a meeting like that one and I see all those production people with their assistants and see the other staff managers with the assistants, and I hear fellows refer to corporate policy that dictates and supports their action at the plant level, I suddenly realize that I'm all alone up there. I can't sit down and fire off a letter to my boss at the division level like the rest of those guys can do. I haven't got any authority at all. It is all based strictly on my own guts and strength. Now Bob is a wonderful guy, I like him and I have a lot of respect for him, but it just so happens that 80 percent of the time he and I disagree. He knows it and I know it; I mean it's nothing we run away from, we just find ourselves on opposite sides of the question and I'm dependent upon his tact and good judgment to keep from starting a war.

Boy, it can get you down—it really can after a while, and I've been at it for—God—20 years. But in production control you've got to accept it—you're an outcast. They tell you you're cold, that you're inhuman, that you're a bastard, that you don't care about anything except your schedule. And what are you going to say? You're just going to have to swallow it because basically you haven't got the authority to back up the things you know need to be done. Four nights out of five I am like this at the end of the day—just completely drained out— and it comes from having to fight my way through to try to get the plant running as smoothly as I can.

And Andrews up there in that meeting. He stands up with his chart and he compliments everybody about how well they are doing on efficiency. You know, he says, "Keep up the good work," and all that sort of stuff. I just sat there— shaking my head. I was so dazed you know, I mean I just keep saying to myself, "What's he doing? What's he saying? What's so great about this?" You know if I could have, I'd have stood up and I'd have said, "Somebody go down to my files in production control and pick out any five customer orders at random— and letters—and bring them back up here and read them—at random, pick any five." You know what they would show? Broken promises and missed delivery dates and slightly off-standard items we've been pushing out the door here. I mean, what is an efficient operation? Why the stress on operating efficiency? That's why I just couldn't figure out why in the world Andrews was getting as much mileage out of his efficiency performance as he was. Look at all the things we sacrifice to get that efficiency. But what could I do?

In early 1964 the report being sent by Fox to division would show, despite the fact that sales had fallen about 3 percent below budget, that profits for 1963 had exceeded the amount budgeted and that operating efficiency and cost reduction had both exceeded the budget by a comfortable margin. This enabled the managers and supervisors at the St. Laurent plant to attain the salary bonuses for which they had been striving.

Case 4–2
Neiman-Marcus
Henry W. Lane, Eileen Morley

BACKGROUND

In late 1974, Richard Marcus, President of Neiman-Marcus, and Neal J. Fox, General Merchandise Manager, were listening to details of a marketing study of the Chicago area, where Neiman-Marcus planned to open a new store. Chicago was the second largest retail market in the country, offering both a strong demand for high-priced quality goods and intense competition for Neiman-Marcus. After the presentation Neal turned to Richard and commented:

Much as I believe that centralized merchandising can work for us as we expand, Dick, I wonder if we shouldn't start thinking about some alternatives for organizing our merchandising activity—not in popular-priced goods, but maybe in furs and couture and gifts. After all, these represent about 25 percent of our sales, and they project our image and personality.

I'm not totally happy with the way our present stores are selling these items now. I wonder what will happen when we get to 18 or 20 stores. Can we continue to buy for them all on a centralized basis, or should we give the stores more autonomy?

History of Neiman-Marcus

Neal's words were an indication of the way the Neiman-Marcus organization had grown since it was first established by Al Neiman, his wife Carrie Marcus-Neiman, and her brother Herbert Marcus, in Dallas, Texas, in 1907. At that time wealthy Dallas women had their clothing custom-made in Paris or New York; other women went to a local dressmaker. The three young entrepreneurs were convinced of the potential of the Dallas market for fine quality ready-to-wear women's apparel, even though such a thought was a daring innovation at that time. Their ideas quickly proved right. Neiman-Marcus grew with the Texas economy. Initially based on cotton and cattle, the source of wealth changed when oil was discovered and Neiman-Marcus found itself located in the heart of the Texas oil fields. Dallas prospered as a banking and trade center. Population grew from 84,000 in 1907 to 260,000 in 1930. The store prospered with the city as Herbert Marcus added other lines—men's and children's wear, giftware, jewelry and furs. Through the expansion however, he maintained the Neiman-Marcus image as a specialty store.[1] During this period Herbert Marcus bought out Al Neiman's share of the business and became President.

In the late 1930s and early 1940s Herbert Marcus wanted to expand and build other stores, but his plans were hampered by temporary financial problems and he never managed to do so. During World War II and the period which followed, industrial activity boomed in Dallas which by 1950 had grown to 538,000 people.

In 1950 Herbert Marcus died, and his son Stanley[2] was elected president. Mr. Stanley immediately began the expansion program his father had wanted. In 1951 he opened his first suburban store in the Preston Center Mall, north of downtown Dallas. The following year he built a central service center for both Dallas stores. In 1955 he opened a store in Houston and in 1963 another in Fort Worth. In the same period he added two hotel boutiques. In 1965 he replaced Preston Center with a new store in the North Park Shopping Mall. Other stores in Bal Harbor, Florida (1971), Atlanta (1972), and St. Louis (1974) followed quickly, and plans were under way to build in Chicago, in Chevy Chase, Maryland, and in two California locations. These were the stores which increased Neal Fox's concern.

Philosophies and policies

Herbert Marcus had defined the Neiman-Marcus policies very early. The store was to concentrate on quality, exclusivity, good value at all price levels, and customer satisfaction.

As far as quality was concerned, he wanted to sell the finest and most fashionable merchandise in the world. He also wanted its selection to be unique. Stanley Marcus referred to this selection as "editing":

The quality that makes one paper like the New York Times really stand out lies in the editing. One paper features its foreign news on the front page, another buries it . . . inside; one plays up violence . . . the other relegates [it] to its local news section. So it goes with stores. Essentially all of us buy in the same market but we select differently.[3]

At Neiman-Marcus exclusiveness meant more than sole representation and reliance on manufacturers' workmanship. It included the improve-

[1] A specialty store sold quality merchandise with highly personalized service and did not carry a range of hard goods such as furniture and appliances which could be found in department stores.

[2] Known throughout the store as Mr. Stanley to avoid confusion with Mr. Herbert Marcus. In the same way his son was known as Mr. Richard.

[3] All of Mr. Stanley's comments are taken from his book, *Minding the Store.* (Boston: Little, Brown and Co., 1974).

ments in style and fabrication which Neiman-Marcus buyers insisted on and paid extra for—such as silk instead of rayon linings, and handmade buttonholes. The principle was always to improve the merchandise, never to reduce its quality in order to lower cost.

Herbert Marcus held actual price to be a poor indicator of value. Whether merchandise cost $5 or $50,000 he expected it to represent a true value to his customer. Despite its image of catering only to the very wealthy, the store always carried popular-priced merchandise. Stanley Marcus called it "a store with a split personality," selling fur coats or jewelry items at $50,000 but also doing a large business in $50 dresses.

Customer satisfaction was Herbert Marcus' final maxim. He believed there was a right customer for every piece of merchandise and that a merchant should match customers and goods, even if this meant losing a sale rather than selling an inappropriate garment or product. Stanley Marcus quoted his father:

There is never a good sale for Neiman-Marcus unless it is a good buy for the customer.

His comment became the Neiman-Marcus "Golden Rule."

Beautiful, spacious, uncluttered store interiors and attentive personal service were also considered by Stanley Marcus to be highly important contributions to shopping pleasure and satisfaction—at a cost which the founders judged worthwhile.

We want to sell satisfaction, not just merchandise . . . This may prove expensive to us and a few may take advantage of this policy unfairly but we are convinced that adherence to this idea will cement our customers' loyalty to Neiman-Marcus.

The second generation: Promotional activities

The values and policies of Herbert Marcus established a strong foundation for the initial store operation. It was Stanley Marcus, however, who turned it into a world-renowned institution through his promotional genius.

My contributions to the business took shape in my ability to translate the store's ideals into ideas that a larger number of potential customers could find credible. Somewhere in my education I had picked up a sense of promotion, and understanding of how to do things that would get a maximum amount of desired publicity, a flair for communicating with people by doing things that commanded attention.

In 1924 Stanley Marcus chose to leave the Harvard Business School after one year to help his father expand the Dallas store. He had worked in many different departments and knew the organization inside out. His first promotional event was a weekly fashion show and luncheon which gave women a reason to shop in downtown Dallas during hot summer months. The shows ran for 28 years. In 1934 Mr. Stanley started a national advertising campaign in *Vogue* and *Harper's Bazaar*—then unknown media for a Texas store. This move enhanced the store's emerging national reputation but was also defensive. Mr. Stanley wanted to get the Neiman-Marcus name under the eyes of his Texan customers, who would otherwise assume that the exclusive merchandise advertised could only be purchased in New York. In 1936 he invited the fashion editor of *Vogue* to visit the store's Texas Centennial Fashion Show, and word of Neiman-Marcus spread even more rapidly. By the end of the 1930s the store had been featured in *Fortune, Collier's* and *Life* magazines. In 1938 Mr. Stanley established the Neiman-Marcus Award for Distinguished Service in the Field of Fashion—presented each year in Dallas at a fashion gala with an invited audience of thousands from the fashion world. All of these promotional activities immensely increased the sense of pride which the Dallas community felt in Neiman-Marcus.

The promotional feature for which Neiman-Marcus was best known originated with "Men's Night"—a pre-Christmas gift show at which men shopped for wives, daughters, lovers, friends. This event provided the original stories of extravagant purchases—such as the entire window display replicated in a customer's playroom on Christmas Eve. Mr. Stanley soon realized that newscasters had picked up these stories, so in order to ensure that he had something for them to publicize each Christmas, he invented unique and extravagant catalog gift offerings. The first such gift was "His and Hers" Beechcraft airplanes. Many others followed, ranging from Chinese junks to camels. Stanley Marcus commented:

We usually sell from one to a dozen of these bizarre catalog offerings, but the important thing is that they help sell millions of dollars of gifts from our under $10 and under $20 pages . . . dresses, sweaters, neckties . . . and toys, of good quality and taste which are sent all over the world.

The most spectacular promotional event was the annual "Fortnight" which Mr. Stanley started in 1957. In each, a particular country was featured both in the store and by the city. Art, music, and entertainers were brought in, and cultural and social events were planned for the Fortnight. This was one of the ways in which Stanley Marcus tied the store closely into Dallas community life.

Merger with Carter, Hawley, Hale

In the mid-1960s, with four stores and an international reputation, Stanley Marcus wanted to expand beyond Texas. As with all expansion programs, financing was an important issue. Would internally generated funds be sufficient to support an ambitious program? Furthermore, while sale of stock would reduce family control of the business, how should the problems of management succession typical of family businesses be dealt with? As a result of these considerations, Stanley Marcus decided that the best course of action was to seek a merger.

The decision was not easy to implement because he insisted on finding a partner who would want Neiman-Marcus to continue doing business in its traditional high style. In 1969, after turning down other offers, Neiman-Marcus sold to Carter, Hawley, Hale, who promised Stanley Marcus the autonomy he sought. In the period 1968–74, Carter, Hawley, Hale exhibited a "hands off" policy, demonstrating faith in Neiman-Marcus management ability.

Carter, Hawley, Hale's business consisted of specialty stores, department stores, bookstores, and a national catalog sales operation (Exhibit 1).

For the fiscal year ending February 2, 1974, Carter, Hawley, Hale sales were over $1 billion, with pre-tax income of $80.1 million. Neiman-Marcus contributed approximately 15 percent of the total corporate sales and Neiman-Marcus pre-tax profit in 1972 and 1973 exceeded the national average for specialty or department stores, which ranged respectively from 4.9 to 6.4 percent of sales in 1973.[4]

Exhibit 1
Carter, Hawley, Hale Stores, Inc., subsidiaries

The Broadway; Los Angeles, California. Thirty-seven department stores in Southern California, Arizona, Nevada, and Utah.

The Emporium; San Francisco, California. Eleven department stores in Northern California.

Capwell's; Oakland, California. Five department stores in Northern California. Capwell's and The Emporium were the dominant general department stores in the Bay area. Five additional stores were planned for that area.

Weinstock's; Sacramento, California. Nine department stores in California and Nevada.

Neiman-Marcus; Dallas, Texas. Seven specialty stores in Texas, Florida, Georgia, and Missouri.

Bergdorf Goodman; New York, New York. A specialty store on Fifth Avenue and one in White Plains.

Holt, Renfrew; Montreal, Quebec. Twenty specialty stores coast-to-coast in Canada.

Sunset House; Los Angeles, California. Nationally distributed catalog and thirty-four gift shops in Arizona, California, Texas, and Utah.

Walden Book Company; Stamford, Connecticut. Three hundred thirty-eight book shops in forty states.

In addition to the subsidiaries listed here, Carter, Hawley, Hale owned 20 percent of the voting stock in the House of Fraser, a department store business in the United Kingdom.

---

[4] Financial Executives Division, National Retail Merchants Association, *Financial Operating Results of Department and Specialty Stores for 1973.*

Expansion outside Texas

Once the merger was accomplished, Neiman-Marcus went ahead with plans to expand. By late 1974 seven stores were in operation; six more on the way or planned, two of which would open in 1975–76; two more in Chicago and one in California were planned but deferred due to economic conditions; three additional California store sites had been located (see Exhibit 2).

Exhibit 2
Neiman-Marcus stores in 1974

The new stores were designed with the same high architectural and interior standards consistent with Neiman-Marcus's image—one of the world's finest specialty stores.

During this period, the downtown Dallas, North Park, and Houston stores continued to provide the major share of sales volume, representing approximately 60 percent of total sales, with the remainder divided equally between branches and catalog sales.

Competition

Competition for Neiman-Marcus came primarily from small specialty store operators. The small store owner had more flexibility than a large chain store in responding to local environment. Store owners knew their customers, selected merchandise for their particular environment and market sector, and gave personal service. Collectively, Neiman-Marcus was trying to do on a grand scale what small stores were doing individually. Neiman-Marcus had proved that it could be done with a small number of large stores. The question now was whether it could continue to be done nationally, in widely dispersed and differing communities.

A different kind of competition came from other major specialty stores such as Saks Fifth Avenue, Lord & Taylor, and I. Magnin. Neal Fox pointed out that he had watched some of these chains grow and could detect variations of quality among stores. In some cities the store had a price point emphasis, merchandise mix, and overall milieu that was inconsistent with their favorable pre-expansion image. He commented that this might well be related to location, and emphasized that it was crucial to choose only those areas where the Neiman-Marcus point of view and standard of quality could be established and maintained.

Reorganization

In 1972, Stanley Marcus reorganized the company in order to orient it toward future demands (Exhibit 3). He became Chairman of the Board— a move designed to allow time to work with a new President before he retired. Richard Marcus, his son, was elected President. He was 35 years old, and had moved successfully through positions in buying, merchandise management, and store management.

Merchandising responsibility was divided between two Senior Vice President-General Merchandise Manager postions, instead of a single traditional role. Stanley Marcus explained that this move was intended to give each manager more time to concentrate on particular merchandise, establish more intimate contact with their departments, and find new market opportunities. In 1974 these two posts were held by Neal J. Fox, who had worked 8 years with Neiman-Marcus after 9 years experience with Brooks Brothers; and by Murray Friedman, who brought 12 years experience from Saks Fifth Avenue.

A new position of Director of Stores was also created at the Senior Vice President level. Richard Marcus commented that store managers had to seek help from many different corporate groups, and it was decided that these efforts should be coordinated as the number of stores increased, and that store management should have a voice at the top. The new Neiman-Marcus organization is shown in Exhibit 3.

HOW THE NEIMAN-MARCUS ORGANIZATION FUNCTIONED

Store management

The Senior Vice President and Director of Stores coordinated activities between the various Neiman-Marcus stores and the merchandising groups

Exhibit 3
Neiman-Marcus organization, December 1974

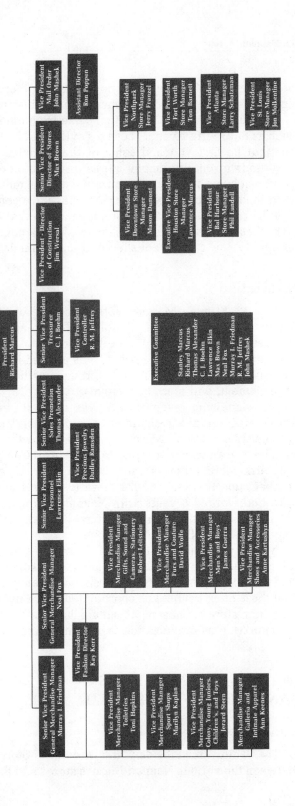

in Dallas. The occupant of this role was Max Brown who had spent 11 years with a multistore chain in Florida.

In Max Brown's opinion tension inevitably existed between buyers and store management personnel.

Buyers may often feel they purchase great merchandise but that the store people don't know what to do with it. Store executives may wonder why buyers don't buy things that sell. It's my job to help synthesize the "buy" and "sell" aspects of the business.

Max Brown and the store managers reporting to him were accountable for the stores' sales, expenses, and profits. Towards these ends store management was responsible for presenting merchandise, for directing the sales effort, and for control of store expenses. Max Brown referred to this process as a "four walls" responsibility.

The separation between Merchandising and Store Management responsibilities was not always clear. Grey areas included initial inventory levels, price changes, and responsibility for taking markdowns. Max commented that:

If store personnel are good communicators, they will provide judgmental input into the buying organization to change faulty distribution mixes. We need this input because customer patterns do change by store over time, so the distribution should change. But some buyers continue to write a standard mix.

The internal organization of typical store is shown in Exhibit 4.

Two important characteristics of the store organization structure were (*a*) separation of operations and merchandising responsibilities, and (*b*) the informal yet expected and critical communications between central Merchandise Managers and Buyers on the one hand, and Store Merchandise Managers and Department heads on the other. The Store Merchandise Managers had direct responsibility for the selling departments. They assisted Department Managers with promoting and presenting merchandise, and coordinated merchandising interactions with the central buying group.

The first store outside Texas was opened in Bal Harbor, Florida. The store manager who opened the Bal Harbor store then moved on to manage the opening of the Atlanta store. He described his job as being the exporter of Neiman-Marcus standards into new areas

It's a challenging experience (not least because) customers expect to find 300 Stanley Marcuses behind the counters and every single piece of merchandise in the building to be different from anything they have ever seen before.

In his store, the Manager and the two Assistant Managers worked as a team, meeting daily to discuss problems. He described changes he had seen during his 17 years with the Neiman-Marcus organization.

Exhibit 4
Typical store organization, Neiman-Marcus 1974

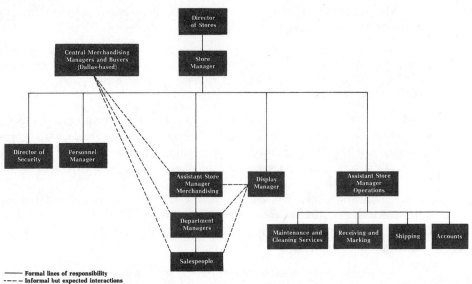

―――― Formal lines of responsibility
―――― Informal but expected interactions

In the old days buyers also had more of a managerial role. While the buyer was involved in the department manager's role, the department manager had no say in buying. It was an overwhelmingly one-sided relationship. Now buyers concentrate on buying and managers on managing.

In addition to maintaining communication with the buyers in Dallas, a department manager's prime responsibility was sales leadership. This meant motivating a sales staff of up to 35 people while ensuring they lived up to the "Golden Rule" laid down by Herbert Marcus. One department manager commented that to accomplish this, she had to keep herself motivated, which took a lot of time and maturity. She also stressed the importance of her sales people:

They're not just clerks; they're important members of the team. Many customers have commented that they shop at Neiman-Marcus because the sales people make them feel special. It's important for the buyers to understand that customers shop here for more than just the merchandise.

On the store operations side, types of expertise were needed which contrasted sharply with the talents of merchandising and sales people. Management and motivation skills were needed in operations as well, but in more diverse areas. Operations managers were responsible for all support functions such as receiving and marking merchandise, accounting, packaging and mailing, maintenance, alterations, and fur storage. An Assistant Store Manager for operations typically controlled an expense budget of around $250,000 per month.

One Assistant Store Manager for Operations found himself involved in improving the design of work areas in the Atlanta store.

In the downtown Dallas store, goods sold on the sixth floor were manually transported to the basement for packing and shipping. Atlanta's system of belt conveyors and chainveyors on which sales people hang garments to be transported three floors to the basement are all great improvements.

The receiving and ticketing area was designed by people who were not totally knowledgeable about work functions. By changing locations and redesigning work flow I was able to reduce the number of employees in that operation from 20 to 12.

There were no work standards when the store opened. I believed a person could make a certain number of tickets and hang a certain number of garments in a day, and I set out to find a standard. We started with 1200 garments a day and increased it to 2500.

The St. Louis store manager also commented on the critical future role of operations.

My Assistant Store Manager for Operations came from the systems and planning area of Neiman-Marcus. He has a real love for the detail of the business— for seeing that standards of productivity are met and improved. He's done a great job staying on top of expenses and the operations part of the store. Thirty to 40 percent of store personnel are in operations and it's a really important area. It can well determine profitability.

Merchandising is the area of the store that's going to keep the doors open, but over the years I think it's been romanticized. I see a great upgrading of the operations end of the business. It used to be almost a stigma. Now it's gained great respectability. However there's still a lot of room for improvement. The nonselling department managers are usually not college graduates and there aren't adequate training mechanisms for operations people.

Merchandising

Reporting to the Senior Vice President-General Merchandise Managers were various Vice President-Division Merchandise Managers. Buyers in turn reported to Division Managers. (Exhibit 5)

Due to differing volumes of business, and different gross margins, different departments commanded different levels of attention and concern, as well as resources.

Richard Marcus spoke of the effect of an economic down turn on problems facing merchandisers in 1974:

Exhibit 5
Merchandising organization, December 1974

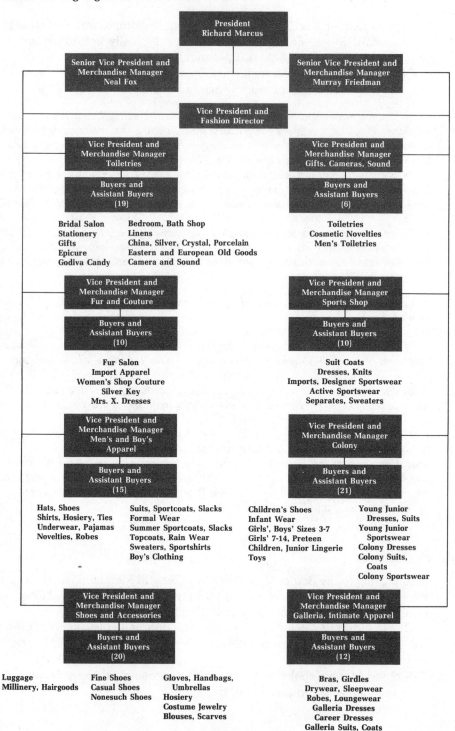

President
Richard Marcus

Senior Vice President and Merchandise Manager
Neal Fox

Senior Vice President and Merchandise Manager
Murray Friedman

Vice President and Fashion Director

Vice President and Merchandise Manager Toiletries

Buyers and Assistant Buyers (19)

Bridal Salon	Bedroom, Bath Shop
Stationery	Linens
Gifts	China, Silver, Crystal, Porcelain
Epicure	Eastern and European Old Goods
Godiva Candy	Camera and Sound

Vice President and Merchandise Manager Gifts. Cameras, Sound

Buyers and Assistant Buyers (6)

Toiletries
Cosmetic Novelties
Men's Toiletries

Vice President and Merchandise Manager Fur and Couture

Buyers and Assistant Buyers (10)

Fur Salon
Import Apparel
Women's Shop Couture
Silver Key
Mrs. X. Dresses

Vice President and Merchandise Manager Sports Shop

Buyers and Assistant Buyers (10)

Suit Coats
Dresses, Knits
Imports, Designer Sportswear
Active Sportswear
Separates, Sweaters

Vice President and Merchandise Manager Men's and Boy's Apparel

Buyers and Assistant Buyers (15)

Hats, Shoes	Suits, Sportcoats, Slacks
Shirts, Hosiery, Ties	Formal Wear
Underwear, Pajamas	Summer Sportcoats, Slacks
Novelties, Robes	Topcoats, Rain Wear
	Sweaters, Sportshirts
	Boy's Clothing

Vice President and Merchandise Manager Colony

Buyers and Assistant Buyers (21)

Children's Shoes	Young Junior
Infant Wear	Dresses, Suits
Girls', Boys' Sizes 3-7	Young Junior
Girls' 7-14, Preteen	Sportswear
Children, Junior Lingerie	Colony Dresses
Toys	Colony Suits, Coats
	Colony Sportswear

Vice President and Merchandise Manager Shoes and Accessories

Buyers and Assistant Buyers (20)

Luggage	Fine Shoes	Gloves, Handbags,
Millinery, Hairgoods	Casual Shoes	Umbrellas
	Nonesuch Shoes	Hosiery
		Costume Jewelry
		Blouses, Scarves

Vice President and Merchandise Manager Galleria. Intimate Apparel

Buyers and Assistant Buyers (12)

Bras, Girdles
Drywear, Sleepwear
Robes, Loungewear
Galleria Dresses
Career Dresses
Galleria Suits, Coats

Inventive buying has become even more important as quality manufacturers go out of business and resources in the marketplace dry up. Many young buyers grew up in an era of declining quality which inevitably affects their standards. At the same time a large segment of manufacturers can no longer produce to old standards at reasonable prices. Everyone is buying from the same source and consequently all the stores look alike. The traditional Neiman-Marcus emphasis on improving merchandise is more critical than ever now.

Buyers still really need to know what a manufacturer can do to improve the product, rather than how to take something out to reduce the price. We will go to market with buyers, and also counsel manufacturers. One of our challenges is not to be tempted to lower our sights, but if anything to raise them. I'm not convinced that when the economy is down, people who have experienced better quality merchandise will step down to something of lower quality—they may well buy fewer pieces instead.

At one time differences in labor costs in Europe made buying there advantageous, but inflation has changed that too. The newer markets are in the Far East and in South America where manufacturers can produce quality. But they haven't developed the fashion flair of Europe. This means that fashion buyers and merchandisers have to spend a lot of time in the market developing design ideas, and not simply buying goods already made. They sit down with manufacturers and create their own styles, and fashion excitement is often created by the items which result.

The Division Merchandise Manager for Gifts talked about his job.[5]

The prime job of a merchandise manager is drawing up the sales operating plan for his departments and following up by working with buyers in individual areas. It's important to be able to make decisions about where to put the money. Am I going to put it into food service or the bath shop? Within food service does it go into conventional things, or into the greatest new line of ashtrays I've seen in years? These are value judgments. Each buyer has to be gutsy and take a chance.

A Division Merchandise Manager is also responsible for setting the taste and quality level in his division and for developing creative merchandising themes.

We start much of it here in-house. A buyer came to me with a great picture of ripe juicy tomatoes. Another buyer suggested we should do a glass with luscious tomatoes on it—maybe a new type of Bloody Mary glass. That was great but we had to use the design in other ways too . . . a new line of tomato red cookware. The bath shop buyer is going to do a beach towel with a big red tomato. The dish buyer remembered dishes in the market that would fit nicely. We also had some tomato-red Haitian coasters. Before you knew it, we had the whole theme for spring—Tomato Red.

In addition to imagination and creativity, the Division Merchandise Manager said that buyers need to be knowledgeable in the field as a whole and about Neiman-Marcus customers.

---

[5] His division included decorative home and hard goods such as china, silver, antiques, bedroom and bath shops, fine linen, and the epicure shop.

Buyers have to have knowledge to back up their creativity. I'm looking for an antiques buyer, a person who has a knowledge of Chinese, Japanese, and European antiquity. That buyer would have to go to market and come back with the decorative accessory antiques of the type Neiman-Marcus wants. Something priced within means of, not necessarily a modest customer, but not a museum either.

They have to have an inventory in proportion to their clientele and really know them. They have to remember that it's easier to buy than sell. I have customers call me directly on specific merchandise. If I have it in inventory and it's a fine piece, I even place it in their home. It's service like this that makes Neiman-Marcus different.

Neal Fox commented that customer knowledge of this kind was equally vital in couture:

It's difficult for a buyer to go to market—even with a great deal of knowledge and preparation, without knowing the customers. It creates confidence to know that the blue dress with sequins coming down the runway is perfect for Mrs. Smith. It might be a $750 dress and there is always a moment of truth when you have to make a decision.

Division of responsibility between merchandising and store management

Unlike many retail organizations, the Neiman-Marcus central buying group was not responsible for displaying or selling merchandise in the stores. The merchants planned inventory levels in different kinds of merchandise, procured and priced it, planned advertising campaigns and determined initial distribution. They also planned sales promotions and provided selling departments with salient information about fabrics or fashion news. Store department managers were responsible for actual display and sales.

Two-way communication was important in a multi-store operation of this kind: information from store branches to buyers about what was selling and being asked for; information from buyers to store sales personnel about what merchandise was coming, and how to treat merchandise at point of sale. One way Neiman-Marcus achieved this was by video-taping fashion shows put on by designers at the downtown Dallas store and sending the tapes to other stores, simultaneously presenting the message firsthand in all locations. Other buyers made training video-tapes on such special topics as varieties of jade, latest men's fashions, or the treatment of damaged merchandise, which were circulated in the same way.

Elements of profitability

Richard Marcus indicated that two basic elements of profitability which concerned him most were gross margin and expenses. A number of factors contributed to achieving gross margin, particularly properly determined markups and inventory levels. Buyers for each department had different individual markup goals depending on merchandise. The buying group also had a collective markup objective. For domestic goods under the retail method of inventory, the markup was approximately 40 percent to 50 percent—standard in the industry. Because of this, buyers needed to find unique merchandise so they weren't tied as strongly to competitive pricing. Richard Marcus also said that the Neiman-Marcus philosophy of value at all prices also meant that buyers were not constrained by a fixed price-line concept covering either a few selected price points or an entire range of prices. Price ranges were determined by the quality of available merchandise, but buyers had to be conscious of the fact that too many inexpensive items would lower the store's average "sale per square foot." Murray Friedman, a Senior Vice President-General Merchandise Manager, commented:

> It's a constant struggle. Do you need the extra volume at the expense of sacrificing a standard that you need to survive? We shouldn't sacrifice standards for the sake of getting other customers.

If inventories got out of line, unplanned markdowns were taken and gross margin diminished. Richard Marcus explained that markdowns were charged against a buyer's performance, because in most cases markdowns exceeding plan resulted from overbuying, not from failure to sell an inventory that was on plan.

> Inventory management is absolutely essential and both buyers and store personnel have to be concerned about it. When a buyer goes into a store and sees merchandise that came in three days earlier still in the stockroom and not on the floor, and it is marked down and sold six weeks later, whose fault is it?

In a similar vein one merchandise manager commented that:

> You often hear stores complain when inventories are below plan, but never when they are above plan, even though excess inventory later gets marked down.

In 1974 the stores were experimenting with a new markdown system. Under the traditional system, initial markdowns (usually 33–40 percent) and second markdowns (50 percent) had been dictated by the buyers and implemented in all stores simultaneously. With the new system, judgment on timing of the second markdown was given to store management because it was difficult for buyers in Dallas to feel the rhythm of sales in different areas, or to know which stores should go to 50 percent immediately. Making this a local procedure also saved buyers' administrative time.

The second determinant of profit was expenses, according to Richard Marcus. These included direct store expenses and a prorated share of nonassigned multistore expenses such as executive salaries, credit, and advertising costs. These were charged as a percentage of sales. Richard Marcus saw a real irony in these interactions.

If the stores went haywire and really exceeded their expense plan substantially we would rarely respond by making cutbacks in the merchandising procedures. But the opposite does occur. If we get over-inventoried and take higher markdowns and lose our gross margin, then we have to make up for it some place fast and the fastest place is in store expenses. The stores say, "Thanks for coming back again. How much blood do you want this time?"

Other interactions between merchandisers and store management

Richard Marcus commented that perhaps the most common confrontation between merchants and store management occurred when a buyer went into a store, didn't like the way the department looked, and started rearranging merchandise.

A wise store manager will find a way to straighten out the buyer and explain that though he wants constructive ideas, "Don't come blowing in here and changing everything." Store managers have to be able to mediate situations like that. It's easy to tell which buyers have had past store management experience—their perspective is different. Those who lack this are apt to get on their high horse too frequently.

He explained that one important aspect of the Store Manager's role was credibility with buyers so he or she could intervene without a fight.

Managing those relationships is a day-to-day challenge that everyone has to work on. I think it would be impossible to try and clear the air forever by mandating these relationships, and anyway such an action would probably be stifling.

One store manager commented on the interaction of buyer and store department manager on inventory:

I see a need for more store autonomy, not in buying but in reordering. I think the ideal would be for the buyer to be a selector and make the initial buy, but have department managers reorder merchandise that is selling. Our reorders now depend on the buyers' funds. Many multistore companies do this by store. We don't.

At the same time he recognized the skills of Neiman-Marcus buyers:

I feel that our buyers are the best in their specialties in the world. I want that knowledge in my stocks.

Another department manager in Couture described the way in which buyers made efforts to keep communications with department managers open.

I make two market trips a year with buyers. Even though markets are thinning and many manufacturers are shutting down, I feel our four buyers are exceptionally selective and this is a primary reason I can build up my business. It helps me a great deal to know how they make their decisions and what to expect.

Several other department managers reported making similar trips with buyers.

Planning and measurement systems

Sales plans were established by the divisional vice presidents (merchandise managers) and their buyers for two separate seasons or six month cycles—February/July and August/January. The planning was done department by department within each division for each store location; and collectively for all stores. For example, Atlanta might have its sales planned at 105 percent of the previous year, while St. Louis was planned at 108 percent, both within an overall corporate sales objective of, say, 106 percent. The merchandise managers and buyers determined the levels of inventory, including receipt of new merchandise required to achieve their sales plan. They planned the dollar value and mix of inventory, and the dollar value of markdowns for each store. They monitored their performance month to month, using stock-to-sales ratios set by the General Merchandise Managers.

The plans for each season were a result of a process which Neal Fox called "plan as you go." At the end of each month when statistical data were available, the buyers and merchandise managers re-evaluated that month in light of their plan and made projections for that same month for the next year. They looked at their performance on sales, inventory levels, and markdowns by location and decided where improvements could be made. They committed these projections to paper and sent them to Neal for review. Neal reviewed performance monthly with his merchandise managers and buyers, and at the end of a 6-month season reviewed their cumulative plans for the following year.

At the end-of-season review Neal told merchandising managers and buyers the overall corporate sales goal as well as the goals for each location so that they could adjust their planning documents accordingly. The corporate goals were established jointly by the General Merchandise Managers, Director of Stores, and Treasurer, under the overall direction of the Chief Executive Officer. Neal Fox did not give his people these goals earlier because he did not want their planning hindered. He said:

I try to encourage my people to think of the business as if it were their own, and make continual efforts to improve, but without undue pressure.

Sales goals were also established by store management as the basis for setting expense goals. Neal commented that the merchandising people tended to set more optimistic goals than did store management:

For instance, I might plan sales at 105 percent of the previous year's sales, while the stores plan expenses at 102 percent of the previous year's sales.

This was an advantage when sales goals were reached, because the differential between the two figures was all profit, but when sales goals were not reached, inventory backed up, creating unplanned markdowns and gross margin erosion. Neal Fox indicated, however, that with the economic slowdown these sales goals were tending to be closer and that eventually both groups would probably use one mutually reconciled sales objective.

Information processing

Richard Marcus, Neal Fox, and Murray Friedman all agreed that they would like their merchandise system to be more refined. Store expansion was beginning to strain the present manual unit control system. Under this system a merchandise position report (MERPO) was produced twice a month by the MIS group at the Dallas Service Center showing basic inventory and sales information for each store location. It was prepared from reports of cash sales, sales audits, accounts receivable and markdowns sent to Dallas by the stores and it usually lagged one week behind actual merchandise sales. The buyers used this report, along with a form showing their consolidated, monthly merchandise orders, to compute their "open to buy"—the amount of money they had left to spend that month. The MIS groups also produced a weekly Markdown Analysis Report, listing markdowns by store and department from worksheets prepared in each store. The report compared the actual dollar amount of markdowns against the sales plan and against the previous year's markdowns. It was used primarily by the buyers during high markdown periods such as the end of a season.

Each merchandising division had a unit control office. In these offices data from ticket stubs were entered in unit control books as merchandise was sold or transferred between stores. While the Unit Sales Analysis Report was an ongoing process, it was recapped and analyzed monthly. The report provided a breakdown of sales by store, department, classification (e.g., cotton dresses, pantsuits, etc.) and gave rate-of-sale information. It facilitated analysis of sales by classification and price points and allowed buyers to reorder in proper volume. This report, like the others, went to the General Merchandise Managers, Merchandise Managers, appropriate buyers, and Store Managers.

The executives at Neiman-Marcus realized that buyers needed almost daily information on how their merchandise was performing; how much stock they had in-house; and how much stock on order. The executives also realized that their system was old and that some of their competitors reported this information on a more timely basis while it was still highly actionable. Neal Fox explained that:

> By "actionable" I mean that a buyer has time to reorder or to move goods from one store to another. If a $250 dress isn't moving in St. Louis where there are four pieces, but three of the four in Dallas have already sold, then she could move them from St. Louis to Dallas.

Richard Marcus commented that improving the information system should allow their basic stock programs to be improved. One way of decentralizing the buying functions would be by delegating maintenance of inventory levels of certain basic items back out to the stores.

> With expansion we can't expect the buyers' offices to process all the routine flow. We need standards and systems to handle that. One possibility might be a separate basic stock unit in Dallas, but outside the buying offices. A buyer would set minimum stock levels and quality criteria for merchandise, but the paperwork traffic would be done outside his office.

For Murray Friedman the need for a new system seemed relatively urgent.

> From a merchandise point of view we are behind the times with the control system. We need a more automated system and we need it fast for merchandise information—date of receipt—rate of sales—on-hand by style and store. You can't operate a multistore operation without it. We're on manual unit control right now. It's going to be difficult to expand properly without a proper system. We can do it but it makes the buyer' jobs tougher—increases reliance on stock counts and escalates communication between buyers and stores, because they have to spend more time getting information about what's happened in the stores.

Rewards and compensation

At Neiman-Marcus everyone except sales people were on straight salary. Until 1971 the Merchandise Group had a bonus system, but this was discontinued because it was considered unfair to offer it only to the merchants. At the time of the change the company added a percentage figure to merchandisers' salaries, based on each person's historical bonus earnings. No changes in the incentive systems were being contemplated. If any improvements in rewards were made, Richard Marcus said that these would probably be in terms of increased benefits.

Some incentive systems lead people into short-term thinking—maximize today and let tomorrow take care of itself. We would like to develop the kind of philosophy whereby people realize they have strong opportunities to earn, based on meeting longer-term objectives.

Plans are there to be met—that's basic. But we also look at other subjective areas as well, such as the level of housekeeping for a store manager. On the more subjective items we try to get concurrence on standards.

One store manager mentioned his own performance evaluation:

I'm evaluated more and more on profit, and that lost gross margin can really hurt. I'm also evaluated on maintaining a good merchandise image and good morale in the store. It's an appropriate procedure. I don't like the thought of someone telling me my whole career is based on profit and loss because in that case I'd have a whole store full of items that delivered the best gross margin, and not a quality store, and that would be an image change that Neiman-Marcus wouldn't like.

Career development

Two separate career paths had previously existed at Neiman-Marcus for merchants and store management. In the past two years a new training program had been introduced in which everyone followed a course alternating between the two. A typical sequence of assignments would be:

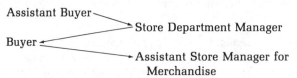

At the Assistant Store Manager level a crossroad was reached and people had to choose either merchandising or management. The senior executives all said they felt this flexible interchange was essential at least through the buyer rank. Richard Marcus said:

It's important for buyers to have experience in the stores so they understand the problems of running departments offering merchandise which five or more buyers are shipping in, and trying to motivate a sales force at the same time. It's also beneficial for store department managers to understand that manufacturers aren't just sitting around with goods waiting to be shipped; that buying involves a lot more than placing orders.

I see a great deal of progress in the previous five years in raising the stature and responsibility of store management as a career. There was a time when buyers and merchandising managers were in all the positions of authority and store management wouldn't consider standing up to them. Now Store Managers and Divisional Merchandise Managers are at the same level of responsibility— Vice Presidents—and are paid accordingly.

Max Brown commented that the Executive Progression Program was capable of producing senior store managers for the new stores at the present rate of expansion.

It is easier to take Neiman-Marcus people and train them to qualify for a job, than to take someone already qualified and teach them Neiman-Marcus.

This resulted in transferring 28 people from Dallas to St. Louis at considerable cost. The policy, which offered many career opportunities, had resulted from experience in opening new stores. Richard Marcus commented:

In all new stores the top management are Neiman-Marcus people. In Bal Harbor many of the department managers were hired from the local area, but they had difficulty "unlearning" their way of operating and learning our way. The result was a complete turnover of department managers within 18 months. In Atlanta 60 percent of the supervisory force came from within Neiman-Marcus, but there another problem showed up. We probably hadn't set our sights high enough in some instances. People were eager to go to the new stores because they were losing ground in their existing position. As a result we took care to staff St. Louis initially with 80 percent strongly performing Neiman-Marcus people.

Training for new store openings

The St. Louis store manager said he was convinced of the importance of training sales and service personnel by experienced Neiman-Marcus managers.

I had 6,000 applications for 393 sales and operations jobs. By the time I finished hiring I had the cream of the crop. I brought every sales and service person into the store 30 days before opening for business and spent that time explaining what Neiman-Marcus was all about and its philosophy for dealing with people. Department managers discussed merchandise, selling points, quality factors, and why the store did or did not carry certain merchandise. I believe a great rapport and ability to communicate developed during this period.

EXPANSION ISSUES

Neiman-Marcus' store expansion program presented challenges at many levels. A key issue was choice of communities in which Neiman-Marcus standards could be established and maintained and where the store could also stand alone and grow as part of that community. While each store would have a different merchandise mix, all had to project a consistent Neiman-Marcus image to customers.

Once a store was designed and constructed another challenge consisted of identifying and responding to local needs and preferences. In Atlanta, the Assistant Store Manager for Merchandise commented that since a different merchandise mix is generally required in each store, communication about local life styles to Dallas was essential: "This is one of my jobs." Sometimes educating the local market was also necessary. The St. Louis store manager remarked that:

This city is probably more traditional and less fashion-minded than Bal Harbor or Dallas. I see an educational process ahead of me. We've proved we can sell some higher priced merchandise but giftware is behind expectations and so is couture.

In Atlanta the store manager commented:

I feel this market perhaps isn't ready for our really total concept of couture. Many customers are probably still convinced they could buy couture at a lower price. The women here have been largely educated by another store in the city, which presented an image of couture which isn't ours.

The store responded to this situation, not by downgrading its couture range but by getting a change in the percentage commitment to a designer whose apparel had been well received, from 10 percent to 25 percent. Local tastes had to be explained very carefully to buyers the first year.

I felt our managers might be guilty of wanting to stock the items the Atlanta customers wanted to buy—even if they weren't altogether our standard—and not trying to educate them. If the buyers bought only lower priced couture, that would lower our standards.

Another problem involved the need to increase the number of central merchandising personnel in order to provide buying support as each new store was added. In 1974 Neiman-Marcus therefore had many new young buyers with departments having a $3 or $4 million sales volume. Richard Marcus commented:

These new young people don't thoroughly know our philosophies. They say they know them but they haven't lived with them long enough to have internalized them. Unless they do, we shall end up looking like everyone else.

The problem was complicated by a shift in economic conditions which Murray Friedman noted:

Buyers in the last ten years have gone to the market and over-bought because they could sell everything they bought. It was a glamor era. Young buyers have never had to face problems. It's a tremendous teaching job, making a buyer a buyer again instead of a market selector. You work one-to-one and train them to Neiman-Marcus. It's basic.

John Mashek, Vice President in charge of the mail order operation uncovered yet another problem:

In talking to buyers about getting a better markup on some exclusive items submitted for mail order, I found they thought the kind of markup which is necessary and normal at Neiman-Marcus to be almost immoral. These young buyers had grown up in the retail business during a period of heavy regulation and price control and had been subjected to more stringent pricing and categorizing of merchandise in the previous four years than perhaps ever before. We now have to educate them in our standards and operations so they will understand our principle of good value at all price levels and that we're not out to gouge the customer.

One Store Manager described a different shift in orientation—of people promoted from Assistant Buyer to department managerships in new stores.

A department manager's prime responsibility in addition to communication, is sales leadership. This means motivating a staff of up to 35 people. For someone who was in a buying office without anyone reporting to them, this is initially a huge change. They have been primarily technicians. Now they have to be aware that everything they say has an effect on other people. Also that they're much more independent and able to structure their way of doing business.

Opening new stores also changed people's perceptions of the Merchandising-Store Management relationship. An Assistant Store Manager commented:

Before we felt that everybody should get along and be very nice—don't make a controversial decision without a lot of memo writing which stifled any change. It certainly made it difficult to react quickly, which is the key to high performance in retailing.

With the opening of this store buyers have listened and been responsive to what we said. In cases where we asked for merchandise they didn't think was right for this store, we were able to go to the Merchandise Manager. He usually indicated that we should do what was right for the store and each side might have to adjust. This is the real change—recognizing that confronting differences of opinion is good and constructive.

When my department managers come to me I try to convince them that confronting the buyers is constructive. They don't have to tell them that the merchandise is fabulous if they don't believe it. There used to be a great tendency to do that. This change really started when we began to expand outside Texas. We built so many stores in other places that buyers needed this information, since we had gone beyond the point where they could watch each store carefully. Now they recognize the value of getting it from us since they can no longer generate it themselves.

As Neiman-Marcus expanded, the size of individual stores remained approximately the same. The Merchandising organization was under great pressure however, to expand to meet the greatly enlarged merchandise needs of the whole organization. The fur Merchandise Manager had already conjectured how he might recommend restructuring his fur department if expansion made it necessary.

If we were to have regional divisions, Washington, Atlanta and Florida would be one; Chicago, St. Louis would be a midwestern division; the Texas complex another; and California the west coast division.

Buyers could basically become technicians concerned with purchasing quality skins, arranging contracts with workrooms to have coats made; finding new markets and being fashion innovators. The decision as to what merchandise went into each area would be up to regional merchandising management.

In a multistore operation, coordinating transfer of expensive merchandise is a headache. It's easy to have a large inventory in transit or even lost or stolen. With a regional structure, buyers could be involved if really big ticket items were transferred between regions—perhaps even get on a plane to make the deal and come back with the merchandise; much better than having a $30,000 fur coat sitting in the mail for a week.

We could also have regional sales. For example, all "fun" furs in the southeast region could be sent to Florida for a week; then moved on to Atlanta.

A china and crystal buyer had already experienced some adverse effects of expansion.

The stores have to find competent people who know the quality of merchandise, and have the expertise necessary to sell it. Just receiving it and getting it onto the selling floor is a problem which will increase with each new store opening. And with expansion, each new store will be more difficult to visit. This is already happening. My Merchandise Manager comes back from a store and asks when I was last there. I tell him the last time was when I was budgeted to go. I have budgets to live with and so do the other buyers. We would like to get out to the stores more often.

Other problems which he reported had to do with the balance between work and personal life. He commented that he had a wife and children at home who liked to see him once in a while, and he wasn't at all certain how he could handle 20 stores. He saw the buying job:

Getting so bloody big that it will probably have to be redefined. I have all I can handle now. The phone never stops ringing. I try to keep in daily contact with the people in the stores but pretty soon it will be humanly impossible.

His biggest problem, however, was inventory. Giftware had a slow turnover compared to apparel, and the maintenance of a basic stock was difficult on two counts.

First I have to convince management, whose experience tends to be in high turnover fashion and apparel items, to invest money in this low-turning inventory. The second problem is the mechanics of getting and maintaining a good basic stock in each of the stores. I operate a large central reserve stock in Dallas for the four Texas stores. They each have their personalities—they're not just extensions of the downtown store. But other locations are so remote that centralized stocks are impossible. This means higher stock-to-sales ratios in the other stores, which management naturally doesn't like. The same thing is happening in our competitors' stores. Many of them just don't maintain good crystal and china departments anyone.

He had discussed these problems with his Division Merchandising Manager. The two of them had agreed that he could probably establish guidelines within which the stores themselves could choose merchandise to fit their regional differences.

For instance, I have bought from Wedgewood and other traditional companies over the years. I could give department managers leeway to choose from a range of items that I selected—put an asterisk next to some basic items that all stores must carry. Then allow some latitude on the fringes. Maybe even let some stores buy a fine quality Swedish crystal with exceptionally clean lines that just doesn't sell in Dallas. But some guidelines are essential to define the look and ambiance.

Murray Friedman summarized some of the problems connected with expansion:

We expect buyers to be wizards now that we have stores all over. Any number of problems can come up that we cannot anticipate.

Remember that the same coat buyer who's trying to find lightweight raincoats for the early warm spring season in Texas and Florida, will at the very same time be looking for heavy coats for promotion in Chicago when the snow's coming down. Multiply that by every ready-to-wear operation in the organization and you certainly have a problem.

Case 4–3
TRW Systems Group* (A and B condensed)

Paul H. Thompson

revised by
Joseph Seher and John P. Kotter

HISTORY OF TRW INC. AND TRW SYSTEMS GROUP

TRW Inc. was formed in 1957 by the merger of Thompson Products, Inc., and the Ramo-Wooldridge Corporation. Thompson Products, a Cleveland-based manufacturer of auto and aircraft parts, had provided $500,000 to help Simon Ramo and Dean Wooldridge get started in 1953.

Ramo-Wooldridge Corporation grew quickly by linking itself with the accelerating ICBM program sponsored by the Air Force. After winning the contract for the technical supervision of the ICBM program, R-W gradually expanded its capabilities to include advance planning for future ballistic weapons systems and space technology and by providing technical advice to the Air Force.

R-W was considered by some industry specialists to be a quasi-government agency. In fact, some of their competitors in the aerospace industry resented R-W's opportunities for auditing and examining their operations.

Because of this close relationship with the Air Force, R-W was prohibited from bidding on hardware contracts. This prevented them from competing for work on mainframes or on assemblies. In 1959, after the merger with Thompson, TRW decided that the hardware ban was too great a liability and moved to free the Systems Group from its limiting relationship with the Air Force.

The Air Force was reluctant to lose the valued services of the Systems Group. But they agreed to a solution which called for the creation by the Air Force of a nonprofit organization, the Aerospace Corporation, to take over the advance planning and broad technical assistance formerly given by the Systems Group. TRW agreed to recruit, from its own person-

---

* In its brief history, this part of TRW, Inc. had had several names: The Guided Missiles Division of Ramo-Wooldridge, Ramo-Wooldridge Corporation, Space Technology Laboratories (S.T.L.), and most recently, TRW Systems Group. Frequently used abbreviations of TRW Systems Group are TRW Systems and Systems Group.

nel, a staff of top technicians to man Aerospace, and in 1960, about 20 percent of Systems' professional people went over to Aerospace.

The Systems Group had to undergo a difficult transition from serving a single customer to a competitive organization. The change involved worrying about marketing, manufacturing, and dealing with different types of contracts. Previously, Systems had worked on a cost-plus-fixed-fee basis, but now worked on incentive contracts rewarding performance and specified delivery dates, while penalizing failures.

Systems thrived in the new competitive arena (see Exhibit 1), winning a number of important contracts. Nestled in the sunny, Southern California region at Redondo Beach, the Systems Group worked in a free and open atmosphere. According to an article in *Fortune,* Systems' competitive advantage was its professional personnel:

Exhibit 1
Comparative profile of TRW Systems Group

	June 1960	Feb. 1963
Customers	8	42
Contracts	16	108
Total personnel	3,860	6,000
Technical staff	1,400	2,100
Annual sales rate	$63 million	$108 million

S.T.L. is headed by 38-year-old Rube Mettler, who holds the title of president of the subsidiary. A Ph.D. from Caltech, he served with Hughes Aircraft, and was a consultant at the Pentagon before coming to Ramo-Wooldridge in 1955, where he made his mark directing the Thor program to completion in record time. Of his technical staff of 2,100, more than 35 percent hold advanced degrees, and despite their youth they average 11 years of experience per man: in other words, most of them have been in the space industry virtually since the space industry began. They are housed mostly in a group of four long, low buildings for research, engineering, and development in the campus-like Space Center at Redondo Beach. Some of them are occupied in the various labs for research in quantum physics, programming, and applied mathematics, inertial guidance and control, etc.; others simply sit in solitude in their offices and think, or mess around with formulas on the inevitable blackboard. But typically, the materialization of all this brainpower is accomplished in one medium-sized manufacturing building called FIT (Fabrication, Integration, and Testing), which has but 800 employees all told. FIT has a high bay area to accommodate its huge chamber for simulating space environment and other exotic testing equipment.[1]

---

[1] *Fortune,* February 1963, p. 95.

THE AEROSPACE INDUSTRY

Observers have described the industry in which Systems competed as a large job shop subject to frequent changes. T. C. Miller and L. P. Kane, experts on the aerospace industry, described it as follows:

Because of rapid changes in technology, in customer requirements, and in competitive practices, product lines in the aerospace industry tend to be transitory. The customers' needs are finite and discrete. . . . Although the aerospace industry as a whole has grown steadily during the last decade, the fluctuations of individual companies underscore the job-shop nature of defense work. Aerospace industry planners must be constantly aware of the possibility of cancellation or prolongation of large programs.[2]

The rapid changes and temporary nature of the programs had several effects on companies within the industry. Sales and profits fluctuated with the number and size of contracts the company had; the level of activity in the company fluctuated, which meant hiring and later laying off large numbers of employees; and each plant went from full utilization of physical facilities to idle capacity.

The fluctuations resulted in a highly mobile work force that tended to follow the contracts, moving from a company which had finished a contract to one which was beginning a new contract. But the employees were highly trained and could find other jobs without difficulty. Miller and Kane pointed out that:

The industry's ratios of technical employment to total employment and of technical employment to dollar volume of sales are higher than those in any other industry. Moreover, 30 percent of all persons privately employed in research and development are in the aerospace industry.[3]

TRW Systems tried to minimize these fluctuations and their effects by limiting the size of a contract for which they might compete. They would rather have had ten $10 million contracts than one $100 million contract; also they had a policy of leasing a certain portion of their facilities in order to maintain flexibility in their physical plant.

In pursuing a conscious policy of growth, they competed for many contracts. By winning a reasonable number of these contracts, the company grew; and when one contract ran out, there were others always starting up. As a result, between 1953 and 1963 Systems did not have a single major layoff.

Another characteristic of the industry was the complexity of the prod-

---

[2] T. C. Miller, Jr., and L. P. Kane, "Strategies for Survival in the Aerospace Industry," *Industrial Management Review*, Fall 1965, pp. 22–23.

[3] Ibid., p. 20.

ucts being produced. There were thousands of parts in a space rocket and they had to interrelate in numerous subtle ways. If one part didn't come up to specifications it might harm hundreds of others. Since the parts and systems were so interdependent, the people in the various groups, divisions, and companies who made and assembled the parts were also highly interdependent. These interdependencies created some organizational problems for the companies in the industry, which forced them to develop a new type of organization called the matrix organization.

TRW SYSTEMS' ORGANIZATION

Exhibit 2 shows an organization chart for TRW in 1963 with the various functional divisions and the offices for program management (the word project is often used interchangeably for program). These different systems interrelated in what was called a matrix organization. The relationship between program offices and the functional divisions was a complex one, but can best be explained in a simple fashion by noting that instead of setting up, for example, a systems engineering group for the Atlas missile and another separate systems group for the Titan missile program, all the systems engineers were assigned organizationally to the Systems Division. This Systems Division was one of five technical divisions, each staffed with MTS (Members Technical Staff) working in a particular functional area. The various program offices coordinated the work of all the functional groups working on their particular programs and, in addition, handled all relationships with the contracting customer. It will be noted that the program offices were, formally, on the same organizational level as the functional divisions.

The engineers in these functional divisions were formally responsible to the director of their division, but they might also have a "dotted line" responsibility to a program office. For example, an electrical engineer would be responsible to his manager in the Electronics Division even though he might spend all of his time working for the Atlas program office. While working on the program he would report to the Atlas program director through one of his assistants.

Functional organization

Each functional division served as a technology center and focused on the disciplines and skills appropriate to its technology. Generally, a number of operations managers reported to the division manager, each of whom was in charge of a group of laboratories dealing with similar technologies. The laboratory directors who reported to the operation managers were each responsible for a number of functional departments which were organized around technical specialties. The engineers in these laboratory departments were the people who performed the actual work on program office projects.

Program office organization

A program manager maintained overall management responsibility for pulling together the various phases of a particular customer project. His office was the central location for all project-wide activities such as the project schedule, cost and performance control, system planning, system engineering, system integration, and contract and major subcontract management. Assistant project managers were appointed for these activities as warranted by the size of the project.

The total project effort was divided into subprojects, each project being assigned to a specific functional organization according to the technical specialty involved. The manager of the functional organization appointed

Exhibit 2
Organization chart, 1963

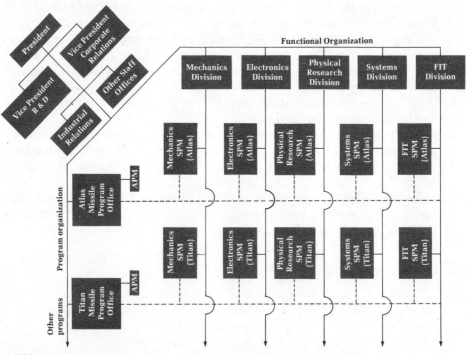

APM = Assistant Project Manager
SPM = Subproject Manager

a subproject manager with the concurrence of the project manager. The subproject manager was assigned responsibility for the total subproject activity and was delegated management authority by the functional division management and by the assistant project manager to whom he reported operationally for the project. The subproject manager was a full-time member of the project organization, but he was not considered a member of the project office; he remained a member of his functional organization. He was accountable for performance in his functional specialty to the manager of his functional area, usually a laboratory manager. The functional manager was responsible for the performance evaluation of the subproject manager. The subproject manager thus represented both the program office and his functional area and was responsible for coordinating the work of his subproject with the engineers within the functional area. Normally each functional area was involved in work on several projects simultaneously. One manager defined the subproject manager's responsibility this way:

> The subproject manager is a prime mover in this organization, and his job is a tough one. He is the person who brings the program office's requirements and the lab's resources together to produce a subsystem. He has to deal with the pressures and needs of both sides of the matrix and is responsible for bringing a subsystem together. He has to go to the functional department managers to get engineers to work on his project, but about all he can say is "Thanks for the work you've done on my subproject." But he does have program office money as a source of power, which the functional managers need to fund their operations. The technical managers are strong people. They are not "yes" men; they have their own ideas about how things ought to be done. You do not want them to be "yes" men either. Otherwise you've lost the balance you need to make sure that technical performance is not sacrificed for cost and schedule expediencies which are of great importance to the program office. The functional managers also are interested in long-range applications of the work they are doing on a particular project.
>
> This often puts the subproject manager in a real bind; he gets caught between conflicting desires. It is especially difficult because it is hard for him not to identify with the program office because that's the focus of his interest. But he is paid by the lab and that is also where he must go to get his work done. If he is smart he will identify with his subsystem and not with either the program office or the lab. He must represent the best course for his subproject, which sometimes means fighting with the program office and the departments at different times during the life of the subproject. If he reacts too much to pressures from either side, it hurts his ability to be objective about his subproject, and people will immediately sense this.

The casewriter asked Jim Dunlap, Director of Industrial Relations, what happened when an engineer's two bosses disagreed on how he should spend his time. He replied:

The decisions of priority on where a man should spend his time are made by Rube Mettler because he is the only common boss. But, of course, you try to get them to resolve it at a lower level. You just have to learn to live with ambiguity. It's not a structured situation. It just can't be.

You have to understand the needs of Systems Group to understand why we need the matrix organization. There are some good reasons why we use a matrix. Because R&D-type programs are finite programs—you create them, they live, and then they die—they have to die or overhead is out of line. Also, there are several stages in any project. You don't necessarily need the same people on the project all the time. In fact you waste the creative people if they work until the end finishing it up. The matrix is flexible. We can shift creative people around and bring in the people who are needed at various stages in the project. The creative people in the functions are professionals and are leaders in their technical disciplines. So the functional relationship helps them to continue to improve their professional expertise. Also, there is a responsiveness to all kinds of crises that come up. You sometimes have 30 days to answer a proposal—so you can put together a team with guys from everywhere. We're used to temporary systems; that's the way we live.

Often an engineer will work on two or three projects at a time and he just emphasizes one more than others. He's part of two systems at the same time.

The key word in the matrix organization is interdependency. Matrix means multiple interdependencies. We're continually setting up temporary systems. For example, we set up a project manager for the Saturn project with 20 people under him. Then he would call on people in systems engineering to get things started on the project. Next he might call in people from the Electronics Division, and after they finish their work the project would go to FIT [Fabrication, Integration and Testing] where it would be manufactured. So what's involved is a lot of people coming in and the leaving the project.

There is a large gap between authority and responsibility and we plan it that way. We give a man more responsibility than he has authority and the only way he can do this job is to collaborate with other people. The effect is that the system is flexible and adaptive, but it's hard to live with. An example of this is that the project manager has no authority over people working on the project from the functional areas. He can't decide on their pay, promotion, or even how much time they'll spend on his project as opposed to some other project. He has to work with the functional heads on these problems. We purposely set up this imbalance between authority and responsibility. We design a situation so that it's ambiguous. That way people have to collaborate and be flexible. You just can't rely on bureaucracy or power to solve your problems.

The casewriter talked to a number of people in various positions at TRW Systems Group and their comments about the matrix could be summarized as follows:

It is difficult to work with because it's flexible and always changing, but it does work; and it's probably the only organization that could work here.

Nearly everyone the casewriter talked with indicated that Systems Group was a "good place to work" and that they enjoyed the freedom they had. However, one critic of the system, a member of the administrative staff, presented his complaints about the system as follows:

People think this is a country club. It's a college campus atmosphere. Top management thinks everyone is mature and so they let them work as if they were on a college campus. They don't have rules to make people come to work on time or things like that. Do you know that 60–70 percent of the assigned parking spaces are empty at 8:30 A.M.? Personnel did a study of that—people are late. It's a good place to work for people who want complete freedom. But people abuse it. They don't come to work on time; they just do what they want around here. It's very democratic here. Nobody is telling you what to do and making all the decisions, but it can border on anarchy.

The management philosophy is that everybody will work harmoniously and you don't need a leader. But I think there has to be leadership, some one person who's responsible.

The casewriter then asked the question: "Isn't the project engineer responsible?" and the reply was:

The project engineer is a figurehead—in many cases he doesn't lead. I know one project engineer who provides no leadership at all. Besides, the matrix is constantly agitating. It's changing all the time, so it's just a bucket of worms. You never know where you stand. It's like ants on a log in a river and each one thinks he's steering—when none of them are. It's true that the top-level managers can make this philosophy work on their level. But we can't on our level. Let me give you an example. Mettler says he wants everything microfilmed, but he doesn't tell others to let me do it. I have responsibility but no authority in the form of a piece of paper or statement that I can do it. I just can't walk into some guy's empire and say I'm here to microfilm all of your papers. It's like an amoeba, always changing so you never know where your limits are or what you can or can't do.

As a contrasting view, one of the laboratory heads felt that the lack of formal rules and procedures was one of the strengths of the organization. He commented as follows:

This is not a company which is characterized by a lot of crisp orders and formal procedures. Quite honestly, we operate pretty loosely as far as procedures, etc., are concerned. In fact, I came from a university environment, but I believe there's more freedom and looseness of atmosphere around here than there was as a faculty member.

I think if you have pretty average people, you can have a very strict line type of organization and make it work, and maybe that's why we insist on being different. You see, I think you can also have a working organization with no strict lines of authority if you have broader-gauged people in it. I like to think that the individuals in the company are extremely high caliber and I think there is some evidence to support that. 6

Another manager supported the matrix organization with the following comments:

The people around here are really committed to the job. They'll work 24 hours a day when it is necessary, and sometimes it's necessary. I was on a team working on a project proposal a few months ago and during the last week of the proposal there were people working here around the clock. We had the secretaries come in on different shifts and we just stayed here and worked. I think that Mettler makes this matrix organization work. It's a difficult job but people have faith that Mettler knows what he's doing so they work hard and it comes out all right.

EVOLUTION OF CAREER DEVELOPMENT

In 1962, TRW Systems Group began a management development program called Career Development. Jim Dunlap, the Director of Industrial Relations, had responsibility for this program along with his other duties in Industrial Relations (see Exhibit 3).

Exhibit 3
Industrial relations

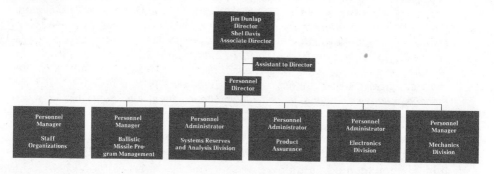

Early history of career development (1957–1965)

"What are we doing about management development?" Simon Ramo was asked in 1957. Ramo replied: "We don't believe in management development. We hire bright, intelligent people and we don't plan to insult their intelligence by giving them courses in courage."

In 1961, as Systems was trying to expand its customer base and cope with its new competitive environment, Rube Mettler became President. Mettler asked a consulting firm for advice on how best to make the transition to a competitive firm. "Systems needs men with experience in business management," the consultants said. "You will have to hire experienced top-level administrators from outside the firm. There aren't any here." Mettler agreed with them about needing top-level administrators. "But we'll develop our own people," Mettler added. Mettler confided in others that he feared that a manager with experience in another organization would have to unlearn a lot of bad habits before he could be successful at TRW.

Mettler put Dunlap in charge of the development program at TRW. Mettler made it clear to Dunlap that he wanted a task-oriented, dynamic development program to fit the special needs of the Systems Group.

Dunlap felt he needed assistance to implement the kind of program Mettler wanted. "The one thing I did was to entice Shel Davis to come into Industrial Relations," commented Dunlap. "He impressed me as a restless, dynamic, creative sort of guy." Davis had worked in a line position in one of TRW's other divisions.

With the help of an outside consultant, Dunlap and Davis began to design a development program. Early in 1962, 40 top managers were interviewed about what they felt was needed. One manager characterized the feelings of the entire group: "We need skills in management. Every time a new project starts around here, it takes half of the project schedule just bringing people on board. If we could have a quicker start-up, we'd finish these projects on time."

Dunlap, Davis, and the consultant went to work on a plan to fit these specific needs. Dunlap set up a two-day off-site meeting to discuss their plans and recommendations with some of the top managers. At the meeting, Dunlap and Davis talked about two, relatively new, applied behavioral science techniques (called team development and T-groups) as ways of meeting the needs of managers.[4] Dave Patterson was there and was impressed by this approach. Patterson had recently been appointed head of a new project and asked for their assistance: "I have a new team and I'm ready to hold a team-building meeting next week. Can you arrange it?"

Shel Davis, along with a consultant, held an off-site team development session for Patterson. After the meeting, Patterson's project group improved its working relationships with manufacturing. The success of this experiment became well known throughout the company. Mettler asked Patterson what effect the meeting had had. "It saved us six weeks on

---

[4] *Team development* (or team building) refers to a development process designed to improve the performance and effectiveness of people who work together. *Laboratory T-groups* (training groups) is a form of experiential learning away from the normal environment. Using unstructured groups, participants attempt to increase their sensitivity to their own and others' behavior as well as factors that hinder group interaction and effectiveness.

the program. About a million bucks," Patterson replied. This impressed people.

Late in 1962 Davis and Dunlap prepared a "white paper" on possible approaches in career development and sent it to the top 70 people. Most of the managers responded that TRW should improve its skills in three areas: communications and interpersonal skills, business management skills, and technical skills. Davis described the conversation he and Dunlap had with Mettler:

Jim and I talked with Mettler about the kind of program we wanted in the company and what we did and didn't want to do. As it turned out, we were in agreement with Mettler on almost every issue. For example, we decided not to make it a crash effort but to work at it and to take a lot of time making sure people understood what we wanted to do and that they supported it. We also decided to start at the top of the organization rather than at the bottom. During these discussions, they decided to call the training effort Career Development rather than organizational development or management development because Mettler didn't want to give the impression that they were going to concentrate on administrative training and neglect technical training.

Shortly after the white paper came out, Shel Davis and Jim Dunlap began to invite people to T-groups run by professionals outside of TRW. About 12 people took advantage of this opportunity between January and May of 1963. Ten of the 12 later reported that it was a "great experience." As a result, Mettler continued to support Dunlap and Davis, telling them: "Try things—if they work, continue them; if they don't, modify them, improve them, or drop them."

In April 1963, Davis and Dunlap decided to hold a team development meeting for the key people in Industrial Relations. The two men felt that once employees at the Systems Group started going to T-groups that there would be a growing demand for "Career Development" activities which the IR group would be asked to meet. The team development session, they felt, would help train the IR staff to meet this demand.

Dunlap and Davis next decided to run some T-groups themselves, within TRW. Dunlap argued for limiting this effort to 20 people. Davis wanted 40, saying, "Hell, let's go with it. Let's do too much too fast and then it will really have an effect on the organization. Otherwise it might not be noticed." Dunlap and Davis eventually decided to run four T-groups of ten people each.

The chain of events following that activity was later described by Frank Jasinski, who became Director of Career Development in 1964:

After that things really started to move. There was a strong demand for T-group experience. But we didn't just want to send people through labs like we were turning out so many sausages. We wanted to free up the organization, to seed it with people who had been to T-groups. The T-groups were to be just the beginning of a continuing process.

This continuing process was in several stages and developed over the three-year period. Maybe I can describe it in terms of one manager and his work group. First, the manager volunteered to go to a T-group (we have kept the program on a voluntary basis). Before he went to the T-group, there was a pre-T-group session where the participants asked questions and got prepared for the T-group experience. Then they went through the T-group.

After the T-group, there were three or four sessions where the T-group participants got together to discuss the problems of applying the T-group values back home. After the manager had been through the T-group, some of the members of his work group could decide to go to a T-group. The next stage was when the manager and his group decided they wanted to undertake a team development process where they could work on improving intragroup relations, i.e., how they could be more effective as a team.

Following a team development effort could be an interface meeting. This is the kind Alan East had. It seems Alan's department, Product Assurance, was having trouble getting along with a number of different departments in the organization. Alan felt if they were going to do their job well they had to be able to work effectively with these other groups. So he got three or four of his people together with the key people from five or six other departments and they worked on the interdepartmental relationship. Still another type of meeting that is similar is the intergroup meeting. If two groups just can't get along and are having difficulties, they may decide to hold an off-site meeting and try to work on the problems between them.

We also started doing some technical training and business management training. As with all of our training we try to make it organic: to meet the needs of the people and the organization. We tend to ask, "What is the problem?" Specific skill training may not be the answer. For example, a manager calls us and says he wants his secretary to have a review course in shorthand because she is slipping in her ability to use it. We might say, "Let's talk about it; maybe her shorthand is slipping because she doesn't use it enough and maybe she wants more challenging work. Why don't we get together with you and your secretary and discuss it." We have held several meetings with bosses and their secretaries to improve boss-secretary relationships. When they understand each other better, the secretary is more willing to help her boss and she is also in a better position to do so.

Such a large increase in Career Development activities required a rapid build-up of uniquely trained personnel. This problem was met in part by the use of outside consultants. Systems Group was able to interest a number of the national leaders in T-group-type activities to act as consultants, to serve as T-group trainers, and to work with the divisions on team building activities. By December 1964, they had built up a staff of 9 outside consultants.[5]

In order for the program to work on a day-to-day basis, they felt a

---

[5] This group consisted of senior professors at some of the largest business schools in the country and nationally recognized private consultants.

need to build a comparable internal staff. It was decided that the personnel manager in each division would not only be responsible for traditional personnel activities but he would also be an internal consultant on Career Development activities. Lynn Stewart, one of the outside consultants working with the Systems Group, described how TRW obtained a group of trained personnel managers.

Systems Group needed to build some internal change agents, which meant expanding the Industrial Relations effort. It required the development of the skills of people in Industrial Relations, especially the personnel managers. They were able to retool some of the people in Industrial Relations by sending them to T-groups. Some were not able to make the transition. They were transferred or fired. All of this was done to provide a staff that could service the needs created when people returned from T-groups.

In December 1964, Jim Dunlap announced that he had been promoted to Vice President of Human Relations for TRW Inc. and would be moving to Cleveland. He also announced that Shel Davis would succeed him as Director of Industrial Relations. (Exhibit 4 presents an organization chart of Industrial Relations as of January 1965).

A number of the personnel managers became concerned about the future of Industrial Relations. They knew Shel Davis had openly referred to the day-to-day personnel activities as "personnel crap," and they wondered what changes he would make. One personnel manager expressed this feeling when he said: "There were some undertones of a threat in Jim's leaving which might break the balance of prudence and loose Shel upon the group, forcing us to work exclusively on Career Development and to neglect our day-to-day personnel responsibilities."

Exhibit 4

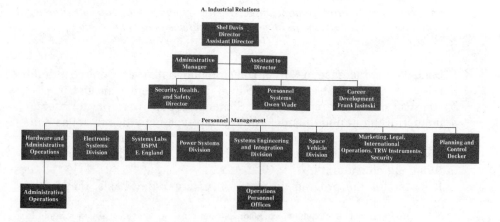

A. Industrial Relations

Exhibit 4 (*continued*)

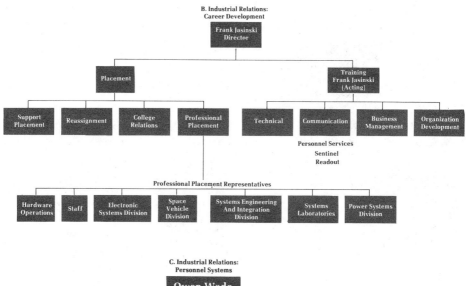

B. Industrial Relations:
Career Development

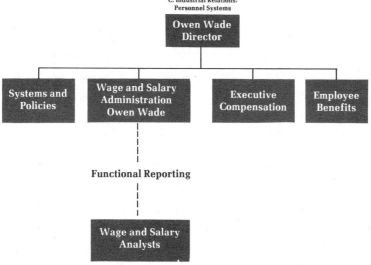

C. Industrial Relations:
Personnel Systems

Exhibit 4 (*concluded*)

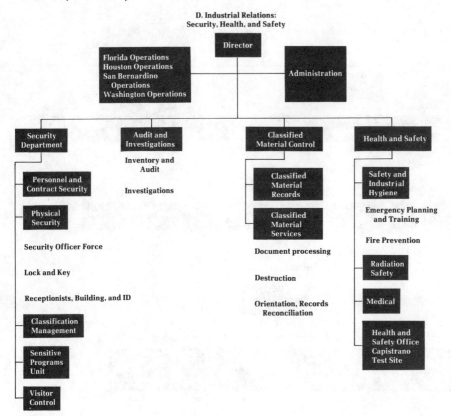

D. Industrial Relations:
Security, Health, and Safety

Director

Florida Operations
Houston Operations
San Bernardino
Operations
Washington Operations

Administration

Security
Department

Audit and
Investigations

Classified
Material Control

Health and Safety

Personnel and
Contract Security

Inventory and
Audit

Classified
Material
Records

Safety and
Industrial
Hygiene

Physical
Security

Investigations

Classified
Material
Services

Emergency Planning
and Training

Security Officer Force

Document processing

Fire Prevention

Lock and Key

Destruction

Radiation
Safety

Receptionists, Building, and ID

Orientation, Records
Reconciliation

Medical

Classification
Management

Sensitive
Programs
Unit

Health and
Safety Office
Capistrano
Test Site

Visitor
Control

By summer, 1966, however, most of the people in Industrial Relations felt that Shel Davis had adjusted to his role as Director of Industrial Relations and was doing a good job of balancing the demands of Career Development and the day-to-day personnel activities.

CAREER DEVELOPMENT IN 1966

By 1966, Career Development activities had greatly increased since their initiation in 1963 (see Exhibit 5). While T-groups continued to be used, the major effort of the department was in facilitating team building and intergroup labs.

Exhibit 5
Career development activities 1963–1965

	1963		1964		1965	
Activities	Courses	Attendees	Courses	Attendees	Courses	Attendees
Orientation	49	627	32	369	32	1,146
Colloquia	51	3,060	31	5,580	7	1,525
Invited lectures	2	800	4	1,600	—	—
Evening courses	12	261	17	438	16	651
Staff education	—	767	—	1,066	—	1,166
Technical courses	—	—	3	97	6	377
Internal leadership laboratories (T-groups) ...	1	45	4	104	4	151
External leadership laboratories (T-groups) ...	—	20	—	17	—	27
Team development meetings	—	—	4	76	44	671

Team development

There were a number of different types of team development activities. One was an effort to get a new team started faster. TRW repeatedly created temporary teams to accomplish recurring tasks. The tasks were quite similar but the team membership changed considerably. One example was a team established to prepare a proposal to bid on a particular contract. More than a dozen organizations would contribute to the final product: the written proposal. On major proposals, the representatives from the administrative and nontechnical areas remained fairly constant. The technical staff, however, varied with the task and usually was entirely new from proposal to proposal. This changing team membership required constant "bringing up to speed" of new members and repeated creation of a smoothly working unit. As the new team came together a team development session, usually off-site, helped to get the team working together sooner and would save time in the long run. A session would last one or two days and the participants would try to identify potential problems in working together and then begin to develop solutions for such problems. Lynn Stewart, an outside consultant, described a team development session for a launch team:

TRW has a matrix organization so that any one man is a member of many systems simultaneously. He has interfaces with many different groups. In addition, he is continually moving from one team to another, so they need team development to get the teams off to a fast start. On a launch team, for example, you have all kinds of people that come together for a short time. There are project directors, manufacturing people, the scientists who designed the experiments, and the men who launch the bird. You have to put all of those men together into a cohesive

*group in a short time. At launch time they can't be worrying about an organiza-
tional chart and how their respective roles change as preparation for the launch
progresses. Their relationships do change over time, but they should work that
through and discuss it beforehand, not when the bird is on the pad. The concept
of the organization is that you have a lot of resources and you need to regroup
them in different ways as customers and contracts change. You can speed up
the regrouping process by holding team development sessions.*[9]

Another type of team development activity was one with an ongoing
group. Typically, the manager would come to the personnel manager in
his division and express an interest in team development for his group.
If both agreed it would be beneficial, they would begin to plan such a
session. First, an effort would be made to identify an agenda for the
one or two-day off-site meetings. This would be developed in one of
two ways. The personnel manager or the consultant could interview, on
an individual basis, all the people who would be attending the session
to identify problem areas on which they needed to work. He would then
summarize the problems identified in his interviews and distribute this
summary to the participants a day or two before the session was held.
Another method sometimes used to develop an agenda was to get all
of the participants together on-site for 2 or 3 hours several days before
the off-site meeting. The participants would then be divided into subgroups
and would identify problem areas to work on. At the extended off-site
staff meeting, the intention was that the group would be task-oriented,
addressing itself to the question, "How can we improve the way our
group works together?" They would look at how the group's process got
in the way of the group's performance. The manager of the group would
conduct the meeting but the personnel manager and an outside consultant
would be there to help the group by observing and raising issues that
the group should look at. There had been a number of similar team development sessions at TRW and the people involved felt that they had been
worthwhile in that they had improved the group's effectiveness.

Another type of team development activity that was carried out on a
continuous basis was the critiquing of the many meetings held in the
organization. The casewriter sat in on a staff meeting of the Industrial
Relations Department which was attended by the personnel managers
and key people in the staff groups of Personnel Systems and Career Development. The purpose of the meeting was to plan the projects to be undertaken by Personnel Systems and Career Development throughout the remainder of the year. This included a discussion of what projects the
personnel managers would like undertaken and priority listing as to which
were most important. Owen Wade, Director of Personnel Systems, led
the discussion during the first hour and one half of the meeting while
the group discussed projects for Personnel Systems. Frank Jasinski, Direc-

tor of Career Development, led the discussion in the last hour of the meeting, in which projects for Career Development were discussed. Near the end of the meeting the following discussion took place:

Shel Davis: *We only have ten minutes left so we had better spend some time on a critique of the meeting. Does anyone have any comments?*

Ed (Personnel Manager): *We bit off more than we could chew here. We shouldn't have planned to do so much.*

Don (Personnel Manager): *I felt we just floated from 10:30 to 10:45. We got through with Frank and his subject and then nothing was done until the break.*

Bob (Personnel Manager): *Why didn't you make that observation at 10:30, Don, so we could do something about it? Do you feel intimidated about making a process observation?*

Don: *No. I felt like I was in the corner earlier. But not after making this observation. Besides, I did say earlier that we weren't doing anything and should move on, but I guess I didn't say it loud enough for people to hear me.*

Ed: *Don, that is the first time you've made a process observation in six months. I wish you'd make more of them.*

Shel: *I think Owen's presentation was very good because he had estimated the number of man-weeks of work required for each of the projects. Frank's presentation was less effective because his didn't have that.*

Jasinski: *I have a question on the manpower requirements. I spent seven or eight hours preparing for this meeting in setting priorities on all the projects we had listed and then it wasn't followed up in this meeting.* [*Two or three people echoed support for this statement.*]

Bob: *I thought we were asked to do too much in preparing for this meeting. It was just too detailed and too much work, so I rebelled and refused to do it.*

Wade (Director of Personnel Systems): *Well, from my point of view on the staff side of the fence, I feel pressured and as if I'm asked to do too much. The personnel managers have a very different set of rules. You don't plan as much as we have to and I think you should plan more.*

One of the participants commented that a large number of the meetings at TRW were critiqued in a similar manner.

Intergroup and interface labs

As a result of the nature of the work at TRW and of the matrix organization, there was a great deal of interaction between the various groups in the organization. Sometimes this interaction was characterized by conflict; the Career Development staff began to work on ways to help groups deal with this conflict. One such effort, the first interface lab, developed out of an experience of Alan East, Director of Product Assurance. Mr. East commented on his experience:

I came to Product Assurance from a technical organization so I knew very little of what Product Assurance was about. First, I tried to find out what our objectives were. I talked to our supervisors and I found there was a lack of morale. They thought they were second-class citizens. They were cowed by the domineering engineers and they felt inferior. I decided one of the problems was that people outside Product Assurance didn't understand us and the importance of our job. I concluded that that was easy to solve: we'd educate them. So, we set out to educate the company. We decided to call a meeting and we drew up an agenda. Then, as an afterthought, I went to see Shel Davis to see if he had some ideas on how to train people. But he just turned it around. He got me to see that rather than educating them, maybe we could find out how they really saw us and why. Well, we held an off-site meeting and we identified a lot of problems between Product Assurance and the other departments. After the meeting, we came back and started to work to correct those problems. [10]

After East's successful interface meeting, the idea caught hold and similar meetings were held by other groups. Harold Nelson, the Director of Finance, held an interface meeting between four members of his department and a number of departments that had frequent contact with Finance. The purpose of the meeting was to get feedback on how Finance was seen by others in the organization. Commenting on the effectiveness of the meeting, Nelson added, "They were impressed that we were able to have a meeting, listen to their gripes about us and not be defensive. The impact of such meetings on individuals is tremendous. It causes people to change so these meetings are very productive."

Del Thomas, a participant in the interface meeting with Finance, represented another department. Thomas observed that, prior to the meeting, his group felt Finance was too slow in evaluating requests and that Nelson and his subordinates ". . . were too meticulous, too much like accountants." Thomas felt the meeting improved the performance of Finance:

I think Harold [Nelson] got what he was looking for, but he may have been surprised there were so many negative comments. I think there are indications that the meeting has improved things. First, Harold is easier to get ahold of now. Second, since the meeting, Harold brought in a new man to evaluate capital expenditures and he's doing a top job. He's helpful and he has speeded up the process. I think the atmosphere of the whole Finance group is changing. They are starting to think more of "we the company" and less of "us and them."

EVALUATION OF THE CAREER DEVELOPMENT EFFORT

Jim Dunlap, the Vice President for Human Relations, was asked to evaluate the effect of Career Development on TRW Systems. Dunlap pulled two studies from his desk drawer. The first, a report by a government official titled "Impulse for Openness," noted in its summary:

It is not our intention, nor certainly that of TRW Systems, to imply that either the company reorganization or the physical progress are results solely of the Career Development program, but it does appear that the program had a substantial impact on the success of the company. The data shown completes the picture of changes in the company during the period under discussion. Employment at 6,000 in 1962 and over 11,000 in March 1966, will most likely double by the end of this year. Sales more than tripled between 1962 and 1965. Professional turnover decreased from 17.1 percent in 1962 to 6.9 percent in March 1966. The average for the aerospace industry in this area of California is approximately 20 percent.

Also, Dunlap revealed the results of a study by a professional organization to which many of Systems Group employees belong. It took a survey of all of its members, asking them to rank 54 firms in the aerospace industry on six different factors. The respondents ranked TRW Systems first in "desirability as an employer," seventh for "contribution to aerospace," and second in "salary."

Dunlap also added his personal comments on the efforts of the Career Development program:

It's very hard to make an evaluation of the program and say it has saved us "X" million dollars. But there are several indications that it has been effective. Turnover is down significantly and I've heard a lot of people say, "I stayed at TRW because of the Career Development activities." Some people make more definite claims for the program. Dave Patterson says our Team Development Process saved us $500,000. Rube Mettler is convinced the program has improved our skills so that we've won some contracts we wouldn't have gotten otherwise. I believe it has improved our team performance. All of our proposal teams spend two days of team building before they start on the proposal. Every program starts with an off-site team development lab. They help build a team esprit de corps and it creates an openness so they are better able to solve problems.

A number of employees were willing to discuss their attitudes towards the Career Development program. Denis Brown, a member of the administrative staff, and a participant in the activities of Career Development, felt the program was valuable. Denis noted:

They took the OGO launch crew off-site and improved their effectiveness. Well, a launch is very tense and if one guy is hostile toward another it may mean a failure which costs $20 million. I don't know how much they spent on Career Development, but say it's a quarter of a million dollars. If one man improves his relationship with another and it saves a launch and $20 million, you've made it back many times over. The company feels it is a good thing, and it has worked well, so they'll continue it.

Jim Whitman, a subproject manager, had high praise for Career Development. Whitman credited the program for making groups more effective in communicating and working with one another. Recounting his own experiences, Whitman added that the program led to better collaboration and working conditions between the design engineer and the fabrication engineer.

But other employees were less enthusiastic. John Ward, a member of a program office, discussed his participation in Career Development activities. Ward felt that some of the off-site sessions were "rather grueling affairs, particularly when you are the center of attention." But Ward added that the session he attended was valuable.

> In my opinion, the reason it was worthwhile is that under the pressure of work people cannot—I use the word cannot when I should say will not—take the time to sit down and discuss some very basic issues to get the air cleared. Even in a small group people tend to wear blinders. You think about your own problems because you have so many of them, so you tend to build up a fence to keep some of the other fellow's problems from getting through. He talks about them but you don't hear them; you don't get the significance of what he's trying to tell you. But if you go away with instructions that people are not to bother you unless it is really important, you create an environment where there is time to work out some of these things.

One member of the administrative staff, Dan Jackson, had very different views on Career Development. Jackson noted:

> Idealistically, it's a good thing. If in the real world people lived that way, were open and sincere and could tell each other their feelings without getting hurt, it would be excellent. But people just aren't that way in the real world. The people who are enthusiastic about this, Mettler, Hesse, Davis, etc., are at a level in the company where they can practice this. They're just dealing with other vice presidents and top-level people. But down on my level it won't work. We've got to produce things down here and people just aren't responsible and we can't just be nice to people all the time. We have to get some work done.
>
> I think that the trainers at the lab live that way and that's all right, but they tend to be frustrated head-shrinkers. They want to be psychiatrists but they don't have the training—so they do sensitivity training. It's kind of like running a therapy group. I think the techniques they use are pretty good, like having one group inside talking and one group on the outside observing, but the people running it aren't well enough trained. They may be the best that are available, but they are not good enough. Frankly, I think these trainers are really just trying to find out their own problems, but they do it by getting mixed up in other people's problems.

Jackson continued, observing that participation in these activities was not completely voluntary:

> Oh, it's voluntary, but you are kind of told you had better go. You aren't fired if you don't but there's pressure put on you to go. One of our Ph.D's walked out after two days at a T-group. I don't think it has hurt his career, but people know he took a walk. He just felt it was a sin, morally wrong, what was going on up there.

While Jackson seemed to express the most negative attitudes toward Career Development, there was a widely circulated story about a man who had suffered a nervous breakdown after attending a T-group. Jim Dunlap was asked to comment on the incident:

Yes, one person had a traumatic experience, or as they say, "cracked up." Very early in the program we decided that the people in personnel should go to a T-group so they'd understand what we were going to do. I asked this fellow if he'd like to go. He took it as an order and he went. But I was only asking him to go. If I'd known more about him, I wouldn't have asked him if he wanted to go. But I just saw him at work and he seemed to be getting along all right, although I knew that he didn't enjoy his job. He wanted to get into education. But I didn't know he was having troubles at home and that things weren't going very well for him in general. He was just kind of holding himself together as best he could. He went to the T-group and it caused him to start thinking about his situation and he fell apart; he had a nervous breakdown. After the T-group was over he came home, but he didn't come to work. He stayed home for a week or two. Finally, he decided he needed help and began to see a psychiatrist. Apparently that was just what he needed because he then decided to get that job in education which he liked very much. He seems to have solved his problems, so everything has turned out for the best. But it scared the hell out of us at the time.

Reading 4–1
Organization design:
An information processing view*
Jay R. Galbraith

The information processing model

A basic proposition is that the greater the uncertainty of the task, the greater the amount of information that has to be processed between decision makers during the execution of the task. If the task is well understood prior to performing it, much of the activity can be preplanned. If it is not understood, then during the actual task execution more knowledge is acquired which leads to changes in resource allocations, schedules, and priorities. All these changes require information processing *during* task performance. Therefore *the greater the task uncertainty, the greater the amount of information that must be processed among decision makers during task execution in order to achieve a given level of performance.* The basic effect of uncertainty is to limit the ability of the organization to preplan or to make decisions about activities in advance of their execution. Therefore it is hypothesized that the observed variations in organizational forms are variations in the strategies of organizations to (1) increase their ability to preplan, (2) increase their flexibility to adapt to their inability to preplan, or (3) to decrease the level of performance required for continued viability. Which strategy is chosen depends on the relative costs of the strategies. The function of the framework is to identify these strategies and their costs.

The mechanistic model

This framework is best developed by keeping in mind a hypothetical organization. Assume it is large and employs a number of specialist groups and resources in providing the output. After the task has been divided into specialist subtasks, the problem is to integrate the subtasks around the completion of the global task. This is the problem of organization design. The behaviors that occur in one subtask cannot be judged as good or bad *per se.* The behaviors are more effective or ineffective depending upon the behaviors of the other subtask performers. There is a design

---

* Reprinted by permission from *Interfaces*, vol. 4, no. 3 (May 1974), pp. 28–36.

problem because the executors of the behaviors cannot communicate with all the roles with whom they are interdependent. Therefore the design problem is to create mechanisms that permit coordinated action across large numbers of interdependent roles. Each of these mechanisms, however, has a limited range over which it is effective at handling the information requirements necessary to coordinate the interdependent roles. As the amount of uncertainty increases, and therefore information processing increases, the organization must adopt integrating mechanisms which increase its information processing capabilities.

1. Coordination by rules or programs

For routine predictable tasks March and Simon have identified the use of rules or programs to coordinate behavior between interdependent subtasks (March and Simon, 1958, chap. 6). To the extent that job-related situations can be predicted in advance, and behaviors specified for these situations, programs allow an interdependent set of activities to be performed without the need for inter-unit communication. Each role occupant simply executes the behavior which is appropriate for the task-related situation with which he is faced.

2. Hierarchy

As the organization faces greater uncertainty its participants face situations for which they have no rules. At this point the hierarchy is employed on an exception basis. The recurring job situations are programmed with rules while infrequent situations are referred to that level in the hierarchy where a global perspective exists for all affected subunits. However, the hierarchy also has a limited range. As uncertainty increases the number of exceptions increases until the hierarchy becomes overloaded.

3. Coordination by targets or goals

As the uncertainty of the organization's task increases, coordination increasingly takes place by specifying outputs, goals or targets (March and Simon, 1958, p. 145). Instead of specifying specific behaviors to be enacted, the organization undertakes processes to set goals to be achieved and the employees select the behaviors which lead to goal accomplishments. Planning reduces the amount of information processing in the hierarchy by increasing the amount of discretion exercised at lower levels. Like the use of rules, planning achieves integrated action and also eliminates the need for continuous communication among interdependent subunits as long as task performance stays within the planned task specifications, budget limits and within targeted completion dates. If it does not, the hierarchy is again employed on an exception basis.

The ability of an organization to coordinate interdependent tasks depends on its ability to compute meaningful subgoals to guide subunit action. When uncertainty increases because of introducing new products, entering new markets, or employing new technologies, these subgoals are incorrect. The result is more exceptions, more information processing, and an overloaded hierarchy.

Design strategies

The ability of an organization to successfully utilize coordination by goal setting, hierarchy, and rules depends on the combination of the frequency of exceptions and the capacity of the hierarchy to handle them. As the task uncertainty increases the organization must again take organization design action. It can proceed in either of two general ways. First, it can act in two ways to reduce the amount of information that is processed. And second, the organization can act in two ways to increase its capacity to handle more information. The two methods for reducing the need for information and the two methods for increasing processing capacity are shown schematically in Figure 1. The effect of all these actions is to reduce the number of exceptional cases referred upward into the organization through hierarchical channels. The assumption is that the critical limiting factor of an organizational form is its ability to handle

Figure 1
Organization design strategies

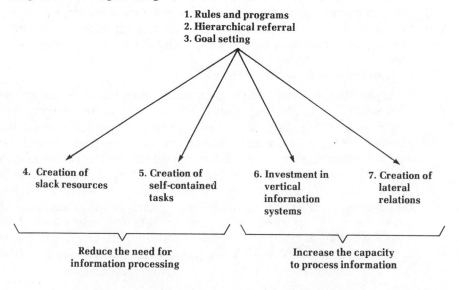

1. Rules and programs
2. Hierarchical referral
3. Goal setting

4. Creation of
   slack resources

5. Creation of
   self-contained
   tasks

6. Investment in
   vertical
   information
   systems

7. Creation of
   lateral
   relations

Reduce the need for
information processing

Increase the capacity
to process information

the nonroutine, consequential events that cannot be anticipated and planned for in advanced. The nonprogrammed events place the greatest communication load on the organization.

1. Creation of slack resources

As the number of exceptions begin to overload the hierarchy, one response is to increase the planning targets so that fewer exceptions occur. For example, completion dates can be extended until the number of exceptions that occur are within the existing information processing capacity of the organization. This has been the practice in solving job shop scheduling problems (Pounds, 1963). Job shops quote delivery times that are long enough to keep the scheduling problem within the computational and information processing limits of the organization. Since every job shop has the same problem, standard lead times evolve in the industry. Similarly, budget targets could be raised, buffer inventories employed, etc. The greater the uncertainty, the greater the magnitude of the inventory, lead time, or budget needed to reduce an overload.

All of these examples have a similar effect. They represent the use of slack resources to reduce the amount of interdependence between subunits (March and Simon, 1958; Cyert and March, 1963). This keeps the required amount of information within the capacity of the organization to process it. Information processing is reduced because an exception is less likely to occur and reduced interdependence means that fewer factors need to be considered simultaneously when an exception does occur.

The strategy of using slack resources has its costs. Relaxing budget targets has the obvious cost of requiring more budget. Increasing the time to completion date has the effect of delaying the customer. Inventories require the investment of capital funds which could be used elsewhere. Reduction of design optimization reduces the performance of the article being designed. Whether slack resources are used to reduce information or not depends on the relative cost of the other alternatives.

The design choices are: (1) among which factors to change (lead time, overtime, machine utilization, etc.) to create the slack, and (2) by what amount should the factor be changed. Many operations research models are useful in choosing factors and amounts. The time-cost trade-off problem in project networks is a good example.

2. Creation of self-contained tasks

The second method of reducing the amount of information processed is to change the subtask groupings from resource (input)-based to output-based categories and give each group the resources it needs to supply the output. For example, the functional organization could be changed to product groups. Each group would have its own product engineers, process engineers, fabricating and assembly operations, and marketing activities. In other situations, groups can be created around product lines, geographical areas, projects, client groups, markets, etc., each of which would contain the input resources necessary for creation of the output.

The strategy of self-containment shifts the basis of the authority structure from one based on input, resource, skill, or occupational categories to one based on output or geographical categories. The shift reduces the amount of information processing through several mechanisms. First, it reduces the amount of output diversity faced by a single collection of resources. For example, a professional organization with multiple skill specialties providing service to three different client groups must schedule the use of these specialties across three demands for their services and determine priorities when conflicts occur. But, if the organization changed to three groups, one for each client category, each with its own full complement of specialties, the schedule conflicts across client groups disappears and there is no need to process information to determine priorities.

The second source of information reduction occurs through a reduced division of labor. The functional or resource specialized structure pools the demand for skills across all output categories. In the example above each client generates approximately one third of the demand for each skill. Since the division of labor is limited by the extent of the market, the division of labor must decrease as the demand decreases. In the professional organization, each client group may have generated a need for one third of a computer programmer. The functional organization would have hired one programmer and shared him across the groups. In the self-contained structure there is insufficient demand in each group for a programmer so the professionals must do their own programming. Specialization is reduced but there is no problem of scheduling the programmer's time across the three possible uses for it.

The cost of the self-containment strategy is the loss of resource specialization. In the example, the organization foregoes the benefit of a specialist in computer programming. If there is physical equipment, there is a loss of economies of scale. The professional organization would require three machines in the self-contained form but only a large time-shared machine in the functional form. But those resources which have large economies of scale or for which specialization is necessary may remain centralized. Thus, it is the degree of self-containment that is the variable. The greater the degree of uncertainty, other things equal, the greater the degree of self-containment.

The design choices are the basis for the self-contained structure and the number of resources to be contained in the groups. No groups are completely self-contained or they would not be part of the same organization. But one product-divisionalized firm may have 8 of 15 functions in the division while another may have 12 of 15 in the divisions. Usually accounting, finance, and legal services are centralized and shared. Those functions which have economies of scale, require specialization, or are necessary for control remain centralized and not part of the self-contained group.

The first two strategies reduced the amount of information by lower performance standards and creating small autonomous groups to provide the output. Information is reduced because an exception is less likely to occur and fewer factors need to be considered when an exception does occur. The next two strategies accept the performance standards and division of labor as given and adapt the organization so as to process the new information which is created during task performance.

3. Investment in vertical information systems

The organization can invest in mechanisms which allow it to process information acquired during task performance without overloading the hierarchical communication channels. The investment occurs according to the following logic. After the organization has created its plan or set of targets for inventories, labor utilization, budgets, and schedules, unanticipated events occur which generate exceptions requiring adjustments to the original plan. At some point when the number of exceptions becomes substantial, it is preferable to generate a new plan rather than make incremental changes with each exception. The issue is then how frequently should plans be revised—yearly, quarterly, or monthly? The greater the frequency of replanning, the greater the resources, such as clerks, computer time, input-output devices, etc., required to process information about relevant factors.

The cost of information processing resources can be minimized if the language is formalized. Formalization of a decision-making language simply means that more information is transmitted with the same number of symbols. It is assumed that information processing resources are consumed in proportion to the number of symbols transmitted. The accounting system is an example of a formalized language.

Providing more information, more often, may simply overload the decision maker. Investment may be required to increase the capacity of the decision maker by employing computers, various man-machine combinations, assistants-to, etc. The cost of this strategy is the cost of the information processing resources consumed in transmitting and processing the data.

The design variables of this strategy are the decision frequency, the degree of formalization of language, and the type of decision mechanism which will make the choice. This strategy is usually operationalized by

creating redundant information channels which transmit data from the
point of origination upward in the hierarchy where the point of decision
rests. If data is formalized and quantifiable, this strategy is effective. If
the relevant data are qualitative and ambiguous, then it may prove easier
to bring the decisions down to where the information exists.

4. Creation of lateral relationships

The last strategy is to employ selectively joint decision process which
cut across lines of authority. This strategy moves the level of decision
making down in the organization to where the information exists but
does so without reorganizing around self-contained groups. There are
several types of lateral decision processes. Some processes are usually
referred to as the informal organization. However, these informal processes do not always arise spontaneously out of the needs of the task.
This is particularly true in multinational organizations in which participants are separated by physical barriers, language differences, and cultural differences. Under these circumstances lateral processes need to
be designed. The lateral processes evolve as follows with increases in
uncertainty.

4.1. *Direct contact* between managers who share a problem. If a problem arises on the shop floor, the foreman can simply call the design engineer, and they can jointly agree upon a solution. From an information
processing view, the joint decision prevents an upward referral and un-
loads the hierarchy.

4.2. *Liaison roles.* When the volume of contacts between any two departments grows, it becomes economical to set up a specialized role to
handle this communication. Liaison men are typical examples of specialized roles designed to facilitate communication between two interdependent departments and to bypass the long lines of communication involved
in upward referral. Liaison roles arise at lower and middle levels of
management.

4.3. *Task forces.* Direct contact and liaison roles, like the integration
mechanisms before them, have a limited range of usefulness. They work
when two managers or functions are involved. When problems arise involving seven or eight departments, the decision-making capacity of direct
contacts is exceeded. Then these problems must be referred upward. For
uncertain, interdependent tasks, such situations arise frequently. Task
forces are a form of horizontal contact which is designed for problems
of multiple departments.

The task force is made up of representatives from each of the affected
departments. Some are full-time members, others may be part-time. The
task force is a temporary group. It exists only as long as the problem

remains. When a solution is reached, each participant returns to his normal tasks.

To the extent that they are successful, task forces remove problems from higher levels of the hierarchy. The decisions are made at lower levels in the organization. In order to guarantee integration, a group problem-solving approach is taken. Each affected subunit contributes a member and therefore provides the information necessary to judge the impact on all units.

4.4. *Teams.* The next extension is to incorporate the group decision process into the permanent decision processes. That is, as certain decisions consistently arise, the task forces become permanent. These groups are labeled teams. There are many design issues concerned in team decision-making, such as at what level do they operate, who participates, etc. (Galbraith, 1973, chap. 6 and 7). One design decision is particularly critical. This is the choice of leadership. Sometimes a problem exists largely in one department so that the department manager is the leader. Sometimes the leadership passes from one manager to another. As a new product moves to the marketplace, the leader of the new-product team is first the technical manager, followed by the production, and then the marketing manager. The result is that if the team cannot reach a consensus decision and the leader decides, the goals of the leader are consistent with the goals of the organization for the decision in question. But, quite often, obvious leaders cannot be found. Another mechanism must be introduced.

4.5. *Integrating roles.* The leadership issue is solved by creating a new role—an integrating role (Lawrence and Lorsch, 1967, chap. 3). These roles carry the labels of product managers, program managers, project managers, unit managers (hospitals), materials managers, etc. After the role is created, the design problem is to create enough power in the role to influence the decision process. These roles have power even when no one reports directly to them. They have some power because they report to the general manager. But if they are selected so as to be unbiased with respect to the groups they integrate and to have technical competence, they have expert power. They collect information and equalize power differences due to preferential access to knowledge and information. The power equalization increases trust and the quality of the joint decision process. But power equalization occurs only if the integrating role is staffed with someone who can exercise expert power in the form of persuasion and informal influences rather than exert the power of rank or authority.

4.6 *Managerial linking roles.* As tasks become more uncertain, it is more difficult to exercise expert power. The role must get more power of the formal authority type in order to be effective at coordinating the joint decisions which occur at lower levels of the organization. This position power changes the nature of the role which for lack of a better name is labeled a managerial linking role. It is not like the integrating role because it possesses formal position power but is different from line managerial roles in that participants do not report to the linking manager. The power is added by the following successive changes:

a. The integrator receives approval power of budgets formulated in the departments to be integrated.
b. The planning and budgeting process starts with the integrator making his initiation in budgeting legitimate.
c. Linking manager receives the budget for the area of responsibility and buys resources from the specialist groups

These mechanisms permit the manager to exercise influence even though no one works directly for him. The role is concerned with integration but exercises power through the formal power of the position. If this power is insufficient to integrate the subtasks, and creation of self-contained groups is not feasible, there is one last step.

4.7. *Matrix organization.* The last step is to create the dual authority relationship and the matrix organization (Galbraith, 1971). At some point in the organization some roles have two superiors. The design issue is

Figure 2
A pure matrix organization

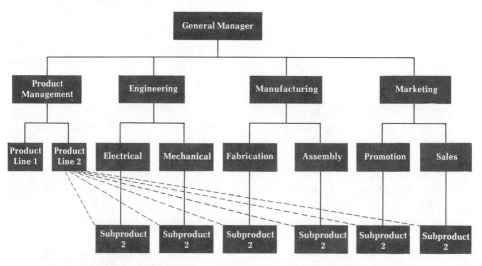

------- Technical authority over product
———— Formal authority over product (in product organization, these relationships may be reversed)

to select the locus of these roles. The result is a balance of power between the managerial linking roles and the normal line organization roles. Figure 2 depicts the pure matrix design.

The work of Lawrence and Lorsch is highly consistent with the assertions concerning lateral relations (Lawrence and Lorsch, 1967; Lorsch and Lawrence, 1968). They compared the types of lateral relations undertaken by the most successful firm in three different industries. Their data are summarized in Table 1. The plastics firm has the greatest rate of new-product introduction (uncertainty) and the greatest utilization of lateral processes. The container firm was also very successful but utilized only standard practices because its information processing task is much less formidable. Thus, the greater the uncertainty the lower the level of decision making and the integration is maintained by lateral relations.

Table 1 points out the cost of using lateral relations. The plastics firm has 22 percent of its managers in integration roles. Thus, the greater the use of lateral relations the greater the managerial intensity. This cost must be balanced against the cost of slack resources, self-contained groups, and information systems.

Table 1*

	Plastics	*Food*	*Container*
Percent new products in last ten years	35 percent	20 percent	0 percent
Integrating devices	Rules Hierarchy Planning Direct contact Teams at 3 levels Integrating dept.	Rules Hierarchy Planning Direct contact Task forces Integrators	Rules Hierarchy Planning Direct contact
Percent integrators/ managers	22 percent	17 percent	0 percent

* Adopted from Lawrence and Lorsch, 1967, pp. 86–138, and Lorsch and Lawrence, 1968.

Choice of strategy

Each of the four strategies has been briefly presented. The organization can follow one or some combination of several if it chooses. It will choose that strategy which has the least cost in its environmental context. (For an example, see Galbraith, 1970). However, what may be lost in all of the explanations is that the four strategies are hypothesized to be an exhaustive set of alternatives. That is, if the organization is faced with greater uncertainty due to technological change, higher performance standards due to increased competition, or diversifies its product line to reduce dependence, the amount of information processing is increased. *The organization must adopt at least one of the four strategies when faced with greater uncertainty.* If it does not consciously choose one of the four, then the first, reduced performance standards, will happen automatically. The task information requirements and the capacity of the organization to process information are always matched. If the organization does not consciously match them, reduced performance through budget overruns and schedule overruns will occur in order to bring about equality. Thus the organization should be planned and designed simultaneously with the planning of the strategy and resource allocations. But if the strategy involves introducing new products, entering new markets, etc., then some provision for increased information must be made. Not to decide is to decide, and it is to decide upon slack resources as the strategy to remove hierarchical overload.

There is probably a fifth strategy which is not articulated here. Instead of changing the organization in response to task uncertainty, the organization can operate on its environment to reduce uncertainty. The organization through strategic decisions, long-term contracts, coalitions, etc., can control its environment. But these maneuvers have costs also. They should be compared with costs of the four design strategies presented above.

Summary

The purpose of this paper has been to explain why task uncertainty is related to organizational form. In so doing the cognitive limits theory of Herbert Simon was the guiding influence. As the consequences of cognitive limits were traced through the framework various organization design strategies were articulated. The framework provides a basis for integrating organizational interventions, such as information systems and group problem solving, which have been treated separately before.

BIBLIOGRAPHY

Cyert, Richard, and March, James. *The Behavioral Theory of the Firm.* Englewood Cliffs, N.J.: Prentice-Hall, 1963.

Galbraith, Jay. "Environmental and Technological Determinants of Organization Design: A Case Study." *"Studies in Organization Design,* ed. p. Lawrence and J. Lorsch. Homewood, Ill.: Richard D. Irwin, Inc., 1970.

Galbraith, Jay. "Designing Matrix Organizations." *Business Horizons,* February 1971, pp. 29–40.

Galbraith, Jay. *Designing Complex Organizations*. Reading, Mass.: Addison-Wesley, 1973.

Lawrence, Paul, and Lorsch, Jay. *Organization and Environment*. Boston, Mass.: Division of Research, Harvard Business School, 1967.

Lorsch, Jay, and Lawrence, Paul. "Environmental Factors and Organization Integration." Paper read at the Annual Meeting of the American Sociological Association, Boston, Mass., August 27, 1968.

March, James, and Simon, Herbert. *Organizations*. New York: John Wiley & Sons, 1958.

Pounds, William. "The Scheduling Environment." In *Industrial Scheduling*, ed. Muth and Thompson. Englewood Cliffs, N.J.: Prentice-Hall, 1963.

Simon, Herbert. *Models of Man*. New York: John Wiley & Sons, 1957.

Reading 4–2
*What kind of management control do you need?**
Richard F. Vancil

Profit centers are a major tool for management control in large industrial corporations. They possess important advantages:

1. Profitability is a simple way to analyze and monitor the effectiveness of a segment of a complex business. For example, a product division competes in the marketplace against several other companies in its industry, and also competes among other divisions in its company for an allocation of corporate resources for its future growth. Relative profitability in both types of competition is a useful decision criterion for top management.
2. Profit responsibility is a powerful motivator of men. Managers understand what profit is all about, and aggressive managers welcome the opportunity to have their abilities measured by the only real entrepreneurial yardstick.

Simple and powerful, profit centers sound like a panacea, the answer to a top manager's prayer. No wonder the concept has been so widely adopted. However, as with many a miracle drug, all too often the side effects of the medicine may be worse than the illness it was intended to cure.

There is an excellent body of literature on the problems that arise in implementing the profit center concept.[1] The question I shall discuss is a more basic one: *When* should profit centers be used? More precisely, what executives below the president of a corporation (who clearly is responsible for profits) should be held responsible for the profits from segments of the business?

Parts of this discussion will come as no surprise to corporate presidents or to their controllers. I shall stress the relevance of corporate strategy and organization structure to profit center systems—an approach that may seem obvious to such executives. But I cannot find a discussion of these considerations in the literature, and thus I am led to believe that a concise statement of the conventional wisdom may be worthwhile.

CHOICE OF FINANCIAL GOALS

The cornerstone of every management control system is the concept of responsibility accounting. The basic idea is simple: each manager in a company has responsibility for a part of the total activity. The accounting system should be designed so that it yields a measurement of the financial effects of the activities that a manager is responsible for. This measurement can be stated in the form of a financial objective for each manager. Specifying that objective helps in delegating authority; a manager knows that the "right" decision is the course of action that moves him down the path toward his financial objective.

But this system does not go far enough. No single measurement, no matter how carefully constructed, can accurately reflect how well a manager has done his job. Part of the failure is simply due to the fact that corporations—and their managers—have multiple objectives. For instance, there is the matter of corporate social responsibility. Good performance toward that goal, even if measurable, cannot be added to the profit equation. Another major inadequacy of a single financial measurement is that it reflects performance during a particular time period, ignoring the effects that current actions may have on future performance. Every manager must make trade-offs between conflicting short-term and long-

---

[1] See, in particular, John Dearden, "Appraising Profit Center Managers," *Harvard Business Review,* May–June 1968, p. 80; "Bonus Formula for Division Heads" (with William S. Edgerly), *HBR,* September–October 1965, p. 83; "The Case Against ROI Control," *HBR,* May–June 1969, p. 124; "Limits on Decentralized Profit Responsibility," *HBR,* July–August 1962, p. 81; and "Mirage of Profit Decentralization," *HBR,* November–December 1962, p. 140.

term needs; examples range all the way from the shop foreman who defers preventive maintenance in order to increase this month's output, but at the expense of a major breakdown next month, to the division manager who cuts his R&D budget in order to improve the year's profits but loses or delays the opportunity to introduce a profitable new product three years from now.

Despite these flaws, oversimplified financial measurements are almost universally used. The reason is not their value in evaluating a manager's performance—the faults noted are too obvious and important to ignore—but their effect on future performance. Specifying a financial objective can help a manager to think realistically about the tough decisions he must make, even if the objective does not always point the way to the right decision.

The selection of the right financial objective for each manager, therefore, can have an important effect on how he does his job. Although the range of *possible* objectives is very great, the financially measurable results of any manager's activities can usually be classified into one of five categories of responsibility centers. As indicated, financial responsibility is simplest in the case of standard cost centers, most complex in the case of investment centers.

How should management measure the financial results achieved? It is not enough simply to say that a particular product division is a profit center; decisions are also required that specify how the profit is to be calculated, focusing in particular on how transfer prices shall be set and how the costs of services received from other organization units shall be charged against the division. Similarly, while the basic concept of an investment center is simple, it is difficult to decide which assets to include in the investment base and how they shall be valued. Therefore, although there may be only five types of financial responsibility centers, there are *many* methods of financial measurement that can be used for specific organizations.

Criteria for selection

Figuring out the best way to define and measure the financial performance for each manager is the corporate controller's most challenging—and analytically demanding—task. Two types of considerations affect each choice. The first is the strategy of the company: its broad objectives, the nature of the industries in which it operates, and the niche it seeks to carve for itself in each industry on the basis of its distinctive competence. The second is the organization structure of the company—the way the total task is divided among the managers to permit delegation of authority and specialization of effort.

Types of financial responsibility

The principal types of financial responsibility can be classified as follows:

Standard cost centers are exemplified by a production department in a factory. The standard quantities of direct labor and materials required for each unit of output are specified. The foreman's objective is to minimize the variance between actual costs and standard costs. He also is usually responsible for a flexible overhead expense budget, and his objective, again, is to minimize the variance between budgeted and actual costs.

Revenue centers are best illustrated by a sales department where the manager does not have authority to lower prices in order to increase volume. The resources at his disposal are reflected in his expense budget. The sales manager's objective is to spend no more than the budgeted amounts and to produce the maximum amount of sales revenue.

Discretionary expense centers include most administrative departments. There is no practical way to establish the relationship between inputs and outputs. Management can only use its best judgment to set the budget, and the department manager's objective is to spend the budgeted amount to produce the best (though still unmeasurable) quality of service that he possibly can.

Profit centers, the focus of this article, are units, such·as a product division, where the manager is responsible for the best combination of costs and revenues. His objective is to maximize the bottom line, the profit that results from his decisions. A great many variations on this theme can be achieved by defining "profit" as including only those elements of cost and revenue for which the manager is responsible. Thus a sales manager who is allowed to set prices may be responsible for gross profit (actual revenue less standard direct manufacturing costs). Profit for a product-line marketing manager, on the other hand, might reflect deductions for budgeted factory overhead and actual sales promotion expenses.

Investment centers are units where the manager is responsible also for the magnitude of assets employed. He makes trade-offs between current profits and investments to increase future profits. Stating the manager's objective as maximizing his return on investment or his residual income (profit after a charge for the use of capital) helps him to appraise the desirability of new investments.

The controller must have a thorough knowledge of his company's strategy and organization structure. He draws on his knowledge to apply two criteria for deciding which measure of financial responsibility to use for each organization unit and how it should be calculated:

1. *Fairness*—Each manager must believe that the summary financial measurement used to report on his performance is appropriate. This means he must see all of the signals he receives about his job as consistent with each other. Moreover, he must believe that the measurement encompasses all the factors he can control and excludes those over which he has no control. And he must be convinced the measurement is calculated in such a way that a "good" decision on his part will be reflected as such by the financial measurement. The "fairness" of a financial measurement is not a fact; it is a perception through the eyes of the manager to whom it applies.

2. *Goal congruence*—The most difficult compromises that must be made in designing a management control system have to do with varying goals.[2] When a manager is assigned a financial objective for his activities and a fair measurement of performance is determined, ideally he should be able to pursue his objective without concern for whether or not his actions are in the best interests of the corporation. But in reality, as we know, that ideal is not easy to attain. The controller, designing a management control system with a corporate-wide perspective, must ensure that managers are not working at cross-purposes. He must select objectives and measurements in such a way that a good decision by any manager is also a good decision for the corporation as a whole.

For the controller, applying these two criteria simultaneously means that he must combine the points of view of both the individual manager and the corporation. That becomes progressively more difficult as the complexity of the organization structure and the business increases. In the balance of this article I shall discuss the use of the two criteria, dealing first with relatively simple organization structures and then with more complex ones.

USE IN SIMPLE STRUCTURES

Discussing the design of a management control system for "simple" organizations is not a theoretical or academic exercise. Some small businesses have simple organization structures, and even the largest corporations progressively subdivide the management tasks to the point where

---

[2] For the original statement of this problem, see Robert N. Anthony, *Planning and Control Systems: A Framework for Analysis* (Boston: Division of Research, Harvard Business School, 1965).

an individual manager is responsible for a single functional activity. Functional units are the organizational building blocks in the most complex corporations.

What varieties of control systems are possible and feasible in simple organizations? When are the criteria of fairness and goal congruence satisfied? How does a company's strategy affect the choice of a system?

Practical alternatives

The simplified organization chart shown in Exhibit 1 is typical of a great many companies or parts of companies. The structure of the organization is simple in two respects:

1. There are only two levels of line managers in the hierarchy (the "general manager" might be thought of as the president of a small company).
2. The subordinate managers each have responsibility for a functional activity, which implies a rather natural distribution of tasks and authority between them.

Exhibit 1
Functionally organized business

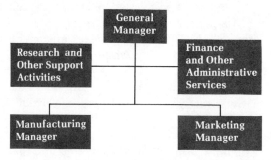

The business also requires some administrative and support activities, but the choice of financial measurements for these orgazational units is less complex and will not be discussed here.

Selecting an appropriate financial measurement for this president's performance is not really a problem. He is responsible for the entire business, its profits, and the investment required. The financial responsibility of his two principal subordinates, however, is not so easily determined. The manufacturing manager, responsible for all production operations in the plant, could be charged with the responsibility of running either a standard cost center or a profit center. And the marketing manager, responsible for all sales and promotion activities, could be treated as the head either of a revenue center or of a profit center. With just two functional units, and two alternatives available for each, there are still four alternatives for the design of a management control system for this business:

Alternative	Manufacturing	Marketing
1.	Standard cost center	Revenue center
2.	Standard cost center	Profit center
3.	Profit center	Revenue center
4.	Profit center	Profit center

These four alternatives are not simply theoretical possibilities; each may be appropriate under different circumstances. The critical circumstances concern the nature of the key decisions to be made and the way decision-making authority is delegated in the organization.

As for the decisions, most of them involve choices in allocating resources. There are questions of *purpose* (e.g., whether incremental marketing expenditures should be used for advertising or for hiring more salesmen) and of *timing* (e.g., when a piece of production equipment should be replaced). In an ideal world, an all-wise and all-knowing president could make every decision, and his decision would always be "right"in the sense that it is the best course of action for the company at the time even though it may turn out to be wrong as future events unfold. The problem is that no president can make all the decisions and that, as he delegates power to subordinates, he runs the risk they will make decisions that are different from those he would make.

Effective decision making in a functionally organized business is hampered by the fact that no subordinate has the same broad perspective of the business that the president or general manager has. Many decisions, and almost all the important ones, affect more than one function in the business. They are seen differently by managers according to the functions they manage. One possible response to this problem is not to delegate authority for important decisions below the level of general manager. Another approach is to broaden the perspective of the functional manager by delegating such authority to him and then holding him responsible for the profitability of his decisions.

The implications of the second approach can best be seen by examining a series of examples. I shall describe a company situation for each of the four design alternatives mentioned.

1. No profit centers. Company A manufactures and distributes fertilizer. It buys chemicals, minerals, and other components from large suppliers and mixes them in various combinations to produce a limited variety of standard fertilizers with specified chemical properties. These are sold to farmers in bulk. Because the quality is specified and subject to verification by chemical analysis, all producers sell at the same price and offer identical volume discounts. Transportation costs are a major factor, and Company A thus enjoys a relative advantage in its local market. Its salesmen call on purchasing agents for large corporate farms and on distributors that sell to smaller farmers. Most orders are placed well in advance of the growing season, so the mixing plant is busy several months of the year, but there is still a large seasonal peak in both marketing and manufacturing.

Prices tend to fluctuate with the cost of the primary chemical components. The result is that an efficient fertilizer producer tends to earn about the same profit, as a percentage of the sales dollar, on each of the products in his line.

In this company the mission of the marketing manager is to sell as much fertilizer as he can. He has no control over product design or pricing, and promotional activities other than direct selling efforts are ineffective. His primary concern is with the effective use of his salesmen's time and with the development and maintenance of good customer relations. His stated objective is to produce as much revenue as he can with the number of salesmen currently authorized. In technical terms he is a "revenue center." He is also responsible for the expense budget for his activities.

The mission of the manufacturing manager, on the other hand, is to produce fertilizer in the required quantities as efficiently as possible. The work force is only semiskilled, and his primary concern is to ensure that they are properly trained and well supervised and that material wastage is held to a minimum. He is a "standard cost center," financially responsible for meeting the standard direct cost of each unit produced and for controlling overhead expenses against a variable budget reflecting the volume of throughput.

The president of Company A is the only man financially responsible for the profit of the company. There are a limited number of key, cross-functional decisions to be made, and he makes them. One concerns the size of the sales force; another concerns the acquistion of equipment to increase the capacity or reduce the labor costs in the mixing plant. Both of these are what are called "capacity decisions." While the evaluation of alternatives for either decision is not easy, it can be handled as well or better by the president than by either of his two subordinates.

2. Marketing profit centers. Company B produces a line of branded consumer toiletries. The products are heavily advertised and made available to consumers in drugstores, supermarkets, and other retail outlets throughout the country. The marketplace is in continual turmoil as competitors jockey for consumer attention through price promotions, premium offers, and "new" formulas and "secret" ingredients announced through both media advertising and point-of-purchase promotion. The company's field sales force is small; salesmen call on distributors and purchasing agents for large retail chains. The producer itself is simple to manufacture, but consistently reliable quality is considered important to maintain customer good will.

Marketing is where the action is in Company B. The marketing manager is responsible for profitability, which is defined as sales revenue less standard direct manufacturing costs and all marketing costs. The president of the company is very interested in the marketing function and devotes much of his time to it. At the same time, he realizes that there are a myriad of marketing decisions to be made, many of them requiring specialized knowledge of local markets and detailed current information on competitors' actions. Therefore, he needs to delegate considerable authority to the marketing manager.

The manufacturing manager, like his counterpart in Company A, is a standard cost center, responsible for standard direct costs and a variable overhead budget.

3. Production profit centers.   Company C produces a line of specialty metal products sold as semifinished components, primarily to manufacturers of high-style lighting fixtures. The company has only a few dozen customers, four of which account for over 50 percent of the sales volume. The business is price-competitive; Company C's equipment is not unique, and other manufacturers are frequently asked to bid against Company C on prospective contracts. Company C is renowned, however, for its technical skills in solving difficult manufacturing problems. Even on relatively routine contracts, the company is sometimes able to charge a slightly higher price because of its consistently high quality and its responsiveness in meeting its customers' "emergency" delivery requirements.

Price quotations on each contract are prepared by an estimator in the plant. The field sales force calls on old customers and prospective new ones, maintaining and developing relationships and soliciting opportunities to bid for their business.

Manufacturing is the name of the game at Company C. The manufacturing manager is responsible for profit, defined as the contribution to overhead after subtracting all direct manufacturing costs. He keeps himself informed of the backlog of orders against each type of equipment in his shop and personally reviews all bids over a nominal amount, estimating the price to quote in view of his desire for the business and his assessment of the customer's loyalty. He is also responsible for meeting his variable overhead budget.

As for the marketing manager, he is a revenue center, like his counterpart in Company A. He endeavors to use his sales force as effectively as possible to turn up attractive bidding opportunities on which the company can compete successfully.

4. Multiple profit centers. Company D is a partly integrated oil refining and marketing organization. The company's refinery purchases crude oil and refines it into gasoline, kerosene, and other products. The company also operates a regional chain of service stations, advertising its brand of gasoline to consumers. The company's strategy is to be less than self-sufficient in producing enough gasoline to meet its retail requirements. Thus the refinery is usually able to operate at capacity, and gasoline is purchased from other refiners as required.

Both the manufacturing (refinery) manager and the marketing manager are responsible for *part* of the profits earned by Company D. The refinery manager sells his gasoline to the marketing department at the same price charged by other refiners; the profit on the refinery is an important measure of the efficiency of his operations. The marketing manager, much like his counterpart in Company B, is also a profit center; he attempts to find the optimum balance and mix of marketing expenditures that will be most profitable for the company.

In this kind of situation, therefore, the president needs to delegate considerable decision-making power to not one, but two subordinates. With respect to each he acts in the way described for Companies B and C.

The foregoing examples, simple as they are, show how difficult it is to generalize on the question of whether or not a functional manager should be held responsible for profit. The first, most obvious, statement is that the decision turns on the nature of the business. The tangible differences between businesses and the unique tasks they imply for management must be reflected in the management control system. The challenge for the controller is to synthesize the characteristics of the business and select a financial objective for each manager that (1) motivates him to achieve the company's objectives, and (2) minimizes unnecessary conflict between managers.

However, the characteristics of a business are not the sole determinants of financial responsibility. In fact, they are not the most important ones. This brings us to the next point: the implications of corporate strategy.

Crucial role of strategy

As an illustration, let us consider the situation of a franchised automobile dealership called Connelly Autos, Inc. The company sells new and used cars and auto repair services. Connelly's organization structure is simple; under the president there are two marketing managers, one for new cars and one for used cars, and a service department manager.

In this case, and in retail distribution businesses generally, it is easy to see the advantages of holding a sales manager responsible for the profits of his department. Moreover, suppose a customer with a certain amount of money to spend is undecided about buying a stripped-down new car or a more expensive model that is a year or two old. If Connelly's two sales managers compete for this customer's business, the result is probably that the customer is better served, in the sense that he has more information about the relative advantages of his two major alternatives and can ultimately make a choice that satisfies him better.

Also, the dealership is probably better off as a result of the competition. There are many other new car and used car dealers, so if the company itself offers both choices in a manner that is as competitive as the two departments would be if they were in separate dealerships, it stands a better chance of getting a customer's business no matter which car he chooses to drive.

The difficult problem is designing a management control system for Connelly's service department manager. What is his financial responsibility? How should Connelly measure his performance in financial terms? The service department is not simply another sales department, delivering retail repair services to customers. It is also a "manufacturing" department producing services for the two automobile sales departments; it prepares new cars for delivery and services them during the warranty period, and it repairs and reconditions used cars to be sold at retail.

The real question becomes: What does Connelly want his service department manager to do? Here are several possible answers:

1. Run the service department as though it were an independent auto repair shop. With this mission, the service department manager would be responsible for profits and should probably sell his services to the new and used car departments at the regular retail price, or perhaps with a slight "dealer" discount.

2. Employ the capacity of the shop to the fullest, using renovation work on used cars as a way of absorbing slack capacity. With this mission, repair services should probably be sold to the used car department at standard direct costs. The used car manager would buy cars needing repair work, at wholesale auctions if necessary, thus providing all the volume the service department could handle. The service department would be essentially a standard cost center, and the profit on retail repairs would be de-emphasized.

3. Run the shop in such a way as to maximize customer goodwill, attempting to build a reputation that will yield regular, repeat customers

for new cars. Under these circumstances, it would be very difficult to calculate a financial measurement that would appropriately reflect the performance of the service department manager. He should not be held responsible for profits, nor should he be expected to run close to capacity if he is to be responsive to customer emergencies. The shop should probably be treated as a standard cost center, but without emphasis being placed on financial performance.

Finding an answer

Thus the answer to the question of what the service department manager should do turns on Connelly's strategy for his dealership. The three alternatives outlined really characterize three different strategies. The first envisions a "balanced" dealership, the second had a strong used-car focus, and the third emphasizes new car sales.

Not all automobile dealers pursue the same strategy, nor should they. Local competitive conditions are a major factor in selecting a strategy, and the quality and type of resources available to Connelly are also critical factors in his choice. (Resources include the location of the dealership, the capital available for investment in new and used car inventories, and the competence and aggressiveness of Connelly's three subordinates.) Finally, the strategy Connelly selects will affect his image in the community as a businessman and a citizen, and his personal aspirations concerning the size and reputation of the business also have a bearing on the problem.[3]

There are thousands of automobile dealers in the United States, and they appear to be identical in terms of the characteristics of their business. Managers adopt different strategies, however, in order to differentiate their business from that of their competitors. The controller, designing a management control system, must understand both the nature of the business and the strategy being pursued if he is to create a set of financial measurements that will motivate functional managers to contribute to the achievement of company objectives. This task is not easy even in simple, functional organizations; it is more difficult still in complex organizations.

USE IN COMPLEX STRUCTURES

As a business grows and the magnitude of the management task increases, its organization structure tends to become more complex. Prod-

---

[3] For a more complete discussion of all the factors influencing the formulation of strategy, see Kenneth R. Andrews, *The Concept of Corporate Strategy* (Homewood, Ill.: Dow Jones-Irwin, Inc., 1971).

ucts come to be manufactured in more than one location and sold in more than one market; new models and lines may be added. Such multiplant, multimarket, multiproduct corporations typically have a multitier organization structure consisting of three or more layers of managers. Naturally, the management control system becomes more complex, too.

Part A of Exhibit 2 is an organization chart for a complex, functionally organized business (it may have started as the company shown in Exhibit 1). As long as the business continues to be functionally organized, much of the discussion in the preceding section about the design of a management control system is applicable.

Exhibit 2
Complex organizations

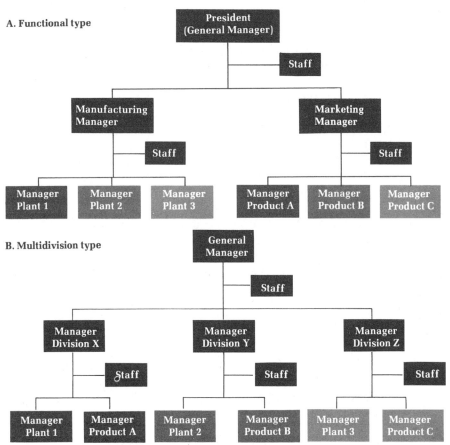

But an important difference should be noted. In the simple organization shown in Exhibit 1, top management has very little choice about how to divide the functional tasks among subordinates. In many situations of the type shown in Part A of Exhibit 2, however, reorganization along the lines shown in Part B of the same exhibit may be feasible and appropriate. In such cases, what pros and cons should be considered in deciding whether to adopt the product division approach? Except in cases where that approach seems a "natural" (for example, a conglomerate that has grown through the acquisition of independent businesses), the answer depends largely on how much management wants to maximize efficiency and on how much it wants to maximize responsiveness to markets. Let us consider this trade-off in some detail.

Turn to product divisions?

Product divisions are almost always treated as profit or investment centers. The responsibility of the division manager is usually broad enough so that he can conceive of his division as though it were an independent company. In addition, the scope and substance of his task and the objective he is to strive for may be delineated clearly. In such circumstances, the task of designing a management control system for the functional subordinates of the division manager is precisely the same as that discussed earlier; the division manager is really the general manager shown in Exhibit 1.

Now, what can functional organizations do that product divisions cannot? Functional organizations have the potential of great efficiency. The efficiency of an activity can frequently be measured in terms of the quantity of inputs required to yield one unit of output. For a great many activities, efficiency increases as the size of the activity grows—at least, up to some point where there are no further "economies of scale" to be realized. The reason that efficiency increases is that large-scale operations permit the utilization of increasingly specialized inputs. For instance, a general-purpose machine tool and a skilled operator may be able to produce 100 parts per hour; but a specially designed piece of equipment might produce 1,000 parts per hour and require no operator at all. Also, specialization of workers can yield economies of scale, as the learning curve of production workers demonstrates.

The arguments, then, in favor of retaining the organization structure shown in Part A of Exhibit 2 might run as follows. While it is technically feasible to equip each plant so that it turns out one of the three products of the company, it would be a great waste to do so. Manufacturing costs would be much lower if each plant specialized in certain aspects of the manufacturing process, doing only a limited number of functions on all three products. Further, the quality of manufacturing supervision and technical services, such as engineering and quality control, is better when those activities are centralized under one manufacturing manager. Scattering such activities across three product divisions would both lower the quality of the personnel that could be afforded and reduce the efficiency of their services. Similar arguments might be made about the efficiency of the marketing organization.

What advantages are unique to product divisions? They hold out the promise of more *effective* management than is the case with functional organizations. (One way of contrasting effectiveness with efficiency is to say that efficiency means doing something right and effectiveness means doing the right something.) The benefits are harder to document or quantify, but the potential for improvement exists both in strategy formulation and in tactical decision making.

In a strategic sense, it is easier for a product division than a functional organization to focus on the needs of its customers, rather than on simply manufacturing or selling the current line of products. The division manager can develop a strategy for his particular business, finding a competitive niche for it that may be different from the strategy being pursued by other division managers with different product lines. Tactically, a product division can also be more responsive to current customer needs. The division manager has the authority to change the production schedule in response to the request of an important customer; in a functional organization, by contrast, such a request must "go through channels," which may be ponderous and time-consuming.

Finally, it can be argued that product divisions are an excellent training ground for young managers, fostering entrepreneurship and increasing the number of centers of initiative in a corporation.

A business organization must be both efficient and effective if it is to survive, be profitable, and grow. The fundamental choice in organizational design is not an either-or question, but one of achieving the best possible balance between the benefits from economies of scale and those from strategic and tactical responsiveness.[4] One approach that is being used increasingly in a variety of settings is the matrix form of organization.

Adopt the matrix form?

This relatively new form of organization apparently was developed first in the aerospace industry nearly three decades ago. Companies in

---

[4] For an excellent treatise on the complex factors that must be considered in making a basic change in organization structure, see Alfred D. Chandler, Jr., *Strategy and Structure: Chapters in the History of the American Industrial Enterprise* (Cambridge, Mass.: The M.I.T. Press, 1962).

that industry had massive capacity, both human and physical, for the design and manufacture of weapons systems, and they were organized according to functional specialties. At any one moment, such a company might have had several large contracts in its shop, each at various stages of completion and each drawing on the various functional departments to a greater or lesser extent.

In these cases, management's focus was on the efficient use of each department's capacity; this meant that inadequate attention was devoted to cost and schedule performance on each contract. The solution was to establish a new set of project managers, one for each contract, and to superimpose them across the existing functional hierarchy. A project manager's responsibility was to coordinate the inputs from each department in such a way that contractual performance requirements would be fulfilled.

Although matrix organizations, in a formal sense, are not widely used in industry, the concept has several attractive features. It holds the promise of both efficiency *and* effectiveness. Functional specialization is retained, thus permitting the efficiencies of economies of scale. But at the same time that program or product managers are viewed as the users of functional skills, they are also charged with producing a result that is competitively attractive to the customer and profitable for the company.

A matrix organization is essentially a functional organization. The six third-level managers in Part A of Exhibit 2 appear in Exhibit 3 and could still report to their respective functional superiors. However, there is an important difference: the relationships between the six managers are much more explicit in Exhibit 3.

The matrix form of organization may be appropriate when much interaction between the functions is necessary or desirable. It can be particularly useful when one function (such as marketing) is concerned with planning for the effective combination of resources, while another function

Exhibit 3
Concept of a matrix organization

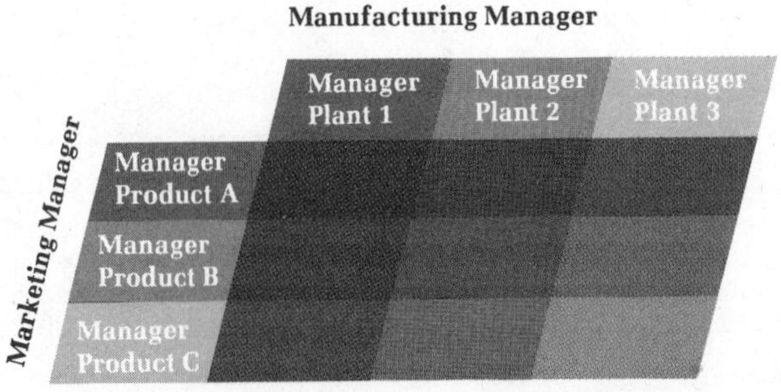

(such as manufacturing) is concerned with acquiring resources and using them efficiently. These two tasks obviously must be integrated and coordinated continuously. The matrix organization is intended to describe the interrelationships between the manufacturing and marketing functions and, without dismantling the old hierarchy, to legitimatize and encourage direct contact between the two parties concerned with any interlocking tasks or "cell" in the matrix. The matrix design does not really represent a structural change; it is simply a more realistic, comprehensive description of organizational relationships.

From the point of view of the designer of a management control system, a matrix organization poses no special problems and may offer an opportunity for a unique type of control system. Selecting the appropriate financial measurement for each functional manager may require nothing more, in some circumstances, than an application of the type of analysis described earlier. But management may need to go a step further if the nature of the business and its strategy are more complex than in those examples previously cited.

Problems in responsibility. In some businesses, both the marketing and the manufacturing functions may be highly interdependent and responsible for activities which have major effects on profits. How can the managers of the two functions be held jointly responsible?

One way is to hold each man responsible for a portion of the profits of the company, using a transfer price to permit a calculation of that profit. The determination of transfer prices in highly interdependent situations may be difficult, but it may be worth the trouble in order to motivate each manager properly.

Another approach is to use the matrix form of organization as an acknowledgment of the interdependence, and to hold each functional manager responsible for the entire profit of the business. This approach requires "double counting" of each profit dollar. In terms of Exhibit 3, the manufacturing manager would be responsible for profit, defined as sales revenues less all manufacturing costs and all direct marketing expenses, for all products manufactured in the three plants. Each plant manager might have a similar responsibility for his plant. The sum of the defined profits for the three plants would be the total contribution to corporate overhead and net profit. Each product manager would also be responsible for profits, defined in the same way, for the products in his line. The sum of the profits for the three product managers would be the same as the total profit of the three plants.

Such a management control system may seem confusing at first, but it can be effective. The intent of double counting the profit is to make clear to all managers involved that they must work together in order to achieve their own individual objective. A profitable action which requires cooperation does not reflect to the credit of only one party, nor does it require a fictitious division of the profit between them. Both men benefit. Thus Plant Manager 1 would work with all three product managers, trying to find ways to use the facilities at his disposal in order to yield the highest profit for his plant. And Product Manager A would work with all three plant managers, attempting to utilize their resources in such a way as to maximize the profitability of his product line.

An intended effect of such a system is a certain amount of tension in the organization—an atmosphere of constructive conflict in which the managers in one function know they are working toward the same goal and must compete among themselves to cooperate with managers from the other functional area. Such conflict, if handled sensitively by a sophisticated top manager, can break down some of the parochialism of a purely functional organization without splintering it into less efficient product divisions.

Because of these potential advantages, we may see increasing use of the matrix concept in companies where functional interdependence is high and the rewards from functional specialization are too great to ignore.

CONCLUSION

Responsibility for the design of a management control system rests inescapably on top management. For one thing, it is top management that decides on the strategy and organization structure of a business. For another, the control system is a major tool for implementing those decisions effectively. The controller, as a member of the top management team, has an important role to play because the design of a control system is too complex a task for the chief executive to undertake without the benefit of staff support.

The president and his controller, joint designers of the management control system, face a great many choices as they try to decide (a) the type of financial objective to be specified for each organizational unit, and (b) how to calculate that measurement. There is a natural bias among corporate executives in favor of responsibility for profit. Profit is a powerful measurement; it provides a clear objective, is easily understood, and is a good motivator of such men. But not all managers are responsible for profits in any meaningful sense of that term. Creating a set of profit centers may cause more problems than it is worth.

Profit should be used as a measure of financial responsibility only when it is possible to calculate it in such a way that a manager's "profit" increases as the result of actions for which he is responsible and which he has taken in the best interests of the company.

Reading 4–3
The human side of the matrix *
Paul R. Lawrence, Harvey F. Kolodny,
Stanley M. Davis

Matrix management and organization have become increasingly common in recent years. If we were pressed to pick one word that characterizes the potential of the matrix organization, it would have to be *flexibility*. The matrix structure offers the potential of achieving the flexibility that is so often missing in conventional, single-line-of-command organizations and of reconciling this flexibility with the coordination and economies of scale that are the historic strengths of large organizations. (See the box on page 238 for the basic elements of matrix design.)

Now that the use of the matrix structure is so widespread, it has become apparent that it calls for different kinds of managerial behavior than are typical in conventional line organizations. This article will identify the key management roles in a matrix organization and describe the essential aspects called for in each of them.

Envision the matrix structure as a diamond [Figure 1]. The general executive, who heads up the matrix, is at the top of the diamond. The matrix bosses, or matrix managers, who share common subordinate(s), are on the sides of the diamond. The person at the bottom is the 2-boss manager.

TOP LEADERSHIP

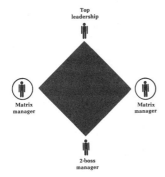

Top
leadership

Matrix
manager

Matrix
manager

2-boss
manager

Figure 1

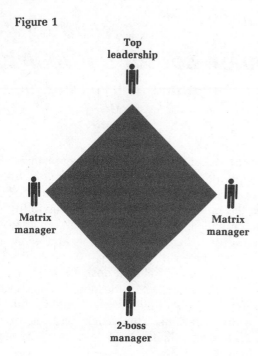

The top leadership is literally atop, or outside of, the matrix organization. This is not generally appreciated. Even in totally matrix organizations, the top executives are not *in* the matrix. Despite this, however, they are *of* it: It is the top leaders who oversee and sustain the balance of power.

In a corporation-wide matrix, the top leaders are the chief executive and a few other key individuals; in a product group or a division matrix, the top leader is the senior manager. This individual does not share power with others and there is no unequal separation of authority and responsibility. Formally, the role itself is the same as in any traditional organization. What distinguishes it from the traditional top slot is the leadership process as it is applied to the people in the next levels down.

The top leader is the one who must "buy" the matrix approach. He must be convinced of its merits to the point that he believes it is the best (although not necessarily the ideal) of all alternative designs. He must also "sell" it; he must be very vocal and articulate in developing the concept and arousing enthusiasm for it among the ranks.

One of the several paradoxes of the matrix approach, then, is that it requires a strong, unified command at the top, to ensure a balance of power at the next level down. In some senses this is the benevolent dictator: "You will enjoy democracy (shared power), and I will enjoy autocracy (ultimate power)"; or "I'm OK, you're OK; but I'm still the boss."

Balancing power as a top leader therefore calls for a blend of autocratic and participative leadership styles. A clear example of this comes from Bastien Hello, head of the B-1 bomber division at Rockwell International. *The New York Times* called his project the most costly and complex plane project in history. In an interview he said:

> *Today I have some formidable people working for me. When you have a group like that, you have two choices, running a Captain Bligh operation, or a Mr. Roberts operation. I would call one autocratic, the other group therapy.*
>
> *If I have to lean in one direction, I would shave a little closer to group therapy. It's not because I, and the fellows who work for me, don't have autocratic tendencies: We do. But if you're going to keep everybody working in the same direction, you've got to have group participation in the decisions.*
>
> *So I like to get my team of managers together and thrash out problems with them, and I like to hear all sides. It's not that I'm a goodie goodie about it; there is malice aforethought to it.*
>
> *Once they have participated in and agreed to the decision, you can hold their noses right to it. It's not that I like group sessions—I don't, they're painful—but they do bring the team along. And once you get them signed up, then you become autocratic about it.*

The general executive of a matrix organization has the unique role of heading up both of its dual command structures, administrative and technical. As we understand this role, it involves three unique aspects: *power balancing, managing the decision context,* and *standard setting.* These three processes, while of concern to any top executive, take on a very special importance in a mature matrix organization. The reason for this importance is not hard to find. It stems directly from three basic reasons as to why a matrix can be a desirable organizational form.

1. The existence of dual pressures calls for balanced decision making that considers both aspects simultaneously. The general executive's critical role in achieving such decision making is to establish and sustain a reasonable balance of power between the two arms of the matrix.

2. The second necessary condition for a matrix organization to be effective is that a very high volume of information be processed and focused for use in making key decisions. If the organization is to cope with such an information processing load, the top leader must be only one among several key decision makers—he must delegate. However, he cannot delegate to other decision makers the job of setting the stage; he must himself manage the decision context.

3. Last, the top executive must set the standards of expected performance. Others contribute to this process, but unless the top individual

has high expectations for the organization, it is unlikely that the matrix organization will respond adequately to the environmental pressure for resource redeployment, which we have identified as a third necessary condition for a matrix organization. Let us look at each of these three special aspects of the top leader's role in the matrix organization in more detail.

Power balancing

The power balancing element of the general executive's role is, in our experience, vital to mature matrix organization performance. Any general manager must of course pay attention to this process, but it is uniquely critical in matrix organizations. If we contrast the pyramid diagram of a conventional hierarchy and the matrix diamond diagram, we have a clue as to why this is true. The diamond diagram, unlike the pyramid, is inherently unstable. For the structure to remain in place despite environmental pushing and pulling that lead to changed administrative and technical requirements, its emphasis and activities must be constantly rebalanced by hands-on top leadership. The analogy is crude by relevant. Managers in a leadership role are usually quite explicit about this requirement of their job. The "tuning" of a matrix organization needs continuing attention.

The basic methods that general executives use to establish a power balance are both obvious and important. The two arms of a matrix organization are, first of all, usually described in the formal documents that establish the structure as being of equal power and importance. The top executive uses every possible occasion to reinforce this message, and one way that is often used is by establishing dual budgeting systems and dual evaluation systems.

Most mature matrix organizations adopt dual budgeting systems, in which a complete budget is generated within each arm of the matrix. As with a double-entry accounting system, the dual budgets count everything twice—each time in a different way and for a different purpose. Functional budgets are primarily cost budgets—unless the functions sell their services outside. The budgets begin with product- and business-area estimates of work required from each functional area, usually expressed in man-hours and materials requirements. Functional groups then add indirect and overhead costs to these direct hours and come up with an hourly rate for services to the product or business managers.

Product or business units accept these rates or challenge them, sometimes by threatening to buy from the outside. This is the time when the difference in outlook is most striking. Business units, for example, have little sympathy for functional desires to hold people in an overhead category for contingencies or for the development of long-term competence. A business unit is hard pressed to see the need to develop competence that may be required three years hence, or for another business when its own central concern is with short-term profit and loss. When the rates are approved for all the different functions, the product or business units develop their own profit and loss budgets for each of their product lines.

The parallel accounting systems provide independent controls that are consistent with the characteristic of the work in each type of unit and that recognize the partial autonomy of each organizational subunit. Each unit has the means to evaluate its own performance and to be evaluated independent of others. The CEO of one organization described the dual control systems in his organization as follows:

The accounting system matches the organization precisely; so that's an aspect the product manager and I don't have to talk about. He can see how he's doing himself. When resources seem to be a problem, then I must get involved.

Both product managers and functional managers get accounting evaluations. The functional shops have budgets but little spending money. They have a cost budget, but in theory it's all released into the projects. From the functional side, the accounting system locates and isolates unused capacity. As soon as the task requirement disappears the excess capacity turns up. The functional shop then has a "social" problem. The key thing is that the excess turns up immediately. There is no place to hide. Matrix is a free organization, but it's a tough organization.

With dual budgets, some interesting possibilities arise in achieving flexibility of organizational response. In the aforementioned organization, the CEO resolved an internal dispute: A product group was lobbying for control of repair and overhaul contracts on products in the field that it had developed and sold over the protests of a functional group that had always managed the organization's field repair and overhaul activity. In the resolution of the dispute, the function remained in charge of the activity, but the product group was credited with the profits from all repair and overhaul contracts on its products. Both sides were satisfied.

Dual personnel evaluation systems go hand in hand with dual budgeting to help sustain a power balance. If a person's work is to be directed by two superiors, in all logic both should take part in that person's evaluation. Occasionally, the duality is nothing more than a product or business group sign-off of an evaluation form prepared by the functional boss. At other times, the initiative comes from the other side, primarily because the individual involved may have been physically situated within the product or business unit and had limited contact with the functional unit during the period covered by the evaluation.

Essential characteristics of matrix organization

The identifying feature of a matrix organization is that some managers report to two bosses rather than to the traditional single boss—there is a dual rather than a single chain of command.

Firms tend to adopt matrix forms when it is absolutely essential that they be highly responsive to two sectors, such as markets and technology; when they face uncertainties that generate very high information processing requirements; and when they must deal with strong constrains on financial and/or human resources. The matrix form can help provide flexibility and balanced decision making but at the price of complexity.

Matrix organization is more than matrix structure. It must also be reinforced by matrix systems such as dual control and evaluation systems, by matrix leadership behavior that operates comfortably with lateral decision making, and by a matrix culture that fosters open conflict management and a balance of power.

Most matrix organizations assign dual command responsibilities to functional departments (marketing, production, engineering, and so on) and to product/market departments. The former are oriented to specialized resources while the latter focus on outputs. Other matrix organizations are area-based departments for either products or functions.

Every matrix organization contains three unique and critical roles: the top manager who heads up and balances the dual chains of command; the matrix bosses (functional, product, or area) who share subordinates; and the 2-boss managers who report to two different matrix bosses. Each of these roles has its own unique requirements.

The matrix organization started in aerospace companies, but now firms in many industries (chemical, banking, insurance, package goods, electronics, computer, and so on) and in different fields (hospitals, government agencies, professional organizations) are turning to different forms of the matrix structure.

Regardless of the particular system design, the person with 2-bosses must know that both have been a part of the evaluation if that person is to feel committed to consider both orientations in his activities. For this reason many matrix organizations insist that both superiors sit in on the evaluation feedback with the employee and that both advise the employee of salary changes so that rewards will not be construed as having been secured from only one side of the matrix.

These basic formal arrangements for setting up a reasonable balance of power are essential in a mature matrix, but they are seldom sufficient. Too many events can upset the balance, and a loss of balance needs to be caught by the general manager or it can degenerate into a major power struggle and even an ill-advised move away from the matrix organization. The matrix can be thrown off balance in many ways, but a common cause of a loss of balance is a temporary crisis on one side of the matrix structure that is used as an excuse for mobilizing resources in that direction. Up to a point such a reaction to a true crisis is certainly appropriate, but it can be the start of a lasting imbalance unless it is corrected by the general manager.

A more lasting source of instability arises from the fact that product- and business-area managers manage a whole business and thereby have that special mystique associated with bottom-line responsibility. This is a source of power. They are seen as the sources of revenue—the people who make the cash register ring. The general manager needs to be alert to this one-sided source of power to avoid its unbalancing potential. The profit center manager is often tempted to argue that he must have complete control over all needed resources, but this argument has no place in a matrix organization.

Given the inherent power instability of the matrix, the general managers of mature matrix organizations use a wide variety of supplemental ways to maintain the balance of the matrix. These methods are not new, but they are worth remembering as especially relevant for use in a matrix. Here are five such means:

1. Pay levels, as an important symbol of power, can be marginally higher on one side of the matrix, thus acting as a countervailing force.

2. Job titles can be adjusted between the two sides as a balancing item.

3. Access to the general manager at meetings and informal occasions is a source of power that can be controlled as a balancing factor.

4. Situation of offices is a related factor that carries a status or power message.

5. Reporting level is a frequently used power-balancing method. For instance, product managers can report up through a second-in-command while functional managers report directly to the general manager.

We have talked about the unbalancing potential possessed by profit center managers. But this imbalance of potential fluctuates from situation to situation. In many cases, the organization traditionally gave top priority to the functional side. Here the general manager employs his stratagems to shore up the prestige and position of the business-area or product managers and to make them in fact as well as in name the equals of the functional managers.

Managing the decision context

There is no substitute in a matrix organization for the sensitive management of the decision context by the top leadership. The existence of a matrix structure is an acknowledgment that the executive leaders cannot make all the key decisions in a timely way. There is too much relevant information to be digested, and too many points of view must be taken into account. But the general manager must set the stage for this decision making by others. He must see that it happens.

We have already seen that dual environmental pressures and complexity make conflict inevitable. To cope with this situation, the top manager must sponsor and act as a model of a three-stage decision process:

1. The conflicts must be brought into the open. This is fostered in the matrix structure, with its dual arms; but beyond this, the given manager must reward those who bring the tough topics to the surface for open discussion.

2. The conflicting positions must be debated in a spirited and reasoned manner. Relevant lines of argument and appropriate evidence must be presented. The executive manager's personal behavior has to encourage this in others.

3. The issue must be resolved and a commitment made in a timely fashion. The leader cannot tolerate stalling by others or passing the buck up the line.

All these decision processes call for a high order of interpersonal skills and a willingness to take risks. They also call for a minimum of status differentials from the top of the bottom ranks. Top leaders can favorably influence these factors by their own openness to dissent and willingness to listen and debate. One of the noticeable features of most leaders of matrix organizations is the simplicity of their offices and the relative informality of their manner and dress. The key point here is that this behavior must start at the top as part of setting the decision context.

Standard setting

The leadership of matrix organizations is where high performance standards start. We earlier identified environmental pressures for high performance as a necessary condition for matrix organizations. But it is all too easy for organizational members to insulate themselves from these outside pressures. The general executive in a mature matrix organization internalizes the outside pressures and articulates them in the form of performance standards. Each subsystem on both sides of the matrix structure will of course be making its own projections and setting specific targets for higher review. But the overall level of aspiration in the organization begins with the general executive. This is a duty, as we said before, that he cannot afford to delegate.

THE MATRIX BOSS

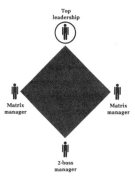

The matrix organization boss shares subordinates in common with another boss. As matrices evolve, this means that the matrix structure boss will find himself positioned on one of the dimensions in the power balance. Whether the dimension is the one that is given or the one that is grown can make a significant difference for the perspective that evolves. Since one of the most typical evolutions is from a functional structure through a project overlay to a business-function balance, let us examine the matrix-boss role for each of these two dimensions in detail. The same lessons, however, apply to matrix structure bosses who are in charge of areas, markets, services, or clients.

The functional manager

One of the greatest surprises of the matrix organization form comes in the changing role of functional managers. In a functional organization, managers have authority over the objectives of their function, the selection of individuals, the priorities assigned to different tasks, the assignment of subordinates to different tasks and projects, the evaluation of progress on projects, the evaluation of subordinates' performance, and decisions on subordinate pay and promotions. They consult or take direction only from their boss in these matters, but much of the function is self-contained.

In a matrix organization, by contrast, none of these responsibilities is the sole responsibility of the functional manager. He must share many of the decisions with program or business managers or other functional managers at his level. Many matrix structures require dual sign-offs on performance evaluations and on pay and promotion decisions. Even when this is not so, consultation on these matters with others is essential for the effective functioning of the matrix and the power balance discussed previously. Tasks, assignments, and priority decisions have to be shared with business managers and indeed often come about as the result of decisions made by project or business teams. Even a function's objectives are partially determined by the resource demands of projects and businesses. The functional manager in his matrix role is responding in areas in which he has traditionally been the initiator. A manufacturing manager, for example, struggled against and for several years resisted the notion that many of the plant managers who reported to him had to set their goals in response to a business team's needs and that review of goal accomplishment, from a time point of view, was the business manager's and team's responsibility. He had difficulty in understanding that his responsibility was to review goal accomplishment from the point of view of a functional specialty.

Thus, for the functional manager, a matrix organization is often experienced as involving a loss of status, authority, and control. He becomes less central and less powerful as parts of his previous role as initiator move from the function to the business manager. The ultimate example of this is the increased confrontation of functional managers by their functional subordinates, who are now also members of a business team that provides the legitimate need and social support for such upward initiation and confrontation. For managers who have been in relative control of their domain, this is a rude awakening that can create initial hostility and a quite predictable resistance to a matrix form of management.

As a matrix organization matures, however, functional managers adapt to these changes, and they find the role not only tolerable but highly challenging. Even though in matrix organizations it is the business managers who tend to control the money that buys human resources, functional managers must engage in very complex people planning.

They must balance the needs of the different product lines and/or businesses in the organization, they must anticipate training needs, and they must handle union negotiations if layoffs or promotions are involved. They must also administer support staff (supervisors, managers, secretaries, clerks) and accompanying resources (equipment, facilities, space, maintenance), many of which must be shared with the business units.

To accomplish this with any degree of efficiency, functional managers must balance workloads to avoid excessive peaks and valleys in resources. They must do this in any organization, but in a matrix, business managers act with relative autonomy, and functional managers cannot be effective by holding to some central plan prepared primarily for budget purposes. It is imperative that they know the product- and business-workload projections and changes well in advance; that they negotiate constantly with these managers to speed up, slow down, schedule, plan, and replan the pace and amount of their activities. In other words, they must go to the business unit managers and be *proactive* if they are to manage their functions effectively.

Some comments from managers in 2 matrix organizations serve to underscore this need for proactive behavior:

Functional managers have to learn that they're losing some of their authority to product units, and they will have to take direction from the product bosses. They have to segment their work along product lines, not functional lines, and they must be willing to establish communication channels with product lines.

Functional managers have to learn to become more aware of the impact of their decisions on our product-market success and become more responsive to the product organization needs that reflect the market. They have to remove their blinders and look around them while they turn the crank.

One functional manager concurred heartily:

We have to learn to serve as well as dictate; become more customer-oriented— where the customer is the product line. We must realize that the function's mission is to perform the function and prove that the function is the best available. There is a burden of proof in matrix that did not exist in functional organization.

The business manager

As we have pointed out, in a matrix organization various functional specialists are brought together in temporary (project) or permanent (business or product) groupings. These groups are led by product or business managers who have the responsibility for ensuring that the efforts of functional members of the team are integrated in the interest of the project or business. In this regard they have the same responsibilities as a general executive; their objective is project accomplishment or the long-term profitability of a business.

However, in a matrix organization these business managers do not have the same undivided authority as does the general executive. People on the team do not report to them exclusively since many also report to a functional manager. Thus, as many such managers have complained, "We have all the responsibility and little of the required authority."

Top leaders in traditional organizations have the benefit of instant legitimacy because people understand that reporting to them means being responsive to their needs. This is because their boss not only has formal title and status, but influences their performance evaluation, their pay, their advancement, and, in the long run, their careers. In a matrix organization these sources of authority are shared with functional managers, thus lessening, in the eyes of team members, the power of the project or business manager. He does not unilaterally decide. He manages the decision process so that differences are aired and trade-offs made in the interest of the whole. Thus he is left with the arduous task of influencing with limited formal authority. He must use his knowledge, competence, relationships, force of personality, and skills in group management to get people to do what is necessary to the success of the project or business.

This role of the matrix organization (business) boss creates both real and imagined demands for new behaviors that can be particularly anxiety-producing for individuals who face the job for the first time. The matrix (business) manager must rely more heavily on his personal qualities, on his ability to persuade through knowledge about a program, business, or function. He must use communication and relationships to influence and move things along. His skills in managing meetings, in bringing out divergent points of view and, it is to be hoped, working through to a consensus are taxed more than the skills of general managers in conventional organizations.

Thus, for individuals who face these demands for the first time, the world is quite different. They can easily experience frustration, doubt, and loss of confidence as they begin to rely on new behaviors to get their job done. They begin to question their competence as they experience what in their eyes is a discrepancy between final and complete responsibility for a program and less-certain means of gaining compliance from others. Some individuals learn the required new behaviors; other never do.

Not only does the actual and required change in behavior create a problem for new matrix organization business managers, but so does their own attitude toward the change. In our experience, individuals assigned to this role must first break through their perception of the job as impossible. Individuals who have spent all their time in traditional organizations have firmly implanted in their minds the notion of hierarchy and formal authority as the source of influence and power. They are convinced that the job cannot be done because they have never had to think through how power and influence, in reality, are wielded in the traditional organization. They cling to the myth that the formal power a boss has is what gives him influence.

This myth remains even after they themselves have developed and used other means of gaining influence. The myth about power and influence is often the first barrier that must be broken before the individual can be motivated to address the real demands for new behavior.

In his relations with his peers in both arms of the matrix organization, a business manager needs to assume a posture that blends reason and advocacy; bluster and threats are out. It is through these relations that he obtains the human resources needed to accomplish his goals. He has to expect that a number of these resources will be in short supply and that competing claims will have to be resolved.

In these dialogues the business manager must stand up for his requirements without developing a fatal reputation for overstating them. He must
search with his peers for imaginative ways to share scarce resources.
He must reveal any developing problems quickly while there is still time
for remedial action. These actions do not come easily to managers condi-
tioned in more traditional structures.

Last, in his relations with the various functional specialists represented
on his team, the matrix organization business manager must establish a
balanced or intermediate orientation. He cannot be seen as biased toward
one function. He cannot have an overly long or short time horizon. His
capacity to obtain a high-quality decision is dependent on an approach
that seeks to integrate the views and orientations of all the various functions. If he shows a bias, team members will begin to distrust his objectiv-
ity and his capacity to be a fair arbiter of differences. This distrust can
be the seed of a team's destruction.

For many individuals, this is a difficult task. A career spent in one
side of the matrix structure creates a bias imperceptible to the individual
but quite obvious to others. The need to wear multiple hats believably
and equally well creates heavy attitudinal and behavioral demands.

It requires of an individual the capacity to have empathy with people
in a number of functional areas and to identify with them while at the
same time maintaining a strong personal concept and orientation that
guides his own behavior and role performance.

Since the heir to the chief executive office is likely to come from this
rank, there is generally a great, though diplomatic, battle going on for
supremacy among the shared-subordinate bosses. The statesman's posture is an ingredient essential to success. The appearance of being threatened by sharing subordinates is fatal: This brands the individual as not
being top-management material.

Top leadership often uses the matrix structure to let the candidates
for the top spar with each other in a constructive arena. The matrix structure is a better form than the pyramid for testing managers' ability to
make things happen because of the strength of their personalities, their
ability to lead, and the validity of their perceptions rather than because
of their superior position in the hierarchy.

The perceptive matrix organization manager is aware that subordinates
have other voices to attend to, other masters to please. Orders that seem
irrational or unfair can more easily be circumvented under the protection
of the other boss, than they can in a single chain of command. More
care is therefore given to making clear the logic and importance of a
directive.

For senior managers who must share their people with other senior
managers, the matrix organization is both a training ground for how to

assume the insitutional reins and an incentive to go beyond having to share those reins equally with anyone else.

The rule for success in this role is to accept that while it can place contradictory demands on people, it is the best solution to accomodate simultaneous competing demands. Assume that there is no one best way to organize; each alternative has equally important claims, and the correct choice is both—in varying proportions.

2-BOSS MANAGERS

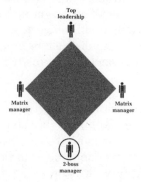

The most obvious challenge built into this matrix organization role is the sometimes conflicting demands of two bosses. For example, a representative from a manufacturing plant on a business team may know that his plant is having profitability problems and that the last thing the plant manager wants is to disrupt ongoing production activities with developmental work such as making samples or experimenting with a new process. Yet, as a business-team member, the plant's representative may see the importance of doing these things immediately to achieve project success.

In this situation the individual in a 2-boss position experiences a great deal of anxiety and stress. These come from the difficulties of weighing the conflicting interests of his function and his project team. Both have legitimate viewpoints. But which is the more important viewpoint from the perspective of the whole organization? This is not an easy question to answer or an easy conflict to resolve. But added to this are the questions of identification and loyalty to the individual's function or business team and the consequences of rejection or even punishment from the side of the matrix organization that perceives it has lost in a given conflict. To compound the problem, even if the plant representative on a project team decides that he needs to go against what he knows is in the interest of his plant, how does he communicate this back to his organization members and convince them of the merits of his views? The same problem would exist if he were to favor his functional orientation and have to persuade the team that sample runs will have to be delayed.

We can see from this description and the earlier discussion that there are problems of dual group membership—new demands for communication, uncertainty about the kinds of commitment that can be made, uncertainties about how to influence other people in the function or team, and uncertainties created by a more generalist orientation not demanded in a conventional functional organization. There are of course differences in the capacity of individuals to deal with ambiguity, but all individuals new to matrix management lack some of the knowledge and the skills needed to navigate through the ambiguities and conflicts generated by a matrix organization.

Remember that this manager is also at the apex of his or her own pyramid—subordinates to this role need not be shared. It is the multiple demands from above and beyond the immediate command that must be managed. But his approach, to be successful, must be no different from that of the top role: Both must pay heed to competing demands, make trade-offs, and manage the conflicts that cannot be resolved. Any skillful politician knows that alternative sources of power increase one's flexibility. It is the unimaginative 2-boss manager who would trade extra degrees of freedom for finite and singular sources of action.

One operating manual for this role, developed after about a year's experience in a matrix organization, included the following points in a section titled "Practices for Managing Matrix Relationships":

- Lobby actively with relevant 2-boss counterparts and with your matrix bosses to win support before the event.
- Understand the other side's position in order to determine where trade-offs can be negotiated; understand where your objectives overlap.
- Avoid absolutes.
- Negotiate to win support on key issues that are critical to accomplishing your goals; try to yield only to the less critical points.
- Maintain frequent contact with top leadership to avoid surprises.
- Assume an active leadership role in all committees and use this to educate other matrix players; share information/help interpret.
- Prepare more thoroughly before entering any key negotiation than you would in nonmatrix situations; and use third-party experts more than normally.
- Strike bilateral agreements prior to meetings to disarm potential opponents.

- Emphasize and play on the supportive role that each of your matrix bosses can provide for the other.
- If all else fails:
    a. You can consider escalation (going up another level to the boss-in-common).
    b. You can threaten escalation.
    c. You can escalate.

Before traveling this road, however, consider your timing. How much testing and negotiating should be done before calling for senior support? Does the top leadership want to be involved? When will they support and encourage your approach? Does escalation represent failure?

This kind of advice relies on managerial behavior, not on organization structure, for success. It sees personal style and influence as more important than power derived from either position or specialized knowledge. Success flows from facilitating decisions more than it does from making them. To remain flexible in this managerial role, it suggests, the manager must minimize the formal elements, move from fixture to actor, from bureaucracy to process.

The role problems of the 2-boss manager can of course become manageable in a mature matrix organization. This happens primarily because for the most part the functional and business managers learn to avoid making irreconcilable demands of their shared subordinates. This will still happen on occasion, however, even in a smoothly functioning matrix organization. In a familiar instance, the 2-boss manager may be directed to be in two places at the same time.

In addition to a balanced structure and shared roles, a matrix organization should have mechanisms for processing information along overlapping dimensions simultaneously. In a product-area matrix organization, a way of dealing with such situations is to establish the norm that the 2-boss individual is expected, and even directed, to convene a meeting between his two bosses to resolve any such conflict. The 2-boss manager is reprimanded only if he suffers such a conflict in silence.

Beyond handling such occasional problems, the 2-boss manager learns in a mature matrix organization that his role gives him a degree of influence not usually experienced at his level in a conventional organization. He not infrequently finds himself striking a balance in a discussion with his two bosses over some point of conflict. If he knows his facts and expresses his judgment on the merits of the particular issue, he often finds it is taken very seriously. This is the heart of training for general management.

This is exactly how the matrix organization is intended to work—with decisions being made at a level where the relevant information is concentrated and where time is available for a thorough airing of the options.

In such a framework a higher percentage of decisions will, in fact, be given careful attention and decided on for their unique merits rather than in terms of a single orientation.

In reviewing the general characteristics of the mature matrix organization, we have emphasized the quality of flexibility. By looking in some detail at the four roles unique to the matrix we have discovered where that flexibility comes from—from the individuals in key roles who have been challenged by the matrix structure to respond to each new situation in a fresh and flexible fashion. This constant pressure for fresh thinking and for learning in the mature matrix organization has, in fact, seemed to greatly increase the organization's productivity, especially at middle-management levels. This may be fine for the organization, but how about the individuals as they initially face new and demanding role expectations? Is this a problem or an opportunity? In most cases it is probably both.

The future of the mature matrix

A matrix organization includes matrix behavior, matrix systems, and a matrix culture, as well as a matrix structure. After years of working with a matrix, some organizations find that they no longer need the contradictory architecture of the matrix structure to accomplish their goals. Instead, they revert to the simpler pyramid for their structural form, while at the same time retaining the dual or multiple perspective in their managerial behavior, in their information processing, and in the culture of their firms.

This interpretation suggests that the matrix organization is not likely to become the dominant feature in the *structure* of American organizations. Its utility is more likely to be in helping organizations become more flexible in their responses to environmental pressures. Structures are intended to channel people's behavior in desired ways. Like laws, they are strongest when they are not invoked or tested. To the extent that managers behave effectively, they have little need to bump up against formal structures and reporting walls. In traditional pyramids, managers were always bumping against something—either the structure was centralized, and there wasn't enough freedom, or it was decentralized, and there wasn't enough control.

Organizations with mature matrix structures therefore appear to follow one of two paths, and the extent to which the structural framework survives depends on the path an organization takes. One is to maintain dual command, shared use of human resources, and an enriched information processing capacity. The other is to maintain matrix behavior, matrix systems, and a matrix style or culture, but without using the matrix's structural form. Some organizations tear down the matrix entirely and revert to the traditional forms, practices, and managerial behavior of the pyramid.

The distinction between a pathological breakdown and an evolutionary rotation, where the matrix is a transitional form, is a matter of interpretation. As we observe the change in these organizations we may ask, was the matrix thrown out or did the firm grow beyond it? The distinction is more than academic. As long as the environmental pressures that initially propelled an organization into a matrix structure remain, the original inadequacies of the pyramid form will reappear if the matrix structure is actually abandoned. Our observations suggest that this would be fairly evident in three to six months and painfully obvious within one to one and a half years.

Because the structural element of the matrix is so fiendishly difficult to many, we observe organizations trying to shed the form while maintaining the substance. Our diagnosis is that it can be done successfully only where appropriate matrix behavior is so internalized by all significant members that no one notices the structural shift. Even then, however, we anticipate that through the years the structual imbalances will increase.

Where we stand on the learning curve

Not too many years ago few managers in our classrooms had heard of matrix organization, and today nearly half of them raise their hands when asked whether they work in a matrix organization. Objectively, this self-reporting is inaccurate. What is relevant, however, is the perception itself. Like Molière's gentleman who was surprised to learn that he had been speaking prose all his life, many managers find that they have been "matrixing" all along. The word is jargon, but the grammar connotes people's behavior more than the form of their organization. The unrealistically high self-reporting also demonstrates an increasing comfort and familiarity with the idea among a very large body of executives.

Our major purposes have been to broaden traditional treatments of the matrix structure by demonstrating its applicability in diverse settings and by suggesting ways to change a seemingly radical conception into a familiar and legitimate design. The matrix structure seems to have spread despite itself. It is complex and difficult, it requires human flexibility in order to provide organizational flexibility. But the reverse is also true. For these reasons, we believe, many managers shied away. The academic literature, until now, has limited the utility of the matrix structure to high-technology project organizations. We have shown how both in organization theory and in application, the matrix structure has a much broader applicability. Behavioral descriptions were replete with words like "tension," "conflict," and "confusion." For many it was not pleasant, but it seemed to improve performance. Success gave it legitimacy, and as the concept spread, familiarity seemed to reduce the resistance.

Matrix structure gained acceptance in the space age of the late 1960s. In fact, for a while in the early 1970s it almost seemed to be a fad. Organizations that should never have used it experimented with the form. It was in danger of becoming another hot item from the behavioral science grab bag for business. When this occurred, the results were usually disastrous, thus fueling the sense that if an organization played with the matrix structure it might easily get burned. Despite many misadventures, however, the matrix structure gained respectability. What was necessary was made desirable.

More organizations are feeling the pressure to respond to two or more critical aspects of their businesses simultaneously—that is, to consider and organize by function *and* by product, by service *and* by market area at the same time. There is also increasing pressure to improve information processing capacity, and recent technological advances make multiple matrix systems feasible. Last, it is clear that there is an increased sense of the scarcity of all resources and hence pressures for achieving economies of scale. As we described, these were the necessary and sufficient conditions for the emergence of matrix organizations in the first place. Because these conditions are increasingly prevalent, we feel that more organizations will be forced to consider the matrix organizational form.

Each organization that turns to the matrix structure has a larger and more varied number of predecessors that have charted the way. Despite our belief that matrix structures must be grown from within, the examples of wider applicability must nevertheless suggest that we are dealing less and less with an experiment and more and more with a mature formulation in organization design. Familiarity, here, reduces fear. As more organizations travel up the matrix structure learning curve, the curve itself becomes an easier one to climb. Similarly, as more managers gain experience operating in matrix organizations they are bound to spread this experience as some of them move into other organizations on their career journeys.

When pioneers experiment with new forms of organization, the costs are high and there are usually many casualties. In the case of the matrix structure, this has been true for both organizations and individuals. As the matrix has become a more familiar alternative, however, the costs and pressures have been reduced. Today, we believe that the concept is no longer a radical one, the understanding of the design is widespread, and the economic and social benefits have increased.

People in the Middle Ages had a very clear view of the world order. Galileo changed that. Newton changed the view of universal order once more, and Einstein did too in a later age. In each period there was certainty of the logic and correctness of the structure of the universe. And each period lasted until a new formulation posed a previously unthinkable question. After varying periods of resistance or adjustment, people become comfortable with the new formulation and in each instance assume it to be the final word.

The organization of large numbers of people to accomplish uncertain, complex, and interdependent tasks is currently nowhere as susceptible to the same exactness in calculation as the physical world. And there are those who would say that to compare the world of physics and the world of organizations is to compare the sacred with the profane. But the process of acceptability and then increased applicability of new formulations is similar, even if rather more humble. We believe, therefore, that in the future matrix organizations will become almost commonplace and that managers will speak less of the difficulties of the matrix structure and will take more of its advantages almost for granted.

SELECTED BIBLIOGRAPHY

Chris Argyris's "Today's Problems with Tomorrow's Organizations" (*The Journal of Management Studies*, February 1967, pp. 31–55) is an empirical study of nine British matrix organizations. The study is positive about the structure, but demonstrates how implementation has been unsuccessful because of traditional management behavioral styles. Arthur G. Butler's "Project Management: A Study in Organizational Conflict" (*Academy of Management Journal*, March 1973, pp. 8–101) contains an excellent review of the project management literature and deals extensively with the conflict faced by professionals involved in project work. David I. Cleland and William R. King's *Systems Analysis and Project Management* (McGraw-Hill, 1968) is one of the best and most thorough books available that explains project management and locates it in the larger setting of systems and organization theory. And Stanley M. Davis's "Two Models of Organization: Unity of Command versus Balance of Power" (*Sloan Management Review*, Fall 1974, pp. 29–40) spells out the basic theories and how they evolved in both domestic and international organizations.

Jay R. Galbraith's "Matrix Organization Design" (*Business Horizons*, February 1971, pp. 29–40) contains a fictitious case through which the author describes the decisions involved in adding a product orientation to a functional organization until an appropriate balance is reached. The article delimits the boundaries of matrix organization. William C. Goggin's "How the Multidimensional Structure Works at Dow-Corning" (*Harvard Business Review*, January–February 1974, pp. 54–65) is a case description of how Dow-Corning expanded a matrix form of organization into one that added an area dimension to the product and function areas plus a fourth dimension to consider organizational evolution. And Sherman K. Grinnell and Howard P. Apple's "When Two Bosses Are Better Than One"

(*Machine Design,* January 9, 1975, pp. 84–87) includes brief but practical guidelines on when to use a matrix organization and how to make it work.

Leonard R. Sayles's recent article in *Organizational Dynamics,* "Matrix Management: The Structure with a Future" (Autumn 1976, pp. 2–18), expresses a viewpoint similar to our own and has developed a suggestive typology that encompasses five different types of matrix structures.

PART III

In this section, our scope of attention once again expands, this time to multibusiness and multinational corporations.

As the cases illustrate, the size, product/market diversity, and geographical dispersion of multibusiness and multinational companies all contribute to presenting managers with organizational issues which can be different from and often more complex than those addressed in earlier sections. However, as the text demonstrates, the basic conceptual framework introduced in Parts I and II can be applied to multibusiness and multinational companies as well.

Two of the cases in this section (ITT and Clark Equipment Co.) are representative of multibusiness *and* multinational organizations, while the third (Texana Petroleum) portrays a domestic multibusiness company. Similarly, the readings focus on specific design issues and solutions for multibusiness companies (Stieglitz), and for those that are both multibusiness and multinational (Davis).

Chapter 5

Organizing human resources for multibusiness and multinational companies

Because of their greater size, the greater diversity of their products and markets, and their greater geographical dispersion, multibusiness and multinational companies face organizational problems that are somewhat different from and often more complex than those faced by single businesses. For example, many companies included in the *Fortune* 500 list of largest industrial corporations operate in dozens of different countries, making and selling hundreds of different products through an organization staffed by thousands of people. In doing so these companies must deal with questions such as:

How can we coordinate and control our divisions and subsidiaries when no one has the necessary breadth of experience and knowledge to fully understand our diverse businesses?

How can we simultaneously cope with the need to adapt our major product lines to the unique cultural and marketing characteristics of each country we operate in as well as the need to achieve economies of scale worldwide and to coordinate all of our new-product development efforts?

How can we make sure that our many dispersed employees do not misuse our significant economic power?

We will discuss these and other questions related to organizational issues in multibusiness and multinational companies throughout this chapter. Initially, however, we will attempt to show that despite differences in size, product/market diversity, and geographical spread, the basic approach of organization design in single businesses can be applied to multibusiness and multinational companies as well.[1]

THE THREE DESIGN QUESTIONS

Question 1: Drawing subunit boundaries

Just as in single businesses, in drawing subunit boundaries for multibusiness and multinational firms one needs to consider: the diversity and interdependence of the activities the corporation is engaged in; the trade-off between the gains of specialization and economies of scale that can occur within subunit boundaries; and the costs of establishing these subunits and integrating across their boundaries.

For example, in one large multinational company, the president's staff reviewed its organization in 1970 in response to numerous complaints and problems within its European operations. Specifically, after an initial period of success in Europe, the company was having great difficulty penetrating new and larger markets. The staff report concluded that its functional organization in Europe should be changed to a national organization—i.e., its major subunit boundaries should include all activities within a country and not all European activities associated with particular functions such as manufacturing, marketing, and so on. Their rationale, in summary, was the following:

When we originally established the European organization, our sales were $10 million. Today they are $300 million. Back then we had to organize Europe by functions because we couldn't afford any other option—our sales just would not support separate manufacturing facilities and sales forces in each country. But today we can afford a country-by-country organization, and we desperately need one. The cultural, economic, and legal conditions in each European country are different. Our current organization serves none of these differences very well. We need an organization that can sell a French variation of our product with a French sales force, for example. If we organize our European operation by countries, we can achieve this.

In another moderate-sized ($700 million in sales) American multibusiness company, a second type of boundary choice problem arose in 1975 regarding long-range planning activities. The chairman of the board be-

---

[1] We are really talking about three different types of companies in this chapter: domestic multibusiness, single-product multinational, and multiproduct/multinational. Although one could devote a chapter to each, as we have done with domestic single-product companies, that is beyond the scope of this book.

lieved that the company had grown to the point where it managed a very large amount of assets for its stockholders, and that it had a duty to do some long-range thinking (10–20 years) to protect those assets. This raised the question of where the long-range planning activity should be carried out. While one executive suggested that long-range planning should be included in all management jobs—that is, that a special function or set of functions should not be created—the suggestion was quickly disregarded. Almost everyone agreed that the long-range planning task was sufficiently different from most of the tasks managers did that it would not be carried out very well, if at all, by line managers. Two options then emerged. In the first, a special long-range planning function would reside at the divisional level. Operationally, that meant a staff person would report to each of the company's six division managers. Their efforts would be coordinated by a planner who reported to the president. In the second option, a corporate long-range planning subunit would be created, reporting to the president, and staffed with seven planners. This latter arrangement was eventually chosen because "the advantages to be gained by having long-range planning better integrated into operating divisions were more than offset, we felt, by the need for a group of a certain minimum size—that is a group that could include a Ph.D. economist, a political scientist, a professional planner, and so on."

Because the situations are sometimes more complex than in single-business contexts, judgments about where to draw subunit boundaries can be more difficult in multibusiness and multinational firms. Nevertheless, the process is the same in both cases.

Question 2: Organizing within subunits

The major subunits of multibusiness organizations are usually single-product companies themselves, or groups of such companies. (You will recall that a number of the cases in Part II concerned divisions of multi-business companies.) The major subunits of multinational companies are sometimes single-business companies, and sometimes functional units or geographical organizations. We have already dealt with the question of internally organizing these units in Part I (subunits specialized by function, area, or product) and Part II (single-business companies).

An example will help demonstrate the applicability of these approaches to an international setting. Consider a company that makes and sells about $20 million a year in specialized electrical equipment. In 1969 it was organized functionally (see Figure 5–1).

When establishing a fourth geographical subunit in the international department, the sales manager had to deal with the following types of decisions:

Should I hire local nationals as salespeople, and train them as best I can? Or should I bring in some of our experienced salespeople from other countries? (He decided the sales task required salespeople to be from the same culture as the buyer, so he hired local nationals and trained them.)

Should I compensate the sales force at the local wage rate and risk upsetting them when they learn how much more their colleagues in the other areas get? Or should I hire them at a higher rate and accept the direct economic consequences? (He decided to set the base salaries above local wages but below salaries for his salespeople in other areas.)

How can I best deal with the culturally based reluctance of most of the nationals to be away from their homes on sales trips? (He eventually decided to draw small sales territories for six salespersons in the six most densely populated areas, which contained about 85 percent of all potential buyers. He then hired six people, each of whom lived within one of the six territories. Thus overnight travel was not necessary.)

Figure 5–1

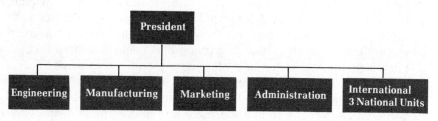

Regardless of the setting, the key to effectively organizing within subunits is a thorough knowledge of the tasks (or the business) and the employees (or the organization) involved, as well as the organizational design tools that can be used. In multibusiness settings, this means understanding a diverse set of businesses. And in multinational settings, this usually means understanding a diverse group of people and cultures.[2]

Question 3: Integrating the subunits

Essentially the same integrating devices that are used by single-business companies are also used by multibusiness and multinational companies. For example, to integrate its 12 product/market divisions, one multibusiness company relies on:

---

[2] For a discussion of the importance of understanding foreign work forces and some of the common problems managers face in doing so, see David Sirota and J. Michael Greenwood, "Understanding Your Overseas Work Force," *Harvard Business Review*, January–February 1971, pp. 53–60.

1. Three key positions in the management hierarchy, called group vice presidents. These managers, who are stationed at corporate headquarters, each have four divisions reporting to them.
2. Goals and plans jointly agreed on each year by corporate headquarters and each of the divisions.
3. A corporate staff that helps the company's president and group vice presidents examine divisions' plans and establish reasonable goals.
4. A monthly meeting of division managers, group vice presidents, the president, and some of the corporate staff to review results to date.
5. A financial measurement system that focuses on each division separately and the company as a whole.
6. A compensation system that rewards division managers for both corporate and divisional results.

Just as in the case of a single business company, the problem of integration is probably the one organizational issue that most plagues multibusiness and multinational managers, despite the fact that subunits in multiproduct and multinational firms are often much less interdependent than the subunits in a typical domestic single-product company. The large volumes of complex information that must move among subunits can sometimes make the nature of the interdependencies very complex. But more important, the high degree of subunit differentiation caused by the diverse products, markets, and cultures these organizations deal with, in addition to the large number of employees involved and their geographical dispersion, all make achieving effective integration very difficult.

ORGANIZATIONAL PROBLEMS CAUSED BY HIGH DIVERSITY, LARGE SIZE, AND GEOGRAPHICAL DISPERSION

In a typical multibusiness organization the problem of achieving effective integration among the subparts operationally means getting thousands of people, most of whom are thousands of miles apart and have never met each other, and none of whom really understand all of the businesses the others are involved in, to behave in ways that facilitate the achievement of corporate goals.[3]

Consider, for example, the case of a diversified American corporation that acquired its first consumer goods manufacturing business. The acquisition came into the company as a division reporting to a group vice president, but since no one at corporate headquarters knew much about

---

[3] See R. N. Anthony and J. Dearden, *Management Control Systems,* 3d ed. (Homewood, Ill.: Richard D. Irwin, Inc., 1976), chap. 8.

this new business, it operated with a fairly high degree of autonomy (a fact which some other division managers quickly spotted and resented). The new division was required to report financial results monthly, and for the first 12 months met its sales and profit objectives each month. In the 13th month, however, sales were off 20 percent and profits were down 35 percent.

The group vice president in charge of the new division requested an immediate report from the division manager outlining the reasons for the declining sales and profits as well as corrective actions being taken. The report arrived three weeks later and satisfied neither the group vice president nor those on the corporate staff who read it. The group vice president asked for a more detailed report. Before this report arrived, the next month's financial figures reported that sales were off 25 percent and profits were wiped out completely. The corporation's president became very concerned at this point because he felt the division's performance could cause the company to miss its overall profit goals for the year. He urged the group vice president to take more aggressive action, so the group vice president and five other corporate staff people immediately went to visit the division. The division manager and his staff resented the "interference" and indicated that they were doing the best they could to deal with an unusual situation; and they were reluctant to talk with the corporate staff. Division and corporate staff did negotiate a new budget as well as a set of specific actions the division manager was to take. The next financial report showed that the division almost broke even; yet the following month it again lost a large amount of money. The corporate president thereupon fired the division manager and replaced him.

The new division manager encountered a variety of unexpected problems. He quickly discovered that his background with the company's other manufacturing divisions had not adequately prepared him to understand this division's business; he found he would have to go through a learning period. He also found a company culture that was very different from those in his past experiences. Meanwhile, the division continued to lose money. The losses increased when another of the company's divisions pulled out of a joint venture, leaving the troubled division with excess capacity in a partially built facility. Despite pressure from the corporation's president, the other division refused to have anything to do with what they referred to as a "snake pit."

After 16 months the corporation did get this situation under control. But the cost was high, even in corporate terms. Although this example illustrates problems resulting from an acquisition, they typify the type of control and collaboration issues that business diversity can cause in multibusiness organizations.

Multinational organizations can sometimes operate in even more diverse environments than the one just illustrated. Not only do they often
have considerable product diversity, they also must cope with cultural
and legal diversity.[4] Successful integration within and among products
and cultures can, as the following example illustrates, be very difficult:[5]

To hear officials of some multinational companies talk, there is a surefire success formula for any large corporation with global facilities. First of all, they
say the multinational should unify its product lines around the world to obtain
mass-production efficiency. Second, it should make its parts wherever such manufacturing is most economical. Third, it should focus its sales efforts on countries
where markets are growing fastest. The result, say the formula's proponents, is
a maximization of profits.

If all this sounds reasonable, not to say obvious, one might consider the fact
that Ford Motor Co. has been following just that formula in recent years and is
finding that the scheme isn't as surefire as it seems. This by no means implies
that the giant auto maker is thinking of abandoning its integrated approach; however, it does mean that Ford is finding some major flaws in the approach—a
finding that is emphasized by talking to Gerd Maletz, an owner of one of the
biggest Ford dealerships in Germany.

"Take spare parts," Mr. Maletz says. "An engine for one Ford model now
must come from Britain, and we may wait months for it. And if the British workers
are on strike—and they're always on strike—we wait and wait and wait. We
could get a German engine in a couple of days."

Ford decided on integration in 1967. At the time the company's rationale for
so doing seemed sound indeed: integration would avoid unnecessarily duplicating
the amount—some $100 million—that it costs to engineer and produce a new
auto model.

So Ford decided to produce just one European line in place of the completely
different cars that used to be turned out by its British and German plants. And
the single line began to reduce costs in another way, since the company began
to buy parts in bigger volumes—meaning lower prices—from its outside suppliers.

To achieve integration, Ford began to weave a complex manufacturing web
that stretched from its big plants in Britain and Germany to its smaller units in
Belgium, France, Ireland, the Netherlands, and Portugal. It was planned that some
units would make parts, some would assemble finished autos and some would

---

[4] For example, many European countries have laws regarding worker participation on
management boards (so-called co-determination), while most of the rest of the world does
not. But even within Europe, each country has slightly different laws regarding worker
participation. See for example, Robert Kuhne, "Co-Determination: A Strategy Restructuring
of the Organization," in *The Columbia Journal of World Business*, Summer 1976, pp. 17–
25.

[5] From William Carley, "A Giant Multinational Finds Unified Activities Aren't Easy to
Set Up." Reprinted with permission of *The Wall Street Journal*, © Dow Jones & Company,
Inc. 1974. All rights reserved.

do both, with the entire operation being directed from Ford of Europe's headquarters in Warley, outside of London.

But even in the very early stages, there were problems. One Ford executive, an American who moved from Detroit to Britain to help set up Ford of Europe, says he quickly ran into nationality differences. "It was easy to get our British people to agree (to a plan), but five minutes later they were always back questioning it," the American recalls. "It seemed almost impossible to get the German Ford people to agree to anything; but once they did, they just kept marching even if they were marching right off the end of the earth."

The first all-new auto launched by Ford of Europe was a medium-sized car that was called the Cortina Mark III in Britain and the Taunus in Germany. The launch, which began in 1970, was a disaster, and the after effects are still plaguing Ford. "There's no question we screwed that one up," one official concedes.

The fiasco stemmed partly from British inexperience with the metric system. Ford's British workers had just converted to that system, long used by Germany and other Continental countries; but, says one of the British workers, "we were still thinking in inches." As a result, the British and German parts often didn't mesh. "The doors didn't fit, the bonnet (hood) didn't fit, nothing fit," says Arthur Naylor, a metal finisher in Ford's Dagenham, England, body plant.

It has also been argued by British workers that some of the German-designed parts were too precise. "Our men often work with a one-sixteenth inch tolerance, but on the German engine suspension system, we had to work down to two- or three-thousandths of a bloody inch," contends Jock Macraw, a union shop steward at Dagenham. "The Germans wanted an engineering job done on the production line, and that's impossible."

Because of all the snafus, the Cortina-Taunus assembly line in Dagenham barely moved along. By January 1971, when some kinks had been ironed out, the line was speeded up—much to the displeasure of some workers, Mr. Macraw says. Coincidentally, Ford's wage contract was expiring at the time; and on January 20, 1971, unions struck Ford in Britain, halting production for nine weeks. It wasn't until September, nearly a year after initial production of the new car had begun, that Dagenham hit peak production. Ford says the peak should have been reached in two months.

Significant geographical dispersion, beyond that found in this example of Ford in Europe, can significantly intensify the organizational problems faced by multinational and multibusiness companies. It is possible for an important message in such companies to pass through dozens of people before it reaches its appropriate destination. Because the potential for distortion and miscommunication increases with each additional person involved, it is relatively easy for information to be lost or distorted.

Perhaps an even more troubling consequence of large size and geographical dispersion relates to the potential for power misuse. The substantial resources of large companies can lead to an inherently dangerous situation. Because a great deal is at stake, because managers have considerable power available to them to protect those stakes, and because there are many geographically separated managers who can be difficult to control, some managers have involved corporations in unethical and illegal activities.[6] The result for large corporations in general, and large multinational enterprises in particular, has been the development of a cadre of vocal critics.[7]

Finally, a problem common to all organizations is that what is best for the whole is not necessarily best for each of its parts. The inevitable conflict, and the problems it can cause, is exacerbated in multibusiness and multinational organizations for two reasons. First, the conflict is often more visible, because the performance measures for the whole and the parts are clearer. For example, one parts plant, instead of separate ones in each European country, might increase a corporation's net income through economies of scale, but it might also reduce the net income of a subsidiary that lost sales while waiting for spare parts. Second, getting the subparts to do what is in the best interest of the corporation is often more difficult, for all of the reasons previously mentioned (e.g., a corporate president might desperately want to enforce a rule that no bribes be paid by his company's employees, but not be able to do it).

COPING WITH EXTREME DIVERSITY, SIZE, AND GEOGRAPHICAL DISPERSION

Multibusiness and multinational organizations rely on a variety of mechanisms to help them cope with difficult integration problems, the most common of which is modern communication and transportation facilities. The airplane and the telephone/telex, which we tend to take for granted today, play an enormously important role in tying together the distant parts of large enterprises. Likewise, future technological advances in transportation and communication could significantly help multinational enterprises in particular.

Other integrating mechanisms which are used more selectively include group structures, corporate staffs, elaborate measurement and reward systems, selective transfers, area structures, and presidential "offices."

Group structures with corporate staff

In addition, multibusiness firms often rely heavily on group structures as integrating devices. In a typical case, product divisions that are related

---

[6] "The Pressures to Compromise Personal Ethics," *Business Week,* January 31, 1977, p. 107. See also Steven N. Bresner and Earl A. Molander, "Is the Ethics of Business Changing?" *Harvard Business Review,* January–February 1977, pp. 57–71.

[7] See Richard Barnet and Ronald E. Muller, *Global Reach: The Power of the Multinational Corporation* (New York: Simon and Schuster, 1974).

because of technology or markets are grouped together under a group vice president. The group vice president then becomes a specialist in that product/market group and attempts to identify and manage any interdependence among the divisions in the group. He also helps the president, with the aid of corporate staff, to make decisions regarding funding requests, financial objectives, and business plans from his divisions. He also works with the president and the staff to monitor division performance on the measurement systems they have developed (which often involve a monthly or quarterly reporting requirement). When designed properly to fit the business situation, these arrangements can significantly increase a corporation's ability to process relevant information and make effective integrating decisions, as well as to take speedy action when problems develop.

The size of a corporate staff group, the complexity of the reporting systems, and the number of decisions made or reviewed at corporate headquarters can vary significantly among companies that use this set of integrating devices. Companies that have relatively little diversity among their businesses and relatively high interdependence among them tend to rely on a large corporate staff and a relatively centralized decision-making system; with more business diversity and less interdependence, corporations often use a smaller corporate staff and more decentralized management. At the extreme, some multibusiness companies with very diverse and independent businesses do not use this device at all, but instead rely on other mechanisms, such as the careful selection and transfer of division managers.[8] In such cases the diversity among the businesses makes it impractical to try to actively manage them from corporate headquarters.

Companies that have varying degress of diversity and interdependence among their divisions will often treat different divisions in different ways. As a rule, the lower a division's interdependence with other parts of the company, the higher the chances are that it will be allowed to operate autonomously, that it will be treated as a profit center, and that the division manager will be offered the opportunity for significant bonuses based on divisional profits.[9]

Selection and transfer of managers

Careful selection and transfer of people into subunit manager slots can be a key integrating device. To facilitate the integration of a subunit

---

[8] Harold Stieglitz, "On Concepts of Corporate Structure," *The Conference Board Record,* February 1974, pp. 7–13; see also Jay Lorsch and Stephen Allen, *Managing Diversity and Interdependence* (Boston: Harvard Business School, 1973).

[9] Richard F. Vancil, *Decentralization,* (New York: Financial Executive Research Foundation, 1978).

into the corporation, for example, the president might select someone with whom he or she has a good relationship, who can be trusted to pass on accurate and timely information, and who also has a background in the area of business that is the focus of the subunit's activities. Similarly, to facilitate the integration of two divisions that are highly interdependent, a company might rotate its division managers.[10] Probably the major reason this solution is not used more frequently is that companies often do not have the type of people needed to make it work. They do not always have someone the president knows and trusts, who has a background in a certain product or area, and who is available to be moved. Some companies systematically try to develop a pool of people who might be used to support such a selection, promotion, and transfer policy.[11] They might, for example, hire some Europeans graduating from a U.S. business school, initially give them assignments at corporate headquarters, and then give them a series of assignments in different European subsidiaries, all in order to prepare them for positions as European division managers. This approach can be quite expensive, however.

Product/area structure

Multinational organizations also rely heavily on a variety of product/ area structures to help with their integration problems. In cases where they feel an area focus is more important than a product focus, companies depend on a geographic structure combined with some type of product management; those that emphasize a product focus rely on a product division structure aided by some type of area coordination.[12] Companies that feel they need to focus equally on products and markets (and sometimes on functions, too) may rely on a product/area matrix. All except the smallest multinational organizations are using one of these three structures or moving toward using one of them.[13]

The trend toward global product/area structures is relatively new, yet because of its advantages it will undoubtedly become more important

---

[10] For an interesting discussion of how corporations use management transfer to aid coordination and control, see Jay Galbraith and Anders Edstrom, "International Transfer of Managers: Some Important Policy Considerations," *The Columbia Journal of World Business,* Summer 1976, pp. 100–112.

[11] Robert A. Pitts, "Unshackle Your 'Comers'," *Harvard Business Review,* May–June 1977, pp. 127–136.

[12] Stanley Davis, "Trends in the Organization of Multinational Corporations," *The Columbia Journal of World Business,* Summer 1976, p. 70.

[13] A typical multinational company evolves in the following way. When it first starts selling internationally, it sets up foreign subsidiaries. When the sales from these subsidiaries become significant, or after its investment abroad becomes significant, the company establishes an "international division." Later it shifts to either a global product division or global area division. Finally, it reorganizes, using some form of product/area matrix.

in the future.[14] The slowness with which companies have adopted this structure is very much a function of the problems it can cause, which are similar to those of matrix structures in single businesses. As a result, one writer has warned that multinational/multibusiness companies not implement a matrix unless:

1. There is diversification of both products and markets requiring balanced and simultaneous attention.
2. The opportunities lost and difficulties experienced by favoring either a product or geographic unity of command cannot be ignored.
3. Environmental pressure to secure international economies of scale require the shared use of scarce human resources.
4. There is a need for enriched information processing capacity because of uncertain, complex, and interdependent tasks.
5. Information, planning, and control systems operate along the different dimensions of the structure simultaneously.
6. As much attention is paid to managerial behavior as to the structure. The corporate culture and ethos must actively support and believe in negotiated management.[15]

Office of the president

Some multibusiness and multinational organizations have recently developed still another mechanism to promote integration. Usually called "the office," this device is most commonly used at the presidential level. Instead of having one person act as president, under an "office" arrangement, three or four people work together in that role. When it is successful, this device fosters faster and more competent information processing.[16] One significant requirement for this arrangement to be successful is that excellent relationships exist among the people in the office.

Corporate culture

Another integrative device that is used by multibusiness and multinational organizations is a corporate "culture" which is developed and main-

---

[14] For a good discussion of the advantages of a complex matrix for a multibusiness and multinational company, see William Goggin, "How the Multidimensional Structure Works at Dow Corning," *Harvard Business Review*, January–February 1974, pp. 54–65.

[15] Stanley Davis, "Trends in the Organization of Multinational Corporations," *The Columbia Journal of World Business*, Summer 1976, p. 70.

[16] For an example of an "office," how it was developed, and how it works, see Gilbert Burck, "Union Carbide's Patient Schemers," *Fortune*, December 1965.

tained by top management. Through their words and deeds, top managers attempt to clearly set norms and values.[17] For example, if a corporate president can establish the norm that "we do not engage in illegal activities even if the countries we operate in expect it," that norm can have an effect more powerful than the most expensive control systems or the most elaborate hierarchies.

That more companies do not actively try to create and maintain an integrating culture attests to its difficulty. Establishing certain norms and values in a global organization is a slow and time-consuming process, and one that may not be practical under many circumstances.

SUMMARY

The approach we outlined for dealing with organizational questions in single-business companies is equally applicable to multibusiness and multinational companies. Nevertheless, because of their greater product/ market diversity, their greater size, and their geographical dispersion, the latter type of company often faces even more difficult integration problems. To cope with these problems, they tend to use all of the integration devices used by single-business companies, plus additional ones that are appropriate for their specific problems (see Figure 5–2).

In designing a solution to an organizational problem in a multibusiness or multinational corporation, one needs to consider, just as in single-business contexts, the diversity and interdependence of the activities the corporation engages in, and the current organization (formal, informal, people). One needs to make judgments about what fits and what does not. And one needs to avoid the temptation to solve troublesome integration problems by ignoring important aspects of the corporation's product/ market diversity and reducing needed differentiation in the organization.

One of the most common mistakes that managers in multinational and multibusiness organizations make is to ignore important aspects of their product market diversity—often because they are not happy with the implications of organizationally taking that diversity into account. Corporate staff managers, for example, often try to implement uniform compensation and performance appraisal systems throughout a worldwide corporation, regardless of important differences among divisions and countries.[18] After acquiring a new division in a different business or in

---

[17] Roger Harrison, "Understanding Your Organization's Character," *Harvard Business Review*, May–June 1972.

[18] See, for example, Howard Perlmutter and David Heenan, "How Multinational Should Your Managers Be?" *Harvard Business Review*, November–December 1974, p. 129.

Figure 5–2

Integrating device	Advantages	Drawbacks
Modern communications and transportation facilities	To some degree, available to everyone.	Cost, especially in time and energy for traveling managers.
Group structures, with corporate staff and elaborate measurement/reward systems	Can significantly increase a corporation's ability to make optimizing decisions and spot problems quickly.	Absorbs subunit manager's time. If businesses are extremely diverse, this option just may not work.
Selection and transfer of subunit managers	Can be less expensive and cumbersome than structural solutions.	It is sometimes not possible to find the types of individuals needed. Extensive transfers can be expensive.
Product/area structure Area subunits with product managers Product subunits with area coordination Matrix	Best when area focus is most important. Best when product focus is most important. Can achieve integration within and across products, areas, and other dimensions (e.g., functions).	Does not provide best product focus. Does not provide best area focus. Can be very difficult to maintain the balance in the system and to manage the tensions and conflicts.
Office of the president	Allows a key "office" to process information faster and more competently than if it were staffed with a single individual.	Requires the development and maintenance of excellent working relationships among the people involved.
Corporate culture	Once established can be much more powerful and less expensive than other solutions.	Difficult and slow to develop.

a different country, corporate managers often try to treat it like the rest of the corporation, regardless of important differences. This type of behavior leads eventually to organizational problems—sometimes very serious ones.

Case 5-1
International Telephone & Telegraph Corporation
Compiled by Stephen A. Allen III

The materials contained in this case were selected primarily to permit the reader to examine the organizational approaches developed by a well-known chief executive to manage a highly diversified, multinational corporation. The major focus is on relationships among (*a*) the goals, corporate strategy, and management assumptions of Harold Geneen; (*b*) the organizational approaches and control systems used by ITT; and (*c*) the behavior of the company's managers. The data also permit a more limited exploration of the organizational integration of newly acquired companies and the role played by executive values and career goals in a large, complex organization.

The materials have been arranged in the following sequence to provide a logical flow to the ideas and issues:

A. *Harold Geneen and ITT*
   1. "ITT: Can Profits Be Programmed?"—*DUN's REVIEW*, November 1965.
   2. Excerpts from "ITT Takes the Profit Path to Europe"—*Business Week*, May 9, 1970.
   3. Excerpts from "How One Man Can Move A Corporate Mountain"—*Fortune*, July 1, 1966.
   4. "The Financial Key at ITT"—*DUN's REVIEW*, December 1970.
   5. Excerpts from "Management Must *Manage*"—An Address by Harold S. Geneen before the Investment Group of Hartford and the Connecticut Investment Bankers Association, February 15, 1968.
   6. "How ITT Tightens Its Spreading Net"—*Business Week*, June 24, 1967.
   7. "They Call It 'Geneen U.' "—*Forbes*, May 1, 1968.
   8. Harold Sydney Geneen from *Who's Who*, 1970.
B. Corporate-Divisional Relationships
   1. Excerpts from "ITT: The View from the Inside"—*Business Week*, November 3, 1973.
C. *Selected Financial and Operating Data*
   Exhibit 1: ITT—Selected Operating Data, 1959–1972.

Exhibit 2:   ITT—Revenues and Net Income by Principal Product
Groups—1971 and 1972.

ITT: CAN PROFITS BE PROGRAMMED?*

In a locked room high up in the Manhattan headquarters of International
Telephone & Telegraph Corp., 50 executives sit around two long, felt-
covered tables. There, from all over the world, they are reporting to Harold
S. Geneen, ITT's combative, contentious chairman who sits at the center
of one table. "John," says Geneen, speaking to one of the executives,
"what have you done about that problem?"

John speaks into the microphone in front of him. *Well, I called him, but I
couldn't get him to make a decision.*
Do you want me to call him?
Gosh, that's a good idea. Would you mind?
I'll be glad to, says Geneen. *But it will cost you your pay check.*
Never mind, says a flustered John. *I'll call him again myself.* (The windup?
John not only kept that pay check, he got action.)

Geneen is confident that he has developed a management system that
literally enables ITT to program its profits. Although it lacks a formal
name (Geneen himself is forever searching for a two-word description,
tossing out such phrases as "momentum management," "informed management," "noninsulated management," and "factual management"), perhaps it is best described as three-pronged. For it combines a powerful
central management group, semiautonomous divisions, and a highly refined system of goals and controls.

You can run a company one of three ways, says Geneen. *There's the old
kind of company you run from headquarters. Then there's the holding company
that owns a bunch of companies and just sits back and waits for them to send
in their dividends. We're neither the first nor the second, but a stage in between.
We support our companies constructively, in the things they can't do themselves.
And if support isn't enough,* Geneen adds bluntly, *we use discipline.*

Management "by the book"

Much of that discipline comes from a bulky, leather-covered looseleaf
book that is seldom out of Geneen's sight. Stamped in gold on its cover
is "H. S. Geneen" and the words, "ITT, General Management Meeting,
System Confidential." The six-inch-thick book, and some 50 others exactly

---

* Reprinted in part by special permission from *Dun's Review*, November 1965.
Copyright 1965, Dun & Bradstreet Publications Corporation.

like it in the possession of ITT top executives around the world, is the very touchstone of the corporation's system of management. "There's more intelligence in these books over a period of time," says Geneen, "than you can buy from 100 services."

Here is how it works: Except for August with its vacations and December with its holidays, each ITT manager throughout the System sends to world headquarters in New York a monthly report detailing all facts affecting the performance of his unit. Often running to 20 single-spaced typewritten pages, the report must contain financial analyses of sales, profits, return on investment, and virtually every other measurement used in business. What is more, it must describe every existing and potential problem affecting the operation ("All hell breaks loose," confides one ITTer, "when a problem that should have been put in the report has not been put in. That's when Geneen gets really livid"). A description of the problem, however, is not enough. The report must also explain how the problem arose and how it will be solved.

One typical report in a recent volume is clearly indicative of the semiautonomous status of even very large ITT-associated companies, and the strictness with which such companies are controlled. The report was submitted by Hermann Abtmeyer, managing director of Standard Elektrik Lorenz Aktiengesellschaft in Stuttgart, Germany. The company, employing 35,000 people, produces a volume of $200 million annually, which, claims Geneen, is equivalent to about $400 million in the United States because of currency valuations. Says Geneen: "Abtmeyer is a sort of Ben Fairless [Benjamin F. Fairless, former chairman of U.S. Steel Corp.] in Germany."

Ben Fairless or not, Abtmeyer's single-spaced report covered both sides of 11 pages, as well as four pages of charts. It minutely described problems in finance, manufacturing, marketing, research, and labor. It even analyzed the status of competition for each of Standard Elektrik's main product lines, on a product-by-product basis.

A translation of Geneen's scribbled marginal comment about two such product analyses: unfavorable. "The thing we really raise hell about," he says, "is something going off the track."

To help keep things on the track, reports such as Abtmeyer's are mimeographed, collated, bound into sets, and then airmailed to each manager. The executive's job is to carefully read them (usually a weekend chore requiring 8 to 12 hours), familiarize himself with the problems of other managers, and then prepare himself for the monthly management meeting that is held not long afterward at world headquarters in New York. And ten times each year, the looseleaf books are emptied and the whole process is repeated.

In addition to a sound system, so that all executives can be heard, the meeting room contains a giant motion-picture screen, projection equipment, and related communications gear. The room is dominated by the two green-felt covered tables, each 60 feet long, that become a monthly battleground where reports are picked apart, discussed and hammered into future "action assignments."

Geneen, naturally, presides at the meetings. And although he usually is the chief questioner, all managers in attendance are expected to participate, discussing not only their own problems but those of others. Because there is so much ground to cover, the meetings often last for several days. Sometimes, too, they run late into the night. One session this past September, for example, lasted from 9:30 in the morning until 11:15 at night. "These are real working meetings," exults Geneen, who seems to relish 16-hour workdays. "There's no substitute for getting the facts, because when you're aware of the problems, you soon think in terms of the solutions."

Some of those solutions are already taking shape in Geneen's mind during the six hours it normally takes him to read the book. Hefting it in his hands and fanning his thumb across the initialed tabs that separate the many sections (CIA, for example, means Controls, Instrumentation, and Automation), Geneen points out pages whose corners have been turned down: "On every page with a dog-ear, there's a problem."

On such pages Geneen has scribbled notations, made X's and even circled whole paragraphs—all in red ink. At the meeting itself, he can then quickly flip to the offending sections, call out the name of the manager responsible and literally put him on the spot. Two cryptic examples from Geneen's September 1965 book:

1. "Japanese in Port." (Japanese companies are moving certain products into Portugal. ITT has plans. Should it hurry up its plans?)
2. Opposite of R.S." (The area manager's economic appraisal differs from the one prepared by economist Raymond J. Saulnier, formerly an economist for the Eisenhower Administration and now with ITT.)

Do Geneen's managers resent being singled out in front of their associates? Whether they do or not, those who have stayed at ITT have come to expect it and are invariably prepared with the right answers.

Still more meetings

But "the book" and monthly world meetings, though key, are only one part of ITT's system of management. Similar airings of problems are regularly held at lower levels of the organization, and as a result there is a constant interplay between ITT goals and ever changing field conditions. Even the method of establishing goals is a sophisticated one. Once a year each ITT company is required to develop a complete business plan covering a five-year period, with main emphasis on the first two years. Each year, in turn, this plan is reviewed by the appropriate area staff (North America; Europe, Middle East, and Africa; South America; Far East and Pacific), then again by the headquarters staff in New York.

What it adds up to: at least 50 meeting days a year and a total of 400, Geneen estimates, during the past six years. "Thus," he says, "there's no lack of communications for setting goals, for following performance, or for taking action between the top echelon of the company and the firing line."

Because that firing line is every bit as lively as its name implies, ITT is obviously not every executive's cup of tea. The pace is grueling, the hours are long, and the demands are stringent. On the other hand, there is plenty of excitement, top pay, and sizable bonuses tied directly to performance. Nor can anyone claim that Harold Geneen expects more of his team members than he does of himself.

Not surprisingly, as ITT has mushroomed, many of its executives have fallen by the wayside. Apart from those whom Geneen himself has fired, many others have simply resigned. Some left because of the pace; others (such as John J. Graham, former director and area vice president for North America, who is now president of Curtiss-Wright) left when the offers from outside became too good to resist. The high turnover notwithstanding, ITT's executive force has grown from about 500 in 1959 to 1,100 today. If the planned redoubling of sales and earnings is achieved on schedule, moreover, Geneen estimates that he will need another 1,200 executives by 1969–70.

But where will they come from? One answer is the considerable number of top executives that have been promoted from ITT ranks, and this will continue to be the case as ITT expands its training programs. The fact is, however, that the company has long relied heavily on outside recruiters, and even today half of all new executives come from the outside. The major change is that many more executives are approaching ITT directly these days, because, as Geneen puts it, "The company that's growing tends to attract people, and the company that isn't, doesn't."

This point is strongly emphasized by John C. Lobb, ITT vice president and group executive for technical and industrial products. "The System," he says, "brings good people to the top very fast. And the bad ones drop out very fast. But the kind of guys that stay with the company like the momentum and the constant expansion. A guy can come in," adds Lobb, who has been with ITT three years, "and start running a $20-million company. An acquisition can bring it to $100 million in a year, and maybe double that in the next two years. At most companies you have to wait until somebody dies before you have an opportunity to run something as large as that."

The ITT way

Naturally, newly acquired companies are, as Geneen puts it, "a little chary" at the beginning. To smooth the way, all changes and modifications—such as personnel and payroll records, engineering and marketing—are channeled through a single ITT staffer for about a year. At the same time, the acquired company's management quickly becomes familiarized with the ITT way of doing things. "By the time we had Avis three months," says Geneen, "we had already held three full-day meetings with them. Give us a year of this working together and we'll understand their problems, and they'll see what we're trying to do." He adds: "We've already advanced Avis' program in Europe by two years."

How does ITT integrate a new acquisition into the system? More important, what steps does it take to improve the unit's profit-producing capability? The one approach that has paid off best, replies group executive John Lobb, has been the organizational one. The way it works, particularly with manufacturing companies: the new company is brought into an industry group (John J. Nesbitt, for example, became part of the heating, ventilating, and air-conditioning group), where functions such as marketing and R&D have been centralized, and where related ITT companies literally pool their resources to serve one broad market.

As a result, ITT has been able to set up a number of multiproduct plants, instead of the great many single-product ones that had been required when each company operated independently. "We take unrelated, heterogeneous companies," says Lobb, "and put them into a multifactory business, with particular emphasis on marketing. The companies don't lose their identity, but they do lose some of their autonomous decision-making power. Because of this approach," he adds, "we've had pretty good luck in improving the return on investment."

Hand in hand with such reorganization goes a technique that Lobb and his managers call "defensive football." Normally, they have found, only 20 percent of an acquired company's products contribute as much as 80 percent of its profits. "We believe," says Lobb, "that if a product line doesn't return 8 percent after taxes on the capital employed, you should get the hell out of the business."

To minimize the number of products that cannot make that 8 percent, ITT's first step with all acquisitions has been to weed out lines that are not profitable. "These are the ones," says Lobb, "that they shouldn't have had in the first place."

With General Controls, for example, the first sharp improvements in profits were achieved by literally cutting $5 million in products from its catalog, closing one plant and shrinking another. Similarly, within six months after ITT acquired Bell & Gossett, it sold off three unprofitable divisions.

"General Controls," says Lobb, "was a loss operation when we bought it. It broke even in 1963 and will earn $1.6 million this year. Bell & Gossett earned $2.4 million in 1963 and will make $4.2 million this year."

Naturally, all of ITT's acquisition activity and subsequent reorganization has required a considerable amount of restaffing. Even though the acquisitions have been harmonious ones, in many areas the lines were foreign to traditional ITT business. So in the last three years the company has had to bring in many new people—especially in marketing and engineering.

That staffing job is nowhere near complete today, but Lobb takes some solace in the fact that "it takes a couple of business generations to get like GM, where you're three deep in every job position. Now, though," he adds, "we do have enough depth so when we start something in Europe we can send someone over for six months or a year to train nationals."

Lobb's last point is an extremely significant one. The ITT system is international to a degree that not one of its competitors can match. More than two thirds of ITT's 195,000 employees live outside the United States, almost all of them nationals of the countries in which they are located. In Europe alone, ITT conducts major manufacturing operations in five of the six Common Market countries (Belgium, France, Germany, Italy, and the Netherlands), also has major manufacturing plants in each of the Outer Seven nations (Austria, Denmark, Norway, Portugal, Sweden, Switzerland, and the United Kingdom), and has still additional operations in Finland and Spain.

ITT TAKES THE PROFIT PATH TO EUROPE*

Robert Townsend and the Justice Department have one dislike in common—corporate bigness as exemplified by International Telephone & Telegraph Corp. Townsend, former chairman of Avis-Rent-A-Car (now an ITT subsidiary) and author of *Up the Organization,* believes that excellence and size are incompatible. He has said: "I would like it on my tombstone, 'Townsend never worked a single day for a company like ITT.'" Less pungent but far more threatening to ITT are the barbs of the Justice Department's suits against the company's purchases of Grinnell Corp. and Canteen Corp. and its proposed merger with Hartford Fire Insurance Co.

Not surprisingly, Harold S. Geneen, the formidable 60-year-old chairman and president of ITT, is grimly determined to turn back the antitrust challenge. Loss of Grinnell and Canteen would strip ITT of sales exceeding $600 million a year and net income of $25 million, while derailment of the Hartford deal would wreck one of the largest corporate mergers ever attempted. Hartford's riches include $1.9 billion in assets and $50 million in earnings.

Taking the longer view, Geneen is intent on preserving ITT's ability to make large acquisitions in future years in case momentum in generating internal earnings begins to slow. Geneen firmly believes that the acquisition route is the only way to move into new areas of operations. Growth is, indeed, his credo. An epitaph for the English-born, former accountant that rivals Townsend's in trenchancy is suggested by Richard H. Griebel, a former ITT executive who is now president of Lehigh Valley Industries: "Three things should be written on Hal Geneen's tombstone—earnings per share, 15 percent growth per year, and size."

Use of diversity

ITT's diversity probably will enable Geneen to maintain his proud string of 43 consecutive quarters of increased earnings. Number 43 was a 13 percent increase in the first quarter of 1970, a period for which many U.S. companies reported massive declines.

Despite this good start, Geneen figures that economic conditions will make his usual target of 15 percent growth unattainable this year. The Nixon Administration, in Geneen's words, appears bent upon "bringing on recession as though it were some sort of vaccination against disease." So he will be satisfied with 9 percent or 10 percent this year.

The word is out from Geneen's 12th-floor suite at Manhattan's 320 Park Avenue that the early 1970s are a time for consolidation and internal expansion. The rapid and diverse expansion of the past decade has stretched ITT's management capabilities to the utmost, despite an increase in the number of executives from 450 in 1959 to 2,200 today. In the past two years alone, just six of ITT's larger acquisitions—Sheraton, Levitt, Rayonier, Continental Baking, Grinnell, and Canteen—have brought in combined sales of $1.8 billion and profits of $60 million. Adding Hartford Fire, the sixth largest U.S. property and casualty company, will be still another stiff managerial challenge.

Still shopping

That does not mean that Geneen won't be rounding out product lines with other acquisitions. In March, ITT paid $40 million in stock for Gwaltney, Inc., whose Smithfield hams will buttress the food operations. European companies also are on the shopping list, though trustbusters are on watch there, too. French government opposition recently forced ITT to give up its attempt to acquire Guinard, a pump maker with sales of $40 million.

Geneen holds that internal diversification into unrelated businesses rarely works. Thus, if a "reasonably sized company" in a wholly new field became available at a bargain price, he would have to be interested in gaining a toehold. "The trouble is that what I call a small toehold, the Justice Department calls a foothold," he adds with a wry grin. "But we don't need to buy any major companies."

* * *

Whatever the outcome of the anti-trust suits, ITT is already well positioned to move into the 1970s without going on a buying spree. With a solid footing on both sides of the Atlantic, it is admirably set up to ride out industry and, to some degree, national economic slowdowns. Last year, 64 percent of ITT's $5.5 billion in sales and 55 percent of its $234 million in profits were generated in the United States and Canada. The North American sales of $3.5 billion break out to 40 percent in manufacturing and 60 percent in services. Foreign sales of $2 billion represented 36 percent of the conglomerate's total but generated 45 percent of the profits. The split in foreign revenues was less even than in the United States, with 85 percent coming from manufacturing and 15 percent from services.

Sea of troubles

When Geneen was hired away from Raytheon Co. in 1959 to take the top spot at ITT, he faced nothing but difficulties. ITT's operations were nearly all overseas and were constantly endangered by rising xenophobia—especially in Latin America. The threat to ITT properties worried American bankers, who were well aware that most of the company's profits were earned abroad.

Geneen's initial solution was to develop ITT's U.S. operations. He is fond of pointing out that "ITT became international by coming back to the U.S." But the trip was complicated by AT&T's near-monopoly in the U.S. telecommunications business. This limited ITT's scope in its traditional business. So Geneen looked at electronics manufacturing, but high price/earnings multiples made acquisitions too costly.

ITT studies next pointed out real growth potential in the service industries, where p/e ratios were lower. ITT started small, buying Hamilton Management Corp., with its mutual fund, and Aetna Finance Corp., a

St. Louis loan company. The first big step came when Geneen swapped $41 million in stock for Avis, No. 2 in car rentals, in 1965. Heftier acquisitions followed: Sheraton, Levitt, and Canteen.

Back to Europe

The push into the service sector rounded out Geneen's U.S. buildup. But the beauty of ITT's global grasp is that these acquisitions now form the cutting edge of Geneen's strategy of raising foreign operations back to parity with those in North America.

Geneen is under no illusion that the road to new successes in Europe will be easy just because it is ITT's traditional stamping ground. ITT-Avis, for instance, moved into Europe soon after it was acquired. "We lost a lot of money in the first two years . . . and made quite a few mistakes," says Avis President Winston V. Morrow. Last year, Avis had European turnover of $30 million and cleared $2 million.

Yet ITT does have a large advantage over most U.S. companies that are just starting to reach into Europe's markets. After all, it began as a European company 50 years ago. It knows the conventions of dealing with touchy governments and foreign currencies (though it did drop $2.3 million on the devaluation of the franc). And ITT-Europe, based in Brussels, gives the parent company a strong logistical base for its supranational subsidiaries.

U.S. challenge

Europe's potential, good as it may be, cannot hide the fact that U.S. operations will continue to account for more than half of ITT's sales. Last year's North American volume of $3.5 billion produced net income of only $129 million, hardly a sparkling return when 60 percent of the business is in consumer services.

ITT management clearly has its work cut out for it at home, as well as abroad. The trick will be to continue to grow at Geneen's advertised rate of better than 10 percent a year while acquisitions are being held to a minimum. A 10 percent rise in volume this year would amount to $547 million, roughly the total sales of, say, Gillette Co. or Quaker Oats Co. Geneen argues that ITT has its hooks in enough of the right growth markets to meet his projections. "I never seem to be able to get across to the analysts that this is not just one large company but a group of smaller companies," he laments.

Synergy

Geneen expects such internal growth to benefit from that much publicized but hard-to-pin-down conglomerate virtue of synergy. ITT's great strength is a central management corps that can help the subsidiaries in finances, research, marketing, and legal work. Homebuilder Levitt, for example, is in a far stronger position than its independent competitors during an economic downturn since it can tug on the financial cord to parent ITT.

The most important kind of synergy exists between Geneen and ITT's diverse operations. All his high-flying growth plans might have run him into a financial bind had he not been able to operate the company successfully enough to pay for his purchases. Nearly all his acquisitions were financed with ITT common and preferred stock rather than the more popular "funny money" packages of debentures, warrants, and the like. Though ITT carries $1.7 billion of debt, it is easily able to service its annual interest charges of $112 million with a healthy $450 million cash flow.

But Geneen has paid some fancy prices for companies. The House Antitrust subcommittee recently presented a table using straight purchasing accounting rather than the pooling-of-interest method employed by ITT and most other conglomerates. The table shows that Geneen paid $60 million above Levitt's net worth of $32 million and $133 million over Sheraton's net worth of $60 million. Under new rules proposed by the accounting profession, such "goodwill" (the difference between price and net worth) would have to be amortized over a maximum of 40 years, thus slicing into earnings. Geneen's reaction: ITT would just have to pay less for future acquisitions.

HOW ONE MAN CAN MOVE A CORPORATE MOUNTAIN*

"If I had enough arms and legs and time," Geneen says, "I would do it all myself." But since he can't, he has evolved a management system at ITT that responds as much as any organization can to the boss's relentless urge for constant improvement. At first glance, ITT's formal structure seems quite traditional. Four executive vice presidents report directly to Geneen. They divide among them nearly all the line responsibilities for the company's operations. Because of the ways ITT's various businesses are concentrated in various parts of the world, any one of these four may be in charge of everything in one geographic area, or all of a group of related activities wherever they are, or a combination of area and operational responsibilities. Defense production, Avis, and some other line operations are run by executives who report to Geneen along with

---

* Excerpts from article by Stanley H. Brown in *Fortune,* July 1966. Reprinted by permission from *Fortune* Magazine. © 1966 by Time, Inc.

the usual staff department heads such as administrative, legal, corporate relations, research, and the controller.

At this point, though, the organizational pattern diverges from the norm. Most companies have a vice president in charge of marketing who reports to the chief executive. Geneen tried that for a while, didn't like it, and went to another conception that brings him a lot more information about ITT's line operations. ITT has eight men, called product-line managers, who divide the worldwide job of product planning and marketing along such lines as telecommunication, components, avionics, consumer products, and so on. These men function, officially at least, as staff men who may not give orders to operating people; they merely offer recommendations. But they, too, generally report directly to Geneen. "We're really extensions of his office," one of them explained. If their recommendations are not accepted by operating managers, they inform Geneen, who then is likely to resolve the conflict personally. Using this group of freewheeling product-line managers as a bridge, Geneen is able to cross most channels with complete freedom.

THE FINANCIAL KEY AT ITT*

Ask Harold S. Geneen to describe how management works at International Telephone and Telegraph Corp., and he remarks, "hard work" and "a lot of scrub-brush methods." Then, without abandoning his modest stance, the 60-year-old president of the nation's ninth-largest industrial company adds, "And I think we run good financial controls."

In a year like 1970, as even Harold Geneen would admit, controls are the key not only to winning an award for financial acumen but also to profitability. A lot of companies thought they had controls, but this year anyway, they will not be able to prove it by their income statements. ITT will. On estimated sales of $6.1 billion, it is expected to earn an estimated $340 million—or 20 percent more than 1969's record profits. These estimates include Hartford Insurance, acquired earlier this year. Without the insurance company's earnings, ITT estimates an 11 percent gain. In fact, any lesser performance would be news. Unique among billion-dollar enterprises, ITT has posted 45 consecutive quarters of gains in sales, earnings, and earnings per share.

The ITT system is founded on three Geneen laws. The first: problems must be highlighted. The annals of ITT are replete with tales of the unwary subordinate who failed to "red flag" a problem, hiding it in hopes of solving it before it came to light. Even insiders confess that bonuses are mercilessly axed for those who neglect to give early warning.

---

* Reprinted by special permission from *Dun's Review*, December 1970. Copyright 1970, Dun & Bradstreet Publications Corporation.

Second: facts must be unshakeable. "I don't believe a man's opinion until I believe his facts," says Geneen. Third: Geneen insists on face-to-face communication.[1]

On the surface, the system itself looks a lot like a management textbook description of controls. It has a business plan, continual reporting of actual results as compared to plan, and a procedure for remedial action when the two diverge. A lot of companies have it. The difference at ITT is its responsiveness. "Many others get the same numbers," says Geneen, "but maybe they don't work as close to them or as quick at them."

That responsiveness starts nearly a year before when the first pass at the yearly business plan is taken. Although it is called a rough cut—or the "O1"—it is by anyone else's standards a complete planning job. In it, each operating manager, called a unit manager, forecasts in dollars every aspect of his business operation—typically including sales, earnings, capital requirements, working capital, cash requirements, inventory, receivables, new products, and all the rest. "Call it a game if you want to," says Geneen. "He's planning and running the business on paper."

From there, the plan goes to step two: scrutiny by the headquarters staff to determine if the manager's estimates are realistic and to judge whether the plan will work.

To bolster such an opinion, ITT employs a huge central staff, numbering perhaps 400 administrative, technical, and financial experts who are free to examine the operations of the unit manager—including delving into his books—any time they feel the need. This goldfish bowl environment of the unit manager is one of the pressures singled out by critics of the system. Yet it is also the thing that enables the 16 product line managers, broad-gauged marketing men to whom the staff reports, to get onto an even footing with the unit men regarding their line of business.

Some time toward the end of March the process of refining expectations begins. The product line manager and the unit manager meet at New York headquarters armed with facts, figures, and logic to support their estimates. If one man expects sales to rise by 5 percent, for example, he has to be able to debate the other who maintains sales will remain, say, even. Geneen says: "After that, we've got a pretty good agreement on what a business unit is going to do. These estimates have withstood the criticisms and arguments of all the people who may have something to contribute." If unreconcilable disputes arise, which is rare, they are arbitrated by the president's office.

From then until fall, the manager's own staff develops the final plan, which he will bring to New York for still another round of testing by

---

[1] *Casewriter's addendum:* "As Geneen explained to me, it is not enough for him to see the figures; he must see the expression of the man who presents them, and how he presents them." From Anthony Sampson, *The Sovereign State of ITT,* (New York: Stein & Day, 1973), p. 100.

ITT's top management group. "But when we're through," says Geneen, "the manager will have a game plan, and that is what he runs on the following year."

As exhaustive as this may seem, there is more. One reason ITT can react as fast as it does, Geneen explains, is that game plans include exigency plans; e.g., what would be done if business ran at only 80 percent of expected sales volume. Or 70 percent. "They won't have all the answers on that," he admits, "but when faced with lower volume, at least the manager has pre-thought through a few of the problems, and when it happens it isn't quite as much of a shock."

"And that's how we worked through 1970," says Geneen. "This year we used the safety approaches and backstops we had been practicing for eight or nine years." In fact, the full repertoire. For the U.S. economy was in a slump. Consumers were not buying. Every other conglomerate saw trouble ahead with sales falling in division after division, and the going got rougher as the General Motors strike loomed.

But the red flags started popping at ITT's Park Avenue headquarters late last year. It was then that sales estimates were lowered and cost-cutting procedures were begun.

When sales go off estimates, the unit manager—there are some 200 of them—has two programs to follow. First he must immediately reduce his costs. "This preserves a good deal of his profitability," says Geneen. Only after this is done does he go out and try to bolster the lagging sales.

Always strict with costs—ITT goes for reductions of 2 percent to 5 percent even in lush years—the company pared $70 million this year. It did it by across-the-board reductions in administrative and general costs and overhead—one cut before the year began and a second during 1970. Still other adjustments were made in individual units as dictated by figures that flow into headquarters weekly.

What Harold Geneen-style financial acumen accomplishes, in sum, is to eliminate surprises and create predictability. The ITT president willingly forecasts earnings progress on the order of 12 percent to 14 percent a year in a healthy economy and 10 percent in a lean year. It could get boring—but don't try to tell that to an ITT unit manager.

MANAGEMENT MUST MANAGE*

We have created new approaches to management methods to meet our needs. For example, take the role of the Product Line Manager. In

---

* Excerpts from an address by Harold S. Geneen, Chairman and President, International Telephone and Telegraph Corporation before the Investment Group of Hartford and the Connecticut Investment Bankers Association, February 15, 1968. Reprinted by permission from the International Telephone and Telegraph Corporation.

our official job designations, he is formally charged with the "competitiveness" of his assigned product lines, although he is not part of the line organization. In this disengaged role he acts as a constant spur and check and help to the line performance.

Quick, responsive

But more important, there's *real* understanding today, because there is *real* communication between this area group and the managements of each of our companies. It is quick, responsive, and on-the-spot. And our Company managers have learned they can trust it, that it is a two-way street, and that the environment we have created not only allows but *welcomes* "feedback," with the resulting setting and acceptance of common and practical goals of performance.

There is no nonsense though. Our staff, who are our specialists in the area or from world headquarters, go *at will*—with the usual courtesies, of course—to and through any and all of our operations: to teach, to train, to monitor our operations, and to improve them. They do not conflict with the line manager by issuing orders to the line operation. But they do provide a clear professional review *with* the manager and higher up— if needed—on a day-in, day-out basis. This accomplishes most of what is needed, and gets the best value from both the manager on-the-spot and from our staff with this disengaged approach.

Now, this open policy has been a great *insurance factor*. It is almost always the well-intentioned manager who is over his head and too proud to ask for help, that constitutes the real problem in business. Our open policy prevents this kind of surprise. No method is foolproof, of course, and we have had our problems. But comparatively, there are fewer of them and they are less severe, with this kind of approach.

More importantly, the communications between the area and the managers and the top of the Company is a working one. I estimate that about 20 of our top New York executives and myself have spent the equivalent of some 350 long working days, in the last eight years, sitting across the table each month with our European company managers and our European area management. Among us, we wrestle *first-hand* with all our problems whether competitive, performance, or otherwise.

Now, this is the equivalent of almost *two full working years*. It does not include all of the other work of the area and World Headquarters staffs that takes place in the plants and in other meetings.

For example, the meeting which went on for four days in Brussels at the end of January had 120 people in the room at one time. In this manner, we not only can accomplish our goals with the most informed facts, but we can also train our young executives in our business and in our goals by their attendance. What would you think that case-study class sessions of this type—and "live," as they say in the TV industry—in our own business are worth to our future management? And they are a mere by-product.

* * *

We also have similar but smaller area groups in South America and the Far East. Our largest similar group is in the United States, where our area management constitutes one of the best consulting firms in the country—also with similar assignments applying to our domestic business.

"Red flag" items

But we don't stop there. Once a month, each manager of every profit-and-loss division—however small—all around the world, writes his own report, following a general format, and sends it to Headquarters. The first and most important part of this report is what we call our "Red Flag" items. These are the problems which, to his mind, are important, which need solving, and which require our help.

In our once-a-month worldwide meeting for two to three days in New York, all of the problems of our areas around the world are taken up and action started. Each of these letters has been read by the entire management group prior to the meeting, and each manager gets the attention his "Red Flag" requires—no matter where it is waving on the globe. These are approaches by what we would call simply, hard work. But in our mind they represent—*insurance.*

For example, on the plane returning from Europe last month and just as part of management reading material, I picked out a memorandum which I thought might be of interest to you tonight. This is a purely routine one from another area, namely our Weekly Staff Reports.

The memo is headed: "Worldwide Industrial Engineering activity report. Week ending February 2, 1968."

There are 38 items reported on. Let me give you samples:

The first item has to do with "hard core" unemployment—a brief report on our early start as to what type of products could be manufactured in plants located in depressed areas under the job program, analysis of the requirements, labor content, skill, etc., and a brief summary of areas that we're going to investigate.

Item 2. A report that we've reduced the capital budget of one of our major plants in Europe by $3,313,000, which reduced budget has been accepted by both the industrial engineering department and plant management.

Item 4. I'll skip around through items to give you an idea. Some work in Chile ensuring that our equipment supply and installation commitments are scheduled properly so that we meet our service commitments under our franchise.

Item 5. A consumer products problem in Germany calling for a re-design of a major chassis with 5 percent cost reduction.

Item 6. A subset program covering four countries in Europe. These are the telephone subsets that you have on your desk. Let me read the percentage reductions in cost for four countries: "Lower by 18 percent, 6 percent, 11 percent, 10 percent."

Item 7. A single product cost leadership seminar in our British plant. This is our program to increase our market penetration by developing the lowest cost in the industry.

Item 8. Working with the Plant Manager in our French plant in connection with moving manufacturing outside of Paris and utilization of the remaining space.

Item 9. A brief progress report on one of our British plants where we are performing order quotation, production materials lists, purchasing, inventory control, and even engineering layout on a computer project which we expect to expand throughout all of our European plants.

Item 10. Development of 1968 year-end inventory targets.

Item 12. A brief report of one division where there appeared to be a weakening of profits. After investigation it now appears that there will be a gain of 16 percent over the first quarter 1967 income. The point is: we went in and checked.

Reducing defects, costs

Item 15. ITT soldering program. In electronics, many people forget the importance of soldering joints. More errors and rejects come from this than any one single source. We estimate that we make 2 billion soldering joints a year and these, because of the nature of the equipment, are mostly made by hand. We figure that it costs 4¢ to correct a solder joint in the plant; once it's in the field it costs us $35 to locate and correct. This is a program to reduce defects and costs by training and proper soldering. First time ever in the history of our companies and, we believe, in Europe.

Item 17. Analysis of the world market for submarine cables. The note says "analysis being re-done in view of market data which indicate an even larger market potential than before reported." This may well lead to capacity requirements that have to be planned in advance to take full advantage.

Item 18. A report on a reed switch appropriation. The key points are the directness of the conclusions:

"A.   The manufacturing build-up schedule is unrealistically optimistic."

"B.   The amounts requested are excessive to the task."

"The detailed report is being prepared."

We'll go into this problem and we'll come up with a fair and sound answer.

Item 19. Refers to the slippage of budgeted output of a division, and goes on to say: "assisted them to develop a schedule to recover output. Unit output will be back on schedule by the end of April."

Item 20. A coordination of interchange of manufacturing and development personnel between two of our companies to assure that efforts are not duplicated and that the exchange of information will be timely and will be followed.

Save $100,000 a year

Items 26, 27, 28, and 29. Reports on national and international purchasing contracts which will save upwards of $100,000 a year. Note the international purchasing contract—something that we have developed.

Item 31. A plan to reduce costs $40,000 a year by use of ITT air pool, developed on the West Coast.

Item 32. A plan to ship roof-top multizone air-conditioning units on trailers aboard flat cars, with subsequent program to store away from plant and time delivery at lower cost.

Item 33. A small item—installation of an 18-foot hydraulic tail-gate for radio-dispatched trucks. Will replace three ITT trucks and drivers.

And so it goes for the rest of the items. This is only one of approximately 15 to 20 weekly staff reports of similar nature and similar direct action.

One of the things that occurred to us was the difficulty in measuring staff dollars-and-cents contribution.

The line manager has a Profit-and-Loss statement to which he can point.

The staff function, as we use it, may well be as responsible at times for profit improvement as a line man himself. You will recall that it is often a meshing of their own observations and decisions which results in our final operating actions.

Effectiveness reports

To partly remedy this and, in part, to give the staff man a chance to be creative in profit contribution, we instituted several years ago a monthly effectiveness report. The rules for this report are very interesting. Nothing can be reported except in terms of dollars-and-cents results accomplished. These may be the elimination of an unnecessary competitive design, or a price rise that was warranted by the market, or in many other areas of imagination and interest. Frequently, these effectiveness reports for a single month will add up to well over $1 million. It is, of course, to be recognized that, in many cases, these gains will also be reported in the line operations. But we're not so interested in keeping score by credit as we are in the fact that these improvements come through with dollars-and-cents results.

Now these are rather small items to take your time up with. But I thought that by dipping down into the unseen stream of our management activities, and coming up with this small sample of the constant levels of action which are going on within the Company, you might get some impression of the broad and necessary continuous surge of activity aimed directly at improving profits.

HOW ITT TIGHTENS ITS SPREADING NET*

The Brussels reckoning comes once a month. Next Tuesday, 60 men will crowd around a 50-ft. conference table, barren of ashtrays but bristling with bottles of soda water. The mood, as always, will be electric. With the air of a surgeon, Harold S. Geneen will begin another of his famous and relentless probes for soft spots in the European theater of International Telephone & Telegraph Corp.'s vast empire.

This month the men on the griddle—buttressed by a 2-in.-thick "bluebook" of financial data that spew from a computer each month—will fire back some heartening news.

F. J. "Tim" Dunleavy, head of ITT Europe, together with his 25-man staff and the managing directors of ITT Europe affiliates, are making a swift rebound from the same blow last year that has ITT's competitors still reeling: a serious downturn in Europe's consumer electronics markets.

The recovery is a stunning example of modern U.S. management techniques—particularly financial management—at work in Europe, where big companies often couple fine technology and modern plant with archaic financial methods that date from the counting house.

Administration. Set up in 1960 to coordinate an amorphous sprawl of enterprises, ITT Europe is now the administrative center for 50 manufacturers and a flock of other types of companies in Europe, Africa, and the Middle East.

Tying the organization together is ITT Europe's "business plan," an elaborately detailed map of targets and timetables spanning two years and projected ahead to the fifth. It is rewritten every year and reviewed every month; in some critical areas—currently consumer product lines, employment, and inventories—it is reviewed weekly.

The business plan, reflecting Geneen's financial background and unique on the European scene, pushes financial goals down through the organization—even to the shop foreman. While most European executives tend to think about earnings on a corporate or continental scale, ITT managers worry about the profit on each individual product line.

Higher return. The plan also emphasizes the U.S. concept of asset reduction—and thus increased return on assets. It constantly presses managers to keep inventories and receivables low and to use borrowed money instead of cash. Since 1962 ITT Europe has reduced assets from $1.07 per sales dollar to 82¢. Said Dr. Gerhard Simons, who managed the business planning process: "If we had several hundred million dollars more in receivables and inventory, at 7 percent interest, it would wipe out a lot of income."

It was the business plan's constant review and coordination of goals and progress reports that revealed the turn in German consumer markets early enough to head off disaster last year.

The first softening in such consumer items as radios and TVs came in Britain early in 1965. ITT Europe kept that year's profits up by cutting back quickly and shifting into telecommunications markets' products such as telephone equipment for government buyers.

German sag. Then, markets went bad in Germany. "In the third quarter of 1965," says Dunleavy, who became president of ITT Europe in 1964, "we faced the decision whether to go ahead with higher production to keep unit costs low, or to pull back." Peering over granddaddy half-rim glasses, he says: "We rightfully chose to cut."

By April, 1966, worse danger signals were leaping from the monthly reports: orders were off, sales forecasts were dropping, and inventories were rising.

To top it off, the telecommunications market went into a temporary tailspin. The German Bundespost, a big customer, ran into a budget squeeze. Money tightened for other clients.

ITT Europe responded by quickly cutting its 37,000-man German work force back by 7,000 and laying off another 3,000 workers outside Germany. It permanently closed three German plants for consumer products, and mothballed surplus telecommunications capacity in West Berlin.

Competitors, slow to react to the softening, compounded the problem by loading up on inventories, then hitting the market with price cuts as deep as 10 percent to 20 percent. "We would have taken a bath if we had been stuck with inventory," says Dunleavy.

Mild decline. As it was, ITT Europe's profits were off a scant 3 percent last year, according to New York securities analysts (ITT Europe itself won't talk numbers).

By contrast, the analysts figure, profits plunged 13 percent for Holland's giant Philips Lamp Co.—which to date has cut back only 6,000 of its 87,000-man Dutch work force; some 12 percent for Germany's Siemens AG; and 25 percent for AEG-Telefunken.

This year, ITT Europe's profits might rise as much as 19 percent, the analysts judge, while the forecast for rivals is that profits will keep dropping.

Aside from the nimble cutbacks, ITT Europe's financial adroitness is best seen in its other maneuver—the quick shift toward strengthening activity in telephone and military communications fields. This push has depended largely on ITT Europe's ability to invest quickly and to help customers get financing.

Quicker controls

The brass at ITT Europe is quick to concede that its early warning system wasn't early enough in ITT's harrowing brush with the downturn in Germany. The ITT control system now faces a tightening.

Two controls were added to the business plan in 1965, during the consumer downturn in Britain:

For each product line, managers had to outline actions to meet the goals set out in the plan—with timetables and the name of the man responsible for each action.

Again for each product line, managers had to present contingency plans showing short-term moves they could make in case of sudden developments.

Now, new early warning tools are going into the upcoming business plan—including leading indicators that apply to markets for each product. This week, economists from all ITT Europe companies meet in Brussels with ITT Corp.'s economic advisor, former Presidential adviser Raymond Saulnier, to work out these indicators.

THEY CALL IT "GENEEN U."*

Graduates of Harold Geneen's ITT hold top jobs throughout U.S. industry. Should Geneen be blamed for the turnover? Or praised for creating so many top executives?

Even those who hate the man admit he's a genius. He gives his executives all the opportunity they could ask to prove themselves, along with salaries and bonuses they never dreamed of making; and still many of them quit.

---

* Reprinted by permission of *Forbes* Magazine from the May 1, 1968, issue.

Geneen looks very much like the harried businessman who lives next door, of medium height—perhaps 5 feet 10 inches—getting a trifle flabby in spite of an almost fanatical daily devotion to the Royal Canadian Air Force Exercises, his shoulders a bit stooped from bending over a desk. And yet he's a most uncommon man. What makes him uncommon is not merely that he's such a complex personality or that he has created a great conglomerate. Complex personalities are everywhere in the complex corporate world of today and others have created conglomerates, too. But in a time when huge prosperity has created opportunities for entrepreneurs to flourish, for ambitious men to achieve, probably no other man has achieved as much as Geneen. So contagious is his energy and enthusiasm that in a few short years he has sent forth into the corporate world literally dozens of men who today either head companies of their own or hold high positions in other great corporations.[1]

Dissenting opinions

Geneen has detractors. They say he develops so many top executives for other corporations only because he can't hold them himself: He either fires them or drives them so hard they finally decide that no amount of money is worth it. So Geneen's detractors say. There is some truth in both these charges. Many executives with whom *Forbes* talked agreed he sent his staff in to put pressure on John Lobb because he became too strong and was being mentioned as a potential ITT president. He fired William Duke when Duke could not solve ITT's long-range problems in defense fast enough to suit Geneen.

The charge about Lobb may be questionable, but there's no question that Geneen is hard to work for. *I left because of hellish pressure I could not endure,* says John T. Naylor, former head of ITT's South American operations and now president of Telectronic Systems, a Philippine telegraph and telephone company. *I did not want a premature heart attack.*

William Marx, former No. Two man at ITT and now executive vice president of Celanese, says he left Geneen because *the pace, the pressure was frenetic. I couldn't see ITT as the sole purpose in life. The environment was a painstaking*

---

[1] These men include Glenn Bailey, Chairman and President, Keene Corporation; Gerhard Andlinger, Chairman, Esterline; and George Strichman—Chairman and President, Colt Industries. The presidents are Richard Griebel, P. Ballantine and Sons; John Lobb, Crucible Steel; Martin H. Dubilier, Kearney-National; Dr. William Duke, Whittaker Corporation; Neil Firestone, Turner Corporation; Chris Witting, Crouse-Hindz Co., and Harry Bowes, McCall Corporation. . . . ex-ITT men are presidents of perhaps half a dozen other major companies or their subsidiaries. In addition, ex-ITT men hold executive vice presidencies at Celanese, Colt Industries, and Electronic Associates. Others hold important vice presidencies in scores of companies, including Singer, General Dynamics, and General Electric. The controller of Litton Industries comes from ITT.

one in which you have to give your all. In my case, it was a problem of never getting home, of never seeing my family. I don't think men work for bread alone.

I can work as hard as he can, but I have a family and Hal has none, says Ballantine's Dick Griebel. *He goes too far—drives people to the wall. Then, suddenly, no matter how much he pays them, the money becomes unimportant.* That is true of outsiders as well as insiders. The consulting firm of McKinsey & Co. now refuses to work for him.

The thing about Geneen is that he doesn't know there is a clock, says Robert S. Alexander, now vice president of Zenith. *He will start a meeting at 5 and maybe realize at 8:30 that it's still running and maybe he ought to send out for some sandwiches and maybe break up at midnight. There aren't many people I know who do that.*

Alexander enjoyed working for Geneen, and part of him obviously wanted to remain in the excitement of ITT. *The reason I left was his schedule—the all-day and all-night meeting,* he says. *My wife and I had to give up all our friends; all we could possibly have were ITT associations. He'd call you for a one-day meeting in Brussels tomorrow. I ended up with a house in Chicago, a house in California, an apartment in New York—and I didn't live in any of them. He's still my friend and I admire him greatly. But I told him, "If you want to know the life I don't want to lead, all you have to do is look at your own."* He said, *"Well, you couldn't have put it any clearer."*

The fact remains that this pressure he puts on men is not the reason for his success: Geneen is successful because he knows how to get more out of people than most other bosses do. Says Gerry Andlinger: *He sets almost unattainable standards that either stretch a person or break him. It stretched me.*

He forces people to think who have never thought in their lives, says Dick Griebel. *Part of it is for survival.*

Geneen made me believe that there is no such thing as impossible, says Lobb, who reports that earnings of all 22 ITT acquisitions in his area were at least doubled within two years.

Andlinger again: *He taught me never to give up. If Mr. Geneen says you should aim for $1 million and you know only half a million dollars is possible, you shoot for $2 million. You come back from Brazil without a contract and he'll say, "Did you see the President?" You think, "What me? Me see the President and be thought a brash young man?" But you go back and you see the President and you get the contract.*

Gambling on people

One of the reasons for Geneen's success both in running ITT and in creating executives for other corporations is the fact that he's willing to gamble on a man. He'll spot a man in his 30s or early 40s working for another company, a man who has talent but who—given the plodding road to advancement in most companies—can't hope to become even a vice president for at least ten years, and offer him a job running an ITT division, being his own boss, at a salary he didn't hope to make in 15 years. To get Dr. Louis Rader, who stayed with him two years, Geneen gave him a salary of $86,500, a bonus of $20,000, plus stock options and a seat on the board. At General Electric, where he was a general manager, Rader had been making about $45,000. Joseph Bokan, now a vice president at Keene Corp., also joined ITT at $35,000 versus his GE salary of $23,000. John Graham left Radio Corp. of America to go to ITT for what he calls "a substantial increase." Kearney-National's Dubilier says: "Geneen will pay a man 50 percent more than he can possibly make anywhere else."

Geneen, incidentally, uses money to attract not only people, but companies as well. His favorite technique for making sure that managements will favor being acquired by ITT is offering management five-year contracts and huge increases. His recent arrangement with Sheraton Corp. is typical. ITT has entered into five-year contracts with Sheraton's top three officers. The trio will be paid a total of $315,000 a year versus their pre-ITT salaries of $172,000. Small wonder so few managements object to being acquired by ITT. Happiest of all are executives about

But more important than money in attracting people is the opportunity that Geneen offers. Says a former ITT executive, now president of his own company, a man who frankly dislikes Geneen: "The rest of my life I'm going to be grateful to that character. Other companies like General Motors or General Electric never would have given me line (operating) experience at my age. He gambled on me, and much as I dislike the man, I'm grateful to him. He's a genius, one of the most brilliant industrialists who has ever come on the American business scene."

In one month, Geneen hired three men from McKinsey. He took four executives with him from Raytheon including Ballantine's Griebel and George Strichman, now chairman of Colt Industries. He plucked Glenn Bailey from Chrysler. Bailey, who is now president of Keene Corp., was vegetating at Chrysler. He desperately wanted line experience, because he someday wanted to run his own show, but, despite his intelligence and ambition and a degree from the Harvard Business School, he couldn't get it. He was too young (only 34). Geneen took a chance on him and put him on the ITT staff. Two years later Bailey got his chance in operations.

Says Celanese's Marx: *That's Geneen's way. He takes a chance on young men who have apparent potential but who have not yet had a chance to demonstrate it. He makes them capable executives. Or they make themselves capable executives. That's closer.*

Door to opportunity

Especially in his early years, when he was in a hurry and had no time to wait for inexperienced men to grow, Geneen pried proven executives from other companies. Zenith Vice President Robert Alexander and Crucible President John Lobb were heads of their own companies when they came to work for Geneen. More recently, Allegheny President Charles Ireland quit his company to move into ITT. Geneen has taken scores of executives from the ranks of General Electric.

Geneen and Bill Marx really combed American industry, says John Graham, an ex-ITT vice president for North America, and now a vice president at General Dynamics. *The first group they took in was of outstanding quality. They looked for bright people with proven reputations.*

Geneen gets the people, but, even more important, he makes them— if they don't break first. For he gives them room to grow. His technique is a strange and contradictory one. He gives them authority, at the same time prodding them, pushing them, badgering them, even screaming at them. The men who have worked for him describe his technique best.

Henry Bowes, now president of McCall Corp. says: *He expected me to put my neck on the line. This was one of his greatest secrets. It's not hard to say we ought to do thus and so, but it's very hard to say that if we do thus we'll increase our business 25 percent and our profits 12 percent.*

Alexander says: *Geneen would assign responsibility and expect you to do it and not run back to him for any little question. He makes you make the decisions and get a job done. He doesn't care how you accomplish something and as long as it is running according to plan you'll have very little communication with the man. But as soon as it's not running according to plan, then you'd better prepare to have a good reason why not and a good suggestion about how to get it back on the track. He expects you to do that and cry for help, too—if you need it—before the ship is sunk.*

What is unusual about Geneen is the detail he demands. He demands monthly reports from all divisions. He discusses them at monthly meetings attended by his key staff people and his important line people. The monthly reports have to include not only major items on why a division is above or below quota, but items as minor as a lost order. To ensure that the reports are made in such detail, Geneen has a staff that is constantly dropping in on operations to check on things. And line people know that if Geneen finds out anything negative about a man's operation, no matter how petty, from anyone else but the man himself, he explodes; so the reports are highly detailed.

Because Geneen might ask a dozen questions on even a minor item in a report, Geneen executives are forced to pay more attention to details than is the case in other companies. Each month Geneen reads all the monthly reports, which fill a book ten inches thick. He has a photographic memory and total recall—not just for numbers but for technical details.

So on one hand, Geneen executives have a good deal of freedom and responsibility. On the other, Geneen is always there, always probing for weak spots. When he detects trouble, he moves in fast. He will frequently get involved in decisions himself. "You could almost call it management by detail," says General Dynamics' Graham. "There are more problems— some quite minor—solved at a higher level in ITT than any other large company I know of."

In some of the descriptions of him, Geneen sounds almost sadistic in the way he drives men. Most who know him, however, agree that it is results he is after, not the feeling of power. Says Geneen: "I delegate, but don't abdicate. I'm no laissez-faire, let-me-know-how-things-are-in-six-months guy. I want to know what's going on. I don't want some proud guy to get into his own Vietnam and then suddenly hand me his resignation. Hell, his resignation can't bring back the $10 million he'd lose. That's why I make everyone tell me about red-flag areas—spots where trouble may be brewing." "He doesn't play politics," says Esterline's Andlinger. "A guy who does very well stands high with him. A guy who does poorly— well, the fall from grace is pretty immediate. In ITT you don't achieve a lot of results by trying to go after some other guys."

His admirers like to compare Geneen with management geniuses like John Patterson of National Cash Register or Alfred Sloan of General Motors. It's probably too early to know whether he'll build the kind of corporate monument they built, but he does resemble them in one way: he doesn't do things the way people are used to having them done in other companies. He's in dead earnest when he says: "Most American companies compete with each other in inefficiency. The major reason so many giant corporations stick basically to one industry is they are headed by men who couldn't run a multi-industry company." One of his favorite sayings is: "Throw away the textbook." Of his days as executive vice president of Raytheon, which he quit to join ITT, Geneen says, "Here was the problem. I was driving at high speed when every so often, without warning, somebody else would try to put their hand on the wheel."

It is this spirit that leads Geneen to throw young executives in over their heads to see if they can swim, that leads him to shrug off executive turnover, to worry very little about whether his subordinates like him as long as they perform for him. "History shows there's nothing unusual about some of the sides to Geneen," says John Lobb. "The guys who are very successful, who are way above everyone else, have got to be concentrated. That guy has got to have a forceful personality. He's got to be a little like Napoleon, like Ernie Weir who made money in steel in 1932. You can't be a nice guy and a real big winner. There are a lot of nice, soft-spoken fellows around who watch their market shares go down yearly."

Not all the men who go to work for Geneen are better off afterwards. After shooting up to become a $65,00-a-year ITT group vice president, Joseph Bokan left under pressure. Discouraged, for a while he ran a profitable but not too exciting liquor store before becoming a vice president at Keene Corp. "Until I went to work for Geneen I had a record of one success after another," says consultant Harry Beggs. "What happened to me at ITT broke that record and took something out of me."

Beggs capitalized on a Geneen quirk—he can't fire a man face to face. When Bill Marx fired him, Beggs said, "Geneen hired me himself, he'll have to fire me himself. I want to see him.' But in the year that Beggs remained on the payroll without any duties, he did not get to see Geneen once.

Others who gambled on Geneen won. Ex-McKinsey consultant, Martin Dubilier says: "Geneen got a lot out of me, but I got a lot out of Geneen. No one else would have given me the job he did at that age without any line experience." As John Lobb points out: "My operations always made more money than they were budgeted to make. Under those circumstances Geneen isn't hard to get along with."

Says Andlinger: "He sets the standards, you meet them and the rewards are fantastic—responsibility at an early age, always being given opportunity after opportunity. I became a vice president at 34. Then I took over Latin America, which is a very large group. Geneen was like a father to me. He had a lot of interest in what challenge would be right for me next." Ballantine's Griebel says, "Hal gives you a chance to either strike out or hit a home run in the world series."

Geneen did not accidentally create this environment. He had a dream, he fulfilled it. "I remember being way down in a highly structured one-industry company long ago," he says. "I couldn't get anyone to listen to my ideas. Now I wasn't asking anyone to make me president overnight. I just wanted to get some action on my ideas. I felt so frustrated, I resolved that someday I'd create an environment where a man would get a chance to contribute and I did."

Geneen has done just that. "We all learned a lot from him," says John Lobb. "Geneen demanded excellence and got his managers to insist on this quality in their subordinates." "Many of us use Geneen's techniques such as his controls, reports, and meetings," says McCall's Bowes. "His cents-per-share works like a charm. It's hard for people to visualize large amounts of money. So when people want to spend, we ask them to tell us how much it will cost in cents per share."

Scientist William Duke of Whittaker says, "He created executives by forcing men to make a decision on the basis of how it would affect earnings, return on sales and investment. There's no question I've taken bits of Geneen along with me such as the necessity to personally face up to each division manager." Crouse-Hinds President Chris Witting says, "The detailed study that Geneen constantly insists on keeps ITT just plowing along, increasing profit every quarter."

The turnover helps

Surface observers and some security analysts have criticized ITT because of the turnover of executives. The textbooks say this is a bad thing. But as General Dynamics' Graham points out, "There are a lot of companies where there hasn't been enough turnover at the top. They're bottlenecked, but no one can say that about Geneen's ITT."

Secondly, John Lobb points out that high turnover has not hurt ITT. Geneen attracts many good men as replacements and gets a lot of others from acquisitions. Thirdly, a lot of good men come to ITT because of the turnover. It means that they will have an opportunity to move up.

Surprisingly, turnover has brought ITT ambitious, aggressive men who wouldn't be career employees in anybody's company except their own. Eager to make big reputations, they've done quite a lot of good for ITT before they move on. "Every major person who went there did something that is still contributing to the growth of the company," says John Graham. "Duke brought in a lot of military work—that's a five- to seven-year cycle. Lobb cleaned out a lot of bad product lines and helped build U.S. operations. Firestone (now president of Turner Corp.) did a lot to formalize ITT manufacturing techniques." Glenn Bailey built a losing operation into one that was making an after-tax profit of $3.2 million. Dubilier took over a $25-million operation and built it into a $125-million one.

Earlier ITT alumni such as Graham, Rader, Bokan, Beggs, and Marx made moves that helped the company. They also brought a lot of good talent into the company and trained it. Many of this group are still at ITT.

Even though the turnover had not been hurting ITT, Geneen has done his best to stop it. He has raised salaries and changed his stock-option plan. "Here's the magic of it," says Geneen, "We've made it possible for you to forget the little company." He figures that an executive who stays with him could be worth over $2 million in ITT stock at retirement.

Geneen also has toned down the pressure he put on his men. He still criticizes them in front of their fellow executives, but he fights his tendency to shout at them now. And he's far more diplomatic. No one lately has seen him so mad that his nose turns white. "After I left, I heard that he calmed down very significantly," says Harry Beggs. "The board was upset about publicity on the turnover."

Geneen himself acknowledges that he has become more diplomatic. In the words of McCall's Bowes, "He mellowed as he got more control over ITT." Says Geneen: "I don't think anyone could have gone through the experience of the last nine years and not changed. Now we're much more diplomatic. When a guy is in trouble, we don't say he's stupid—we try and see how we can help him."

But of course Geneen has not changed in his ambition or the pace he sets. The more he succeeds, the more ambitious he gets. "ITT will continue to earn 10 percent more annually. That is my promise to stockholders, that is my pressure, my goal. We want it every year."

Geneen flatly denies that there are no good men left in ITT who could run it if he died. He points out he has a president's office "composed of myself, Executive Vice President Tim Dunleavy, a real leader, and Rich Bennett, a bear cat on operations."

Yet even if critics are correct and there is no strong No. Two man left in ITT, that doesn't mean ITT would be a better company if it had one. Geneen probably feels more comfortable and is more effective without one. That way he can interact directly with the young men he has running line operations. With Geneen at the top, inspiring, probing, demanding, and his young executives doing the impossible in the line jobs, ITT should continue to perform brilliantly.

In the event of Geneen's death, what? "You can't kill a big company," says John Graham. "If Geneen died tomorrow, that company would go right on. There's enough built-in momentum. There are quite a few people in the U.S. who could run the company. Specifically what will happen behind Geneen is that someone will formalize the place and it will be a much more conventional operation than it is today."

What the books will say

When the history books and novels are written, it is probable that Geneen will be criticized—as National Cash's Patterson is—for losing so many key executives. He is more likely to be remembered as a ruthless, over-powering character than as a "statesman of industry." But could statesmen of industry do the job that Geneen is doing?

HAROLD SYDNEY GENEEN FROM *WHO'S WHO 1970**

Harold Sydney Geneen—mfg. exec; b. Bournemouth, England, Jan. 22, 1910; s. S. Alexander and Aida (DeCruciani) G.; brought to U.S., 1911,

---

* Reprinted from *Who's Who in America* (36th edition) by permission of Marquis Who's Who, Inc.

naturalized (derivative), 1918; B.S., N.Y.U., 1934; LL.D. (honorary), Lafay-
ette College, PMC Colleges; m. June Elizabeth Hjelm, Dec. 1949. Accountant and analyst Mayflower Assoc., 1932–34; sr. accountant Lybrand, Ross
Bros. and Montgomery, 1934–42; chief accountant Am. Can Co., 1942–
46; director, v.p., controller Bell & Howell Co., Chgo, 1946–50; v.p., controller Jones & Laughlin Steel Corp., Pitts., 1950–56; exec. v.p., dir. Raytheon
Mfg. Co., Waltham, Mass., 1956–59; pres., chief officer, dir. International
Tel. and Tel. Corporation, 1959– , also mem. exec. com, former chmn.
bd.; dir. foreign subsidiaries, affiliated cos.; dir. Nat. Shawmut Bank. Re-
gional leader Nat. Alliance of Businessmen. Decorated grand officer Order
of Merit (Peru); commander Order of the Crown (Belgium); Grand Cross
of Civil Merit, Grand Cross of Isabella Catholic Mothers of the Americas
(Spain). Registered C.P.A., N.Y., Illinois. Mem. Am. Inst. C.P.A.s, Financial
Execs. Inst., Soc. C.P.A.s N.Y. Episcopalian. Clubs: Duquesne (Pitts.); Saint
Bartholomew Community House, Oakmont Country, Braeburn Country,
Oyster Harbours, Union League (N.Y.C.); Harvard (Boston). Office: 320
Park Av. N.Y.C. 10022.

ITT: THE VIEW FROM THE INSIDE*

ITT manages about 265 companies. Most of them make money, and
most of them make more money than they did when Harold Geneen
acquired them or inherited them. They have undergone massive—though
not often visible—changes since then. They seem to run on plans, budgets,
reports, meetings, ITT visits, and phone calls. The stories that follow
tell something of how ITT nurses and cajoles several of those companies—
from giant Hartford Fire Insurance to Groko, a tiny Dutch food company—
to produce the 10 percent to 12 percent annual earnings growth that Geneen demands.

Sheraton's James:
Teaching ITT the hotel business

You could not believe the number of meetings we were required to
attend," recalls a former Sheraton Corp. of America officer, describing
the first three years following ITT's 1967 acquisition of the Boston-based
hotel chain. "There were constant reviews. There must have been 30-
odd ITT task forces. We had reports coming out of our ears. The ITT

---

people wanted to know too much. They were overdoing it, and our people, especially operating people such as hotel managers, rebelled. We lost a lot of them before ITT saw the light."

It was an educational acquisition for ITT, however. Until it picked up such companies as Avis, Inc., Hartford Fire Insurance Co., and Sheraton, ITT was primarily a manufacturer.

"We replenish our inventory at midnight, every day," explains Howard P. "Bud" James, the man ITT eventually brought in to run Sheraton. "You close your books every night, and there's a day-to-day profit-and-loss statement. If you are free and able to make decisions, you can correct the mistakes right away."

For a year after the acquisition, ITT retained President Ernest Henderson III, son of the Sheraton founder. But Henderson was largely inactive. To no one's surprise, he left after a year and went into the nursing home business. ITT then tapped Philip L. Lowe, an investment specialist in the New York office.

He started selling off the old downtown hotels, cut out Sheraton's costly in-house architecture, engineering, and maintenance services, and kicked off a $700-million expansion into new hotels—all needed changes. But Lowe also zealously injected ITT's intensive meeting and manufacturing-derived control procedures. And the massive layoffs accompanying the services ITT terminated created bitter morale problems. Sheraton was losing money, and the debt it had incurred for the expansion threatened further losses.

Experience needed. Finally, ITT resolved that Sheraton should best be run by a hotel man. Lowe left to form an investment company. ITT moved in James, the president of the Sahara-Nevada Corp. hotel chain in Las Vegas. "They recognized the need for a professional," says James.

James demanded and was given unprecedented autonomy to run Sheraton. He reported directly to the ITT president's office, bypassing the group vice-president level. When the comptroller's office measured Sheraton's performance, James insisted that ITT distinguish between hotels operated strictly to make money and those run in part to fulfill pledges to other countries.

Another issue was Sheraton's big expansion, which Geneen himself had announced. "How soon do you want that $700 million back?" James recalls asking Harold Geneen. Geneen answered, "What do you mean?"

"Let somebody else pay for the land," James says he told him, "and stop spending hundreds of millions of dollars on real estate for company-owned properties." James urged instead that others build the hotels and that Sheraton run them under management and licensing agreements. Geneen agreed, and this basic policy change was settled before James took the job.

Reorganizing the reorganization. There were still some surprises. In May 1970, before returning to Las Vegas to pack, James stopped in Boston for a routine monthly operations review at Sheraton. He found 100 persons there—from ITT in New York, from Sheraton's Boston headquarters, and from Sheraton's divisions. They met from 8 A.M. to 11 P.M. "There were so many people," he says, "that we had to meet in a nearby hotel property."

Within a month or two, James had chopped the attendance figure at such meetings to seven—three top ITT officers, James, and his three division chiefs—and had moved the meeting to New York, where it precedes the general management meeting. Sheraton is still not profitable, says ITT President Francis M. Dunleavy, but it will be next year. "The hotels we want to stay in are much more profitable," he says. "The others are less of a loss, and the startup hotels are on plan."

ITT operatives no longer swarm over Sheraton as they did in the past. In the 13th floor executive office lobby of Sheraton's Boston headquarters, there is a new sign: "Visitors—including ITT personnel—please register."

Hartford's Schoen:
Selling insurance the ITT way

"The entrepreneur-type who wants to captain the ship won't be happy in the ITT system," says Herbert P. Schoen, president and chief executive officer of Hartford Fire Insurance Co. As top man in the pride of the ITT fleet, which contributed 26 percent of profits in 1972, 60-year-old Schoen must at least rate commander bars. He is an ITT director and meets four times a month or more with the company's undisputed captain—and only entrepreneur—Harold Geneen, who is also on the Hartford's board.

A soft-spoken, Harvard-educated lawyer, Schoen was elevated from executive vice-president in December 1972, when Henry V. Williams moved up to chairman. He has been with the Hartford for 27 years.

Even before consummation in 1970 of the big, controversial merger, the Hartford was initiated into the ITT fold. In 1969, the company asked ITT to tutor the insurer in its famous planning techniques.

Once ITT-ized, the Hartford, in turn, designed planning systems for ITT's European insurance subsidiaries. The Hartford supervises Abbey Life Insurance Co. in England, as well as other ITT insurance holdings in Europe.

Soothing disbelievers. Initially, Geneen faced stiff resistance not only from the Connecticut Insurance Dept. and the Justice Dept., but from skeptical Hartford employees as well. The settlement with Justice has been well documented, though questions about alleged political intrigues linger on. The state's insurance department, after its initial resistance, allowed the merger to go through once ITT assured it that the Hartford would keep its identity.

But there were still the disbelievers within the Hartford. To ease their apprehensions, Geneen himself made an unusual appearance at the Asylum Avenue headquarters. He pressed the flesh, asked questions, listened to presentations, learned and remembered names and faces. The doubters were converted by Geneen, who also sought to assure top management that he was going to learn the insurance business. According to Schoen, he got it down cold. Says the executive, "you only have to tell him something once."

Coincidental with the merger, the Hartford began an intensive drive to write new business. Premiums from its biggest line, property and liability insurance, have risen from $898 million in 1968 to $1.6 billion last year. The Hartford rates No. 3 in property and casualty volume, behind State Farm and Allstate.

Its competitors charge that the Hartford has been cutting rates to increase volume and improve cash flow. That claim, however, is tough to prove since the big property and casualty contracts are all tailor-written. But clearly, the Hartford is not alone in shaving rates. The whole industry has recently engaged in a rate war, but the Hartford has been in the spotlight because of its affiliation with ITT.

Capital gains. If ITT has been pushing the Hartford—and Schoen heatedly denies any such pressure—then the conglomerate must be disappointed with this year's performance. While the Hartford's business has been growing at a handsome average of 15 percent annually in the past few years, the growth of premiums written slowed to only 9.2 percent in the first half of 1973. Schoen argues that the whole industry is suffering one of its inevitable downturns, and adds: "Not even Geneen can change the cyclicality of the insurance business."

One major change at the Hartford since ITT took over is that the insurer has begun to realize hefty capital gains from its portfolio. In pre-ITT 1968, the Hartford took capital gains worth only $832,000; by contrast, in 1972, the figure was $41.8 million. As a result, fully one third of the Hartford's 1972 net income of $126.7 million came from realized capital gains, which gave ITT a hefty boost in per-share earnings.

Providing that the recent binge of new business does not come back to haunt the Hartford in the form of an avalanche of claims, and providing the stock market does not go into a deadly spiral, the insurance company should continue to contribute handsomely to its parent's bottom line. And that, after all, is why ITT has fought so hard to buy and to keep the 163-year-old insurance company.

Cannon's von Harz:

The taming of a reluctant tiger

Every November, the ex-ITT (pronounced "exit") Club meets at a Santa Ana (Calif.) restaurant for drinks. Some members claim that as many as 70 persons attend, all formerly affiliated with Cannon Electric Co., a 1963 ITT acquisition.

ITT bought the Santa Ana maker of multicontract electrical connectors from the Cannon family for $30 million. It proved difficult to swallow.

Behind the indigestion was a conflict between ITT's demand for performance and ITT's characteristically cautious avoidance of the ruinous disruptions that can accompany a bull-in-a-china-shop takeover. As part of the merger agreement, President Robert Cannon left the company, and ITT elevated Roger Bowen, then executive vice president.

But Bowen left in five months. Over the first two years under ITT, Cannon lost three of five vice presidents, many general managers, and more than half its regional sales managers. William C. Esteras, who was a divisional manager then, recalls working for "six or seven" general managers in the first 14 months.

The success of an acquisition, says Frank J. McCabe, ITT's vice president for personnel, "is often directly a function of the attitude of the previous management." McCabe suspects that Bowen never really intended to stay, which Bowen confirms.

In addition, Cannon harbored structural weaknesses that took years to overcome. ITT found Cannon locked into the peaks and valleys of the aerospace market, deriving only 20 percent of its sales from commercial customers. Further, Cannon's productivity was sub standard for ITT.

When Bowen left, ITT moved in James Yunker, then executive vice president. After four years in the job, he was moved again, to a group vice presidency. Wenzel Wochos, a longtime Cannon man, took over and stayed until he retired in 1971. Then ITT installed the current chief executive, James L. von Harz, whom ITT recruited from Transitron Electronics Corp.

On the upswing. Only with von Harz is the company showing good results. Sales have doubled to about $100 million from the 1963 level, with most of the growth in the past two years. Cannon has introduced 100 new products, 80 percent of them commercial. Cannon says it now gets 50 percent of its sales from automotive, telecommunications, and data processing markets. Despite its growth, Cannon has cut employment from 3,000 to 2,300.

Von Harz, 58, had doubted that he would like working for ITT. "At first, I just said I wasn't interested in any numbers jungle," he says he told the company when approached about the job. "As it turns out, it's not at all like the image." At his monthly meeting with his Defense-Space Group vice president, for example, "we spend only 20 percent of our time on numbers," he says. "The rest of it goes on people, products, markets, and long-range problems."

Just after the takeover, Cannon was treated to a two-month honeymoon. Cannon officers were whisked to New York, and top ITT officers, including Harold Geneen, flew out West. "Geneen recognized all of us by name," recalls James H. Anderson, then director of operations at Cannon. "You could tell he had really done his homework."

Then ITT got down to business. Continues Anderson: "New York staffers came in and filled us in on all the procedures. At about the same time, we had to get to work on our five-year and one-year plans. Maybe the hardest thing for all of us to digest was that the financial man, from then on, reported directly to New York."

PGS' Andrews:
Changing to suit the family image

The only visible indication of ITT's corporate presence in bucolic Berkeley Springs, W. Va., is a sign on U.S. Route 522. It reads simply: "PGS Corporation/A member of the ITT system/Executive offices." Moreover, PGS' 46-year-old President Hale E. Andrews says ITT "didn't ask for the sign, we put it up." But now in its sixth year under ITT control, Andrews' company is a prime example of how subtly yet significantly companies change after joining Harold Geneen's corporate family.

Until ITT's 1968 stock-swap acquisition of PGS, formally known as Pennsylvania Glass Sand Corp., the company's top management had for years come largely from two families: The Andrews and the Woods. Solid and conservative, PGS avoided debt and paid cash dividends ($1.60 per share in 1967). It is the only industrial and the biggest single employer in Berkeley Springs (pop. 875), where it has its main plant. Corporate headquarters was moved there from Lewistown, Pa., in 1965. Three years later in a major management reorganization, Andrews was promoted from executive vice president to president, succeeding his father, who became chairman. William J. Woods, who had held that post, retired but his son, William J. Woods, Jr., continued as an executive vice president.

Then ITT made its bid to take over the supplier of raw materials for glass, whose customers include Ford Motor Co., PPG Industries, Inc., and Bausch & Lomb, Inc. The younger Woods, whose family owned an estimated 7 percent of PGS' stock, was opposed to the merger. "I hated to see PGS go into that ITT conglomerate," he says. "PGS was not a sick company that needed selling out." In 1966, PGS netted an impressive $5.4 million on sales of $25.7 million.

Geneen's request. But PGS's board favored the ITT offer, which was just fine with the younger Andrews, a Princeton graduate who had joined the company in 1950 and whose family owned very little PGS stock. "I like to think of myself as a professional manager, not an owner," he says. But the disgruntled Woods resigned from PGS eight months after the June 1968 merger and founded a competitive sand glass company, Unisil Corp., which he now runs from an office on New York's Park Avenue. Some other PGS personnel have since joined him. "They [ITT] fired no one," says Andrews. "If there was any firing to do, I would do it. But I didn't."

The day after PGS became part of ITT, Geneen requested the company's business plan for 1969, and he wanted it by November. "We were changing the management of PGS when ITT came along," says Andrews. "So in some ways, it was a propitious time for us to adopt their reporting."

Initially, Andrews' only contacts with ITT were with Geneen, the office of the president, and the liaison man. "ITT did not bring an influx of its people to Berkeley Springs," says Andrews. "The opposite is true. People wondered when ITT would show up."

After the first year, J. Ronald Goode, product line vice president of ITT's natural resources group, started monitoring PGS, taking over the liaison role. "His responsibility is to see that the planning is done to assure the unit's continued growth and progress," says Andrews. PGS files a batch of reports to ITT ranging from monthly financial results to five-year plans, all kept neatly in huge brown three-ring binders. Andrews also says ITT and PGS executives meet several times a month.

"I don't think there's much question that the acquisition stimulated strategy for growth," says William H. Lawyer, PGS' director of planning and organization. PGS' growth had slowed in the early 1960s, but now Andrews says the company is "growing at a rate comparable to the 1940s and 1950s," when sales and earnings were climbing an average of 10 percent per year.

Solid commitment. By regularly reporting to ITT, says Andrews, "you're always focusing on potential opportunities and problems. And the moment you do that, you're thinking of solutions." PGS, which had 15 plants in 10 states when acquired by ITT, has completed three major expansions in five years, most of it financed internally, and will have four more completed by year-end. And it is breaking ground for a new Western plant that is scheduled to start up in 1974. "This level of activity far exceeds anything we've done in the past," says Andrews. "The climate we live in with ITT not only permits expansion, it encourages it. This is what ITT is interested in, not what our profits were last month."

"The emphasis is on new product development, and new uses for existing products," says Lawyer. PGS' lines of silica sands and fuller's earth have grown from 185 to 202 since its acquisition.

Most PGS customers see little change in the way the company does business. But one 20-year customer says: "PGS pushes us much harder for finalized contracts because, to justify expansion to ITT, it has to have the bird in the hand. It used to be just a handshake, and go ahead and build your plant because we're going to buy from you." But he concedes, "They have to sell service, and they are excellent at it, and that has not deteriorated."

"There's no question that there's a certain overhead price you must pay, being a member of ITT or any other large company," says Andrews. "But our problems all boil down to little ones." He also says, "You know how hard Geneen is reputed to be. [But] they're pleased with our rate of growth."

Groko's de Bruyn:
A total overhaul of a tiny company

Groko, a Dutch foods company, may be the most metamorphosed of any ITT acquisition. A tiny company by ITT standards, Groko has changed its product mix, distribution, markets, and management.

ITT's Continental Baking unit bought Groko in 1969 as an early move into the European food market. The company was then run by Aart Zuiderent, who founded it just after World War II at the age of 24. He had previously diversified from canning into frozen foods and had bought a minority share in a French food distribution company, René Lampe. Groko was a volume-oriented company, selling primarily to institutions and caterers. Its products had a low-quality image.

Now Groko is out of canned foods entirely and has expanded into prepared and more frozen foods. It has moved into retailing and pushed beyond the Netherlands into France and Belgium. It is now doing private-label food retailing as well, serving the supermarket chains that have begun to sweep through Europe. Groko has taken control of the French distributor, renamed Groko-France.

The new style. Zuiderent, 48, is out, but only in the ITT sense. He is now a consultant to ITT's expanding food division in Europe. A colleague describes him as "a highly individualistic, rather dictatorial, self-made man who ran the company with wet-finger planning and a financial control department consisting of a bookkeeper and two assistants." Zuiderent, who had always worked for himself, tended to toss ITT's reporting forms onto the desk of his sales manager, Leo de Bruyn.

Typically, ITT's first move as the new proprietor was to install its financial reporting system and appoint the bookkeeper comptroller. ITT introduced a rigid quality control system where there was next to none and began limited R&D. De Bruyn was made manager of the company.

The move to private labeling was partly a Groko idea, and it met some resistance in New York. It was feared that the company would become too dependent on one or two supermarket chains. So Groko now limits private label sales to any one chain to no more than 15 percent of its output.

ITT's arrival seems to have been good for Groko so far. Sales have risen 58 percent since 1970 and should be more than $10 million this year. De Bryun expects an after-tax profit margin of 3 percent or 4 percent, a respectable return in the food business.

SELECTED FINANCIAL AND OPERATING DATA

Exhibit 1

International Telephone and Telegraph Corporation and Consolidated Subsidiaries selected operating data (dollar amounts in millions except per share figures)*

	1972	1971	1970	1969	1968	1967	1966	1965	1964	1963	1962	1961	1960	1959
Sales and revenues	$8,556.8	7,345.8	6,364.5	5,474.7	4,066.5	2,760.6	2,121.3	1,782.9	1,542.1	1,414.1	1,090.2	930.5	811.5	765.6
Income before extraordinary items†	$ 476.6	406.8	353.3	234.0	180.2	119.2	89.9	76.1	63.2	52.4	40.7	36.1	30.6	29.0
Earnings per share before extraordinary items‡	$ 3.80	3.45	3.17	2.90	2.58	2.27	2.04	1.79	1.55	1.35	1.21	1.09	.98	.95
Return on stockholders equity	% 13.7	13.3	13.0	11.8	12.2	11.7	11.5	10.8	9.9	9.1	8.6	8.0	7.3	7.0
Gross plant additions	$ 718.4	653.6	615.2	513.2	362.1	238.1	168.0	145.6	119.3	123.2	114.6	105.3	67.0	64.0
Provision for depreciation	$ 265.9	231.1	210.5	190.2	158.3	116.1	73.9	63.7	50.7	39.4	30.8	31.3	25.1	27.4
R&D expenditures§	$ 328.0	288.0	257.0	236.0	210.0	210.0	220.0	182.0	174.0	170.0	150.0	131.0	n.a.‖	n.a.‖

* The above data are as reported in the ITT Annual Reports for the respective years, except that earnings per share amounts have been adjusted for 2-for-1 stock split effective January 26, 1968.

† Extraordinary items in 1972, 1971, 1968, 1967, 1961, and 1960 amounted to $6.7 ($70.0), $12.2, $3.5, $7.6 and $7.9 million respectively.

‡ On a fully diluted basis, earnings per share before extraordinary items for 1972 and 1971 were $3.72 and $3.36 respectively.

§ ITT makes no deferrals of R&D expenditures; income is charged with all costs of such activities during the period when the costs are incurred.

‖ n.a. = not available.

Exhibit 2
Revenues and net income by principal product groups—1971 and 1972 (dollar amounts in millions)

	Sales and revenues				Income†			
	1972		1971*		1972		1971*	
Manufacturing:								
Telecommunication equipment	$1,909	22%	$1,588	21%	$111	23%	$ 71	17%
Industrial products	1,562	18	1,409	19	61	13	58	14
Automotive and consumer products	1,008	12	864	11	43	9	36	8
Natural resources	355	4	313	4	38	8	28	7
Defense and space programs	469	6	469	6	11	2	11	2
	5,303	62	4,643	61	264	55	204	48
Consumer and business services:								
Food processing and services	1,013	12	971	13	6	1	19	4
Consumer services	602	7	553	7	13	3	12	3
Telecommunication operations	186	2	173	2	26	6	24	6
Business and financial services	413	5	387	5	28	6	24	6
Hartford Fire	—		—		126	26	105	24
	2,214	26	2,084	27	199	42	184	43
Divestible operations (all or part of earnings may be replaced by reinvestment of proceeds):								
Under consent decrees	1,040	12	937	12	14	3	33	8
Chilean companies	—		—		—		6	1
	1,040	12	937	12	14	3	39	9
Total	$8,557	100%	$7,664	100%	$477	100%	$427	100%

* Restated for pooling of interests in 1972.
† Excludes gain in 1972 on divestments under consent decrees of $6.7 million or $.05 per common share and provision in 1971 for losses on investment in Chilean operations of $70 million or $.57 per common share.

Case 5–2
Texana Petroleum Corporation
Jay W. Lorsch, Paul R. Lawrence, James A. Garrison

During the summer of 1966, George Prentice, the newly designated Executive Vice President for domestic operations of the Texana Petroleum Corporation, was devoting much of his time to thinking about improving the combined performance of the five product divisions reporting to him (see Exhibit 1). His principal concern was that corporate profits were not reflecting the full potential contribution which could result from the close technological interdependence of the raw materials utilized and produced by these divisions. The principal difficulty, as Prentice saw it, was that the division general managers reporting to him were not working well together:

As far as I see it, the issue is where do we make the money for the corporation? Not how do we beat the other guy. Nobody is communicating with anybody else at the general manager level. In fact they are telling a bunch of secrets around here.

Exhibit 1
Texana Petroleum Company—partial organization chart, 1966

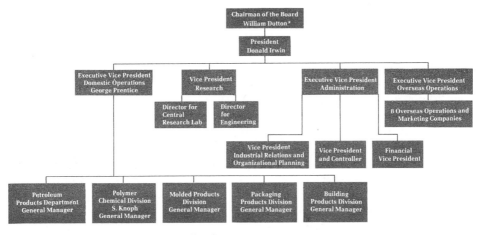

* Names included for persons mentioned in the case.

RECENT CORPORATE HISTORY

The Texana Petroleum Corporation was one of the early major producers and marketers of petroleum products in the southwest United States. Up until the early 1950s, Texana had been almost exclusively in the business of processing and refining crude oil and in selling petroleum products through a chain of company operated service stations in the southwestern United States and in Central and South America. By 1950 company sales had risen to approximately $500 million with accompanying growth in profits. About 1950, however, Texana faced increasingly stiff competition at the retail service station level from several larger national petroleum companies. As a result, sales volume declined sharply during the early 1950s and by 1955 sales had fallen to only $300 million and the company was operating at just above the break-even point.

At this time, because of his age, Roger Holmes, who had been a dominant force in the company since its founding, retired as President and Chief Executive Officer. He was replaced by Donald Irwin, 49, who had been a senior executive with a major chemical company. William Dutton, 55, was appointed Chairman of the Board to replace the retiring Board Chairman. Dutton had spent his entire career with Texana. Prior to his appointment as Chairman he had been Senior Vice President for Petroleum Products, reporting to Holmes.

Irwin and Dutton, along with other senior executives, moved quickly to solve the problems facing Texana. They gradually divested the company's retail outlets and abandoned the domestic consumer petroleum markets. Through both internal development and acquisition they expanded and rapidly increased the company's involvement in the business of processing petroleum for chemical and plastics products. In moving in this direction they were rapidly expanding on initial moves made by Texana in 1949, when the company built its first chemical processing plant and began marketing these products. To speed the company's growth in these areas, Irwin and Dutton selected aggressive general managers for each division and gave them a wide degree of freedom in decision making. Top management's major requirement was that each division general manager create a growing division with a satisfactory return on investment capital. By 1966 top management had reshaped the company so that in both the domestic and foreign market it was an integrated producer of chemicals and plastic materials. In foreign operations the company continued to operate service stations in Latin America and in Europe. This change in direction was successful and by 1966 company sales had risen to $750 million, with a healthy rise in profit.

In spite of this success, management believed that there was a need for an increase in return on invested capital. The financial and trade press, which had been generous in its praise of the company's recovery, was still critical of the present return on investment, and top management shared this concern. Dutton, Irwin, and Prentice were in agreement that one important method of increasing profits was to take further advantage of the potential cost savings which could come from increased coordination between the domestic operating divisions, as they developed new products, processes, and markets.

DOMESTIC ORGANIZATION, 1966

The product division's reports to Mr. Prentice represented a continuum of producing and marketing activities from production and refining of crude oil to the marketing of several types of plastics products to industrial consumers. Each division was headed by a general manager. While there was some variation in the internal organizational structure of the several divisions, they were generally set up along functional lines (manufacturing, sales, research and development). Each division also had its own controller and engineering activities, although these were supported and augmented by the corporate staff. While divisions had their own research effort, there was also a Central Research Laboratory at the corporate level, which carried on longer-range research of a more fundamental nature that was outside the scope of the activities of any of the product divisions.

The *Petroleum Products Division* was the remaining nucleus of the company's original producing and refining activities. It supplied raw materials to the Polymer and Chemicals Division and also sold refining products under long-term contracts to other petroleum companies. In the early and mid-1950s this division's management had generated much of the company's revenue and profits through its skill in negotiating these agreements. In 1966 top corporate management felt that this division's management had accepted its role as a supplier to the rest of the corporation, and felt that there were harmonious relations between it and its sister divisions.

The *Polymer and Chemicals Division* was developed internally during the late 1940s and early 50s as management saw its share of the consumer petroleum market declining. Under the leadership of Seymour Knoph (who had been General Manager for several years) and his predecessor (who was in 1966 Executive Vice President—Administration) the division had rapidly developed a line of chemical and polymer compounds derived from petroleum raw materials. Most of the products of this division were manufactured under licensing agreement or were materials the formulation of which was well understood. Nevertheless, technical personnel in the division had developed an industry-wide reputation for their ability to develop new and improved processes. Top management of the division took particular pride in this ability. From the beginning, the decisions of what products to manufacture were based to a large extent upon the requirements of the Molded and Packaging Products Divisions. However, Polymer and Chemicals Division executives had always attempted to market these same products to external customers, and had been highly successful. These external sales were extremely important to Texana since they assured a large enough volume of operation to process a broad product line of polymer chemicals profitably. As the other divisions had grown, they had required a larger proportion of the division's capacity, which meant that Polymer and Chemicals Division managers had to reduce their commitment to external customers.

The *Molded Products Division* was also an internally developed division, which had been formed in 1951. Its products were a variety of molded plastic products ranging from toys and household items to automotive and electronic parts. This division's major strengths were its knowledge of molding technology and particularly its marketing ability. While it depended upon the Polymer and Chemicals Division for its raw materials, its operations were largely independent of those of the Packaging Products and Building Products Divisions.

The *Packaging Products Division* was acquired in 1952. Its products were plastic packaging materials, including films, cartons, bottles, etc. All of these products were marketed to industrial customers. Like the Molded Products Division, the Packaging Division depended on the Polymer and Chemicals Division as a source of raw materials, but was largely independent of other end-product divisions.

The *Building Products Division* was acquired in 1963 to give Texana a position in the construction materials market. The division produced and marketed a variety of insulation roofing materials and similar products to the building trade. It was a particularly attractive acquisition for Texana, because prior to the acquisition it had achieved some success with plastic products for insulation and roofing materials. Although the plastic products accounted for less than 20 percent of the total division sales in 1965, plans called for these products to account for over 50 percent of division sales in the next five years. Its affiliation with Texana gave this division a stronger position in plastic raw materials through the Polymer and Chemicals Division.

Selection and recruitment of management personnel

The rapid expansion of the corporation into these new areas had created the need for much additional management talent, and top management had not hesitated to bring new men in from outside the corporation, as well as advancing promising younger men inside Texana. In both the internally developed and acquired divisions most managers had spent their career inside the division, although some top division managers were moved between divisions or into corporate positions.

In speaking about the type of men he had sought for management positions, Donald Irwin described his criterion in a financial publication:

We don't want people around who are afraid to move. The attraction of Texana is that it gives the individual responsibilities which aren't diluted. It attracts the fellow who wants a challenge.

Another corporate executive described Texana managers:

It's a group of very tough-minded, but considerate, gentlemen with an enormous drive to get things done.

Another manager, who had been with Texana for his entire career, and who considered himself to be different from most Texana managers, described the typical Texana manager as follows:

Texana attracts a particular type of person. Most of these characteristics are personal characteristics rather than professional ones. I would use terms such as cold, unfeeling, aggressive, and extremely competitive, but not particularly loyal to the organization. He is loyal to dollars, his own personal dollars. I think this is part of the communication problem. I think this is done on purpose. The selection procedures lead in this direction. I think this is so because of contrast with the way the company operated ten years ago. Of course I was at the plant level at that time. But today the attitude I have described is also in the plants. Ten years ago the organization was composed of people who worked together for the good of the organization, because they wanted to. I don't think this is so today.

Location of division facilities

The Petroleum Products, Polymer and Chemicals, and the Packaging Products Divisions had their executive offices located on separate floors of the Texana headquarters building in the Chicago "Loop." The plants and research and development facilities of these divisions were spread out across Oklahoma, Texas, and Louisiana. The Molded Products Division had its headquarters, research and development facilities, and a major plant in an industrial suburb of Chicago. This division's other plants were at several locations in the Middle West and East Coast. The Building Products Division's headquarters and major production and technical facilities were located in Fort Worth, Texas. All four divisions shared sales offices in major cities from coast to coast.

Evaluation and control of division performance

The principal method of controlling and evaluating the operations of these divisions was the semiannual review of division plans and the approval of major capital expenditures by the executive committee.[1] In reviewing performance against plans, members of the executive committee placed almost sole emphasis on the division's actual return on investment against budget. Corporate executives felt that this practice together with the technological interdependence of the divisions created many disputes about transfer pricing.

In addition to these regular reviews corporate executives had frequent discussions with division executives about their strategies, plans, and operations. It had been difficult for corporate management to strike the proper balance in guiding the operations for the divisions. This problem was particularly acute with regard to the Polymer and Chemicals Division, because of its central place in the corporation's product line. One corporate staff member explained his view of the problem:

> *This whole matter of communications between the corporate staff and the Polymer and Chemicals Division has been a fairly difficult problem. Corporate management used to contribute immensely to this by trying to get into the nuts and bolts area within the Polymer and Chemicals organization, and this created serious criticisms; however, I think they have backed off in this manner.*

A second corporate executive, in discussing this matter for a trade publication report, put the problem this way:

> *We're trying to find the middle ground. We don't want to be a holding company, and with our diversity we can't be a highly centralized corporation.*

Executive vice president—domestic operations

In an effort to find this middle ground the position of Executive Vice President—Domestic Operations was created in early 1966, and George Prentice was its first occupant. Prior to this change, there had been two Senior Domestic Vice Presidents—one in charge of the Petroleum and Polymer and Chemicals Divisions and the other in charge of the end-use divisions. Mr. Prentice had been Senior Vice President in charge of the end-use divisions before the new position was created. He had held that position for only two years, having come to it from a highly successful marketing career with a competitor.

At the time of his appointment one press account described Mr. Prentice

---

[1] The executive committee consisted of Messrs. Dutton, Irwin, and Prentice, as well as the Vice President of Research, Executive Vice President—Administration, and the Executive Vice President of Foreign Operations.

as "hard-driving, aggressive, and ambitious—an archetype of the self-actuated dynamo Irwin has sought out."

Shortly after taking his new position Prentice described the task before him:

I think the corporation wants to integrate its parts better and I am here because I reflect this feeling. We can't be a bunch of entrepreneurs around here. We have got to balance discipline with entrepreneurial motivation. This is what we were in the past, just a bunch of entrepreneurs and if they came in with ideas we would get the money, but now our dollars are limited, and especially the Polymer and Chemical boys haven't been able to discipline themselves to select from within ten good projects. They just don't seem to be able to do this, and so they come running in here with all ten good projects which they say we have to buy, and they get upset when we can't buy them all.

This was the tone of my predecessors (Senior Vice Presidents). All of them were very strong on being entrepreneurs. I am going to run it different. I am going to take a marketing and capital orientation. As far as I can see, there is a time to compete and a time to collaborate, and I think right now there has been a lack of recognition in the Polymer and Chemicals executive suite that this thing has changed.

Other views of domestic interdivisional relations

Executives within the Polymer and Chemicals Divisions, in the end-use divisions, and at the corporate level, shared Prentice's view that the major breakdown in interdivisional relations was between the Polymer and Chemicals Division and the end-use divisions. Executives in the end-use divisions made these typical comments about the problem:

I think the thing we have got to realize is that we are wedded to the Polymer and Chemicals Division whether we like it or not. We are really tied up with them. And just as we would with any outside supplier or with any of our customers, we will do things to maintain their business. But because they feel they have our business wrapped up they do not reciprocate in turn. Now let me emphasize that they have not arbitrarily refused to do the things that we are requiring, but there is a pressure on them for investment projects and we are low man on the pole. And I think this could heavily jeopardize our chances for growth.

*   *   *   *   *

I would say our relationships are sticky, and I think this is primarily because we think our reason for being is to make money, so we try to keep Polymer and Chemicals as an arm's length supplier. For example, I cannot see just because it is a Polymer and Chemicals product, accepting millions of pounds of very questionable material. It takes dollars out of our pocket, and we are very profit-centered.

*   *   *   *   *

The big frustration, I guess, and one of our major problems, is that you can't get help from them [Polymer and Chemicals]. You feel they are not interested in what you are doing, particularly if it doesn't have a large return for them. But as far as I am concerned this has to become a joint venture relationship, and this is getting to be real sweat with us. We are the guys down below yelling for help. And they have got to give us some relief.

*   *   *   *   *

My experience with the Polymer and Chemicals Division is that you cannot trust what they say at all, and even when they put it in writing you can't be absolutely sure that they are going to live up to it.

*   *   *   *   *

Managers within the Polymer and Chemicals Division expressed similar sentiments:

Personally, right now I have the feeling that the divisions' interests are growing farther apart. It seems that the divisions are going their own way. For example, we are a Polymer producer but the molding division wants to be in a special area, so that means they are going to be less of a customer to us, and there is a whole family of plastics being left out that nobody's touching, and this is bearing on our program. . . . We don't mess with the Building Products Division at all, either. They deal in small volumes. Those that we are already making we sell to them, those that we don't make we can't justify making because of the kinds of things we are working with. What I am saying is that I don't think the corporation is integrating, but I think we ought to be, and this is one of the problems of delegated divisions. What happens is that an executive heads this up and goes for the place that makes the most money for the division, but this is not necessarily the best place from a corporate standpoint.

*   *   *   *   *

We don't have as much contact with sister divisions as I think we should. I have been trying to get a liaison with guys in my function but it has been a complete flop. One of the problems is that I don't know who to call on in these other divisions. There is no table of organization, nor is there any encouragement to try and get anything going. My experience has been that all of these operating divisions are very closed organizations. I know guys up the line will say that I am nuts about this. They say to just call over and I will get an answer. But this always has to be a big deal, and it doesn't happen automatically, and hurts us.

The comments of corporate staff members describe these relationships and the factors they saw contributing to the problem:

Right now I would say there is an iron curtain between the Polymer and Chemicals Division and the rest of the corporation. You know, we tell our divisions they are responsible, autonomous groups, and the Polymer and Chemicals Division took it very seriously. However, when you are a three quarter billion dollar company, you've got to be coordinated, or the whole thing is going to fall apart—it can be no other way. The Domestic Executive Vice President thing has been a big step forward to improve this, but I would say it hasn't worked out yet.

*   *   *   *   *

The big thing that is really bothering [the Polymer and Chemicals Division] is that they think they have to go develop all new markets on their own. They are going to do it alone independently, and this is the problem they are faced with. They have got this big thing, that they want to prove that they are a company all by themselves and not rely upon packaging or anybody else.

*   *   *   *   *

Polymer and Chemicals Division executives talked about the effect of this drive for independence of the divisional operating heads on their own planning efforts:

The Polymer and Chemicals Division doesn't like to communicate with the corporate staff. This seems hard for us, and I think the [a recent major proposal] was a classic example of this. That plan, as it was whipped up by the Polymer and Chemicals Division has massive implications for the corporation both in expertise and in capital. In fact, I think we did this to be a competitive one-up on the rest of our sister divisions. We wanted to be the best-looking division in the system, but we carried it to an extreme. In this effort, we wanted to show that we had developed this concept completely on our own. . . . Now I think a lot of our problems with it stemmed from this intense desire we have to be the best in this organization.

*   *   *   *   *

Boy, a big doldrum around here was shortly after Christmas (1965) when they dropped out a new plant, right out of our central plan, without any appreciation of the importance of this plant to the whole Polymer and Chemicals Division's growth. . . . Now we have a windfall and we are back in business on this new plant. But for a while things were very black and everything we had planned and everything we had built our patterns on were out. In fact, when we put this plan together, it never really occurred to us that we were going to get it turned down, and I'll bet we didn't even put the plans together in such a way as to really reflect the importance of this plant to the rest of the corporation.

A number of executives in the end-use divisions attributed the interdivisional problems to different management practices and assumptions within the Polymer and Chemicals Division. An executive in the packaging division made this point:

We make decisions quickly and at the lowest possible level, and this is tremendously different from the rest of Texana. I don't know another division like this in the rest of the corporation.
Look at what Sy Knoph has superfluous to his operation compared to ours.

These are the reasons for our success. You've got to turn your guys loose and not breathe down their necks all the time. We don't slow our people down with staff. Sure, you may work with a staff, the wheels may grind, but they sure grind slow.

Also, we don't work on detail like the other divisions do. Our management doesn't feel they need the detail stuff. Therefore, they're [Polymer and Chemical] always asking us for detail which we can't supply, our process doesn't generate it and their process requires it, and this always creates problems with the Polymer and Chemicals Division. But I'll be damned if I am going to have a group of people running between me and the plant, and I'll be goddamned if I am going to clutter up my organization with all the people that Knoph has got working for him. I don't want this staff, but they are sure pushing it on me.

This comment from a molding division manager is typical of many about the technical concerns of the Polymer and Chemicals Division management:

Historically, even up to the not-too-distant past, the Polymer and Chemicals Division was considered a snake pit as far as the corporate people were concerned. This was because the corporate people were market-oriented and Polymer and Chemicals Division was technically run and very much a manufacturing effort. These two factors created a communication barrier, because to really understand the Polymer and Chemicals Division problems, they felt that you had to have a basic appreciation of the technology and all the interrelationships.

Building on this strong belief, the Polymer and Chemicals Division executives in the past have tried to communicate in technical terms, and this just further hurt the relationship, and it just did not work. Now they are coming up with a little bit more business or commercial orientation, and they are beginning to appreciate that they have got to justify the things they want to do in a business or commercial orientation, and they are beginning to appreciate that they have got to justify the things they want to do in a business sense rather than just a technical sense. This also helps the problem of maintaining their relationships with the corporation as most of the staff is nontechnical; however, this has changed a little bit in that more and more technical people have been coming on and this has helped from the other side.

They work on the assumption in the Polymer and Chemicals Division that you have to know the territory before you can be an effective manager. You have got to be an operating guy to contribute meaningfully to their problems. However, their biggest problem is this concentration on technical solutions to their problems. This is a thing that has boxed them in the most trouble with the corporation and the other sister divisions.

These and other executives also pointed to another source of conflict between the Polymer and Chemicals Division and other divisions. This was the question of whether the Polymer and Chemicals Division should develop into a more independent marketer, or whether it should rely more heavily on the end-use divisions to "push" its products to the market.

Typical views of this conflict are the following comments by end-use division executives:

The big question I have about Polymer and Chemicals is what is their strategy going to be? I can understand them completely from a technical standpoint, this is no problem. I wonder what is the role of this company? How is it going to fit into what we and others are doing? Right now, judging from the behavior I've seen, Polymer and Chemicals could care less about what we are doing in terms of integration of our markets or a joint approach to them.

* * * * *

I think it is debatable whether the Polymer and Chemicals Division should be a new product company or not. Right now we have an almost inexhaustible appetite for what they do and do well. As I see it, the present charter is fine. However, that group is very impatient, aggressive, and they want to grow, but you have got to grow within guidelines. Possibly the Polymer and Chemicals Division is just going to have to learn to hang on the coattails of the other divisions, and do just what they are doing now, only better.

* * * * *

I think the future role of the Polymer and Chemicals Division is going to be, at any one point in time for the corporation, that if it looks like a product is needed, they will make it. . . . They are going to be suppliers because I will guarantee you that if the moment comes and we can't buy it elsewhere, for example, then I darn well know they are going to make it for us regardless of what their other commitments are. They are just going to have to supply us. If you were to put the Polymer and Chemicals Division off from the corporation, I don't think they would last a year. Without their huge captive requirements, they would not be able to compete economically in the commercial areas they are in.

A number of other executives indicated that the primary emphasis within the corporation on return on investment by divisions tended to induce, among other things, a narrow, competitive concern on the part of the various divisional managements. The comment of this division executive was typical:

As far as I can see it, we [his division and Polymer and Chemicals] are 180 degrees off on our respective charters. Therefore, when Sy Knoph talks about this big project we listen nicely and then we say, "God bless you, lots of luck," but I am sure we are not going to get involved in it. I don't see any money in it for us. It may be a gold mine for Sy but it is not for our company; and as long as we are held to the high profit standards we are, we just cannot afford to get involved. I can certainly see it might make good corporate sense for us to get it, but it doesn't make any sense in terms of our particular company. We have got to be able to show the returns in order to get continuing capital and I just can't on that kind of project. I guess what I am saying is that under the right conditions we could certainly go in but not under the present framework; we would just be dead in terms of dealing with the corporate financial structure. We just cannot get the kinds of returns on our capital that the corporation has set to get new capital. In terms of the long run, I'd like very much to see what the corporation has envisioned in terms of a hook-up between us, but right now I don't see any sense in going on. You know my career is at stake here, too.

Another divisional executive made this point more succinctly:

Personally I think that a lot more could be done from a corporate point of view and this is frustrating. Right now all these various divisions seem to be viewed strictly as an investment by the corporate people. They only look at us as a banker might look at us. This hurts us in terms of evolving some of these programs because we have relationships which are beyond financial relationships.

The remarks of a corporate executive seemed to support this concern:

One of the things I worry about is where is the end of the rope on this interdivisional thing. I'm wondering if action really has to come from just the division. You know, in this organization when they decide to do something new it always has been a divisional proposal—they were coming to us for review and approval. The executive committee ends up a review board; not us, working downward. With this kind of pattern the talent of the corporate people is pretty well seduced into asking questions and determining whether a thing needs guidelines. But I think we ought to be the idea people as well, thinking about where we are going in the future, and if we think we ought to be getting into some new area, then we tell the divisions to do it. The stream has got to work both ways. Now it is not.

Case 5–3
Clark Equipment Company
Stephen A. Allen III

During 1971 the Clark Equipment Company moved from an area to a product form of organization for its European subsidiaries. Exhibit 1 contains an article from the August 1972 issue of *International Management* describing this organizational change and its rationale. Exhibits 2 and 3 are the casewriter's representation of reporting relationships for Clark's major operating units in 1970 and 1971, respectively.

BACKGROUND INFORMATION

With 1971 revenues of $760 million, the company described itself as a "highly integrated, multinational manufacturer and distributor of capital goods." Although perhaps best known for its line of fork-lift industrial trucks, Clark Equipment derived 68 percent of its 1971 revenues from four other classes of products—automotive parts and components, construction machinery, truck trailers, and refrigeration and food-service equipment—and was also in the business of financing purchases of its equipment (see Exhibits 4 and 5 for revenues by product line and product descriptions.) Clark's corporate office is faced with the task of managing a world-wide organization consisting of 7 major product divisions, 43 manufacturing facilities, a number of licensees and affiliates, and a distribution network of over 1,000 independent dealers and factory branches.

One business magazine has described the company in the following manner:

> Clark is less well-known than most large U.S. corporations even at home; partly because it is headquartered in Buchanan, Michigan, which is a sleepy little rural community in the southwest corner of the state, about a two-hour drive from the Chicago airport. . . . Top Clark executives are all self-consciously proud of their peculiar corporate domicile. The financial vice president says that when he is in Europe he introduces himself jokingly to strangers as a simple old Michigan country boy. . . . Such statements would generally be a private matter, if they did not also profoundly express the company's temperament and orientation, or the corporate culture, if you will. . . . From Buchanan a handful of low-keyed, stolid Mid-Western executives run, without much fuss or business ritual, what is perhaps the second most successful company in the capital goods industry—after Caterpillar Tractor, a company that is in a class by itself.[1]

Corporate strategy

The company's 1970 annual report devoted considerable space to a discussion of the rationale behind its expanding activities. The following excerpts provide insights into the corporation's overall strategy:

> . . . It's one thing to do well in boom times; it's quite another to perform in difficult times. This is particularly true of the capital goods industry which is historically cyclical in nature. Since World War II, the year-by-year performance chart on capital goods companies has resembled a roller coaster. While the trend generally has been up, the downward dips have sometimes been as severe as the upward curves. In the past, Clark has been no exception to this historical trend [see Exhibit 6].

---

[1] John Thackray, "Clark's Quiet Americans," *Management Today,* December 1969, pp. 88–91.

On an annualized average three-year basis, Clark has shown significant, uninterrupted gains [see Exhibit 7]. However, the entire thrust of Clark's planning and development has been to even out the cycles, and to stabilize our growth on a year-to-year basis.

As Clark entered the 1950s, our business consisted of two major product lines—power train components for the automotive and agricultural equipment industry and fork-lift trucks for material handling. All but a small percentage of these products were sold in the United States. As a result, Clark's fortunes rested almost entirely on the health of two product lines in one national economy. The swings in these two markets inevitably swung Clark's own performance.

To counteract this vulnerability, Clark began an extended program of diversification, both into other product areas and businesses and into other world markets. One purpose was to allow Clark, through additional product lines, to participate in a broader sector of any single country's economy. Even though these product lines are in the area of capital goods, and subject to cycles, the markets do not necessarily follow the same cyclical periods. There is a tendency, in fact, for the cycle of one of these markets to overlap another. The total business, therefore, is better protected against deep dips in operating performance.

Cyclical variations also exist among the various national and regional economies of the world. International expansion not only broadens the total market for Clark products, it also provides a hedge against softening trends that periodically affect individual economies.

Clark's product diversification both expanded our existing businesses and added entire new product lines.

In 1950, for example, our industrial truck business was concentrated almost exclusively in gas-powered fork-lift trucks and tow tractors with less than 10,000-pound capacity. Today, a broadly expanded line includes electric-powered lift trucks, a major line of trucks with capacities of 10,000-70,000 pounds, van carriers to transport containers, and completely automated storage and retrieval systems. Our automotive activities have added new lines of heavy-duty off-highway power shift transmissions and planetary axles to our lines of axles and axle housings, medium-duty transmissions, torque converters and related drive units.

Construction machinery, which married Clark's automotive heavy-duty power trains to a line of rubber-tired earthmoving equipment, now comprises our second largest product line, accounting for more than a quarter of our sales. Trailer products, which include truck trailers, truck bodies and shipping containers, and refrigeration and food service equipment each account for approximately 8 percent of total sales.

Clark also has improved and expanded two other realted, but independently managed, businesses: replacement parts and credit operations. Both have played a key role in the growth and success of Clark's major product lines, especially industrial truck and construction equipment. Both also return a profit in their own right.

With the exception of automotive products, which are sold directly to OEM customers, Clark's product lines reflect a common pattern. All are industrial end-use products, so that Clark is able to respond directly to the markets' needs and demands and to build supplementary businesses, such as parts, service, and credit. These product lines are sold through a network of independent dealers and some factory branches, numbering more than 1,000 throughout the world. The retail outlet is the key to Clark's marketing organizaion. It not only represents the prime outlet for Clark products, but also serves as a finger on the pulse of the market, complementing the company's own marketing intelligence and enabling Clark to respond quickly to shifts in market demand.

Internal expansion paralleled product diversification. In 1950, Clark operated three manufacturing facilities, all in the United States. Today, there are 23 Clark manufacturing facilities in the United States and Canada, plus 12 additional manufacturing facilities operated by Clark overseas subsidiaries in seven countries

Table 1
Major acquisitions since 1955

Company	Date of acquisition	Size of acquisition
Brown Trailer, Inc.	1958	Specific data unavailable (1955 sales were less than $20 million)
Tyler Refrigeration Corp.	1963	1963 sales of $20 million
Hancock Mfg. Co. (self-loading scrapers, land levelers)	1966	Added $22 million to Clark's 1966 sales
Chicago Malleable Castings (malleable iron castings)	1966	
Melroe Co. (loaders, agricultural implements)	1969	Added $30 million to Clark's 1969 sales
Delfield Co. (food service equipment)	1969	
Lima and Austin-Western Divisions of Baldwin-Lima-Hamilton Corp. (truck and crawler-mounted cranes, hydraulic excavators, portable crushing/screening plants, asphalt plants, road graders, mobile hydraulic cranes)	1971	1970 sales of $79 million

on three continents. We also have manufacturing agreements with 22 overseas licensees and affiliates in 16 countries. Clark also has some 390 international distributors with outlets in more than 150 countries.

Clark's diversification was accomplished both through internal development and through selected acquisitions. As Table 1 suggests, acquisitions were an important, but not the predominant, source of company growth.

A final dimension of Clark's overall strategy is the use of the following six yardsticks against which to measure its financial strength and soundness:

1. A minimum current ratio of 2 to 1.
2. A profit goal of 6 percent on sales.
3. A dividend payout of between 40 percent and 50 percent.
4. A capital base consisting of 70 percent equity and 30 percent long-term debt, with a variance of 5 percent from the norm considered acceptable in any given year.
5. A ratio of sales to fixed assets of 7.5 to 1.
6. The use of credit subsidiaries to support company sales effort.

Management viewed these yardsticks as "simple and flexible, subject to adjustment in light of changing conditions."[2]

Organization and control

The 1970 Annual Report outlined Clark's organization and operating policies as follows:

The basic organizational philosophy developed at Clark is one of decentralized management. We are not a conglomerate, but neither do we believe in being monolithic. Responsibility is placed at the lowest possible level it might logically be assumed. Authority and the means to get the job done accompany this responsibility. For example, the general managers of the U.S. divisions are totally responsible for engineering, manufacturing and marketing of their products. They are charged not only to serve today's market, but also to prepare for tomorrow's. We believe these operating people are more sensitive to their own market needs than a corporate staff concerned with five or more markets and bearing no direct responsibility for success or failure in the marketplace.

The corporate staff exists to guide, to plan, and to serve. It includes only those functions which provide service to all of the Clark group, and which provide necessary coordination and control where required, such as legal, finance, tax, and accounting. There is a conscious effort to keep the lines of communications between corporate and line management as short as possible. Corporate management is determinedly accessible. Red tape is studiously avoided. The emphasis is on information and recommendation flowing up, not opinion and dictate flowing down.

To assure this interchange, corporate and line management meet monthly to review on a 30-day basis the results of the previous month and the expectations for the next. Frequent short-term corrections are made; production schedules may be raised, lowered, or revised according to the latest marketing information. These meetings, by taking stock of the business each and every month, provide an automatic discipline against sliding—by not allowing unfavorable situations or trends to continue unnoticed and uncorrected. Similar sessions are held monthly within the operating organizations.

These monthly sessions bridge what Clark considers to be our two most impor-

---

[2] 1970 Annual Report, pp. 8–9.

tant planning sessions of the year—the semiannual Profit Planning meetings, held in December and again in July. At these sessions, each operating group makes a formal presentation on its past performance versus plan and its expectations for the forthcoming 6- and 12-month periods. The key managers from both the operations and corporate level take part, so that there is staff to staff, as well as manager to manager involvement. Although the presentations may be formal, the discussion is not. There is give and take at all levels. The object is not to win or lose an argument, but to produce the best information and the most realistic plan. While such sessions may not be unique to Clark, we believe our atmosphere for open and candid exchange is of utmost importance.

While this approach to organization placed considerable emphasis on the individual division's managing relationships with its particular markets and customers, an examination of the company's recent annual reports indicated several important types of interunit relationships at Clark:

1. Approximately one-half of the output of the automotive plants is transferred to other product plants, being used primarily in the production of industrial trucks and construction machinery.
2. The company's financing subsidiary and its central parts operations represent central services drawn on by many of the product divisions.
3. While the divisions are responsible for product development and redesign, a central R&D organization—consisting of research, development, testing, and manufacturing research units—has prime responsibility for basic research and provides specialized services in the other areas.
4. Outside the United States, there is increasing use of single manufacturing facilities to produce several classes of products.

Management Today provides the following description of Clark's approach to organization:

A few years ago somebody asked the then chairman, and the major architect of Clark's growth, George Spatta, what the company policy was on a particular subject. "The Clark policy is to have no policy," was the reply, which has since become a catch phrase among Clark executives. But an unwritten policy of Spatta and Clark is to load up executives with heavy burdens of responsibility, and then to reward them accordingly. Many companies, of course, claim to do likewise. Few of them, however, can demonstrate the principle so convincingly as Clark can in the monthly salary cheque.

Spatta once told a young trainee, "Stick with me and I'll make you a millionaire." He made several millionaires. Schirmer (Clark's current chairman) earns over $320,000 a year, excluding stock options, about double the salary scale for his position at International Harvester or Caterpillar Tractor. A senior vice-president gets about $200,000. Andrews (Vice President-European Operations) and the other key executives in Europe earn about three times what they could command at other companies.

Few policies, big bundles of cash for the successful manager, as few corporate procedures as possible, bluntness in communication—the Clark style seems something of a throwback to more innocent, uncluttered days in management. At Clark there are no job descriptions, in the United States or in Europe. An executive can often voluntarily assume areas of responsibility if there is a vacuum. Protocol and hierarchically patterned behaviour has been contained to a minimum. At one group management meeting a young executive in his 20s once scathingly criticized an aspect of the company operations to Schirmer's face, in the presence of the entire high command. The European managers who were present thought the roof would fall in. Schirmer laconically accepted the criticism.[3]

In 1971 the ten top corporate officers had an average age of 54 and their years of service with Clark averaged 22. The ranges were 40 to 63 and 12 to 34, respectively.

EVOLUTION OF INTERNATIONAL OPERATIONS

Clark began licensing overseas manufacturers to produce certain popular models of fork-lift trucks in 1948. It also held small equity interests in some of these operations. This early development of overseas activities was described as happening

. . . almost by accident. During the war the company manufactured about two thirds of United States production of fork-lift trucks. When the war ended, thousands of these little trucks were left behind on the docks in Britain, France, and Australia. Europeans requested Clark's help in reconditioning the machines. . . . Clark management felt that here was a chance to do a little business in Europe, but on a very temporary basis. The board allocated the grand sum of $200,000 to set up licensing agreements and joint partnership deals with European manufacturers. Schirmer explains that partly because of the insular culture of Buchanan, "the board went into this very, very carefully."[4]

In 1952, sales of Clark products by overseas affiliates and licensees amounted to $7 million, compared to the company's total revenues of $125 million.

Continued growth of overseas revenues during the 1950s began to raise a number of management issues. *Management Today* notes,

By the mid-1950s it became evident to Clark that the European business was not after all a temporary one. Seen in this new light, the licensing and partnerships agreements immediately had several disadvantages, particularly concerning long-term growth. What Clark had once saved in terms of capital investment, or maximum sales coverage at minimum cost, weighed less heavily than the limitation of working through a string of smallish, mostly family-owned European concerns,

---

[3] Thackray, in *Management Today*, December 1969.

[4] Ibid.

many not particularly well-managed, in competition with International Harvester, or Caterpillar Tractor, both with long-established, strong European operations.

The licensing arrangements, moreover, lacked permanence. Each license contract usually ran for about ten years. When it expired there was always doubt if either party wanted to renew, and on what terms. The licensee, knowing Clark's dependence on him, would always try and knock down the terms of renewal. If the contract could not be renewed for lack of agreement, it usually could not be replaced with another licensee in a hurry. Clark then faced the loss of market representation. And then Clark always had inadequate managerial control over these license operations. There was one occasion when the German company, which was then owned in the majority by Hugo Stinnes, started deviating from the Clark standardized engineering specifications, and there was nothing Buchanan could do about it. (Clark seeks as complete as possible worldwide standardization of design and parts, for obvious reasons.) Then, if Clark wanted a licensee's plant engineer to visit Buchanan for consultations, permission from his employer would have to be obtained.[5]

In 1958 the company created Clark Equipment International, C.A. to establish and manage overseas manufacturing operations, still depending mainly on limited equity participation. The company noted,

> The dropping of trade barriers and the birth of the European Common Market, the relaxation of import restrictions in some countries, the general stabilization of world markets—all were factors in the establishment of our new wholly owned subsidiary. . . . Continued growth in industrialization in many lands abroad has intensified the need for equipment. World conditions have become such that it is now desirable to serve these needs from overseas plants. . . . Most of the overseas plants limit their production to those sizes and models which have the broadest appeal in their own markets. The cost of tooling makes such a procedure necessary. Any sizes or models not manufactured locally are shipped from Clark plants in the United States.

By 1961 sales by affiliates and licensees were over $65 million and Clark exports were over $20 million, compared to the company's total revenue of $177 million. In 1962 a Zurich office was organized "to provide marketing services for Clark products overseas and technical liaison and engineering services for licensees."

During the 1960s Clark acquired either full or controlling interest in several of its affiliate and subsidiary companies. The most notable examples were Clark Maschinenfabrik GmbH (1963), Clark Equipment Limited (1964), Clark Equipment France S.A. (1966), and Clark Equipment Australia Pty., Limited (1969). Table 2 shows the importance of overseas sales both to Clark's consolidated revenues and to its network of affiliates.

The following provide some indication of the relationship between

---

[5] Ibid.

Table 2
Recent trend in overseas sales ($ million)

	1964	1965	1966	1967	1968	1969	1970	1971
Total overseas sales by subsidiaries and affiliates ...	124	140	160	164	183	234	270	300
Amount consolidated into Clark accounts	n.a.*	n.a.	n.a.	n.a.	n.a.	132	186	195
Export sales.................	24	30	36	32	35	n.a.	n.a.	n.a.
Total Clark revenues	353	430	517	517	539	657	684	760

* n.a. = not available.

Clark's European operations and the parent company prior to the 1971 organizational changes.

European operations are something more than a corporate dumping ground for company technology and excess cash flow. The now wholly owned Clark Stacatruc Ltd. in Birmingham developed a small, three-wheel utility industrial truck for the British market, which is now being manufactured and sold in the United States, and which uses a large number of European components. A German subsidiary exports its compaction equipment know-how around the world, and its technology has gone to Buchanan. The company expects one day soon to enter the compaction equipment market in the United States. Then, as a last illustration, the British operation has much greater sophistication of product and design than the U.S. parent in the large multiple van carriers.

*   *   *

"Clark gives us certain guides on what they want to earn on their money, and after that Schirmer couldn't care less how we run our business," says John Andrews, the company vice president who runs the European operations from Camberly. "The only area where we slavishly follow the U.S. standards is in finance and accounting."

*   *   *

Andrews and other European managers are included in long-term planning and where-are-we-going sessions at Buchanan. None of the European plant managers are American. And Americans are for the most part only to be found at the central European staff offices in Brussels, where they are about half the total complement. Although the Clark U.S. engineering force does most of the basic and conceptual designing of products, the Europeans do interpretative designing for their markets. "The U.S. engineers show meticulous care in development and conception," says Andrews. "Basically their great strength is in the care in conception. And this helps us minimize the cost of guarantee in the first and second years in which a new machine is being used in the market."[6]

---

[6] Ibid.

In 1969 *Management Today* summed up its view of Clark's European activities as follows:

Although the company has one of the most profitable European operations of any U.S. corporation, Clark executives readily admit that the company could be an even better money-spinner; because factories scattered in to too many locations prevent a realization of the full economies of large-scale production. There are three industrial truck plants. One in Britain (Birmingham), another in France, another in Germany. There is separate production in all three countries for construction equipment, at different locations from the industrial trucks. There are two plants making refrigeration equipment, one in Britain (Prestcold Tyler Refrigeration), another in Germany.[7]

Exhibit 1

Clark Equipment Alters Its Overseas Strategy*
by
Roy Hill, Senior Editor
International Management

About two hours' drive from Chicago, in the sleepy-looking town of Buchanan, Michigan (population 6,000), there's a modest sign in the main street announcing Clark Equipment Company. In the company's grounds, the first thing the visitor sees is a notice warning "slow, beware of the ducks."

Beyond this duck pond in Midwestern America lie the unpretentious offices of a company that last year had consolidated sales of $741 million worldwide, of which $195 million was achieved outside the U.S.

Clark is a conservative company that became international almost by accident. It manufactures and sells capital goods such as fork-lift trucks, construction machinery, lorry trailers, automotive parts and food refrigeration equipment.

Unlike some international companies, it has not been over-ruthless or over-dogmatic in its handling of foreign partners and subsidiaries. Says Frederick Bechtel, the slow-speaking president for international operations, in his office in Buchanan: "We made every effort not to disturb the local managements beyond what we thought was good for them and for us in the long term."

Clark still hasn't brought all of its international operations under one organizational system. But in Europe it has reached a stage in its evolution which other parts of Clark's world are expected to follow.

In its slow evolution in Europe, first Clark licensed European partners to manufacture its products and use its name.

Then it acquired European manufacturing companies which it wholly owned and whose managers reported to a British vice-president, who in turn reported to Bechtel in Buchanan.

Only in the last two years has Clark evolved its present structure. Plant managers report, via European general managers in their own product lines, to the appropriate product divisions in the U.S. There is a European headquarters in Brussels, as there has been since the early 1960s. But today it is essentially an administrative office, without direct operating responsibilities.

Yet despite the time it has taken Clark to develop a structure along product lines, the sales growth of the company has been unimpaired. In the ten years from 1961 to 1971, Clark sales worldwide expanded from $173 million to $741 million. Net income, which in

---

[7] Ibid.

Exhibit 1 (*continued*)

1961 was $7.8 million, was $29 million in 1971. But here there was a sharp fall from the 1969 income peak of $38.6 million.

Clark's management ascribes this decline in the last two years chiefly to the cyclical nature of the capital goods industry. Officials point out that, taken together, the three years 1969–71 were the most profitable in the company's history.

However, the tighter trading and profit picture illustrated by the 1971 results supported Clark's top management's view that organizational change was necessary. Says Walter E. Schirmer, Clark's chairman and chief executive officer: "The debate in the top echelons of the company before we brought Europe into the divisional line of control was not so much about structure as about objectives.

"I think our primary objective was to make maximum use of what is any company's most valuable asset, top management talent. We decided that the best way was for corporate vice-presidents to have worldwide responsibilities instead of just concentrating on the U.S."

Clark got into its two main product lines in Europe by entirely different routes. Industrial trucks, including fork-lift trucks, were exported in large numbers during World War II. After the war they needed servicing, and Clark set up licensing arrangements and joint partnership deals in Germany, France, Belgium and Britain. Some of these licensees were small and indifferently managed, but Clark secured a firm foothold in the European market at minimum cost.

In construction machinery, in contrast, Clark only got into the business in the U.S. in the early 1950s. It decided from the beginning that despite the competition from established giants, such as Caterpillar Tractor Company and International Harvester Company, it would manufacture overseas.

The way Clark moved into Britain in construction machinery says a great deal about the company's preferred business methods at a time when it was relatively small.

Englishman John Andrews owned and ran a small thriving company, All-Wheel Drive, which specialized in converting trucks to four-wheel drive for desert operations. He visited Buchanan looking for a supplier of axles, and there he met Schirmer.

As Andrews recalls: "He asked whether my company would become Clark's licensee in Britain. I said, 'Fine, but we only have a tin shed.' He replied that with our record we must have good management, and that it was management he was interested in, not tin sheds.

"So there and then, within a few hours, we fixed a licensing arrangement which proved to be incredibly successful, both from a business angle and from a pleasant relationship angle. He didn't even ask to see our balance sheet. We worked on the details of the deal on the back of an envelope, and I returned home with the engineering drawings for their new construction equipment."

In the early 1960s Bechtel, who had joined Clark as a general counsel but had some international experience with the U.S. General Electric Company, was appointed to head the international division. "I had to play it very much by ear," he recalls. "The success of our international operations was my responsibility, but I couldn't just lay down the law with licensees, in situations where we had minority holdings, even if I wanted to.

"Everyone was doing their own thing in Europe and, with the advent of the European Common Market, I wanted to construct a European holding operation and organize the management to run it on a multi-plant basis. But our European friends had many reservations. We never made any grand strategic plan."

In the early 1960s, therefore, Clark was patient even while it suffered. When the German company deviated from the standard engineering specifications there was nothing that the Buchanan headquarters could do except complain. But when the German majority owner went bankrupt, Clark swiftly bought control from the banks.

In Britain Andrews, who held 60 percent of the joint company against Clark's 40 percent, sold his share to the British group Vickers Ltd. on the advice of his bankers. But neither he nor Clark was happy with the new partner. "We struggled along for a year and a half,

Exhibit 1 (*continued*)

absorbing overheads we had never experienced before," Andrews says. "Then Clark bought out the Vickers interest and took control."

In Belgium the majority partners at first refused to be dislodged. But in exchange for taking over their industrial truck operations, Clark offered the Belgians a 30 percent investment in a new $7-million plant to make axles and power shift transmissions, among other things. The Belgians accepted.

"When we acquired companies," Bechtel says, "we had to take them as they were. The construction machinery facility at Limburg, in Germany, was on a hillside at three or four levels. Anybody in the trailer handling business would have told you to stay as far away from that plant as possible.

"But it was in the package. So we took it and sold the plant to the German government for a computer center; we moved down the railway a few kilometers, employed the same people and doubled the output."

Even before it bought control, Clark had organized a U.S. staff to transfer information to licensees. And because the Clark name was involved, it had quietly sent engineers to Europe to check that quality standards were maintained.

By the mid-1960s, Bechtel was sending other managers to Europe "to get their feet wet. I wanted to bring the staff functions of the company into a sense of responsibility for things globally."

One area that needed attention was accounting procedures. Says Bechtel: "I would go to the German plant and they would proudly display a set of books that was two and a half months old. In Buchanan, we were producing monthly results of the domestic operations on the fifth working day of the following month.

"But you couldn't write a letter to a European controller who was two months behind with his figures and have him suddenly change his schedules. He would say it was impossible. So I had to send someone over there to show him the way it was going to be done."

In financing, too, Clark judged it was essential to use U.S. managers. Says Bechtel: "In the U.S. we had helped our dealers financially, helped our customers with retail purchases, developed a whole set of approaches for leasing and for leasing with option to buy. That was something the Europeans knew very little about at that time."

But the European plants continued to function under their own managements, and to select their own methods of reaching the broad earnings objectives provided by Clark headquarters. It was a European—Andrews—who "did a foreman's job," as he puts it. Under Bechtel he was a vice-president and general manager for Europe. Operating out of Camberley, near London, and from Brussels, he was, as he says, "continually in the air, helping with all the problems that were arising in all the factories."

This was an invigorating time, Andrews says. The company was so loosely structured there were no restrictive job descriptions: "People would gladly fill in and tackle other people's jobs."

Bechtel concedes: "We were prosperous. We had good relationships and informal communications. But increasingly our products faced tougher global competition.

"For example, in the materials handling field in the U.S. there are about 30 fork-lift truck companies. But if you go to a European trade fair there are more than 50. These people are generating concepts, product designs, that you had better be aware of. So it's better that our chief engineer for materials handling begins to feel this responsibility and look at things globally on a product basis."

The feeling grew at Clark headquarters that the U.S. domestic divisions should get involved overseas directly, instead of just lending executives to the international division for overseas duties.

A start was made when, about two years ago, marketing was put on a global basis. The European marketing managers no longer reported to Andrews and through him to Bechtel, but directly to their divisions in the U.S.

There were other things in Europe that caused unease at headquarters in the U.S. Says

Exhibit 1 (*continued*)

Bechtel: "We had, in construction machinery, trends of optimistic forecasting. We began to think maybe it was better to have a boss not connected to a plant, who wasn't involved in employment levels and therefore didn't wait three or four months to see what, in hindsight, was real after 45 days—that the trend was down and there wasn't any input from the dealers to tell you any different."

So about a year ago the divisions in the U.S. were made fully responsible for their products in Europe. The international division ceased to have functional and operating responsibilities. Bechtel became, in his own words, "an arm of the presidential office, aiding those people who don't have the time to travel on a global basis to look at everybody."

The European headquarters in Brussels continues to function. But Andrews, having reached retirement age as a vice-president, has stepped down. He has been replaced by an American, who reports to Bechtel as Andrews did. But Brussels these days is concerned mainly with legal, tax and financing matters.

Andrews still comes into his Camberley office, and he is vice-chairman of the Zurich-based holding company, which controls external revenues from licensing and services.

Naturally, though without animosity, he regrets the changes at Clark. He says: "I believe that the way to run an outfit like this is to have a very strong general manager on the spot. I feel that the person-to-person control which we previously enjoyed was an easier thing for the company as a whole. Now it's the domestic divisional managers who make the decisions."

Bechtel, in contrast, believes that whatever may be lost by remoter decision-making is gained in other directions. "The president of a domestic division is a very knowledgeable guy in his field," he points out. "Previously, I couldn't get his full attention. Now he's involved in Europe directly. He has got to think globally. So this broadens his approach to management, and he has to take more active steps to develop his successor, who can take charge in the U.S. when he is away."

Against this, Andrews argues that "in a time of crisis the very first thing a U.S.-based manager will do is go straight to his American problem. When problems crop up in the U.S., a guiding hand will often put them right and the under-management knows precisely how to carry on from that point onwards. But internationally that is not so. We might be denied continuity of guidance from the U.S."

Clark's European managers, though, remain intensely loyal to the company. This is due in part to personal rewards which Andrews describes as "quite unusual." He says European key executives can earn three times what they might command at other companies. But the loyalty of the managers is also a tribute to the good human relationships built up over the years.

The number of executives who stay with Clark is almost an embarrassment. "Fortunately," says Andrews, "we are growing at a speed where we are able to demote people without actually demoting them, simply by letting them stay where they are. And for those who have what it takes, so long as we keep on growing, promotion chances are good."

Thus the German head of the fork-lift truck plant in Germany suddenly found himself general manager for Europe in industrial trucks, which has annual sales around $60 million. And the Briton who ran the construction machinery plant at Camberley is now responsible to his division for the British, French and German construction machinery plants.

Andrews, though, thinks that the separation along divisional lines has been carried too far. "True," he says, "the products are utterly different. They are handled differently and have different sales people. But well over 55 percent of the total activities are identical."

Perhaps it is absurd that people who work at the industrial truck and construction machinery plants in Camberley, on opposite sides of the same small road, have very little to do with one another. Even a joint executive dining-room, which is one way of helping to foster a "total company" atmosphere, doesn't exist.

But Bechtel points to practical steps, designed to improve efficiency, which are being implemented now, though some of them were thought about before divisional control was established.

For instance, Clark is reducing production areas to a minimum. Thus Clark's fork-lift

Exhibit 1 (*concluded*)

truck operation, which has remained near Birmingham ever since it was purchased from the then British Motor Corporation, has been relocated at Camberley.

In Chicago, Clark has a parts warehouse that dispenses about $90 million of parts a year. "It's a computerized marvel" Bechtel says. "The technique of operating that, of relating the computer to what you have got and what you should buy and where you should buy it, printing the tickets and invoices and tying it in to your distribution in one big electronic package, takes a lot of know-how. And now we are trying to make it compatible with our operations in Europe."

By U.S. standards, Bechtel says, the British and German ends of the company never had their warehouses organized in a modern, efficient way. But on May 30 this year a central parts operation was inaugurated at Mulheim, in Germany, to which most distributors and branches will be linked by telex.

Says Bechtel: "These themes of rationalization and of the product divisions taking a direct responsibility are going to be around for quite a while. It is going to mean a continuous refining and perfecting and adjustment."

Clark, the company that evolved slowly in organizational terms while sprinting in terms of growth, has managed to get the best of all worlds. It took over from its licensees without offending them, and it succeeded internationally despite tough competition.

Now it has dovetailed its European with its U.S. operations on product lines. In the process the line of command has become more lengthy, stretching all the way back to the Midwestern state of Michigan. But there is little sign that, because of this, Clark has lost the goodwill of its foreign managers.

Clark aims for worldwide sales of $1,000 million by the end of fiscal 1973. That will be the time to judge whether the company that lies beyond the duck pond really has made a wise organizational choice.

---

* Reprinted from the August 1972 issue of *International Management* by special permission.

Exhibit 2
Basic organization—1970*

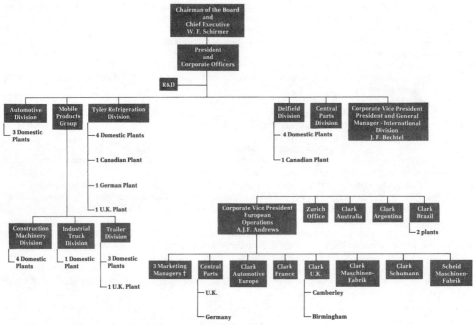

* Prepared by casewriter on basis of 1970 Annual Report.
† Separate European marketing organizations for Automotive, Industrial Trucks, and Construction Equipment.

Exhibit 3
Basic organization—1971*

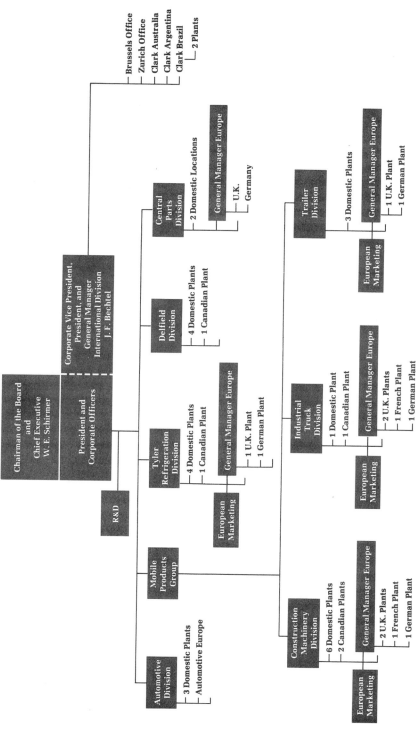

* Prepared by casewriter on basis of *International Management* article and 1971 Annual Report. The term "plant" does not always indicate separate physical locations. For example, management responsibilities for the operations of Clark Equipment France were split on a product line basis between the Construction Machinery and Industrial Divisions. A similar split was used for Clark U.K. The new organization also reflects the 1971 domestic acquisitions by Clark.

Exhibit 4
Sales and revenues—1970 and 1971

	Amounts in thousands					
	1971				1970	
	Reported consolidated		Pro forma ex Lima & A-W		Consolidated	
Sales by classes of products	Amounts	%	Amounts	%	Amounts	%
Automotive parts and components....	$111,028	15.0	$111,028	16.1	$107,985	16.1
Industrial trucks	272,990	36.8	272,990	39.5	280,924	41.9
Construction machinery	241,085	32.5	190,817	27.6	181,332	27.0
Truck trailers	57,678	7.8	57,678	8.3	51,145	7.6
Refrigeration and food service equipment	58,687	7.9	58,687	8.5	49,621	7.4
Total net sales	$741,568	100.0	$691,200	100.0	$671,007	100.0
License fees and dividends from foreign associates	4,812				3,772	
Pre-tax income of finance subsidiaries not consolidated	10,887				7,025	
Other income	3,186				2,906	
Total revenues	$760,353				$684,710	

Exhibit 5
Description of products by location*

UNITED STATES

Automotive products

Buchanan, Mich.: Axles, axle housings, steel castings, sheet metal fabrication, hydraulic products. *Chicago, Ill.:* Malleable castings. *Jackson, Mich.:* Transmissions, differentials, torque converters, winches.

Central parts

Chicago, Ill.: Parts warehouse and distribution center.

Mobile products

Battle Creek, Mich.: Industrial trucks, straddle carriers, horizontal transporters, towing tractors, material handling systems. *Benton Harbor, Mich.:* Tractor shovels, tractor dozers, backhoe loaders. *Cooperstown, N.D.:* Agricultural implements. *Gwinner, N.D.:* Industrial loaders. *Lubbock, Tex.:* Conventional and self-loading tractor scrapers. *Michigan City, Ind.:* Truck trailers, truck bodies. *Reading, Pa.:* Truck trailers, truck bodies, freight containers, container chassis. *Sedalia, Mo.:* Truck bodies. *Spokane, Wash.:* Truck trailers, truck bodies, container chassis.

Refrigeration and food service products

Niles, Mich.: Commercial refrigeration equipment. *Cadillac, Mich.:* Food service equipment. *Detroit, Mich.:* Food service equipment. *Grand Rapids, Mich.:* Shelving and checkout counters. *Waxahachie, Tex.:* Commercial refrigeration equipment. *Seattle, Wash.:* Environmental chambers. *Smyrna, Del.:* Food service equipment, ice-making equipment.

_____
* From 1970 Annual Report. Does not reflect 1971 acquisitions.

Exhibit 5 (*continued*)

Research and development

Buchanan, Mich.: Corporate Test Center, Manufacturing Research Laboratory. *Cassopolis, Mich.:* Corporate Development Center.

CANADA

Clark Equipment of Canada, Ltd.

St. Thomas, Ont.: Construction machinery, industrial trucks, log skidders,

Canadian Tyler-Refrigeration, Ltd.

Barrie, Ont.: Commercial refrigeration equipment. *Agincourt, Ont.:* Food service equipment.

EUROPE*

Clark Automotive Europe (81 percent owned)

Bruges, Belgium: Universal and power shift transmissions, torque converters, axle components.

Clark Central Parts GmbH

Mulheim (Ruhr), West Germany: Parts warehouse and distribution center.

Clark Central Parts Limited

Camberley, Surrey, England: Parts warehouse and distribution center.

Clark Equipment France S.A.

Strasbourg, France: Industrial trucks, construction machinery.

Clark Equipment Limited

Camberley, Surrey, England: Construction machinery, industrial trucks, van carriers. *Birmingham, Worcestershire, England:* Industrial trucks.

Clark Equipment (Trailer Division) Limited

Bridgend, Glamorgan, South Wales: Truck bodies.

Clark Maschinenfabrik GmbH

Mulheim (Ruhr), West Germany: Industrial trucks.

Clark Schumann Fahrzeugfabrik GmbH

Kirchheimbolanden, West Germany: Truck trailers, truck bodies.

Sociétè de Vente de Materiel d'Enterprise (Genemat) (25 percent owned)

Paris, France: Construction machinery.

Macmor, S.A. (40 percent owned)

Madrid, Spain: Distributor of construction machinery.

---

* Foreign plants are wholly owned subsidiaries unless otherwise indicated. Operations in which Clark holds less than one fourth equity are not listed.

Exhibit 5 (*concluded*)

EUROPE (*continued*)

Prestcold Tyler Refrigeration, Limited (50 percent owned)

Bedford and Kempston, England: Commercial refrigeration equipment.

Scheid Maschinenfabrik GmbH

Aumenau, West Germany: Compactors, road rollers, industrial trucks, industrial loaders.

Tyler Refrigeration International GmbH

Schwelm/Westfalen, West Germany: Commercial refrigeration equipment.

LATIN AMERICA

Equipamentos Clark S.A.

Valinhos, São Paulo, Brazil: Gears, transmissions, construction machinery, industrial trucks.

Eximia Industrias Clark Argentina S.A.I.C.I.F.

Buenos Aires, Argentina: Industrial trucks, construction machinery, commercial refrigeration equipment, trailers, truck bodies.

Industrias Campos Salles Ltda. (95 percent owned)

São Paulo, Brazil: Commercial refrigeration equipment.

Productos Industriales Metalicos, S.A. (40 percent owned)

Queretaro, Mexico: Industrial trucks, construction machinery.

Refrigeracion Ojeda, S.A. de C.V. (45 percent owned)

Mexico D.F., Mexico: Commercial refrigeration equipment.

Transmisiones y Equipos Mecanicos, S.A. (36.5 percent owned)

Queretaro, Mexico: Transmissions.

OTHER

Clark Equipment Australia Pty., Limited

Hornsby, New South Wales, Australia: Industrial trucks, construction machinery, truck bodies, industrial loaders.

Okamura Tyler Co., Limited (40 percent owned)

Tokyo, Japan: Commercial refrigeration equipment.

Premier Metal Company of South Africa, Limited (25 percent owned)

Johannesburg, Republic of South Africa: Industrial trucks, construction machinery, truck bodies.

Exhibit 6
Selected financial data*

Year	Total revenues†	Net income	Depreciation	Capital expenditures	Earnings per share‡	Return on net sales	Return on shareholders' equity
1957	145,494	8,229	2,503	4,262	.89	5.8%	14.7%
1958	144,660	6,449	2,664	3,964	.67	4.5	10.7
1959	210,578	12,402	2,780	3,501	1.30	6.0	19.0
1960	199,626	6,742	2,964	3,384	.70	3.4	9.7
1961	178,429	7,821	3,083	3,542	.81	4.5	10.9
1962	236,219	13,675	3,632	3,527	1.34	5.9	17.6
1963	270,928	15,847	3,702	5,509	1.54	6.0	15.8
1964	352,978	21,125	5,361	7,719	2.03	6.1	18.5
1965	429,659	23,993	5,925	10,272	2.08	5.7	18.8
1966	516,647	29,367	7,373	27,248	2.52	5.8	20.2
1967	517,024	24,179	8,805	14,514	2.05	4.8	14.5
1968	539,447	28,960	9,985	16,029	2.43	5.5	16.0
1969	657,164	38,605	11,137	22,492	3.21	6.0	19.3
1970	684,710	35,281	12,383	26,668	2.92	5.3	15.7
1971	760,353	29,016	14,749	22,764	2.36	3.9	11.8

* First four columns are in $ thousands. From 15-year summary in 1971 Annual Report.
† Restated to include pre-tax income of finance subsidiaries previously reported net of tax.
‡ Adjusted for stock splits.

Exhibit 7
1971 performance review*

Notwithstanding the cyclical nature of the capital goods industry, Clark has generated continuing growth in sales, net income, cash dividends and net worth. Such progress is shown in the following tabulation which averages these key indicators over three-year periods to even out the peaks and valleys characteristic of the heavy equipment business.

		Average annual		
Period	Sales	Net income	Cash dividends	Year-end net worth
1951–53	$119,647,000	$ 5,319,000	$ 2,602,000	$ 35,585,000
1954–56	122,581,000	8,216,000	4,204,000	48,740,000
1957–59	164,622,000	9,027,000	5,118,000	62,898,000
1960–62	200,055,000	9,413,000	5,887,000	77,977,000
1963–65	344,955,000	20,322,000	8,070,000	116,613,000
1966–68	515,413,000	27,502,000	12,478,000	172,607,000
1969–71	685,974,000	34,301,000	16,831,000	247,097,000

* From Annual Report, p. 14.

Reading 5–1
On concepts of corporate structure: Economic determinants of organization*
Harold Stieglitz

Just about 25 years ago, General Motors announced one of its most important products—the GM Formula. Its wage escalation clause negotiated then with the UAW provided for a 1¢ increase in hourly wages for each 1.14 point rise in the BLS index. Confronted with the inflationary period of Korea, many company negotiators copied GM and adopted the 1 for 1.14 formula for escalating wages. The fact that the formula had a specific relevance to GM's employees—that it reflected the ratio of average wages of the GM employees to the cost-of-living index at the time of adoption—seemed beside the point. The fact that a different formula might have more appropriately reflected the wage-cost-of-living relationship of their employees deterred few from just going ahead with 1 for 1.14. Evidently what was good enough for the sophisticates at GM was good enough for most of its emulators.

More than 50 years ago, however, GM had developed another product that proved to have an even larger impact. This was a management concept labeled "centralized coordination, decentralized administration"— or, "decentralization with coordination and control." While adoption of this concept came less rapidly, many companies turned to it—especially in the post–World War II growth period, when diversification and greater complexity characterized an increasing number.

In application, the concept meant reorganizing operations into divisionalized profit centers that operated with a high degree of decentralization; setting up corporate staffs to provide centralized coordination and control under corporate-wide policies. Initially, the ambiguities and vagaries of the concept were not seen as deterrents to its adoption. GM's success in the marketplace showed it must be doing something right. If "decentralization with centralized control" was good enough for GM, it was good enough for others.

Since the early 1920s, however, the concept was subject to adaptation and development at GM itself. Even during Alfred P. Sloan's tenure,

---

* Reprinted by permission from *The Conference Board Record*, February 1974.

changes in technology and the marketplace brought an ebb and flow to the degree of decentralization versus centralized coordination—and, retrospectively, it's been more ebb than flow. But those who borrowed the concept sometimes missed the nuances of GM's later experience, so what seemed to work there didn't always work for them.

Emulation in structuring organization is not, of course, dead. Upon hearing of a major company that operates very effectively with a very small central staff, many a chief executive has envied the cost savings implicit in such a structure. Some have tried it. Similarly, the prospect of putting some young tigers at the head of their own decentralized profit centers has led others to reorganize. However, in more recent years, there is evidence that a more mature approach to organization planning has displaced such "me-too-ism."

The reasons for structuring organization

Sloan, the prime mover in the development and adaptation of GM's concept of organization, at the close of his long career, remarked, "An organization does not make decisions; its function is to provide a framework, based upon established criteria, within which decisions can be made."[1] The modifying phrase "based upon established criteria" is crucial, and maturity in corporate organization structuring has only developed as more top executives have been able to identify those criteria that condition the framework.

Admittedly, many a pragmatic top executive denies that there are any basic criteria that dictate key elements of the organization structure. The "situation," the "personalities," the "management style," and a host of other factors are presumably enough to make each organization and its structure unique.[2] Over the long run, however, one may observe that constant reorganizations and adaptation tend to move the structure in directions that seem almost independent of particular personalities or styles or whims.

Demonstrably, the spectrum of organizational structures throughout industry remains quite broad. It stretches from companies that are organized virtually like holding companies to those that operate, basically, like one-man businesses. There are companies that operate in a highly centralized manner, others that are highly decentralized—and all shades in between. Similarly, some are functionally organized, some have certain

---

[1] Alfred P. Sloan, Jr., *My Years with General Motors* (New York: Doubleday, 1964).

[2] See *The Chief Executive and His Job*, Studies in Personnel Policy, No. 214 (The National Industrial Conference Board, 1969).

elements set up as divisions, some are mixed. And staff within these companies come in all shapes and sizes.[3]

Still, the patterns of organization structure that have emerged indicate that there are company characteristics that are at the root of the developments, and they are primarily economic. Moreover, those that are evidently most influential in shaping organization structure can be specified:

1. *Degree of diversification* in terms of the variety of goods and services produced and/or markets served.
2. *Degree of interdependency,* integration or overlap among the diversified operating components.

Such other factors as economies of scale, dispersion, or absolute size are significant, but largely to the extent that they affect diversification and overlap.[4]

The extent to which a company is diversified tends to determine whether its major operating activities will be structured by division or function and the nature of the groups that come into existence.

The extent to which the operations overlap—in terms of markets, technology, sources of supply, etc.—emerges as the key determinant of the degree of decentralization and the types and role of corporate staff.

In short, the emergence of the divisionalized decentralized form of organization is less a matter of managerial sophistication, more a matter of economic necessity. In an organizational sense, sophistication amounts to recognition of the inevitable.

A continuum of organizations

Relating structure to economic variables is more readily seen when the varieties of types of companies and apposite key structural elements are arrayed. Looking at diversity and overlap of operations, it's quite evident, for example, that companies range from those engaged in the production and/or sale of one good or service to those involved in a multiplicity of related and unrelated businesses. Indeed, when so arrayed, it is clear that the myriad variations form a continuum with no real discontinuities [see Figure 1].

A company at point 1 of the continuum may be substantially different

---

[3] For documentation of major organization trends see *Corporate Organization Structures,* Studies in Personnel Policy, Nos. 183 and 210 (The National Industrial Conference Board, 1961 and 1968), and *Corporate Organization Structures: Manufacturing* (1973). Also see *Organization Planning: Basic Concepts, Emerging Trends* (The National Industrial Conference Board, 1969).

[4] See, for example, *Staff Services in Smaller Companies: The View from the Top,* Report No. 592 (The Conference Board, April 1973).

Figure 1
A continuum of corporations and related organization structures

Elements of organization	Single businesses I (1 2 3 4)	Multiple businesses related II (5 6 7 8)	Multiple businesses unrelated III (9 10 11 12)	Multiple businesses unrelated (no corporate identity) IV (13 14 15 16)
Structure of operations	Functional	Divisionalized	Divisionalized	Divisionalized (subsidiaries)
Functional elements within divisions	—	Production and sales (little staff)	Production and sales (more staff)	Production and sales (more complete staff)
Degree of decentralization	More centralized	Decentralized	Highly decentralized	Highly decentralized (virtual autonomy for divisions)
Corporate Staff Type	Administrative and operational	Administrative and operational	Administrative	Administrative (if any)
Role	Services Advisory control	Advisory control	Advisory (consultant)	—
Groups	—	Super-divisions	Liaison	Unlikely

from one at point 10, but to distinguish too sharply between companies at points 4 and 5 would be fatuous. Even so, the continuum, as represented in the chart, can be divided for analytical purposes into four categories— each of which, in itself, covers a spectrum of companies:

I **Single businesses**—one company producing a single or homogeneous product for a single or homogeneous market.

II **Multiple businesses, related**—one company producing a variety of products for a variety of markets, but with a high degree of overlap in markets for the various products and/or a high degree of integration in materials or technology involved in manufacturing the products.

III **Multiple businesses, unrelated**—one company producing a variety of products for a variety of markets, but the overlap is absent. There are virtually no common denominators—no overlap—in the markets served or the resources or technology employed in producing the variety of goods or services.

IV **Multiple businesses, unrelated (no corporate identity)**—one company but little or no attempt to manage the unrelated businesses; little or no attempt to project a company identity. This, of course, is the holding company defined by Sloan as "a central office surrounded by autonomously operating satellites."

This continuum is not designed to suggest a strategy for growth. Nor does it imply that normal growth occurs through movement across the continuum. A company's growth pattern may keep it in Category I, move it from I to II, or from IV to III.

It bears repeating that the array is a continuum—there are no sharp discontinuities. For analytical purposes, a company can only be characterized as having "more or less" of the economic qualities of a particular category. Similarly, the key organizational elements that relate to these categories can also only be referred to in terms of degree—more or less— i.e., more or less decentralized, more or less divisionalized. Overall, the tendency to divisionalize increases as one moves from Categories I to IV; more significantly, the degree of decentralization decreases as one moves from IV to I. The major related structural elements—makeup of the divisions, types and roles of staff, nature of the groups—also vary.

Functional versus divisional form of organization

It is no accident that companies, regardless of size, that fall into Category I tend to be organized on a functional basis. At the extreme left of the spectrum there is usually little basis for coordinating specialized activities in any other way. Thus, inasmuch as all manufacturing and engineering activities serve a common product, they are organized under one head. Inasmuch as all marketing activities are designed to promote one product, they too are most effectively coordinated by one head.

As the company finds either its product or market spectrum broadening—as it diversifies—it often is able to segregate either its production activities or its marketing activities by product or market. But in terms of who is accountable for what, it's still functional—until such time as increased diversity allows both marketing and production of a given product for a specified market to be linked.

This move to link production and sales of a given product under one head—thus divisionalizing and forming a "profit center," as opposed to a "cost center"—characteristically occurs in companies whose diversification efforts result in (a) more discrete technologies for each product, (b) more discrete markets for each product. Under these circumstances, whether diversification has come from internal product development or external mergers or acquisition, product divisions emerge as the more effective operating components. Again, it is no accident that companies whose operational characteristics are those of Categories II, III, or IV tend to organize them into product or so-called market divisions. In short, they divisionalize.[5]

However, the divisions that are so characteristic of the more diversified companies vary in terms of the more specialized functional components that are assigned or report to the division head. In Category II, for example, the divisions undoubtedly have their own production and sales units; they may very well have their own accounting and engineering units. But it is most likely that corporate units in various areas, e.g., marketing, manufacturing, purchasing, or research and development, will exist, in part, to supply certain services that are common to several divisions. Thus the divisions of companies in Category II tend to truncate; they are not complete in terms of all the functions necessary to carry on their operations.

The divisions that make up companies in Categories III and IV, on the other hand, tend to be more self-sufficient, less reliant on common services. Indeed, in Category IV, many of the operating components exist as virtually self-sufficient subsidiaries. Obviously, the greater interdependence and overlap of markets, technology and resources in Category II accounts for the more truncated divisions in this class; the lack of common-

---

[5] For a more complete analysis of divisionalization, see *Top Management Organization in Divisionalized Companies,* Studies in Personnel Policy, No. 195 (The National Industrial Conference Board, 1965).

ality between the divisions or subdivisions of Categories III and IV makes
for far greater self-sufficiency—at least in terms of functional components.

Centralization-decentralization

Degree of overlap is even more closely related to the varying degrees
of decentralization that are evident at various points in the continuum.
Decentralization, in this context, has a specific meaning: the extent to
which decision-making authority is delegated to lower levels of the organization and, by implication, the degree of constraint—of centralized control
in the form, for example, of corporate-wide policies—that curtails the
area of discretion left to lower-level managers.

Generally, it can be observed that three factors have a major effect
on the degree of delegated authority and/or decentralization:

1. *The confidence factor*—the confidence of superiors in the competence
   of subordinates.
2. *The information factor*—the extent to which the organization has developed mechanisms to feed information to the decision-making
   points, and the extent to which feedback systems have developed
   that allow accountable managers to evaluate results of their decisions.
3. *The scope-of-impact factor*—the extent to which a decision made by
   one unit head affects the operations of another unit.

It is this third factor—the scope-of-impact of decision—that, in the
long run, becomes the key ingredient in determining the degree of decentralization. And, clearly, the scope-of-impact of decisions is directly related to the degree of integration, or overlap, or interdependence of the
company's varied operations. With a greater degree of interaction, less
decentralization is possible. As the operations become more highly varied
and opportunities for operational synergy decrease, the greater the possible degree of decentralization, the greater the toleration of differences
in approaches to personnel, customers, and the public.[6]

In terms of the continuum, it is evident that the operation of companies
in Category I encourages a higher degree of centralized decision making
than takes place in Category II. Similarly, companies in Category III can,
and do, tolerate more decentralization than those in Category II. And
while the operations, or the divisions of companies, in Categories III and
IV might be very similar in terms of diversity and minimum overlap,
the fact that companies in Category IV are not intent on projecting a
corporate identity—and thus can eschew corporate-wide policies—makes

---

[6] Ibid.

for a degree of decentralization that verges on virtual autonomy for the operating divisions or subsidiaries.

Corporate staff: Functions and roles

Size is undoubtedly a key factor that determines whether and when a particular staff unit will emerge within the corporation. Until there is a continuing need for a particular functional expertise, the company may well make use of outside or part-time consultants or services. But once the need is felt and a full-time staff unit is created, whether it be one person or a larger unit, the nature of the operations and the degree of decentralization tend to be strong determinants of the types of specialized staff that come into being and their role relative to the rest of the company.

For analytical purposes, it is useful to distinguish between: (*a*) administrative staff, the functional (staff) units that derive from the fact that a corporation exists as a legal and financial entity (the legal, financial, and public relations staff are typical), and (*b*) operational staff, the functional (staff) units that emerge because of the peculiar nature of the companies' operations (e.g., manufacturing, marketing, purchasing and traffic).

An even more substantive distinction can be drawn between the various roles that characterize staff in its varied relationships. Again, for analytical purposes, whether it be administrative or operational staff, three roles can be distinguished.[7]

1. *Advisory or counseling role*—the staff unit brings its professional expertise to bear in analyzing and solving problems. In this role, staff acts as a consultant; its relationship is largely that of a professional to a client.
2. *Service role*—the staff unit provides services that can be more efficiently and economically provided by one unit with specialized expertise than by many units attempting to provide for themselves. Its relationship in this role is largely that of a supplier to a customer.
3. *Control role*—because of its professional or specialized expertise in a given functional area, staff is called upon to assist in establishing the plans, budgets, policies, rules, standard operating procedures that act as major constraints on delegated authority; that set the parameters of decision making at lower levels. And it sets up mechanisms to audit and evaluate performance vis-à-vis these controls. In exercising this role, its relationship to the rest of the organization is that of an agent for top management.

---

[7] For a more complete discussion, see also *Top Management Organization in Divisionalized Companies* [footnote 5], especially chap. 7, "Staff."

By combining the elements—type of staff and role—it is possible to draw a profile of corporate staff. And that profile tends to vary with companies in each of the four categories.

Thus the fact that Category I includes companies that are organized functionally, that are more centralized than decentralized, narrows the options for the character of staff units that come into being. Of necessity, staff units of both administrative and operational types become part of corporate structure—with the operational staff elements often reporting directly to the accountable operational head of manufacturing or sales. And while some staff units may be more service-oriented than advisory, others more advisory than control, the fact that the functional organization is virtually one large profit center makes advice, service, and control a part of every staff unit's job.

Among Category II companies, whose diversification has fostered divisionalization and greater decentralization, the profile of corporate staff changes. The change is largely one of role rather than type.

Because the divisional operations are interdependent and overlap, there may well be need for operational staff as well as administrative units at the corporate level. But divisions may also have their own staff units to provide services that are unique to the division. Thus, in a divisionalized company there may be, for example, R&D at both corporate and division levels, with divisional staff emphasizing development, corporate staff emphasizing longer-range research. However, because more staff is created within the divisions of Category II companies to provide services locally, the service role of the corporate staff declines. As a result, the advisory and control roles of the corporate staff units assume primary emphasis.

However, this is not to suggest that the advisory and control role become dominant merely as residual factors. To the contrary, they gain emphasis because: (a) In companies with the economic characteristics of Category II, corporate top management becomes relatively more future-oriented; the divisions remain more oriented to the near term. The future emphasis underscores the corporate staff's advisory role in planning. (b) The decentralization occasioned by multiple profit centers heightens the need to discern areas of overlap as well as matters of overriding corporate concern that require consistency in decision making, i.e., the generation of corporate policies. And it puts greater emphasis on discerning and establishing more sophisticated control procedures. Thus the greater emphasis on staff as an agency of control.

Moving to companies whose economic characteristics are those of Category III, the profile of corporate staff again changes—this time in both type and role. Because the operating divisions have little in common, they share no markets; they don't overlap in technology and resources; there is little need for corporate staff in operational areas. Rather, operational staff units are more often housed within the divisions or at the group level. The corporate staff units more often are those in the general areas of administration—financial, legal—and often those that are closely tied to future development of the corporation.

More significantly, the corporate staff's role as a control agency, prominent in both Categories I and II, fades among Category III companies. The far greater degree of decentralization possible in any such company is synonymous with fewer overall constraints in the form of corporate policies and procedures. This fact accounts for the change in role. For the most part, staff units in Category III companies, with the possible exception of finance and planning, are primarily advisory in role—captive consultants.

The diminished need for operational staff and the shift to a primarily consulting relationship that characterizes corporate staff in Category III companies becomes even more pronounced in Category IV. Indeed, it becomes difficult even to see corporate staff—in the sense so far discussed—in the company that operates like a holding company. The parent corporation may have a strong financial unit and legal unit, but these exist primarily to serve the parent. Since the divisions or subsidiaries are encouraged to operate in a manner that verges on autonomy, they establish their own controls, have their own staffs whose profile undoubtedly varies with the economic characteristics of the particular division or subsidiary. If there is such a thing as "corporate staff" in companies at the extreme of Category IV, it may very well exist as a separate "management service" subsidiary from which the other divisions may purchase services as required.

Group structures

The increased use of groups, headed by group executives, is relatively recent. The increase has resulted largely from the proliferation of operating divisions within corporations. It's another level of management introduced to secure better coordination of several presumably separate divisions.[8] Almost by definition, the group mechanism is confined to the divisionalized companies of Categories II and III. But not quite.

There are ambiguities in the group concept and variations in the structure of groups that can be linked to the same factors accounting for variations in the role of corporate staff.

Starting with Category IV, in this instance, there is little evidence of attempts to link operating units into groups headed by a group executive. This seems consistent with the parent corporation's hands-off approach to the highly independent divisions or subsidiaries.

---

[8] Ibid., chap. 4, "Group Executives."

In Category III companies, on the other hand, diverse though the divisions may be, there is an attempt to link the operations more closely with guidance from the corporation. There is an attempt to devise a corporate strategy and to project a corporate identity. Divisions very often are assembled into groups. But for the most part, the divisions within the groups have little in common—other than that they serve the "industrial market" or "consumer market" or operate under some such similarly broad umbrella. The group executive, in such instances, may serve as an advisor, a reviewer of plans, an appraiser of performance. But he is essentially a link pin between the division and their objectives and the corporation. His primary function may well be to plug the communication gap that emerges when the proliferation of divisions has caused too broad a span of control for the chief executive. Chances are that such a group will have no staff at the group level, or possibly just a controllership function that reports to the group executive.

Move to Category II companies and the character of the group and the function of the group executive change. Here, the groups that emerge tend to be more closely knit, comprised of divisions that invite synergistic development. Indeed, in many such situations the group structure develops as a pragmatic mechanism for dealing with the fact that the "discrete and separate" divisions are not really all that discrete or separate. In many such companies, the divisions do share markets or do overlap in technology. The pulling together of these overlapping divisions makes it more possible to develop a business strategy for a total market, or to pool certain production facilities, or share common staff services.

The group, in such instances, actually becomes more of a super-division composed of truncated or even functional divisions. And the group executive, rather than providing liaison between a series of unrelated divisions, becomes the head of a more encompassing profit center.

In Category I companies, the definition of group seems to preclude its existence—except possibly at point 4 in the spectrum where beginning attempts to diversify may lead to the creation of a group that pulls together newer businesses emerging as product divisions. The closest approximation of the group executive in the functionally organized company is the high level executive who coordinates related staff and operating functions—e.g., an executive vice president whose domain covers manufacturing, engineering, R&D, and purchasing. However, he is still primarily a functional executive.

The models in perspective

These major elements of structure, when assembled by category, reveal organizational profiles that are significantly different. Each structural model is rooted in the dominant economic characteristics of the corporation as a total entity. It is worth underscoring the point that each category in itself covers a spectrum. The "more or less" caveat referred to earlier applies to each as well as the overall continuum. The profile of a company at point 13 may be more like one at point 12 than one at 16; or 5 and 4 may be more similar than 5 and 8.

Developments in organization structure make clear that companies, structurally, are trending toward more congruence with the economic realities of their businesses. But obviously there are many companies whose current structures seem to be at odds with their economic models. Indeed, complete congruence is more an ideal than a realizable goal.

In some companies, shorter term pressures, or more immediate advantages take priority over what seems more logical in the longer term. Immediate pressure to penetrate special markets may induce a divisionalized structure even though there are longer-term advantages to greater integration on a functional basis. Or one phase of the company's operations, accounting for perhaps the larger part of the company's total sales and profits, may be so significant that the overall structure is organized functionally to accommodate it. Or the lack of management talent may require higher level management to make more decisions and thus force a greater degree of centralization than seems warranted by the character of the operations. For these and many more highly practical reasons, the longer-term optimum organization structure is less than optimum to those whose performance is evaluated in the short term.

However, there is another set of factors, equally real, that impede achievement of the best fit. These lie in the psyche of the human organization. The incumbent staff may be so thoroughly familiar with the more specific organization problems of various elements of the organization that they have difficulty seeing the total corporation because of its divisions.

Even more inhibiting to achievement of the optimum structure are the inertial factors that restrict any major organization change—the comforts of sticking with past habits and traditions, of applying past practice to new situations.[9] A company's growth may be of a character that it moves from Category I to Category II. But the operating and staff personnel who move with it know how to operate in the environment of a functional organization with greater centralization and don't willingly assume new roles. As a result, some of the more poignant managerial tragedies, particularly those of chief executives, can be traced to their inability to mate individual "management styles" with the economic verities of the total company.

---

[9] For elaboration, see *Organization Change—Perceptions and Realities*, Report No. 561 (The National Industrial Conference Board, July 1972).

Reading 5–2
Trends in the organization of
multinational corporations*
Stanley M. Davis

Methods of organizing and managing multinational industrial corporations have matured considerably in the last five years, and the basic rules are now rather well understood. Changes in the external environment, however, together with new complexities that arise from corporate responses to these changes, continually reduce the effectiveness of these basic structures and practices. The result is that new methods and forms evolve in response to the new exigencies. My purpose in this article is to chart and explain these recent trends in the evolving patterns of global organization among U.S.-based corporations.

We will examine the problems arising from the well-recognized patterns and the refinements that are being made to cope with them. Basic design involves three different organizing units: *functions, products,* and *geography.* Neat distinctions between the three, however, have been found inadequate because they only optimize along one of these dimensions. Here are some of the trends:

Worldwide functional structures show definite instabilities.

Corporations organized by country are exploring how and where to place product management more adequately in their framework.

Firms with worldwide product groups require better coordination within countries and regions than their structures provide.

Corporate planning and development activities have led some companies to organize around markets, not geography.

Some companies experiment with global matrix management and structure.

These developments all point to a trend of learning to integrate and manage diversity in ways that were not possible with the early generations of multinational organization design. This article is intended as a guide to those who are seeking innovative adjustments to organizing the complexities of global corporations.

---

* Reprinted with permission from the Summer 1976 issue of the *Columbia Journal of World Business.* Copyright © 1976 by the Trustees of Columbia University in the City of New York.

The basic patterns

There are many variations in organizational design of an international business, but the general tendency among U.S.-based industrial corporations is quite clear.[1] Initial development of foreign markets occurs through exports, and little attention is paid to either the management or organization of this activity. Investment in local manufacturing facilities is generally triggered as a response to the threat of lost market share caused by the growing sophistication of local enterprise. Management and control of the new operations remains independent, perhaps reporting only dividends and considered by the parent as a portfolio gamble. As growth occurs, and increased capital investments are called for, the more formal procedures and controls used for the domestic operations are applied to the operations abroad.

When a corporation has four or more foreign manufacturing operations it is likely to place them all into an international division, reporting to a single executive. While the structure of the domestic company is laid out along product and/or functional lines, the international division is organized around geographical interests. The head of the division is on a hierarchical par with the heads of the domestic product groups, and all report directly to the president. General managers of each foreign unit report up to the boss of the international division, sometimes through an intermediary regional level, and the units themselves reflect the same functional organization as exists in the domestic product divisions. For the foreign units, the creation of the international division provides guidance and support, but it also increases the control of headquarters over the subsidiaries and reduces some of their previously enjoyed autonomy.

Product versus geography

Once the international division grows large enough to rival the largest domestic product division, capital budgeting and transfer pricing become

---

[1] This article assumes a general knowledge of global corporate design on the part of the reader, and focuses on trends and developments after a brief description of basic structural alternatives. For those who wish to cover the basics in depth, see:

Gilbert H. Clee and Wilber M. Sachtjen, "Organizing a Worldwide Business," *Harvard Business Review*, November–December 1964.

Michael Z. Brooke and H. Lee Remmers, *The Strategy of Multinational Enterprise* (New York: American Elsevier Publishing Co., 1970).

John M. Stopford and Louis T. Wells, *Managing the Multinational Enterprise* (New York: Basic Books, 1972).

Michael G. Duerr and John M. Roach, *Organization and Control of International Operations* (The Conference Board, 1973).

Stanley M. Davis, "Unity of Command versus Balance of Power: Two Models of Management," *Sloan Management Review*, 1975.

substantial issues. Pressures to create a new organization design that bridges the domestic-international split become irresistible. The two dominant choices involve maximizing either the product or the geographic dimension.

In the global product structure, the international division is carved up, and its products are fed back into the rest while domestic units become worldwide product groups. Products that require different technologies and that have dissimilar end-users are logically grouped into separate categories, and the transfer of products into various world markets is best managed within each distinctive product classification. The product diversification may be in related or unrelated lines. A strategy of global product diversification requires heavy investment in R&D; and the global product structure facilitates the transfer and control of technology and new products between domestic and foreign divisions.

To create a global structure based on geography, the domestic business is labeled as the North American area and the regional pieces in the international division are elevated to similar status. In contrast to the diversity and renewing growth phases of the product-structured firms, companies that elect an area mold tend to have a mature product line that serves common end-user markets. They generally place great reliance on lowering manufacturing costs by concentrating and specializing production through long runs, in large plants, using stable technology. They also emphasize marketing techniques as the competitive basis for price and product differentiation. Industries with these characteristics that favored the area structure include food, beverage, container, automotive, farm equipment, pharmaceuticals, and cosmetics.

The worldwide area structure is highly suited to mature businesses with narrow product lines, because their growth potential is greater abroad than in the domestic market where the products and brands are in later phases of their life cycles. Since they derive a high proportion of their total sales from abroad,[2] intimate knowledge of local conditions, constraints, and preferences is essential. Many of these firms rely heavily on advertising and benefit from standardizing their marketing as well as production techniques worldwide. But standardization and area variegation are sometimes incompatible. In one classical gaffe, for example, advertisement for a major U.S.-based banking firm used a picture of a squirrel hoarding nuts. The idea was to convey an image of thrift, preparedness, and security. When the same advertisement appeared in Caracas, however, it brought a derisive reaction, since Venezuela has neither winters nor squirrels as we know them. Instead, the image evoked a

---

[2] Stopford and Wells report that when foreign sales reach 40 percent of the total, most firms turn to some form of direct area coordination (*Managing the Multinational Enterprise,* p. 64).

thieving and destructive rat. The major advantage of a world-wide area structure, then, is its ability to differentiate regional and local markets and determine variations in each appropriate market mix. Its disadvantage as a form of organization is its inability to coordinate different product lines and their logistics of flow from source to markets across areas.

Alternative global organizations include a mixture of product and area structures, and in some cases the use of functions as the defining element in the macro-design. All designs, however, represent trade-offs in which the one that is ultimately selected appears to have the greatest advantages. But what about the advantages that are lost by not having chosen the other designs? In the following sections we will see how global corporations are attempting to answer this question and achieve the advantages of several designs simultaneously. We will look at how various industrial corporations have juggled the functional, product, and geographic dimensions around in their attempts to get the best global organization design. The first step generally involves elimination of the international division.

Eliminating the international division

Through time, the disjunction between a corporation's product structure in its domestic divisions and a geographic basis for organizing its overseas activities creates difficulty. Ironically, the more successful the international division, the more rapidly these difficulties occur. Strategically, the posture shifts from that of a domestic firm with international activities to that of a global corporation. Structurally, the pressures build to reflect this new unity. Although the emergent design is rather predictable in rational economic terms, the speed, clarity, and success with which it is accomplished depends mainly on history, power, and personalities in the firm. As Stopford points out,[3] the major players are bound to have different structural priorities:

Domestic Priorities
Products
Functions
Areas

International Priorities
Areas
Products
Functions

Central staff may compound the conflict by its predominantly functional orientation. While managers are looking for ways to maximize the advan-

---

[3] Ibid., p. 77.

tages of all three dimensions simultaneously, resolution is delayed by the need to defend their interests and perspectives. In the process, the existing organization lags behind the evolving strategy; usually catching up in a large quantum jump known as a "shake up," only to begin lagging behind again.

The detailed study by Beer and Davis[4] is an example of the conflict and cost experienced during the phase when the international division is dismantled. The process generally takes years, and even then the international division may survive for political and quasi-rational reasons. Clark Equipment is another company that has been in the process of shifting to a global organization, and reducing the scope of its international division, for several years.

Clark is a highly integrated manufacturer and distributor of industrial end-user products that are sold through a global network of independent dealers. It has sales of over $1 billion, and international sales represent about a third of this amount. In 1970 they operated with seven domestic product divisions and an international division. At that time, there were many discussions about U.S. versus European sourcing and facilities expansion, and about the need for continent-wide product planning. Clark needed a global perspective for its various product lines, but lacked information systems and a formal structure with which to realize this goal. As part of a rationalization program to realize these needs, they separated marketing and operations as independent "profit" centers functioning worldwide. They rationalized manufacturing facilities to eliminate multiproduct plants, and to develop product-centered operating subsidiaries. Next, the domestic divisions assumed worldwide profit responsibility, and the European headquarters lost its profit and loss responsibility.

Still, in 1976, the international division has survived. Within Clark it is seen as a group of "area-based, entrepreneurial generalists." Their job is to enter new markets and to develop global dealer networks; they are not expected to have functional or product expertise. They play a staff role with regard to established operations, yet they maintain operating and profit responsibility for Clark's Latin American and Asian activities. Two continuing questions for the firm are:

1. Organizationally, when is the right time to shift responsibility to the worldwide product divisions?
2. Strategically, is there sufficient reason to maintain the international division rather than fold it into corporate planning?

In the world of organization theory the pure answer to the second question is probably "no," but historical and political conditions are compelling.

---

[4] Michael Beer and Stanley Davis, "Creating a Global Organization: Failures Along the Way," *Columbia Journal of World Business*, Summer 1976.

Many international divisions such as the ones at Clark and the one examined by Beer and Davis continue to exist, some as useful anomalies and some as mere anachronisms. The general model assumes that the international division will be replaced by regional or product divisions, while in practice international divisions die hard and often linger on in residual roles, sometimes continuing to play important though reduced roles. In all cases, the transfiguration is a struggle to piece together the dimensions of a new global structure. Even firms as sophisticated as IBM have been very slow to break up their international division. Although there are no quantitative data to prove it conclusively, it appears that firms who diversify their products before they diversify the countries they operate in attempt to disband their international division sooner, but may have more difficulty doing so. Corporations that expand globally without or before becoming multiproduct, on the other hand, seem to retain the international division structure longer but are able to make the transition more smoothly, as the IBM and Pfizer examples will show in the next section.

The moral of the tale is that firms assuming a global strategy would do well to adopt a global structure. When they don't it is likely to be because of history, politics, and personalities in and of the firm. Companies that want to avoid domestic-international splits among their management should avoid the same in their structure.

Given: Geographic organization
Needed: Global product management

The international division, and the extension of the geographic basis to a worldwide area structure, improves the coordination of all product lines within each zone, but at the expense of reduced coordination between areas for any one product line. The unwillingness to make this trade-off leads corporations with a geographic structure to introduce global product line management into their organization design. Narrow product line companies that embark on a diversification strategy, for example, have drifted away from earlier typical methods of integrating the new lines into the existing geographic set-up. These new lines, generally small when considered as a proportion of the whole, tend to drift upward in the geographic hierarchy, gathering product/management identity and independence as they become more centralized. IBM's office products division and Pfizer's international diversification efforts are examples of this phenomenon.

IBM

IBM was one of the last holdouts for the international division (IBM World Trade Corporation) structure long after its international sales suggested that a dichotomous structure of "here and abroad" was inadequate. Shortly after it broke up its international division and created a worldwide area structure, it began to differentiate the global structure for its office products (OP) business. OP is a substantially different business than the very large data processing (DP) operations, and the head of this division wanted it to be one profit center independent of the geographic profit centers for data processing. In less than three years, between 1972–75, the locus of OP in the IBM hierarchy moved upward from a role subordinate to DP in each country unit, to that of a product division with worldwide responsibility.

Until 1972, there was a single composite sales and profit objective at the country level for both DP and OP. Since as much as 90 percent of a country's business was DP, OP usually would be slighted in any trade-off. Also, staff at World Trade Headquarters were shared and, on critical functions like pricing, OP did not get the support it needed. Steps were taken in 1972 to correct this problem when the country manager was no longer allowed to make OP-DP trade-off decisions; they were to be made at the group (Europe, Americas/Far East) level. For a brief while the OP country managers reported to the OP group managers, but then the reporting line was further centralized and they reported directly to World Trade Headquarters. Under that arrangement OP became a separate profit center within the international side of IBM, and the reporting lines effectively bypassed the area and country levels of the old structure. In what must have been read as a moderate challenge to the hegemony of the country managers, who were generally DP types, the OP country manager now had to rely on him only for non-marketing staff support on a dotted line basis.

The third structural change in three years took place in mid-1975 when OP was centralized once again. It was taken out of the three geographic groups (United States, and Americas/Far East) and set up with the new minicomputers and software as part of a worldwide General Business Group. The General Business Group, an almost $4 billion unit, then set up its own international division based on country management units.

Pfizer

Pfizer, one of the world's leading pharmaceutical companies, has followed a similar path. With about half of its sales and more of its earnings coming from abroad, it has still held onto its international division rather than shift to a global area design. Beginning in the early 1960s it embarked on a diversification program to counter the decline in new drugs due to the harsh regulatory climate and severe technological obstacles. Its program was both ambitious and haphazard. They made about 60 acquisitions in a dozen years and strayed far afield of their basic business: drugs and health care products in a science-based company. Organizationally, most of these new product lines were fit into the existing geographic structure of country management. During the period from acquisition, through adjustment, and often to divestiture, these units would be moved up and down the geographic hierarchy looking for the appropriate way of placing diversified product lines in a geographically differentiated structure. Many, of course, were dumped along the way, including pesticides, plastics, protein fish meal, door-to-door cosmetics, and baby foods. Those fitting into the more traditional Pfizer offerings finally survived within the international division. Significantly, the more distinct businesses were ultimately organized as separate worldwide product divisions, bypassing the international-domestic split, and reporting directly to corporate headquarters. These included Quigley refractories, Howmedica orthopedic supplies, and Coty consumer products.

The reasons and conditions for pulling a product line out of its geographic moorings are similar to the reasons for creating a global structure based on product lines in general. Among the most important are:

Sharp differences in marketing or production and supply.

Little or no interdependence between the main line and the new one.

Currently small, but potentially large, growth of the separated product.

To avoid rivalry and hostility among managers in the different products.

The lessons of IBM and Pfizer are repeated in other firms that move outside their original, narrow product base:

1. Pure geographic structures do not permit sufficient integration of any one different product line.
2. The more differentiated a new product line is from the main business the more centrally (globally) it should be managed.
3. The need to introduce product differentiation into a geographically specialized hierarchy increases the managerial and the structural complexity by geometric proportions.

Given: Global product management
Needed: Geographic coordination

Global corporations that are organized along product lines have the opposite problem: how to coordinate their diverse business activities within any one geographic area. Having made the strategic choices to carry a diversity of products to new areas, their structures reflect the need to maximize technological linkages among the far flung plants in each business unit. This has been done, however, at the cost of duplicating management and organization in each area. To cope with problems of coordinating and simplifying these parallel managements, firms must reach through their existing product structure and weave an additional dimension across the organizational pattern. In the language of this metaphor, those who do it successfully will have a blend rather than a plaid fabric as the result. Eaton Corporation offers one example of a global firm that has successfully woven a few threads across the straight grain.

Eaton

Eaton is a highly diversified company in the capital goods and automotive industries. It has sales of over $1.5 billion, employs over 50,000 people and operates over 140 facilities in more than 20 countries. In 1974 each of its four worldwide product groups had a Managing Director for European operations. Each of the firm's 29 manufacturing facilities and 6 associate companies in Europe reported to one of these 4 people. In addition, 18 service operations, a finance operation, and an R&D center in Europe reported to their functional counterparts in the parent company. Senior management was concerned about how well it was coordinating these activities in Europe.

It was important for Eaton to be able to evaluate and respond to significant trends and developments in European countries, such as tariffs, tax matters, duties, government legislation, currency fluctuations, environmental controls and energy conservation, co-determination and industrial democracy, labor matters, nationalization, and government participation in ownership. Its current organization structure did not provide a regular and convenient means of communication among its European units, either for exchanging information, for building a positive corporate identity, or for assessing corporate needs and coordinating programs and procedures to meet them.

Rejecting the notion of country managers, and/or of one Vice President for Europe, they instituted a European Coordinating Committee (ECC) together with coordinating committees in each country where they had major involvement. The four European Managing Directors were permanent members of the ECC and each served as a coordinator for one or more of the country committees; Europeans representing various functions were appointed to one-year terms; and the firm's Executive Vice Presidents and Group Vice Presidents were all made ex-officio members, with one being present at each ECC meeting on a rotating basis. Meetings are held monthly, midway between the monthly meetings of the corporate Operating Committee, and minutes are sent to world headquarters within five working days. Attendance is required, the chair rotates periodically, and the location rotates among the major facilities. The President and the four Group Vice Presidents flew to Europe to formally launch the new coordinating committees, and the corporate newsletter devoted an entire issue to the new developments.

Six months later Eaton formed a Latin American Coordinating Committee, and about a year after that they created a U.S. and Canadian Division Managers' Council, using the same model. The same attention was paid to details of the committees' operations and to their implementation. The European committee, then, served as a model for realizing better coordination across business lines in each of the firm's major geographic concentrations, and it is probable that the capstone in the future will be a council of councils that will take the form of annual or semi-annual worldwide coordinating committee meetings.

This example is a moderate step, in structural terms, towards complementing the warp of a traditional product line organization with the woof of geographic coordinates. The fabric of the organization is not significantly altered, rather it is reinforced. Little is done to increase the complexity of the global design or management practices. Success depends on thorough implementation of a plan that least disturbs the existing managerial style and corporate culture. The change is supplementary, rather than radical, and it has the desired effect of managing *both* product and country diversity.

Firms that are organized along global product lines will probably experience similar needs to coordinate their activities within a foreign country when:

1. They have at least two significant but organizationally independent business units there.
2. There are economies to be gained from pooled information.
3. There are benefits derivable from a more unified corporate identity.
4. There is a discernible need for assessing and coordinating corporate programs and their implementation.

The functional dimension in global terms

The product and area structures, and any combinations, all treat the functional dimension in tertiary fashion, locating it in the various parts of the structure after the deck already has been cut twice. The extractive raw material ventures are an exception to this rule.

Functional activities play a critical role, for example, in the petroleum industry because of the scale required for economy, the technological complexity involved, and the importance of captive markets for the sale of crude. All major petroleum companies encompass exploration, crude production, tanker and pipeline transportation, manufacturing (refining), and marketing, in addition to the logistics of worldwide supply and distribution at each step in these process and product flows. These may be managed directly through centralized functional departments acting with worldwide line responsibility, and supplemented by corporate staff who coordinate the functions within areas; or, conversely, through area management, with staff coordination for the functions. In any one petroleum company, the structure is either a mixture of the two or else it shifts back and forth. Conoco, for example, dropped its area division and returned to a functional structure last summer. It reasoned that environmental changes, such as the oil import program and the Arab oil embargo, no longer made it feasible to think of domestic and foreign markets separately.

Most oil companies have a petrochemical products division reporting directly to the president, and since they have diversified into other energy sources they also have a unit for that at the top of the hierarchy. The result is usually a three-dimensional mixture of parallel hierarchies: some functions, some regions, and some products all reporting directly to the chief executive. Each of the hierarchies then has its own particular structural sequence: for example, a functional division will be subdivided by regions, whereas a region reporting directly to the top would subdivide by functions; a product division might subdivide by functions or by regions. The result is a complex array of different hierarchies [see Figure 1].

Whichever dimension is chosen as the organizing principle for a corporate division, that unit will confront problems integrating the other dimension(s) in its lower levels. Also, the corporation as a whole faces the problems of integrating each dimension as it is variously located in different countries, different hierarchical levels, and different divisions. By varying the primary building blocks, rather than using only one as the basis, the coordinating dilemmas are compounded rather than resolved, no mat-

Figure 1

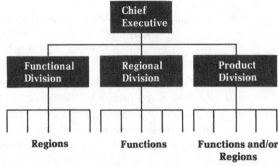

ter how intelligent is the choice of mix. It is an open question whether management is ultimately backing into structural diseconomies; each structural choice is rational, but the totality nevertheless creates complexities that often negate the gained advantages. The structural choice at these macro levels of design is also motivated by whether they are politically more or less vulnerable to dissection by the government in the event of moves to break up the big oil companies.

The aluminum industry is another example where functional activities continue to play a primary role in fixing the structure. Alcan, for example, organized their activities in 1970 around the three major steps in the making and selling of their single product line. Reporting directly to the president were three executive vice presidents for raw materials, smelting, and fabricating sales; and within each of these functional divisions, foreign subsidiaries then grouped around area managers. Where a national subsidiary is itself vertically integrated, as in Brazil and India, they report up the fabricating line. A worldwide functional structure, however, is not very stable and in 1973 Alcan subsumed its ore activities under the executive vice president—smelting. Their concern was with the vulnerability of their sources of supply. This left the company with a global dichotomy between production and sales in line operations, which continues to drift to an area format with problems of integration for supply and distribution on a global basis.

The lesson is, don't organize global structures around business functions unless you are in extractive raw materials industries, and even then you will find that they are unstable and will have to share primacy with geographic factors and, in some instances, with product differences. For global industrial corporations, basic functions such as manufacturing and marketing are and should be subsumed under product or geographic units. Even European-based companies, who have tended to emphasize functional structures in their domestic activities far more than U.S.-based ones, give this dimension lesser importance in their multinational design.[5]

Organizing around markets, not geography

Although the basic organizing dimensions for multinational corporations are functions, products, and geographic areas, some firms have begun to think in terms of market differences as a more important basis for determining their global structure. A market is conceived as an identifiable and homogenous group that has a similar pattern of need, purchasing behavior, and product use. Taking this definition and applying it to the

---

[5] Lawrence G. Franko, "The Move Toward a Multidimensional Structure in European Organizations," *Administrative Science Quarterly*, p. 493–506.

nations of the world, companies are less likely to divide the globe on the basis of physical proximity than on the basis of needs and abilities to satisfy them. The traditional categories of Latin America, Far East, Europe, and the like lose their power, and the new categorization is derived from development economics. Here, the oversimplified dichotomy between developed and less-developed has yielded to the current preference for dividing the globe into five "worlds." The first world includes the familiar capitalist economies of the industrialized world, and the second world includes the 1.3 billion people in the centrally planned communist economies. The third world is comprised of developing countries that have a modern infrastructure and/or have exceptional wealth in natural resources. Able to attract foreign investment and to borrow on commercial terms, they need time and technology more than foreign aid. They include OPEC members, Brazil, Mexico, South Korea, Taiwan, and Turkey. The fourth world countries have similar characteristics but in much less generous amounts and therefore need injections of both trade and aid. The fifth world countries are the complete have-nots, without resources or the likelihood of ever improving their lot.

Business planners and marketers have taken these distinctions and, together with their own companies' historical record have redrawn their organizational lines. One firm begins with Stanford Research Institute's economic projections for 1975–90, and plans a growth-market group around ten countries that are expected to have annual growth rates averaging 6 percent or more. Brazil, Iran, Taiwan, Korea, Indonesia, Mexico, Venezuela, Japan, Turkey, and Spain. Richardson-Merrill, another multinational, has maintained its Latin America/Far East unit, but has reorganized the country groupings within it to reflect the same market differentiation:

Group 1: Andean Common Market, S.E. Asia, Philippines, and the Caribbean—representing small, noncomplex, and underdeveloped markets for their products, in places they have chosen to operate.

Group 2: India, Indonesia, and Iran—representing large, noncomplex, and high potential growth markets.

Group 3: Mexico, Brazil, and Australia—representing large, complex markets to them, with proven records for their company as well as satellite markets in neighboring countries.

Group 4: Japan—stands by itself as another large, complex, and mature market that requires specialized attention.

Ingersoll Rand distinguishes between offensive and defensive strategies when establishing manufacturing plants abroad: "offensive" plants are to be used for exports as well as for sales in that country, whereas "defensive" location decisions are mainly to protect against erosion of market share in that country. Other firms are finding it useful to define area managements in terms of a composite scale of key factors: examples include labor-capital intensity of the technology employed, the level of anticipated competition, the character of government (e.g., a socialist bloc group), the cost of energy, and the availability of skilled personnel.

Market-centered thinking is making deeper inroads into planning and development than into operations, but the evolutionary trend is clear nonetheless. General Electric carries the idea into its planning around "strategic business units," which easily translate into families of businesses laid out on a product/geography grid. Again, the older and already tested structure acts as a supportive framework, while new strategies evolve some kinds of metastructures as an overlay. As the new language developed in central staffs gets absorbed, and as the future orientation becomes operating reality, it is not unlikely that we will witness a new generation of structural form in global corporations.

The basic principle in this approach is that geography is an obfuscation for conceptualizing global growth strategy and for organizing and managing the multinational corporations' response. This avenue is far from new as regards market segmentation for domestic activities. A common differentiation in a domestic structure, for example, is between a government sector, an industrial sector, and a consumer sector. Organizing around markets, rather than geography, is recent, however, as applied to worldwide corporate structuring. The country, or nation-state, is kept as the basic unit of analysis, but the grouping together of countries is done on the basis of a different set of questions and assumptions: not on the assumption that understanding management in Mexico helps one to start a business next door to Guatemala; but that demographic, income, natural resource data, and the like are more relevant criteria, and also are ones that lend themselves to country cluster analysis and hence to market-determined organization design.

The patterns and problems discussed above for the global industrial corporations are also reflected in the multinational spread of service corporations. Here, market segmentation around clients and services is analogous to the product dimension in a manufacturing firm, and management searches for ways to integrate this dimension with the familiar geographic design.

The market-center concept is useful to all firms, though few thus far have actually structured their worldwide activities around it. Companies might want to do so when:

1. Operations in neighboring countries are totally independent of each other.

2. Communication networks are good, and the technology for processing information rapidly and accurately is present or is not important.
3. There already exists a marketing orientation with the parent company.
4. A set of markets can be identified that have more managerial validity than do sets of countries with geographic regions.
5. The concept is already familiar to managers through the planning process.
6. Management is not locked in to defense of territories.

Global matrix organization

The trends in organization that we have discussed above all start with a primary structural dimension—either functions, products, or geography—and then try to compensate for the benefits lost by not choosing another of these dimensions as their major organizing theme. All of them involve trade-offs. When a company shifts from organization form A to form B, many benefits of the old form linger on because they have been deeply ingrained. At some imaginary fleeting moment there is a balance of benefits, but over time the advantages of the abandoned form are bound to atrophy. This imbalance frequently worsens until there is a sense that the trade-off has gone too far. Companies then either swing back to the earlier form, as in the familiar centralization/decentralization/recentralization cycles, or else they introduce subordinate coordination schemes such as the ones described in the sections above.

In other words, when companies face multiple goals, they often deal with them in sequence rather than simultaneously. Or else different parts of the company organize around the different subgoals. Translated into structural terms, there is an implicit assumption that the entire organization cannot specialize by two or three dimensions simultaneously. It is this assumption that some firms are rejecting. In doing so, they must reject a pattern of organization based on a hierarchy of power and a unity of command, and they replace it with a dual or plural model that involves a balance of interest and power. One structural design is not overlaid with elements of another, rather, the two are blended and given coequal weight. The general manager of a French subsidiary, for example, will report to a vice president for a worldwide product line as well as to vice president for Europe. This is the essence of global matrix organization.

Dow Chemical Company is perhaps one of the first industrial corporations to use the matrix form in its global macro-structure. Although Dow does not publish organization charts, for internal or external consumption, its 1968 annual report nevertheless did publish a matrix diagram of sorts

Figure 2

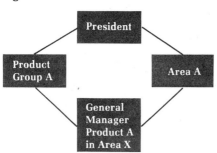

in the form of a photo cube. Along each dimension of the cube were photos of the key managers for the various functions, product groups, and geographic areas in the Dow organization. At that time the Dow organizational philosophy was that they managed with a three dimensional matrix. Shortly after that, in fact, one of Dow's senior managers, William Goggin, became President of Dow Corning and introduced there what he called a four-dimensional matrix, by adding "time" into the sense of structure.

While these ambitious notions of multidimensional structuring grappled with managing global complexities simultaneously, they proved exceedingly difficult to keep in balance. By 1970, it was apparent that Dow Chemical's matrix was effectively two-dimensional, a worldwide grid of product and geography with functions variously located at different levels in the grid hierarchies. In 1972 the matrix became further imbalanced when the product dimension lost line authority and was kicked upstairs in the form of three Business Group Managers who reported to Corporate Product Development. They were to be separate channels of communication for their product group across the areas, and their clout came from their control over capital expenditures. Life Sciences was the only product division that maintained worldwide reporting control.

Around 1974 Dow Chemical held a meeting of its senior managers worldwide. During an anonymous question-and-answer period with the Chairman, Carl Gerstaker, the question was asked: "Which dimension of the matrix do you consider to be most important?" The very fact that the question was asked demonstrates that the matrix had deteriorated significantly. Gerstaker's answer was to the point: the most important dimension in a matrix organization is the weakest and/or the most threatened. Despite the Chairman's understanding of multidimensional structures, however, the matrix continued to decompose. In 1975, the Life Sciences Division lost its worldwide reporting line and was subsumed under each of the geographic "operating units." Whereas each product used to have an identifiable team linking its business through the areas, the basic locus of these teams now exists within each area. Today, Dow Chemical would be described more appropriately as using a geographically-based structure. In retrospect, it should be noted that, with the exception of Life Sciences, only the areas ever had their own letterhead stationery. Although the ideology of global matrix management still exists in some corners of Dow, the ethos and spirit of it is not to be found.

The example of Dow is not to be read as a failure. As Peter Drucker says, the matrix structure "will never be a preferred form of organization; it is fiendishly difficult."[6] He concludes, nevertheless, that ". . . any manager in a multinational business will have to learn to understand it if he wants to function effectively himself."[7] Dow's global matrix was a valiant and creative effort, a radical approach to structuring a multinational corporation. Some European firms, such as Phillips, have operated with a matrix organization for years, and some U.S.-based non-industrial corporations have also relied on the matrix form. Global construction and engineering firms, such as Bechtel Corporation, and one bank, Citibank, are examples that have been more successful than Dow Chemical.

Dow Corning, a twentieth the size of Dow Chemical, has been more successful in maintaining its global matrix. A relatively smaller size may be one reason, but far more important is that Dow Corning pays great attention to the behavioral requirements of matrix management in addition to the structural ones. The Chairman is an overt enthusiast of the matrix, amiably stressing to his managers that they will be democratic and share power. The balance of power and shared decision making is translated into non-concrete form, for example, by the elimination of walls and corridors in favor of office landscaping around family groupings. Since the organization is purposefully built around a paradox of competing claims, stability rests in managers' behavior more than in structural form. Matrix is a verb.

Corporations need not organize their domestic activities around a matrix in order for the form to be used in their global framework. But if they are going to attempt implementing a matrix design, they should only do so when:

1. There is diversification of both products and markets requiring balanced and simultaneous strategy decisions.
2. The opportunities lost and difficulties experienced by favoring either a product or geographic unity of command cannot be ignored.

---

[6] Peter Drucker, *Management: Tasks, Responsibilities, Practices* (New York: Harper & Row) p. 598.

[7] Ibid.

3. Environmental pressure to secure international economies of scale require the shared use of scarce human resources.
4. There is a need for enriched information processing capacity because of uncertain, complex, and interdependent tasks.
5. Information, planning, and control systems operate along the different dimensions of the structure simultaneously.
6. As much attention is paid to managerial behavior as to the structure. The corporate culture and ethos must actively support and believe in negotiated management. They have to think matrix.

Conclusions

In summary, the basic patterns of organization for global corporations are rather standard by this time. While the posture of a firm is domestic with only some foreign activities, the latter are generally grouped into an international division. Once a global orientation is assumed by the firm, either a worldwide product structure or worldwide geographic divisions are the most common alternatives. Functional specializations are seldom used as the organizing basis for a global structure; natural resource industries are sometimes the exceptions to this rule.

When organizations experience significant diversification in both their products/services and markets, the singular structure based on *either* global product division *or* geographic area divisions becomes inadequate. Diversification has led to experiments in global organization design which simultaneously structures a corporation by product/service *and* by geography. This occurs through a variety of forms, although the principles of design are the same in each.

In its simpler form, corporations develop an overlay of the second organizing dimension across the basic dimension used in the global structuring. Examples include using area coordinating committees in a product structured firm; shifting the level of product line reporting, according to the unique requirements of each, between country, region, zone, and worldwide in a geographically structured firm; and using the corporate planning function to negotiate product-market interdependencies.

In its more complex form, corporations are using global matrix management and matrix structures. These involve some manner of dual reporting lines between the product/service and market dimensions; dual accounting and planning; and a sense of shared responsibilities in which trade-offs have to be negotiated at the point of interface, rather than sent up to a common boss for resolution. Global matrices, as is also the case with their domestic counterparts, are structurally unstable. Conflict is inherent in the design, and managed as an acceptable cost for having the best of both forms of organization.

The general trend is clear. Traditional structures, with their simple choice of functional, product, *or* geographic design, are relied on less and less by global industrial corporations because they optimize along only one dimension. Changes in the external environment and the strategic responses to these changes, however, led global corporations to develop and manage more complex organization designs than were possible only a decade ago. The new designs attempt to integrate and manage competing needs simultaneously. As the new patterns are understood more clearly, it becomes evident that their success does not lie in having made the most rational choice of structure in any given case. Instead, success with the new patterns depends more on managerial ability to live with a paradox.

ORGANIZATIONAL CHANGE

Chapter 6

Managing organizational change

Even an appropriate organizational design has a limited lifetime. Inevitable changes in a company's environment, whether cultural, economic, or technological, create misfits and their associated problems. Consequently, an important aspect of managerial work involves the *process* of managing changes in organizational design. The remainder of this book focuses on such processes.

Organizational change strategies and tactics

Just as there are many different types of job designs, compensation systems, and training programs, there are also many different approaches to planning and implementing changes in those systems.

Strategically, managers sometimes try to introduce organizational change very quickly—in a matter of days or weeks, perhaps even before people realize what has happened. At other times they proceed much slower; change efforts have been known to take years before they are successfully completed. Managers sometimes involve virtually no one but themselves in the planning and execution of a change; at other times they involve many people—perhaps everyone who will be affected by the change.

In dealing with specific individuals or groups of individuals, managers can employ a large number of tactics to implement an organizational change. These tactics include: persuading people of the merits of the change; forcing or coercing people to accept the change without resistance; offering people some form of compensation in lieu of what they will lose as a result of the change; supporting people emotionally or with education to help them accept the change; scaring people into accepting the change; asking people to participate and help in the design or implementation of the change; and co-opting people—making them feel as if they are participating. The appropriateness of any of these tactics varies significantly in different change efforts.

Problem-solving change versus developmental change

Organizational change efforts can be thought of as existing on a continuum where at one extreme a company attempts solely to solve some current organizational problem and at the other extreme attempts solely to prevent problems from emerging in the future. Most change efforts will, of course, be somewhere between the extremes, but will usually be aimed mainly at solving a current problem or developing the organization for the future.

Distinguishing between problem-solving and developmental change is also important because managers tend to approach these two different kinds of change efforts using different strategies and tactics.

Choices

In managing organizational change, managers are confronted with many choices. They must decide:

1. How much change to try to bring about.
2. How much effort will be directed at problem-solving versus developmental change.
3. What specific strategy and tactics to use.

The difficulties inherent in making these choices are increased by the number of options that are possible in any instance.

The remainder of this book is designed to help you develop your decision-making abilities in these areas. Part IV focuses mostly on problem-solving change, while Part V focuses on developmental change.

PART IV

Section four shifts our attention from questions of organizational design to issues associated with implementing changes in design tools to solve organizational problems, regardless of the type of organization involved.

Managers who attempt to introduce major organizational changes often run into problems of human resistance. The text in this section provides a framework for analyzing such resistance and for selecting appropriate change strategies and tactics. The cases present examples of a variety of different change strategies and tactics. The readings provide specific discussions of two very different approaches to change: those aimed at minimizing any resistance (Tagiuri) and those aimed at overcoming resistance (Machiavelli).

Chapter 7

Organizational change strategies and tactics

Solving and avoiding organizational problems inevitably involves the introduction of organizational change. When the required changes are small and isolated, they can usually be accomplished without major problems. However, when they are large and involve many people and subunits, they can often bring about significant problems.

The following scenario illustrates a common pattern in the process of organizational change:

1. Some factors in a business situation change over a period of time.
2. A number of aspects of the organization that once fit the situation and worked well no longer are appropriate.
3. Organizational problems begin to surface.
4. Managers become aware of the problems and attempt to take some corrective actions.
5. The management initiative runs into resistance.
6. The managers eventually overcome the resistance, but at a large cost to the organization (and often to themselves).

Though managers may encounter many potential problems while initiating an organizational change, the one that seems to emerge most often is related to human resistance.[1] To understand how managers can successfully manage organizational change, we must begin by examining this central problem area.

---

[1] See Jay Lorsch, "Managing Change," in *Organizational Behavior and Administration*, ed. Paul Lawrence, Louis B. Barnes, and Jay Lorsch (Homewood, Ill.: Richard D. Irwin, Inc., 1976), pp. 669–72.

HUMAN RESISTANCE TO CHANGE

Human resistance to change takes many forms, from open rebellion to very subtle, passive resistance. And it emerges for many reasons—some of which are rational and some of which are not. Some reasons are primarily self-centered; others are relatively selfless.

Politics and power struggles

One major reason that people resist organizational change is that they see they are going to lose something of personal value as a result of the change. Resistance in these cases is often called "politics" or "political behavior," because people are focusing on their own best interests and not that of the total organization.[2] For example:

After a number of years of rapid growth, the president of one organization decided that its size demanded the creation of a new staff function—New Product Planning and Development—to be headed by a vice president. Operationally, this change eliminated most of the decision-making power that the vice presidents of marketing, engineering, and production had over new products. Inasmuch as new products were very important in this organization, the change also reduced the status of the marketing, engineering, and production VPs. Yet status was important to those three vice presidents.

During the two months after the president announced his idea for a new-product vice president, the existing vice presidents each came up with six or seven reasons why the new arrangement might not work. Their objections grew louder and louder until the president "shelved" the new job idea.

A manufacturing company had traditionally employed a large group of personnel people as counselors, "father confessors," and friends to its production employees. This group of counselors exhibited high morale because of the professional satisfaction they received from the "helping relationships" they had with employees. When a new performance appraisal system was installed, the personnel people were required to provide each employee's supervisor with a written evaluation of the employee's "emotional maturity," "promotion potential," etc., every six months. As some of the personnel people immediately recognized, the change would alter their relationship with most employees—from a peer/friend/

---

[2] For a discussion of power and politics in corporations, see *Power and the Corporate Mind*, chap. 6, by Abraham Zaleznik and Manfred F. R. Kets De Vries, (Boston: Houghton Mifflin, 1975); and *Macro Organizational Behavior*, chap. 4, by Robert H. Miles (Santa Monica, Calif.: Goodyear Publishing, 1978).

helper to more of a boss/evaluator. Predictably, they resisted the new system.

While publicly arguing that the new system was not as good for the company as the old one, they privately put as much pressure as possible on the personnel vice president until he significantly altered the new system.

"Political behavior" emerges in organizations because what is in the best interests of one individual or group is sometimes not in the best interests of the total organization or of other individuals and groups. The consequences of organizational change efforts often are good for some people and bad for others. As a result, politics and power struggles often emerge throughout these change efforts.

While this political behavior sometimes takes the form of two or more armed camps publicly fighting it out, it usually is much more subtle. In many cases it occurs completely under the surface of public dialogue. In a similar way, although power struggles are sometimes initiated by scheming and ruthless individuals, they more often are fostered by those who view their potential loss as an unfair violation of their implicit, or psychological, contract with the organization.[3]

Misunderstanding and a lack of trust

People also resist change when they incorrectly perceive that it might cost them considerably more than they will gain. Such situations often occur when people are unable to understand the full implications of a change or when trust is lacking in the change initiator/employee relationship.[4]

For example, when the president of a small Midwestern company announced to his managers that the company would implement a flexible working schedule for all employees, it had never occurred to him that he might run into resistance. He had been introduced to the concept at a management seminar and decided to use it to make working conditions at his company more attractive, particularly to clerical and plant personnel. Shortly after the announcement to his managers, numerous rumors began to circulate among plant employees—none of whom really knew what flexible working hours meant—and many of whom were distrustful of the manufacturing vice president. One rumor suggested that "flexible hours" meant that most people would have to work whenever their super-

[3] Edgar Schein, *Organizational Psychology,* (Englewood Cliffs, N.J.: Prentice-Hall, 1965), p. 44.

[4] See Chris Argyris, *Intervention Theory and Method,* (Reading, Mass.: Addison-Wesley, 1970), p. 70.

visors asked them to—including weekends and evenings. The employee association, a local union, held a quick meeting and then presented the management with a nonnegotiable demand that the flexible hours concept be dropped. The president, caught completely by surprise, decided to drop the issue.

Few organizations can be characterized as having a high level of trust between employees and managers; consequently, it is easy for misunderstandings to develop when change is introduced. Unless misunderstandings are surfaced and clarified quickly, they can lead to resistance.

Different assessments of the situation

Another common reason people resist organizational change is that their own analysis of the situation differs from that of those initiating the change. In such cases, their analysis typically sees more costs than benefits resulting from the change, not only for themselves, but for their company as well.

For example, the president of one moderate-size bank was shocked by his staff's analysis of their real estate investment trust (REIT) loans. Their complex analysis suggested that the bank could easily lose up to $10 million and that possible losses were increasing each month by 20 percent. Within a week, the president drew up a plan to reorganize that part of the bank that managed REITs. However, because of his concern for the bank's stock price, he chose not to release the staff report to anyone except the new REIT section manager. The reorganization immediately ran into massive resistance from the people involved. The group sentiment, as articulated by one person, was "Has he gone mad? Why in God's name is he tearing apart this section of the bank? His actions have already cost us three very good people (who quit), and have crippled a new program we were implementing (which the president was unaware of) to reduce our loan losses."

Those who initiate change sometime incorrectly assume that they have all the relevant information required to conduct an adequate organizational analysis. Further, they often assume that those who will be affected by the change have the same basic facts, when they do not. In either case, the difference in information that groups work with often leads to differences in analysis, which in turn can lead to resistance. Moreover, insofar as the resistance is based on a more accurate analysis of the situation than that held by those initiating the change, that resistance is obviously "good" for the organization, a fact which is not obvious to some managers who assume that resistance is always bad.[5]

---

[5] See Paul R. Lawrence, "How to Deal with Resistance to Change," *Harvard Business Review*, May–June, 1954.

Fear

People sometimes resist change because they know or fear they will not be able to develop the new skills and behaviors required of them. All human beings are limited in their ability to change their behavior, with some people much more limited in this respect than others.[6] Organizational change can inadvertently require people to change too much, too quickly. When such a situation occurs, people typically resist the change—sometimes consciously, but often unconsciously.

Peter Drucker has argued that the major obstacle to organization growth is managers' inability to change their attitudes and their behaviors.[7] In many cases, he points out, corporations grow to a certain point and then slow down or stop growing because key managers are unable to change as rapidly as their organizations. Even if they intellectually understand the need for changes in the way they operate, they sometimes are unable to make the transition.

In a sense, all people who are affected by change experience some emotional turmoil, because change involves loss and uncertainty—even changes which appear to be "positive," or "rational."[8] For example, a person who receives a significantly more important job as a result of an organizational change will probably be very happy. But it is possible that such a person also feels uneasy. A new and very different job will require new and different behavior, new and different relationships, as well as the loss of some current activities and relationships that provide satisfaction. It is common under such circumstances for a person to emotionally resist giving up certain aspects of the current situation.

Still other reasons

People also sometimes resist organizational change to "save face"; to go along with the change would be, they think, an admission that some of their previous decisions or beliefs were wrong. They may resist because of peer group pressure, or because of a supervisor's resistant attitude. Indeed, there are many reasons why people resist change.[9]

Because of all the possible reasons for resistance to organizational change, it is hardly surprising that organizations do not automatically

---

[6] For a discussion of resistance that is personality-based, see Goodwin Watson, "Resistance to Change," in *The Planning of Change* by Warren Bennis, Kenneth Benne, and Robert Chin (New York: Holt, Rinehart, and Winston, 1969), pp. 489–93.

[7] *The Practice of Management* (New York: Harper & Row, 1954).

[8] See Robert Luke, "A Structural Approach to Organizational Change," *Journal of Applied Behavioral Science*, 1973.

[9] For a general discussion of resistance and reasons for it, see chap. 3 in Gerald Zaltman and Robert Duncan, *Strategies for Planned Change* (New York: John Wiley & Sons, 1977).

and easily adapt to environmental, or technological, or strategic changes. Indeed, organizations usually adapt only because managers successfully employ strategies and tactics for dealing with potential resistance.

TACTICS FOR DEALING WITH RESISTANCE

Managers may use a number of tactics to deal with resistance to change. These include education/communication, participation, facilitation and support, negotiation, co-optation, coercion and manipulation.[10]

Education/communication

One of the most commonly used ways of dealing with resistance to change is education and communication. This tactic is aimed at helping people see the need for the logic of a change. It can involve one-on-one discussions, presentations to groups, or memos and reports. For example, as a part of an effort to make changes in a division's structure, measurement system, and reward system, the division manager put together a one hour audio-visual presentation that explained the changes and the reasons for the changes. Over a four-month period, he made this presentation no less than a dozen times to groups of 20 or 30 corporate and divisional managers.

Education/communication can be ideal when resistance is based on inadequate or inaccurate information and analysis, especially if the initiators need the resister's help in implementing the change. But this tactic requires at least a minimally good relationship between the initiators and the others, or the resisters may not believe what they hear. It also requires time and effort, particularly if a lot of people are involved.

Participation

Participation as a change tactic implies that the initiators involve the resisters or potential resisters in some aspect of the design and implementation of the change. For example, the head of a small financial services company once created a task force to help design and implement changes in the company's reward system. The task force was composed of eight second and third level managers from different parts of the company. The president's specific request to them was that they recommend changes in the company's benefits package. They were given six months and asked

---

[10] Conceptually there are a number of ways that one can label change tactics. This list of seven tactics is one useful approach. Other writers on this subject have used different variations on that list.

to file a brief progress report with the president once a month. After making their recommendations, which the president largely accepted, they were asked to help the firm's personnel director implement them.

Participation is a rational choice of tactics when change initiators believe they do not have all the information they need to design and implement a change, or when they need the whole-hearted commitment of others in implementing a change. Considerable research has demonstrated that participation generally leads to commitment, not just compliance.[11] But participation does have its drawbacks. Not only can it lead to a poor solution if the process is not carefully managed, but also it can be enormously time-consuming.

Facilitation and support

Another way in which managers can deal with potential resistance to change is through facilitation and support. As a tactic, it might include providing training in new skills, giving employees time off after a demanding period, or simply listening and providing emotional support.

For example, one rapidly growing electronics company did the following to help people adjust to frequent organizational changes. First, it staffed its human resource department with four counselors, who spent most of their time talking to people who were feeling "burned out" or who were having difficulty adjusting to new jobs. Second, on a selective basis, it offered people "mini sabbaticals," which were four weeks in duration and which involved some reflective or educational activity away from work. And finally, it spent a great deal of money on education and training programs conducted in-house.

Facilitation and support are best suited for resistance due to adjustment problems. The basic drawback of this approach is that it can be time-consuming and expensive, and still fail.[12]

Negotiation

Negotiation as a change tactic essentially involves buying out active or potential resisters. This could mean, for example, giving a union a higher wage rate in return for a work rule change. Or it could involve increasing an individual's pension benefits in return for an early retirement.

Effective use of negotiation as a change tactic can be seen in the activi-

---

[11] See, for example, Alfred Marrow, David Bowers, and Stanley Seashore, *Management by Participation* (New York: Harper & Row, 1967).

[12] Zaltman and Duncan, *Strategies for Planned Change*, chap. 4.

ties of a division manager in a large manufacturing company. The divisions in this company were very interdependent. One division manager wanted to make some major changes in the division's organization. Yet, because of interdependencies, she recognized that she would be forcing some inconvenience and change on other divisions. To prevent top managers in other divisions from undermining her efforts, she negotiated with each division a written agreement that promised certain positive outcomes (for them) within certain time periods as a result of her changes, and in return, specified certain types of cooperation expected from the divisions during the change process. Later, whenever other divisions began to complain about the changes or the change process itself, she pulled out the negotiated agreements.

Negotiation is particularly appropriate when it is clear that someone is going to lose out as a result of a change and yet has significant power to resist. As a result, in some instances, it can be a relatively easy way to avoid major resistance. Like the other tactics, negotiation may become expensive—and once a manager makes it clear that he will negotiate to avoid resistance, he opens up the possibility of being blackmailed by others.[13]

Co-optation

A fifth tactic managers use to deal with potential or actual resistance to change is co-optation. Co-opting an individual usually involves giving him or her a desirable role in the design or implementation of the change. Co-opting a group involves giving one of its leaders, or someone it respects, a key role in the design or implementation of a change. A change initiator could, for example, try to co-opt the sales force by allowing the sales manager to be privy to the design of the changes, and by seeing that the most popular salesperson gets a raise as part of the change.

To reduce the possibility of corporate resistance to an organizational change, one division manager in a large multibusiness corporation successfully used co-optation in the following way. He invited the corporate human relations vice president, a close friend of the president's, to help him and his key staff analyze some problems the division was having. Because of his busy schedule, the corporate VP was not able to do much of the actual information gathering or analysis himself, thus limiting his own influence on the diagnoses. But his presence at key meetings helped commit him to the diagnosis and the solution the group designed. The commitment was subsequently very important because the president, at

---

[13] For an excellent discussion of negotiation, see Gerald Nierenberg, *The Art of Negotiating* (New York: Cornerstone, 1974).

least initially, did not like some of the proposed changes. Nevertheless, after discussion with his human resource VP, he did not try to block them.

Co-optation can, under certain circumstances, be a relatively inexpensive and easy way to gain an individual's or a group's support (less expensive, for example, than negotiation and quicker than participation). Nevertheless, it has its drawbacks. If people feel they are being tricked into not resisting, they obviously may respond negatively. And if they use their ability to influence the design and implementation of changes in ways that are not in the best interests of the organization, they can obviously create serious problems.

Manipulation

Manipulation, in this context, refers to covert influence attempts. In a sense, therefore, co-optation is a form of manipulation. Other forms do not have specific names, but involve, for instance, the selective use of information and the conscious structuring of events so as to have some desired (but covert) impact on the participants.

Manipulation suffers from the same drawbacks as co-optation, but to an even greater degree. When people feel they are not being treated openly, or that they are being lied to, they often react negatively. Nevertheless, manipulation can be used successfully—particularly when all other tactics are not feasible or have failed.[14] With one's back to the wall, inadequate time to use education, participation, or facilitation, and without the power or other resources to use negotiation, coercion, or co-optation, a manager might resort to manipulating information channels to scare people into thinking there is a crisis coming, which they can avoid only by change.

Coercion

The seventh tactic managers use to deal with resistance is coercion. Here they essentially force people to accept a change, explicitly or implicitly threatening them with the loss of jobs, or promotion possibilities, or raises, or whatever else they control. Like manipulation, coercion is a risky tactic, because people strongly resent forced change. Yet coercion has the advantage of overcoming resistance very quickly. And in situations were speed is essential, this tactic may be one's only alternative.

For example, when assigned to "turn around" a failing division in a

---

[14] See John P. Kotter, "Power, Dependence, and Effective Management," *Harvard Business Review,* July–August 1977, pp. 133–35.

large conglomerate, the chosen manager relied mostly on coercion to achieve the organizational changes she desired. She did so because she felt, "I did not have enough time to use other methods, and I needed to make changes that were pretty unpopular among many of the people."

Using change tactics

Effective organizational change efforts are almost always characterized by the skillful use of a number of these change tactics. Conversely, less effective change efforts usually involve the misuse of one or more of these tactics.

Managers sometimes misuse change tactics simply because they are unaware of the strengths and limitations of each tactic (see Figure 7–1). Sometimes they run into difficulties because they rely only on the same limited number of tactics regardless of the situation (e.g., they always use participation and persuasion, or coercion and manipulation).[15] Sometimes they misuse the tactics simply because they are not chosen and implemented as a part of a clearly considered change strategy.

CHANGE STRATEGIES

In approaching an organizational change situation, managers explicitly or implicitly make strategic choices regarding the speed of the effort, the amount of preplanning, the involvement of others, and the relative emphasis of different change tactics. Successful change efforts seem to be those in which these choices are both internally consistent and in which they fit some key situation variables.

The strategic options available to managers can be usefully thought of as existing on a continuum (see Figure 7–2).[16] At one end of the continuum, the strategy calls for a very rapid implementation of changes, with a clear plan of action and little involvement of others. This type of strategy mows over any resistance, and at the extreme would involve a fait accompli. At the other end of the continuum, the strategy would call for a much slower change process that is less clearly planned from the start and that involves many people in addition to the change initiators. This type of strategy is designed to reduce resistance to a minimum.[17]

With respect to tactics, the farther to the left one operates on the

---

[15] Ibid., pp. 135–36.

[16] See Larry E. Greiner, "Patterns of Organizational Change," *Harvard Business Review,* May–June 1967; and Larry E. Greiner and Louis B. Barnes, "Organization Change and Development," in *Organization Change and Development,* ed. Gene Dalton and Paul Lawrence (Homewood, Ill.: Richard D. Irwin, Inc., 1970), pp. 3–5.

[17] For a good discussion of an approach that attempts to minimize resistance, see Renato Tagiuri, "Notes on the Management of Change," Working Paper, Harvard Business School.

Figure 7-1
Tactics for dealing with resistance to change

Tactic	Best for	Advantages in using this tactic	Drawbacks
Education/communication	Resistance based on lack of information, or inaccurate information and analysis.	Once persuaded, people will often help with the implementation of the change.	Can be very time-consuming if large numbers of people are involved.
Participation	Situations in which initiators do not have all the information needed to design the change and where others have considerable power to resist.	People who participate will be committed to implementing change. And any relevant information they have will be integrated into the change plan.	Can be very time-consuming. Participators could design an inappropriate change.
Facilitation and support	Dealing with people who are resisting because of adjustment problems.	No other tactic works with adjustment problems as well.	Can be time-consuming, expensive, and still fail.
Negotiation	Situations where someone or some group will clearly lose out in a change, and where they have considerable power to resist.	Sometimes is a relatively easy way to avoid major resistance.	Can be too expensive in many cases. Can alert others to negotiate for compliance.
Co-optation	Very specific situations where the other tactics are too expensive or are infeasible.	Can help generate support for implementing a change (but less than participation).	Can create problems if people recognize the co-optation.
Manipulation	Situations where other tactics will not work or are too expensive.	Can be a relatively quick and inexpensive solution to resistance problems.	Costs initiators some of their credibility. Can lead to future problems.
Coercion	When speed is essential and the change initiators possess considerable power.	Speed. Can overcome any kind of resistance.	Risky. Can leave people angry with the initiators.

Figure 7–2
Strategic options for the management of change

Rapid changes   Slow changes
Clearly planned   Not clearly planned initially
Little involvement of others   Lots of involvement of others
Attempt to overcome any resistance   Attempt to minimize any resistance

Key Situational Variables

- The amount and type of resistance that is anticipated.

- The position of the initiators vis-à-vis the resisters (in terms of power, trust, etc.).

- The locus of relevant data for designing the change, and of needed energy for implementing it.

- The stakes involved (e.g., the presence or absence of a crisis, the consequences of resistance and lack of change).

continuum in Figure 7–2, the more one tends to use coercion and the less one tends to use the other tactics—especially participation. The opposite is true the more one operates to the right on the continuum—the less coercion tends to be used and the more the other tactics tend to be used.

Exactly where a change effort should be strategically positioned on the continuum in Figure 7–2 seems to be a function of four key variables:

1. *The amount and type of resistance that is anticipated.* The greater the anticipated resistance, other factors being equal, the more appropriate it is to move toward the right on the continuum.[18] The greater the anticipated resistance, the more difficult it is to simply overwhelm it, and the more one needs to find ways to reduce some of it.
2. *The position of the initiator vis-à-vis the resisters, especially with regard to power.* The greater the initiator's power, the better the initiator's relationships with the others, and the more the others expect that the initiator might move unilaterally, the more one can move to the left on the continuum.[19] On the other hand, the weaker the initiator's position, the more he or she is forced to operate to the right.

---

[18] Jay Lorsch, "Managing Change," in *Organizational Behavior and Administration,* ed. Paul Lawrence, Louis Barnes, and Jay Lorsch (Homewood, Ill.: Richard D. Irwin, Inc., 1976), pp. 676–78.

[19] Ibid., pp. 676–78.

3. *The locus of relevant data for designing the change, and of needed energy for implementing it.* The more the initiators anticipate they will need information from others to help design the change and commitment from them to help implement it, the more they must move to the right.[20] Gaining useful information and commitment requires time and the involvement of others.
4. *The stakes involved.* The greater the short-run potential for risks to organizational performance and survival, the more one must move to the left.

Organizational change efforts that are based on an inconsistent strategy, or ones that do not fit the situation, tend to run into predictable problems, For example, an effort that is not clearly planned, but is implemented quickly, will almost always run into unanticipated problems. Efforts that attempt to involve large numbers of people, and which at the same time try to move quickly, will virtually always end up sacrificing either speed or involvement. Efforts in which the change initiators do not have all the information they need to correctly design a change, but which nevertheless move quickly and involve few others, sometimes encounter enormous problems.

IMPLICATIONS FOR MANAGING ORGANIZATIONAL CHANGE

Organizational change efforts can be greatly aided by an analysis and planning process composed of the following three phases:

1. Conducting a thorough organizational analysis—one which identifies the current situation, any problems, and the forces which are possible causes of those problems. The analysis must clearly specify:
   a. The actual significance of the problems.
   b. The speed with which the problems must be addressed if additional problems are to be avoided.
   c. The types of changes that are generally needed.
2. Conducting a thorough analysis of factors relevant to implementing the necessary changes. This analysis focuses on questions of:
   a. Who might resist the changes, why, and to what extent.
   b. Who has information that is needed to design the change, and whose cooperation is essential in implementing it.
   c. The position of the change initiator vis-à-vis other relevant parties in terms of power, trust, normal modes of interaction, etc.

---

[20] Ibid.

3. Selecting a change strategy based on the analysis in phases one and two, and a set of change tactics, and then designing an action plan that specifies:
   a. What must be done.
   b. By whom.
   c. In what sequence.
   d. And within what time frame.

It is conceivable that some or all of these steps will need to be repeated when initiating and managing an organizational change if unforeseen events occur or if new and relevant information surfaces. At the extreme, in a highly participative change, the process might be repeated a dozen times over a period of months or years. The key to successful organizational change is not whether these steps are repeated once or many times, but whether they are done competently and thoroughly.

Case 7–1
First National City Bank Operating Group (A) and (B)*
John A. Seeger, Jay W. Lorsch, Cyrus F. Gibson

John Reed paced along the vast glass walls of his midtown Manhattan office, hardly noticing the panorama of rooftops spread out below his feet, baking in the September sun. One of 41 Senior Vice Presidents of the First National City Bank, Reed, at 31, was the youngest man in the bank's history to reach this management level. Reed headed the bank's "Operating Group" (OPG)—the back office, which performed the physical work of processing Citibank's business transactions and designing its computer systems, as well as managing the bank's real estate and internal building services. Today, musing to himself about the forthcoming 1971 operating year and his plans for the next five years, John Reed was both concerned and angry.

He was concerned that his recent reorganization of the Operating Group, though widely recognized as a success, was not sufficient. His area still followed the traditional working procedures of the banking business, and OPG continued to be seen by the rest of the bank as a "necessary evil" which, given enough tolerance by its more intelligent brethren, should "muddle along" the way it always had. After a year and a half with the Group and five months as its head, he still had few concrete measures of its performance. But most of all, John Reed was concerned that his initial concept of what the Group needed—massive new computerized systems for coping with a growing mountain of paper-based transactions— might be both impractical and irrelevant. Reed's new staff assistant, Bob White, had been pushing hard for a change in management approach, to emphasize budgets, costs, and production efficiency instead of system development.

And, uncharacteristically, John Reed was angry. He looked again at the management report he had received the day before. Here it was, September of 1970, and he was only now learning that his manpower had grown by 400 people in July and August. Maybe Bob White really had something in his stress on control and management.

First National City Bank

The Operating Group was one of the major divisions established in a reorganization of Citibank at the end of 1968. The five market-oriented divisions, shown in the organization chart in Exhibit A1, generated varying demands for OPG services; all of them were looking forward to continued growth in 1971, and all were pressing for improved performance by the Operating Group.

Citibank's Personal Banking Group (PBG), with 181 branches and 6,000 employees, provided a full range of services to consumers and small businesses in the metropolitan New York area. As the area's leading retail bank, PBG projected a 3 percent annual growth in checking account balances, and a 2 percent annual growth in savings accounts over the next several years; in addition to an increase in number of accounts, PBG anticipated continuation of the recent trend toward more activity *per* account.

The Investment Management Group, with 1,700 employees, managed assets for personal and institutional investors, and provided full banking services to wealthy individuals. In this latter category, the group currently

Exhibit A–1
Institutional Organization, 1970

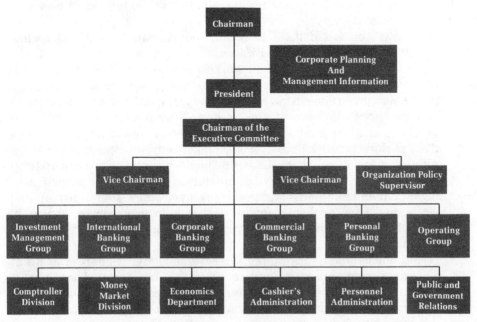

carried some 7,000 accounts, and hoped to increase its customers by 25 percent in the next four years.

The Corporate Banking Group, itself subdivided into six industry-specialist divisions, served big business (generally, companies with more than $20 million in annual sales), financial institutions, and government accounts within the United States. CBG aimed at an annual growth rate over 5 percent, but qualified its ambitions: in order to gain market share in the increasingly competitive world of the major corporations, the bank would have to improve both its pricing structures and the quality of its services. Operating Group errors, CBG said, had irritated many major accounts, and their reputation for slow, inaccurate service made expansion of market share very difficult.

The Commercial Banking Group operated 16 Regional Centers in the New York area to serve medium-sized companies, most of which did not employ their own professional finance executives and thus relied upon the bank for money advice as well as banking services. The fastest-growing group of the bank, Commercial Banking projected an annual growth rate of about 10 percent.

The International Banking Group operated some 300 overseas branches in addition to managing several First National City Corporation subsidiary units concerned with foreign investments, services, and leasing. Although IBG conducted its own transaction processing at its overseas centers, still its rapid growth would present new demands on the Operating Group in Manhattan. All business originating in New York was handled by John Reed's people, and the IBG complement of 160 New York–based staff officers was expected to double in five years.

Worldwide, First National City Corporation had shown assets of $23 billion in its financial statement of December 31, 1969. Earnings had been $131 million, after taxes (but before losses on securities traded). The corporation employed 34,000 people, having doubled its staff in the previous ten years, while tripling its assets. Citibank's published goals for financial performance presented another source of pressure for improvement in the Operating Group: Board Chairman Walter B. Wriston had recently committed the bank to an annual growth rate of 15 percent in earnings per share of common stock. President William Spencer had made it clear to John Reed that OPG was expected to contribute to this gain in earnings.

The operating group's functions

As the bank had grown, so had its back office. Increases in services offered, in customers, in volume per customer, and in staff all meant added transactions to be processed by the Operating Group. As the volume of paper flowing through the bank increased, so did the staff and budget of the back office. In 1970, John Reed had some 8,000 people on his group payroll, and would spend $105 million on the direct production of the bank's paperwork. For several years, transaction volume had increased at an annual rate of five percent; the Operating Group's total expenditures had grown faster, at an average of 17.9 percent per year since 1962.

Operating Group's headquarters was a 25-story building at 111 Wall Street, several miles south of the bank's head offices at 399 Park Avenue. The volume and variety of work flowing through this building was impressive; in a typical day, OPG would:

1. Transfer $5 billion between domestic and foreign customers and banks.
2. Process $2 billion worth of checks—between 1.5 and 2 million individual items. (A stack of 1.5 million checks would stand as tall as a 66-story building.).
3. Start and complete 900 jobs in the data processing center, printing 5 million lines of statements, checks, and other reports.
4. Process $100 million worth of bill and tax payments for major corporations and government agencies. (And during the 16 weeks between February 1 and May 30, the group also processed 50,000 income tax returns per day for the City of New York.).
5. Handle 102,000 incoming and outgoing telephone calls and 7,000 telegrams and cables.
6. Mail out 30,000 checking account statements and 25,000 other items, accounting for $10,000 a day for postage.

Operating Group Organization

In 1969, John Reed had transferred into OPG from the International Banking Group, to become a vice president of the bank and to set up a task force pointed toward reorganization of the group. He had assembled a team of young, technically oriented managers (most of them relatively new to OPG) to analyze and rearrange the basic functions of the group. Systematically, this task force had examined the structure and function of each OPG sub-department, working with the line managers to question where the subgroups fit in the organization; to whom their managers reported and why; what processes and technologies they shared with other groups; and how the physical output of each group affected the operation of the next sequential processing step. The result of this study was a complete realignment of reporting responsibilities, pulling together all those groups doing similar work, and placing them under unified management.

A leading member of OPG's "systems management" team during this reorganization effort was Larry Small, who had followed John Reed from the planning staff at the IBG in 1969. Small, a 1964 graduate of Brown University (with a degree in Spanish literature), set the keynote for the task force approach with his concept of basic management principles. Small elaborated:

Managing simply means understanding, in detail—in meticulous detail—where you are now, where you have to go, and how you will get there. To know where they are now, managers must measure the important features of their systems. To know where they are going, managers must agree on their objectives, and on the specific desired values of all those measured factors. And, to know how to get there, managers must understand the processes which produce their results. Significant change demands the participation of the people involved, in order to gain the widespread understanding required for success. Management is essentially binary; all change efforts will be seen as either successes or failures. Success follows from understanding.

Few major changes in equipment or physical space were required by the new organization, and the approach characterized by Larry Small's statement made the transition an easy one. By late 1969, the Operating Group was running smoothly under a four-area structure as shown in Exhibit A-2.

Area I was the "operating" part of Operating Group; these were the people who processed the transactions which constituted the bank's business. Area I operated the computer systems, processed checks for collection from other banks, posted the accounts for Citibank's customers, transferred funds from one customer to another, and prepared customers' bank statements.

Area II encompassed system design and software for computer operations. It was the "intellectual" side of Operating Group, developing new computer systems for the use of Area I. The subgroups in charge of operations analysis, management information systems, and data control also belonged to Area II, as did the programming group in charge of "ALTAPS," a new automated loan and time payment processing system.

Area III, quite removed from the paper-oriented processing groups in Operating Group, was a free-standing organization in charge of Citibank's real estate, physical facilities, and building services. (When he was not concerned about processing transactions in the back office, John Reed could worry about the quality of cafeteria food, and the cleanliness of the bathrooms.)

Exhibit A–2

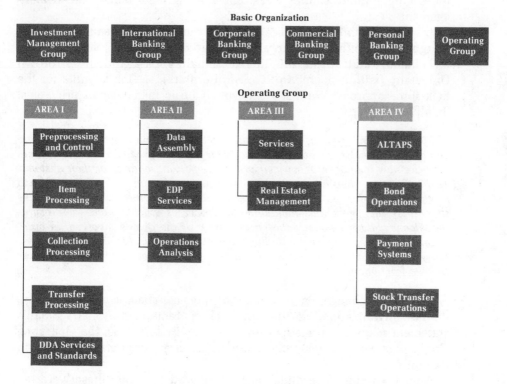

Area IV was composed of the relatively low-volume, high-value, transaction processing departments—stock transfer, corporate bonds, corporate cash management, mutual funds, and government services.

In addition to the routine of day-to-day operations, Reed was responsible for the long-range development of both hardware and software systems. For several years, a subsidiary of the bank, with operations in Cambridge, Mass., and in California, had been working on the kind of online systems and terminals which would be required to·support the "checkless society" which the financial community expected would replace paper-based record processing in the long-range future. Reed had decided to maintain the separation of this advanced research and development activity from the Operating Group. "Let's face it," he said, "the computer systems we have now will never evolve into the systems needed for point-of-sale transaction processing. When those new systems come, they'll come as a revolution—a total replacement of existing technology. We should develop the new systems, sure. But we shouldn't let them screw up the systems we need today and tomorrow in the meantime."

In September of 1970, John Reed, feeling comfortable with the overall structure of OPG but impatient with its lack of measured progress, had assigned Larry Small to head Area IV. Small's demonstrated skills in management of change held out the promise that this highly sensitive area, where any errors could cause major problems for the bank's most important customers, would soon be under more effective control. Now Reed was considering the future course of Area I, where even more people and dollars were involved.

Area I: The demand deposit accounting system

The largest single job performed by the Operating Group was Demand Deposit Accounting (DDA), the complex process of handling the physical flow of paper and communications, posting transactions, distributing processed items, and producing the bank's daily statement of condition. Some 2,000 employees of OPG's Area I performed this work. The process was composed of three parts: The "front end," which received, encoded, and read transactions onto magnetic computer tapes; the data center, which sorted the data and printed statements; and the "back end," which microfilmed and filed the checks of Citibank's own customers, prepared and mailed their statements, and handled accounting exceptions.

Around the clock, mail sacks containing checks, deposit slips, travellers' checks, transfer vouchers, credit memos, and other paper transaction records arrived in the eighth floor receiving room at 111 Wall Street to enter the "front end" of the Demand Deposit Accounting system. The first step of that process was to weigh the bags, in order to gauge the volume of work coming in: one pound of mail equaled about 300 items to be processed.

Each incoming mailbag contained a control sheet, listing the various bundles of checks in that shipment and the aggregate totals of the bundles. As each sack was opened, its contents were checked against its control sheet, to ensure that all the bundles listed were actually received. This marked the first step in Citibank's system for proving the books; from this point onward in the DDA system, each batch of material was signed for whenever it moved from one area of responsibility to another. The records of these transfers, together with any changes in batch totals as discrepancies were discovered or generated, were accumulated by a "proof clerk" on each operating shift. The following morning, these proof worksheets were consolidated into the bank's daily report of its operating condition, as required by the Federal Reserve System.

Materials arriving from other banks and check clearing houses were already partly processed, but items from domestic Citibank branches, the head office, mail deposits, and lockboxes had to be encoded with machine-readable information. These papers were distributed to one of the 150 magnetic ink encoding machines, where operators would key the dollar amounts into a keyboard. The machines would print these amounts on the checks, accumulating batch totals for each 300 checks processed. Some machines had several pockets, and sorted the work into different pockets for different kinds of media, adding up separate control totals for each pocket. As the pockets filled up, the paper was unloaded into conveyor trays, to be transported to the next operation, where the checks were read by machines and sorted by their destination, while the information from them was recorded on computer tape.

Encoder operators were generally women, who worked on an incentive pay arrangement and processed 800 to 1100 items per hour. No direct record of keypunching accuracy was kept, and operators were not penalized for errors.

At the read/sort machines, on the floor above, the paper media were sorted into two major classifications. "On-us" checks—those written against the accounts of Citibank's own customers—were directed to the "back end" of the DDA system; "transit" checks, written on other banks, were directed to the various check clearing houses and exchanges. Firm deadlines held for these exchanges. For example, the major Manhattan banks met at ten each morning to trade checks with each other, and to settle the differences between the checks paid and collected for other banks. This meeting had been a New York tradition for well over a hundred years; banks were not late for the exchange.

About 600,000 checks each day entered the back end of Citibank's process, where they were microfilmed, screened for exceptions, and filed by customer for rendering and mailing of statements.

Overdrafts, stop payment orders, and "no-post" items were listed by the computer and referred to exception clerks, who searched through the incoming paper for the offending items, in order to route them to the proper offices for special handling. No-posts were especially troublesome; about 1300 items per day, with an average value of $1,000 each, would flow into the back end, destined for accounts which had been closed, or were burdened by attachments, or had invalid numbers, or belonged to recently deceased owners, or were suspected of fraudulent activity. On a typical day, the exception clerks would fail to find between 50 and 100 of these checks, and the cases would be referred to the investigations unit.

In the filing and signature checking section, women worked at 158 large filing machines, where each operator was responsible for 5,000 to 7,500 accounts. In addition to simply filing the day's flow of checks, each operator handled telephoned check-cashing authorizations; reconciled "full sheets" (the first pages of multi-page monthly statements); compiled the daily activity of medium-volume accounts (between 25 and 125 items per day) into "SMUT listings"[1]; and ruled off the accounts scheduled for next-day statement rendering.

Nine clerks in the breakdown section received the checks for tomorrow's statements from the filing clerks, collated them with the statements arriving from the computer printer, and prepared the work for the rendering group the next day. The 60 women in rendering confirmed the count of checks to go with each statement, observed special mailing instructions, and sorted the outgoing mail into heavy, medium, and lightweight classifications.

Throughout the DDA process, errors could be generated in a variety of ways. Any of the machines could eat a check if the machine were out of adjustment. Multi-pocket encoders could add a check into the total for one pocket, but sort the paper into a different pocket, creating a shortage in one batch of material and a corresponding overage in another. Conveyor trays could be spilled, and loose paper could be stored in desk drawers, or shoved under furniture, or swept out in the trash. The bank's proofing system recorded variances in all the processing steps, and accumulated the errors in the "difference and fine" account—commonly called the "D&F."[1]

The operating group staff

By tradition, the Operating Group was a service function to the customer-contact divisions of the bank. Citibank's top management attention was directed outward—toward the market. Operations was expected to respond to change as generated and interpreted by the customer-contact offices. As a consequence, tradition held that the career path to the top in banking led through line assignments in the market-oriented divisions. "The phrase 'back office' is commonly assumed to mean 'backwater.' " said John Reed. "Operations is a secure haven for the people who have grown up in it; it's a place of exile for people in the other divisions."

In 1970, most of the Operating Group's management was made up of "career men" who had spent 15 to 25 years with OPG, often beginning their service with several years of clerical level work before advancing to supervisory jobs. Through years of contact with "their" outside divisions of the bank, managers had built up rich personal acquaintanceships with the people they served. Frequent telephone contacts reinforced these

---

[1] The Citibank executives interviewed for this background material were generally young men who had served with OPG for only two or three years. They did not know the antecedents of the acronym "SMUT-list." Similarly, the source of the name "D&F" for the variance account was obscure—although one manager thought there might once have been a monetary fine levied against the bank which failed to balance its accounts perfectly.

relationships. Dick Freund, OPG's Vice President for Administration and a veteran of 42 years' service with the group, commented on the close interaction between OPG people and the customer-contact offices:

> *Problem-solving here is typically done on a person-to-person basis. For example, an account officer in International Banking, faced with tracing some amendment to a letter of credit, would know that Jerry Cole, an assistant vice president on the 22nd floor, could find the answer. He'd call Jerry, and yes, Jerry would get him an answer. Whatever else Jerry was doing in the Letter of Credit Departments could wait; when a customer needs an answer, our men jump. They're proud of the service they can give.*

Recruits for the managerial ranks of the bank typically came directly from the college campus. Dick Freund described the process:

> *We hire people straight out of college—most of them without business experience—and shuttle them around in a series of low-level jobs while they learn the bank. The Yale and Princeton and Harvard types eventually settle in the customer-contact offices; the Fordham and St. John's and NYU types come to Operating Group. We don't have the glamorous jobs that IBG and Corporate can offer, but even so there's a lot of prestige to working for First National City, and the security we offer means a lot to some of these people. I know one officer who bases his whole employment interview on security. "You come to work for us," he says, "and put in a good day's work, and you'll never have to worry about your job. Never."*

While management ranks remained stable, the characteristics of the clerical staff had changed dramatically over the previous decade. Through the 1950s OPG relied on the local parochial high schools as a source of well-trained clerical applicants. Those women would typically work for one to five years before leaving to raise a family; some stayed on to form the experienced core of the staff. By 1970, however, applicants for work in lower Manhattan were predominantly Black and Puerto Rican.

MANAGEMENT SUCCESSION AND THE CHANGING ROLE OF OPERATING GROUP

Dick Freund traced the recent succession of top managers at the Operating Group:

> *From 1964 to 1968, when he retired, we had a top man who convinced the Policy Committee that our operating capabilities were becoming more and more important—that we simply couldn't afford to take them for granted. There was a tidal wave of paperwork coming—the same wave that swamped so many brokerage houses in '68—and we had to pay attention. Until 1968, nobody cared much.*
>
> *The first clear signals that management attitudes towards the Operating Group were changing came in 1968, when Bill Spencer was appointed Executive Vice*

President in charge of Operations. Mr. Spencer was generally regarded as a prime candidate for the bank's presidency. It was plain that his appointment wasn't some form of punishment. He had to be here for a reason, and the reason had to be that Operations was, after all, an important part of the corporation.

It was Mr. Spencer who recruited John Reed to move from the International Banking Group to Operations, and who promoted Reed to Senior Vice President, later in 1969.

And that was another sign that things were changing, Reed said. For one thing, nobody my age had ever made SVP before. But more important, I wasn't a "banker" in the traditional sense. Most of Operations' management had been in the group for 15 to 30 years; I'd only been with Citibank for five, and none of that was with OPG.

John Reed's undergraduate training had been in American literature and physical metallurgy. After a brief job with Goodyear Tire and Rubber, and a tour in the United States Army, he had taken a masters degree in management at MIT, and then joined the IBG planning staff, where he applied systems concepts to the international banking field with impressive results. That his rise in the organization was atypical was illustrated by the following comments from other bank officers:

I've spent all my life in the bank, said a gray-haired senior vice president from the Corporate Banking Group. *I was trained by assignment to different departments every two years; then, when I went into a line position, I had enough experience to correct something by doing it myself. At the very worst, I always knew people in the other departments who could straighten out any problem.*

I started with Citibank as a night clerk in Personal Banking, said a PBG vice president. *It was ten years before I reached supervisory ranks, and by then I'd had a lot of experience in credit and in operations as well.*

I joined the bank as a naïve liberal arts graduate, and spent three years in clerical work before making first-line supervision, said a newly-appointed assistant vice president in the Operating Group. *After eight years as a supervisor, you get a pretty good feeling for what's happening around you.*

In May of 1970, to the surprise of no one, William Spencer was named President of First National City Corporation. John S. Reed—youth, non-banking background, and all—was selected to head the Operating Group.

Operating group costs

By tradition, the method of meeting increased work loads in banking was to increase staff. If an operation could be done at the rate of 800 transactions per day, and the load increased by 800 pieces per day, then the manager in charge of that operation would hire another person. It was taken for granted. Financial reports would follow, showing in the next month-end statement that expenses had risen, and explaining the rise through the increased volume of work processed.

But in the late 1960s the work load began to rise faster than the hiring rate could keep up, and in addition there was a decrease in productivity per operator. Backlogs of work to be done would pile up in one OPG department or another, and would require overtime work in order to catch up. Even with extensive reassignment of people and with major overtime efforts, some department would periodically fall behind by two or even three weeks, generating substantial numbers of complaints from customers. Three or four times a year, special "task forces" would be recruited from other branches of the bank to break the bottlenecks of these problem departments. Trainees, secretaries, junior officers, and clerks would be drafted for evening and weekend work, at overtime pay rates. "The task force approach is inefficient, annoying, and expensive, but it gets us out of the hole," said Dick Freund. "A lot of these people don't *want* to work these hours, but it has to be done." In 1970, OPG spent $1,983,000 on overtime pay.

There were other sources of expense in the Operating Group, which did not show up on financial reports. John Reed described a major area of hidden costs:

> If we have cashed a $1,000 check drawn on the Bank of America in California, we are going to be out $1,000 until we send them the check. If we miss sending the check out today, it will wait until tomorrow's dispatches to the West Coast, and we'll wait a day longer for that $1,000. There are rigid deadlines for each of the clearinghouses; even a relatively small number of checks missing these deadlines can cost us a great deal of money. If each day only three percent of the $2 billion we handle is held over, then we will lose the interest on $60 million for one day. That turns out to be something like $3 million a year in lost earnings. We call it "lost availability."
>
> That's a big number. Yet, until a few months ago we were making no effort to reduce it, or even to measure it. No one had thought of it as a cost. Check processing has always been treated as a straight-line operation, with bags of checks going through the line as they were received. Whatever wasn't processed at the end of the day was held over, and cleaned up the following day. It was just another clerical operation.

In 1970, lost availability amounted not to three percent of the value of checks processed, but to four.

Operating group quality

"Quality is something we really can't measure," said Dick Freund. "But we can get perceptions that the level of service we're providing isn't acceptable. For all our outlay of expenses, it seems we are not improving, or even maintaining, our performance."

Indications of poor service came to the Operating Group in the form of customer complaints, usually voiced through Account Officers from the market-contact divisions of the bank. Failures could take many forms, including loss of checks after they had been posted, late mailing of statements, mis-coding of checks, payment of checks over stop orders, misposting of transfers, and, on occasion, loss of whole statements. Since any kind of error could cause inconvenience to the customer, the people in direct touch with the market were highly sensitive to quality. These Account Officers frequently assumed the role of problem-solvers on the customer's behalf, traveling to the 111 Wall Street office to work directly with Operating Group staff to remedy specific errors affecting their accounts. A separate section had been set up to analyze and correct errors in customer accounts; its backlog of unsolved inquiries was a major indicator to management of OPG's quality level. In the fall of 1970, this investigations department faced a backlog of 36,000 unsolved cases.

The importance of error-free operation to the customer-contact officers was pointed out by several officers from outside the Operating Group:

Sure, I know the volume of paper has gone up, said a vice president from Corporate Banking Group. *I know we have 750,000 accounts, and most of them are handled for years without a mistake. But Operations has to perform at 100 percent, not at 99 percent. Errors can be terribly embarrassing to the customer; repeated errors can lose customers for us. I have 600 checks missing from last month's statement for a major government account . . . and there were 400 missing from the previous month's statement. Now, how can I sell additional services to that account, when we can't even produce a correct monthly statement for him?*

We tell the customer that his canceled check is his legal receipt, said an assistant vice president from Personal Banking, *and then we lose the check. What am I supposed to tell the man then? I can get him a microfilmed copy of the check, but that's not very useful as a legal document, is it?*

Just getting a simple transfer through the books can generate a whole family of problems, said an Account Officer in International Banking Group. *Here's a typical case. A translator at 111 Wall Street miscodes the original transaction (it was written in Portuguese), and the transfer goes to the wrong account. When that customer inquires, we trace the error and reverse it. But before the correction goes through, a follow-up request comes in from Brazil; it's a duplicate of the first request, and our people don't catch the fact it's a follow-up, so they put through another transfer. Now the same item has gone through twice. Where does it all end? My customer is tired of writing letters about it.*

If our operations were perfect, sighed a CBG vice president, *we'd have a tremendous tool to go out and sell against the competition.*

The "technological fix"

"The customer-contact side of the bank," said John Reed, "and to some extent the top management group, shows a natural tendency to press in the direction of great, massive, new, total computer systems—bringing the ultimate promise of technology into instant availability. It has been natural for all of us to blame mistakes and daily operating problems on inadequate systems; after all, if the systems were perfect, those mistakes would be impossible. But maybe we've all been brainwashed. Maybe we expect too much."

Fifteen years before, Citibank had acquired its first computer—a desk-sized Burroughs machine used to calculate interest on installment loans. For the four years following, the Operating Group had cooperated in an extensive research program on automated check processing, based on equipment developed by International Telephone and Telegraph to encode and sort mail in European post offices. This experimental system had progressed to the point of pilot use on the accounts of First National City's own employees when, in 1959, the American Banking Association adopted Magnetic Ink Character Recognition (MICR) as an industry-wide standard approach to check processing. Citibank immediately dropped the ITT system, and installed MICR equipment.

Although the computer facilities had grown immensely in the ensuing decade, the basic process performed by the Operating Group remained the same. "For example," said Reed, "people used to verify names and addresses against account numbers by looking them up in paper records. Now they sit at cathode-ray tubes instead, but they're still doing the same operation."

Reed's computer people had reported to him that Citibank's use of machines was already highly efficient. Operating Group was—and had been for several years—at the state-of-the-art level of computer usage. A new survey by the American Bankers Association seemed to verify this conclusion: where the average large bank spent over 30 percent of its back-office budget on machine capacity, OPG spent less than 20 percent.

Reed paused beside his corner window. "Think about this for a minute," he said. "We've been running this operation as if it were a computer center. We've been hoping for some Great Mother of a software system to come along and pull the family together. Well, she's slow. None of us children has heard one word from her. Maybe she's not coming.

"What if it's *not* a computer center we have here? What other point of view could we take, that would result in running the Operating Group differently? Better?"

Reed turned. "What if it's a *factory* we've got here?"

The "factory" concept

Through much of August 1970, John Reed had worked with Larry Small and Bob White to develop the implications of viewing the Operating Group as a high speed, continuous process production operation. White, working without an official title, had just joined Reed's staff after six years' experience with Ford Motor Co., most recently as manager of engineering financial analysis for Ford's Product Development Group. At the age of 35, with an Ohio State Bachelor of Science degree and an MBA from the University of Florida behind him, Bob White brought to the Operating Group a firm conviction that the McNamara philosophy of budgets, measurements, and controls was the only way to run a production operation.

Now, in early September, Reed was trying some of these ideas on Dick Freund to get a sense of their impact on the traditional banker. Freund, with more than four decades in the organization, was serving as a sounding board; Reed had almost decided to carry a new program to the Policy Committee of the Bank, and wanted to anticipate their reactions:

We know where we want Operating Group to be in five years' time. For 1971 and 1972 we want to hold expenses flat; in spite of the rising transaction volumes we'll keep the same $105 million expense level as this year, and after that we'll let costs rise by no more than six percent a year. By 1975, that will mean a $70 million annual saving compared to uncontrolled growth at 15 percent. At the same time, we want to improve service, and eliminate our bottlenecks and backlogs, like the jam-up in investigations.

To accomplish those goals, though, we will have to put over a fundamental change in outlook. We must recognize the Operating Group for what it is—a factory—and we must continually apply the principles of production management to make that factory operate more efficiently.

It is not important for the people in the factory to understand banking. We'll take the institutional objectives and restate them in terms of management plans and tasks that are quite independent of banking. The plain fact is that the language and values we need for success are not derived from banking, and we couldn't achieve what we want in terms of systems development and operations if they were.

To control costs, we must think in terms of costs. That means bringing in management people trained in production management—tough-minded, experienced people who know what it is to manage by the numbers and to measure performance against a meaningful budget. We have to infuse our management with a new kind of production-oriented philosophy, and the process has to start with new, outside points of view. Good production people in here can provide a seed crystal and the present management staff can grow around the seed. Some of them will make it; others won't. Our headhunters can find the top factory management people to start the reaction. From there on, it's up to us.

Our costs are out of control because we don't know what they are, let alone what they should be. Our quality is criticized when we don't have any idea what quality really is, or how to measure what we're already doing. Our processes run out of control and build up backlogs because our efforts are aimed at coping with transactions instead of understanding what made them pile up in the first place.

I'm not talking about turning the Operating Group into a factory. I'm talking about recognizing that it is a factory, and always has been. The function isn't going to change, but the way we look at it and manage it must.

Reed turned to Dick Freund, who had been listening intently. "What will they say to that, Dick?"

Freund smiled, and his eyes sparkled. "They'll go for the stable budget idea, and in spite of skepticism they will hope you can do it. They'll love the idea of improved service, but they'll know you can't pull that one off if you're holding costs down. And the factory management idea?

"There's one other bit of history you should know, John. The first engineer we ever hired came to work here in 1957, the year after we bought our first little computer. He was an eager guy, really impressed by the challenge of managing back office operations. He poked around for a few days, and then came back to the head office to declare that this wasn't a bank at all. It was a factory, he said. Nothing but a goddam paperwork factory.

"That was after just two weeks on the job.

"It was his last day on the job, too."

Reed grinned broadly, and turned to face Bob White. "Are you ready to move out of the office, Bob? This concept is going to fly, and we're going to need someone down at Wall Street who can make it happen. Why don't you get yourself ready to take over Area I?"

First National City Bank Operating Group (B)

Picture a high-pressure pipeline, five feet in diameter, carrying money to dozens of different distribution pipelines. Your job is to make a lot of plumbing changes in the pipes, but you can't shut off the flow of money while you work. If anything goes wrong and the pipe breaks, all those dollars are going to spill out on the floor. In a week's time, you'll be wading around in ten billion dollars. You'll be up to your eyebrows in money. Other people's money.

John S. Reed, one of six executive vice presidents of Citibank and the officer in charge of the bank's Operating Group, was reflecting on the process of change in a continuous-process, high-volume production operation. It was January of 1973, and Reed was reviewing the accomplishments of the past two and a half years. On the surface, it was easy to document progress; the Operating Group had numbers to show for its efforts. But Reed was anticipating criticism, too, as he prepared for the Policy Committee meeting at the end of the month. After all, the Group's performance hadn't been perfect; the money pipeline had broken, for the second time, only four months ago. Several customer-contact divisions still complained that service and quality levels in OPG were going downhill, in spite of numeric measurements that showed substantial improvement. And John Reed's fellow EVPs and division heads on the Policy Committee had tenacious memories.

Added to his other concerns was a new situation, highly visible to the bank as a whole. Organizers for the Office and Professional Workers Union were handing out thousands of leaflets to workers at 111 Wall Street, OPG's office building. Citibank's pay scales were competitive with other Manhattan employers' rates, but there were some indications of dissatisfaction in the work force. The previous year, for example, 125 women had walked off the job with a list of grievances; bringing the situation back to normal had required four months' full-time effort of one of OPG's most experienced assistant vice presidents. There was little feeling among top management that unionization was an immediate threat, but still the OPWU leaflets couldn't be ignored.

How, Reed wondered, could changes in the bank's "back office" be evaluated in terms of their impact on the rest of the institution? How could the new nonbanking approach of the Operating Group be made meaningful to the traditional bankers from the market-oriented divisions? For that matter, how could Reed himself picture the full impact of his changes on the Operating Group and on the bank?

He stood at the window of his Manhattan office, high above the early-morning traffic on Park Avenue. Behind him on his huge desk lay the two documents he had studied the night before. One was a draft of a speech which Robert B. White, Senior Vice President in charge of the production areas of the Operating Group, would soon deliver to the American Bankers Association. The speech outlined the management approaches Citibank had applied to its back-office operations over the previous two years. Citibank's success in gaining control of its paper work had attracted industry-wide attention; in 1971 and 1972, OPG had handled substantial increases in volume of work while reducing its expenditures below the 1970 level. The chairman of the First National City Corporation had been widely quoted as crediting the Operating Group for a major share of the bank's increased earnings. Judging by the numbers, John Reed had few reasons for concern.

The second document on his desk, however, seemed to tell a different story. It was a consultant's report, which Reed had commissioned in order to hear an outside viewpoint on the effects of the changes he and his colleagues had engineered in the past two years. The report was based largely on interviews the consultants had conducted with some 70 officers of the bank, both inside OPG and in the market-contact divisions; it focused sharply on some undesirable side effects of OPG's changes. The imposition of tight control policies, the report suggested, could lead to anxiety and insecurity in middle management. These fears could lead, in turn, to establishment of unrealistic goals (as an effort to please the new bosses), and to increased resistance to change (as middle management's effort to protect itself). The consequence of these two factors could be poor performance, seen as missed deadlines and crises, and as a sensed need by top management for still tighter controls. It was a classic vicious circle.

Placed side by side, the two documents made interesting reading. Reed wondered how OPG could learn from the comparison—how they could avoid unanticipated consequences of change in the future.

Change in the operating group, 1970–72

Soon after his promotion to head OPG in May of 1970, John Reed had faced the question of defining just what OPG was. Was it, as banking tradition dictated, simply a mechanical support group for the customer-contact offices of the bank? Or could it be seen as an independent, high-volume production operation—a factory—which designed and controlled its own processes and products in the style of a manufacturing organization?

Operating Group, Reed decided, was a factory. As such, it badly needed managers who knew how to run factories—men skilled in planning and controlling mass production processes. Dick Freund, OPG's Vice President for Administration and a veteran of 45 years' service with the bank, described the group's first effort to recruit professional production management:

What industries do you think of when you want examples of outstanding factory management? Well, automotives have to be close to the top of the heap. And what companies do you think of? The winners: General Motors and Ford. The first headhunter Reed turned loose on the job happened to have his foot in the door at Ford. You should have seen the first man who came to interview; we really went all the way to impress him. Reed had the fellow out to his home to talk, and so did Mr. Spencer (the bank's president). The guy was obviously impressed, and went back to Detroit to think it over. Then he told us "no." His family was well established in their present home, and he didn't want to bring them to New York. His kids had put on a very convincing flip-chart presentation, he told us. Can you imagine it? Reed and Spencer were just incredulous—couldn't believe it. Here's a really top guy, and he lets his kids decide what he's going to do. We were flabbergasted.

Succeeding efforts at recruiting production-oriented executives were more fruitful, and OPG began to fill its management ranks with young, aggressive talent. One of the early arrivals was Bob White, who left Ford Motor Company to work as John Reed's assistant. For several months, the two men worked intensively to build a specific action framework around the 1971 goals of OPG. Then White, supported by other newly recruited executives (three of them from Ford), moved into the line organization to take charge of the transaction processing responsibilities of OPG's Area I.

"Tops-down management"

The draft of Bob White's speech for the ABA explained how the change process began with a fundamental look at the group's whole philosophy of management:

In general terms, we can say that "administering" connotes a passive mode, while "managing" bespeaks an active mode. An administrator is, in a sense, a bystander, keeping watch on a process, explaining it if it goes awry. But managing means understanding your present world, deciding what you would like it to be, and making your desired results happen. A manager is an agent of the future, of change.

The fact is that, traditionally, banking operations are not really managed at all. In a sense, the people in charge are running alongside the processing line, instead of being on top of it pressing the process levers. All you can do in such a situation is react. At Citicorp, we decided that this was unacceptable. We wanted to manage our back office, not administer it.

There are two critical prerequisites for this: conviction, and orientation toward results. Each manager must be absolutely convinced that he *can* control *all* factors relevant to his operation. That conviction must begin at the top, and must carry with it a willingness to spend for results. I am talking about spending in terms of change to the organization, its structure, its fabric. About the amount of top management time and energy expended, and about the type of people you are willing to accept in your culture.

To ensure an environment that will foster the kind of dedication and commitment we need, we use a pass/fail system as a management incentive. A manager passes or fails in terms of result objectives he himself has set within the top-down framework. He is rewarded or not rewarded accordingly. No excuses or rationalization of events "beyond one's control" are accepted. . . .[1]

---

[1] (*Note to the reader:* Italicized quotations are used throughout this case to interject representative comments of *other* managers who were involved in or affected by the OPG reorganization, as reported to the consultants whom Reed had hired. These quotations, of course, did not appear in the ABA speech.)

I've been treated better in the past three years than in all of the previous nine years.

Reed has been very fair with everybody who has produced, in a salary sense. . . .

The feeling was we should do things, especially make or beat budget, and that if we didn't we should expect to be out. . . .

The ABA speech continued:

The style of management we sought was tops-down management. Each manager sets his own objectives for his own level in translating objectives set from above. Although people felt initially constrained by a tops-down approach, I am fully convinced that it is the ONLY approach. Each manager is not only free to exercise his vision—he is expected to do so. He is unfettered by what is traditional, by what is the norm. Nothing is sacred. The real problem is that the tops-down system "strains" people, but it does not "constrain" them. "Good" people thrive in such an environment. . . .

This job is exciting, like working for a glamour company, almost like having your own company. I really like being a "maverick." . . .

I like the opportunity to work for change, and to have responsibility for it. What I don't like is the incompetence of those who resist. . . .

I work ten to twelve hours a day. I guess Reed works twenty-four. . . .

OPG has lived in crisis for the past six years, but it's worse now, especially the hours and pressure that everyone is under. I spent the whole summer working six days a week, and never saw the kids. Finally got up the courage to tell my wife I was working Labor Day weekend. She put it to me . . . said . . . well, I called and said I wasn't coming in. The guys I used to work with say to me now, "congratulations," even though my new job isn't a promotion. They see me as being better off, just to be out of that place.

If you start your management process with the first-line supervisors and accumulate upward, you are assuming that the smartest people and the strategic direction for the business come from the bottom of the management pyramid . . . if this is true, we need to reverse the present salary structure so that the first-line people are paid the most money. It is not a question of brightness or ability, it is rather that top management has a better view of the overall organization, its direction, goals, strengths, weaknesses, and so forth. . . .

The speech went on to outline the basic management theories which Operating Group had formalized and applied to its functions in the past three years. "Management 101," it was called, and it was simply stated as "knowing WHERE WE ARE, WHERE WE WANT TO BE, and HOW WE PLAN TO GET THERE." Each responsible manager was expected to know, in formal terms, the current state of his world and all the processes that were producing his current results; the *desired* state of his area and the processes that would produce *those* results; and finally the changes he would make to today's processes, to turn them into tomorrow's processes. "It is not results we are managing, but processes that achieve the results." After defining the 1970 situation of the Operating Group and its three goals for 1971 (flat costs, improved service, and elimination of the investigations backlog), the speech proceeded:

What was left was to design the action plan—the processes that would get us to the results we wanted. (See the accompanying reproduction of a slide shown to the audience at this point in the speech.)

PHASE I ACTION PLAN:
NOVEMBER 1970—JUNE 1971

- Hire the right "top management" people to build up a new style of management team

- Squeeze out the "Fat"

- Implement major new computer systems

- Develop a Financial Control System that forecasts
    People and annual salary rates
    Overtime
    Lost availability
    Inventory

- Define the "Rock" cleanup process
    Separate backlog from current work
    Do today's work today

We planned to build a strong management team, to hire managers who had the conviction and motivation to control their own operations with "management" skills as opposed to "administrative" skills.

We planned in 1971 to cut out all the "fat" accumulated during the prior 10 years of 18 percent annual cost rises—at that rate we knew there *was* some fat.

We planned to develop and install a financial control system, emphasizing simplicity and the major cost elements; (1) people, (2) overtime, (3) process float, or lost availability, and (4) equipment and computers.

We planned to define a process for cleaning up rocks, such as the 36,000 backlogged investigations, so that we could come out from under the crisis environment and get control of our processing. This meant designing the techniques to separate rocks out from current work so that we could both dissolve the rock AND do today's work today so that the "rock" would not grow.

In fact, the real significance of the Phase I action plan was that it enabled us to get a handle on the operating environment. With this program, we started to get on top of the back office so as to control and manage it.

> *The whole management team was brought in cold, predominately from Ford. So you had this whole new team applying industrial concepts to paper flow. It has worked. But people took affront that these bright young stars were coming along and changing the whole new world.*

> *The number of people actually severed from the bank was actually very small for the organization . . . only 179 . . . but the image is very negative. . . .*

> *The fear of a cut—a layoff—wasn't a very realistic one. In fact, there have been very few—but the perception of it was the important thing.*

> *The key issue in the bank today is job security. . . .*

> *There was a language problem. The buzz words used by the new guys differed from the language the old managers used and understood.*

> *Lots of people close to retirement retired early. People at the AVP level are running scared. . . .*

> *The bank no longer offers "security" to old-timers. My chance to become a VP is almost nil, regardless of performance; I just don't have the right background. . . .*

> *People have really put out in this place . . . some of them have really worked. But when some old-timers were pushed out, it hurt a lot of us. We said, "Is that what's in store for us if we keep going here?" Also, when the old timers who knew other parts of the bank left, we lost a way to get a lot of contacts with the other groups.*

To gain control of costs, it was necessary to forecast what our expenditures would be *before* we were committed. We developed a one-page expense summary report based on forecast, rather than on history. (See Exhibit B–1.) The manager is in control of all his variables. We do not recognize any type of expense as uncontrollable or institutional. Forecasts are updated monthly and are met.

> *We have a tendency now to try to meet due dates at all costs. . . .*

> *Due dates for changes are in most cases absurd. Time commitments are ridiculous, and the consequences of not meeting due dates aren't made known beforehand.*

> *People try to be optimistic to please the boss. When they miss the milestones, they get screwed.*

But when we set about implementing new computer-based systems, we learned a very important lesson: we hadn't gone back to basics enough. We found we did not really understand the present processes completely.

AREA | **AREA 1**   **DIVISION**   **DDA RECAP**   **DATE**   **EXHIBIT**

	Month of January			Month of February			March–December			Full year 1973			
	Actual	Actual (0)/U Budget	Actual (0)/U Forecast	Actual (0)/U 1972 Actual	Forecast	Forecast (0)/U Budget	Forecast (0)/U 1972 Actual	Forecast	Forecast (0)/U Budget	Forecast (0)/U 1972 Actual	Forecast	Forecast (0)/U Budget	Forecast (0)/U Prior Forecast	Forecast (0)/U 1972 Actual
Salaries														
Official & nonofficial														
Part time														
Fringe benefits														
Overtime														
Temporaries														
Severance														
Subtotal salaries														
Other Operating (incl. 799s)														
Education & training														
Computer time—Outside vendors														
Consultants														
Computers														
Furniture & equipment														
Insurance & legal														
Postage														
Stationery & supplies														
Telephone, telegrams & cables														
Travel membs. & subs.														
Business, prom. & ent.														
Food														
Operating losses & losses not insured														
Difference & fine														
Lost availability														
Rent														
Rental income														
OPC occupancy expense														
Real estate taxes														
Building depreciation														
Utilities														
Freight & cartage														
Other														
1972 related expense														
Provisions														
Subtotal Other Operating														
TOTAL EXPENSE														

And so a second action plan, Phase II, was devised in June of 1971. We called it the Performance Criteria System, PCS. What we were aiming at was breaking up the operations into manageable, controllable, understandable pieces. These were the key approaches to defining the back office dynamics.

One: Define the products/services as recognized by the customer.
Two: Develop a customer-to-customer flowchart and procedures for processing each product/service.
Three: Develop the organization to match and support the product definition and process flow on a customer-to-customer basis.
Four: Develop our physical layout into a closed-room/one-floor layout that matched the flows, procedures, and organization so as to enhance control and minimize movement.
Five: Decentralize all peripheral equipment.
Six: Incorporate support functions into the responsible line organization.

Our processing had always been conceived of in functions, rather than in system processes. All the work flowed into one pipeline of processing functions; for example: preprocessing, encoding, read-to-tape, sorting, reconcilement, repair, and dispatch. You can visualize the functions along a vertical axis, and the people and timeframe along a horizontal axis (see Exhibit B–2), giving us a very wide pipe carrying two to three million transactions per day. If the one pipe breaks, all the work in the pipe before the break stops or spills out. That shouldn't happen often, but when it does, the whole operation stops.

We aimed to break down that pipeline into several smaller lines, each carrying a different product and each supervised by a single manager who controlled every aspect of his process, from the time a customer originates a transaction all the way through a straight line until we dispatch the results back to the customer. (For an example of this straight-line flow, see Exhibit B–3.)

We began by breaking the operations out on the basis of six separate input streams: two flows from our domestic branches, separate domestic and international mail deposit flows, one flow from our head office department and one from incoming exchanges. Each of these became a separate processing line. (See Exhibit B–4.) These flows are not mere theory; they exist in documented fact.

> In came flowcharting and the product line concept. We had a flowchart that stretched across the room and back. White had an incredible ability to understand the whole thing—to point to something and just ask the critical question about how something worked, or why it was part of our activity and not somewhere else. The result was a definition of eleven different products, and a full reorganization in one month. It's the only way to run a bank.
>
> Changes were viewed differently by different people. People started flowcharting everything, and Bob White was going over everything, step-by-step. But lots of people got the feeling that they didn't know what to do. They didn't "fit" in this new environment. . . .

Exhibit B-2
Functional organization: Pipelines

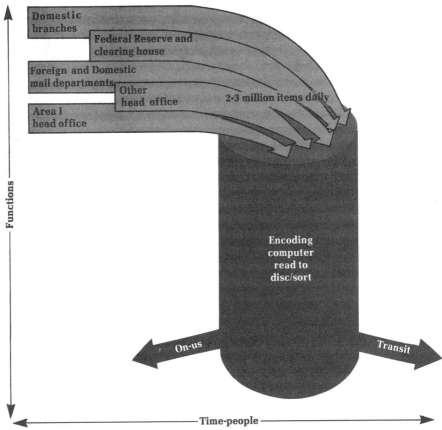

The blowup: September 1971

In August of 1971, Bob White decided it was time to act on the new organization of Area I. "We had been talking a lot about reorganizing the flows," he said, "but nothing was actually happening. We had spent months with people, talking about implementation, and we thought they understood. It was time to move."

On a hot September Friday evening, when the regular working shift went home, equipment crews began the job of rearranging the facilities of 111 Wall Street. By Monday morning the physical layout was set up for six separate lines, each with its own full complement of peripheral

Exhibit B–3
Straight-line flow

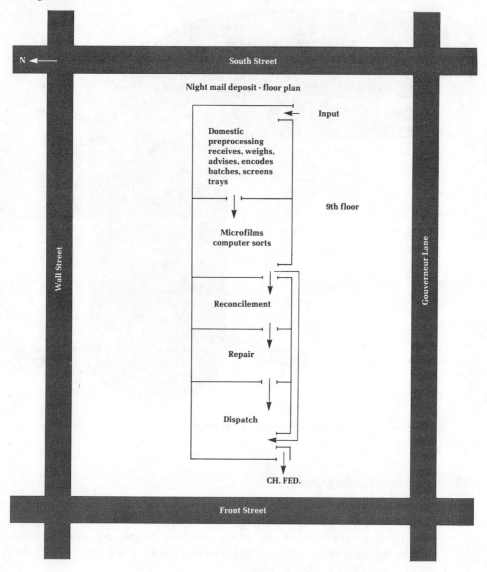

Exhibit B–4
Product/process organization: Pipelines

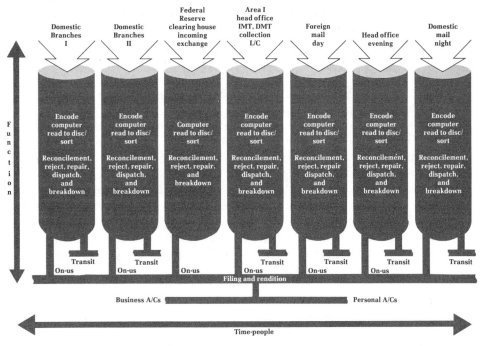

equipment, ready to begin work. And, soon after the work force reported on Monday, it became clear that the Demand Deposit Accounting system had problems. Equipment had been moved and connected, but technicians had not had time to check its operation before it went back into service; some of the machines refused to operate at all. Machine operators, informed on Friday that they would still have their same machines but they would be in different locations on Monday, arrived at work with questions, and there were not enough supervisors to answer them. Leftover work from Friday's processing, tucked away in accustomed corners by machine operators, was nowhere to be found; the customary corners were gone.

The money pipeline creaked and groaned under the strain.

As the week wore on new problems came to light. The three proofing clerks who had handled three shifts of consolidated front-end operations could not keep up with the load generated by decentralized work streams. With new people in charge of new areas, proof clerks did not know whom to call to resolve apparent discrepancies; the "Difference & Fine" account of accumulated variances began to grow alarmingly. By the end of the week, it was apparent that Citibank's problems were greater than just "de-bugging" a new system. OPG's managers were inventing new systems on the spot, attempting to recover. By the second weekend of September, the disturbance had grown to tidal wave proportions. The D&F account hit $1.5 billion on each side of the ledger before heroic week-end work by the group's middle managers brought it back down to $130,000,000. First National City Bank failed to meet the other New York bankers at the 10 A.M. exchange, and failed to file its Federal Reserve reports.

The money pipeline had burst.

Geoffrey MacAdams, the grey-haired head of the proofing operation, walked into the computer room, waving his hands in the air. "Stop the machines," he said haltingly to the computer operations head. "Stop the machines. It's out of control."

"I remember walking through the area and finding a pile of work, out on a desk-top, with a note on the top saying, 'This is out by a million, and I'm just too sleepy to find it'," said one manager. "There was maybe twenty or thirty million dollars in the stack. At least the girl was good enough to put a note on it. We were learning, the hard way, not to put papers like that into desk drawers."

Larry Stoiber, Operations Head for four of the six processing lines, looked up slowly one morning when Bob White greeted him, and delayed several seconds before showing signs of recognition. Stoiber had been at work for 55 hours without a break. White sent him home in a Citibank car, with instructions not to let him back into the bank until he was coherent.

In two weeks' time the new production processes began to work. Within a month of the change, routine operations once more ran routinely (note the difference between the Bob White memo of August 30 and the status report of October 6 on lost availability, attached as Exhibits B–5 and B–6). But it was five months before the backlog of work and problems generated by the DDA blowup were resolved.

In early October, as the DDA system began to return to normal and its managers turned their attention to the problems of cleaning up the side effects of the blowup, John Reed visited the Wall Street building to talk to Larry Small and Bob White. "I wanted to be the first to tell you this news," he said. "The Promotions Committee met this morning. You have both been named Senior Vice Presidents of the bank." He smiled broadly. "Congratulations."

> *The design for change from the top just cannot anticipate all the prob-*
> *lems that are going to arise at the first-line supervisor level; those*
> *people have to know more than just the before and after job*
> *description. . . .*

Exhibit B–5

MEMORANDUM TO: MESSRS. J. CAVAIUOLO, OPERATIONS HEAD
                        L. STOIBER, OPERATIONS HEAD
                        F. WHELAN, OPERATIONS HEAD

Effective Tuesday, August 31, I would like a report (attached) from each of you showing Lost Availability and deferred Debits and Credits for each of your operations:

    —Branch—Whelan
    —Domestic Mail—Stoiber
    —Foreign Mail—Stoiber
    —Head Office—Stoiber
    —Lock Box—Stoiber
    —Exchanges—Cavaiuolo

The first Lost Availability report should cover the period from the first City Country deadline on Monday to the New York, New Jersey deadline on Tuesday. The deferred debits and credits report should be based on one DDA update to the next.

The report should be completed and on my desk by 1:45 p.m. daily. Initially the report will be in addition to the regular Lost Availability daily report—I assume you will insure the report will tie. You are now each *personally* responsible for insuring that all lost availability is measured. I would rather not *ever* find anymore "undiscovered" lost availability.

If you have any questions or any problems in meeting this deadline, see me today. If not, I will expect the first report at 1:45 p.m. on Tuesday.

Bob

Robert B. White
Vice President
August 30, 1971

I'll tell you why people didn't protest the change, or question their instructions. We were scared—afraid of losing our jobs if we didn't seem to understand automatically.

The changes were accompanied by a great fear that people would get fired. Most lower managers and clerical workers felt management—that's AVP level and above—was highly insensitive to people. . . .

Reed and White and the new guys know what they're doing; they're good at setting up cost and quality measures, and conceptualizing the system. But at the practical level, things haven't worked. In the past, new instructions would be questioned, and worked through until they were either understood, or the designer was convinced there

Exhibit B–6

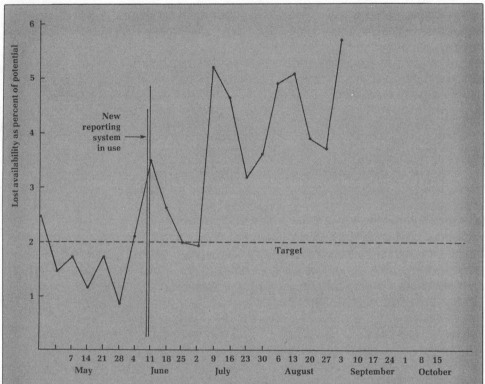

Excerpt from October 8, 1971, internal report on the status of "rocks" in the Demand Deposit Accounting system.

Float

Float statistics for the month of September were not available due to incomplete data as a result of procedural changes caused by the recent reorganization. A data-capturing network has now been developed and implemented; and reliable and complete data were reported on October 1 and thereafter, indicating an average 3.2 percent lost availability for the three-day period October 1–5.

was a problem. For example, if I go out there and tell Mary to start writing upside down and backwards on what she is doing, she'll look at me and say "why?," because she knows me and to her it doesn't make sense. If one of the new guys tells her to write upside down and backwards, she'll do it and not say a word. If anything a little unusual starts to happen, she won't know why it's important, and she won't say a word about it. When the Ford kids say do it, people do it. But they're scared.

It hurt us, credibility-wise, with the rest of the bank. The sharks smelled blood in the water, and came at us from all directions. But things are better now—an order of magnitude better.

Just a year later, in September of 1972, the Demand Deposit Accounting System blew up again, this time centered in the back end of the process, where the filing and telephone authorization process was being changed to anticipate the installation of computer voice answer-back equipment. The changes altered the way accounts were "ruled off" in preparation for statement rendering, making it impossible for the file clerks to select the proper checks to match with the computer-printed last pages of customers' statements. Unlike the 1971 crisis, this blowup affected customers directly and immediately. "The problem looked critical to the branch people, who had customers standing in line at the tellers' windows waiting for answers that never came. And it seemed critical to account officers in corporate banking, who couldn't get statements for their customers. But it was actually much less serious than the 1971 episode, because it didn't involve the proofing system," said Bob White. "We were able to react much more quickly, and we were pretty much recovered from it within a month and a half."

Achievements in the operating group

The draft speech for the American Bankers Association summarized the results of Operating Group's improvement efforts in two charts which would be reproduced as full-color slides (see Exhibits B–7 and B–8). By the end of 1973, according to the forecast, personnel in the group would be reduced by 30 percent from 1970 levels; overtime would be down by 71 percent; lost availability would be down by 75 percent; and the backlog of investigations would be shrunk from 36,000 to 500 cases—one day's load. The speech would elaborate:

The real achievement here, though, is that we forecasted what we would achieve and then made it happen. Moreover, we *did* put together the kind of management team we wanted, and we *did* get hold of the processes within our shop. At the same time, we developed a control system to measure the two facets of service to our customers: quality and timeliness. Quality measures error rate; it is the number of errors as a percentage of the total work processed on a daily basis.

We currently measure 69 different quality indicators, and we are meeting the standards 87 percent of the time. When a given indicator is met or beaten consistently, we tighten the standard; we expect to continue this process indefinitely.

Timeliness is the percentage of work processed in a given time period—generally a 24-hour time period. At the moment, we have defined 129 different standards for timeliness, and we expect that number to continue to grow. Today, we are

Exhibit B–7
Expense forecast summary

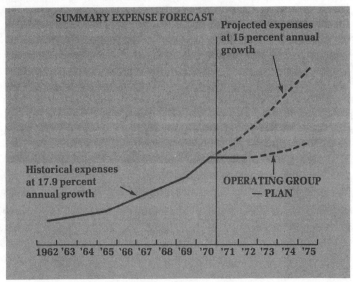

meeting 85 percent of these standards. Moreover, we also continually tighten these standards as soon as we prove they can be consistently met. I think it is fair to say that our service performance has improved greatly since we began to hold costs flat—if for no other reason than that we now *really* know what we are doing.

> *In order to make progress, we had to be firm with the other divisions of the bank. We used to interrupt anything in order to handle a special request. No more. We consciously shut them out, so we could work on the basic processes here. Now we have no people wandering in here to distract our clerks.*

Exhibit B–8
Results: 1970–73

	RESULTS					
	Headcount		Overtime		Lost availability	
Year	Number of employees	Cumulative percent decrease from 1970	$ (000)	Cumulative percent decrease from 1970	$ (MMs)	Percent of potential
1970	7,975	—	1,983	—	56.4	4.0
1971	6,610	17	1,272	35	32.8	2.0
1972	5,870	26	845	57	26.5	1.8
1973	5,528	30	564	71	14.2	0.5

From outside the Operating Group, changes were also evident. Three officers from the customer-contact divisions commented as follows:

> *My frustration is I wish there were more old-time bankers in there, and fewer systems and organization types. There is a huge loss of old guys I can turn to for help in getting things done, people who know banking. Maybe they should keep just a few. Some. A few cents a share might well be worth it.*

> *People over here do say that if those guys are so good, why do they keep screwing up. You'd think they'd learn something in two years. . . .*

> *In the old days, when the old guys were running things, you knew who to go to. Now we don't know. Even if we find somebody, he's faced with a process where he couldn't give special service even if he wanted to.*

Bob White's speech concluded:

These, then, were the achievements of two years of fundamental change. They are, I think, substantial, and they provide us with the solid base we need to focus in on the future.

> *One of John Reed's magazine articles that came around said something about people being replaceable, like machines. That hurt. You lose solidarity.*

> *Somebody asked me once if I liked it that we were working in what Reed called a factory. That really struck home. So, maybe it is like a factory. Why do they have to say it?*

Case 7–2
Inland Steel Corporation
John J. Gabarro, Jay W. Lorsch

revised by
John P. Kotter and Leonard A. Schlesinger

In December of 1967 Mr. Grant Ambrose, assistant general manager for mills of Inland Steel Corporation's Lake Michigan Works, was considering the computerization of several proposed rolling mills. Inland Steel Corporation, seventh largest steel manufacturer in the United States, had pioneered the application of computer control to the rolling of steel with a computerized hot strip rolling mill in 1965. Ambrose was interested in seeing what Inland could learn from that experience as an aid to future planning of new mills and the implementation of computer control.

The Lake Michigan Works also had two manually controlled hot strip mills, as well as a number of cold strip, tin, shaping, and plate mills. Mr. Ambrose was responsible for all of these mills, as shown in Exhibit 1. The Lake Michigan Works complex employed 22,000 people and was the third largest steel manufacturing site in the country. Over half of Inland Steel's production was located at this site.

Inland's computerized 80-Inch Hot Strip Rolling Mill was the first computer-controlled hot mill in the industry, and it had been the subject of widespread attention and numerous tours by industrial and educational groups. The 80, as it was referred to by Inland personnel, incorporated many advancements in the state of the art as well as a computer-controlled process, and it differed in many respects from the company's older 76-inch and 44-inch hot mills. The 80's rolling mill was nearly half a mile long, over twice as long as the 76 and was also three times as fast.

Six hundred and eighty employees worked in the 80's three-shift operation. Thirty men were directly involved in operating the process—ten on each shift's operating crew, as opposed to 20 per shift in the older 76. The remainder of the 680 employees were involved in supervisory, maintenance, administrative, and supporting functions. All of the 80's employees had been transferred from the older hot mills and were experienced in steel manufacture.

Exhibit 1
Simplified organization chart—Lake Michigan Works

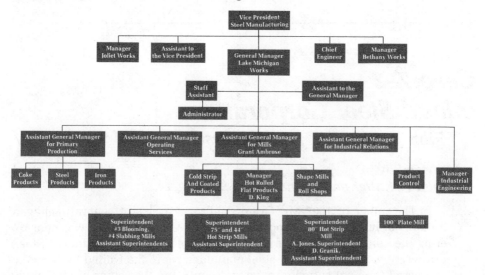

The hot strip rolling process

The hot strip rolling process was one of a series of processes in the making of strip steel. As shown in Exhibit 2, steel ingots were rolled into slabs by a slabbing mill before they entered the hot strip rolling mill. Hot Strip mills were called hot mills because the slabs were reheated to about 2,200° F in furnaces and then rolled into strip steel while still red-hot. The coils of strip steel from the hot mills were then either sold directly to the customer or sent to the cold mills for further rolling and surface finishing. The steel was eventually used in thousands of end products such as cars, washing machines, and filing cabinets.

The slabs which entered the hot mill were relatively large—averaging about 8 inches in thickness, 30 feet in length, and of varying widths (up to 74 inches). These slabs were reheated for two to three hours and then put through a series of roughing mills (each set of rolls was called a mill) for reduction in thickness and rolling to proper width.

The slabs moved along a long, conveyor-like mill table which passed through the roughing and finishing mills, and terminated at the coiler. After going through the roughing mills, the slabs were called bars. They continued along the mill table into the finishing mills where they were rolled to the required thickness. The bar would enter into one end of the finishing train (a series of finishing mills) and emerge from the other end as strip steel. The final process along the mill table was the winding of the strip into coil.

Exhibit 2
Simplified diagram—steel coil manufacturing

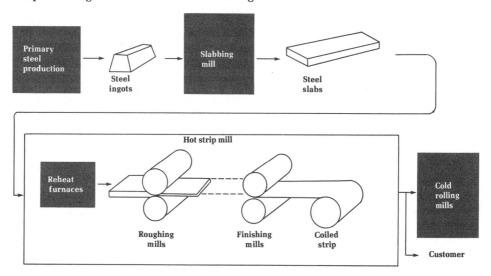

Inland Steel's 76-inch hot mill, built in 1932, was typical of manually controlled mills. Exhibit 3 shows its layout and the locations of members of the operating crew. To the uninitiated, such a hot mill was a noisy and dramatic place, with glowing hot slabs entering each of the rolling stands with a boom. The constant noise in the mill necessitated the use of hand signals for most communication on the mill floor. Normally a hot mill such as the 76 was housed in a large, unheated building which was hot in the summer and cold in the winter. Thus, in the winter time, operators who were stationed along the mill table, were alternately exposed to the intense heat of the bars going through the mill and the cold of the winter day. Often the area adjacent to the rolling stand was wet from sprays used in the process and from water which cooled the rolls. "Warming" stoves were placed along the mill table to alleviate these conditions in the winter.

Each slab which entered a rolling mill (whether computerized or not) was designated for a specific customer order, with specified finished coil dimensions for thickness, width, surface quality, and metallurgy. Inland Steel's central production planning department prepared a "rolling schedule" for each hot mill, giving the rolling sequence and dimensions of the slabs and the finished specifications on the orders to be rolled in a turn (shift). The rolling schedules were arranged in order of decreasing widths to obtain even wear on the rolls. Orders of similar widths and other dimensions were arranged together and called "sections."

Traditional mill work roles

There were two key people in a manually controlled mill such as the 76: The *roller* who, as seen in Exhibit 3, operated the finishing mills, and the *rougher,* who operated the roughing mills.

The roller's job was the most critical to rolling good steel, and unlike the other members of the crew, he was salaried. His role was important because he determined the settings on each finishing mill for every bar processed. Since each bar and order was different, the roller had to call on his experience and judgment for setting up the mills. Often he was able to judge the settings for each of the finishing mills from "feel," while at other times he calculated them in the roller's shanty. Bad settings would result in unacceptable dimensions for the order and, more important, incorrect settings could cause "cobbles" or "wrecks" in the mill. (Cobbles occurred when the mills damaged the steel being processed so that it was unusable. A wreck was a cobble where not only the steel was ruined but the mill itself or the rolls were damaged.) A cobble spoiled the steel in the mill, but could also cause the scrapping of bars coming down the mill table behind it, if these bars cooled too much while the

Exhibit 3
Simplified layout of the manually controlled, 76-inch hot strip mill

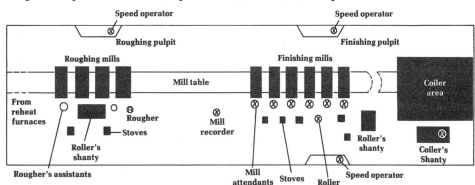

cobbled bar was being removed and scrapped like cobbles. The decision whether to roll or scrap a cooling bar was made by the roller, since steel that was too cold to roll could cause a wreck in the mill, and wrecks meant the expense of damaged equipment (rolls cost about $20,000 a pair), and costly down time. Hence, the roller's judgment and his ability to make decisions quickly had a great effect on productivity and cost.

Most rollers had come up through the ranks and had a great deal of experience, the majority having worked 30 years or more in the steel mills. These men had "strong mill sense," which enabled them to determine how the steel would react under varying settings and conditions of pressure and temperature. The rollers often recorded unusual situations in little books which they carried on their person.

The "art" still left in steel manufacture made the roller a valuable person, as reflected by the $20,000 to $25,000 a year in salary and incentive, which rollers of large hot mills normally received in 1965.

Each of the mills in the finishing train had a *finishing attendant,* except for the last mill. These men set up the mills for each slab according to the roller's hand signal instructions. The roller set the last and most critical mill himself. The speeds and accelerations of the finishing train were operated by the *finishing speed operator* who sat in the finishing pulpit, an enclosed room attached to the front wall about 30 feet above the mill floor with windows overlooking the finishing mills. The speed operator also received his instructions from the roller's hand signals. Because this job required considerable experience and skill, it was one of the highest paid jobs on the operating crew.

The rougher served much the same function for the roughing train as the roller did for the finishing train, although less skill was required to operate the slower and less complex roughing mills. This position was considered the top nonsalaried job in the mill. Roughers usually had worked in every job in the mill's operating crew and for the most part had over thirty years of experience.

The rougher had two *roughing assistants* who helped him set up his mills. There was also a *roughing mill operator* who worked in the roughing pulpit, similar to the finishing pulpit, overlooking the roughing mills. He set the rolling rate of the mill and observed the operation of the roughing mills and table.

The *coiler* and several *coiler's helpers* operated the coiling machines. Correct coiling had an effect on the finished coils' quality, and was, therefore, a critical part of the process.

With each new section (change in width or gauge), the *mill recorder* walked alongside the mill table ahead of the first slab of the new section and advised each operator of the change. The rougher and the roller then checked the change in section with their rolling schedules and calculated the necessary setups; each then walked along his train and informed his mill attendants and speed operators of the new setups by hand signals.

All of the operating crew were paid on a base rate plus incentive based on tonnage, and all but the roller were nonsalaried.

Each turn had a *mill turn foreman* who supervised the coil operations, the roughing train, and the furnace operations. Historically, these foremen had relied heavily on the rollers, who were theoretically under their direction, for the technical aspects of setting the mills and rolling the steel. Foremen tended to concentrate on the maintenance and administrative aspects of the operating crew.

Considerable coordination was required along the mill table. The roller was dependent on the roughing mills for proper width and suitable dimensions of the bars, and both the roughing and finishing trains had to be coordinated for good pacing of production. Coordination was especially important when a cobble or wreck occurred, so that the cobble could be removed rapidly enough to minimize the loss of other steel. Once a bar or slab was in a mill it could not be stopped, and the ability of the mill personnel to act rapidly and correctly during a cobble was very important.

The computerized work process in the 80-inch hot mill

The 80 had begun rolling steel manually in early 1965 and had first gone "on computer" in July of 1966. The computer was not the only difference between the 80 and the older 76 and 44. The 80's equipment was faster and larger, as evidenced by the 80's half-mile length, considerably larger than the 76's 920-foot length. The 80 was also capable of strip speeds of more than 3,800 feet per minute at the last finishing stand, which was over three times as fast as the 76. In addition, the mill included a large enclosed slab yard, as shown in Exhibit 4, and several adjacent support building.

Because of greater maintenance needs, the 80 averaged 25 percent down time, and the older mills averaged 20 percent down time.

The 80's production output averaged 3,000 tons/turn by December 1967, compared to 1,400 tons/turn of the 76. This greater output was achieved by the 80's 680 employees as compared to the 76's 900 employees. This increased productivity was due to the greater mechanization in the rolling and peripheral operations, as well as to the computer.

By late 1967, the computer calculated and set up almost all of the variables in the process, including all operations from the furnace to the coiling operation. The setup computations for all the mill stands were made by the computer, and the 80 had no rougher or roller. The computer also performed the section changes automatically, drastically changing the mill recorder's role. In the 80, the mill recorder worked in one of the pulpits, keeping records and announcing section changes over a public address system. His latter function was performed only as a safety precaution in case the computer failed to perform the change properly.

Since the mill operated on a three turn (shift) per day basis, each turn had a senior turn foreman who was responsible for the entire hot rolling process, which included the furnaces, the roughing train, finishing train, and the coiler. Reporting to him was the heating and roughing foreman who supervised the furnaces, roughing train, and the 80's water treatment plant. (See Exhibit 5.) The senior turn foremen and the senior control systems analyst reported to the general foreman–hot mill through the foreman–hot mill. There were about 120 men working under the general foreman–hot mill. He and the five other general foremen (Coil Storage Finishing and Shipping, Mechanical, Electrical, etc.) reported to Don Granik, the mill's assistant superintendent, and then to Oscar Jones, the mill's superintendent. Jones reported to Mr. Dwight King, manager of hot rolled flat products, who in turn reported to Ambrose.

The general foreman–hot mill was responsible for the operation of the rolling process for all shifts, and as such was the most influential of the general foreman. The 80, unlike the other hot mills, had a foreman–hot mill, directly below the general mill foreman. It was felt that this additional level of supervision was needed to integrate the programming and the computer room activities with the mill's operational needs.

In actuality, both the general foreman–hot mill and the foreman–hot mill were involved in both mill and computer room affairs, though the general foreman–hot mill was more heavily involved in production activities and the foreman–hot mill in the computer room. In the realm of pro-

Exhibit 4
Simplified layout of the computer-controlled, 80-inch hot strip mill

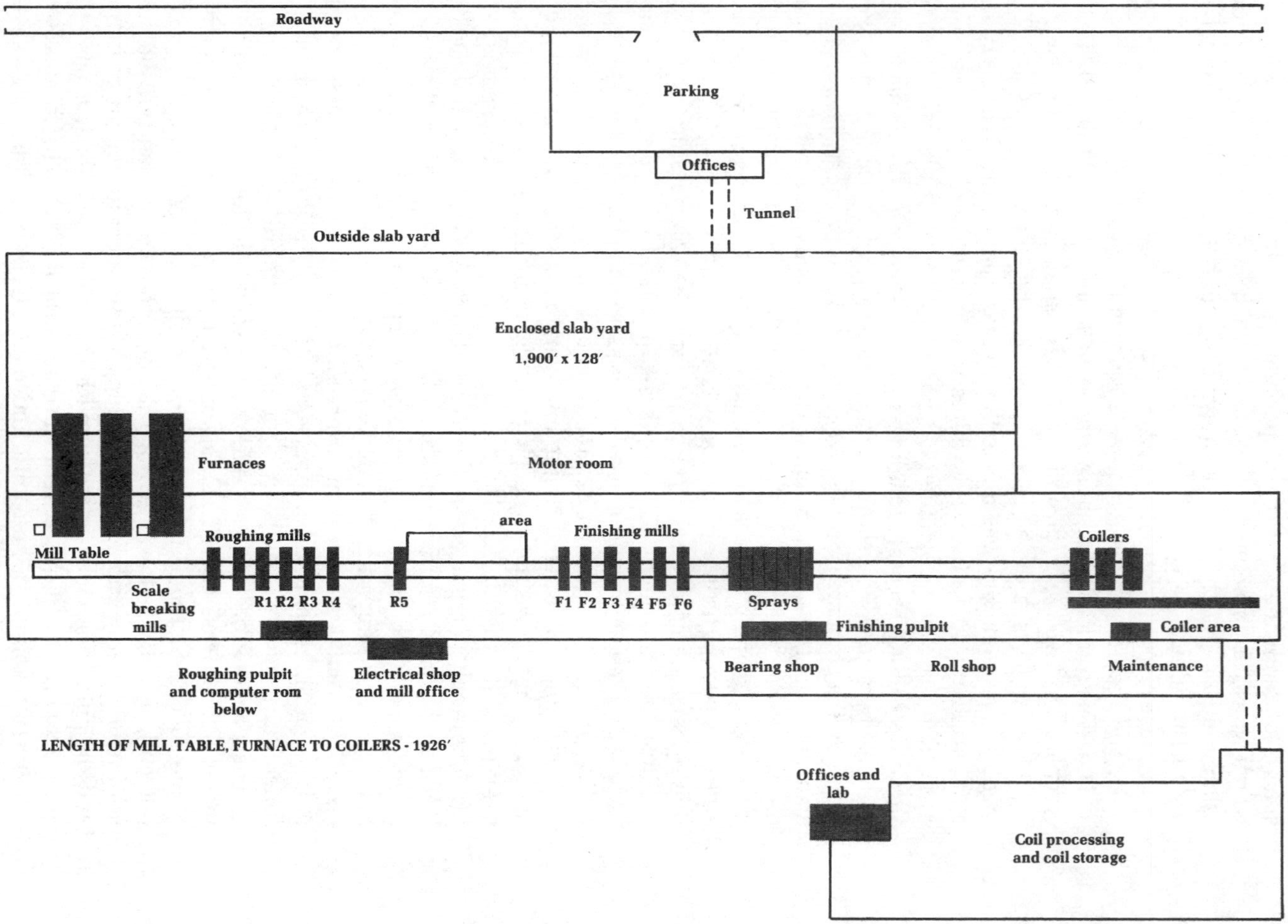

Roadway

Parking

Offices

Tunnel

Outside slab yard

Enclosed slab yard
1,900' x 128'

Motor room

Furnaces

Roughing mills

R1 R2 R3 R4

Scale
breaking
mills

Mill Table

Roughing pulpit
and computer rom
below

Electrical shop
and mill office

R5

area

Finishing mills

F1 F2 F3 F4 F5 F6

Sprays

Bearing shop

Finishing pulpit

Roll shop

Maintenance

Coilers

Coiler area

Offices and
lab

Coil processing
and coil storage

LENGTH OF MILL TABLE, FURNACE TO COILERS - 1926'

Exhibit 5
Organization chart–80-inch hot strip mill department

duction, the general foreman–hot mill concentrated on the more complex finishing end operations, and the foreman–hot mill on the preparatory and initial operations.

The rolling schedule for the 80 was prepared by the plant's centralized production planning department, as were the rolling schedules for the 76 and 44. Production planning also prepared a punch card for each slab to be rolled by the 80, giving the slab's initial dimensions and the specifications of the finished coil to be rolled from the slab. These cards were then arranged according to the rolling schedule and fed to the computer in correct order.

The operating crew on the 80 included a roughing attendant and a utility man at the roughing pulpit (see Exhibit 4), a finishing attendant, an assistant finishing attendant, the mill recorder, and two utility men in the finishing pulpit. The coiling operation included a coiler and a utility man in the coiler's pulpit, and an inspector and several coiler utility men in the coiler area. The pulpits were attached to the front wall about 30 feet above the mill floor overlooking the process. All of the pulpits were heated and, unlike those in the older mills, air-conditioned. Although the operating crew was housed in these pulpits, most of the area adjacent to the mill table was heated by large heaters.

As seen in Exhibit 4, these pulpits were approximately one-sixth mile apart from each other. The roughing attendant monitored all of the steps which the computer calculated for each slab before it entered a roughing mill. These computer-calculated settings were displayed on a control panel in the roughing pulpit. The computer also displayed the actual settings of each of the six roughing mills. The roughing attendant intervened manually in the process any time the computer and actual settings did not match. (A nonmatch caused the background of the incorrect setting to become red on the display panel.) He also intervened whenever he felt that the computer's settings were incorrect on any of the 30 variables he monitored.

In the finishing pulpit, the finishing attendant operated the last three finishing mills and his assistant, the first three. The speed and acceleration were usually set manually by these men, although the computer calculated and displayed speed and acceleration settings for each bar. They also monitored the displays for all other settings on the six finishing mills. As part of his responsibilities, the finishing attendant determined whether or not to roll steel that had cooled while a cobble was being removed. He often operated the mills manually for very wide widths of steel.

One of the utility men in the finishing pulpit operated a crop shear which cut off the tip of each bar before it entered the finishing train. The other utility man operated the sprays which were used to cool the strip to specified temperatures before it entered the coiler. Neither the crop shear nor the spray functions had been completely computerized.

The 80's electrical and mechanical groups were organized differently than in other mills. Traditionally, the electrical and mechanical crews were matched to the various operating crews in a mill. In the 80, however, each group was organized into areas by equipment. For example, there were three electrical areas. The first included the least sophisticated equipment in the 80 such as cranes, furnaces, and the simpler equipment on the first part of the mill process. The second area included the 80's more sophisticated water treatment works, and the roughing mills. The third area included the computer room and the very complex equipment in the finishing end of the mill. The mechanical function was divided into two areas, rolling equipment and all other equipment.

All the employees in the 80 were paid on a base rate plus incentive based on production output. The operating crew shared in the same incentive, which was computed for each turn, based on that eight-hour period's output. The electrical and mechanical support groups shared in another incentive based on each preceding two-week period's output. The furnace and slab yard crews shared an incentive based on a week's output. The other occupational crews, such as crane and general labor, coil handling, and shipping, also shared in incentives based on the output over the period of time influenced by their performance.

The operating crews, as in the older 76, included the personnel actually operating the rolling mills and the people in the coiler area. In late 1967, their pay, including incentive, ranged from $3.90/ hour for a utility man to $5.42/ hour for a finishing mill attendant. Incentive pay accounted for roughly 30 percent of the operating crew's total pay; the incentive pay earned by crews on different turns varied, with some crews making more than others. The crews worked eight hours per turn and ate when they could during the turn, since no formal lunch period was observed.

Mill management's philosophy on the computer

As shown in the biographic data in Exhibit 6, the 80's management team had substantial steel-making experience. Oscar Jones had been superintendent of several mills before the 80, and the assistant superintendent, Don Granik, was one of the few men who was a college graduate and a member of management to have been a roller on an important mill. Granik had rolled the 76 for over six years and was generally acknowledged to be a "top steel-maker with good practical knowledge of the business." The general foreman–hot mill, Ron Danville, was experienced mainly in production also, although he had received considerable computer training and had presented a paper on the computer control of the 80 to a technical society.

Jones summarized the attitude prevalent among the 80's management by saying:

Our philosophy is that the computer is a tool which helps us make better steel. The computer is online about 95 percent of the running time, and the operators are now glad to use it. But we want them to be responsible for the job. Our attitude has been not to be computer-dependent. We want to be able to go off-computer and keep rolling steel if we have to. Some of the newer computerized mills in other companies are not like this. When the computer's down, the mill goes down.

Exhibit 6
Biographic data—key management personnel—80-inch hot strip mill

Oscar Jones, 44, Superintendent, BS Mechanical Engineering. Began career in the electrical department.

Electrical General Foreman	#3 & #4 Slabbing Mills
Electrical General Foreman	#3 Cold Mill
Mill General Foreman	76" Hot Strip Mill
Mill General Foreman (for pre start-up planning) 1 yr.	80" Hot Strip Mill
Assistant Superintendent (for start-up operations) 6 mos.	80" Hot Strip
Superintendent, 1–1/2 yrs.	76" and 44" Hot Strip
Superintendent, 9 mos.	#1, #2 Cold Mills
Superintendent, 3 mos.	80" Hot Strip

Donald Granik, 41, Assistant Superintendent, BS Business Administration. Began career as turn foreman on the 76" Hot Strip.

Turn Foreman / Relief Roller / Roller } 6 yrs.	76" Hot Strip
Mill General Foreman, 1 yr. 6 mos.	76" Hot Strip
Assistant Superintendent, 2 yrs.	80" Hot Strip

Ronald Danville, 31, General Mill Foreman, BS and MS Engineering, Columbia University. Joined Inland Steel on its training program from college.

Turn Foreman	76" Hot Strip
Turn Foreman	80" Hot Strip
Senior Turn Foreman	80" Hot Strip
Foreman—Hot Mill (for phasing-in of online computer control)	80" Hot Strip
Mill General Foreman	80" Hot Strip

Paul Owens, 29, General Mechanical Foreman, BS Mechanical Engineering. Joined Inland Steel after college. Considerable engineering and supervisory experience in mechanical area before being assigned to the 80.

James Rodriguez, 31, General Electrical Foreman, BS Electrical Engineering. Joined Inland Steel after college. Varied experience in engineering and supervisory positions. General electrical foreman in a mill before being assigned to the 80.

Mr. Jones pointed out that one of the reasons that the computer room and the programmers reported to the general mill foreman was that Inland felt that those operations should be an integral part of the manufacturing operation.

Jones further commented:

In my opinion it's not yet feasible to run the mill on computer 100 percent of the time because the computer doesn't have every possible situation programmed into it. We want the operator to intervene when he can handle a situation better than the computer. The reason for our attitude is that we have literally hundreds of analog signals which feed the computer information. They all come from input devices which sense the process. These input devices can deteriorate, and when they do, they give wrong signals. If the computer gets a bad signal it stays tilt. When this happens you have to be able to keep rolling steel without the computer, because when you're working with hot metal you can't just stop, you've got to get it out of whatever part of the process it's in and quickly.

Mr. Granik elaborated on the fact that not all parts of the process were yet computer-controlled:

It hasn't been possible to put every single function on computer because some settings in the process are so variable and are affected by so many things that our program can only cover part of the normal situation. Our approach is to continue to refine these programs based on what we learn. When something can be done better manually than by the computer, we do it that way.

Ron Danville summarized his feelings simply by saying:

I tell the men that the computer is a tool to use. They're still making the steel. When we can do something better with manual control, we do it that way until the program is improved.

Background on the computer's start-up

The 80 began rolling steel in February of 1965 under manual control. The setups themselves were made manually, but were calculated by the computer offline. The computer was not put in online control of the process until July of 1966. During the year and a half period of manual control, the original programs were debugged and rewritten, based on the results of actual rolling experience. Mr. Jones amplified on this by saying:

It's important to understand that we began rolling the 80 without a roller or an online computer. People used to ask, "How the hell is that mill rolling?" We rolled by using the computer's offline calculations, trying them out and improving on them. We kept a data log of these settings and their revisions, which we called the "butcher book." These improvements were fed back into the program. The offline operation allowed us to concentrate on the steel-making process before taking on all the problems of an online computer. We still use the "butcher book" whenever we go to manual control.

Mr. Danville described this period and his role in the following way:

During this period we were finishing the writing of the computer to the process, improving the program, and learning to roll the mill manually. I was a turn foreman and later a senior turn foreman throughout this time. I worked pretty closely with the computer room people on the debugging of the program and also whenever we tried the computer online. On these occasions the systems analyst and I would go up to the pulpit and take the controls while the operators sat back and watched us. The operators didn't show any antagonism but I think they were skeptical. They'd give us a lot of good-natured kidding.

Little conflict or direct interaction occurred between the operating personnel and the computer room during this period except at Mr. Danville's level. There was, however, resentment on the part of some turn foremen to claims made by one of the senior systems analysts that eventually the direction of mill practices would originate in the computer room.

In preparation for putting the computer online, the mill went down for four days. Concurrent with the transition, Mr. Danville was promoted to foreman–hot mill and became responsible for both the mill operations and the computer room; two senior systems analysts were promoted out of the computer room to other assignments. Mr. Danville described the preparation for the transition to online computer control in the following way:

We brought in all the finishing and roughing attendants and the assistant finishing attendants and trained them in the pulpits using ghost slabs (slabs which the computer simulated). We tried to explain how their roles would change and we tried to give them an understanding of how the total system worked, which included taking them down to the computer room.

When we first went to the online operation, we had a lot of problems with the program as you'd expect. There were complaints that the computer had cut down production. I had to try and sell them on the short-term losses for long-term gains. The online wasn't hurting them in the pocketbook, though, because the crew was on an interim incentive during the start-up, which was a flat plan that paid some incentive from the first ton of output. This was because Inland didn't want to commit itself to an incentive rate until we knew what the true capacity of the mill was.

After the mill had gone online, the 80 became the subject of much trade press attention because it was the first completely computerized hot mill. Trade journals were more than generous in making claims for the computer's capabilities, with the result that some personnel in the mill felt that the part played by operating and support crews and mill supervision was being overlooked.

In general, however, the acclimation to an online process went on without major hostility to the computer. Mr. Danville described the attitudes of the operating crews in the following way:

We had problems and the computer got blamed for a lot of things which it didn't cause. There were also some problems between the turn foreman and the computer room, especially when I wasn't around. But I don't think that there was ever any serious resistance to the computer. To begin with, we'd always been reliant on the computer for setups and calculations even when we were controlling the mill manually. The original setup calculations were good, better than most people felt they could have done themselves. So the initial performance was good enough to inspire confidence in the program.

I don't think that the turn foremen resented the new role of the computer because the 80 is so much bigger and more complex than the 76 or the 44 that coming here was a big step up in responsibility for the foremen. Their responsibility has increased as our tonnage has gone up and so has the foremen's esteem in the eyes of the people in the mill; so I don't feel they lost any prestige in the transition. Neither have the attendants, because they now control much more equipment than they did before.

People became much more interested in the computer when we tried to operate it online and learn what could be done with it. Don Granik was a big influence in this because he took a close interest in the program and in seeing how it could be manipulated and improved. There are a lot of people who are interested in improving it now. Now that the system is more stable, the operating crews rely on it and can produce much more online than manually.

A number of supervisors in the 80 agreed that the greatest difficulty during the phasing-in of the computer's online operation was in getting the operating personnel to understand the capabilities and limitations of the computer's program.

Process operation

The computer had been improved by late 1967 to perform the pacing of production coming down the mill; and since it had already performed most of the setup operations, there was much less need for interdependence between operators than in the old mills during normal operations. However, when a wreck or cobble occurred, part of the mill would go off computer, and the pacing function stopped. This required rapid coordination, especially between the coiler and the finishing attendant if the cobble occurred in the coil area, and between the finishing and roughing attendants if it occurred in the finishing train.

All of the pulpits were connected by a public address system which could be heard throughout the mill on loudspeakers. The PA was a key link during a cobble and also served as a means for informal bantering between pulpits, including some needling when production was being lost because of problems at one of the areas. "O.K. you guys, why don't you get your hand out of my pocket," or, "It looks like you want to give all the tonnage to the next turn," were remarks characteristic of the kidding that went on. It was the mill's policy for operators to use their judgment in intervening with the computer. Often when an operator encountered a slab which was not behaving as expected, he would use the PA to warn the stations farther down the mill about it.

The PA was also used by the mill recorder to announce the next section coming down the mill as a back-up net in case the computer failed to perform its integration function; this was a holdover procedure from the days when the computer was first put online. The mill recorder also posted the delay reports on down time and did other paper work.

The finishing pulpit was the busiest of the three, since the senior turn foreman had his desk there and a quality control man was also stationed there to record rolling information. Exhibit 7 shows a layout of the pulpit and lists the people who came into the pulpit in a typical 90-minute period. A blackboard for posting turn information was located at the end of the pulpit. The blackboard was also used by the crew to spoof one another or management. As an example of this, the casewriter found a reference to a recent trade article about the mill's automatic roll changing equipment on the blackboard which read:

> Welcome to Fantasyland
>
> Our role changes are completely automatic and they only take two minutes!

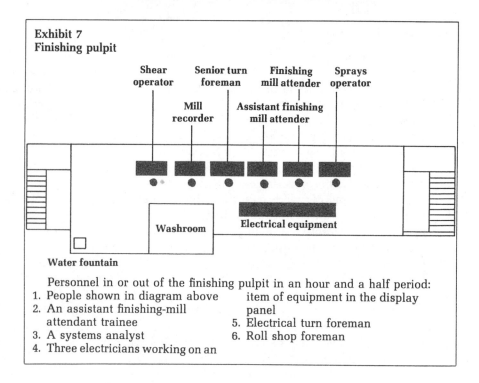

Exhibit 7
Finishing pulpit

Shear operator   Senior turn foreman   Finishing mill attender   Sprays operator

Mill recorder   Assistant finishing mill attender

Washroom   Electrical equipment

Water fountain

Personnel in or out of the finishing pulpit in an hour and a half period:
1. People shown in diagram above
2. An assistant finishing-mill attendant trainee
3. A systems analyst
4. Three electricians working on an item of equipment in the display panel
5. Electrical turn foreman
6. Roll shop foreman

In contrast to the finishing pulpit, which a number of people entered over the course of a day, the roughing pulpit was often only occupied by the roughing attendant, joined occasionally by the utility man. The tone in all of the pulpits, however, was generally hushed except for the intermittent comments over the PA.

Compared to the older mills, there were relatively few people on the mill floor, except when an equipment problem occurred with one of the rolling stands, and in the words of one operator, "People seem to come out of the walls." When such problems occurred, the first person seeing the problem would call for mechanical or electrical personnel by sounding a horn which could be heard all over the mill or by using the mill's PA.

An example of the sense of immediacy in such a situation was observed by the casewriter during an early visit to the mill. Ron Danville, the mill general foreman, a utility man, the roughing operator, and some visitors were in the roughing pulpit when Danville noted that a bar was not entering a roughing stand properly. Danville and the utility man immediately ran to the roughing stand, while the operator pulled the bar out of the stand and called to stop more bars from coming. At the roughing stand, Danville determined that one of the rolls was not turning; and using hand signals, he communicated this up to the operator who sounded the horn for some mechanical assistance. While the repair was being made, the operator called for a crane to remove the cooled bar from the table. The necessary adjustment was made, and the mill was rolling again in less than five minutes' time.

The computer room

The computer room was directly below the roughing pulpit and housed the activities of the senior systems analyst, a control systems analyst, two programmers, a programming trainee, and four console operators—one for each turn. A large schematic display of the computerized process, arranged as a flow diagram showing the succession of operations, was built into one of the walls. This display had a light representing each location in the process where input devices tracked the slabs. The console operator monitored the complete process by watching the display. He also monitored the interventions made by the various operators and any "alarms." "Alarms" were printouts by the computer indicating that something was wrong, such as an input sensor not operating, or that some parameter of the process was incorrect.

Whenever one of these situations occurred, the console operator would call the pulpit involved and warn them of the problem. Communications also initiated in the pulpit when an automatic adjustment failed to occur. The pulpit affected would call the computer room to inform them of the malfunction, in order to see if it was a program or computer problem. Any of the above situations would normally result in the affected part of the process going off computer control. Generally the communications between the computer room and the pulpits were not of a routine nature and occurred only around problems. Calls from the computer room were customarily made over a telephone line, rather than over the PA, although the computer room was connected to the PA.

Operators' reactions to the computer

As suggested by the description above, the operators' roles in the 80 were considerably different from those in the older mills. Eli Smith, a finishing attendant, explained the differences:

The biggest difference is that with a computerized process a man has a lot more responsibility than in the old mill, a lot more to worry about if he does this job the way it should be done. Maybe you do less physical work than before, but there are lots of things that you have to check on, be on top of. In the old mill there was a speed operator, and an attendant for each mill in the finishing end. And the roller told them all what to do. Each man was responsible for concentrating on one part of it except for the roller. Well now, me and the assistant attendant watch all of it. It's a strain; you always monitor the computer because you know it isn't right 100 percent of the time. A good operator catches it before there's a problem.

With the computer on the process, any one of a hundred little things that isn't right, like a bad heat detector or a slipping motor some place, affects the process. The program does the right thing only when everything is right. Most of the time the computer is O.K. But you have to be watching for the one time that something goes wrong. That's the difference between the good operator and a guy who isn't so good.

Now if a guy doesn't give a damn, and a lot of them don't, he doesn't feel the strain. The computer's great for him. He just sits back and doesn't worry about it until he has a wreck in the mill.

Just the opposite thing happens if you get a man like Slovak (an assistant finishing attendant) who worries a lot. In a job like this he has real troubles because there are a lot of things to follow on the panel. He gets very anxious, so that when something does go wrong he panics and he makes a mess. He's all nerves. This morning we were having troubles—all morning—and Slovak was so nervous I wouldn't let him touch a control. I had one of the trainees work the first three mills.

. . . We worry about a lot of the things the roller does in the old mill and we have to do the watching that the five mill attendants do in the other mill. I guess you could say that the finishing operators and the computer have replaced the roller.

But people haven't changed. You got a guy who is interested in making good steel, he was good in the old mill and he makes good steel here, too. He uses the computer to help him. The guys who were weak or didn't give a damn in the old mill are the same ones who have troubles here.

Tom Slovak, the assistant finishing mill attendant referred to above, described his feelings in the following way:

It gives you a different kind of fatigue. You're mentally tired; it's not physical. I get all strung up at the end of a day. In the other mill I could get along on five hours' sleep and once I got in the mill I was wide awake. But here, I can't do the job unless I've had eight hours' sleep because it's constant concern— watch everything and it moves quick—everything is faster than the old mill.

Another operator commented about the men's attitudes by saying:

Most of the men like the computer. But when things go haywire you'll hear them say it's because of the "goddamn computer." Things will be better when the programmers gain a little more experience. Every time something goes wrong and the mill goes off computer, the reasons go down to the computer room. Eventually all this information will make the programs better. We've got some good supervision here—guys who know the computer business and understand the steel end of things. That's what's going to make this baby work—bringing the computer know-how together with the experience of running the mill. With the competition we're getting from outside the United States in the steel industry, we're going to need top notch operations like this. Most of the men recognize this—management and the union especially.

Management's reaction to the computer

The computer not only posed changes in the concerns of operators, but, as implied above, in the concerns of the mill's management. Mr. Jones discussed some of the differences in managing a computerized mill by saying:

We have all the concerns they have in the older mills plus all the problems that are unique to a computer. The older mills have been shaken down but we're dealing with new problems. The decisions are not as clear cut. You now have to determine whether the cause of a problem is internal to the computer, or because of our mill practice, or a combination. You constantly have to be asking if the computer is really helping you.

One thing it's done is make everything more interdependent. The computer requires that everything electrical and mechanical be in pretty top shape. Before, the roller could keep rolling with a mill limping along because he knew from experience how far he could go. The computer is much more sensitive and has narrower limits, and it won't work with bad equipment. Don Granik and the general foremen get together in a daily meeting to coordinate around mill problems and sort out what's causing what.

There are so many more interdependencies now that responsibilities are not so clear cut. In the old mill I could pin the responsibility on someone. Here it's hazier. But I know I'm responsible for everything.

One of the problems in managing a computerized operation is that we have a tendency as a society to (a) oversell process computers and (b) feel that the computer will take care of everything. For example, people on the top don't understand the limitations. They tend to say, "How the hell can you be off gauge— you've got a computer!" The salesmen sell its capabilities to the customers, and this results in closer and closer manufacturing tolerances.

Don Granik further elaborated on the issue of people's expectations of a computerized process:

Sometimes people in higher management and in other parts of the company just don't have awareness of the limitations of a computerized mill or what it takes to make it run well. People expect such unrealistic things from the mill, that it's hard to get a sense of personal achievement, especially if you pride yourself on being a steel-maker. You know what you're doing, but not too many people outside really appreciate what's involved.

One of the problems is that no one had a computerized hot mill before Inland. Our sales force developed a good story based on "a computerized process." Most of our competition reacted by also building computerized mills, some of which are now finished. The general result was that everyone's sales force attempts to oversell their capabilities to top the competition.

The whole industry has talked itself into severe restrictions. And everyone is forced to talk it up when in fact many are having a rough time. You don't hear this through official channels, but over a couple of beers from the guys who run the mills, after a conference, or after a visit to their mill.

As implied in Mr. Jones's comments, the computerized process had resulted in a greater interdependence between the electrical, mechanical, and mill crews. Both the electrical and mechanical general foremen felt this had affected their jobs.

Mr. James Rodriguez, electrical general foreman of the 80, attempted to describe these differences in the following way:

Electrical is much more important to the successful operation of the 80 than in a noncomputerized mill. It means that we have to understand the process of making strip from slab, because the electrical is now so interwoven with the process that the operating crew has to rely on us more. It also means that we may get blamed for quality which in other mills would be unheard of. You'd blame some operators for being off gauge. But here it could reasonably be our fault. We also have a greater effect on the pacing of tonnage because it's automated.

The computer has also made us work closer with mechanical because the automatic control requires that machines be better mechanically than in the old mills. This makes the problems a little fuzzier and it's harder to determine the cause. It's not so clear whether it's a mechanical or an electrical problem, so we often have to work at it jointly.

Owens (mechanical general foreman), Danville, and I get together with Granik every morning and go over the delays of the past 24 hours and decide who attacks what. It's normal for mechanical or electrical to try to minimize his effort and move it on the other, so that's where Don (Granik) comes in; he assures that the right decision is made.

The electrician's life here is also different from the older mills. Our men have to deal with some pretty sophisticated equipment so they need to be highly trained. In fact, the Inland Apprenticeship Program[1] partially resulted from our need for better-trained electricians. Most of the electricians have a strong interest in electrical things and they like to study on the side. A lot of them transferred here because they wanted to work on the equipment. But we also have a few people just looking for a job.

Some of them are still afraid of the monster and feel relieved when a foreman or an engineer arrives when they have a problem. A guy has to have a lot of confidence in himself not to feel afraid of it.

Paul Owens, mechanical general foreman, described the influence of the computerized process on his group:

Automation affects us more than the computer aspect of it. To do something automatically, everything has to be mechanically right. And to do things automatically you need more mechanical equipment. This requires more inspection, preventive maintenance, and actual maintenance.

In the old mills you could just go out on the floor to see what the problem is. Our problems show up in the read-out or feedback from the computer. It can be a gear that's wearing, and the slight wear has to be fixed or the computer won't react correctly. In an old mill the part could go until it broke down completely. This means you have to prethink and anticipate problems and the foreman has to then plan the shutdown turns in much more detail.[2]

In other mills, electrical have their problems and mechanical theirs, and they can work pretty independently. But here we can't. We meet every morning at 9:00 with Don Granik to decide whose problem is what.

For example, the computer calls for a section change and the sideguides don't move to the new position. The operator calls an electrician and he sees it's not the electrical switches that are causing it. So they tell us and we investigate to see if it's the gears or some other mechanical problem. We can narrow it down pretty much by looking at it more closely. That will generally give us an area to look at on the down turn. We also get this kind of thing from the mill people. But in an older mill you'd never hear about it until it physically broke down because it wouldn't make any difference until then.

The demands on the mechanics are different also. The problems here are

---

[1] This was a program whereby mechanical and electrical apprentices attended special sessions taught by a large well-known midwestern university for Inland, which covered a number of basic sciences and advanced subjects. Completion of various portions of this program enabled these personnel to advance rapidly to senior skilled job levels.

[2] The shutdown turn was a weekly eight-hour period when the mill was closed for preventive maintenance and repairs.

not obvious. When a finishing attendant calls for a mechanic it's usually not a problem that he can see. The older mechanics are stumped about where to look. They're not used to figuring things out. He has to have the mental ability to put things together and figure things out. The Inland Apprenticeship guys can do this. The older guys aren't threatened because they're so secure, but they're probably a little bitter because it took them so long to make top grade, and the Inland Apprenticeship Program allows men to go up rapidly.

Management's concern for the future

The mill's management had a number of concerns about the future and related problems. Mr. Jones described the generally greater reliance on the computer by the operating crew as a mixed blessing:

Now that the programs are all running well enough so that we're on computer most of the time, we find that when we do have to go off computer we don't produce as much as we used to in the manual, off-line days. People are no longer used to coping with all the details they used to. Should we arrange it so that people perform some functions manually when we're online so that they can better handle these situations when they occur?

Another problem is building the men we need to run computerized mills. You have to have someone who can talk everybody's language at the general foreman, assistant superintendent, and superintendent's level. How do you build this kind of man? What kind of experience should he get?

Mr. Granik also had some concerns for the future:

Most of the people in the 80 came with plenty of mill experience. A lot of them had good mill sense. But the next generation will be completely computer-dependent and they will have very little mill sense. Can you give people mill sense in a computerized process? I think you can, but how do you do it?

Both Jones and Granik were aware that these questions had some bearing on the larger issue facing Mr. Ambrose and Inland's top management in assessing future computerized mills. They also wondered what could be learned from the 80's successes and difficulties which would be of assistance in planning new computerized operations.

Case 7–3
Stop & Shop Supermarket Co. (A)
Paul R. Lawrence

revised by
Constance Bourke and John P. Kotter

In 1956 Stop & Shop operated over 100 supermarkets in and around the Boston metropolitan area. Although a few small, "neighborhood" stores remained in the chain, most stores were large, modern supermarkets consisting of complete grocery, meat, and produce departments and offering up to 5,000 different items to the shopper. Since the early 1950s the company had added six to ten stores a year, many of them in new suburban shopping centers. See Exhibits 1 and 2 for recent sales and earnings data.

Exhibit 1
Selected operating data ($ 000)

Year	Sales	Net income	Wages	Shareholders' equity
1948	$45,879.1	$ 645.0	$4,502.8	$5,554.6
1949	50,227.2	758.0	5,278.2	6,137.1
1950	50,039.3	874.0	5,469.9	6,777.4
1951	56,453.8	780.0	5,642.6	7,316.0
1952	62,576.8	749.0	6,630.6	7,912.4
1953	66,791.9	827.0	7,482.5	8,439.5
1954	79,651.0	802.0	9,158.9	8,908.2
1955	82,430.3	1,003.0	9,710.0	9,561.7

The food distribution industry had witnessed a number of changes in the post–World War II period. These included a trend away from neighborhood ("mom and pop") stores and toward modern supermarkets, increasing population migration to the suburbs, a trend from service to self-service stores, and rapid growth in the number of different items handled by supermarkets. Merchandising methods had also undergone considerable revision with the advent of prepackaged meat and produce; increasing use of promotion premiums, stamp plans, and give-aways; and growing emphasis on both newspaper advertising and point-of-sale merchandising. During this same period, the industry had experienced a continued trend toward lower operating margins, which reflected both severe competition and the need for increasing emphasis on cost reduction and effective control of payroll expenses.

Exhibit 2

Consolidated Income Statements
($ 000)

	Fiscal year *ended* *6/29/57*	*Fiscal year* *ended* *6/30/56*
Sales (at retail)	$123,106.2	$98,189.3
Less—Cost of sales and operations	119,643.8	95,345.6
	3,462.4	2,843.7
Add other income		
Cash discounts on purchases, interest,		
income, etc.	810.9	682.2
Gain on sale of capital assets, etc.	100.4	83.4
Income before depreciation, interest,		
and federal income taxes	4,373.7	3,609.3
Deduct		
Depreciation of buildings, equipment,		
trucks, and automobiles	1,039.2	841.4
Interest on unsecured loans, etc.	203.1	127.7
Total	1,242.3	969.1
Income before federal income taxes	3,131.4	2,640.1
Less—federal income taxes	1,373.6	1,265.7
Net income	$ 1,757.8	$ 1,374.4

THE 1954 ORGANIZATION

Exhibit 3 shows the 1954 management organization of Stop & Shop. A central merchandising function negotiated purchases, set prices, and developed company-wide merchandising programs. The typical Stop & Shop supermarket, along with its parking lot, covered nearly half a city block and employed upward of 50 people (counting both full- and part-time workers). Each store had three separate departmental managers (for grocery, meat, and produce), each of whom was given direct and detailed supervision by a district manager or by his two assistant district managers (one for meat and one for produce). Final decisions as to new equipment, merchandise displays, employee promotions and demotions, work assignments, and much of the merchandise ordering were made almost entirely by one or more of the members of these district supervision teams. Each district manager and his assistant managers supervised 10 to 12 stores.

TOP MANAGEMENT'S REAPPRAISAL

By 1954 Stop & Shop's top management was becoming increasingly concerned with the pressures that both growth and changing industry conditions were placing on its current organizational arrangements. While

Exhibit 3
Partial organization chart, 1954

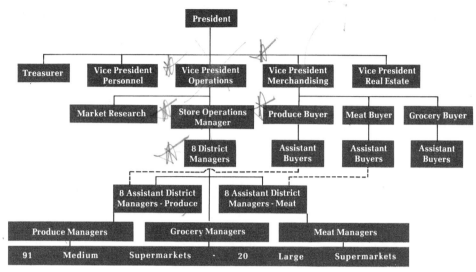

considerable "centralization" had been useful during Stop & Shop's earlier years, new stores were now being built farther and farther away from the headquarters, to handle an increasingly wide variety of merchandise, and for minimum volumes of $2 million a year. Management was also concerned with its competitive posture via-à-vis modern supermarket chains, particularly those run by strong, local independents. One executive noted:

> Our toughest competition is from local independents. Chains don't bother us too much, but when a fellow is right there on the spot and can battle with local conditions, he's got an edge on us if we can't move quickly enough. What we've got to do is to be sure that we're always in a good competitive position relative to the other people in this business. We think the important thing in doing this for the next few years is to be a little more flexible and a little more aggressive in our stores, and in order to do that we have to have a clear-cut organization behind those stores. We want the advantages of the independent in being able to take quick appropriate action on the local scene, combined with the advantages of big business—merchandising specialists, high-volume purchasing, area-wide advertising, well-known names, and that sort of thing.

On the basis of these concerns a group of five high-ranking executives set out to study organizational approaches of other supermarket chains, to conduct extensive interviews with Stop & Shop personnel at all organizational levels, and to devise an improved organization for the company.

1955 REORGANIZATION PLAN

Based on the recommendations of its management study team, Stop & Shop instituted a set of major organizational changes in 1955. The objectives of this reorganization plan, which included altering the company's basic structure and developing new control and communication procedures, were cited as "decentralization" and "systematic management procedures."

Changes in structure and personnel

The first step in the reorganization plan was to make certain structural and personnel changes at the top management level. The management study team had been particularly concerned that a split command at the top had frequently led to lack of consistent follow-up on programs as well as to conflicting signals to department managers in the stores. To help remedy this problem the jobs of vice president of operations and vice president of merchandising were combined into the single job of vice president of sales (see Exhibit 4). The former vice president of merchandising was transferred to a different post in the company. The former store operations manager left the company and was replaced by one of the members of the management study group, and the newly created

Exhibit 4
Partial organization chart, 1955

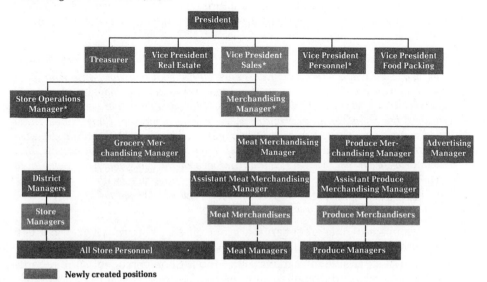

job of merchandising manager was filled by another member of the group. These moves at the top level put the executives who initiated the reorganization plan in a position to exercise the formal authority to implement the plan.

These executives believed the most important part of the reorganization plan was the development of a new position, the store manager, who would be responsible for all departments in his store. These jobs were to be staffed by people chosen from among the ranks and given a two months' training program in which they would spend time in each of the three departments in a variety of stores. Initially, these store managers would be assigned to newly opened stores; however, the ultimate goal was to have all stores headed by such managers.

Management hoped to gradually build a cadre of "strong" store managers who would play a key role in Stop & Shop's strategy of combining the advantages of a large business with those of a strong, local chain. More specifically, management believed that effective store managers could ultimately

1. Provide their stores with unified administrative leadership.
2. Improve communications between the stores and the headquarters.
3. Develop more creative local merchandising methods.
4. Formulate and work toward systematic, planned objectives.
5. Deploy store personnel more effectively and keep payroll costs in line.

One executive summarized these goals by noting, "We want some day to have real administrators running our stores—not just errand boys."

Closely related to the idea of developing strong store managers were certain changes in the supervisory link between the home office and the stores. Assistant district managers were shifted from the line function of directly supervising the perishables departments in each store to the staff job of acting as field merchandisers (see Exhibit 4). Where these men had been reporting to the district managers, they were now to report directly to their respective merchandising managers (formerly called buyers). The objective of this change was to build a single, unified chain of command from the store operations manager through the district managers directly to the new store managers, while still providing the perishables departments with staff merchandising help through the new merchandisers. Some of the "old school" district managers, whose profit performance under the old system was poor, were reassigned as managers of large stores or as product merchandisers because management thought the "transition" would be particularly difficult for them. A number of other individuals were promoted to district manager and store manager positions.

New control procedures

In addition to changes in structure, Stop & Shop began budgeting sales volume and payroll expenses in each of the stores. Prior to the start of each three-month period, each district manager was expected to work out with his store managers or department managers a target for sales volume and payroll. In turn, the store operations manager worked out his own targets for each of the stores. The two sets of targets, which were independently developed, were then reconciled through discussions between the store operations manager and the district managers. Once these targets were agreed upon, they were used as a comparison against actual operating results, which were reported to the stores by four-week and again by three-month periods. The new merchandising manager simultaneously worked out sales targets by product classification (grocery, meat, and produce) with his different managers.

Management was also working on a more systematic way of evaluating field personnel. They looked to the new budgeting procedures as one source of information, but they were also adopting systematic forms for the periodic review of performance of each person in the organization. A program was also under way to write up more complete and accurate job descriptions for all positions. Management felt that the discussions which would have to precede reaching an agreement on job descriptions would help the people in the organization to clarify in their own minds just what was expected of them. Also, the resulting descriptions would be useful in training people who were new to Stop & Shop or moving into new assignments. Management was particularly concerned that the descriptions arise out of meetings that were to be held at different levels so that greater agreement would be reached on the content and nature of different jobs.

A final program initiated by management was a new system for ordering merchandise in the stores. This procedure centered around a mathematical formula which used the previous week's sales for each item in a store as a basis for determining the next week's order for that item. The system was designed to keep each store's inventory at a minimum while also providing safeguards against its stocking out of any item. As part of this system, procedures were also developed for allocating shelf space for many of the items carried.

New communication procedures

As a part of its reorganization plan, management developed several new routine communication procedures. Every other week all district managers were called to a meeting at the headquarters, which consisted of two parts. The first part was a session with the merchandising manager and his key people to discuss future merchandising plans. The second part was conducted by the store operations manager to discuss with his district manager group some of their current problems. On alternate weeks it was planned to call all the store managers into a meeting at headquarters to have discussions of their common problems with the store operations manager. The new merchandising manager also conducted weekly meetings at headquarters with each of his major merchandising groups. Managers were encouraged to speak up to their superiors and were protected from unfavorable consequences of doing so.

In addition to this schedule of meetings, top management developed systematic approaches for keeping in touch on an individual basis with people in the field. For instance, the store operations manager scheduled three days of every week to travel with his district managers as they made their supervisory tours of the stores. The other top people also scheduled a considerable number of days to travel with the district managers.

New training programs

As a final part of its reorganization plan, management conducted formal training programs, first for district managers, and later for combined groups of store managers and merchandisers. Discussions in these programs were divided between cases on organizational change in other firms and the specific changes made in the Stop & Shop organization.

THE REORGANIZATION IN ACTION: DISTRICT MANAGERS AND STORE MANAGERS

Some six months after the reorganization plan was announced, a researcher from the Harvard Business School asked to observe some of the store situations in which organizational changes were occurring. The researcher talked with and observed several district managers over a period of several weeks and in a variety of contexts. The following data on District Managers 1 and 2 are representative of the range of responses of this group to the reorganization plan.

District manager 1

Beliefs about himself as a district manager

One thing I've done lately is stop worrying about being fired. When I was sick last summer I had a lot of time to think. I decided that it wasn't worthwhile worrying about things like that and I might as well go ahead and do what I was going to do. I also decided to speak up more when I disagreed with something. So now, I go ahead and say what I want and I'm perfectly willing to take what follows. I don't think I'm going to get fired because actually I think I'm doing a pretty good job as a district manager.

I don't think any of us should be too proud to use the good ideas that somebody else has. The important thing is to teach yourself the new tricks first. Then you might have a chance to teach someone else.

Attitudes toward subordinates

My notion of a good supervisor is one who doesn't talk any more than his subordinates do. Of course, you've got to do some of the talking to explain what he ought to know about the company and his responsibilities, but you also have to give him plenty of time to talk about his problems and the things he has on his mind or you are not going to get very far.

I don't do the same thing every time I go into a store; if I did I would blow my brains out after a while because this job would be so dull. Of course, I don't do things the way I used to a few years ago. Even in the stores without store managers I've been letting the department managers handle more matters, like working out displays, than I used to, more than I imagine some of the other district managers do. Besides, how the hell am I going to develop my men if I don't let them do things like that?

I believe that if a store manager can come up with his own answer to a problem, it is going to be the best answer in almost every case. I may not agree with the way he would do it, but, unless he is really wrong, you ought to go ahead and let him do it his own way and he'll be better off. That is the only way you can teach them to take the initiative.

Attitudes toward reorganization

The store manager program is still pretty new . . . but I think it is already showing that it is paying for itself. We can add the store manager's salary to our store payroll and still show a better overall performance in that store. He can give us a lot of valuable supervision in there.

I have to keep forcing myself to work consistently through the store manager. Every once in a while I slip back into the habit of speaking to whomever happens to be handy when I see something I don't like, but you really lose the effectiveness of what you are trying to do if you do that. Sometimes I have to remind other people, too, that come into the store to deal with the store manager.

District manager

Beliefs about himself as a district manager

I think the first thing you are here for is to make some money for the company. To do that you have to go out and get a volume of business. You've got to be selling things and selling them in a way that doesn't run your costs up too much.

To do that you have to keep your shelves filled with good merchandise properly presented. These are the fundamentals. If you do those things right, it will show up in the figures.

I'm getting paid to have good merchandising ideas. Anybody who is a district manager must be interested in merchandise and selling merchandise, and to do this, you have to work with people to get them to understand your goals so they can do it themselves.

Attitudes toward subordinates

You really have to train store managers to look after details and then you have to follow up to make sure it is done. For example, I've written complete notes about everything I talked to this store manager about today so there will be no excuse for his not doing something about them. Then I'll check these notes with him when I come back. You have to spend a lot of time with some of these people explaining things to them.

I find that I can work much better with the people under me who've learned to accept criticisms, even welcome them, instead of those who seem to be fighting them.

You heard my discussion with that store manager about what I want done on that drug counter. I've gone into all those details before. He told me it couldn't work out there and I showed him how to make it work, and then today we have to go right back through the whole thing all over again. Now that's not the way you should have to treat the manager. I shouldn't have to spell things out that way. If I had [store manager X] here I would just say to him, "Put the drug counter up there" and that would be the end of it. It would have been done. That is my idea of a good store manager.

Attitudes towards reorganization

I'm one of the few people who doesn't like this new inventory control system. I thought the old way was much better. Also, I had a team with my two assistant district managers operating in my territory that you just couldn't beat. But, I'm perfectly willing to live with the way things are. You sort of have to learn to do that. The company has reasons for doing what they are doing. I don't happen to think it is right, but I'm perfectly willing to live with it.

Interactions Between District Managers and Store Managers

The following are selections from interactions observed between the two district managers and their respective store managers.

District manager 1

On one occasion District Manager 1, the Store Manager, and the Grocery Department Manager were having a discussion about the new inventory control methods.

DM 1: *I understand your complaints, but when our methods consultant sends in a report that we should mark merchandise when it goes on the selling floor and not in the basement I've got to listen to him, because I'm not a technician and I don't know about these things. My point is—let's not close our minds to this system. When an expert comes up with a recommendation, I think we've got to consider it.*

Grocery Mgr.: *What about the payroll in the stores that have changed their control system? Is it the same?*

DM 1: *Yes, it is. It doesn't cost any more, and as a matter of fact, it costs a little bit less and they cut down the inventory.*

SM: *Well, our problem here is that our shipment from the headquarters warehouse comes in on Thursday. Everybody in the store is on the selling floor waiting on customers, and you can't concentrate on the storage area. You simply couldn't handle a demand marking system here, because our part-timers come in Thursday at three o'clock for three hours. If they had to mark merchandise, they simply wouldn't be able to get it on the shelves by six o'clock.*

DM 1: *I can certainly see that, and it is obvious that every store is not the same. But you don't have the new shelf allocation system here. When you do, though, you can go through a whole week on all but a very few items by putting them up just once. That is all part of the new inventory control system that is coming in. Your shelves won't look as good—I know that and I don't like it. But it will cost you a lot less to put out merchandise on Monday, Tuesday, and Wednesday than on Thursday, Friday, and Saturday, when your whole selling area is packed with people. I think you're right: when you don't have the shelf allocation system, you can't go to demand marking. In spite of the difficulties you've done a tremendous job in this store.*

Grocery Mgr.: *Yes, but it's all guesswork, though.*

DM 1: *That's right, but we've seen in the other stores that you can cut your labor way down if you're on the shelf allocation system, no matter how good your guesses have been in the past about what you need and when you need it.*

SM: *When they put us on that shelf system, I'll believe it.*

DM 1: *You're right. I think that is the time to consider it. Nevertheless, you've done a great job.*

Grocery Mgr.: *It's not just me, it's also guys like Bobbie. [Points to a young man who is opening a carton.]*

District manager 2

On one occasion the researcher observed the opening day of a new store. During the morning the only interactions between DM 2 and his new store manager were as follows:

DM 2 *[To SM]: You better keep an eye on the front entrance where they are passing out carriages and keep the flow in and out going steadily.*

The store manager nodded, and for the next four hours remained at the task almost continuously.

DM 2, on a different occasion, told a store manager to get some merchandise out of the employees' lunch room. After the store manager carried it out and set it in the hall, DM 2 told him to take it to the store office. The following exchange then occurred:

SM: *The office is too full to put them in.*

DM 2: *What have you got down there?*

SM: *Some cases of cash register tapes.*

DM 2: *Well, that shouldn't be. Move that tape out of there and then you can put this merchandise down there.*

After discussing some further points with this SM, DM 2 continued:

DM 2: [To SM]: *What I suggest you do is get yourself a notebook like the one I take notes in about our discussions. You do the same thing. Then you'll have them in one place and you'll be able to keep track of them. I guess that's all I've got. Any questions?*

SM: *No.*

Comments by store managers

The researcher talked to various store managers who worked for DM 1 and DM 2. The following comments were typical.

SM [who worked for DM 1]: *I've really got a good deal in this store, because I've got good boys and we work together pretty well. There's a lot of little things that go together that make a good store. The district manager has to be on your side. He can't be doing things that will keep you from moving in as boss, but there's a lot more to it. You've also got to have good personalities in the store on a department head level and on the store manager level and, if your district manager is going to criticize somebody, or pay somebody a compliment, he should have you along and mention it was the store manager's idea. If you get all these things working together, even though they are just little things, you're going to have a good store.*

SM [who worked for DM 2]: *You know DM 2 really goes by the book on things like special displays. He does things the way the company wants, and that's the way they have to be done here. That's the way it should be, because, of course, if you go by the book, you're going to keep out of trouble. I know there's a lot of DMs who wink at stuff like that; they realize a fellow has a few cases of junk that he wants to move, and island wings are usually a good way to do it. I know that Charlie has got a hell of a lot of stuff down there in the back room that he'd like to clean out but if I ever let him start putting up carriages of merchandise around the store, he'd have them all over the place. They don't stay in one place long. You put a carriage by the drug table, and in a half hour some damned little kid has pushed it*

Exhibit 5
DM—SM interaction analysis by classification of speech and topics

Category	DM 1	SM	DM 2	SM
Average percent of talking time	58	42	75	25
Asking questions	9	4	9	2
Giving information	17	23	26	17
Giving opinions	17	10	12	4
Giving suggestions/directions	15	5	28	2
Average percent of new topics initiated	77	23	86	14
Average percent of total talking time of both DM and SM spent on:				
People		48		11
Merchandise		16		32
Record systems		22		47
Physical plant		7		10
Small talk		7		0.5

Notes:

1. Topics were classified as follows: Such questions as, "Is Joe doing a good job?" "What would you think of transferring Mary?" "Is Bill still asking for more money?" "Why did you assign that work to John?" were considered as "discussion of people." Under "merchandise" fell communications about the amount, kind, handling, and explaining of merchandise. Under "record systems" came all discussions of payroll records, procedures for scheduling people, sales figures, and so on. Under "physical plants" were included discussions of store maintenance, housekeeping, new equipment, etc. "Small talk" was all joking, kidding, and talk not related to business.

2. The records of DM 1 covered 227 minutes of which 157 minutes occurred during early days of the week and 70 minutes late in the week. The number of separate comments were 1,115 recorded on nine separate store visits with three different store managers.

The record of DM 2 covered 456 minutes, of which 293 were early, and 173 late in the week. The number of separate comments was 2,092, recorded on four separate store visits with three different store managers.

way over to the coke machine. It's the same sort of thing in any job. You have to figure out what kind of person your boss is and then play the game his way.

See Exhibit 5 for a more systematic comparison of the behavior of DM 1 and DM 2.

THE REORGANIZATION IN ACTION: PRODUCT MERCHANDISERS

Another important aspect of the Stop & Shop reorganization was redefining the roles of the former assistant district managers. This entailed their moving from a "line" job to a staff role as product merchandisers advising and consulting with the perishable department managers in the stores while reporting to the merchandising managers of meat and produce at the headquarters. This shift in job function, title, formal authority, and reporting relationships affected a group of 18 people.

Management was well aware that it would be difficult for those men to make an effective transition into their new organizational roles. Many of them were older, long-service employees. Furthermore, their new superiors, the merchandise managers, were senior company executives who would be accustomed to giving orders and pushing their subordinates to achieve high sales volumes and quick turnover on the perishable items. However, top management, and especially the vice president of sales (46,24)[1] was convinced that this move was necessary to build up the proper role for the store manager without losing the merchandising know-how of the old Assistant District Managers (ADMs). The store operations manager (38,16) also stated that one of his big jobs with his district managers and store managers was in getting them to work together with the product merchandisers in such a way as to develop the merchandising ability of the store managers as well as to ensure good merchandising in the perishables departments.

Observations at Antioch

The researcher spent a considerable amount of time in a new store at Antioch before and after its opening. The following series of events center around the produce department in this store.

At about 9:40 one morning the researcher saw the No. 2 man in the fruit department having a cup of coffee out in front. He whispered, "You should have been around a few minutes ago. Things are already happening." When asked what was going on, he put his finger up to his lips and walked into the store. The researcher followed him and saw the produce merchandiser rearranging the fruit and vegetables and the produce department manager following behind. There was no talking going on. The produce merchandiser was rearranging all the produce on the display table. A second later the produce department manager walked up and started rearranging the same boxes, trying to line them up perhaps even a little neater. The produce merchandiser said nothing during the next ten minutes except at one point when he said, "Tell your boys not to put these price tags on the baskets," and the produce department manager nodded.

The researcher walked up after a while and introduced himself to the produce merchandiser:

Researcher: *Looks like you have some problems here?*

Produce merchandiser: *You leave this place alone for one day and everything goes to hell.* [He turned away after this comment.]

---

[1] Numbers indicate the age and years of service with Stop & Shop, respectively, of the individual involved.

Later, in a conversation with the store manager, the researcher learned that the store's district manager (DM 2; 55,33) had been in the store on the previous day at the same time as the assistant produce merchandise manager.

Researcher: *What did DM 2 do when those head office guys were chewing out the fruit department?*

Store Mgr.: *He agreed with them all along. I guess it did look pretty sloppy over there.*

Researcher: *DM 2 joined in with them? I thought the merchandisers were supposed to come to you if they had any problems and not raise hell with the men in the stores.*

Store Mgr.: *It all depends on the person. It's different under each one of them. Each DM is different too. This was a pretty drastic change for the old ADMs. They've had complete charge of their own departments for 20 years. This store manager program is a pretty big change, and I don't think they're used to it yet. Also, I don't think they've gotten together with the DMs and ADMs and the store managers and really spelled out how this new program is supposed to work and particularly how these ADMs are supposed to behave in the store now.*

How we're all supposed to act under this new program isn't written down anywhere. Let me give you an example. On the training program, when I was assigned to a store manager, he went into his fruit department one morn- ing and asked to see one of the clerks. The other clerk told him he wasn't there anymore, that the produce merchandiser had transferred him to a differ- ent store the previous night. The manager hadn't even been consulted. We went back to his office, and he was pretty upset. He figured, "How's the store manager program going to work if I don't even know what's going on in my own store?" He said it made him look like a fool to everybody and it tore down the store manager's authority in the eyes of the fruit department.

But, those guys did have a point yesterday. Those watermelons looked pretty sloppy, but I don't know how many watermelons are supposed to be cut at the beginning of the week. I figure the fruit man should know, or he wouldn't be a fruit man. All I can do is look at the department through the eyes of the customer like they told us on the training program, and if things look okay to me, that's all I can do about it. But then these fruit guys come in here and tear everything apart.

Researcher: *Have you ever talked to them about it?*

Store Mgr.: *No. Maybe it's good to have these outside guys prodding the fruit people now and again. After all the guys in the fruit department see me every day. Besides, I don't know the details of this fruit business. I couldn't go up to the produce ADM and say, "Look, if you've got any trouble bring it to me, I'm the store manager here." They'd go to DM 2 and he'd think I had a swelled head or something with my new title.*

As long as things run fairly smoothly and we're making a profit, that's all I can ask for. It'll take time, and we'll just have to sweat it out. But it's tough for those guys to change just like it was tough for me to change from being a grocery manager to being a store manager. After all, I had been in the business 23 years as grocery manager, and they must feel sort of the same way about it. I don't know what's in the company's mind, you never know. Maybe they'll do away some day with ADMs, you don't know.

DM 1 and produce merchandising

At about the same time, the researcher learned of an incident that involved conflict between the produce executives and the store executives. In this instance it centered around the produce merchandise manager and another district manager, DM 1 (48,22). This episode gave the researcher a chance to observe the store operations manager (SOM) handling a conflict between two important groups. DM 1 introduced the subject during a conversation with SOM in one of the stores.

DM 1: *I suppose you had a lot of fireworks in your merchandise meeting yesterday at headquarters?*

SOM: *No, not particularly.*

DM 1: *I thought you would have heard a lot from the produce merchandise manager.*

SOM: *I heard a lot from the PMM afterward about some of the troubles you have been giving his stomach.*

DM 1 [with strong feeling]: *Well, that's nothing compared with what he's been doing to us. The produce merchandise manager dug into an issue here that for once I don't intend to give an inch on. I think I'm right, and I don't intend to back down.*

SOM [to researcher]: *Let me give you a little background on this issue . . . We first got interested in prepackaging produce during the war. The traditional practice was to sell by the unit—a dozen oranges, and so on. But the best way of measuring most kinds of fresh produce is by weight. Recently DM 1 has been turning completely to the prepackaging of fresh produce in some of his stores and not using the scales at all on the selling floor. The current problem with PMM is partly this prepackaging thing with some other issues thrown in. As I got the impression from talking to him, he ran into a number of situations while he was out looking at some stores of DM 1's on Wednesday that were an odd combination of circumstances. Partly they reflected matters of bad judgment on the part of some of our people in the stores. But, the whole combination of events sparked PMM into blaming prepackaging for the whole problem and he got very upset. I'm sure it's true that he couldn't eat a thing for lunch Wednesday because what he saw bothered him so much.*

DM 1: *He wasn't the only one that was bothered.*

SOM: *That's true, but you know PMM is sort of an artist about his work. He thinks almost constantly about trying to get the best possible produce into the stores. He also has worked very closely with most of the men who are handling produce in our stores. He thinks of them as "his boys" because he's trained a lot of them. When he sees something going on he doesn't think is right he interprets it as a personal reflection on him. I think there are two or three comments in his whole barrage of statements about what happened on Wednesday that have some logic to them. He mentioned one thing that is a potential problem in prepackaging. It's not a good argument for dropping the prepackaging, but it's an argument for something we've got to be careful about. He pointed out that when you have to prepackage, you're tempted to prepackage some of it the day before so that it's ready to set out the first thing in the morning when the store opens. He said if they start prepackaging too much of it the night before it will come out in worse shape than if they put it up fresh on the day they're going to sell it. I think he's got something there. Of course, we have given our people instructions that they are to prepackage only a minimum amount the night before so that most of it will be freshly packed the next day. If they are not rushed the night before there is always a temptation to package too much and avoid the rush the next morning.*

DM 1: *That's right, but it just wasn't what he ran into on Wednesday. I admit that the store he went into wasn't in very good shape, but it was the day right after the holiday. He was dealing with a fruit man who likes to put all the stuff away when he closes down for holidays, so he didn't have everything in good shape when PMM went in there Wednesday morning. But he hadn't prepackaged a lot of that stuff before—it had just gone out that morning.*

SOM: *In his mind though, there was too much prepackaging the night before.*

DM 1: *But it really wasn't so.*

SOM: *That's right, but you know PMM, he could have talked our produce man into agreeing with him.*

DM 1: *Yes, that department manager would probably say, "yeah, yeah" to PMM, just to get rid of him and avoid an argument.*

Researchers: *What does PMM do when he sees something that bothers him?*

SOM: *He just starts talking to the nearest person. You ought to hear him, he really blows up. He goes at it full force, swearing and yelling.*

DM 1: *The worst part of this is that it was his own assistant merchandise manager who gave us the idea of going to complete prepackaging in the stores. It saved us a lot of money. One thing that PMM was upset about was that we were selling some junk peppers for the price of higher quality peppers. He was right on that and that was a mistake. But the mistake was made in the warehouse when they sent us out junk peppers when we ordered quality peppers; and they charged us for the high quality peppers, too. My produce men should have noticed that, but we didn't make the initial mistake.*

At this point the produce merchandiser (PM 1; 39,19) who covered most of DM 1's stores walked up and joined the conversation. DM 1 left to take care of some other business.

SOM [to researcher]: *DM 1 here is right in the middle of this whole problem. He works for PMM's organization but he has to get along with all the people in the stores.*

DM 1 [coming across the floor]: *Take a bit of this pear* [to PM 1].

PM 1: *No, thanks.*

DM 1: *Isn't that an awful looking pear? We've got a whole bunch of these out in the back room.*

PM 1: *That's nothing, we've got an awful lot more down in the warehouse. We'll be spending a long time getting rid of those. We've been trying to do it in small baskets, in individuals, and in big baskets but we can't get rid of them.*

DM 1: *You said that PMM is an artist and a terrific buyer. I could make a few comments about his buying.*

SOM: *Just hold on* [to DM 1]. *That's not the issue here.*

PM 1: *You know, PMM got upset because he didn't find things the way he wanted when he came into one of our stores. But he got there at 11 o'clock the day after a holiday and was surprised that things weren't in good shape. He went out and came back at 1:30 and everything was fine by then. He just hit a store where our produce manager was really conscientious and put all his produce away for the holiday. That meant it took him longer to get it out on the shelves when he started out on Wednesday.*

DM 1: *I think we should have had one more man in that store that morning and that was my fault. But those mistakes happen once in a while, and PMM's got to expect that. Besides, if we let him have his way, he'd have so many people in the produce department that it would run our payroll out of control. Another problem is that he thinks that all the produce men ought to get up at 2 o'clock in the morning to start setting up their merchandise. He doesn't realize that these people are working on hours these days.*

PM 1: *During Easter week I was out with him at 6:30 one morning lining up some plants to sell in our flower shops. He told me at 6:30 to call up the Highland Park store about the plants. I started to go to the telephone before I suddenly realized that nobody would be at the stores at that time in the morning. I went back and told him that. He thought I ought to call anyway. He really couldn't get it through his head that people wouldn't be there.*

SOM: *He knows that we're on hours now, but he finds it very hard to accept. What's important now, however, is to do something to smooth over the present problem with PMM. Some of the things he was upset about are valid complaints, and we ought to do something about them. One thing we can do is leave scales on the produce floor instead of putting them in the back room. Then we could use them in the few instances when we have to get started fast some mornings. Instead of stopping to prepackage some items, we could just sell in bulk.*

DM 1: *That makes sense. As a matter of fact, the only reason we took them into the back room was that we thought we might use that space for something else. But that isn't important.*

PM 1: *I think that's a good idea, too. We can bring the scales out and use them for those special times.*

DM 1: *I want to make sure that everybody understands though* [to PM 1], *that they'll just use them that way during an emergency period, and as fast as possible we're to get on a prepackaged basis on all items so we can stop having a man look after the scales.*

SOM: *Another thing we could do is lean over backward to get out produce people to understand that they are not to prepackage any more than the bare minimum to get them started the next morning. They could get into some sloppy habits on that. I think PMM is right. It's something we can take care of if we check up on them, give them close supervision, and train them right to do this job.*

PM 1: *I will make that clear to them.*

DM 1: *Then you want no other changes?*

SOM: *No, aside from those things I think we ought to run just the same. I want you to tell your men it's better not to take orders from anyone but you as the district manager or, of course, the store manager. There's no reason you can't have them say that very politely to anybody who starts trying to give them instructions.*

DM 1: *I always tell them to be very polite about it but, nevertheless, to make it clear that they aren't in a position to take instructions from anyone but me or the store manager.*

The District Managers' meeting

A few days later SOM told the researcher that he was going to discuss the relationship between the meat and produce merchandisers and the DMs at the next bi-weekly district managers' supervisory meeting. The researcher attended this meeting and toward the end of it, SOM raised the topic. In the discussion that followed, DM 2 reported that he seemed to be getting somewhat slower action on the problems the produce merchandisers should be solving. DM 1 reported that after working through some initial problems the new arrangement had been going very well. The rest of the district managers were either mildly positive or noncommittal about their experience.

At about this time the vice president of sales entered the meeting and sat quietly near one end of the table.[2] After a few minutes of general discussion a district manager trainee, who was attending the meeting, spoke up.

DM trainee: *One of the things I've noticed while I've been with some of the produce merchandisers is that they're having a lot of trouble convincing*

---
[2] The vice president of sales often came to these meetings late so that committee members would have "plenty of time to warm up" without his presence.

some store department heads to give them enough space for their merchandise. Last week, for instance, I was assigned to a PM who was trying desperately to get space for a special on roses.

DM 1: *Now hold on there. I don't think he had such a tough time.*

Vice President of Sales: *I'm glad to hear he had a tough time. I'd much rather hear that people are fighting for space than are apathetic about it. I like to see some of that kind of fighting going on in the organization over who is going to have the space. It's only when that stops that I begin to worry about it.*

Reading 7-1
Notes on the management of change: Implications of postulating a need for competence*
Renato Tagiuri

This note concerns *resistance to change in organizational settings*, change that would appear beneficial to the organization, and that in the long run would not seem to injure the individual resisting it. Management interested in introducing it feels it is a sensible change, and that the resistance to it is incomprehensible and irrational. An example would be the resistance by some admirals to the introduction of the continuous-aim gun mounting in the U.S. Navy, a change that offered a 2,000 percent improvement in naval gun fire effectiveness.[1] The type of change which management expects to imply a permanent loss for the individual who resists it is not treated here.[2]

BASIC REACTIONS TO CHANGE

Many feel that it is characteristic of people to resist change. This may well be correct. There is, however, plenty of change going on, and lots of people are involved in bringing it about. However, when people resist change, why do they?[3]

It is well to begin with the observation that man, in order to survive, learns to deal with his environment—social, physical, and technical—in ways that ensure him the greatest possible satifaction of his needs under the circumstances. Another way of putting it is that, in order to satisfy his own needs, whatever they are, man sets up as favorable an *exchange relationship* as possible with his environment. This he does by acquiring

---

* Reprinted by permission of the author from John Glover, Ralph Hower, and Renato Tagiuri: *The Administrator: Cases on Human Aspects of Management,* 5th ed. (Homewood, Ill.: Richard D. Irwin, Inc., © 1973).

[1] For an account of this episode, which took place around 1900, see E. E. Morison, "A Case Study of Innovation," *Engineering and Science Monthly,* April 1950.

[2] The thinking appropriate to managing this form of change is substantially different from that discussed here, and involves such notions as managing superfluous personnel, moral obligations of the firm to employees, handling others' hostility toward one, and dealing with one's own guilt feelings.

[3] Common answers to this question: ignorance, fear of unknown, vested interests (anticipated loss), honest differences of opinion.

competence in managing himself in the environment—competence in a myriad of skills and techniques, and in a great many forms of knowledge. For the average man these kinds of competences vary all the way from walking and speaking, to particular work skills, to an understanding of how social relationships operate in his culture.

Depending on the degree and range of his various competences, the individual is able to attain a more or less favorable exchange relationship with his environment. This relationship with the environment, social or technical, becomes very complex. An adult working in an organization must have a great variety of competences in order to act effectively in the sphere of his private life and in his world of work, given the many technologies and skills required by each.

Man acquires the necessary competences and reaches this more or less favorable balance with his environment by making very large and prolonged investments of time and energy. Indeed, the first third of his existence is almost entirely devoted to acquiring the competences needed in life. When his competence is adequate to deal effectively with the environment, the individual has the comfortable experience of being in fair control of the relationship with his immediate world. When his competence is inadequate to the requirements, he feels a loss of control, a sense of danger, and experiences anxiety. The sense of control comes not necessarily from having control *over* the environment, but from being in control of the behaviors and skills required of him in his relationship *to* the environment.

Through investments of time and effort man works out his *technical* role, his *power* position, and his *sentiments* in his relationships with others. Two or more persons, with their different needs on the one hand and different resources and competences on the other, eventually work out who should do what (technical), who controls whom and what (power), and who gets along well or poorly with whom (sentiments). Until the relationship has been worked out along these lines, no one knows just what to do when, what is expected of him, what power he has or is subject to, who are his allies and his foes. This is a very uncomfortable state of affairs for the person. On the other hand, once the system has stabilized along these lines, with some members gaining more advantageous positions than others, coordination, planning economies of energy and time become possible. Individuals can then turn to developing those forms of competence that will make them more effective and perhaps enable them to improve their lot.

When human life is viewed in this way the need for stabilization of the exchange relationship between man and his environment is seen to be basic and powerful. Much human effort has gone and goes into achieving such stability; many human inventions can be understood as serving this need. Tools, social forms, customs and norms, the law, the insurance business, the thermostat, planning, domestication of animals, codes of professional conduct—these are but a few examples of stabilizing mechanisms drawn from widely different areas of endeavor. The important thing to recognize is that once a man reaches a stable level of interdependence with his environment, the stability itself is a great reward to him, for through it he acquires a certain comfort of mind and body and realizes economies of time and energy. These are basic rewards, and their opposites are basic threats and experiences to be avoided. He achieves this stability through competence.

When change is introduced in a stable social system, the component parts have to adapt. The process just described has to start again: New forms of competence may be necessary, new arrangements may need to be worked out, new alliances may form. The previous web is broken; it must be mended and redesigned. Some losses may have to be suffered in the process. Time and energy that before were used for other desirable ends, or were kept in reserve, now must be devoted again to preparing for and adjusting to the new interdependencies. The members of the system who had been particularly comfortable in the previous balance of exchanges, and who tend to have more power than others, may view change with special misgivings. Changes in procedures, in equipment, in methods; changes in the form of the organization; the introduction of new members in the group, or the removal of some—all such changes have the potential of requiring readjustments, of making necessary the expenditure of additional time and effort for the acquisition of new competences.

People's reactions to change, or to anticipated change, may vary from actively seeking the change, through accepting it, to resisting it, depending upon the balance of the potential perceived benefits to the potential perceived costs deriving from the change. Thus, the potential efficiencies resulting from the introduction of an electronic data-processing system may appear to be rather small gains to an employee or executive in comparison with the cost of such change to him in time and effort, and to the changes that such an EDP system would bring about in his technical, power, and social spheres.

The interdependence of technical innovation and organizational and social relationships has been known for a long time. Arnold Toynbee has a tale on this. He points out that resistance to innovation is a very old problem and that it tends to be strongest under conditions of social stability:[4]

---

[4] A. Toynbee, "How Did We Get This Way and Where Are We Going," in *Management Mission in a New Society*, ed. D. H. Fenn (New York: McGraw-Hill, 1959).

. . . the Mediterranean world for the 200 years after Augustus was less insecure and less unhappy than it had been during the 200 years immediately preceding. But all things, and especially good things, have to be paid for; and, in the Mediterranean world under the Augustan Peace, the price of orderliness and justice was uncreativeness and dullness.

Under the Augustan regime, creativeness was deliberately discouraged and in extreme cases was victimized, because the activities of creative personalities are a disturbing factor in society. That is the price of creativeness, but Augustus and his successors were intent on *freezing* society as a precaution against the resurgence of disorder and violence. They looked askance at all manifestations of independent-mindedness and private initiative. They frowned on aristocracies; they frowned on private associations, even those as remote from politics as burial societies; and they frowned, for the same reason, on inventors. For instance:

There is a thrice-told tale of the horrid fate of an inventor of unbreakable glass. The foolish fellow proudly reported his invention to the authorities and suggested to them that he deserved a reward; and the junior officials concerned were sufficiently impressed to send the case to the Emperor.

"Sir," said the European's secretary to his master one morning, "I have been directed to inform you that a man has made the astonishing invention of unbreakable glass, and to ask what action it pleases you to take." "Oh, have the man put to death," said the Emperor, without raising his head from the pile of papers on his desk. The secretary supposed that he had misheard. "I do not think, Sir," he went on, "that I can have managed to make quite clear what I have been instructed to tell you." "You did make it perfectly clear, so have him put to death." "But, Sir," the kindhearted secretary persisted, "the poor man has made a most remarkable and most useful invention, and we were wondering whether you wouldn't think him worthy of a reward."

At this point the overworked Emperor lost his temper. "How dare you plague me," he snapped out, "by forcing me to explain the obvious when it is your duty simply to carry out my orders. Don't you see that if this man's invention is put on the market, it will throw the makers of ordinary glass out of employment, unemployment will lead to unrest, and unrest to revolution and civil war? My predecessor's and my own immense labors for bringing happiness to the human race will run the risk of being undone. You will understand that we can't have that, so I tell you for the third time, see that the man is put to death, and, still more important, see that the blueprint of his invention is incinerated."

For the Ordnance Admirals the continuous-aim gun mounting was not just a technical innovation: It potentially affected their entire way of life.

In a schematic way, reactions to anticipated or actual change can be represented as in the accompanying chart.

COMPETENCE ACQUISITION AND RESISTANCE TO CHANGE

A schematic representation of the reaction to change

1. To obtain what he needs from the environment, the person has to have certain competences or skills.

2. To acquire these competences (which are means to gratifying needs) the person has to invest much time and energy.

3. This investment leads to the necessary competences and, through them, to the gratification of needs.

4. And to a state of acceptable equilibrium between needs and required competences, or to some control over one's situation.

5. Energy and time needed to keep up the required competences drop to a maintenance level. Some energy and time can now be put on reserve.

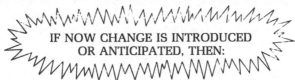

IF NOW CHANGE IS INTRODUCED
OR ANTICIPATED, THEN:

6. The person anticipates (based on other experiences) that his present competences will not or may not be adequate or appropriate for the situation that will result from the change; new competences will be needed. His thinking might proceed as follows:

   a. What will this situation really be like?

   > I am not sure
   > Resist the change

   b. Will I be able to maintain the control, equilibrium I have achieved?

   > I am not sure, probably not
   > Resist the change

   c. What additional competences do I need to maintain the control, equilibrium I have now?

   > I am not sure, I don't exactly know
   > Resist the change

   d. Do I have time, energy to spare, with which to find the answers to the above three questions?

   > Probably not without withdrawing time and energy from current commitments (with possible failure) or from reserves
   > Resist the change

   e. If I can answer the above three questions, do I have the time and energy to acquire the competences that will be required with the change?

   > Probably not without withdrawing time and energy from current commitments (with possible failure) or from reserves
   > Resist the change

Introducing change

There are many approaches to the introduction of change, and they can often be combined to obtain faster and more enduring results. Among the major approaches are:

a. Showing need for the change.
b. Involving the people concerned in the determination of the problem, the development of possible solutions, and their implementation.
c. Obtaining the support of opinion leaders.
d. Having a "champion" for the innovation.
e. Realistic considerations of consequences.
f. Trade-offs.
g. Rewards for risk-tasking.
h. Modification of organizational structure, or technology.
i. Dramatic demonstrations.
j. Shock.
k. Coercion.

In the analysis summarized in the scheme, there are many other practical implications for how to manage change. The essential ideas are to introduce change with minimum threat:

a. To the equilibrium which the person has established with his environment through his competence, i.e., to his control; and
b. To the person's time and energy investments, and reserves.

These objectives are achieved by helping the person to maintain an adequate level of competence as the change takes place and after. This he can do, if he is able to acquire the new necessary forms of competence. In order to do so he must:

a. Identify the *nature* of change.
b. Identify the *implications* of the change for what new competences he will need.
c. Invest *time* and *energy* to acquire these competences.

How can the superior help his subordinate take these steps? The theory (and scheme) suggest the following possibilities. No single thing will do, rather, an effective approach will involve many elements, including:

1. Clearly recognize:
    a. The psychological connection between the need for competence, competence acquisition, and normal reactions to change (real or anticipated).

    b. The importance to the person of maintaining the equilibrium and control in the domains of work, power, and sentiments, which he has painstakingly, slowly, and effortfully developed.

    c. That anticipation of disruption of this equilibrium is reacted to with anxiety and resistance (proactively and in exaggerated forms).

2. Analyze gains and losses:
    a. Carefully analyze the actual and perceived losses and costs which the change may cause the person (but consider also what it would cost him *not* to change).
    b. Carefully analyze the actual and perceived benefits and gains which the change may offer the person.
    One cannot do the above two things without entering into a dialogue with the people involved.

3. Maximize stability around the change:
    a. Introduce as little change as possible which affects the person's basic equilibrium.
    b. Introduce changes in work skills, power relationships, and social relationships one at a time, whenever possible. (Massive change: massive anxiety: massive resistance).
    c. Keep teams intact.
    d. Keep titles, offices, routines the same, if possible.
    e. Clarify continuously goals, policy, strategies, direction.
    f. Increase sense of corporate belonging.
    g. Increase supervision, dialogue, interaction with the person involved.
    h. Clarify the relationship between change and stability (i.e., change is often the means of maintaining stability).
    i. Offer support and assistance through the preparation, introduction, and stabilization of the change and its effects.
    j. Alternate changes with stability (change—stability—change—stability) instead of having continuous change.
    k. Be sure you develop a relationship based on trust.

4. Maximize opportunities for acquisition of competence. Do everything possible to help the person acquire the competences necessary to operate in the changed situation. Wherever possible do this in advance of the change:
    a. Keep people current on what is going on in their field.
    b. Get them involved in situations in which they can learn about new developments, new ways of doing things (e.g., reading, lectures, courses, conferences, visits to other companies, inclusion in important company meetings).
    c. Give *long* forewarning of possible changes.

      d. Get people involved in examining what changes are needed, in making recommendations about this.

      e. See to it that people have the opportunity, time, and energy to acquire needed new competences.

      f. Clarify the nature of the change and thus check people's tendency to fear the worst.

      g. Clarify what new competences (in all three domains, work, power, and social), if any, will be demanded by the change.

5. Supply time and energy equivalents:

      a. Relieve person of some duties.

      b. Change deadlines.

      c. Assign assistants.

      d. Give personal support; more supervision, time, etc.

      e. Make available specialists, consultants.

      f. Do not fire people soon after changes.

      g. Insist on people taking time off (if they do not, send them away on an easy assignment).

If the superior approaches his subordinates in the manner suggested above, and manages to make them trust him, then he is well on his way toward reducing as much as possible *unnecessary* resistance to change.

The way we teach children to swim provides a good illustration of some of these principles. The child needs to adapt to a new situation. His laboriously acquired land skills do not serve him much in the water. The adult helps the child learn about the properties of the new medium. Unlike the ground, water does not hold one up; unlike air, it does not let one breathe. Some motor skills slowly develop that eventually permit effective handling of the new medium. While this learning progresses, the adult, by giving of his own time, energy, and skills, supplies support and continuity with the old ways of doing things, so that the child never entirely feels out of control of the situation. Gradually, as his competence develops, the child needs less and less support. After considerable investment of time and effort on the part of both the adult and the child, the child's competence becomes such that the adult is no longer needed. At this point, the child may actually enjoy the water, the *new* situation. He has control over the necessary competences.

CONCLUSION

This, then, is a way of looking at the very essence of the processes underlying some reactions to change, and at the relevance of this for the management of change.

In fact, a manager who is sophisticated in his knowledge of normal reactions to change can see his role as that of an agent of stability rather than a disturbing agent of change. When we change from winter clothing to summer clothing there is change, but the change actually serves to maintain stability—the stability of the body's temperature. The manager might well think of himself as one who helps maintain stability in certain aspects of the situation by introducing necessary modifications. "The art of progress," wrote Alfred North Whitehead, "is to preserve order amid change, and to preserve change amid order."

Not much was said that is new for the experienced manager, although some order may have been imposed on the many thoughts about managing resistance to change that he has developed as a result on his experience. Also, the discussion has proceeded as if executives had more control over change than they really have. But change is difficult to introduce, fraught with unknowns, costly of material and of human resources. The best men not infrequently get sacrificed in the course of experimenting with innovation. As Robert Frost, the poet, put it in "A Masque of Reason," where he has God speaking to Job:

> Society can never think things out:
> It has to see them acted out by actors,
> Devoted actors at a sacrifice—
> The ablest actors I can lay my hands on

Reading 7–2
On producing change*
Niccolo Machiavelli

. . . It must be considered that there is nothing more difficult to carry out, nor more doubtful of success, nor more dangerous to handle, than to initiate a new order of things. For the reformer has enemies in all those who profit by the old order, and only lukewarm defenders in all those who would profit by the new order, this lukewarmness arising partly from fear of their adversaries, who have the laws in their favour; and partly from the incredulity of mankind, who do not truly believe in any-

---

* From Niccolo Machiavelli's *The Prince*, translated by Luigi Ricci, revised by E. R. P. Vincent (1935). Reprinted by permission of the Oxford University Press.

thing new until they have had actual experience of it. Thus it arises that on every opportunity for attacking the reformer, his opponents do so with the zeal of partisans, the others only defend him half-heartedly, so that between them he runs great danger. It is necessary, however, in order to investigate thoroughly this question, to examine whether these innovators are independent, or whether they depend upon others, that is to say, whether in order to carry out their designs they have to entreat or are able to compel. In the first case they invariably succeed ill, and accomplish nothing; but when they can depend on their own strength and are able to use force, they rarely fail. Thus it comes about that all armed prophets have conquered and unarmed ones failed; for besides what has been already said, the character of peoples varies, and it is easy to persuade them of a thing, but difficult to keep them in that persuasion. And so it is necessary to order things so that when they no longer believe, they can be made to believe by force. Moses, Cyrus, Theseus, and Romulus would not have been able to keep their constitutions observed for so long had they been disarmed, as happened in our own time with Fra Girolamo Savonarola, who failed entirely in his new rules when the multitude began to disbelieve in him, and he had no means of holding fast those who had believed nor of compelling the unbelievers to believe. Therefore such men as these have great difficulty in making their way, and all their dangers are met on the road and must be overcome by their own abilities; but when once they have overcome them and have begun to be held in veneration, and have suppressed those who envied them, they remain powerful and secure, honoured and happy.

*   *   *   *   *

Whence it is to be noted, that in taking a state the conqueror must arrange to commit all his cruelties at once, so as not to have to recur to them every day, and so as to be able, by not making fresh changes, to reassure people and win them over by benefiting them. Whoever acts otherwise, either through timidity or bad counsels, is always obliged to stand with knife in hand, and can never depend on his subjects because they, owing to continually fresh injuries, are unable to depend upon him. For injuries should be done all together, so that being less tasted, they will give less offense. Benefits should be granted little by little, so that they may be better enjoyed.

PART V

Section V expands our scope from relatively short time periods (a few months to a few years), to much longer time periods. Like section four, it addresses change in any kind of organizational unit, but focuses on change that is directed at developing an organization which is capable of being effective in the long run.

Managing the development of organizations, as the text, cases, and readings illustrate, usually involves attempts to increase adaptability so that the organizations can cope with future growth and/or environmental changes. The text in this section identifies the characteristics of highly adaptive and flexible organizations, as well as the tools and strategies available to managers for developing these characteristics. The three cases describe managers whose primary interest is in ensuring long-term positive outcomes as an outgrowth of necessary immediate organizational decisions. The readings provide an overview of organization development, a long-term managerial and organizational effectiveness strategy, as well as frameworks for conceptualizing and managing the growth of organizations over the long run.

Chapter 8

Developing an organization that contributes to long-run effectiveness

"Effective management" is more than the production of immediate results. For companies that want to continue operating in the future, effective management includes creating the potential for achieving good results over the long run. The manager who, as president of a company, produces spectacular results for a three- to ten-year period, but at the same time allows plant and equipment to deteriorate, creates an alienated and militant work force, gives the company a bad name in the marketplace, and ignores new-product development, can hardly be considered effective.

Our focus up to this point—dealing with current problems or potential problems of the immediate future—reflects a key reality of managerial behavior in almost all modern organizations. That is, coping with the complexities associated with today and the immediate future absorbs the vast majority of time and energy for most managers.[1] In this chapter, however, we shift our concern to a longer-run time frame: How do managers develop their human organizations to assure that they have the potential for facilitating organizational effectiveness in the long run?

---

[1] See Henry Mintzberg, *The Nature of Managerial Work* (New York: Harper & Row, 1973), chap. 3.

THE LONG RUN

Most managers will readily admit that their ability to predict their company's future is very limited. Indeed, with the possible exception of death and taxes the only thing that seems entirely predictable is that things will change. Even for the most bureaucratic company in the most mature and stable environment, change is inevitable.[2]

Over a period of 20 years, it is possible for a company, even one that is not growing, to experience numerous changes in its business, its product markets, its competition, government regulations, the technologies available to it, its labor markets, and its own business strategy. These changes are the inevitable product of its interaction with a world that is not static.

Growing organizations tend to experience even more business-related changes over a long period of time. Studies have shown that they not only increase the volume of the products or services they provide, but also they tend to increase the complexity of their products or services, their forward or backward integration, their rate of product innovation, the geographic scope of their operations, the number and character of their distribution channels, and the number and diversity of their customer groups. And while all of this growth-driven change occurs, competitive and other external pressures also increase.[3] Companies that grow rapidly experience even more and faster changes.[4]

From a manager's point of view, these types of business changes are important because they generally require organizational adjustments. For example, a company's labor markets might change over time, subsequently requiring it to alter its selection criteria and make other adjustments to fit the new type of employee. New competitors might emerge with new products, thus requiring renewed new-product development efforts and a new organizational design to support that effort. In a growing company, business changes tend to periodically require major shifts in all aspects of its organization (see Figures 8–1 and 8–2).

The inability of an organization to anticipate the need for change and to adjust effectively to changes in its business or in its organization causes problems, as we have seen in the previous examples in this book. Sometimes these problems take the form of poor collaboration and coordination. Sometimes they involve high turnover or low morale. Always, however, they affect the organization's performance, in that goals are not achieved and/or resources are wasted.

---

[2] Warren Bennis, *Changing Organizations* (New York: McGraw-Hill, 1966), chap. 1.

[3] Donald K. Clifford, Jr., "Growth Pains of the Threshold Company," *Harvard Business Review,* September–October 1973, p. 146.

[4] George Strauss, "Adolescence in Organizational Growth: Problems, Pains, and Possibilities," *Organizational Dynamics,* Spring 1974.

Figure 8–1
Greiner's summary of required changes in organization practices during evolution in the five phases of growth

Category	Phase 1	Phase 2	Phase 3	Phase 4	Phase 5
Management focus	Make and sell	Efficiency of operations	Expansion of market	Consolidation of organization	Problem solving and innovation
Organization structure	Informal	Centralized and functional	Decentralized and geographical	Line-staff and product groups	Matrix of teams
Top management style	Individualistic and entrepreneurial	Directive	Delegative	Watchdog	Participative
Control system	Market results	Standards and cost centers	Reports and profit centers	Plans and investment centers	Mutual goal setting
Management reward emphasis	Ownership	Salary and merit increases	Individual bonus	Profit sharing and stock options	Team bonus

Source: Larry E. Greiner, "Evolution and Revolution as Organizations Grow," *Harvard Business Review*, July–August 1972, p. 45.

Figure 8–2 Summary of changes during three stages of organizational development

Company characteristics	Stage I	Stage II	Stage III
The business			
1. Product	Single product or single line	Single product line	Multiple product lines
2. Distribution	One channel or set of channels	One set of channels	Multiple channels
3. R&D	Not institutionalized—oriented by owner-manager	Increasingly institutionalized search for product or process improvements	Institutionalized search for *new* products as well as for improvements
4. Strategic choices	Needs of owner versus needs of firm	Degree of integration / Market share objective / Breadth of product line	Entry and exit from industries / Allocation of resources by industry / Rate of growth
The organization			
1. Organization structure	Little or no formal structure—"one man show"	Specialization based on function	Specialization based on product-market relationship
2. Product-service transactions	Not available	Integrated pattern of transactions ▢→▢→▢→ Market	Not integrated Ⓐ Ⓑ Ⓒ →→→ Markets
3. Performance measurement	By personal contact and subjective criteria	Increasingly impersonal, using technical and/or cost criteria	Increasingly impersonal, using *market* criteria (return on investment and market share)
4. Rewards	Unsystematic and often paternalistic	Increasingly systematic, with emphasis on stability and service	Increasingly systematic, with variability related to performance
5. Control system	Personal control of both strategic and operating decisions	Personal control of strategic decisions, with increasing delegation of operating decisions based on control by policies	Delegation of product-market decisions within existing businesses, with indirect control based on analysis of "results"

Source: Adapted from Bruce Scott, "Stages of Corporate Development" (Intercollegiate Case Clearing House, 1971)

Because change is inevitable, and because it can so easily produce problems for companies, the key characteristic of an effective organization from a long-run point of view is that it is able to anticipate needed organizational changes and to adapt as business conditions change. Anticipatory skills can help prevent the resource drain caused by organizational problems, while adaptability helps an organization avoid the problems that change can produce. Over long periods of time, this ability to avoid an important and recurring resource drain can mark the difference between success and failure for an organization.

A case of organizational decline

To fully appreciate the importance of anticipatory skills and adaptability in the long run, consider this somewhat extreme case. The company involved was founded in the late 1920s, primarily through acquisitions. It was created as the response of an entrepreneur to a variety of changing market conditions. Over a five- to ten-year period, he established an enormously successful venture; in its market it became the largest and most profitable organization of its kind.

It is difficult to tell from historical records how much, if anything, the entrepreneur did to develop the company's long-run organizational adaptability. Two facts, however, are known. The ongoing operations were so profitable that he submitted to the demands of the national union just to avoid a disruption of operations. This resulted in the establishment of innumerable "work rules" and the entry of first-line supervisors into the union. Second, he did almost nothing to bring in or develop middle- and top-level managers. As an extremely talented person, capable of making a large number of effective business decisions himself, he saw no need for assistance from others.

In the mid-1940s the entrepreneur died. His brother took over as president and tried to maintain the company's existing policies and profitability. For the first few years of his tenure, everything seemed to work well.

Nevertheless, the company's industry, like many others, began to undergo significant changes after World War II. These changes occurred gradually but continuously over at least a ten-year period. During this time the company made very few organizational adjustments to adapt to these changes for what appear to be a number of reasons. First, the few people who had any real decision-making authority in the company did not seem to see any need for many changes. They simply did not have the information that would have showed them what was happening in their industry and in their market area. Second, when they did have information on the changes that were occurring, they often had difficulty deciding how to adjust to them. They were, for example, completely unaware of the typical developmental sequences shown in Figures 8–1 and 8–2. The intuitively brilliant leadership once supplied by the original entrepreneur was gone, and nothing had taken its place. Finally, when they did identify a change and saw what response was needed, the managers were generally unable to implement it. For one thing, union rules prohibited a great deal of change; for another, there was no middle management to help them implement it. The firm was not at all flexible.

Some of the company's competitors were successful in identifying and reacting to the industry and market changes. As a result, the rate of increase of this company's sales and profits began to decrease. At the same time, problems with employees and the union began to surface.

The company's president initially focused his efforts on trying to stop the profit decline. In this endeavor, he was somewhat successful, yet in slowing the profit decline, he was forced to hold salaries and maintenance budgets down, thereby adding to the problems with his employees and the union. A climate of antagonism and distrust developed.

Between 1956 and 1965 the company's real (noninflated) annual growth in sales declined from 5 percent to 0 percent. Its profits leveled out and then fell to a net loss in 1965. By that time, the company's stock price was so low that a larger corporation successfully acquired a controlling interest. This corporation brought in its own top management group (which included a number of extremely successful managers) and predicted a quick turnaround.

The company resumed profitable operations in 1969, and with the exception of 1973, has remained profitable to this time. Nevertheless, its profitability levels remain below the industry average, and its 1975 sales were, in real dollars, about the same as in 1965. It has gone through two more presidents since 1965, and the current one has been quoted in the business press as saying that the job of organizational "renewal" that is ahead of them is still very large.

The characteristics of an effective organization—from a long-range point of view

It is possible to infer the characteristics that contribute to long-run effectiveness by looking for what was missing in the previous example. If we consider our discussion of the difficulty of organizational change in the Citibank cases, we can deduce other characteristics. The picture that emerges is one of an organization where changes in its business are anticipated or quickly identified, where appropriate responses are quickly designed, and where the responses are implemented at a minimum cost.[5] This behavior would be possible because the company is staffed with talented managers who are skilled at organizational analysis as well as with relatively adaptable employees. Informal relations among these people would be characterized by trust, open communications, and respect for others' opinions. The formal design would include effective integrating devices, sensitive and well-designed measurement systems, reward systems that encourage adaptability, and selection and development systems that help support all the other characteristics (see Figure 8–3).

Figure 8–3

The Characteristics of a Highly Effective Organization: A Long-Run Point of View

A. *Employees*
1. The company is staffed with more than enough managerial talent.

2. Managers are skilled at organizational analysis, and understand typical stages of organizational development.

3. A large number of employees are relatively adaptive and have skills beyond a narrow specialty.

4. Employees have realistic expectations about what they will get from and have to give to the company in the foreseeable future.

B. *Informal relations*
1. There is a high level of trust between employees and management.

2. Information flows freely with a minimum of distortion within and across groups.

3. People in all positions of responsibility are willing to listen to and be influenced by others who might have relevant information.

C. *Formal design*
1. The organizational structure includes more than enough effective integrating mechanisms for the current situation, and relies minimally on rules and procedures.

2. Measurement systems thoroughly collect and distribute all relevant data on the organization's environment, its actions, its performance, and changes in any of these factors.

3. Reward systems encourage people to identify needed changes and help implement them.

4. Selection and development systems are designed to create highly skilled managerial and employee groups and to encourage the kinds of informal relations described above.

---

[5] The many social scientists who have approached the topic of organizational adaptability from different perspectives all tend to agree, in general terms, with this conclusion. See, for example, Edgar Schein, *Organizational Psychology* (Englewood Cliffs, N.J.: Prentice-Hall, 1965), p. 99.

Unlike the declining company described earlier, an organization with the characteristics listed in Figure 8–3, as well as other characteristics that specifically fit its current business, could successfully respond to growth, industry changes, top management turnover, and virtually anything else that came its way. Its adaptability would allow it to continue changing its organization to fit its changing business, and it would both survive and prosper over long periods of time.

Bureaucratic dry rot

Very few companies or nonprofit businesses have organizations with characteristics even close to those described in Figure 8–3. This fact has been emphasized by a number of social scientists who, in the past decade, have expressed serious concern over what they call "bureaucratic dry rot."[6] We all pay a heavy price, they note, for the large, bureaucratic, unadaptive organizations that are insensitive to employees' needs, that ignore consumers' desires, and that refuse to accept their social responsibilities.

Existing evidence suggests that although most contemporary organizations cannot be described as very adaptive, many managers nevertheless appreciate the benefits of adaptability. When polled, managers often respond that "ideally" they would like to have the kind of organization suggested by Figure 8–3, but they also admit that their current organization does not have some or all of these characteristics.[7]

There are at least five reasons for the inflexibility and short-sightedness of most contemporary organizations. The *first* and most significant is related to resources. Creating a highly adaptive organization requires time, energy, and money. For example, in the case of the company that went into decline, creating an adaptive organization early in its history might have required:

Hiring, assimilating, and training a management team, both at the top and in middle-level ranks.

Careful selection and training of all other personnel.

Concentrated effort from the managers to develop integrative devices, measurement systems, and the like.

Steady effort from the managers to develop and maintain good informal relationships among themselves and their employees.

---

[6] See Warren Bennis, *Beyond Bureaucracy* (New York: McGraw-Hill, 1966), chap. 1.

[7] Rensis Likert's "System 4" organization is very similar to what we have called a highly adaptive organization. He asked many managers, via a questionnaire, what type of organization they would like to have, and they usually answered "System 4." See Likert's *The Human Organization: Its Management and Value* (New York: McGraw-Hill, 1967), p. 28.

Possibly the organization did not have the resources to invest in these systems. Had it tried, it might have been necessary to divert resources from some of its current operations; and if its competitors did not choose to follow its lead, but continued to invest as heavily as possible in current operations, perhaps the company would have lost market share and income, and even gone out of business long before it could enjoy the benefits of its long-term investment in adaptability.[8]

A *second* reason for the unadaptive and bureaucratic behavior of modern organizations is that their managers are not very skilled at producing the characteristics of an effective organization in the long run. Because organizations generally invest resources in current operations and not in producing adaptive human systems, the on-the-job education of managers is usually focused on current operations, not on producing adaptability. Generating the characteristics shown in Figure 8–3 requires skills that have to be developed and nurtured.[9]

Still a *third* reason for the inflexibility of many contemporary organizations is that some people clearly benefit from a static situation. The entrepreneur who established the unadaptive organization described earlier, thoroughly enjoyed the way he ran the company. It is doubtful that he would have invested resources in developing a management team, even if it cost him nothing. Furthermore, financial backers approved of how he ran the business, which included passing on a large share of the firm's earnings in dividends. Had he tried to cut the dividends to invest more in something as nontangible as adaptability, they undoubtedly would have protested.

A *fourth* reason for unadaptive behavior can also be seen from the case of decline. Once an organization reaches a certain size, if it has not developed a certain minimally adaptive human organization, it becomes very difficult to turn things around without a gigantic infusion of resources. Considerable effort is required simply to overcome the "organizational entropy"[10] that makes the organization even more unadaptive and rigid.

A *fifth* reason why more companies do not have organizational characteristics like those in Figure 8–3 is that their management has decided they are unnecessary. Based on their projection of what the future has in store for their company, they estimate how much adaptability they will need and then invest resources that produce only that level of adaptability. If they are growing very quickly, or if they are in a very volatile

---

[8] See John P. Kotter, *Organizational Dynamics* (Reading, Mass.: Addison-Wesley, 1978).

[9] Chris Argyris, *Increasing Leadership Effectiveness,* (New York: John Wiley & Sons, 1976).

[10] Chris Argyris, *Intervention Theory and Method,* (Reading, Mass.: Addison-Wesley, 1970), chap. 3.

market, and if they expect that rapid changes will continue in their business, they invest considerable resources in creating an adaptive human organization. If they are not growing, if they are in a stable market, and if they feel the future will not demand many changes from them, they invest relatively few resources.

In short, the forces that prevent organizations from developing a high level of adaptability are strong. The forces that can push successful organizations into decline are numerous as well. As a result, one of the most difficult of all management tasks involves developing an organization that has *enough* adaptability to promote effectiveness in the long run.

ORGANIZING FOR THE FUTURE

Developing an organization that is adaptive enough to ensure a company's continued success requires, most of all, a dedicated and skilled top manager or top management group—one both willing and able to make decisions that will balance the needs of the present and the needs of the future. Deciding whether to use an available resource to solve a current problem or to develop flexibility for the future is generally very difficult.[11] Without serious dedication to success in the long run, short-run pressures often take precedence.

Deciding exactly how to develop future adaptability best, but at minimum cost, can also be difficult. Obviously the words and deeds of the people on top are important. If they stress learning, planning, adaptability, open communications, and the like, that behavior will clearly help set norms for others. Training and development activities are also undoubtedly important. So are periodic reviews of the state of the human organization, which identify more and less adaptive components. In each of these cases, however, managers have many options regarding exactly how to stress learning, or to design training, or to review the organization.

Organizational development (OD)

A new management specialty called organization development (OD) has emerged in the past 15 years. OD specialists focus mostly on methods for increasing the adaptability of human organizations.[12] Although the total number is still relatively small, more and more businesses have established OD functions, usually within the personnel or human re-

---

[11] See Peter Drucker, *Management* (New York: Harper & Row, 1976), pp. 43–44.

[12] People who call themselves OD specialists sometimes also help solve short-run organizational problems and involve themselves in other activities as well.

sources department.[13] People who work in these functions utilize a variety of techniques to help managers develop human organizations with the characteristics shown in Figure 8–3. The most commonly used techniques include:

1. Kepner-Trego clinics,[14] phase one Managerial Grid sessions,[15] T-groups,[16] and other training seminars designed to improve a manager's ability to work with others, solve problems, and lead.
2. Methods of resolving conflict and improving relationships in organizations, such as team building,[17] intergroup labs,[18] confrontation meetings,[19] and third-party consultations.[20]
3. Methods for designing formal organizational structure,[21] spatial arrangements,[22] pay systems,[23] jobs,[24] and performance appraisal systems.[25]
4. Methods for measuring the current state of employee attitudes,[26] small group functioning,[27] organizational climate,[28] and organizational processes.[29]

---

[13] Fred Luthans, "Merging Personnel and O.D.," *Personnel*, May 1977.

[14] Kepner-Trego Inc., Princeton, N.J., Problem solving–decision making classes.

[15] R. R. Blake and J. S. Mouton, *Building a Dynamic Corporation through Grid Organization Development* (Reading, Mass.: Addison-Wesley, 1969).

[16] Chris Argyris, "T-Groups for Organizational Effectiveness," *Harvard Business Review*, March–April 1964, pp. 84–97.

[17] Shel Davis, "Building More Effective Teams," *Innovation*, 15 (1970), pp. 32–41.

[18] R. R. Blake, H. A. Shepard, and J. S. Mouton, *Managing Intergroup Conflict in Industry* (Houston: Tex.: Gulf Publishing, 1964).

[19] Richard Beckhard, "The Confrontation Meeting," *Harvard Business Review*, March–April 1967, p. 45.

[20] Richard Walton, *Interpersonal Peacemaking: Confrontations and Third-Party Consultations* (Reading, Mass.: Addison-Wesley, 1969).

[21] Paul R. Lawrence and Jay W. Lorsch, *Developing Organizations* (Reading, Mass.: Addison-Wesley, 1969).

[22] Fritz I. Steele, *Physical Settings and Organizational Development* (Reading, Mass.: Addison-Wesley, 1973).

[23] F. G. Lesieur, ed., *The Scanlon Plan: A Frontier in Labor-Management Cooperation* (M.I.T., Industrial Relations Section, 1958).

[24] W. J. Paul, K. B. Robertson, and F. L. Hertzberg, "Job Enrichment Pays Off," *Harvard Business Review*, March–April 1969, pp. 61–78.

[25] H. H. Mayer, E. Kay, and J. R. P. French, "Split Roles in Performance Appraisal," *Harvard Business Review*, January–February 1965, pp. 123–29.

[26] M. E. Shaw and J. M. Wright, *Scales for the Measurement of Attitudes* (New York: McGraw-Hill, 1967).

[27] J. K. Hemphill, *Group Dimensions: A Manual for Their Measurement* (Columbus: Ohio State University, Bureau of Business Research Monograph 87, 1956).

[28] G. H. Litwin and R. A. Stringer, *Motivation and Organizational Climate* (Boston: Harvard Business School, Division of Research, 1968).

[29] Likert, *The Human Organization*.

5. Broad approaches to the whole development process such as process consultation,[30] and survey feedback.[31]

Applied appropriately, all of these techniques can help develop more adaptive human organizations although they are not a panacea for long-run effectiveness and can be misused like any other managerial tool.[32] Organizations that have been most successful in using these techniques have generally had a competent OD staff or set of OD consultants, as well as a talented top management group that generally guided their efforts.

OD change efforts

Efforts to change an organization for developmental purposes, using any of the techniques previously listed, tend to be different from organizational change efforts aimed at solving a current problem in two important ways.

First, developmental change efforts are of a more ongoing nature. Unlike problem-solving organizational change, they tend not to begin and end in a period of months.

Second, developmental change efforts generally use coercive tactics to a lesser degree than other change efforts. For a variety of fairly obvious reasons, coercion simply cannot be used constantly over long periods of time to create an effective organization.

SUMMARY

Developing a human organization that contributes to long-run effectiveness means developing enough flexibility and anticipatory ability so that the organization can adapt to inevitable changes in its environment. Creating and maintaining such an organization requires that managers be willing to invest resources in its human organization beyond what is needed merely for current operations. It also requires skill in making decisions that affect the human organization's adaptability.

A process that can help managers make effective developmental decisions requires periodic consideration of the following questions:

---

[30] Edgar H. Schein, *Process Consultation: Its Role in Organization Development* (Reading, Mass.: Addison-Wesley, 1967).

[31] P. Chase, "A Survey Feedback Approach to Organization Development," *Proceedings of the Executive Study Conference* (Princeton: Educational Testing Service, November 1968).

[32] For a good general discussion of OD, see Raymond E. Miles, "Organization Development" in *Organizational Behavior: Research and Issues,* ed. George Strauss et al. (Industrial Relations Research Association, 1974).

1. How much change is our organization likely to experience in the next 5, 10, 20 years? In what directions will these changes probably take us? How certain are we of our estimates of change? How much flexibility is needed to respond to these estimated changes?

2. How flexible is our human organization currently—that is, what is its current state on the dimensions shown in Figure 8–3? Is this adequate to cope with the change estimates?

3. If more flexibility is needed, how much is needed and how quickly? Where is additional flexibility needed—everywhere, in top management, or in just the formal systems?

With perceptive answers to those questions, managers can develop and implement over time a set of interventions that keeps a company's organization adaptive enough to cope with its probable future.

Case 8–1
Webster Industries (A)
R. Roosevelt Thomas, Jr.

On Friday, October 17, 1975, Bob Carter, a 32-year-old graduate of the Amos Tuck School, was observing his first anniversary as Manufacturing Manager in the Fabrics Division of Webster Industries. Excluding two years spent earning his MBA, he had been with Webster for ten years. Carter was very satisfied with his Webster experiences. Before being selected for his current position, he had spent two years as a plant production superintendent, three years as a plant manager, and two as assistant to the President, Abe Webster. On a day that should have been one of celebration, Carter sat at home in a very somber mood and started on his third martini of the afternoon.

Earlier in the day, Ike Davis, head of the Fabrics Division, had told Carter that Fabrics would have to reduce its personnel by 20 percent and that the manufacturing department, in particular, would have to make a cut of 15 percent at the managerial level. This meant that Carter would have to trim his 289 managers by 43 individuals. Davis' request stemmed from reduction plans presented to him by Abe Webster. Because Abe had set the following Friday as the deadline for the submittal of termination lists, Davis wanted his top divisional managers as a group to begin a review on the preceding Wednesday of all proposed Fabrics separations. Davis had concluded his conversation with Carter by listing the five guidelines that Abe had provided:

1. No one with over 20 years of Webster service or over 50 years of age should be terminated without review by the President.
2. Since the last reduction approximately one year ago had primarily affected hourly and weekly workers, this "go around" was to focus on managerial levels.
3. Seniority was not to be a major determining factor as to who would be separated.
4. Early retirement should not be counted upon as a mechanism for meeting reduction targets.
5. Blacks, women, and other minorities were not to be terminated more aggressively than other employees.

After speaking with Davis, Carter went home to ponder the situation.

Carter spent the afternoon in his den thinking about the task before him. He remembered the first time he had terminated a subordinate. Early in his career he had fired a secretary—it had taken him a week to muster enough courage to do it and a week to recover. However, since that experience he had found each successive termination increasingly easy. But never before had he been involved in releasing so many individuals at once, especially so many people with whom he had worked and developed social relations. Though he had been in his present position for only a year and had no previous experience in the Fabrics Division, Carter knew most of his managers by name and considered several to be friends. Further, he and his family interacted with many of these individuals and their families in various community and civic activities. In addition to the likelihood of having to recommend the termination of personal and family friends, Carter worried about the possibility of having to release employees with significant service. He knew that any person with over ten years of Webster employment would be very surprised by termination. While pondering the possible consequences of the reductions, Carter became more and more anxious as he realized that he had few firm ideas on how the cuts should be made. The only certainty was that he must conform to Abe's guidelines.

General information on Webster Industries

Location. Located on 17 acres of rolling red Georgia hills at the northern outskirts of Clearwater, Georgia, Webster's headquarters resembled a college campus with plantation-like buildings. Top management was housed in the refurbished "Big House" of the old Webster Plantation, while middle-level corporate managers were situated in a modern three-story office building that was known as the "Box." Built a thousand yards from the Big House, the modern structure appeared out of place in the plantation setting. The Big House and the Box comprised the heart of one of America's most successful textile companies.

Clearwater was unabashedly a company town. Of its population of about 35,000, half the employed residents worked for Webster, one third engaged in "serious farming," and the remainder labored in several small factories around the town. Not only was Webster the dominant employer, Websterites held all "important" community positions. The company stressed community involvement and encouraged its people to accept civic responsibilities.

Because Webster attracted highly educated employees from a variety of places, Clearwater differed from the typical small, rural Georgia town. For example, Georgia educators ranked its school system ahead of Atlanta's. The town had experienced much success in attracting quality teachers by offering generous salary schedules and excellent facilities. Another unique feature of the town was a thriving set of cultural and entertainment events, from regular appearances by the Atlanta Symphony and various theater groups to exhibition games featuring the Atlanta professional athletic teams. As one Clearwaterite put it, "Clearwater is not your run-of-the-mill mill town."

Company history. Colonel Jeremiah Webster, an officer in the Confederate Army, founded the company after the Civil War. When the Colonel retired from the operations, his youngest son assumed the leadership. He in turn was followed by his oldest male offspring, Mark Webster, who presided over the company from 1941 to 1960. Under Mark's tenure, Webster grew and branched into other fabric markets. By 1960 the company produced fibers for carpeting and for home and industrial furnishings. Sales rose from $150 million in 1941 to approximately $900 million in 1960. During this period Webster opened its first plants outside of Clearwater. Growth and geographical dispersion of operations greatly strained the company's management.

In the fifties Mark recognized his company's need for skilled management. Convinced of the importance of management for the future of Webster, in 1955 he set out to attract MBAs to his organization. Though trained as a lawyer, he had considerable respect for "professional" business education. This respect had been fostered by consulting relationships with professors from some of the leading national and regional business schools. Also, Mark encouraged his son, Abe, to attend the Wharton School.

After earning his MBA at Wharton, Abe served five "experience years" before assuming the presidency. Until that time, Webster's President had also served as Chairman of the Board of Directors. However, after Abe's five years of experience, Mark decided to split the jobs. Abe became president and Mark concentrated on the chairmanship. Mark still kept regular hours, but emphasized that Abe was running the business. Under Abe the company continued to grow, primarily through diversification by acquisition of several small furniture and carpet manufacturers. Following these acquisitions, Webster's management adopted a divisional structure. (See Exhibit 1.)

Despite its diversification Webster was very much a textile company. Of its present sales of approximately $1.7 billion, 70 percent came from the Fabrics Division. The carpet and furniture lines each accounted for 15 percent.

The Fabrics Division's products were categorized as fibers for apparel, home furnishings, carpeting, and industrial furnishings. Organizationally, Fabrics had a functional structure of sales, manufacturing, distribution, and research. Within sales, the organization was by markets; the sales force was organized around the different fiber classifications. Comparable

Exhibit 1
Partial Webster Industries corporate organization chart

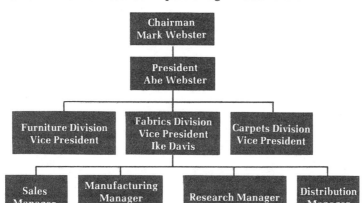

to sales, the manufacturing plants were grouped by markets with three in apparel and two in each of the other areas. Each group reported to a production manager, who in turn reported to the Assistant Production Superintendent, Cecil Stevens. (See Exhibit 2.)

Organizational climate.   Websterites described the company as a "first class" place to work. Employees took great pride in the company's nationally known products and frequently remarked, "You can tell Webster fabrics from a mile away!" The organization consistently won industry awards for superior products, which were displayed in the Big House lobby. Webster also maintained excellent relations with its employees.

Management spared little in its efforts to make work at Webster rewarding *and* productive. The organization's facilities and working conditions excelled by far those of its competitors. Webster's pay and fringe benefits systems offered attractive financial packages and served as models for several firms located throughout the country. Further, because of its rapid growth, Webster had been able to provide its people with challenging work and opportunities for advancement. The company pioneered in establishing a Human Resources Division which performed the regular personnel functions along with a number of activities intended to facilitate the employees' growth and development. As part of its development projects the Human Resources Division designed both a performance appraisal system (PAS) and an information system capable of tracking each employee's career and development. Top management gave the Division much credit for the fact that no Webster plant was unionized.

Company officials also pointed to the firm's paternalism as another

Exhibit 2
Fabrics Manufacturing Department organization chart

factor contributing to good employee relations. These individuals used the term "constructive paternalism" when describing the organization's attitudes and activities.

For example, there were the annual company picnics, luncheons, dinners, and parties around special occasions. The employees' "belief structure" reflected paternalism. Typically, the Webster employee believed, "If you make it through the tenth year, you can be reasonably assured that Webster always will have a place for you." Many employees expected this reciprocal agreement to hold even for individuals who had developed drinking and/or emotional problems. In more than one instance Webster had kept an employee long after alcoholism had impaired his effectiveness, primarily because of top management's feelings that the person had no other place to go. Similarly, the company had paid the psychiatric bills of several employees, rather than dismiss them as ineffective performers. Some viewed the open door policies of the Chairman and the President as another illustration of paternalism. All decisions could be appealed to the highest levels. A few managers expressed concern that employees with the appropriate connections had tended to use the open door policies to secure undeserved promotions. Finally, the company on several occasions had financed the education of local youths—obviously with hopes that they would return to Clearwater and Webster, but also with no strings attached. Two benefactors of this practice were the present Montgomery plant manager (Harvard: BA, MBA) and the chief corporate counsel (Yale: AB, JD). Neither had ever worked for any other organization.

Clearwaterites openly spoke of the firm's paternalism. In the words of one plant controller,

There is a sense of family here. An expectation that if you are loyal to the company, it will be loyal to you. An expectation that if you have a problem, you can take it to Pappa Webster [the company] and it will be at least seriously considered. Twelve years ago, a tornado came through and fiercely hit Clearwater. The company stepped in and gave considerable aid. Those new houses you see along Webster Drive are a result of the company's generous response.

I could go on and on. Fringe benefits also reflect how the company takes care of its people. The whole fringe benefits package is oriented toward taking care of the employee's family. We were the first to ensure the education of a worker's children should he or she die. We continually upgrade retirement benefits to offset inflation. The company's hiring and promotion practices are also paternalistic. The offspring of employees always have first shot—if they are qualified—at openings. Webster—along these same lines—promotes from within. Rare is the case of someone being hired from the outside for a top position.

What more is there to say? Webster is a darn good company.

The Webster employees.   Webster's managerial employees came from several areas of the United States. Typically, they had received degrees from schools on the East Coast. The MBAs were from the top national and regional schools. Managers without MBAs had sophisticated technical training. The backgrounds of Webster's managers differed significantly from those of its typical plant laborers, who tended to come from the area around the plant and to have at least a high school diploma or at most an Associate Degree from a community college. Despite these differences, Webster had experienced little class conflict. Most attributed this harmony to the Human Resources Division, the many opportunities for advancement, and Webster's practice of having MBAs (especially those in manufacturing) spend some time in low-level plant positions.

Manufacturing in the Fabrics Division had 1,787 people located at headquarters and in the nine plants. Of these, 289 served as managers. Managers worked either at corporate headquarters on the manufacturing manager's staff or functioned in a managerial, supervisory, or staff capacity at one of the plants. The background of manufacturing managers was similar to that described above for Webster managers in general. Of the 289 managers, 160 lived in and around Clearwater.

Webster's current troubles

The symptoms that set off the alarm at Webster were second-quarter earnings of less than 50 percent of the prior year's earnings and a threatened cash position. The economy and Webster's sloppy growth habits contributed to each of these difficulties.

The economy, especially the slowdown in the construction industry, hit Webster's furniture and carpeting businesses hard. The softening of the demand for furniture and carpeting caused Webster's sales to decline from a 1973 peak of $2.1 billion. Simultaneously, inflation exerted upward pressure on costs. The dips in sales and earnings reduced Webster's cash flow considerably, so much so that money became extremely tight for the first time in 35 years. Though Mark and Abe Webster had expected the current earnings and cash troubles, they were unnerved by the extent of the problems. In addition to the economy the firm's phenomenal growth had complicated matters further.

The plant production manager in the largest Clearwater plant offered the following observations:

We grew too fast. We wanted diversification but were not ready to handle it. With the acquisitions of the sixties we became a different company almost overnight. Truthfully, we definitely were not prepared to break the billion dollar level in sales. We grew too fast to consolidate. Only now are we learning the basics of managing a multibusiness enterprise. Controls were poor, especially in some of the plants we acquired. Staffing was done sloppily, so we ended up with a lot of fat. Plus we were—in my opinion—lax in our evaluation of performance.

The economy and the problems of diversification combined to slow Webster's growth and to threaten its financial integrity.

Bob Carter's evening

By 6 P.M. Carter began to overcome his initial shock and to realize that, while painful, the reduction was probably needed and probably best for the company. He had known for some time that his department had "fat" at the managerial levels. Just six months earlier he had sought to demote three individuals—including his second-in-command. In denying his recommendation Davis had told Carter, "These men have too much service to be treated as you have proposed." So Carter was stuck with them; at least that had been the case until today. Carter reasoned that one benefit of the reduction in force would be an opportunity to make some long-needed changes. He perceived his task as that of making the best reductions possible in the least painful manner.

After dinner Carter returned to his den to address the issue of how to cut 43 individuals from his managerial payroll. Because of his relatively brief tenure, he wanted to consult at least one other individual. The logical choices were the number two and three persons in his hierarchy. However, Carter wanted to demote the Production Superintendent, Russell Brown, and to promote the Assistant Production Superintendent, Cecil Stevens. He had been impressed with Stevens and had decided some time back that he should have Brown's job. The reduction presented an opportunity to make the change.

Carter concluded that Stevens should be involved initially and perhaps others later on some basis. At 8:30 P.M. he called Stevens, who lived four miles away, and asked him to come over to discuss a "critical" situation. Cecil arrived an hour later. Carter informed him of the reduction plans and of his intention to recommend him for promotion to Production Superintendent. Predictably, Stevens was delighted by his promotion and shocked by the magnitude of the proposed separations. After relating details of his session with Davis, Carter asked Stevens to aid him in developing a strategy for determining the individuals to be released. Specifically, he requested that Stevens be prepared by Monday morning to identify and discuss issues that should be considered in formulating a reduction plan.

Carter and Stevens spent about 45 more minutes discussing their perceptions of the company's situation and the need for the reduction. Also, they raised some questions about Webster's Performance Appraisal System (PAS). Stevens wondered how much weight should be given to performance ratings. Carter admitted that he had not gotten around to using PAS on a regular basis, but indicated that he would be interested in hearing Stevens' perceptions of the system and its use in the department. Stevens asked if they should consider inviting others to the session on Monday morning. After some discussion they agreed to invite the production managers with the exception of the home furnishings manager, who was a likely candidate for demotion or termination. Carter and Stevens ended their meeting by agreeing on a timetable:

Monday, 8 A.M.—Develop strategy.

Monday, 1 P.M.—Begin to implement strategy.

Wednesday, 2 P.M.—Present list to divisional managers.

The Monday morning meeting

On Monday morning Carter, Stevens, and three of the four production managers met as planned. Stevens began the meeting by presenting his thoughts on possible criteria for developing a termination list. His remarks are reproduced in part below.

The following represents my thinking on possible options open to us. I see five.

The first is seniority. *Though guidelines prohibit much use of this criterion, there are a few individuals who might be receptive to offers of early retirement.*

The second is fairness. *Should this be a criterion? Operationally, I do not know what it means except that we would not do anything that would be perceived as grossly unfair. I do know, however, that our people will expect fairness.*

The third is fat. *The list would be determined by the elimination of "fat" or excess positions. This approach has legitimacy. The difficulty, however, is that some good people are in "fat" positions. The use of this criterion alone could result in a net quality downgrading of manufacturing personnel.*

The fourth is performance. *The basic question here is, "How do we measure performance?" How much weight do we give to PAS data? Some individuals feel that the PAS data are hopelessly biased, because of the managers' tendency to give everyone "good" ratings. How much weight do we give to the personnel audit data?[1] If we were to give significant weight to the audit data, would we be compromising the future effectiveness of the auditor? When making field visits, the auditor not only gathers data on performance from managers, but also talks to individuals about their careers and problems. Many employees have been very frank with the auditors. If we use audit data as input in making termination decisions, the employees may feel betrayed and become reluctant to trust the auditors in the future. This would be especially likely if managers tried to make the auditors scapegoats. I can hear a manager telling a terminated employee, "I wanted to keep you, but our auditor Jack had too strong a case against you."*

Finally, to what extent are we constrained by past practices? In the past, few managers have been diligent and responsible in talking with their people about performance; as a consequence, many employees are not aware of their relative standing with respect to performance. If these individuals are terminated, they will likely be shocked and feel that they have been treated unfairly. Can we fairly terminate on the basis of performance?

The fifth is potential. *Again, the basic questions are around measurement and the weights to be given to PAS and audit data. How do we measure potential? How much weight do we give to PAS data? Audit data? Should we terminate an individual with little potential but capable of doing his or her present job fully satisfactorily? I am thinking about one plant controller in particular. He is an excellent Assistant Plant Controller, but does not have the potential to advance further. Would he be a candidate?*

I consider this large reduction to be a one shot deal. As such, the reduction represents a beautiful crisis opportunity to make moves that would be difficult under "normal" circumstances. We can seize the opportunity not only to meet our termination target, but also to upgrade our department. Other divisions are releasing competent people. Some will be better than those that we will propose to keep. This means that we could upgrade by reducing a larger number than our target, and then hiring replacements from our sister divisions' terminations. For example, our target is 43. If after meeting this target we identified five available individuals who were better than persons we were planning to keep, we could

---

[1] Personnel Auditors from the Human Resources Division visited each manager at least once a year to discuss his or her subordinates' performance. During these discussions they obtained a performance rating for each employee. This process was separate from Webster's performance appraisal system (PAS).

terminate 48 and hire the five former employees of the other divisions. However, if we are to seize this opportunity, we will have to develop sound ways of evaluating performance and potential.

A lively discussion of PAS and the Personnel Audit followed Stevens' remarks. During these deliberations the group relied heavily on Stevens' memorandum on performance appraisal at Webster. (See Exhibit 3.)

Exhibit 3
Memorandum on performance appraisal

Memorandum

TO: Bob Carter

FROM:.   Cecil Stevens

RE: Performance Appraisal at Webster
DATE: October 20, 1975

Since leaving your home on Friday evening, I have had an opportunity to talk with a number of individuals. Specifically, I saw Ed Johnson, the designer of our Performance Appraisal System, at the Club and had a good conversation; talked with Jack Bryant, our personnel auditor, about his work with the division; and spent two hours after church discussing the reduction with the manufacturing managers of the other divisions. Immediately below are my impressions of PAS and also the Personnel Audit function of the Human Resources Division.

PAS

Bob, PAS was designed three years ago and has been used primarily on a voluntary basis. My discussion of the system is based primarily on conversations with its designer, Ed Johnson.

Purpose

The system is intended to help the manager act as a:

1. Manager, responsible for attaining organizational goals.
2. Judge, responsible for evaluating individual performance and making decisions about salary and promotability.
3. Helper, responsible for developing subordinates.

One problem in the past has been a failure to recognize the three roles cited above, or a tendency to emphasize one over the others. PAS is based on the assumption that each role is equally important and is intended to help the manager do justice to each.

Components

PAS components are three in number: Management By Objectives (MBO), a developmental review, and an evaluation and salary review.

MBO. This component focuses on results and is intended to help the manager realize organizational goals. Though each manager is expected to adapt MBO to his or her situation, there are typically six steps.

EXHIBIT 3 (continued)

1. *Identification of Objectives.* Here, objectives are identified and prioritized. Also, review periods are set.

2. *Establishment of Measurement Criteria.* The basic question here is, "What monetary measures, percentages, and/or other numbers will be used to measure the achievement of objectives?" For example, if we in manufacturing were to establish "greater production effectiveness" as one of our objectives, we would have to decide how to measure the extent of achievement. Total unit costs? Total direct labor unit costs? Total production?

3. *Planning.* Plans are made for achieving the identified objectives. What is to be done? Who is to do it? When is it to be done? How is it to be done?

4. *Execution.* Plans are implemented.

5. *Measure.* Secure actual monetary figures, percentages, and/or other numbers so that results may be reviewed.

6. *Review Results.* Compare actual measurements to plan. The frequency of measurement and review will depend on the number of review points within a year. Typically, the entire MBO cycle is repeated once a year, with intermittent reviews in between.

MBO is essentially a system for identifying what is to be done and ensuring that it is done. As such, MBO has a major weakness in terms of the managerial role: It does not aid the manager in observing, evaluating, or improving the behavior of subordinates. If the manager is to help his employees improve their behavior, he will need a behavior-oriented tool. The developmental review was designed to meet this need.

THE DEVELOPMENTAL REVIEW.   As indicated above, the review is intended to help the manager observe, analyze, and improve subordinate behavior. There are three subcomponents: the Performance Description Questionnaire, the Performance Profile, and the Developmental Interview.

1. *Performance Description Questionnaire.*   The questionnaire contains 100 questions. Each question has been determined through research to be descriptive of a behavior associated with a component of effectiveness at Webster. Examples of the components covered are openness to influence, priority setting, formal communications, organizational perspective, decisiveness, delegation/participation, support for company, unit productivity, and conflict resolution. The manager is asked to complete a questionnaire for each subordinate. He or she is asked to indicate on a 6-point rating scale how descriptive the statement is of the employee's actual behavior. Also, under each statement is space for the recording of any critical incidents supporting the manager's judgment. (See Attachment 1.) The performance profile is produced by computer from the questionnaire data.

2. *Performance Profile.*   The profile is intended to serve as a tool to help managers discriminate among a subordinate's performances on a number of performance dimensions. An individual's profile shows net strengths or weakness for each dimension in terms of the person's own average. The profile line represents the average of the employee's ratings on all performance dimensions. The number and location of X's show the extent to which the employee's score for a particular dimension is below or above his or her average for all dimensions. Dimensions with X's to the left of the profile line are those where the individual is relatively weak (compared to his or her average). Dimensions with X's to the right are those where the subordinate is relatively strong. The number of X's indicates the extent of the weakness or strength. (See Attachment 2.) The tool is designed to facilitate analysis of a subordinate's performance and is not valid theoretically for comparison of individuals.

EXHIBIT 3 (*continued*)

3. *Developmental Interview.* The purposes of the developmental interview are to provide the subordinate with a performance analysis based on the performance questionnaire and profile, to identify areas of weaknesses, and to translate these weaknesses into an appropriate developmental program. Tools are available to help the manager and subordinate in designing developmental plans.

The reasoning behind the design of the Developmental Review was a hope that the Performance Description Questionnaire and Profile would help the manager and his subordinates distinguish development from MBO and evaluation, and thereby reduce subordinate defensiveness that typically characterizes feedback sessions where developmental and evaluative issues are handled simultaneously.

EVALUATION AND SALARY REVIEW. This review is separate from the MBO and developmental reviews. Its basis is a form which asks the manager to rate the employee's overall performance and his or her potential. (See Attachment 3.) The overall rating should reflect the MBO sessions and the Developmental Review data and interview. In short, the two other components of PAS provide important inputs for the Evaluation Review. Possible overall ratings are unsatisfactory, fair, fully satisfactory, excellent, and outstanding.

Once the overall rating has been given, the salary matrix may be used as a *guide* in determining recommendations for salary adjustments. The matrix approach is straightforward and used by several organizations. Under this method salary adjustments are a function of the subordinate's rating and the relative standing of the employee's salary within his or her pay range. (See Attachment 4.)

Use of PAS

Bob, as I indicated earlier, the system has been used on a voluntary basis so far. In the corporation as a whole, the usage rate is 29 percent; in manufacturing it is 40 percent. The only group using it 100 percent is Fabrics' sales force.

The Personnel Audit

In addition to PAS the Human Resources Division is also responsible for conducting the personnel audit. The purposes of the audit are to secure performance data that will facilitate corporate manpower planning, to encourage and improve communications between superiors and subordinates, and to provide career development counseling. There is a potential conflict among the purposes in that the auditor is required to perform both evaluative and counseling roles. Some individuals who "pour out their souls" to the auditors are unaware of their evaluative function.

Our auditor, as you know, is Jack Bryant. At least once a year Jack visits each manager and talks about his subordinates. He also talks with subordinates about their development and their perceptions of where they stand. Where there are discrepancies between a subordinate's perception and what his or her manager has said, Jack works with the manager in developing a plan for correcting the employee's misperceptions. Jack, however, has no enforcement power; consequently, some managers fail to give accurate—if any—feedback to their employees. The audit has been very successful in securing information for the central corporate data bank, but has had somewhat less success in getting managers to be honest with subordinates. Though individual employees may see their central file, few avail themselves of the opportunity; consequently, many subordinates remain in the dark as to how they are actually perceived by their bosses. I, however, understand that a computer-based system capable of providing each employee with performance data has been designed and implemented below managerial levels. Reportedly, the system annually provides each employee with a printout showing—among other things—performance ratings

Exhibit 3 (*continued*)

and career history. April 1, 1976, is the target data for full implementation in the managerial ranks.

Currently, the form used by the auditors asks for a rating of the individual's performance and potential. There also are sections dealing with the employee's strengths and weaknesses and the manager's recommendations for future reassignments. (See Attachment 5.)

I have checked with Jack, and he has assured me that there are audit ratings on file for at least 97 percent of our personnel.

Bob, I hope these remarks on PAS and the Personnel Audit will stimulate discussion leading to an appropriate reduction plan.

Attachment 1

<table>
<tr><td colspan="2" align="center">Sample Items from Performance Description Questionnaire</td></tr>
<tr>
<td>1. Involves subordinates in decision-making process _____</td>
<td>6. Selects and places qualified personnel _____</td>
</tr>
<tr>
<td>2. Makes a special effort to explain Webster policies to subordinates _____</td>
<td>7. His or her subordinates accomplish a large amount of work _____</td>
</tr>
<tr>
<td>3. Molds a cohesive work group _____</td>
<td>8. Objects to ideas before explained _____</td>
</tr>
<tr>
<td>4. Fails to follow up on work assignments given to others _____</td>
<td>9. Is accurate in work _____</td>
</tr>
<tr>
<td>5. Works closely with subordinates who lack motivation _____</td>
<td>10. Gives poor presentations _____</td>
</tr>
</table>

RATINGS

Number	Definition
1	Strongly Agree
2	Agree
3	Somewhat Agree
4	Somewhat Disagree
5	Disagree
6	Strongly Disagree

Exhibit 3 (*continued*)
Attachment 2

SAMPLE PROFILE INTERPRETATIONS

Dimension	*A*		*B*		*C*	
1. Openness to influence	xx		xxxxx		xx	
2. Priority setting		xx		xxx		xxxxxx
3. Formal communications		xx		xxx	xxxxxx	
4. Organizational perspective	xx		xxxxxxxxxx		xx	
5. Decisiveness		xx		xx	xx	
6. Delegation/participation	xx			xx	xxxxxx	
7. Support for company		xx	xx			xxxxxx
8. Unit productivity	xx			xxx	xx	
9. Conflict resolution		xx	xx		xx	
10. Team building	xx			xxx	xx	
11. Control		xx		xx	xxx	

A. Implication is that this manager is well balanced *dimensionally*.

B. Implication is that this manager has one *very* significantly weak *dimension*, another relatively weak *dimension*, contrasted to the remaining favorably balanced *dimensions*.

C. Implication is that this manager has two relatively weak dimensions, two relatively strong *dimensions*, with remaining *dimensions* relatively balanced.

> CAUTION: Remember that you are only comparing the individual to himself and *NOT* with other people. IF an individual is "well balanced dimensionally," it means there is not much difference between what he does best and what he does the poorest; it does *not* necessarily mean he is a "well-balanced manager."

Exhibit 3 (*continued*)
Attachment 3

DETACH AND SEND TO: P R I V A T E

POSITION PREFERENCE   DATE _____

EMPLOYEE NAME _____   EMPLOYEE NUMBER _____

DIVISION _____   LOCATION _____

POSITION _____   SUPERVISOR _____

Supervisor and subordinate develop *together*. Indicate below subsequent positions for your subordinate *that you both can agree* are realistic, appropriate, and interesting. Specify both functional area (e.g., Sales, Personnel, etc.) and, whenever possible, type of job.

ORDER OF PREFERENCE FOR NEXT JOBS:

    Short-Term
        First choice:

        Second choice:
  Long-Term (within next 5 years)
        First choice:

        Second choice:

Exhibit 3 (*continued*)
Attachment 3 (*continued*)

SUPERVISOR'S SUMMARY: Supervisor fills in by himself *after* the developmental interview. The subordinate should be shown these ratings after the supervisor has coordinated the ratings with the *second* level supervisor.

A. CHANGE OF STATUS: Indicate by your choice of the statements below (check one) the change of status you recommend for this person during the next twelve months.
____ Should be separated as soon as possible. (SEP)
____ Should be reassigned to position with decreased responsibility. (DEM)
____ Should be reassigned to a position with a similar level of responsibility. (LAT)
____ Needs more experience before reassignment can be considered. (EXP)
____ Should be reassigned to a position with more responsibility. (RDY)
____ Should remain in present position. (STA)

B. *CAREER POTENTIAL:* Based on current knowledge, indicate in the spaces below (check one) the level this person has the greatest probability of achieving. Note: Potential ratings do *NOT* imply a person's readiness for promotion now.
____ Potential Division Manager or equivalent. [Must be Group 50 or above.] (BLUE)
____ Potential to higher supervisory/managerial level. (GREEN)
____ Potential is best utilized within a specialty or as an individual performer. (BROWN)
____ Good performer; no indication to date of potential for a higher level. (YELLOW)
____ Questionable performance. (RED)

C. *OVERALL JOB PERFORMANCE* during the past 6–12 months may be characterized as: (check scale)

Unsatisfactory	Fair	Satisfactory	Excellent	Outstanding

D. *COMMENTS:*

. . . .

ENDORSEMENT OF SECOND LEVEL SUPERVISOR

____ I agree with all of the above recommendations.
____ I disagree with some (or all of the above recommendations) and would make the following recommendations:

_____
                                        Signature

Exhibit 3 (*continued*)
Attachment 4

Comparative ratio 1.20 (Max) 1.10	SALARY MATRIX				
	6%	4%	2%	—	—
1.00	8%	6%	4%	—	—
.90	10%	8%	6%	—	—
.80 (Min)	12%	10%	8%	6%	—
	Outstanding	Excellent	Fully Satisfactory	Fair	Poor

Ratings

Note: Comparative ratio equals actual salary divided by the mid-point of the individual's salary range. Salary adjustment is a function of individual's ratio and rating. An employee with an .85 ratio and a rating of excellent would receive an adjustment of 10 percent.

Exhibit 3 (*concluded*)
Attachment 5

Employee Name _____ Supv. Name _____ Date _____

PERFORMANCE   (See Definitions Attached)   *POTENTIAL*

1 2 3 4 5 NR (Circle One)   (Circle One) 1 2 3 4 5 NR

COMMENTS: (Supervisor should define significant strengths and weaknesses [development needs] and accomplishments.)

CHANGE OF STATUS: (for the next 12 months) (Check One)
1. ____ Should be separated as soon as possible (termination).
2. ____ Should be reassigned to a position of decreased responsibility (demotion).
3. ____ Should be reassigned to a position with a similar level of responsibility (lateral move).
4. ____ Needs more experience before reassignment can be considered (not ready).
5. ____ Should be reassigned to a position of more responsibility (promotion).
6. ____ Will probably remain in present position indefinitely (leveled).

Which function(s) (comment) _____

_____

_____

Which function(s) (comment) _____

_____

_____

Which function(s) (comment) _____

_____

_____

PERFORMANCE

Number	Definition
5	Outstanding
4	Excellent
3	Fully Satisfactory
2	Fair
1	Unsatisfactory

POTENTIAL

Color	Number	Definition
Blue	5	Potential division manager or equivalent (for individuals currently at the "A" payroll level).
Green	4	Potential to higher supervisor position.
Brown	3	Potential is best utilized within a specialty or as an individual performer.
Yellow	2	Good performer; no indication to date of potential for a higher level.
Red	1	Questionable performer.

Case 8–2
Century Paper Corporation
Leonard Schlesinger, John P. Kotter, Richard Walton

In August 1976, John Murphy, manufacturing manager for Century Paper's Michigan Pulp Mill operations, reflected on his past two years' experiences. It had been an exciting period of activity for the Pulp Mill; an $11-million capacity-increase project moved toward completion, and a joint labor-management committee had recently designed and instituted several substantial changes in work schedules, task assignments, and technical training requirements. These changes were directed at further improvement of what was already generally recognized as one of Century's best-managed operations.

While most managers and hourly employees were recognizing significantly improved outcomes from the new changes, the Pulp Mill foremen were experiencing considerable difficulty in adapting themselves to their new work situation. The four foremen felt that the organizational changes required them to adopt a whole new set of skills in order to "survive." Over the next month John Murphy, along with his two department managers, planned to devote a great deal of their attention to the foreman issue. They hoped that well-planned and executed remedial action could improve the situation and bring the foremen "up to speed."

BACKGROUND OF THE PULP MILL PROJECT

The Michigan operations of the Century Paper Corporation included one sulfite pulp mill, nine papermaking machines, and a number of end-product converting operations. Until 1974 the pulp mill had served as the sole supplier of the sulfite pulp used in the paper making process.

Rising sales of Century's products resulted in an expansion of paper-making and converting operations throughout 1974 and 1975. These expansions raised the total amount of sulfite pulp used to 300 tons per day. The pulp mill, however, was able to produce only 240 tons per day, even when operating a 7-day-a-week, 24-hour-a-day schedule. As a result, Century was presented with a major make-or-buy decision relative to future pulp needs.

Despite an oversupply of sulfite pulp on the world market in 1974, Century chose to authorize an expenditure of $11 million to increase the capacity of the Michigan pulp mill to 310 tons per day. Bob Jensen, the Michigan operation's General Manager, reflected on the appropriation:

The $11-million appropriation was a testament to our ability to manage well. However, given that this appropriation is the largest single upgrade expenditure in the company's history, there is even greater pressure on us to pull it off without any hitches.

THE PULP MILL PROCESS

Pulp Mill operations were housed in a series of 20 interconnected buildings of various shapes and sizes which encompassed a concentrated area of approximately four large city blocks. The complex represented a capital investment in excess of $35 million.

Exhibit 1 represents a flow diagram of the pulp mill manufacturing process which can be briefly described as follows:

1. Wood is purchased from area foresters in 100-inch lengths and is peeled prior to entering the woodroom where the logs are chipped and placed into storage.

2. The wood chips are removed from storage as needed and transferred to the digesters. Digesting is a high-temperature, high-pressure chemical cooking process designed to break down the tree material (lignin) which holds the wood's cellulose fiber together. The digester cooking solution (ammonia bisulfite) is manufactured in the acid plant located within the pulp mill complex. The digester cooking process is critical to the successful flow of pulp production. An error at this stage of the process affects all of the other processes downstream and limits production. However, as a continuous flow process, breakdowns at almost any stage of the process can slow down or shut down the mill.

3. At the conclusion of the digester cooking process, the now pasty wood solution is transferred to a knotting and screening operation where the tree knots and incompletely digested wood are removed as rejects.

4. Next the "brown stock" washing process begins. A series of high-pressure showers "wash" the wood "paste" to separate the cellulose fiber from the remaining digester cooking solution. The recovered digester cooking solution in turn is sent to the evaporators where it is converted to fuel to be burned in the mill's boilers.

5. From the washers the "paste" undergoes a purification process called centricleaning, which removes sand, grit, and foreign material present.

6. Next, the paste goes through a thickening process designed to increase the consistency of the pulp stock.

7. The pulp is oxidized in a bleaching process to achieve a desired whiteness. The bleach "liquor," as it is called, is a mixture of lime, chlorine, and water, which is produced on site.

Exhibit 1
Pulp Mill process flow design

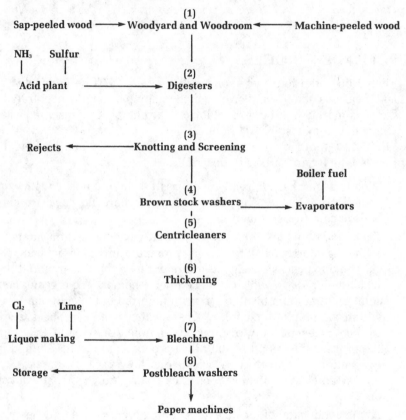

8. The stock goes through another washing process and is either placed into storage for later use or sent on to the paper machines for use in the paper making process.

   The technology used in this manufacturing process continually changed in incremental ways through the installation of new equipment. The direction of this change was consistent; the Pulp Mill had been becoming more of an automatic process control facility.

THE PULP MILL ORGANIZATION

Structure

   Exhibit 2 contains an organization chart for the Pulp Mill Management group. The Pulp Mill *manufacturing manager* assumed overall responsibility for operations and liaison with the rest of the Michigan facility. Reporting directly to the Pulp Mill manufacturing manager were the chemical engineer, industrial engineer, and the two department managers.

The *chemical engineer* had various responsibilities, including process improvement, chemical usage and management, quality monitoring, and control. Any new chemical materials entering the Pulp Mill were tested and approved by him. In addition, the chemical engineer played a major role in cost reduction programs through adopting chemical substitutes or reductions in usage rates.

The *industrial engineer* served as the Pulp Mill's fiscal and budgetary officer. A good deal of his time was spent in the preparation of budgets and forecasts and in the preparation of cost information data. In addition the Pulp Mill Industrial Engineer coordinated the Mill's cost reduction programs.

The two *department managers* subdivided the task of managing the Pulp Mill's daily operations by dividing the mill into a pulp-making part (up through centricleaning) and a pulp-finishing part (up until the pulp is accepted by the paper machines). Each of the department managers had a maintenance manager, two area managers, and two foremen reporting to them. A good deal of the department managers' attention was devoted to supervising and developing the managers who reported to them. Regular performance feedback discussions were routinely held.

The *maintenance managers* each supervised a crew of from six to eight mechanics and maintained responsibility for the upkeep and maintenance of the machinery and equipment within their area of the mill.

The *area managers* were technical experts in complex portions of the pulp mill process. There was one for the digesters, one for the brown stock washers and acid plant, one for bleaching, and one for all of the

Exhibit 2
Pulp Mill management organization

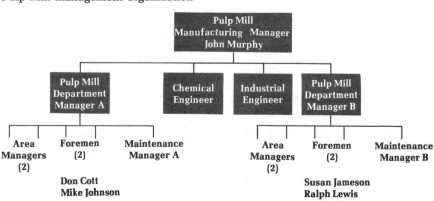

screening, centricleaning, and so forth. In the role of the technical experts the area managers worked with the maintenance managers on equipment upkeep and trouble-shooting, designed process improvements or equipment alterations, and now coordinated the capacity increase project work in their areas. The area manager's job was a fairly new position in the Pulp Mill (begun in 1973). As the technology of pulp production became increasingly complex, such a position was deemed necessary to "keep on top" of process changes and improvements. However, the area managers as a group lacked the official authority to secure maintenance and managerial assistance and relied heavily on interpersonal skills to accomplish these tasks.

The *foremen* were responsible for shift coverage of pulp mill operations. Although they reported to a single department manager they were responsible for supervision of the whole pulp mill on their shift. A common shift's duties included several tours of the pulp mill to check on equipment, employees, etc. and responding to calls on equipment problems by inspection, contacting maintenance employees, supervising repair work, and documenting their actions. In addition foremen were the primary disciplinarians and "monitors" of hourly employees. They checked attendance and lateness, followed up on employees absent from work, admonished employees for sub-par performance, etc.

The foreman's job served as the entry-level position for those interested in careers in manufacturing management. All of the area managers and maintenance managers, along with one of the department managers, the Pulp Mill manufacturing manager, and the chemical engineer had been Pulp Mill foremen earlier in their careers.

The Pulp Mill operated with three shift crews with at least 10 hourly employees on each shift. Exhibit 3 contains an hourly organization chart.

The employees were spread throughout the Pulp Mill and relied mainly on an internal telephone system for communication. However, many employees had the flexibility to visit with the employee(s) nearest to their work area.

The work schedule

Each Pulp Mill employee was assigned to work a six-day week with a rotating day off. Employees also had the opportunity to work each Sunday at double-time premium pay. This alignment of work schedules resulted in an average paid work week for pulp mill employees of 56 hours versus the 40 to 48 hours that was common in other parts of the Michigan facility. With each employee having differing days off Pulp Mill employees were distributed among three shift crews which changed virtually every day.

Exhibit 3
Pulp Mill hourly organization (pre-changeover)

1. Digester Cook	Responsible for the wood-chip cooking process. Controls input, cooking cycle, and flow of pulp stock through the four digesters. Basically tasks are process-control-oriented. Mistakes at this level are the most costly to production.
2. Acid Maker–Brown Stock Washer	Responsible for the manufacture of digester cooking acid and the brown stock washing process. Monitors process flow and controls mixing equipment.
3. Digester Cook Helper	Assists the digester cook in the function of his/her duties.
4. Bleacher	Responsible for the bleaching process. Conducts frequent quality and brightness tests on the pulp stock in addition to calibrating bleaching equipment.
5. Bleach Liquor Maker	Responsible for the manufacture of the bleach liquor used in the bleaching process. A process control activity.
6. Digester Cook Helper Relief	As a result of the six-day-on-rotating-day-off schedule, the digester cook helper relief's role was to serve as a "fill in" operator on other employees' days off.
7. Evaporator Operator	Responsible for controlling the process by which used-up digester cooking solution is converted to boiler fuel.
8. Rejects Operator	Responsible for the accumulation and storage of reject stock eliminated in the knotting and screening process. Fairly routine tasks with heavy direct labor component.
9. Pulp Storage Operators (2)	For pulp which does not go directly to the paper machines there are two pulp storage operators responsible for preparing the pulp for storage. Tasks are highly routine and mechanical. Job involves continuous heavy lifting.

Pulp Mill managers (aside from the shift foremen) generally worked a regular Monday to Friday work week. Shift foremen worked under a "Southern Swing" rotation which was common for the rest of the Michigan facilities. The "Southern Swing" work schedule called for 7 days on then 4 days off, 7 days on then 2 days off, and 7 days on then 1 day off.

The schedule resulted in the shift foreman providing the only supervision in the Pulp Mill outside of regular daytime work hours. Other Pulp Mill managers were "on call" 24 hours a day and could get into the plant on a half hour's notice.

Compensation

All managers were compensated on a salaried basis with a regular provision for salary reviews at least yearly. Salaries were generally regarded as being among the highest in the paper industry.

Pulp Mill employees were compensated on an hourly basis with rates negotiated with the local union. In 1975 the lowest-rated Pulp Mill job paid just under $5/hour with the top Pulp Mill hourly rate approaching $6.60/hour.

There was no bonus or incentive compensation program for either managers or hourly employees.

Selection and development

Century Paper recruited nationally for college graduates interested in careers in Paper Manufacturing Management. The bulk of their new managers were degreed engineers from Midwestern schools. Century practiced a strict promote-from-within policy, with virtually all new hirees beginning their careers as shift foremen. This initial assignment generally lasted from one to three years. In addition to recent college hirees, several longer-term foremen had been promoted from the ranks of the hourly work force. Century believed that these individuals served to provide a sense of continuity in the first level of supervisory management.

Most of the hourly employees were born and raised in the plant community with newer employees being attracted from local high schools. The community was rural in character with its citizens strongly influenced by a European Catholic background. This background was evident in the people's strong work ethic, in the pride they took in their work, and in the importance they put on relationships and on liking the people they worked with, who were often the same people with whom they socialized. It could also be seen in their strong family orientation and respect for those older and more experienced. A significant number of the older employees owned and operated local farms in addition to working at Century.

The pulp mill had a considerable age range among its employees. At one extreme were men with 20 to 25 years' experience, at the other, young men and women who had just started at Century. Many of the older employees could be found discussing "the ways things used to be" and were often drawing comparisons with their past experiences at Century.

The union

The Pulp Mill employees were represented by the International Paper-workers Union. Union-management relations were generally perceived as being positive at the Michigan facility. They had suffered no strikes or work stoppages in the past 30 years. However, recently, the union had decided to clog up the existing grievance machinery in many of the departments by reporting virtually all indications of contract infractions (the Pulp Mill was not affected). Much of the tension in the relationship could be attributed to the large amount of change occurring at the plant and the continuing pressure it placed on the union to "look after the interests of its members." However, communications with union officials were continuing; they were being notified by management well in advance of changes in order to jointly discuss them, and each operating department, as well as the plant as a whole, had developed formal mechanisms for ongoing union-management dialogue.

THE WORK RESTRUCTURING PROJECT

Prior to 1974 all changes in the Pulp Mill operations, both technical and environmental, were met with what could best be described as "patch work" changes to the mill social system. A good example of this phenomenon was the schedule with stable crews working 5-day weeks. The 1960s brought increasing demands for pulp and a 6-day operating schedule. The employee work week was simply extended to 6 days, again with stable crews. In the late 1960s the Pulp Mill moved to a 7-day operating schedule, and Pulp Mill management simply introduced the rotating-day-off concept; a simple solution which led to the crew instability described earlier.

Now there was a great deal of pressure on the Pulp Mill management to make the capacity increase project an enormous success. With this in mind, managers expressed a desire to go beyond upgrading, replacing, or adding equipment and were beginning to look at making some inroads to changing the Pulp Mill work climate. Especially at the department and manufacturing manager levels, there were strong feelings that the capacity increase project provided a vehicle for making some fundamental work improvements. Highest on the management agenda was changing the work schedule for all employees to the Southern Swing schedule. Other items managers wished to address were:

1. Upgrading the employee's technical expertise.
2. Maximizing the employee's job flexibility.
3. Promoting teamwork.
4. Providing employees with jobs that are "meaningful."
5. Attracting and keeping talented employees.

After several months of management discussion on these issues, the union leadership was invited to participate in a joint union-management committee to design and implement "social system" changes in conjunction with the capacity increase project. The union, desirous of having input into any such process, readily agreed to participate in the joint venture.

From February to September 1975 a joint union-management committee, consisting of the Pulp Mill Manufacturing Manager, the two Department Managers, the Michigan Facility Industrial Relations Manager, the local union President and Vice President, the Pulp Mill Committeeman and the two Pulp Mill Shop Stewards, met regularly to discuss potential changes. In addition, area managers and employees participated in various task forces designed to provide input to the joint committee. The changes finally agreed upon included:

1. Schedule change to Southern Swing.   As was indicated, management entered the process determined to change the employee work schedule to the "Southern Swing" work schedule more common to the rest of the plant. Such a shift would allow for the formation of four stable work crews which rotated regularly along with a foreman who worked the same schedule. As Bob Jensen stated:

Our existing work schedule was designed in the late 50s for a 5- or 6-day operation. Times have changed and our existing schedule no longer made sense. Perhaps we should have changed earlier but now is clearly the time to update the way we schedule our people for work.

A common work schedule would also allow for the development of foreman-operator teams which was viewed as being extremely desirable.

2. New job designs.   The Michigan plant had traditionally relied upon detailed, task-oriented job descriptions which always ended with the catchall phrase "and any other duties as assigned by management." The vagueness of statements such as this had resulted in several unnecessary disputes between line managers and employees over the years. In the new job descriptions, however, the committee agreed to drop such detailed task listings in favor of one which simply listed the processes the employee was accountable for, the outcomes which the company expected from the employee's efforts, and the skills necessary for performance of the job. In addition, to assist management in setting new wage rates, for each position a "Project Job Change Summary" was completed which detailed the equipment changes and their impact on the performance of each job.

It was determined that seven of the current jobs were to be replaced by eight new or revised ones:

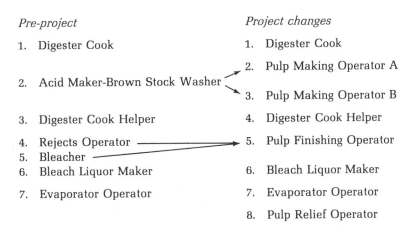

Pre-project

1. Digester Cook

2. Acid Maker-Brown Stock Washer

3. Digester Cook Helper

4. Rejects Operator
5. Bleacher
6. Bleach Liquor Maker

7. Evaporator Operator

Project changes

1. Digester Cook

2. Pulp Making Operator A

3. Pulp Making Operator B

4. Digester Cook Helper

5. Pulp Finishing Operator

6. Bleach Liquor Maker

7. Evaporator Operator

8. Pulp Relief Operator

There were three major changes in the job structure: the change to Pulp Making Operator A & B, the addition of a Pulp Relief Operator, and the combination of the Rejects Operator and Bleacher jobs into a Pulp Finishing Operator.

Equipment additions in the Acid Plant and Brown Stock Washers area necessitated breaking the job up into two separate jobs. The A and B operator concept was designed to gain maximum flexibility from and for the employees affected. The new job descriptions increased the flexibility an employee had in the performance of his/her duties and the A and B concept called for cross training, mutual assistance, and overlap of responsibilities. It was envisioned that a successful test of this concept would lead to further efforts of this nature.

Process improvements justified merging the Rejects and Bleacher jobs into a single all-encompassing position.

The addition of a Pulp Relief Operator was designed simply as an outgrowth of the desire to see what could productively be accomplished with an extra person on each shift. It was expected that this individual could be used to free up other employees for training, committee work, or special projects. In addition, the Union agreed that it was a viable option to utilize this operator to cover for absent employees so that the company would not have to pay overtime.

3. Compensation changes. Inherent in the schedule change to Southern Swing was a wage loss averaging 8 hours pay per employee per week. Plant management was concerned about how this could possibly create resistance to a schedule change. At the same time, however, they did not want to give the impression that they were going to place themselves in the position of simply increasing salaries to "grease the wheel" for smooth implementation of the changes agreed upon. They finally decided that a management task force consisting of the plant industrial relations manager, the plant industrial engineer, and three Pulp Mill managers would review all plant jobs in light of recent equipment and process changes and adjust salaries accordingly. The adjustments were to be made by comparison with the original jobs, other comparable plant jobs and similar jobs in the paper industry in the area.

As a result of the evaluation, the committee recommended wage increases ranging from 5 percent to 8 percent (28¢ to 45¢) on most of the new jobs. The wage increases represented approximately 50 percent of the wages which employees would lose through the schedule change. The Union appeared pleased with the results, and (with the exception of a few minor concerns which were dealt with immediately by the management) accepted the changes in their entirety. The ease in gaining Union acceptance of the revised wage rates could be explained by the fact that the raises granted represented the largest (outside of collective bargaining) wage increases ever given at the Michigan facility. In addition, employees generally were very willing to "trade off" some loss of earnings for their new free time.

4. Shift Teams. The schedule change and revised job descriptions provided for the establishment of shift teams under the guidance of the foremen. It was jointly agreed that overtime, training, and education efforts in the area of team development and effectiveness would be directed at the Pulp Mill employees.

5. Training. A $60,000 appropriation was approved for the development of new training materials to significantly upgrade the knowledge of Pulp Mill employees of the pulping process in general and their area in particular, beyond their present knowledge base of, "If A happens, push Knob B."

6. Additional items. In addition, it was agreed that in many areas equipment would be provided to allow operators to begin performing their own quality tests as a means of gaining more control of the process.

There were few, if any, difficulties in the joint union-management resolution process. A significant proportion of the Pulp Mill employees had demonstrated their desire to participate in the project via their work on the committee or the various task forces, thereby resulting in a good deal of joint ownership in the outcomes.

Implementation and development

All prior events appeared to set the stage for a smooth transition to the new system in the Fall of 1975. No one was able to foresee, however, that technical problems would plague the first phase of the start-up. Managers worked day and night over a six-week period to attempt to stabilize the new processes, and employees were instrumental in assisting their troubleshooting efforts. Employees also exhibited much concern over the status of the process and the lost production. They appointed a group of employees to approach the plant management and volunteer the crews to work through the Thanksgiving holiday rather than shut the Pulp Mill down. They indicated that their "new" understanding of the business (generated via participation in task forces) convinced them of the desirability of not shutting the mill down when production levels had been so low.

Each week, Pulp Mill management-union committees continued to meet to work out some of the details and fine-tune the various changes. Union grievances dropped, too. Morale was high as was the energy level of employees.

Project outcomes

The results of the project clearly matched the expectations of the joint committee; employee morale improved, employees became more active in problem troubleshooting and technical process work, attendance improved, and desired production improvements were steadily being recognized. Much of the positive outcome of the project was ascribed to the broad-based participation in the development of the changes. Exhibit 4 contains an assessment of the Pulp Mill social system in March of 1976. Managers and employees alike viewed the bulk of the changes in a fairly positive light. Representative comments included:

Bleacher operator:

It's about time that managers around here realized that I don't have to turn off my mind when I come to work. I'm enjoying the opportunity to solve problems on my own and get recognized for it.

Union representative:

What we've accomplished here in the past few months is really good. The employees are generally happy with the wage increases and really like the new schedule. We keep solving problems before they blow up into big things.

Chemical engineer:

If someone told me we could have pulled off such a big change a year ago I would have told him he was crazy. But we did it and it seems to work.

However, one area of continuing concern surrounded the role of the foreman in the new operating system. Foremen were not an important part of the original design process and it appeared that employees were more aware of the flexibility inherent in the new operating system than were their supervisors. The simple change of having stable work crews day in and day out fostered a strong team spirit and placed the foreman

Exhibit 4
Pulp Mill system assessment—March 1976 data generated by pulp mill department managers

I. *Job Designs*

Positives

1. There is a great deal of flexibility that is being utilized—people are no longer saying "that's not my job."
2. Employees housekeeping their own areas.
3. Operators can be seen assisting each other regularly.

Negatives

1. Foremen are still not comfortable with the system and are not utilizing the flexibility to its most productive ends.
2. Operators are still not comfortable doing on-the-job problem solving to the extent desired.

II. *Teams*

Positives

1. People are always talking about *their* team.
2. Some teams have already begun safety and clean-up programs.
3. Foremen are now taking more responsibility to communicate with employees—operators say they are getting more information and are informed of the status of follow-up items.
4. The Union continues to give the effort its active support by continuing to work on task forces, solving problems before they become grievances, and making flattering comments about Pulp Mill management at Union meetings. The general membership does not perceive the project as a threat because of the lack of "buzz words," technically difficult behavioral science concepts, and outside interferences by corporate staff.

Negatives

1. Area teams haven't developed to work on some parts of the technical process.
2. Foremen are having a difficult time in coping with their new role.

III. *Foremen*

Positives

1. They are enthusiastic and *want* to understand.
2. They are not waiting for engineers to solve technical problems, but are working on them jointly with their crews.

Negatives

1. They still need to develop better skills in leading meetings, handling conflict and change.
2. They have difficulties in communicating from shift to shift.
3. Foremen, unlike their teams, are not taking the responsibility of making timely decisions when they are needed.
4. They spend a great deal of time as "go-fers" for operators.

Exhibit 4 (*continued*)

IV. *Union Management Interaction*

Positives

1. Successful schedule change.
2. Union and management members are above board and do what they say—they feel part of an important team and take ownership in their actions and decisions.

Negatives

1. Need to expand the membership base for joint activities (foremen, shift team representatives).

V. *Management of Change*

Positives

1. Getting results (with more to come).
2. Communication channels are wide open.

Negatives

1. Often have problems reaching timely resolution on issues.
2. There is often no explicit direction on several items to be worked.

VI. *Union*

Positives

1. Officials take ownership in the changes and have received a large part of the credit for the positive outcomes.
2. The membership rates Union activity on this project as excellent—they are satisfied with the salary changes.
3. The union can point to this project in other operating areas when complaining about conditions.

VII. *Hourly Operators* (Quality of working life)

Positives

1. Information is now reaching the operator level more often.
2. Workloads and the distribution of dull tasks are better balanced.
3. Operators have been able to upgrade their technical competence.
4. A reasonable work schedule which provides for more leisure time exists.
5. They have a greater say in how the Pulp Mill is run.

Negatives

1. Operators need more training to develop these skills even further.

in a position where the traditional role of supervisor, disciplinarian, and technical problem solver in all areas no longer fit. One foreman related a recent occurrence:

On the night of the mill manager's picnic we ran the mill without a foreman on the premises. A serious injury occurred to an employee on the shift. One

*employee coordinated coverage of the equipment while another escorted the em-
ployee to the hospital for treatment. It wouldn't have been any smoother had a
foreman been here. In fact, it might not have been as smooth.*

It was obvious to managers and employees alike that the new systems
required the foremen to have "people development" skills which were
not present within the existing foremen ranks. One foreman responded:

*Foremen need to work on several skills that weren't crucial to being successful
before:*
1. *Team building—both for our crews and ourselves.*
2. *Communication skills.*
3. *One-to-one feedback skills.*

Unfortunately, the existing work schedule for Pulp Mill foremen precluded
their spending additional work hours on developing these skills.

FOREMAN MEETING—JULY 1976

Three of the four foremen attended a meeting in July 1976 where they
presented their views of the situation as it currently existed. (See Exhibit
5 for biographical data on the four foremen and other Pulp Mill managers.)

Susan Jameson:

*There are closer relationships now between the foremen and their crews. You
get a chance to get acquainted with your people rather than working with different
people almost every day. The foreman now knows how the people react in different
situations, how quickly they respond to changes, and how they "troubleshoot"
problems. Thus the foreman can manage more and supervise less. Knowing the
crew better, along with their strengths and weaknesses allows the foreman to
develop his/her people and ultimately to abolish the foreman's job completely!*

Mike Johnson:

*The traditional image of the Pulp Mill foreman is rapidly fading away. In
months to come, if we develop our people's skills, we will be fighting far fewer
"fires" and thus managing the business better. Our role is changing from a foreman
to a manager where we will be training our crews to do our job. So the shift is
from meeting crises to teaching. Now we're caught in the transition and are doing
a pretty lousy job of both. We don't want to continue doing all of the problem
solving but our crews haven't really developed their skills in this area to the
point that they can do it alone. And because of that situation we can't get off
of shifts to get the necessary training to improve our "people skills."*

Donald Cott:

*The foreman is still necessary today as the crews aren't developed enough
to take on full responsibility. But this is changing, perhaps more rapidly than
we know. They are making more and more decisions on their own and doing*

> ### Exhibit 5
> ### Biographical data on selected Pulp Mill managers
>
> *Foremen*
>
> Donald Cott— 55 years old, 30 years with Century Paper, local High School graduate, promoted to management from hourly ranks in 1965, Pulp Mill foreman since 1965.
>
> Mike Johnson— 28 years old, 2 years with Century Paper, two years of college, promoted to management from clerical work force in 1975, Pulp Mill foreman since May 1975.
>
> Susan Jameson—25 years old, 1 year with Century Paper, 1975 graduate of Purdue with Bachelor's in Chemical Engineering. In training September to December 1975, assumed crew responsibilities January 1976.
>
> Ralph Lewis— 47 years old, 1 year with Century Paper, 20-year veteran of U.S. Air Force. In training June to September 1976, assumed crew responsibilities September 1975.
>
> *Pulp Mill Manufacturing Manager*
>
> John Murphy— 32 years old, 9 years with Century Paper, graduate of Indiana with Bachelor's in Chemical Engineering. Previous assignments as paper machine foreman, paper machine chemical engineer, Pulp Mill department manager. Pulp Mill manufacturing manager since December 1974.
>
> *Michigan Operations General Manager*
>
> Bob Jensen— 37 years old, 12 years with Century Paper, graduate of General Motors Institute, MBA from Michigan. Previous assignments as Pulp Mill foreman, Pulp Mill maintenance manager, Pulp Mill department manager, paper machine department manager, converting department manager, Pulp Mill manufacturing manager. Michigan General Manager since 1972.

their own troubleshooting and problem solving. There are many nights when the mill would have run quite nicely without me. But there have been other nights when my crew needed me there if for nothing more than to bolster their confidence. Eventually shift foremen will be obsolete. A coordinator on shifts, especially days, however, might still be desirable. This could be a crew member though or perhaps a rotating job so everyone could do it.

One Pulp Mill department manager, while recognizing the positive tone of most of the foremen's comments, stated the following:

I think they're wrong when they talk about eliminating their job. The foreman's job, no matter what level their crew is at, is essential as a learning experience for Century Paper management careers. This experience provides reality training that we all need regularly. It allows the manager the opportunity to develop in areas like group effectiveness, problem solving, priority setting, standards commu-

nication, motivation, and so forth. It allows the foreman a first good look at everything that is production management.

Now, I do see the foreman's role changing in the coming months and years. I see them as taking the key role in lowering decision making to the hourly employee level. This must be a total Pulp Mill effort but the implementation of going from a foreman to a resource must come from the foreman. The move to Southern Swing is a first step. The second step is to make people development a goal for the Pulp Mill. The third step is to implement.

THE SITUATION IN AUGUST 1976

Foremen had been meeting regularly as a group over the past three months in an attempt to come to grips with the new operating system as individuals and as a group. However, these meetings appeared to have had little or no impact on their performance as managers.

In an analysis of the situation as it presently existed John Murphy viewed a number of options to remedy the situation:

1. *Work toward a rapid elimination of the foreman's job*—This appeared to be an attractive option. However, Century Paper utilized a "promote from within" policy and relied heavily on the foreman's position as a training spot for promotions to higher level manufacturing positions. In addition, it was likely that the existing foremen could not be integrated into the Pulp Mill organization and would be transferred to the papermaking or converting areas as foremen.
2. *Emphasize additional training for foremen over the next several months*—John wondered about the benefits of a crash training effort and was concerned about the time investment it would take.
3. *Let foremen work out a role for themselves*—Such a laissez-faire approach might be costly in terms of continuing ambiguity and dissatisfaction for foremen but had its advantages.

John planned to have several meetings with other Pulp Mill managers over the next several weeks before settling on an alternative.

Case 8–3
Litton Microwave Cooking Products (C)
Vijay Sathe

In October 1976 Bill George, President of Litton Microwave Cooking Products, one of 112 divisions of Litton Industries, was concerned about several issues related to the company's middle and lower management levels. The division had grown from $19 million in sales in 1971 to $186 million in the fiscal year just ended. This tremendous and sustained growth, averaging 60 percent compounded annually, had created stresses and strains for people, particularly those in lower and middle management levels. Their jobs were growing faster than the ability of many of them to keep up. This not only created frustration and anxiety for these people but also had serious implications for the company's well-being in the future. With projections of the extremely rapid rate of growth of the past five years continuing into the late 1970s, the company would soon approach the half billion dollar sales mark. It was clear to Bill that as the division grew to this size and beyond, the nature of the business would require considerable delegation of authority to middle and lower management levels. Would these managers be ready to handle the new responsibilities?

NATURE OF THE BUSINESS

Litton Microwave Cooking Products was the world's largest manufacturer of microwave ovens. In 1976, it commanded 30 percent of the rapidly expanding U.S. consumer market, and 70 percent of the U.S. commercial market for microwave ovens. Saturation in the U.S. consumer market was estimated to be a mere 6 percent, and the industry forecast was for galloping sales into the late 1970s. The current market for microwave ovens was often compared to that for color television in the mid-sixties). The outstanding performance of the microwave oven against the backdrop of the lackluster major-appliance industry was attracting the attention of several domestic and foreign manufacturers. Amana, Tappan, GE, Panasonic, and Sharp were already in the market as strong competitors, and others could conceivably decide to enter the market. Although competition was expected to intensify in the years ahead, market saturation and an industry shakeout was not expected until the mid-1980s.

The spectacular success story of the microwave oven business could

be attributed largely to three factors. First, the initial concerns about
the safety of microwave ovens had been largely laid to rest. In 1973,
Consumer's Union had raised the possibility of radiation leakage but
the FDA's Bureau of Radiological Health (BRH) had not supported the
charge. The BRH had set tough standards on allowable leakage in 1971
and had followed up with strict enforcement. Manufacturers' facilities
were inspected every six months, and all new designs had to be reviewed
by the BRH. Second, rising energy costs had given the microwave oven
the advantage of economy over conventional ovens. With its low power
consumption and cool operation, the energy savings amounted to about
50–75 percent over conventional ovens for the average family of four.
Finally, new features had greatly increased the microwave oven's versatil-
ity. Variable power settings, special browning devices, and temperature
controls permitted the microwave oven to cook almost as broad an array
of foods as conventional devices and permitted its positioning in the
market as a *complete* cooking device.

Litton's position of leadership in this market was attributed to its aggressive marketing and distribution programs backed up by innovative
product design and competitive prices. About 90 percent of the company's
business was in consumer ovens (70 percent in countertop models and
20 percent in ranges); the remaining 10 percent of the business was in
commercial ovens. The countertop business included some private-label
sales, mainly under the Sears label. (Pictures of a representative sample
of the company's products are shown in Exhibit 1).

Litton was a recognized leader in the technology of microwave cooking.
Patent protection was of limited value since the technology was changing
rapidly and success hinged on the ability to be the first on the market
with product innovations. An important determinant of Litton's technological leadership was its engineering design department, believed to be the
"world's largest microwave engineering group." The company's task team
organization, comprising members drawn from various functional areas,
had been credited with offering the flexibility needed to achieve a rapid
response to the demands of the marketplace. In contrast, major competitors were characterized as being in the "appliance industry tradition"—
conservative, and slow to respond to market changes. The committee
structure in GE's appliance division, for example, was described by Litton
Microwave executives as an organization where things tended to get
"bogged down."

Production of ovens involved the subassembly and assembly of parts
purchased to design specifications. About 80 percent of the cost of the
manufactured product was in the purchase price of parts. The direct labor
component, involving relatively unskilled labor, was small. Thus manufacturing cost depended largely on design specifications and the ability to

Exhibit 1
Pictures of products

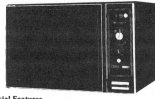

Litton 419 Minutemaster® microwave oven

Litton 460 Memorymatic™ microwave oven

Special Features

- Solid state Vari-Cook oven control for slow-cooked goodness at microwave speeds
- Vari-Temp automatic food temperature control
- 99-minute Micro-Timer digital timer
- Bright, easy-clean acrylic interior
- Sealed-in ceramic shelf
- See-through oven door
- Modern, attractive styling
- Extra-large 1.2 cubic foot usable oven interior

Special Features

- 99-minute electronic timer
- Solid state Vari-Cook oven control
- Vari-Temp control
- Memorymatic oven control with an additional 99 min. of memory time
- Solid state touch control
- Lighted digital display
- Minute Timer
- Automatic on/off control
- Extra-large 1.2 cubic foot usable oven interior
- Easy-clean acrylic interior and sealed in ceramic shelf
- Separate Time and Temp, Memory, and Vari-Cook touch controls
- Free Vari-Cook Microwave Cookbook

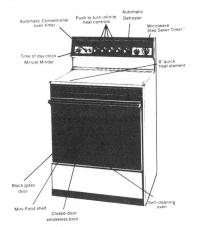

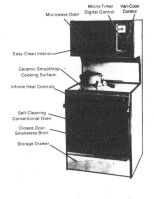

Litton Combination 650 microwave range

("Single Oven Cavity" Range)

Litton Micromatic 989 microwave range

("Double Oven Cavity" Range)

obtain low prices from suppliers. Production efficiencies were only a secondary determinant of cost efficiencies. The Litton division had more microwave oven production experience than any other competitor. And the dedication to microwave ovens offered the company a point of focus and considerable pride in having manufactured "more microwave ovens than anyone else." In contrast, other major competitive manufacturers were more diversified.

HISTORY

Microwave cooking

The principle of microwave cooking was discovered by Dr. Percy Spencer in 1941 while doing war research on radar for Raytheon. By 1946, Raytheon had developed and patented the first microwave oven under the trade name Radarange. The company also licensed others to manufacture cooking devices based on the same principle. By using micro-waves generated by a magnetron vaccum tube as the heating source, rather than the electrical elements or gas flames used in conventional ovens, cooking time was considerably reduced because energy reached the interior portion of food much faster.

Microwave ovens were first sold in 1959 mainly to commercial institutions such as hospitals, schools, restaurants, and vending machine companies. Prices were in the $3,000 range. By 1964 prices for commercial units had dropped closer to $2,000 but total industry sales were still only about 3,000 units.

The consumer market for microwave ovens remained relatively undeveloped through 1965. In 1966, sales reached 12,000 units. In 1967 Amana, a newly acquired subsidiary of Raytheon, introduced the first 115-volt countertop microwave oven and by 1969 the demand for consumer units had grown to an annual rate of 45,000 units. The subsequent growth of the consumer oven business had been spectacular and the high growth rate was expected to continue through 1980 (see Exhibit 2).

The Litton division

Litton Industries was founded in 1953 by Tex Thornton, Roy Ash, and another colleague at Hughes Aircraft who quit their jobs to strike out on their own in the electronics business. Their first acquisition was a small company owned by an engineer named Charles Litton that manufactured magnetron and klystron tubes for military radar installations. Eleven years later, in 1964, the company formed the Atherton division by combining personnel from the original magnetron tube company and a newly acquired Cleveland firm owned by Bob Bruder, that made infrared ovens for vending applications. Mr. Bruder became the division's president. A year later, in 1965, the division introduced its first commercial microwave oven. Within a year, Litton had captured 70 percent of the 9,000 unit commercial market due to the reliability and low price (about $1,000) of their product.

In late 1969, Litton began "Phase 1" of its long-range plan for entering the consumer microwave oven business. Countertop units were produced

Exhibit 2
Industry sales of consumer ovens

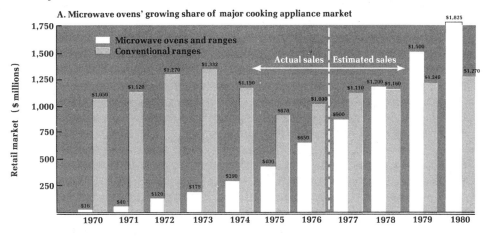

A. Microwave ovens' growing share of major cooking appliance market

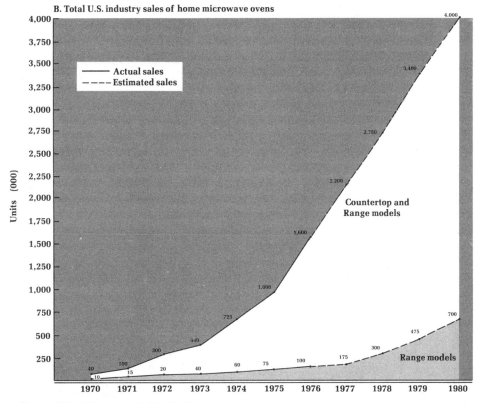

B. Total U.S. industry sales of home microwave ovens

Source: Litton Microwave Cooking Products.

for sale under private label for Admiral, Tappan, and Montgomery Ward. In 1970, public concern over possible microwave radiation leakage and the economic recession put a damper on industry sales. As a result, Litton's sales under the private label program fell short of the company's projections in its first year in the consumer oven market.

In August 1971, 28-year-old Bill George was appointed executive vice president of the Litton division with responsibility for all internal activities, including profitability. (Bob Bruder remained president and in overall charge of the division.) After completing a bachelor's degree in industrial engineering from Georgia Institute of Technology, and an MBA from Harvard Business School, Bill George worked as a civilian in the Department of Defense, first as an assistant to the Assistant Secretary of Defense (comptroller) and then as Special Assistant to the Secretary of the Navy. During the transition of administrations in 1969, Bill was contacted by Bob Bruder and asked to join Litton as director of long-range planning for the company's food services group. His first assignment was to study whether Litton should enter the consumer microwave oven business. Shortly after its entry into the private-label end of the consumer business, Litton had encountered start-up problems and Bill was asked to move to the Atherton division as vice president in early 1970. He had responsibilities at this level for each major area of the business prior to his appointment as executive vice president in August 1971. Excerpts from magazine articles on his career are included in Exhibit 3.

One of the most significant events under the leadership of Bob Bruder and Bill George was the decision to enter the consumer microwave oven market under the Litton brand name despite the disappointing results in the private-brand market in 1970. This represented the first entry in the consumer products field for Litton Industries. While the division continued to have a strong position in the commercial microwave oven market, that represented an entirely different type of sale, to different people, and for different reasons. The biggest concern regarding the decision to enter the consumer market centered on the division's ability to compete successfully with a powerful force like GE.

In January 1971, Bill George selected Dan Cavalier to spearhead the company's entry into the consumer field. Dan's long track record included extensive experience in consumer marketing with companies such as RCA, Philco, Caloric, and GE. Within three weeks of joining Litton, Dan hired his former associate, Si Ware, who had been with Westinghouse for 20 years, to assist him as national sales manager of consumer products.

By the end of 1971 the division had established a 20 percent share of the consumer market through the combination of marketing its own brand and private-label sales. Although some competitors, notably Amana, had the advantage of possessing greater consumer brand awareness, Litton

Exhibit 3

"YOUNG TOP MANAGEMENT: THE NEW GOALS, REWARDS, LIFESTYLES"*

How dedicated under-40 executives are making it big—and richly-running some
of the country's major corporations

The new organizations built by these young executives are often more participative
than traditional businesses. "I don't want to be controlled by an organization, and I
don't want my organization to control other people," says 32-year-old William W. George,
president for two years of Litton Industries, Inc.'s Microwave Cooking Products Div.
"We get together as peers. It doesn't matter whether you're president or an engineer.
Authority goes to competence." George holds what he calls "sensing sessions" at least
monthly with the company's 600 hourly employees. "I don't believe in waiting for contract
time. I want to avoid a we-they attitude."

*   *   *

Change is bound to come in the flexible new organizations. As a rule, major-appliance
makers take 24 to 40 months to introduce a new product. "That's just the way it is in
the industry and nobody changed the rules," says George. "I insisted we make product
introductions in 9 to 18 months. I can afford to take the risk and break the rules. I'm
at an age where if I make a major mistake, I have time to go out and redeem myself."

*   *   *

Acceptance of a youthful executive outside the company is sometimes more difficult
still. "My age is no problem within the company," says Litton's George. "But on the
outside people often have trouble accepting me. They ask pointed questions like: 'Who
was your father?' " George has found being a president at 32 so cumbersome that on
social occasions he evades the issue. "When someone asks, I just say I'm in general
management."

*   *   *

Litton's George practices transcendental meditation 20 minutes every morning and
afternoon to unwind.

*   *   *

Many young executives make special efforts to allocate more time for their families,
which often has the side effect of providing some needed rest and recreation. Some,
like Litton's George, have even found time to help with the chores. Since his wife puts
in a 55-hour week as an educational psychology teacher at the University of Minnesota,
he cooks 40 percent of the family's meals and makes about one-third of the trips to
the babysitter's and day-care centers where the Georges leave their two-year-old son.

*   *   *

Litton's George, who makes more than $75,000 a year, takes a different approach.
"No matter what our income, I should be able to live on $20,000 a year," says George,
who lives in a 40-year-old house valued at about $50,000. "I don't want to be locked
into a high income. Someday I may want to go into teaching or government service
and live on that kind of income."

Exhibit 3A

"BUSINESSMEN IN THE NEWS"*

The major-appliance industry is pretty slow these days, but microwave ovens are burning up the business. An insignificant seller five years ago, they fetched about $300 million at retail last year.

In this youthful business a young man is king. William George, 32, heads the Microwave Cooking Products division of Litton Industries, which ranks No. 1 in sales of home and commercial units. Litton's microwave sales are expected to reach $85 million in 1975, and George says his group has been a "very strong profit contributor." Litton, which lost $40 million as a whole last year, can use the money.

An engineer and Harvard Business School graduate, George worked at the Defense Department for three years before joining Litton. "Every business today is affected by the government," he says. "I wanted to understand governmental processes from the inside."

As it happened, the night he was packing to join the division in Minneapolis in 1970, he heard a government warning on the radio that microwave ovens might be hazardous. For the next six months at Litton, George worked with HEW to establish acceptable safety standards. These days, the government reviews all new designs and inspects Litton's factories twice a year.

---

* Reprinted from the August 1975 issue of *Fortune Magazine* by permission. Copyright © Time, Inc.

---

was able to penetrate the market by emphasizing salesman training, retail demonstrations, special cookbooks, and the introduction of new convenience features. The company then employed about 400 people, half of them hourly workers. Total revenue was $19 million, and the division made a profit contribution to Litton Industries.

In 1972, 300,000 consumer microwave ovens were sold in the United States and Litton maintained its 20 percent share of the market. The division had established an impressive national distribution network for its consumer products via 50 distributors and about 2,000 dealers. It had also completed a new production plant in Plymouth, Minnesota (a suburb of Minneapolis), separate from the one that produced commercial ovens. In early 1973, extensions to the Plymouth facility were made, tripling its production capacity. The older plant was sold and the commercial oven assembly operation was moved to the new Plymouth plant.

In the fiscal year ended July 31, 1973, revenues almost doubled over the previous year and the division continued to maintain its share of the market. Total employment increased 37 percent during the year. In August 1973, Bill George was promoted to president, the name of the division was changed to Litton Microwave Cooking Products, and Bob Bruder was made a group vice president of the Litton Industries Medical Products Group.

In the fall of 1973 Litton decided to enter into production of both double oven[1] and combination oven ("single cavity") microwave ranges with the intent of capturing from 20 to 25 percent of this rapidly growing segment of the consumer market. Up to that point Modern Maid had assembled the double oven unit for Litton, but the company decided on in-house design and assembly of a new product line in both double oven and combination oven ranges. Litton had already developed considerable expertise in microwave oven technology but the combination, or single cavity, oven was a completely new product and involved a great deal of design innovation. For example, the cooking area would have to be much larger than in existing countertop units and the microwave energy pattern would have to be uniform throughout this entire area. It would also be necessary to design an oven door (to prevent microwave leakage) that would not be damaged by the higher cooking temperatures experienced when the electric or gas heat element was in use. Despite the higher design risks involved, the combination oven range represented an attractive investment. Bill George felt that ultimately this model would become the most salable product. It would allow the user to bake, broil, microwave, or perform any combination of these activities without removing the food from the oven.

Both revenue and total employment doubled between July 1973 and July 1975. Revenues totaled $99 million for the fiscal year ended July 31, 1975, and the division made a strong profit contribution to Litton Industries, which was recovering from a $40-million net loss the previous year. Revenues and total employment almost doubled again between July 1975 and July 1976 and the Microwave division continued its position of leadership among divisions of Litton. The trends in revenue, production capacity, and employment over the years are shown in Exhibit 4. In August 1976 Bill George was elected a corporate vice president of Litton Industries and continued as President of Litton Microwave Cooking Products.

The division forecasted a continuation of the success story of the recent past into fiscal 1977. It expected to sell about 450,000 units in the anticipated 1.5-million-unit countertop market and about 55,000 units in the 100,000-unit market for ranges, giving it a 30 percent share of the domestic consumer market for microwave ovens. In addition, it expected to hold its commanding 70 percent share of the $30-million commercial microwave oven market. If these projections were accurate, total revenue would reach $260 to $290 million in fiscal 1977.

---

[1] "Double oven" refers to any range with two separate oven cavities, one of which is strictly for microwave cooking. "Combination oven" refers to a range with a single oven cavity that can be used for microwave cooking and gas/electric cooking.

Exhibit 4
Trends in revenue, unit production, and employment

		Fiscal year				
	1971	1972	1973	1974	1975	1976
Revenue						
Millions of dollars	19	32	53	72	99	186
Percent increase over previous year		68	66	36	38	88
Production capacity						
Thousands of units	43	79	202	288	432	936
Percent increase over previous year		84	56	43	50	116
Employment at end of fiscal year						
Indirect (Managerial, Professional, Secretarial and Support)						
Number	200	389	495	567	812	1167
Percent increase over previous year		95	27	15	43	44
Direct (Hourly workers—unionized)						
Number	213	290	434	482	957	1994
Percent increase over previous year		36	50	11	99	108
Total employment at end of fiscal year	413	679	929	1049	1769	3161
Percent increase over previous year ...		64	37	13	69	79

CORPORATE—DIVISIONAL RELATIONS

Divisions were the fundamental building blocks of Litton Industries. They were decentralized and acted as individual profit centers. As such, the division manager played a key role in the Litton system and enjoyed a great deal of autonomy. With the exception of capital expenditure decisions above $35,000 and executive salary decisions above $45,000, decisions made at the divisional level did not require specific corporate approval. Nor was the division manager required to buy from other Litton divisions. All mandatory interaction in the Litton organization was vertical; horizontal interaction developed based on the mutual self-interest of divisions. Thus, there was no attempt by corporate to interfere with the division on the basis of any ideas of centralized planning efficiencies. It was felt that the advantages from increased motivation due to the increased divisional autonomy outweighed any benefits that could be gained by imposing "slide rule" efficiencies from the corporate office.

There was no human resources function at corporate headquarters.

The industrial relations department was staffed with lawyers concerned mainly with labor negotiations and employment contracts.

Planning at Litton was considered to be a line rather than a staff activity. The genesis of the majority of Litton's plans took place at the division level. Once a year, the division manager was required to submit to his or her corporate group vice president a business plan describing proposed activities during the coming 12-month period. It included projected revenue, profit, and capital requirements. The plan was discussed, evaluated, and modified at the group level before being submitted for corporate approval. Once approved, the division generated a set of detailed and interlocking financial plans to execute the business plan. These plans contained profit and loss statements, balance sheets, and supporting data for the coming 12-month period on a month-by-month basis. Financial data were also included for a 24-month period on a quarterly basis and for a 36-month period on a yearly basis. Once checked for accuracy by corporate headquarters, these plans became the "charter" for the division's operations and were updated quarterly.

In addition to the business and financial plans, the division submitted a monthly report to corporate headquarters showing actual performance against the financial plan. Corporate expected each division to meet the monthly targets. Four performance indicators received special attention: profits, cash generated or used, return on gross assets (including capitalized leases), and return on capital utilized (net assets minus current liabilities). If performance was out of line, the division was expected to immediately notify the corporate management rather than wait for the monthly report to be sent in. In addition, corporate executives visited each division periodically to keep in touch with divisional activities. Telephone meetings were frequently arranged to discuss problems and exchange information.

The division had autonomy only so long as it met its performance targets. If it missed its monthly targets, the division would receive increasing corporate attention, including more than the usual number of corporate visitors. Continued inability to meet targets would result in replacement of the division's general manager, unfavorable corporate resource allocation and, possibly, even divestiture of the division.

The Litton Microwave division was a consistent high-performer and had met its monthly targets for profit, cash generation, and return on investment during each of the past 24 months.

ORGANIZATION AT LITTON MICROWAVE

Between August 1971, when Bill George joined the division as executive vice president, and August 1976, revenue and total employment increased ten-fold and profits increased seventeen-fold at Litton Microwave. The company's organization played an important role in ensuring this dramatic success. Although the formal organization chart consisted of the traditional functional departments under the president (see Exhibit 5 for a list of these departments, and for background information on the department heads), most of the key activities of the division were managed by informal task teams that did not appear on the formal organization chart but operated within the functional structure.

Bill George explained:[2]

Back in 1971 our long-range plan called for building our sales volume to $100 million in five to seven years, representing a compound growth rate of 40 percent per year. I was convinced that the only limitation on our revenue and profit growth was our organization's ability to grow as rapidly as the market opportunities. The organizational challenge was to create a structure and climate which would facilitate such growth. In evaluating whether our functional organization could meet these needs, I became concerned about the ability of this structure to respond to changes in a volatile market and to encourage and stimulate creativity. Functions tended to take a narrow view of their respective roles rather than to see the overall needs of the business. On the other hand, the functional organization was simple and efficient. It provided specialists a point of focus and a feeling of security. As such, we developed the concept of using task teams composed of people from the various functional areas to carry out the bulk of the work.

Each team had a designated leader, generally a member of middle management, representatives from several functional areas, and members of top management on an "as required" basis. Bill George spent a great deal of time attending task team meetings. Examples of task teams included those for new-product development, manufacturing of products, new marketing programs, cost reduction activities, facility planning, private-brand sales, and new business ventures.

Although task teams cut across the various functional areas, they tended to become associated with one functional area more than with others. For example, a majority of individuals on the new-product development teams tended to be engineers, and these teams were under the general supervision of the engineering vice president. Similarly, manufacturing teams were under the vice president of operations and new marketing programs teams were under the marketing head. The activities of several of these teams will be discussed in the context of the appropriate functional department in the sections that follow.

---

[2] This passage, and several others, were taken from an article by Bill George, "Task Teams for Rapid Growth," *Harvard Business Review,* March–April 1977.

Exhibit 5
Backgrounds of functional heads

Doug Baker—Vice President of Human Resources. 42 years old. Bachelor of Business Administration (Texas), MBA (Stanford). Joined Litton Microwave in present position in July 1973. Responsible for all activities involving employee planning, development, and organizational structure. Prior experience included positions as Senior Associate with Willson Associates, Vice President of Jones and Byrd, Manager of Training for Pillsbury Company, and Assistant to the President at the Kitchell Corporation.

Jack Blake—Vice President of Engineering. 48 years old. Bachelor of Science in Business and Engineering (Minnesota), MBA (Minnesota). Joined the division in 1970, promoted to current position in July 1972. Responsible for engineering research, new-product development, product engineering, and all technical support of the division's operations. Previous experience included position as Director of Manufacturing at Litton's Applied Science Division and key engineering-management positions with General Mills and General Motors.

Dan Cavalier—President of Marketing and Sales Division. 58 years old. Undergraduate education at the University of Maryland and the University of Georgia. Joined the division in 1971, received present position in July 1975. Responsible for marketing, sales, and sales-related activities for the company's consumer, commercial, and private-label activities. Past experience included positions as VP and General Manager at Salespower, Manager of Market Development at GE, VP of Marketing for Caloric, and Merchandising Manager for Consumer Products at Philco Ford.

Don Colt—Vice President of International Division. 40 years old. AB (Stanford), MBA (Harvard). Joined Litton Microwave in current position in October 1975. Responsible for all of the division's international activities. Prior experience included marketing and general management positions with the international group of Lawry's Foods for a total of 14 years.

Richard Jones—Senior Vice President of Finance and Administration. 34 years old. Bachelor of Science in Engineering (Michigan), MBA (Michigan). Joined the division as Assistant Controller in 1969, promoted to current position in April 1973. Responsible for all financial activities within the division, including financial control, data processing, financial planning, and international finance. Prior experience included position of Financial Analyst with Litton's Corporate Staff in Beverly Hills from 1967 to 1969.

Paul Westgard—Vice President of Operations. 40 years old. Bachelor of Science in Industrial Administration (Minnesota). Joined the division in April 1974, promoted to current position in December 1974. Responsible for the division's manufacturing operations, materials, and facilities expansion. Previously he was Director of Operations for Josten's, Inc.

Engineering

The 90-person engineering department was composed of 14 task teams working on approximately 40 new-product development projects. These projects were in one of four areas: advanced engineering, design engineering, product engineering, and commercial engineering. Each area was headed by a department manager. The design engineering area was the largest of the four and included managers for the range line, the Litton countertop line, and the private-label countertop line, who reported to a director of design engineering.

Advanced engineering represented the company's research activity. This area originated a few projects that eventually proceeded to the appropriate engineering product group (commercial, range, countertop, or private label). The majority of the design activity originated in these respective areas and represented refinement, modification, and development of the existing product lines.

The progress of a typical product development project is charted in Exhibit 6. A team usually began with an engineer and two technicians. A designer, a stylist, a buyer, a home economist, draftspeople, and quality and manufacturing personnel were added as the project developed. The transition from pre-production to production following the final product review was typically handled by personnel in the product engineering area, but engineers on the original design team would stay on board as needed. The product engineering group was also involved with "firefighting projects." These developed when engineering design or redesign was needed on an emergency basis to overcome problems in an existing product. In addition, members of the product engineering group were involved with cost reduction and product improvement projects. As such, this group handled the bulk of the day-to-day interface activity between engineering and operations. The quality of this interface relationship was described as being "as good as can be expected between engineering and operations." The majority of the problems were with products in the range line, which was undergoing constant development.

The major concern with engineering centered on the ability to expand

Exhibit 6
Product development system*

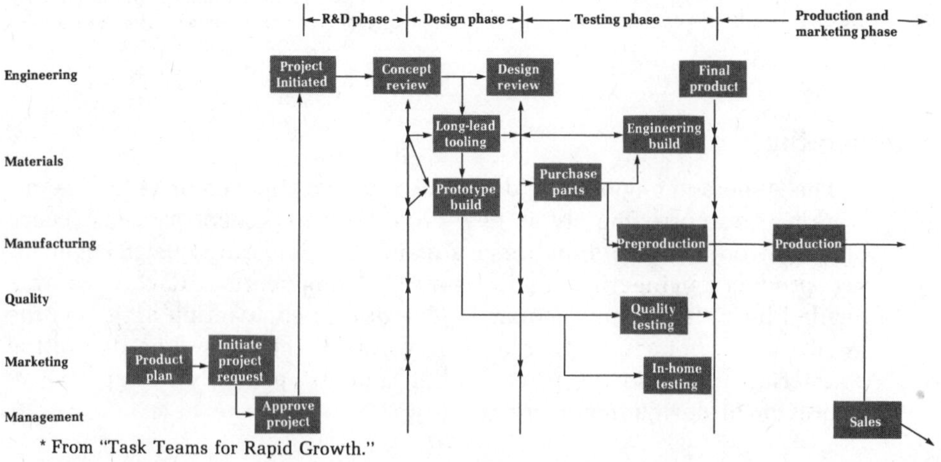

* From "Task Teams for Rapid Growth."

the organization rapidly enough to keep up with the new product development requirements being generated by marketing. On the average, it took six months to fill authorized openings because of the tight hiring market for engineers. In the words of one engineering executive:

Individuals will give you twelve hours a day for only so long. Then batteries begin to discharge. If they are not recharged, a lot of them will leave. It is the inflow of new people that keeps this place charged with energy.

An engineering manager who had been at Litton Microwave for many years had this reaction, however:

I work more hours than perhaps anyone else in engineering. I wouldn't want it any other way! The average engineer is putting in about 50 hours per week. There is some complaining, but not a great deal. This is an exciting place to work because we are at the forefront of microwave engineering technology.

Jack Blake, Vice President of Engineering, attempted to put the problem in perspective:

We have not been able to staff up to the authorized level because the hiring market for engineers is extremely tight and we are very demanding in selecting the people we want. Typically, about ten candidates are interviewed in Minneapolis for every one that we hire. Only two engineers have left in the last three years. About a year ago a competitor hired one of our best engineers away by offering him a $10,000 salary increase. Two months ago this person called me and asked if he could return to work with us at his old salary. He said he missed the professional excitement of being at the forefront technologically. I was glad to have him back.

The engineering department generally recruited persons with prior work experience. For project manager positions, it sought MBAs with engineering backgrounds and 7 to 15 years work experience. Others hired typically had three to five years of experience. Fewer than five percent were fresh engineering graduates. As such, newspaper advertisements and the services of "head hunters," rather than campus visits, were used to locate the needed talent. A human resources manager assigned to engineering assisted in the recruitment process.

Bill George participated in several engineering task team meetings and there were differing opinions regarding his presence in these meetings. One engineer observed:

Bill George is an active participant and attempts to assist in the development of middle management by asking probing questions and encouraging thorough analysis.

Others, however, wondered whether his presence in the meetings actually impeded the development of the very managers he hoped to assist.

His high formal power within the organization coupled with the fact that he was right "ninety percent of the time" made it very difficult for middle management to challenge his analysis. In effect, they had no opportunity to translate their own thinking into actions and learn from the consequences of those actions. According to the critics, there would be definite costs in the short run (in the form of errors) if these managers were allowed to make more decisions, but the development of middle management would be enhanced in the long run. This would become a crucial factor when the company reached $500 million in sales and beyond, as was expected to happen within the next few years. Due to the sheer size and technological complexity of the business, any one person, no matter how bright and energetic, would be then unable to oversee all the important business decisions. One manager remarked:

> An informal organization with one man in firm control can work under the $50 million sales level. The transition from $50 to $100 million is gear-wrenching. The organization becomes formalized. Beyond $500 million the organization becomes totally structured. Bill George is a "hands on" manager and has done an exceptional job so far with his attention to detail. He must now learn to adopt a different style. It calls for sitting in the office and managing people via budgets and numbers rather than by direct involvement in operating decisions.

Operations

Each of the product lines, for example, range, commercial, and countertop, was headed by a plant manager who reported to the vice president of operations. Reporting to the plant manager were one or more "unit managers" responsible for all aspects of manufacturing one or more of the company's product lines. Each unit manager was in charge of a self-contained task team. The typical task team was composed of two to four first-line supervisors, a product engineer, production engineers, quality inspectors, material handlers, schedulers, and from 75 to 200 production workers. It was the task team under the unit manager that made the day-to-day decisions involved in the manufacturing process. They were responsible for product quality, direct and indirect costs, product schedules, scrap, etc., and were assisted on an "as required basis" by specialists in design and product engineering (under VP-Engineering), manufacturing engineering, purchasing, and quality (under VP-Operations), cost accounting (under VP-Finance), and human resources.

Production workers were paid on an hourly basis, with no incentive compensation. For most the job was a relatively low-skill assembly operation, and wage rates ranged between $4.00 and $5.50 an hour. The 1,400 members of the hourly labor force at Litton Microwave were represented by the United Electrical and Machine Workers Union, which had successfully negotiated a new 41-month contract with the company, effective May 10, 1976. Union and management had always had a good working relationship. About 60 percent of the workers were women, most of whom were providing a second source of income for their families. The remainder of the work force were mostly young males between 18 and 25 years of age. There was some management concern about the presence of a drug problem in this segment of the labor force, but it was not considered to be more serious than the national average.

Turnover among the hourly workers had always been rather high, averaging 25 percent per year. It was not difficult to find the needed replacements locally and it did not take long to get new workers "up to speed" given the relatively low level of required skill for the light assembly work to be done. Capable first-line supervisors were, however, extremely hard to recruit. Because of the task and composition of the hourly work force, good supervisory interpersonal skills were needed in addition to technical skills. One unit manager commented:

Most jobs are growing faster than we can define or staff them. What is unique to growth is that experience is measured in months rather than years. Because of the tight market for good first-line supervisors, many of those we recruit are not only new to Litton but new to the trade and new to the job as well.

New supervisors were sent to short outside training programs, both technically oriented ones and others such as leadership training. The prevailing view among managers, including Bill George, was that more needed to be done to strengthen the first level of management.

There was a general concern among managers in the operations area about the adequacy of the various information and control systems, for example, bills of materials, inventory control, materials requirement planning, and other systems. Many of these systems had been automated recently using in-house expertise, and the designers of these systems had encountered difficulty in getting users to change from the old manual system. The new production control system, for example, required operators of fork-lift trucks to carefully document production as goods were transferred from one station to the next, whereas they had not been required to do so under the old manual system.

In general, the tremendous growth of the past two years had made it very difficult to design and implement the various new systems as rapidly as was necessary. In particular, production control was considered to be very weak. Work stoppages due to materials shortages had resulted in several unfavorable cost variances in the recent past. Since production was principally an assembly operation, the company was critically dependent on its parts suppliers for quality and delivery. The division had cultivated more than one supplier for over 85 percent of the parts it required, and supplier relations were generally viewed as being good. However, many suppliers were small vendors who did not have the capacity to keep up with Litton's ever increasing parts requirements. Some parts frequently ran into quality problems. Another reason for parts shortages was that inventory levels were maintained to meet the planned production schedule over the next two months; if production plans were altered on short notice, certain parts could run out.

Some managers within the operations area were concerned about top management involvement in task team meetings. One of them observed:

I have the responsibility but not the authority to make decisions. We go through a lot of turmoil because the president and the vice presidents have failed to delegate authority.

Another pointed to a related concern:

Growth offers the unwritten promise of advancement opportunities, but the promotion we anticipate may never come. There is no time to train us and untested people are being brought in from outside. That's frustrating. If this keeps up, there may be a mass exodus of middle management.

Within operations, there was no consensus over the adequacy of staffing authorizations. One manager dwelled on the virtues of running lean:

You need tight budgets. I feel secure running lean. I feel good running lean.

Another manager remarked:

Obtaining staffing authorization is no problem if I can justify my needs. The difficulty is in finding the right people soon enough after I get staffing approval. That has been a problem.

One senior manager with a broad overview of the operations area held a somewhat contrary view:

Our plans are more aggressive than the resources that are available. Marketing and Finance have been staffed in such a way that their organizations are now in place. One of the last areas to go that way is Operations.

Marketing and sales

Reporting to the President of the Marketing and Sales Division, Dan Cavalier, were Directors of Market Planning, Marketing Communication, Marketing Services (including consumer affairs, sales administration and transportation, and service and parts warranty), and a VP for each of commercial, private-brand, and consumer sales.

Si Ware, who had been recruited by Dan Cavalier back in 1971 to assist in the launching of the consumer sales program, headed the biggest group within marketing and sales as VP-Consumer Sales. Consumer sales, comprising both countertops and ranges were handled by 52 independent distributors as well as by appliance dealers in 12 major metropolitan areas. The consumer sales force was organized into four regions (west, central, east, and south) each headed by a regional manager (in Los Angeles, Chicago, New York, and Dallas). Each region had from four to seven district managers, one or two distributor sales managers, and a home economist. The district managers, who were the field salespersons, were responsible for "direct market" sales in the major metropolitan areas. Forty percent of Litton's consumer sales were via this channel. The remaining 60 percent were through independent distributors in other markets. Distributor sales managers called on these accounts. The home economist handled product demonstrations.

Each independent distributor was called on once a month and was encouraged to purchase in accordance with a quarterly sales plan. District managers each handled between 30 and 40 accounts. They had to spend time with the dealer demonstrating microwave ovens, helping to plan the merchandizing of the products and training retail salespeople. Scheduling calls on accounts was entirely up to each district manager but the company insisted that all calls be preplanned. It ensured compliance via a monthly call report plan sent in advance to the regional manager. Follow up was done via daily call report sheets sent to the regional manager at the end of each week.

Finance

The Senior VP-Finance and Administration reported directly to Bill George. He did, however, have a "dotted line" relationship with Litton's corporate vice president for finance. Reporting to Litton Microwave's Senior VP-Finance were a Director of Business Planning, an Operations Controller, a General Controller, and a Director of Management Information Systems.

The Director of Business Planning was responsible for developing the details of the division's annual business plan. A distinction was made between the "sales plan" which represented the volume level that could be realized with "aggressive marketing" and "Plan I," a more conservative estimate for which corporate approval was sought.[3] Except for the engineering and sales departments, staffing authorization levels were based on the Plan I sales level rather than on the sales plan. Bill George explained the rationale for adopting this procedure:

---

[3] In fiscal 1976, for example, the sales plan level was $176 million and Plan I was $125 million. Actual sales in fiscal 1976 were $186 million.

We are staffing based on a conservative level of sales because if we staffed at the sales plan level and the projected increases of 60 percent–70 percent were not realized, we would have to lay people off. I believe management has a strong obligation not to lay people off. That is one of the reasons I admire the management at IBM—they haven't had a layoff in 37 years.

In January of 1976 a new manpower planning and flexible budgeting procedure had been introduced. Essentially, function heads were asked to estimate their staffing requirements for several revenue levels, e.g., $250, $350, and $500 million rather than at Plan I levels only. It was hoped that this procedure would make it easier and quicker to obtain additional staffing authorization as the business grew. In the past, function heads had been reluctant to seek "budget exceptions." When they did, it usually took some time to justify the need for additional personnel and obtain approval. The flexible budgeting procedure did not constitute a staffing approval but was designed to expedite such approval by forcing function heads to look ahead and anticipate their staffing needs at various volume levels. Except in engineering and sales, staffing authorization at the beginning of the fiscal year continued at Plan I level.

Litton Microwave was audited annually by a "big eight" CPA firm. Because this audit took three months in fiscal 1976, the division was contemplating installing a position of internal auditor to cover both financial and operational auditing.

International

Exports of consumer countertop ovens and commercial units to Canada and several industrialized nations in Europe accounted for approximately ten percent of the company's total revenue. There were no assembly operations outside the United States.

At the beginning of fiscal 1976 Litton mounted an ambitious effort to carve a niche for itself in the Japanese market, which at the time was the largest market for microwave ovens in the world. An office was opened in Tokyo with a Japanese executive as senior managing director. The division's finance manager, who had developed the Japanese plan, was designated managing director. The market failed to grow as rapidly as anticipated and sales did not reach forecasted levels. The company could not establish adequate distribution in that country. Some blamed this on the senior managing director who was in overall charge as general manager and marketing head, arguing that he had not been aggressive enough. In late 1976, Litton was looking for a new Japanese executive to take over the business.

Human resources

The presence of a human resources department at the same organizational level as operations, finance, engineering, and marketing gave formal recognition to Bill George's conviction that human resources were every bit as important as physical, fiscal, technological, and market resources. Human resource managers were assigned to work with each of the functions, with responsibility for all the people issues in that function. Each function was responsible for hiring, performance review, compensation, promotion, and termination decisions in its own area. The human resources manager assigned to that function provided staff assistance. In addition, the department of human resources handled team building sessions, training, and career development.

Team building. The task team concept used at Litton Microwave had its beginning in the team-building program which Bill George initiated soon after becoming executive vice president of the division in August 1971. The program began with a series of off-site seminars with the top management group, conducted by Doug Baker, a local consultant. The purpose of the program was to develop the general management skills of top managers and facilitate communication between the various functions. A variety of learning devices was used, including an exercise written especially for the company, general management case studies, and a questionnaire on organization issues. Reflecting on these sessions, Bill George observed:

Particular attention was directed to my management style and to my willingness or unwillingness to delegate greater decision-making authority. The inputs from these sessions helped me adapt my style to the needs of the emerging organization.

The initial program was so successful that it was extended to all managers within the company and expanded to include a broad range of organizational development activities. Soon after Bill George was promoted to president of the division in August 1973 he convinced Doug Baker, the outside consultant, to join the company on a full-time basis to set up the human resources function and to extend the team-building program throughout the division. (See Exhibit 7).

As of October 1976, all five function heads and several managers reporting to these heads had held team-building sessions for their own groups. The top four levels of management had met several times for group team-building sessions. In addition, the team concept had been spread to other levels of the organization through a series of meetings involving all employees—crew meetings held by unit managers, dialogue sessions between the president and 12–15 employees at various organizational levels,

Exhibit 7
Organizational development at Litton Microwave

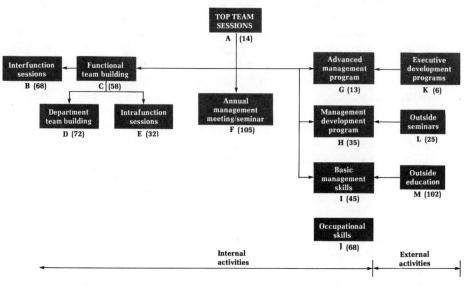

Note: Numbers in parentheses indicate the number of people that participated in each of the activities during fiscal 1976.

* Explanatory notes keyed to alphabetical designations:

A. Team building sessions for president and functional heads.
B. Team building sessions involving managers from two different functions. One day or less in duration.
C. Functional head and the department managers reporting to the functional head. One day or less in duration.
D. Department head and key managers reporting to the department head. One day or less in duration.
E. Team building sessions involving a functional head, department managers, and other managers in the functional area. One day or less in duration.
F. President, functional heads, department managers, and lower level managers. One day in duration. Dealing with issues of organization, use of time, etc. Frequently involved an outside consultant.
G. Functional heads and key managers. Six days spread over several weeks using a couple of outside consultants. Dealt with "high level" managerial skills.
H. Orientation program for new managers. Three and a half days in duration.
I. First-line supervisors. Four and a half days in duration. Interpersonal skills and leadership training.
J. Secretarial and factory personnel (e.g., fork-lift truck operators). One to three days in duration.
K. Such as Harvard's two-week summer programs (e.g., Management of Organizational Effectiveness, Production Management, etc.).
L. Such as American Management Association's one- or two-day programs for management development.
M. Tuition reimbursement for evening courses.

quarterly business reviews for production and office workers, and other meetings. A recent addition by the Human Resources department was interaction sessions between two functions. Five to ten key managers from each function got together for a day to identify and work on overcoming barriers between them. The top management group continued off-site team-building sessions about twice a year.

The meetings at the various organizational levels amounted to a considerable investment of time not only for Bill George (who spent in excess of 75 percent of his working time in all types of meetings) but for other managers as well. Many individuals, including all of top management, believed that this investment of time had been instrumental in fostering a feeling of openness and "one-ness" within the company and had played a crucial role in the company's dramatic success. Comments such as the following were common:

Jealousy is almost nonexistent in this company. Individuals feel free to share their problems and frustrations with others.

There is very little "politics." People are open and direct rather than scheming and spiteful.

Although most credited the team-building sessions with developing the feeling of openness, there were some skeptics. One engineering manager commented on the team-building sessions:

Jobs are growing faster than people. How do you handle those without the needed horsepower as the job grows? Training programs can help, but Human Resources needs to first get their own show together and then begin to do more follow-up with other functions. Last month, for example, we had a three-day meeting of all eight engineering department heads. The Human Resources manager was invited to come along but it was a meeting arranged at our initiative and by us. It went very well.

Recruitment, selection, and training. Human Resources had to spend a great deal of time in recruiting and staffing the ever increasing number of positions to be filled. The hiring market for experienced engineers and first-line supervisors was extremely tight and these positions were hard to fill. Most of the recruiting was done in the Midwest. The division's location in Minneapolis-St. Paul proved to be a selling point in recruiting. Several individuals who had been recently hired commented on how pleased they were with their new community. A typical comment was the following:

It is a great place to raise a family. We have good schools, clean air, low crime, and plenty of activities outdoors. The Twin Cities metropolitan area also provides excellent cultural events.

Many people who had initial reservations liked the Minneapolis-St. Paul area once they moved in and settled. Several of those recently hired were either from the area originally or had lived there before and had chosen to return.

The selection process was generally perceived as being effective. Even those who regretted the numbers of people that were being brought in from outside to fill top jobs agreed that those hired were capable and productive. A recently hired unit manager observed:

The selection process is as thorough as I have seen it anywhere. I was interviewed on four different occasions, including sessions with Doug Baker (VP-Human Resources), Ron March (Manager of Human Resources—Operations Area), Steve Dill (the recruiter), and Paul Westgard (VP-Operations).

Several managers, especially those in operations and engineering, complained bitterly about the length of time it took to fill key positions. One of them in operations remarked:

It has sometimes taken six months to fill supervisory and managerial positions under me and I have had to raise holy hell with Human Resources.

A manager in engineering echoed the same theme:

The average time taken to fill authorized staff openings in engineering is six months. It should take no longer than three months in spite of the relatively tight job market in engineering.

The lag in hiring in fiscal 1976 was generally attributed to the inability of the Human Resources department to fill requests for staff as rapidly as was necessary because they were themselves lean on staff. In July 1976, Bill George gave permission to greatly expand the employment department within the Human Resources function.

An issue related to staffing concerned the bringing in of outsiders to fill high positions. During the past three years, 43 percent of all managerial openings had been filled by hiring from the outside. The remaining positions were filled by promotions from within the division. Managers who were passed over in filling new openings felt doubly frustrated. They were not being promoted on the one hand and had to run lean on the other hand. Bill George was well aware of this predicament:

Above-average performers have problems when we bring people in from the outside to fill positions that they aspire to. We like to promote from within whenever possible but I do not believe in putting people in positions for which they are not qualified. With our rapid growth we have to be sure the individual can handle the position in two or three years when it will likely double in size and complexity.

We should do more to help our people develop. For example, by providing lateral moves when promotion is not possible. But the rapid growth we are experiencing prevents us from promoting as much as we would like to from within.

The large influx of people from the outside presented the division with the problem of socializing the newcomers and bringing them up to speed rapidly. Hard data on the length of tenure of the average non-hourly employee at Litton Microwave were not available but estimates varied between 12 and 18 months for the nonmanagerial staff, and between 18 and 24 months for the 180 managerial employees.

New hires were given a general orientation by Human Resources, with sessions from one to three days in duration, depending on their level in the organization. Those at higher levels were given longer sessions. Most new recruits found these sessions to be very useful. One manager who had been recently hired commented:

> The company is extremely open to the newcomer and that helps speed up the socialization process. But we need a more formalized training program for new hires. At present, the company uses on-the-job training only. Some form of job rotation training would help.

Doug Baker, Vice President of Human Resources, responded as follows:

> Every new managerial employee participates in a three-and-a-half-day off-site team-building seminar no later than six months after joining us. The seminar has a very strong orientation flavor and involves about 18–25 persons who are new to their jobs, to Litton Microwave, or both. It would be nice to have a formalized training program that goes beyond this, but we cannot afford that luxury. We run a tight ship and a fast pace around here and on-the-job training provides the most efficent means of getting a new employee up to speed.

Career development.   In early 1976, a comprehensive career development program was introduced along with the manpower planning and flexible budgeting procedure. The program was aimed at developing the management, professional, and staff capabilities required to support the growing needs of the company. It brought together the career desires and interests of the individual with the future job requirements identified in the annual manpower planning process. At the heart of the program was a job posting system to enable the individual to participate actively in his or her own career planning. Although the career development program was generally well received, both employees and management had some concerns. Employees felt they did not always get a good explanation of why they weren't selected for a given position they had sought. Some top managers, including Bill George, were concerned about employees and young managers developing unrealistic expectations about just how much a growth company could offer in terms of career opportunities. Because of this "fear of unrealistic expectations," one department head chose not to discuss with his subordinates potential career paths and openings he had in mind for them in advance of their actual appointment to these positions.

Performance evaluation.   The evaluation program was used both as a communication and counseling tool in performance planning, and as a basis for performance evaluation. Its specific objectives were: (1) to achieve an understanding with the employee as to what is expected, how expectations are being met, and ways to improve performance, (2) to establish a written record of employee accomplishments, future job expectations, training and development needs, and career goals, and (3) to provide the manager a means of rating the employee's overall performance as a primary consideration for salary purposes. There was a general sense of satisfaction with the performance evaluation program.

Rewards. Employees generally described the pay scales as being "competitive, but not great." However, several persons felt a sense of intrinsic satisfaction in working at Litton Microwave, and saw a potential for considerable pay-off from the company's growth in the future (e.g., in the form of growing responsibilities and career advancement opportunities).

Most of the professional and managerial personnel were paid a straight salary. Only a few key employees were selected for participation in an incentive compensation program tied to individual contribution and company profitability. Selection criteria included: (1) scope of managerial responsibility (generally department heads and above qualified), (2) relative level of earnings, and (3) the individual's potential contribution to division profits.

Those selected for the incentive compensation program were advised of their eligibility at the beginning of the fiscal year and informed of their "base award percentage" (i.e., percentage of the individual's annual base salary that would be paid as incentive compensation). The actual base award percentage used in computing incentives was dependent on the level of actual pre-tax profit achieved (no awards were made if profits fell below 85 percent of Plan I target) and was tied explicitly to the individual's performance rating. Those in the marketing area participated in a similar program except that the base award percentage was influenced equally by the ability to meet profit and sales targets.

THE SITUATION IN OCTOBER 1976

A University of Minnesota research team had conducted an employee attitude survey of all nonunion employees at Litton Microwave in May 1976. Using the results of this survey, a number of feedback sessions were conducted during August and September of 1976. The purpose of these sessions was to feed the results of the survey back to the employees and to ask them to define specific problems and solutions.

The substantive issues raised by most groups during these feedback sessions revolved around questions of delegation, staffing, and compensation. The delegation issue was expressed as a general employee perception that not enough decision-making authority was delegated downward to allow middle managers the latitude necessary for solving the problems of a rapidly growing organization. The inadequate staffing situation was generally attributed to budgeting based on too conservative a level of sales. The compensation issue was primarily manifested in the form of unmet employee expectations and a feeling that individual contributions to divisional success were not properly recognized. These findings were presented to Bill George and the various function heads by the research team on October 4, 1976.

In a memo to all function heads dated October 22, 1976, Bill George described in detail the areas requiring review and approval by various executives (Exhibit 8) and ended with the following paragraph:

Comments we receive from middle management indicate to me that this delegation system (and its intentions) is not well understood by them. I hope you will take advantage of this opportunity to review the delegation within your function, develop the delegation of authority and responsibility to get the job done, yet retain control for yourself of the most crucial areas.

The University of Minnesota survey had indicated that some employees attributed the delegation problem to the management level immediately above them. Others, however, pointed higher. Bill George responded:

We are delegating not out of necessity as growth occurs but as management talent develops and broadens its outlook.

When I took over this division back in 1971, my first order of priority was to build a strong top management team. We did that by 1973. Since then we have been concentrating on the middle management level. With the actions to date, this area is now okay in my view. Our need today is for building a strong first-line supervisory level.

Overall, the key issue is managing growth under control. Our growth has not only been high over a long period of time, it is in a technologically complex business. Rapid growth in a simple business like the manufacture of metal chairs is one thing. Continuing rapid growth in a business requiring constant innovation is a different game altogether. About 90 percent of our products are new every year!

Looking to the future in October of 1976, Bill George was wondering whether a change in structure to a product line organization would help alleviate some of the difficulties the division was experiencing. Under this arrangement, each major product line (range, commercial, and countertop) would be headed by a "mini general manager" with the appropriate engineering, marketing, operations, and human resources personnel reporting directly to him or her. Such a change would thus represent a major reorganization.

Bill George had given serious consideration to this alternative earlier

Exhibit 8

Areas Requiring Review (R) and Approval (A) by Various Executives
Fiscal Year 1977

	Presi-dent	President mktg./sales division	VP & GM Intl*	Function head	Sr. VP finance and admin.	VP human resources
A. Hiring						
1. *Requisitions*						
In Plan I, approved sales plan or flexible budget				A		R
Head count or budget exceptions	A			A		A
2. *Salary offers*						
$24,000 base salary and up	A			A		A
$15,000–$24,000				A		A
3. *Interviews*						
Managers on I.C. or mktg. comm.	A			A		A
B. SALARY/COMPENSATION						
1. *Salary increases*						
$24,000 and up	A			A		A
$15,000–$24,000				A		A
2. *Incentive compensation or marketing commission*						
Eligibility	A	A	A	A		R
Payout	A	A	A	A		R
3. *Sales commissions*						
Plan		A	A		A	A
Payout						
C. JOB CLASSIFICATIONS						
1. *New positions and changes in existing positions*						
Grade 60 and above	A			A		A
Grade 59 and below				A		A
D. BUDGETS						
1. Plan I	A			A	A	
2. *Budget exceptions*						
Advertising						
In sales plan		A			R	
Above sales plan	A	A			A	
Department						
In approved sales plan or flexible budget				A	R	
Exempt managers	A			A	R	
Other than exempt managers					A	R
Not in approved sales plan or flexible budget	A				A	
3. *Budget transfers* (Other than Adv.)						
Over $25,000	A			A	A	
Under $25,000				A	A	

Exhibit 8 (*continued*)

		Presi-dent	President mktg./sales division	VP & GM Intl*	Function head	Sr. VP finance and admin.	VP human resources
	4. *Advertising budget Transfers*						
	Over $100,000	A	A			A	
	Under $100,000		A			A	
E.	CAPITAL AND TOOLING EXPENDITURES						
	1. *Within department* Plan I Budget						
	$25,000 and up	A			A	A	
	$10,000–$25,000				A	A	
	2. *Above Department* Plan I Budget						
	Above $10,000	A			A	A	
	Under $10,000				A	A	
F.	ENGINEERING PROJECTS In Plan I						
	$15,000 and up	A			A		
	Under $15,000				A		
	Not in Plan I Over $5,000	A			A		
	Under $5,000				A		
G.	MARKETING PROGRAMS						
	1. Marketing plans (Annual)	A	A	A		R	
	2. *National advertising* Creative concept	A	A				
	Budget Media schedules		A				
	Creative implementation		A				
	3. *Sales promotions* In Plan I/Sales Plan Budget						
	$300,000 and up	A	A	A		R	
	Under $300,000		A	A		R	
	Not in Plan I/Sales Plan Budget						
	$30,000 and up	A	A	A		A	
	Under $30,000		A	A		A	
H.	PRICING						
	1. Suggested list prices	A	A	A		A	
	2. New discount schedules	A	A	A		A	
	3. Price exceptions		A	A			
	4. Customer classifications		A	A			
I.	WARRANTIES						
	1. Revisions to terms	A	A	A		A	
J.	TERMS OF SALES		A	A		A	
K.	COMPUTER PROJECTS (Major)						
	1. In Plan I					A	
	2. Not in Plan I	A				A	

Exhibit 8 (*concluded*)

	Presi-dent	President mktg./sales division	VP & GM Intl*	Function head	Sr. VP finance and admin.	VP human resources
L. *12-MONTH PRODUCTION PLAN*	R			A (VP Ops)	R	
M. *PURCHASE ORDERS* Over $500,000				A(VP Ops)		
N. *PRESS RELEASES* National	A	A	A			
Local Trade		A	A			
O. *PRODUCT PLANNING AND DEVELOPMENT* Product plans	A	A	A	R (VP Engr)		
Feature decisions	A	A	A	A (VP Engr)		
Styling	R	A	A	R (VP Engr)		
Major technical decision	R			A (VP Engr)		
Schedules	A	R	R	A (VP Engr)		
				R (VP Ops)		
Costs	R	R	R	A (VP Engr)		
				R (VP Ops)		

* Outside the United States.

but had decided against it for two main reasons. First, he had felt that the size of the division was not large enough to make a product-line organization economically viable. Second, he had felt that the needed management talent just wasn't available. Now that the company was much larger and top management was built up, Bill George was once again weighing the relative advantages of moving to a product-line organization:

> *In this business, the key organization question is how one achieves integration between the functions. Delegating authority within a given function is relatively easy to do. Achieving the necessary coordination across the various functions is much more difficult. So far, I have played that key role, with much of the integration at lower levels being carried out by task team leaders. We are now reaching the point at which we may need four or five top-level integrators like myself. I am wondering whether a move to a product-line organization will help achieve the necessary cross functional coordination in the most efficient manner.*

Reading 8–1
Organization development*
Raymond E. Miles

Much of the organizational behavior literature discusses circumstances under which managers may wish to redesign jobs, move toward a more participative style of supervision or decision making, attempt to realign the structures of their organizations to meet changing environmental conditions, or adopt different approaches for reducing conflict. These discussions imply that changing any of these organizational features is an extremely complex process involving a host of individual and situational variables and that change in any one area—for example, job design, leadership, interdepartmental conflict—has implications for all the others. How, then, are such changes to be made?

The answer that has been voiced most frequently over the past ten years is OD—Organization Development, a term which has swept into prominence perhaps as pervasively as did "human relations" and "participative management" in earlier eras. Broadly defined as the effort to improve organizational effectiveness through long-term, planned, systematic applications of behavioral science knowledge and techniques with the collaborative aid of skilled consultants, OD has a complex lineage. While some key components of the OD movement (e.g., sensitivity training and action research) can be traced back to the 1940s, the term Organization Development itself was probably not used with any distinct meaning until the late fifties, and much of the broader conceptualization associated with the movement has occurred within the last ten years (French and Bell, 1973, chap. 3). Numerous academic programs and courses focusing on OD have emerged within the last few years and the final academic annointment—the appearance of textbooks using Organization Development in their title—occurred in the 1969 Addison-Wesley Series (Beckhard, 1969; Bennis, 1969; Blake and Mouton, 1969; Lawrence and Lorsch, 1969; Schein, 1969; Walton, 1969).

Despite its youth, however, and despite the lack of substantial hard evidence attesting to its value, OD has already acquired most of the accoutrements of an established field. Many leading firms and agencies have OD departments (French and Bell, 1973), practitioners have their own accrediting agency, the field is represented by several professional

---

* Reprinted by permission from George Strauss et al., eds., *Organizational Behavior: Research and Issues.* © 1974 by Industrial Relations Research Association.

associations and divisions (Friedlander and Brown, 1974, p. 314; French and Bell, 1973, pp. 28–29), and the Conference Board has prepared two bulletins surveying prominent OD accomplishments (Rush, 1969, 1973). Perhaps most significantly, it is becoming increasingly common in articles, in texts (Margulies and Raia, 1972; French and Bell, 1973), and in reviews (Friedlander and Brown, 1974) to find established areas of concern such as leadership, job design, conflict resolution, etc., incorporated within the framework of OD theory and concepts.

OD is thus an evolving field whose boundaries and issues are not yet precisely defined. In this chapter, therefore, we attempt to define OD, outline and trace the origins of its major approaches and their underlying theories, consider the major criticisms which have been raised, and weigh the available empirical evidence as to its utility.

Three major OD approaches

While I will argue below that OD in practice seldom matches the definition cited earlier, three approaches incorporating many of these "ideal" characteristics have been designed. It may be useful to look briefly at these as illustrations of the scope and methods of OD efforts before we turn to a comprehensive discussion of the issues.

The Managerial Grid. The Grid approach (Blake and Mouton, 1968) is based largely on a "style" of management which attempts to jointly maximize concern for production and concern for people. (The "Grid" itself refers to a graph with two perpendicular axes, each of which is marked off in nine intervals. One axis is labeled "concern for people" and the other "concern for production." An ideal manager is one who rates high on both scales; that is, one who is at the 9.9 position on the graph.) Building on this framework, instruments and exercises have been developed through which managers can appraise their own managerial styles. In addition, the exercises permit managers to receive feedback from and provide feedback to their peers concerning these appraisals. These analyses and discussions, plus training in problem solving, communication, and group process skills are included in Phase 1 of the six-phase Grid OD program, which moves from development of the immediate work group to improvement of intergroup processes, to an organization-wide improvement plan, to the implementation of this plan, and finally to a review of the total effort and planning for new action steps.

Survey feedback. The survey feedback approach, pioneered and developed at the Survey Research Center at the University of Michigan, is built around the collection and discussion of perceptual and attitudinal data concerning organizational processes and relationships between and across hierarchical levels. The first step in this approach involves orienting

he top management group and obtaining their support along with that
f various internal "resource" persons (change agents). Following this,
reparations are made for the administration of a detailed questionnaire
o employees at all levels. Survey findings are processed so that the data
or each work group are available only to that group. Feedback of these
lata is handled on a group-by-group basis in sessions run by the group
eader with the assistance of an outside consultant (Mann, 1961). Feedback
s intended to stimulate discussion of the work group's behavior and to
uggest areas for immediate action or further analysis. Subsequent admin-
strations of the questionnaire provide opportunities for measuring im-
rovement on key behavioral dimensions both within and between work
roups.

Team training. The system-wide team development approach pro-
ides "group problem-solving" and "interpersonal process" training for
work teams throughout an organization. Utilizing a variety of techniques,
team development specialists lead a superior and his immediate subordinates through analyses of "how" and "why" they relate to one another
as they do as they carry out their work assignments. The focus is on
identification of and removal of barriers (e.g., unexpressed feelings, mis-
communications, conflicting priorities, etc.) to effective performance and
the development of behavior patterns which will aid the group in dealing
with present and future problems.

Advocates of this approach (Schein, 1969; Davis, 1967) argue that team
development training and consultation should usually begin with the top
executive teams and then flow down the hierarchy. With high-level groups,
it is typical for the outside consultant first to interview top managers
and then to use data gathered from these interviews to stimulate discussion of group processes in one or more initial training sessions. The consultant then meets regularly with the group as they address current organizational problems, "intervening" to encourage insight and learning
concerning the ongoing dynamics of the group. As the program moves
toward lower levels, training efforts usually become shorter and more
heavily structured (i.e., they take on the appearance of traditional leadership training courses) and more use is made of "inside" OD consultants—
members of the organization's OD department or training staff.

A synthesized example. In order to visualize these approaches in action (and capture their common features) consider the following synthesized example:

A top manager of organization A hears about a presumably successful utilization of behavioral science concepts and techniques in another firm. He arranges
a meeting with (or attends a seminar held by) the consultant involved and is
further intrigued (convinced, sold). He and the consultant plan an initial conference
(meeting; seminar, learning session, demonstration) with the executive team of

organization A. Entry of the OD effort thus occurs at or near the top of the organization with a level of involvement (and, hopefully, a level of understanding) that
goes well beyond that associated with most training and development programs.
Out of these initial meetings a *change strategy* emerges (jointly designed or simply
approved) which may begin with either the top executive team or some other
receptive unit or department.

Change strategies vary around a central theme—data on attitudes toward and
perceptions of current policies, practices, and processes are collected ("surfaced")
through interviews, questionnaires, group meetings, or experiential learning formats and are discussed and analyzed by the group involved with the aid of the
consultant (who frequently provides an interpretive framework of concepts and
theory). These data and their discussion provide targets for change which may
include individual or group behaviors which impede decision making or coordination, role pressures or reporting relationships which have dysfunctional consequences, policies which require rethinking, etc. The group, with the aid of the
consultant, determines how these changes will be introduced, implemented, and
evaluated. Evaluation may include further data collection at periodic intervals,
a series of sequenced review and planning sessions, or some other *sustaining
mechanism*.

By this point, an internal OD group or department has frequently been created
(developed, expanded), and OD work in subsequent areas (usually modeled after
the initial efforts) may rely heavily on these resources, with the outside consultant
returning for planning (and learning sessions) with top management and with
the internal OD staff.

BASIC OD CONCEPTS

The Managerial Grid, survey feedback, and team training represent
only three of the more advanced and widely known OD approaches. In
practice, the term OD is regularly applied to a host of training and development activities which fit only *poorly* my definition of "real" OD, including
traditional programs such as classroom training for middle managers and
the use of standardized job satisfaction surveys. In some organizations
new high-level groups have been formed which are headed by heavily
credentialed professionals (frequently Ph.D.'s) with substantial experience
in one or more approaches to system-wide development; in others, however, the scrape of a blade and a few strokes of a lettering brush have
transformed what were previously known as management training departments into "OD units" without other changes. Most OD practitioners have
their own set of prescriptive concepts, definitions, and change or training
strategies. To this point, the field has applied far more energy to the
development of techniques than to the structuring of descriptive theory
and research.

Nevertheless, out of the confusing array of techniques, approaches, and concepts labeled OD there seem to be some emerging areas of agreement, especially as to (1) the kind of organization OD should develop, (2) the critical necessity of change, (3) the means to be utilized in effecting change, and (4) the role of OD consultants.

The normative model of effective management

As French and Bell (1973) note, the assumptions, values, and concepts of Argyris (1962), Likert (1967), Maslow (1970), McGregor (1960, 1967), and others have become an integral part of the OD literature. Out of the writings of these theorists has been gleaned not only a common image of the main processes characterizing an ideal organization but also a set of specific, desirable underlying behavioral mechanisms. For example, trusting, open relationships are viewed as essential to meaningful participation in decision making and goal setting. Similarly, the provision of nonevaluative feedback and the sharing of feelings as well as thoughts and facts are deemed crucial to cooperative, self-directed performance. Further, openness to feedback and the willingness to confront issues are required if conflicts are to be creatively and thoroughly resolved.

While various terms have been used to identify the end state toward which OD aspires—for example, a "Theory Y" organization (McGregor, 1960, 1967) or a "System IV" organization (Likert, 1961, 1967)—the key dimensions are seldom dissimilar. For many if not most OD theorists and practitioners, OD is development toward an organization characterized by wide employee participation in decision making and goal setting, individual and group self-direction and self-control based on jointly decided goals and objectives, and creative resolution of conflict between and across hierarchical levels—a setting which is expected to provide the opportunity for individual growth and fulfillment while at the same time removing barriers to effective performance. . . .

Turbulent environments and the necessity of OD

A second area of convergence among OD theorists relates to OD's justification. The environment, as they see it, is becoming increasingly turbulent and this, they argue, makes it especially important that organizations adopt the kinds of structure and processes mentioned above. As do open-systems theorists (Burns and Stalker, 1961; Emery and Trist, 1965), OD writers tend to believe that the linkages among the elements in most organizational environments are becoming more numerous and more complex, that the rate of change in environmental conditions is increasing, and that traditional bureaucratic structures are becoming less and less adequate. It is argued that new and more adaptive structures and processes are required and that these in turn demand new levels of interpersonal skill and awareness which OD can best provide.

As mentioned earlier, Bennis (1966) went beyond most of his predecessors, holding that changing organizational environments and societal values doomed all bureaucratic organizations to extinction within a few decades. Bennis (1969) completed the argument a few years later in his pioneering book on OD by stating that "basically, organization development is one of the few educational programs I know of that has the potential to create an institution vital enough to cope with the unparalleled changes ahead" (p. 82). Some variation of this theme appears in most recent OD texts (e.g., French and Bell, 1973, pp. 197–200), which imply an urgent need for fundamental changes in organizational systems, their components, and their relationships, a sweeping mandate not claimed by earlier management and employee development proponents.

Achieving effective management through training

There is a third area of convergence in OD writing: a faith in the value of training as a means of obtaining the changes desired. OD can be viewed as an outgrowth from what had previously been known as "management training and development." The techniques now associated with OD—such as those discussed earlier—have themselves developed over the years, in part as a result of trial and error, as training and development experts struggled to make their programs more effective. For this reason a brief history of organizational training and development efforts may help put OD in perspective.

Technical and human relations training. In the early part of this century, training efforts were aimed almost exclusively at the shop-floor level and at the immediate job skills required to operate an emerging rationalized organizational technology. The bulk of the training was done on the job, augmented by apprenticeship programs incorporating some classroom sessions.

Once the organizational structure was operating, attention turned to maintaining it—keeping friction down and promoting stable performance. With this need, the training spotlight moved up a rung on the organizational ladder and focused on the foreman or first-line supervisor. Beginning in the twenties and thirties and expanding dramatically during World War II, the bulk of this training effort focused on human relations problems—leadership, discipline, the handling of complaints and grievances, etc. Much of this training was carried out in classroom settings, and as effective performance in these areas required major changes in the trainees' attitudes and behavior, it quickly became apparent that training approaches other than the traditional lecture and discussion modes would be required. Case studies, and later role-playing situations, were early products of this search for more intensive forms of training and gained wide usage in the forties and fifties. However, research on the efficacy of these training efforts soon documented a second dilemma that has proven to be strong and persistent—the problem of transferring changes in attitude and behaviors from the training sites (e.g., the classroom) back into the work setting. While supervisors might learn to express consideration toward their subordinates during a leadership training course, once out of the supportive atmosphere of the classroom and back on the job, a supervisor's attitudes and behaviors might well revert back to whatever pleases his boss (Fleishman, 1953).

Management training. While the problems of how to change supervisory behavior and transfer these changes back to the work setting were being debated, major development attention began to shift upward again. In many organizations, work procedures at the lower levels had long been rationalized, and the line was at least being held with regard to work group problems. The most visible problems were no longer those of building and maintaining large-scale production processes but the coordination of increasingly complex organizations and the facilitation of orderly growth. Thus, while training of rank-and-file employees and their supervisors continued to expand in scope and quality, the leading edge of training and development efforts moved into the middle and upper management ranks.

Reflecting this shift in attention, executive development programs spread through major universities across the country during the fifties. The purpose of these usually lengthy (three weeks to six months) programs was to increase the manager's awareness of and ability to respond to the increasing complexity of his organizational world; their curricula included both human relations topics and new techniques for planning and problem solving.

Sensitivity training. Paralleling these developments, a group of psychologists (most notably Kurt Lewin, Kenneth Benne, Leland Bradford, and Ronald Lippitt) were also experimenting with new training approaches aimed specifically at increasing awareness and responsiveness to immediate interpersonal relations. Working from a base of theory and experience created by Kurt Lewin (Marrow, 1969), these psychologists argued that the improvement of interpersonal skills required attitudinal and behavioral changes that could best be accomplished through experiential learning in unstructured "laboratory" settings, where the participant's own behavior served as the curriculum. Out of these experiments was born the T-group (the "T" is for training) (Bradford, 1967; Bradford, Gibb, and Benne, 1964), perhaps the most influential training development in recent decades and the cause of a least a minor social movement.

The original T-group design called for 10–12 participants (called "stranger" groups) from different work or life arenas and one or more "trainers," psychologists skilled in intrapersonal and interpersonal dynamics. Participants gathered in an informal setting with no set agenda of activities—a purposely created vacuum which their own behaviors were to fill. These behaviors then became topics for consideration by the group. Group members were encouraged, by discussion and by the behavior of the trainer, to provide open, direct feedback to one another concerning their "here and now" feelings and responses. Such feedback fulfilled the "unfreezing" step of Lewin's three-phase change model which called for "unfreezing" old attitudes and behaviors, "changing," and then "refreezing" the newly adopted patterns. That is, members first receive feedback which frequently "disconfirms" the image they hold of themselves and how others respond to them. This feedback, hopefully, then motivates them to search for alternative behaviors to which more positive responses will be forthcoming—the "change" phase in the Lewinian model. If new behaviors are positively reinforced by the group, then the final Lewinian phase is accomplished—the new behaviors are "refrozen."

Organization executives followed teachers and counselors as T-group participants, and through the fifties and sixties the T-group phenomenon spread in ever varying formats (Strauss, in press; Back, 1974) across the country and across occupational, sex, and status categories—housewives in Texas, ministers in Kansas, and ex-drug addicts in California attempted to help one another gain insights into themselves and their impacts on others and to experiment with behaviors which were more effective and rewarding.

Almost from the beginning, the T-group movement came under criticism on two counts. The first of these was the charge that T-groups might well be too powerful—that participants risked real emotional damage from direct feedback, unmediated by the usual social amenities, concerning their attitudes and behavior (Odiorne, 1962; Strauss, in press). Allied with this indictment was the charge that even for those for whom T-group training did not prove unhealthy, it was still immoral. That is, this criticism holds that organizations have no right to "brainwash" members' basic attitudes and values—to manipulate changes in their patterns of relating to others and thus in their total life style. This criticism notes that there are few true volunteers for attitudinal and behavioral training— that most members are at least subtly coerced into attendance and even more subtly led to the belief that they have freely chosen new attitudes and behaviors.

T-group advocates responded that participants, under the guidance of an accomplished trainer, might well be in less emotional danger during supportive training sessions than in their typical work-life space (McGregor, 1967). Further, they argued, if training is mandatory and manipulative, it is little more so than any other aspect of managerial life—a process which always demands that the individual sacrifice some freedoms in the interest of effective joint action. Concern over possible damage from participation in a T-group continues to be raised periodically, particularly with regard to some of its more intensive variations and the frequent use of poorly qualified trainers. The concern over trainer qualification is widely acknowledged, and accrediting procedures are available (Friedlander and Brown, 1974, p. 314). Concern regarding the more exotic variants of the T-group format can only be verified or dispelled by major, difficult-to-design research which is unlikely to be forthcoming. Finally, the issue of manipulation has been repeatedly raised and has subsequently been applied to all OD activities. Most OD consultants are sensitive to this issue, as we shall see in a later section, but the underlying ethical questions remain unanswered.

A second, essentially unrefuted criticism holds that traditional T-group formats have not proved effective in providing a carryover of behavioral changes from the protective atmosphere of the training group and site to the harsh realities of the organizational world. More specifically this charge holds that there is little evidence of increased group and organizational effectiveness directly resulting from attitude and behavior changes acquired in T-group type sessions outside the organization (Campbell and Dunnette, 1968). This is essentially the same criticism that was leveled earlier at human relations courses for supervisors.

A number of early T-group supporters were concerned with this "transfer dilemma" and clearly recognized the difficulty that participants might have in maintaining their newly adopted posture of openness, directness, and willingness to acknowledge feelings as well as facts unless their peers, subordinates, and particularly their superiors were also trained along the same lines. Thus, in the 1950s McGregor, Shepard, Blake, and others took T-group concepts inside organizations and began working directly with actual superior-subordinate management teams (French and Bell, 1973, pp. 23–29). By the late sixties, traditional "stranger" T-groups had given way to "family groups" consisting of managers in a single or related set of departments. Greater concern was also shown for improving managers' relations with each other in their *managerial* roles, with less attention being given to individual feelings as such. (The critical question is whether managers can work together; whether they like or respect each other is a related but subsidiary consideration.) This new approach, which has been discussed above, is often called team training and is designed to minimize the transfer dilemma. Here the focus is on the work group as it deals with its ordinary, day-to-day problems, as the consultant seeks to direct the group members' attention to the kinds of social and psychological processes which may be preventing the group from reaching its maximum potential.

As a consequence of all these developments, today it is not uncommon to find organizations which may have moved step by step from the practice of sending individual executives to off-site T-groups, to the practice of placing numerous executives from different organization units in the same T-group, to the current practice of on-site team training (Davis, 1967; Rush, 1969).

Organization development. The training evolution took its most recent step with the growing recognition through the fifties and sixties of a broader, though more subtle, version of the transfer dilemma. The work team, like the individuals in it, is embedded in a larger system. And, just as individual attitudinal and behavioral changes acquired through intensive, experiential learning may be discouraged by the responses of other work group members, modifications in the attitudes and behavior of a work team may also be rejected by other organizational units and levels. A host of incidents in which work group development efforts were damaged if not destroyed by organizational forces external to the group (e.g., Strauss, 1955) led to widespread agreement among training specialists that the development target should not be the individual manager or even the work group, but must be the organization as a whole—thus the term, in its current meaning, Organization Development.

The role of the OD consultant

The final area of convergence relates to the role of the OD consultant. OD consultants have adopted a view of their role which differs greatly from that associated with many accepted consultancy practices. Traditional consultants frequently operate under what I have called the Syndicate Model (Strauss, 1973; Miles, in press). Under this model, someone in the organization "lets a contract" on some portion of the organization (other than his own). Unobtrusively clad outsiders arrive carrying the ominous tools of their trade, briefcases. Units (victims) are studied (cased), briefcases are opened and closed (the report is filed), and the outsiders leave as silently as they arrived. Frequently in their wake are missing names in the organization chart and perhaps major realignments of power and processes.

The new concept of consultancy rejects, in theory if not always in practice, the prescriptive, solution-oriented role of the traditional consultant. Instead, the OD consultant describes his role as (1) *collaboration,* working *with* the client rather than for him; (2) *research,* assisting the client in collecting the information necessary to diagnose and solve his *own* problems; and (3) *process expertise,* focusing on *how* decisions are made (the dynamics of work group behavior) rather than on the nature or quality of the decisions themselves (Schein, 1969; Bennis, 1969).

These values, as suggested, are built into the role of the T-group trainer, who is presumed to teach by example and by participating with the group, rather than by unilaterally diagnosing problems and prescribing solutions. Similarly, close ties can be seen between this emerging concept of consultancy and the role of the behavioral scientist engaged in "action research" (French and Bell, 1973, pp. 84–95)—action research that attempts to "bring together in a single cooperative adventure the skills and resources of both men of science and men of action . . ." (Lippitt, 1951, p. ix). The concept of action research crystallized in the 1940s—Kurt Lewin (1946) was again a leading figure—out of work in the area of ethnic and community relations. Complex attitudinal and behavioral phenomena, it was reasoned, could only be changed if they were understood—and understanding could be achieved only through collaborative research. The action researcher's role was defined as that of helping the client system (a community, a social work agency, an organization, etc.) to (1) assess existing patterns or attitudes, perceptions, and behavior (through interview, questionnaire, and observational methods); (2) set targets or goals for change or further learning; and (3) monitor (feedback) evidence related to progress toward these goals.

Note that in this role the behavioral scientist aids rather than directs; he gathers information for but does not determine action steps. Similarly, the OD consultant utilizes a full range of behaviorally sound techniques to help clients understand their own behavior and that of their organizational unit, surfacing unspoken concerns such as "no one listens to anyone else around here," or "priorities are never really made clear, we just guess and go."

Finally, since training and development efforts focus on the enhancement of the capabilities of organization members and groups, and since OD advocates hold that interpersonal skill turns largely on the extent to which trustworthiness, supportiveness, and openness are displayed, it follows that these behaviors must be key elements of the consultant's role. Therefore, if the new consultant is to gain and build trust, he must protect those he works with from damage (e.g., the work group being studied must have the right to decide how information collected about it will be used). He must share freely of all that he learns and knows, for his effectiveness does not center on the quality of *his* solutions to organizational problems but on the extent to which those he works with develop their own capabilities for solving present and future problems.

In practice, this new concept of consultancy is compromised by the consultant's own ego (his need to prove his expertise in solving as well as clarifying problems) and the demands of clients accustomed to the more comfortable roles prescribed in the traditional model (which allow them to delegate problem solving to the consultant and then simply accept or reject his solutions). Nevertheless, to the extent that the new model is approached in practice, it represents one of the most distinctive and unique features of Organization Development.

SOME AREAS FOR DEBATE

Is OD a distinct field?

Despite the accumulation of the paraphernalia associated with a field and despite considerable agreement among its supporters as to its aim and techniques, OD's first and continuing problem is that of proving that it represents something really new. Cynical observers allege that OD is little more than human relations, participative decision making, and management development banded together and marching under a new banner; OD advocates, in response, insist that OD is not merely a passing fad but a substantive, lasting field of research and practice (French and Bell, 1973, p. 198). Yet identifying the nature of this field is difficult.

If, for example, OD is defined simply in terms of techniques such as attitude surveys or participative/group problem-solving, then, according to the recent Conference Board survey, many organizations not listed by experts as involved in OD look much like their "OD" counterparts (Rush, 1973, pp. 18–41). On the other hand, if OD involves more than a specific set of techniques, as most of its advocates would argue, but is instead "a process," "a system of values," "applied behavioral science," etc. (Rush, 1973, p. 2; French and Bell, 1973, chap. 4), it is even more ephemeral and difficult to identify. Finally, if OD, as at least some of its proponents suggest, encompasses or can encompass all organizational change activities aimed at improving performance (Friedlander and Brown, 1974), it runs the risk of falling into the category of concepts such as "communications" which are so all-pervasive as to become almost useless, unless strictly delimited, for theory building or research.

The question of OD's identity as something distinct and different is one of more than merely academic or professional interest. OD, its supporters and critics agree, demands a level of managerial support (time and money) well beyond that given to "human relations" and other training movements and involvement which cannot be delegated or assigned to some staff unit or department and forgotten. This support and involvement is unlikely to occur if OD is viewed as simply this year's model of an old training vehicle.

At this point, there is probably no adequate response to the criticism that OD is essentially an amalgamation of earlier concepts and some variations on existing training techniques. The key leadership and decision-making models and concepts which OD attempts to implement on a system-wide basis have, as indicated above, been around for at least a decade and have been "sold" under a variety of titles other than OD. Moreover, these universalistic theories have come under heavy attack in recent years for their failure to take into account situational and individual differences (Perrow, 1972; Fiedler, 1967), a point to which we will return later.

Similarly, the principal development methods utilized in OD, particularly the T-group and its variants, are *(a)* no longer new and *(b)* were originally offered as techniques for developing *managers* rather than *organizations.* In fact, as stated above, one of the major difficulties faced by OD advocates is that of differentiating OD as a body of theory and practice from the change techniques it employs. The term Organization Development was probably first used by consultants employing variations of T-groups with existing management teams and has since been eagerly adopted by almost everyone who has engaged in any form of experiential training with one or more managers from any organization. Thus, to many, T-groups and OD are synonymous, and the criticism of and disillusionment with T-groups (now widespread in organizations and within the OD fraternity) carries over to OD. Finally, many OD practitioners are essentially technique-oriented and have continued the practice of referring to whatever training methods they are currently employing (at the moment it appears that transactional analysis (Rush and McGrath, 1973) is in vogue) as OD.

To further compound the problem of establishing OD's identity, the two distinguishing characteristics which apply somewhat exclusively to OD, the collaborative role of the OD consultant and the requirement of a long-term investment in the self-renewal capacity of the organization to meet changing environmental demands, are most often missing in OD practice. The typical OD activity in most organizations is still a training effort begun without the full, uninfluenced endorsement of all its participants and carried out by someone unlikely to have a long-term collaborative relationship with the individuals or unit involved. The image of consultant and client jointly defining problems and utilizing a wide range of behavioral science research techniques to generate and evaluate their solution is more often honored from the podium than in practice. To the extent that this is the case, it is difficult to defend the claim that OD is a special field existing apart from a collection of training activities. More-over, the same set of problems hampers efforts to demonstrate that OD, whatever it may be, is in fact helping to make organizations more effective.

Does OD deliver on its promises?

The question of whether OD leads to improved organizational perfor-mance is almost impossible to answer unless there is an agreed upon, sharply defined concept of what constitutes OD. The Weldon Company case illustrates this dilemma. In the midst of economic distress, the Wel-don Company, a sleepware manufacturer, was acquired by the Harwood Company, a competitor known for its highly participative management philosophy and for its sponsorship of behavioral science research. The new management embarked on an ambitious program to develop, or, if you will, redevelop the Weldon Company's work processes, control and reward systems, and other managerial processes. Subsequent to these efforts, there was a clear-cut change in the organization's "profile" toward Likert's System IV. These changes have been exhaustively documented by Marrow, Bowers, and Seashore (1967).

Nevertheless, even with this evidence in hand, it is difficult to obtain agreement that Weldon represents a triumph for OD. At Weldon, not only were a series of efforts made to change managerial attitudes and behaviors through experiential learning techniques, but in addition, equip-ment was updated, work procedures were revised, skill training was pro-vided for many work group members, and some poor performers were "weeded out" (discharged). The simultaneous change of so many variables made it impossible to identify separate effects, and thus unless the total effort, including changes in structure, process, procedure, rewards, person-nel, and managerial style is accepted as OD, then the Weldon data are open to a number of interpretations.

At the other extreme, efforts to measure the effects of more limited, "accepted" components of OD, such as team development, also tend to produce findings which are hard to interpret. Many of the components are difficult to define or to measure, a conceptual fuzziness which makes research much harder and also provides a built-in excuse for the OD man who fails to attain his objectives. It is very easy for him to claim that OD was unsuccessful in a given situation because the parties just didn't develop a sufficiently high degree of trust.

Case study evidence detailing attitudinal and behavioral changes, cou-pled in many instances with improved output and/or profit figures, have been offered in support of each of the major OD approaches described in the beginning of this review, i.e., Managerial Grid (Blake *et al.*, 1964), survey feedback (Marrow, Bowers, and Seashore, 1967; Waters, 1971), and team training (Davis, 1967, 1971). Case studies are highly vulnerable to criticism, however. They seldom provide adequate controls for Hawthorne effects and "external" causation. Moreover, most OD case studies have been carried out and reported by those involved with or supportive of the development efforts. Acknowledging these shortcomings, along with the fact that successes are probably reported more frequently than failures, it is still almost impossible to deny the fact that major performance improvements have accompanied many of these efforts. Friedlander and Brown (1974), reviewing a number of studies, conclude:

> Though none of the research designs is flawless, there is convergent evidence that group development activities affect participant attitudes and sometimes their behavior as well. These effects may also "spill over" in some fashion to other organization members. It remains unclear, however, what mechanisms operate in successful team development activities, or what critical conditions must be satisfied for successful generalization of learning outside the team, or what effects group development has on actual task performance (p. 329).

As Friedlander and Brown (1974) also point out, performance improvements may also come from non-OD approaches, and definitive research to fairly compare the efficacy of OD versus non-OD change efforts is extremely difficult, if not impossible, to design and carry out. This fact alone probably accounts for Kahn's (1973) critical assessment of the OD literature: "Of the 200 items in Franklin's (1973) bibliography of organizational development, only 25 percent include original quantitative data; the remaining 75 percent consist for the most part of opinions, narrative material, and theoretical fragments" (p. 4).

Which approach? These criticisms notwithstanding, if one believes that OD can and does produce desired attitudinal and behavior changes and performance results, the subsequent research question is which approach is most effective and/or efficient. Perhaps the most detailed analysis of various change techniques to date is that of Bowers (1973). His findings appear to indicate that the survey feedback approach and interpersonal-process consultation had more positive effects on the attitudes of organization members than did task process consultation and T-group related techniques. Moreover, survey feedback appeared to lead more directly to perceived changes in the total organization climate (decision making, communications, willingness to change, acceptance of influence from below, etc.) than did any of the other approaches, and perceptions of changes in these areas were, in turn, crucial to the success of any of the change techniques. Still, the question of whether each of the change techniques had an equal opportunity to succeed in the settings covered by the Bowers review cannot be answered definitively.

In sum, the evidence to date does not provide reliable answers to questions concerning OD's effectiveness or the comparative advantages which one OD approach or change technique may have over another. This is not an unusual situation, however, in the field of organizational behavior, where cause-effect relationships are extremely complex and where few concepts are ever definitively proven or rejected. Some measure of acceptance is evident, however, when the main thrust of criticism moves from a theory, concept, or approach as a whole to issues of its limitations or misapplications. On the basis of such evidence, the basic concept of OD may well be near acceptance, for much of the most recent criticism in and outside of the field has been directed at the variables which OD tends to neglect, most prominently structure and power and the question of under what conditions OD may be most successful. These criticisms are our next concern.

Structural change

Does OD give too little emphasis to structure? The question of whether and/or how OD leads to changes in organization structure is one of the most interesting issues facing the field today. Few of the OD critics have been as pointed in their comments regarding this concern as has one of its chief advocates, Warren Bennis, who states:

> I have yet to see an organization development program that uses an interventional strategy other than an interpersonal one, and this is serious when one considers that the most pivotal strategies of change in our society are political, legal, and technological . . . (Bennis, 1969, pp. 78–79).

While Bennis, who has never been known for excessive moderation, may overstate the case, it is clear that early OD advocates placed too much emphasis on the primacy of interpersonal (as opposed to structural) change strategies. As noted earlier, the OD consultant tends to reject the idea of prescribing structure and process changes, the solutions to organizational problems most often offered by traditional consultants. Instead, the original OD approach, stated or implied, was to attack attitudes and perceptions first, working toward actual changes in interpersonal behavior patterns; then, if necessary, changes in roles, procedures, and perhaps structure would follow as their need was recognized by enlightened organizational members. This was in direct opposition to the socio-technical approach which was emerging during the same period at the Tavistock Institute in England and which sought to work with organization members in the redesign of roles and man-machine systems, assuming that this would lead to. changes in attitudes and behavior (Trist and Bamforth, 1951; Rice, 1958).

More importantly, perhaps, the emphasis on interpersonal issues has appeared "soft" and ambiguous, in the face of a rebirth of interest in structural determinancy—the search for lawful relationships between types of task environments, types of technology, and particular patterns of organization structure and process. In fact, OD's emergence may have widened the already visible gap between primarily social psychological investigations of organization behavior (e.g., Likert, 1967; McGregor, 1960) and concepts offered primarily by sociologists and political scientists (Perrow, 1970, 1972).

While this interdisciplinary debate continues (Argyris, 1972), probably having reached the point where acrimony rather than clarity is the primary outcome, the dialectic has already produced its synthesis, at least in the case of the recent OD literature which considers job and socio-technical systems design as part of its domain. Friedlander and Brown (1974) include both technostructural change efforts and human-processual development approaches as appropriate forms of Organization Development. And they conclude that "increased integration of the two approaches, we feel, will increase the present capacity of OD to influence organizational effectiveness toward both human fulfillment and task accomplishment" (p. 334). More pointedly, they specify the need for this integration in their citations of resistance and failure resulting from an attempt to change structure, technology, or human behavior alone, without considering other factors (p. 314). What they do not specify, however, is how and on what basis this integration is to proceed, which leads us to the question of power.

The problem of power

The allocation of power and its use presents problems for OD theorists and practitioners which may not be as easily dealt with as those associated with the issue of structure. The OD consultancy model, described earlier, eschews the use of coercive power and instead aims at a collaborative relationship in which experiential learning rather than prescription produce the desired changes. The key question is, How is such a relationship established? How does an OD consultant create a collaborative relationship with someone who does not share this expertise and who, even if concerned about some aspect of performance may see little need to change his own behavior or the structure and processes within his unit?

Most prominent OD consultants claim to work "only by invitation" (Schein, 1969; Bennis, 1969), but many others, if not actively "selling" their approaches and services, are in no sense shy about having their availability widely known. All but the most naive are aware that the conditions under which they begin their work with a client (entree) are crucial to their relationship and the overall success of their approach; thus they struggle hard to establish enlightened endorsement and approval from key people in the client system, particularly top management. True collaboration is difficult even at this point, however, because the client ordinarily does not know enough to evaluate alternatives, if indeed any are presented. The more formalized the consultant's approach (e.g., survey feedback, the Grid, etc.), the fewer the alternatives available, other than acceptance or rejection of the total effort. Moreover, even if the consultant makes an elaborate effort to build a base for informed collaboration with top management, as I have advocated he should (see Strauss, 1973), the sheer number of individuals and situations involved makes it increasingly difficult to obtain purely voluntary participation as OD moves down the hierarchy. At the lower levels, members sense the implicit if not explicit power of higher management behind the OD effort, and many persons are coerced into participation despite any tactic which the consultant may employ to prevent this from occurring. Finally, organization members well schooled in the "advancement" game utilize their usual political ploys around an OD effort just as they have learned to do around any organizational activity.

While the use of power or coercion by top management may at times be functional—for example, where reluctance to participate in an OD program is based on apathy rather than on fear or conviction—many unintended dysfunctions may occur if the consultant deemphasizes OD's "learning" goal. Recall that a key objective of OD is not simply one-time behavioral and process change but the development of increased capacity for continuous, self-directed, organizational renewal (Bennis, 1969). While all OD theorists and most practitioners pay homage to this goal, the pressure to move ahead, to show results, and to prove one's expertise is seductive even to a financially secure consultant—and frequently overpowering to members of an OD unit inside an organization. Unchecked, these forces push OD efforts toward the status of "just another management program" aimed at short-term results, dependent on pressure, and devoid of much learning. My current belief is that every major OD effort should have an outside consultant who takes no part in the effort, is not employed for his expertise in change strategies or to verify performance goals, but is simply there to raise questions and concerns regarding the pace of the effort and the extent to which learning is maintained as a goal (Miles, in press).

The second point at which power issues are raised with regard to OD concerns intergroup relations. Early OD theorists and practitioners, particularly those who emerged from the T-group movement, tended to view most conflict, whether between individuals or between adjacent groups or hierarchical levels, as failures in communication and understanding. Presumably, persons or groups who understood one another's situations and were aware of the impacts of their behaviors would choose more mutually rewarding alternatives. Where alternatives exist for increasing the gains to all concerned ("variable sum games") and where interdependence is real and lasting, it makes sense to prescribe "problem solving" approaches to conflict resolution (Lawrence and Lorsch, 1967). However, where such alternatives do not exist (zero-sum situations) or where interdependence is either not recognized or not valued, efforts to create understanding and improved communication may either be repulsed or simply serve to raise the conflict to a more sophisticated level.

When does OD succeed?

The statements that conflict resolution is probably most amenable to productive solution when it is contained, when the issues are discernible, and when alternatives are available (Walton, 1969) leads us to a final question: When and under what conditions is OD most likely to succeed? Despite OD's emphasis on feelings and emotions and despite its claimed value in creating coping capability, OD probably requires a moderately stable set of organizational and environmental conditions if it is to succeed. The principal reason for this requirement is that OD takes time. Friedlander and Brown (1974), reviewing the available reports of major (system-wide) OD efforts, note that "these cases took years to bear fruit" (p. 333), a point generally made by OD advocates though not sufficiently stressed in practice. All but the most shallow or limited OD efforts require extensive, time-consuming interventions at various levels and across numerous units. The development of awareness of organizational processes beyond simple face-to-face interactions cannot be accomplished quickly, nor can collaboration in the choice of new procedures and structures be maintained in the face of intensive internally or externally generated pressures for immediate action.

The organization whose very existence is threatened can probably not afford to wait for a long-term payoff. Potentially disastrous market threats must be countered, all but the most necessary operations curtailed, and other similar dramatic actions must be taken rapidly and often unilaterally, simply to survive. Such crises, of course, are frequently manufactured by managers (Miles and Ritchie, 1971), but when they are real, OD is unable to produce a quick solution.

Furthermore, any successful change effort, including OD, probably requires that the parties involved strongly recognize the need for change (Greiner, 1967). In line with the Lewinian change model mentioned earlier, some discontent with present processes and performance is probably necessary before managers will begin to search for alternative modes of behavior. Most successful major OD efforts appear to have occurred in organizations which were already successful by most standards, but which recognized that growth, market change, or some other anticipated events might be likely to exacerbate existing problems and create new dilemmas requiring new capabilities (Rush, 1969). (The Weldon Company example discussed earlier may be viewed as an exception, but there the OD effort emanated from its stable, successful purchaser, Harwood). Of course, the fact that successful OD programs may require a relatively stable organizational and environmental setting does not destroy the argument that OD can lead to greater responsiveness under conditions of uncertainty. One can argue that a long history of OD activity during stable periods can make an organization much more successful in anticipating and coping with future turbulence. Proof of this argument awaits that rarest form of research, comparative longitudinal studies.

OD's future

Just as with the weather, the best short-run prediction for the future of OD is that of "little change." The amazing growth and adaptiveness of Organization Development have already belied the here today, gone tomorrow predictions of its most cynical critics. At the same time, there is little sign that OD is likely to move quickly toward fulfilling the promises of its more extreme supporters. Instead, there are competing trends and forces which, in combination, appear likely to keep OD alive and even growing, but not in the flourishing, forceful fashion that its advocates desire.

On the positive side, OD has momentum. It has accumulated the accoutrements of a professional field, and those who are associated with the field are, logically enough, devoted to its growth and expansion. OD has a firm foothold in the private sector and growing acceptance in the public, where problems are in abundance and where established, guaranteed solutions are at a minimum. In corporations, public agencies, schools, and hospitals, OD is an accepted if frequently misunderstood term, and OD practitioners are busily accumulating clients. Further, many of the techniques and approaches associated with OD have spread to organizations which do not have full OD efforts (Rush, 1973), and this spillover may prepare the way for further expansion.

On the negative side, OD's momentum may be its own worst enemy. As Burke puts it, OD has a future if ". . . it can avoid premature formulation [of concepts and methodology] . . . and avoid being co-opted by traditional organization pressures" (in French and Bell, 1973, p. 195). OD is a continuing and evolving process that requires substantial investments of resources (especially management time and energy) over a lengthy period of time in order to produce major results. But it is particularly vulnerable to being oversold as a quick, painless solution for every organizational problem and thus being naively purchased. The search for quick solutions, particularly to "people problems," is a way of life in most organizations and is fueled by managers' needs to demonstrate accomplishments rapidly in order to move on and up. The troublesome possibility is that the sellers of OD will attempt to meet the buyers' demands, resulting in the further proliferation of shallow, limited efforts. To the extent that this occurs, OD will grow, but its accomplishments will be limited. Ineffective OD is unlikely to do the organization major damage; rather, it may lead to what I have called an "inoculation effect"; that is, groups and organizations which engage in short-term, ineffectual OD "programs" will be unlikely to engage in more serious efforts in the future. This phenomenon is neatly summarized in the statement a manager made to me recently. "OD?" he said, "we went through that a couple of years ago."

The Conference Board survey cited earlier (Rush, 1973) identified fewer than 50 major organizations which experts agreed were substantially involved in OD (i.e., in which there was a level of involvement likely to lead to sustained, long-term accomplishments). Given the problems mentioned above, I think it unlikely that this number will increase substantially. The growth of genuine OD programs probably does not depend on the development of improved training approaches. Instead, it is more likely to be a function of the extent to which (a) high-level officials in organizations become knowledgeable about what OD can and cannot do, and (b) practitioners move beyond an exclusive focus on interpersonal processual change to a concern with structural questions.

These two determinants of meaningful OD growth are by no means independent. One reason why OD efforts have focused so closely on interpersonal rather than structural or policy issues is because this is exactly as far as many organizations want them to go. In the minds of many managers, OD should not go beyond a concern for improvements in communication, trust, cooperation, etc. In other words, managers too often look upon OD as a means for improving the present system—not for changing it. To the extent that OD practitioners accept the notion that OD produces a need for and an approach to major changes in roles, procedures, departmental reporting relationships, etc. and demand similar awareness from the top administrators with whom they are working, they are likely to achieve fewer, though perhaps more productive, opportunities to engage in OD.

If nothing else, the current focus on OD's failure to take structural and power issues sufficiently into account could have an unanticipated positive effect. That is, it could be that the attention given to structure and task processes, for example, will focus greater attention on the behavioral effects of changes in technology, procedures, roles, reporting relationships, etc. If managers and consultants who regularly prescribe unilateral change in major organizational variables began to take interpersonal processual issues into account to the same extent that OD's critics demand that it focus on organizational variables, OD's impact may well be great.

CONCLUDING COMMENTS

In their review of the Organization Development literature, Friedlander and Brown (1974) offer a most important observation: "We have generally failed to produce a theory of change which emerges from the change process itself" (p. 336). They note that instead of focusing on the change process, the bulk of research to date has sought to "prove" the efficacy of OD or its components (an effort that is no more likely to succeed than attempts to prove or disprove the value of participative management, mediation, job enrichment, or any other complex process influenced by a wide array of difficult to measure and control forces). OD's basic thrust, particularly as it incorporates concern for organizational variables, is, I believe, behaviorally sound, but this belief is likely to remain beyond definitive proof.

This comment is not intended to place OD beyond criticism or to discourage research, for many of its concepts and practices merit concern and are researchable, though at a high cost. Instead, it is intended to focus attention on what we can learn from the successes and failures, in practice, of essentially sound concepts. Friedlander and Brown (1974) call for a closer merging between research and practice and particularly for research which illuminates the processes of change as well as its results. As they point out, we still have much to learn if we are to make effective use of the behavioral sciences in solving problems in either work organizations or in society generally. We still know very little about how to initiate change, about the roles which change demands of those who participate in it, or about how change energy may be sustained. OD may not be the answer to improving organizational and societal change processes, but it is perhaps the best arena for learning and experimentation presently available.

REFERENCES

Argyris, Chris. *Interpersonal Competence and Organizational Effectiveness.* Homewood, Ill.: Dorsey, 1962.

Argyris, Chris. *The Applicability of Organizational Sociology.* New York: Cambridge University Press, 1972.

Back, Kurt W. "Intervention Technique." *Journal of Applied Psychology* 59 (July 1974), pp. 367–87.

Beckhard, Richard. *Organizational Development: Strategies and Models.* Reading, Mass.: Addison-Wesley, 1969.

Bennis, Warren G. *Changing Organizations.* New York: McGraw-Hill, 1966.

Bennis, Warren G. *The Nature of Organization Development.* Reading, Mass.: Addison-Wesley, 1969.

Blake, Robert R., L. B. Barnes, and L. E. Greiner. "Breakthrough in Organizational Development." *Harvard Business Review* 42 (November–December 1964), pp. 135–55.

Blake, Robert R., and Jane S. Mouton. *Building a Dynamic Corporation through Grid Organization Development.* Reading, Mass.: Addison-Wesley, 1969.

Blake, Robert R., and Jane S. Mouton. *Corporate Excellence through Grid Organization Development.* Houston, Tex.: Gulf, 1968.

Bowers, David G. "OD Techniques and Their Results in 23 Organizations: The Michigan ICL Study." *Journal of Applied Behavioral Science* 9 (January 1973), pp. 21–43.

Bradford, Leland P. "Biography of an Institution." *Journal of Applied Behavioral Science* 3 (April–May 1967), pp. 127–43.

Bradford, Leland P., Jack R. Gibb, and Kenneth D. Benne. *T-Group Theory and Laboratory Method.* New York: John Wiley & Sons, 1964.

Burns, Tom, and G. M. Stalker. *The Management of Innovation.* London: Tavistock Publications, 1961.

Campbell, John P., and Marvin D. Dunnette. "Effectiveness of T-Group Experiences in Managerial Training and Development." *Psychology Bulletin* 70 (February 1968), pp. 73–104.

Davis, Sheldon A. "An Organic Problem-Solving Method of Organizational Change." *Journal of Applied Behavioral Science* 3 (January 1967), pp. 3–21.

Davis, Sheldon A. "Laboratory Training and Team Building." In *Organizational Development, The State of the Art.* Ann Arbor, Foundation for Research on Human Behavior, 1971.

Emery, Fred, and E. L. Trist. "The Causal Texture of Organizational Environments." *Human Relations* 18 (February 1965), pp. 21–32.

Fiedler, Fred G. *A Theory of Leadership Effectiveness.* New York: McGraw-Hill, 1967.

Fleishman, Edwin A. "Leadership Climate, Human Relations Training, and Supervisory Behavior." *Personnel Psychology* 6 (1953), pp. 205–22.

French, Wendell L., and Cecil H. Bell. *Organization Development.* Englewood Cliffs, N.J.: Prentice-Hall, 1973.

Friedlander, Frank and Dave L. Brown. "Organization Development." *Annual Review of Psychology* 25 (1974), pp. 313–41.

Greiner, Larry E. "Patterns of Organizational Change." *Harvard Business Review* 15 (May 1967), pp. 119–28.

Kahn, Robert L. "The Work Module—A Tonic for Lunchpail Lassitude." *Psychology Today* (February 1973), 35 ff.

Lawrence, Paul R., and Jay W. Lorsch. *Developing Organizations: Diagnosis and Action.* Reading, Mass.: Addison-Wesley, 1969.

Lewin, Kurt "Action Research and Minority Problems." *Journal of Social Issues* 2 (1946), pp. 34–46.

Likert, Rensis. *New Patterns of Management.* New York: McGraw-Hill, 1961.

Likert, Rensis. *The Human Organization: Its Management and Value.* New York: McGraw-Hill, 1967.

Lippitt, Ronald. *Training in Community Relations.* New York: Harper & Row, 1951.

Mann, Floyd C. "Studying and Creating Change." In W. C. Bennis, K. D. Benne, and R. Chin, *The Planning of Change.* New York: Holt, Rinehart, and Winston, 1961.

Margulies, N., and A. P. Raia. *Organization Development: Values, Process and Technology.* New York: McGraw-Hill, 1972.

Marrow, Alfred J. *The Practical Theorist: The Life and Work of Kurt Lewin.* New York: Basic Books, 1969.

Marrow, Alfred J., David G. Bowers, and Stanley R. Seashore. *Management by Participation.* New York: Harper & Row, 1967.

Maslow, Abrham H. *Motivation and Personality,* rev. ed. New York: Harper & Row, 1970.

McGregor, Douglas. *The Human Side of Enterprise.* New York: McGraw-Hill, 1960.

McGregor, Douglas. *The Professional Manager.* New York: McGraw-Hill, 1967.

Miles, Raymond E. *Theories of Management: Implications for Organizational Behavior and Development.* New York: McGraw-Hill, in press.

Miles, Raymond E., and J. B. Ritchie. "Participative Management: Quality versus Quantity." *California Management Review* 13 (Summer 1971), pp. 48–56.

Odiorne, George. "Managerial Narcissism—the Great Self-Development Binge." *Management of Personnel Quarterly* 1 (Spring 1962), pp. 20–25.

Perrow, Charles. *Complex Organizations: A Critical Essay.* Glenview, Ill.: Scott, Foresman, 1972.

Perrow, Charles. *Organizational Analysis: A Sociological Perspective.* Belmont, Calif.: Wadsworth, 1970.

Rice, A. K. *Productivity and Social Organization: The Ahmedabad Experiment.* London: Tavistock Publications, 1958.

Rush, Harold M. F. *Behavioral Science Concepts and Management Application.* New York: The National Industrial Conference Board, 1969.

Rush, Harold M. F., and Phyllis S. McGrath. "Transactional Analysis Moves into Corporate Training." *The Conference Board Record* (July 1973), pp. 38–44.

Schein, E. H. *Process Consultation: Its Role in Organization Development.* Reading, Mass.: Addison-Wesley, 1969.

Strauss, George. "Organization Development." In *Handbook of Work Organizations in Society.* ed. R. Dubin. Chicago: Rand McNally, in press.

Strauss, George. "Organization Development: Credits and Debits." *Organizational Dynamics* (Winter 1973), pp. 2–19.

Strauss, George. "Group Dynamics and Intergroup Relations." In *Money and Motivation,* ed. William F. Whyte. New York: Harper & Row, 1955.

Trist, E. L., and K. W. Bamforth. "Some Social and Psychological Consequences of the Longwall Methods of Coal-Getting." *Human Relations* 4 (February 1951), pp. 3–38.

Walton, Richard D. *Interpersonal Peacemaking: Confrontations and Third Party Consultation.* Reading, Mass.: Addison-Wesley, 1969.

Waters, Charles A. "The Scientific Data-Based Approach to 'O.D.'" In *Organizational Development, The State of the Art.* Ann Arbor: Foundation for Research on Human Behavior, 1971.

Reading 8–2
*Evolution and revolution as organizations grow**
Larry E. Greiner

A small research company chooses too complicated and formalized an organization structure for its young age and limited size. It flounders in rigidity and bureaucracy for several years and is finally acquired by a larger company.

Key executives of a retail store chain hold on to an organization structure long after it has served its purpose, because their power is derived from this structure. The company eventually goes into bankruptcy.

A large bank disciplines a "rebellious" manager who is blamed for current control problems, when the underlying cause is centralized procedures that are holding back expansion into new markets. Many younger managers subsequently leave the bank, competition moves in, and profits are still declining.

* *Harvard Business Review,* July–August 1972, Copyright © 1972 by the President and Fellows of Harvard College; all rights reserved. This article is part of a continuing project on organization development with the author's colleague, Professor Louis B. Barnes, and sponsored by the Division of Research, Harvard Business School.

The problems of these companies, like those of many others, are rooted more in past decisions than in present events or outside market dynamics. Historical forces do indeed shape the future growth of organizations. Yet management, in its haste to grow, often overlooks such critical developmental questions as: Where has our organization been? Where is it now? And what do the answers to these questions mean for where we are going? Instead, its gaze is fixed outward toward the environment and the future—as if more precise market projections will provide a new organizational identity.

Companies fail to see that many clues to their future success lie within their own organizations and their evolving states of development. Moreover, the inability of management to understand its organization development problems can result in a company becoming "frozen" in its present stage of evolution or, ultimately, in failure, regardless of market opportunities.

My position in this article is that the future of an organization may be less determined by outside forces than it is by the organization's history. In stressing the force of history on an organization, I have drawn from the legacies of European psychologists (their thesis being that individual behavior is determined primarily by previous events and experiences, not by what lies ahead). Extending this analogy of individual development to the problems of organization development, I shall discuss a series of developmental phases through which growing companies tend to pass. But, first, let me provide two definitions:

1. The term *evolution* is used to describe prolonged periods of growth where no major upheaval occurs in organization practices.
2. The term *revolution* is used to describe those periods of substantial turmoil in organization life.

As a company progresses through developmental phases, each evolutionary period creates its own revolution. For instance, centralized practices eventually lead to demands for decentralization. Moreover, the nature of management's solution to each revolutionary period determines whether a company will move forward into its next stage of evolutionary growth. As I shall show later, there are at least five phases of organization development, each characterized by both an evolution and a revolution.

KEY FORCES IN DEVELOPMENT

During the past few years a small amount of research knowledge about the phases of organization development has been building. Some of this research is very quantitative, such as time-series analyses that reveal patterns of economic performance over time.[1] The majority of studies, however, are case-oriented and use company records and interviews to reconstruct a rich picture of corporate development.[2] Yet both types of research tend to be heavily empirical without attempting more generalized statements about the overall process of development.

A notable exception is the historical work of Alfred D. Chandler, Jr., in his book *Strategy and Structure*.[3] This study depicts four very broad and general phases in the lives of four large U.S. companies. It proposes that outside market opportunities determine a company's strategy, which in turn determines the company's organization structure. This thesis has a valid ring for the four companies examined by Chandler, largely because they developed in a time of explosive markets and technological advances. But more recent evidence suggests that organization structure may be less malleable than Chandler assumed; in fact, structure can play a critical role in influencing corporate strategy. It is this reverse emphasis on how organization structure affects future growth which is highlighted in the model presented in this article.

From an analysis of recent studies,[4] five key dimensions emerge as essential for building a model of organization development:

1. Age of the organization.
2. Size of the organization.
3. Stages of evolution.
4. Stages of revolution.
5. Growth rate of the industry.

I shall describe each of these elements separately, but first note their combined effect as illustrated in Exhibit 1. Note especially how each dimension influences the other over time; when all five elements begin to interact, a more complete and dynamic picture of organizational growth emerges.

---

[1] See, for example, William H. Starbuck, "Organizational Metamorphosis," in *Promising Research Directions*, ed. R. W. Millman and M. P. Hottenstein (Tempe, Ariz.: Academy of Management, 1968), p. 113.

[2] See, for example, the *Grangesberg* case series, prepared by C. Roland Christensen and Bruce R. Scott (Case Clearing House, Harvard Business School, Boston.)

[3] *Strategy and Structure: Chapters in the History of the American Industrial Enterprise* (Cambridge, Mass.: The M.I.T. Press, 1962).

[4] I have drawn on many sources for evidence: (a) numerous cases collected at the Harvard Business School; (b) *Organization Growth and Development*, ed. William H. Starbuck (Middlesex, England, Penguin Books, Ltd., 1971), where several studies are cited, and (c) articles published in journals, such as Lawrence E. Fouraker and John M. Stopford, "Organization Structure and the Multinational Strategy," *Administrative Science Quarterly*, vol. 13, no. 1, 1968, p. 47; and Malcolm S. Salter, "Management Appraisal and Reward Systems," *Journal of Business Policy*, vol. 1, no. 4, 1971.

Exhibit 1
Model of organization development

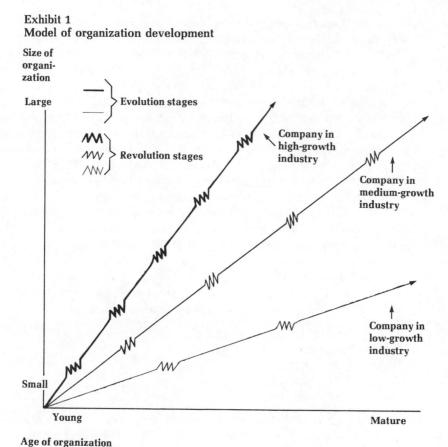

Age of organization

After describing these dimensions and their interconnections, I shall discuss each evolutionary/revolutionary phase of development and show (*a*) how each stage of evolution breeds its own revolution, and (*b*) how management solutions to each revolution determine the next stage of evolution

Age of the organization

The most obvious and essential dimension for any model of development is the life span of an organization (represented as the horizontal axis in Exhibit 1). All historical studies gather data from various points in time and then make comparisons. From these observations, it is evident that the same organization practices are not maintained throughout a long time span. This makes a most basic point: management problems and principles are rooted in time. The concept of decentralization, for example, can have meaning for describing corporate practices at one time period but loses its descriptive power at another.

The passage of time also contributes to the institutionalization of managerial attitudes. As a result, employee behavior becomes not only more predictable but also more difficult to change when attitudes are outdated.

Size of the organization

This dimension is depicted as the vertical axis in Exhibit 1. A company's problems and solutions tend to change markedly as the number of employees and sales volume increase. Thus, time is not the only determinant of structure; in fact, organizations that do not grow in size can retain many of the same management issues and practices over lengthy periods. In addition to increased size, however, problems of coordination and communication magnify, new functions emerge, levels in the management hierarchy multiply, and jobs become more interrelated.

Stages of evolution

As both age and size increase, another phenomenon becomes evident: the prolonged growth that I have termed the evolutionary period. Most growing organizations do not expand for two years and then retreat for one year; rather, those that survive a crisis usually enjoy four to eight years of continuous growth without a major economic setback or severe internal disruption. The term evolution seems appropriate for describing these quieter periods because only modest adjustments appear necessary for maintaining growth under the same overall pattern of management.

Stages of revolution

Smooth evolution is not inevitable; it cannot be assumed that organization growth is linear. *Fortune's "500"* list, for example, has had significant turnover during the last 50 years. Thus we find evidence from numerous case histories which reveals periods of substantial turbulence spaced between smoother periods of evolution.

I have termed these turbulent times the periods of revolution because they typically exhibit a serious upheaval of management practices. Traditional management practices, which were appropriate for a smaller size and earlier time, are brought under scrutiny by frustrated top managers and disillusioned lower-level managers. During such periods of crisis, a number of companies fail—those unable to abandon past practices and effect major organization changes are likely either to fold or to level off in their growth rates.

The critical task for management in each revolutionary period is to find a new set of organization practices that will become the basis for managing the next period of evolutionary growth. Interestingly enough, these new practices eventually sow their own seeds of decay and lead to another period of revolution. Companies therefore experience the irony of seeing a major solution in one time period become a major problem at a later date.

Growth rate of the industry

The speed at which an organization experiences phases of evolution and revolution is closely related to the market environment of its industry. For example, a company in a rapidly expanding market will have to add employees rapidly; hence, the need for new organization structures to accommodate large staff increases is accelerated. While evolutionary periods tend to be relatively short in fast-growing industries, much longer evolutionary periods occur in mature or slowly growing industries.

Evolution can also be prolonged, and revolutions delayed, when profits come easily. For instance, companies that make grievous errors in a rewarding industry can still look good on their profit and loss statements; thus they can avoid a change in management practices for a longer period. The aerospace industry in its infancy is an example. Yet revolutionary periods still occur, as one did in aerospace when profit opportunities began to dry up. Revolutions seem to be much more severe and difficult to resolve when the market environment is poor.

PHASES OF GROWTH

With the foregoing framework in mind, let us now examine in depth the five specific phases of evolution and revolution. As shown in Exhibit 2, each evolutionary period is characterized by the dominant *management style* used to achieve growth, while each revolutionary period is characterized by the dominant *management problem* that must be solved before growth can continue. The patterns presented in Exhibit 2 seem to be typical for companies in industries with moderate growth over a long time period; companies in faster growing industries tend to experience all five phases more rapidly, while those in slower growing industries encounter only two or three phases over many years.

It is important to note that *each phase is both an effect of the previous phase and a cause for the next phase.* For example, the evolutionary management style in Phase 3 of the exhibit is "delegation," which grows out of, and becomes the solution to, demands for greater "autonomy"

Exhibit 2
The five phases of growth

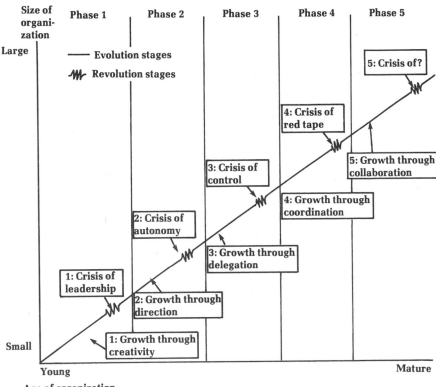

in the preceding Phase 2 revolution. The style of delegation used in Phase 3, however, eventually provokes a major revolutionary crisis that is characterized by attempts to regain control over the diversity created through increased delegation.

The principal implication of each phase is that management actions are narrowly prescribed if growth is to occur. For example, a company experiencing an autonomy crisis in Phase 2 cannot return to directive management for a solution—it must adopt a new style of delegation in order to move ahead.

Phase 1: Creativity

In the birth stage of an organization, the emphasis is on creating both a product and a market. Here are the characteristics of the period of creative evolution:

The company's founders are usually technically or entrepreneurially oriented, and they disdain management activities; their physical and mental energies are absorbed entirely in making and selling a new product.

Communication among employees is frequent and informal.

Long hours of work are rewarded by modest salaries and the promise of ownership benefits.

Control of activities comes from immediate marketplace feedback; the management acts as the customers react.

The leadership crisis. All of the foregoing individualistic and creative activities are essential for the company to get off the ground. But therein lies the problem. As the company grows, larger production runs require knowledge about the efficiencies of manufacturing. Increased numbers of employees cannot be managed exclusively through informal communication; new employees are not motivated by an intense dedication to the product or organization. Additional capital must be secured, and new accounting procedures are needed for financial control.

Thus the founders find themselves burdened with unwanted management responsibilities. So they long for the "good old days," still trying to act as they did in the past. And conflicts between the harried leaders grow more intense.

At this point a crisis of leadership occurs, which is the onset of the first revolution. Who is to lead the company out of confusion and solve the managerial problems confronting it? Quite obviously, a strong manager is needed who has the necessary knowledge and skill to introduce new business techniques. But this is easier said than done. The founders often hate to step aside even though they are probably temperamentally unsuited to be managers. So here is the first critical developmental choice— to locate and install a strong business manager who is acceptable to the founders and who can pull the organization together.

Phase 2: Direction

Those companies that survive the first phase by installing a capable business manager usually embark on a period of sustained growth under able and directive leadership. Here are the characteristics of this evolutionary period:

A functional organization structure is introduced to separate manufacturing from marketing activities, and job assignments become more specialized.

Accounting systems for inventory and purchasing are introduced.

Incentives, budgets, and work standards are adopted.

Communication becomes more formal and impersonal as a hierarchy of titles and positions builds.

The new manager and his key supervisors take most of the responsibility for instituting direction, while lower-level supervisors are treated more as functional specialists than as autonomous decision-making managers.

The autonomy crisis.   Although the new directive techniques channel employee energy more efficiently into growth, they eventually become inappropriate for controlling a larger, more diverse and complex organization. Lower-level employees find themselves restricted by a cumbersome and centralized hierarchy. They have come to possess more direct knowledge about markets and machinery than do the leaders at the top; consequently, they feel torn between following procedures and taking initiative on their own.

Thus the second revolution is imminent as a crisis develops from demands for greater autonomy on the part of lower-level managers. The solution adopted by most companies is to move toward greater delegation. Yet it is difficult for top managers who were previously successful at being directive to give up responsibility. Moreover, lower-level managers are not accustomed to making decisions for themselves. As a result, numerous companies flounder during this revolutionary period, adhering to centralized methods while lower-level employees grow more disenchanted and leave the organization.

Phase 3: Delegation

The next era of growth evolves from the successful application of a decentralized organization structure. It exhibits these characteristics:

Much greater responsibility is given to the managers of plants and market territories.

Profit centers and bonuses are used to stimulate motivation.

The top executives at headquarters restrain themselves to managing by exception, based on periodic reports from the field.

Management often concentrates on making new acquisitions which can be lined up beside other decentralized units.

Communication from the top is infrequent, usually by correspondence, telephone, or brief visits to field locations.

The delegation stage proves useful for gaining expansion through heightened motivation at lower levels. Decentralized managers with greater authority and incentive are able to penetrate larger markets, respond faster to customers, and develop new products.

The control crisis. A serious problem eventually evolves, however, as top executives sense that they are losing control over a highly diversified field operation. Autonomous field managers prefer to run their own shows without coordinating plans, money, technology, and manpower with the rest of the organization. Freedom breeds a parochial attitude.

Hence, the Phase 3 revolution is under way when top management seeks to regain control over the total company. Some top managements attempt a return to centralized management, which usually fails because of the vast scope of operations. Those companies that move ahead find a new solution in the use of special coordination techniques.

Phase 4: Coordination

During this phase, the evolutionary period is characterized by the use of formal systems for achieving greater coordination and by top executives taking responsibility for the initiation and administration of these new systems. For example:

Decentralized units are merged into product groups.

Formal planning procedures are established and intensively reviewed.

Numerous staff personnel are hired and located at headquarters to initiate company-wide programs of control and review for line managers.

Capital expenditures are carefully weighed and parceled out across the organization.

Each product group is treated as an investment center where return on invested capital is an important criterion used in allocating funds.

Certain technical functions, such as data processing, are centralized at headquarters, while daily operating decisions remain decentralized.

Stock options and company-wide profit sharing are used to encourage identity with the firm as a whole.

All of these new coordination systems prove useful for achieving growth through more efficient allocation of a company's limited resources. They prompt field managers to look beyond the needs of their local units. While these managers still have much decision-making responsibility, they learn to justify their actions more carefully to a "watchdog" audience at headquarters.

The red-tape crisis. But a lack of confidence gradually builds between line and staff, and between headquarters and the field. The proliferation of systems and programs begins to exceed its utility; a red-tape crsis is created. Line managers, for example, increasingly resent heavy staff direction from those who are not familiar with local conditions. Staff people, on the other hand, complain about uncooperative and uninformed line managers. Together, both groups criticize the bureaucratic paper system that has evolved. Procedures take precedence over problem solving, and innovation is dampened. In short, the organization has become too large and complex to be managed through formal programs and rigid systems. The Phase 4 revolution is under way.

Phase 5: Collaboration

The last observable phase in previous studies emphasizes strong interpersonal collaboration in an attempt to overcome the red-tape crisis. Where Phase 4 was managed more through formal systems and procedures, Phase 5 emphasizes greater spontaneity in management action through teams and the skillful confrontation of interpersonal differences. Social control and self-discipline take over from formal control. This transition is especially difficult for those experts who created the old systems as well as for those line managers who relied on formal methods for answers.

The Phase 5 evolution, then, builds around a more flexible and behavioral approach to management. Here are its characteristics:

The focus is on solving problems quickly through team action.

Teams are combined across functions for task-group activity.

Headquarters staff experts are reduced in number, reassigned, and combined in interdisciplinary teams to consult with, not to direct, field units.

A matrix-type structure is frequently used to assemble the right teams for the appropriate problems.

Previous formal systems are simplified and combined into single multipurpose systems.

Conferences of key managers are held frequently to focus on major problem issues.

Educational programs are utilized to train managers in behavioral skills for achieving better teamwork and conflict resolution.

Real-time information systems are integrated into daily decision making.

Economic rewards are geared more to team performance than to individual achievement.

Experiments in new practices are encouraged throughout the organization.

The ? crisis. What will be the revolution in response to this stage of evolution? Many large U.S. companies are now in the Phase 5 evolutionary stage, so the answers are critical. While there is little clear evidence, I imagine the revolution will center around the "psychological saturation" of employees who grow emotionally and physically exhausted by the intensity of teamwork and the heavy pressure for innovative situations.

My hunch is that the Phase 5 revolution will be solved through new structures and programs that allow employees to periodically rest, reflect, and revitalize themselves. We may even see companies with dual organization structures: a "habit" structure for getting the daily work done, and a "reflective" structure for stimulating perspective and personal enrichment. Employees could then move back and forth between the two structures as their energies are dissipated and refueled.

One European organization has implemented just such a structure. Five reflective groups have been established outside the regular structure for the purpose of continuously evaluating five task activities basic to the organization. They report directly to the managing director, although their reports are made public throughout the organization. Membership in each group includes all levels and functions, and employees are rotated through these groups on a six-month basis.

Other concrete examples now in practice include providing sabbaticals for employees, moving managers in and out of "hot spot" jobs, establishing a four-day workweek, assuring job security, building physical facilities for relaxation *during* the working day, making jobs more interchangeable, creating an extra team on the assembly line so that one team is always off for reeducation, and switching to longer vacations and more flexible working hours.

The Chinese practice of requiring executives to spend time periodically on lower-level jobs may also be worth a nonideological evaluation. For too long, U.S. management has assumed that career progress should be equated with an upward path toward title, salary, and power. Could it be that some vice presidents of marketing might just long for, and even benefit from, temporary duty in the field sales organization?

IMPLICATIONS OF HISTORY

Let me now summarize some important implications for practicing managers. First, the main features of this discussion are depicted in Exhibit 3, which shows the specific management actions that characterize each growth phase. These actions are also the solutions which ended each preceding revolutionary period.

In one sense, I hope that many readers will react to my model by calling it obvious and natural for depicting the growth of an organization. To me this type of reaction is a useful test of the model's validity.

But at a more reflective level I imagine some of these reactions are

Exhibit 3
Organization practices during evolution in the five phases of growth

Category	Phase 1	Phase 2	Phase 3	Phase 4	Phase 5
Management focus	Make and sell	Efficiency of operations	Expansion of market	Consolidation of organization	Problem solving and innovation
Organization structure	Informal	Centralized and functional	Decentralized and geographical	Line-staff and product groups	Matrix of teams
Top management style	Individualistic and entrepreneurial	Directive	Delegative	Watchdog	Participative
Control system	Market results	Standards and cost centers	Reports and profit centers	Plans and invest-ment centers	Mutual goal setting
Management reward emphasis	Ownership	Salary and merit increases	Individual bonus	Profit sharing and stock options	Team bonus

more hindsight than foresight. Those experienced managers who have been through a developmental sequence can empathize with it now, but how did they react when in the middle of a stage of evolution or revolution? They can probably recall the limits of their own developmental understanding at that time. Perhaps they resisted desirable changes or were even swept emotionally into a revolution without being able to propose constructive solutions. So let me offer some explicit guidelines for managers of growing organizations to keep in mind.

Know where you are in the developmental sequence

Every organization and its component parts are at different stages of development. The task of top management is to be aware of these stages; otherwise, it may not recognize when the time for change has come, or it may act to impose the wrong solution.

Top leaders should be ready to work with the flow of the tide rather than against it; yet they should be cautious, since it is tempting to skip phases out of impatience. Each phase results in certain strengths and learning experiences in the organization that will be essential for success in subsequent phases. A child prodigy, for example, may be able to read like a teenager, but he cannot behave like one until he ages through a sequence of experiences.

I also doubt that managers can or should act to avoid revolutions. Rather, these periods of tension provide the pressure, ideas, and awareness that afford a platform for change and the introduction of new practices.

Recognize the limited range of solutions

In each revolutionary stage it becomes evident that this stage can be ended only by certain specific solutions; moreover, these solutions are different from those which were applied to the problems of the preceding revolution. Too often it is tempting to choose solutions that were tried before, which makes it impossible for a new phase of growth to evolve.

Management must be prepared to dismantle current structures before the revolutionary stage becomes too turbulent. Top managers, realizing that their own managerial styles are no longer appropriate, may even have to take themselves out of leadership positions. A good Phase 2 manager facing Phase 3 might be wise to find another Phase 2 organization that better fits his talents, either outside the company or with one of its newer subsidiaries.

Finally, evolution is not an automatic affair; it is a contest for survival. To move ahead, companies must consciously introduce planned structures that not only are solutions to a current crisis but also are fitted to the *next* phase of growth. This requires considerable self-awareness on the part of top management, as well as great interpersonal skill in persuading other managers that change is needed.

Realize that solutions breed new problems

Managers often fail to realize that organizational solutions create problems for the future (i.e., a decision to delegate eventually causes a problem of control). Historical actions are very much determinants of what happens to the company at a much later date.

An awareness of this effect should help managers to evaluate company problems with greater historical understanding instead of "pinning the blame" on a current development. Better yet, managers should be in a position to *predict* future problems, and thereby to prepare solutions and coping strategies before a revolution gets out of hand.

A management that is aware of the problems ahead could well decide *not* to grow. Top managers may, for instance, prefer to retain the informal practices of a small company, knowing that this way of life is inherent in the organization's limited size, not in their congenial personalities. If they choose to grow, they may do themselves out of a job and way of life they enjoy.

And what about the managements of very large organizations? Can they find new solutions for continued phases of evolution? Or are they reaching a stage where the government will act to break them up because they are too large?

CONCLUDING NOTE

Clearly, there is still much to learn about processes of development in organizations. The phases outlined here are only five in number and are still only approximations. Researchers are just beginning to study the specific developmental problems of structure, control, rewards, and management style in different industries and in a variety of cultures.

One should not, however, wait for conclusive evidence before educating managers to think and act from a developmental perspective. The critical dimension of time has been missing for too long from our management theories and practices. The intriguing paradox is that by learning more about history we may do a better job in the future.

Reading 8–3
The need to prepare for growth*
Peter F. Drucker

Growth requires internal preparation. Because IBM had prepared for growth for many years, it was able to take off as soon as the dead hand of the past had been removed. Without such preparation even the desire to grow, even the understanding of what was needed for growth in the new computer industry, would hardly have sufficed to turn, almost overnight, a maker of simple products without much engineering content into the leader in a technically advanced industry.

When the opportunity for rapid growth will come in the life of a company cannot be predicted. But a company has to be ready. If a company is not ready, opportunity moves on and knocks at somebody else's door.

The IBM story shows that a company, to be able to grow, must, within itself, create an atmosphere of continuous learning. It must be managed in such manner that all its members—down to the lowest-ranking employees—are willing and ready to take on new, different, and bigger responsibilities as a matter of course, and without trepidation. A company can grow only to the extent to which its people can grow.

Of course—at least in the West—one can bring in this or that expert, this or that specialist, this or that capacity, competence, or talent. But fundamentally growth, even growth by acquisition has to come from within and has to be based on the strengths of a company. A growth policy requires that a human organization establish the atmosphere of continuous learning and acquire the readiness to do different and bigger things.

Financial planning for the demands of a bigger business is also needed. Otherwise, when growth comes, the company will find itself in a financial crisis that is likely to frustrate growth. This applies to the small, but also to the fair-sized business. For even fairly moderate growth soon outruns the financial foundations of a business. It soon creates financial demands in areas to which no one, as a rule, has paid much attention. It soon makes obsolete capital structure or existing arrangements for obtaining short-term loans and working capital. Financial strategy is essential to growth—as essential as product strategy, technological strategy, or market strategy.

But the key to the ability to grow is a human organization that is capable of growth.

Top management: The controlling factor

The controlling factor in managing growth is top management—again a lesson of the IBM story. For a company to be able to grow, top management must be willing and able to change itself, its role, its relationship, and its behavior.

This is easily said—and very hard to accomplish. The very people—and usually, the very man—of whom such a change is demanded are also as a rule the people to whom the success of the company so far can be attributed. Now, when success is within their grasp, they are asked to abandon the behavior that has produced it. They are asked to give up the habits of a lifetime. They are asked—or so it seems to them—to abdicate their leadership position. They are asked, above all, to hand over their "child" to others. For growth always requires that the management of one man—or of a small handful of men—be replaced by a genuine top-management team.

Most top-management people in the growth company which somehow does not seem to be growing—that is, in the great majority of small and fair-sized companies with growth potential—know rationally what is needed. But, like Watson, they lack the will to change.

Top management therefore has to start preparing itself for growth at a very early stage. Specifically, it has to take three steps:

1. It has to define the key activities and build, in effect, a budding top-management team to take care of them.
2. It has to be aware of the symptoms of the need for change in basic policy, structure, and behavior so that it knows when the time for change has arrived.
3. It has to be honest with itself and decide whether it really wants to change or not.

IBM worked for long years on making itself look like a big company, internally as well as externally. It worked on its appearance to the outside world, in the design of its products and in the design of all the graphics with which it communicated to its own people and to the outside world. It did not spend a great deal of money on advertising and promotion. But when it did, it tried to make a "big splash."

But at the same time, IBM was run internally on a basis of managerial austerity. There were no staffs. There was no research and development. There were no vice-presidents of this and that. There was a top man—Thomas Watson. There was a strong field sales organization. And there was, as the only staff officer, an educational director. Even engineering was unknown until the late thirties—which seems almost unbelievable today.

IBM, in other words, had analyzed its key activities. It supplied them with resources far in excess of what seemed appropriate to the small company IBM still was in the late thirties and early forties. But it did not do anything else.

There is a paradox to growth. "If you want to be a big company tomorrow, you have to start acting like one today" is said to have been Thomas Watson's favorite aphorism. The company that wants to be able to grow has to support the key activities on the level on which they will be needed *after* the growth has taken place. Otherwise it will lack competence, ability, and strength in the areas in which it needs them the most. But at the same time, such a company does not have the resources. Only by starving all but the truly essential can it balance the conflicting requirements of the present business, i.e., a business with very limited resources, and those of the business of tomorrow, i.e., a business that will demand fairly heavy support in major areas.

One way in which the chief executive of a small or fair-sized business that has growth ambitions can prepare himself for the day when the company will have outgrown management by one man is to build a top-management team at the earliest possible moment. The one way in which he himself can learn to be a true manager, rather than "the boss," is by analyzing first the key activities the business needs and his own personality. There will always be key activities that do not fit the top man, key activities which others can do better—and then others should do them.

When Rosenwald took over Sears he analyzed the key activities and built a top-management team of three people. As long as he stayed in the company, he was the undisputed leader and chief executive. But from the beginning, decisions on the location, organization, and layout of the mail-order plants—a key activity for Sears in those days—were made by Otto Doering and not by Julius Rosenwald. Basic decisions on finance and personnel were made by Albert Loeb. Rosenwald was close to every decision. He did not hesitate to express his opinion and occasionally to overrule his associates. But these men, even in the fairly small company which Sears was in the early days, were "associates" and not "subordinates."

Similarly, the first thing George Merck of Merck & Co. did when, at the end of World War II, he decided that the pharmaceutical industry would grow very rapidly and that his company would be a major factor in it was to bring in Vannevar Bush as chairman of the board, and as an associate. Merck knew that he and his company were innocent of basic scientific knowledge and organized research. But he also knew that this was a key activity.

The top man—or the top men—in a company that has ambitions to grow has to know when the time for a change has come. He has to know the symptoms that indicate that a company has outgrown its traditional structure, its traditional management behavior, and, above all, the traditional role of the top man.

There is *one* reliable symptom.

The top man in a company—especially in a small or fair-sized company that has been growing fast—is typically exceedingly proud of the men who work with him. And yet—and this is the infallible symptom of the need for change—not one of the "boys" is "quite ready yet." When the time for change comes, he always finds good reasons for not moving this man to that bigger responsibility, for not turning over a key area to another man, and so on. He always says "so and so is the best man—but he is not quite ready." This is a clear indication that the top man himself is not ready.

The chief executive, the top man, in the small and fair-sized—but also in the big—company that wants to grow has to impose on himself a change in his own role, behavior, and relationships.

The resistance of the top man to change is often blamed on his age. Ford and Thomas Watson, Sr., were indeed well along in years when their companies outgrew the way they were managing them; Ford was in his sixties, Watson in his seventies. But the resistance to the change in behavior, goal, and relationship which growth elicits from the top man can be just as great among younger men. The Siemens sons were young men, for instance; and so were the Boston bankers who blocked Vail at the Bell Telephone System in the 1890s. On the other hand, many older men are capable of imposing change on themselves. Julius Rosenwald was past sixty when he decided to bring in General Wood and step down. So was George Merck when he decided his own role had to change.

A company may even be fortunate to have an old or aging chief executive when the time for change in his role and behavior arrives. It is much easier to get a man in his sixties or seventies to step down gracefully than to force out a man in his prime who is unwilling to change.

What is demanded of the top man is indeed a great deal. He has to accept that he no longer can be the virtuoso performer. Instead he has to become the "conductor." Where he prides himself, as did Thomas Watson, Sr., on knowing everybody in the company, on knowing every customer, on knowing everything that went on, and on making every decision and solving every problem, he now has to manage by objectives for managers and through their self-control. Where formerly he was the

court of last resort—and very often the court of first resort as well—he
now has to have a management structure. Where he "knows how to do
everything," he now has to let people do it their own way.

To expect of anybody that he can make such a change suddenly is
to expect the miracle of conversion. And even conversions in retrospect
always have a long history of preparation. The top man who wants his
business to grow has to accept the role which he will have to play in
the bigger business long before it becomes a necessity.

First, he has to think through whether he really wants his company
to grow, and whether it is really capable of growth. A great deal can
be said for the "middle class" in business as well as in society. Not to
be a big company is often more enjoyment, more satisfaction, and certainly, for the people at the top, a great deal more personal achievement
and personal freedom. There is no reason to believe that Luxembourg
or Switzerland is less happy, less achieving, or less valuable to humanity
than today's superpower.

No company needs to strive to be "bigger" beyond the minimum growth
needed to stay abreast of its market. Growth beyond this must be based
on capacity to contribute. But a company that decides that it is happy
in its niche, satisfied with the contribution it makes and the market it
serves, and content with doing a good job is not, by this token, a "less
good" or a "less valuable" company. In economic terms it may well be—
and often is—a far more productive company than the giant. Growth as
a goal, to repeat, is delusion. William James, the American philosopher,
talked of the "bitch goddess success." A philospher of business today
might well talk of the "bitch goddess growth."

But even if the top man decides that his company needs growth, he
still has a second question—and a more difficult one: "Do *I* want growth
of the business for myself?"

Thomas Watson apparently knew that he did not want to work in a
big company, even though his whole life was spent in building one. He
lacked, however, the wisdom or the strength of character to face the
consequences. Julius Rosenwald apparently did not. He realized that he
did not want to run a giant company. He also knew that Sears could
and should become one—and he knew the correct conclusions for himself.

The top man who concludes that his company needs to grow but who
also then realizes that he does not want to change himself and his behavior
has, in conscience, only one line of action open to him. *He has to step
aside.* Even if he legally owns the company, he does not own the lives
of other people. A company is not a child—and even with a human child,
the time comes when the parent has to accept that the child has grown
up and needs to be independent and on his own.

A business is a human achievement. And a business, no matter what its legal ownership, is a trust. The top-management man who realizes that he does not want to change also realizes that he will stifle, stunt, and throttle the very thing he has loved and built, his business. If he cannot face up to the demands of his own achievement, he owes it to himself and to his company to step aside.

PART VI

Chapter 9

Organizational analysis and action planning: A summary

Managing organizational design and change in the systematic manner discussed in this book requires an analytical planning process that can be summarized in the following way:

A. Basic organizational analysis
   1. First one needs to identify the company's key activities, their diversity, and their interdependence. This business analysis can be accomplished only by thoroughly examining the company's external environment, its technology, and its strategy or goals. It is important to be specific regarding the important characteristics of the key activities, their differences, the nature of the interdependence among them, and the critical success factors.
      If your focus is primarily on one of the company's subunit's, then it is also important to identify the subunit's tasks in detail.
   2. One needs also to identify the company's current human resource organization in terms of staff characteristics, formal arrangements, and informal relationships. It is essential to go beyond an analysis of the formal design. What is important is the actual human resource organization that has emerged in the situation. And that organization is very much a function of not only the formal design, but also of informal relations and employee characteristics.
   3. One needs next to make a judgment regarding how well the organization fits the company's business. If your focus is primarily

on a subunit, you need to judge how well the subunit design, the subunit's tasks, and its employees fit together. This judgment can be compared with one's knowledge of the existence of any recurring problems. If the analysis is sound, the logical consequences of the misfits should actually exist as problems in the organization.

4. One also needs to make an assessment regarding how flexible and adaptive the human organization is relative to probable changes that the company will experience in the next 5, 10, and 20 years. A judgment is then necessary regarding the adequacy of the adaptiveness.

5. Next, one needs to identify the key historical dynamics that have led to the situation as it has been analyzed so far. What changes have occurred in the business and in the organization? Why have they occurred? How successful has the organization been? Why have problems developed?

6. Finally, one needs to make judgments regarding the actual importance of any identified problems, the speed with which they need to be addressed, and the types of changes that are generally needed.

B. Action planning

1. First, one needs to conduct a thorough analysis of factors relevant to producing the needed changes. This analysis must focus on questions such as: who might resist the changes, why, and how much; who has information that is needed to design the change, and whose cooperation is essential in implementing it; what is the position of the change initiator vis-à-vis other relevant parties in terms of power, trust, normal modes of interaction, and other factors.

2. Then one needs to select a change strategy (based on the above analysis) and a set of change tactics that are internally consistent and follow logically from the analysis.

3. Finally, one needs to design an action plan that specifies what must be done, by whom, in what sequence, and within what time frame.

The effective use of this analytical planning process is an important part of management. It is a skill that can be developed.

Case 9–1
Corning Glass Works (A):
The Electronic Products Division
Michael Beer

In July of 1968 Don Rogers, Vice President and General Manager of the Electronic Products Division (EPD) of Corning Glass Works met with Corning's Director of Organization Development at his request. He began the discussion by reflecting on the state of his organization.

I asked you to get together with me so that I could discuss a serious problem. We have had some difficult times in my division over the past two years. (See Exhibit 1 for EPD's operating data.) Sales have been down due to the general economy and its effects on the electronic industry. But our problems are greater than that. Our business is becoming fiercely competitive. To deal with the downturn in business we have reduced the number of people and expenses sharply. This has been painful, but I think these actions have stemmed the tide. We are in control again. But, the business continues to be very competitive, morale is low, and there is a lot of conflict between groups that we can't seem to resolve. There is a lack of mutual confidence and trust. The organization is just not pulling together and the lack of coordination is affecting our ability to develop new products. Most of my key people believe that we are having conflicts because business is bad. They say that if buisness would only get better we will stop crabbing at each other. Frankly, I am not sure if they are right. The conflicts might be due to the pressures we are under but more likely they indicate a more fundamental problem. Can you and your group determine if the conflict between groups is serious and if so what I might do about it? . . .

THE LARGER CORPORATION

Corning's business

The Electronic Products Division was one of eight line divisions in Corning Glass Works (CGW). (See Exhibit 2.) Corning was recognized as a leading manufacturer of specialty glass. Its growth and reputation were based on a strong technological capability in the invention and manufacture of glass products. This technological capability was supported by a Technical Staffs Division which conducted basic and applied, as well as product and process, research in glass and related technologies. The company had been the first to establish an industrial laboratory in the early 1900s and by 1968 its investment in R&D as a percent of sales

Exhibit 1
Electronic products division sales and operating margin (in $000's; 1961–1968)

	1961	1962	1963	1964	1965	1966	1967	1968
Sales	12,723	21,745	22,836	20,036	25,320	26,553	23,852	24,034
Operating margin*	3,011	5,449	5,826	2,998	5,075	4,170	1,559	1,574

* Operating margin equals sales less manufacturing, administrative and sales expenses.

was quite significant when compared with other companies in the industry. The company's growth, which had been running at an average of 10 percent a year over the previous ten years, was based on its capacity to invent new glass products which had a technological uniqueness or capability its competitors' products did not have. Many of these products were invented in response to a request from original equipment manufacturers (OEMs) who wanted Corning to apply its research and development strength to meet their needs. The technological edge was not limited to its product capabilities as it also had strength in manufacturing. Thus Corning was in the unique position of growing profitably without substantial competitive pressures. Patents, technological know-how in manufac-

Exhibit 2
Organization chart

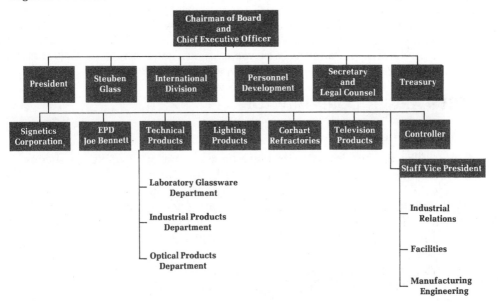

turing, and the requirement of substantial capital investment prevented others from offering serious threats.

Corning's R&D capability led to major businesses in the manufacture of glass envelopes[1] for incandescent lamps and television tubes. Other businesses included glass lenses for optical and opthalmic use, laboratory glassware, refractories for glass and steel furnaces, and many other specialty glass items sold to a wide variety of industries in a wide variety of markets. A major exception to its OEM business was their position in the manufacture and sales of household consumer products for use in the kitchen. Pyrex® pie plates were an early entry into this business, followed in the 1950s by the development of Corning Ware® (heat-resistant cook-and-serve oven ware) and Centura® (break-resistant table-ware).

Corning's unique technological strengths resulted in very profitable growth for the firm in the 20 years preceding 1968, though this growth was uneven due to a dependence on invention in the laboratory. In 1968 Corning was in a strong financial and profit position. (See Exhibit 3 for financial history.)

How the corporation operated

The trend of growth through technological breakthrough led to a number of unique corporate characteristics. The Technical Staffs Division (R&D) was regarded as very important by top management. Its VP reported directly to the Chairman of the Board. Next to R&D, Corning's strongest functional area was manufacturing. Many of the company's top executives had been promoted from the manufacturing ranks and it was widely regarded as the function through which one could advance to the top. To complement a strong manufacturing orientation, the company had developed a control system in which plants were viewed as profit centers. Thus bottom-line results were measured by gross margin (plant sales less cost of manufacture) at the plant level and operating margin at the divisional level (total gross margin for the division less selling and administrative expenses). Financial results were reported every 28 days and were reviewed 13 times a year. These period reviews were conducted at all levels of the corporation.

The nature of Corning's business called for most divisions to maintain relatively small sales departments where a few salesmen would service key accounts. Because there were only a few key customers, virtually all the information needed by a division about its markets could be ob-

---

[1] Glass envelopes are glass bulbs that encapsulate the electrical wiring and filaments which make up an electric light bulb or television tube.

Exhibit 3
Financial history (1959–1968)

Consolidated statement of income	1968	1967	1966	1965	1964	1963	1962	1961	1960	1959
Net sales	$479,089*	$455,220	$444,139	$340,471	$327,612	$289,217	$262,200	$229,569	$214,871	$201,370
Dividends, interest and other income	17,733	15,639	15,404	12,489	10,093	10,554	9,593	8,835	10,160	8,071
Total	496,822	470,859	459,543	352,960	337,705	299,771	271,793	238,404	225,031	209,441
Cost and expenses										
Cost of sales	335,957	310,798	291,669	237,048	229,432	199,211	184,100	160,773	158,293	138,128
Selling, general and administrative expenses	67,251	63,253	61,172	45,612	44,525	40,012	35,088	28,972	25,538	25,380
Interest, state taxes on income, and other charges	8,961	9,210	6,333	2,622	1,505	1,708	1,408	1,243	1,119	1,297
U.S. and foreign taxes on income	37,886	37,779	47,195	28,989	27,221	27,264	23,100	21,490	18,026	20,300
Total	450,055	421,040	405,369	314,271	302,683	268,195	243,696	212,478	202,976	185,105
Net income	$ 46,767	$ 49,819	$ 54,174	$ 38,689**	$ 35,022	$ 31,576	$ 28,097	$ 25,926*	$ 22,055*	$ 24,336

* All figures in thousands.
* Exclusive of nonrecurring net gain of $1,279,499 in 1965 and net loss of $2,334,024 in 1960 on contribution and sales, respectively, of investments in associated companies.

tained by these salesmen who maintained close relations with their customers. Thus many of the divisions had limited marketing efforts. Major sales transactions between Corning and its customers were conducted at high levels of the Corning organization since major investments were often involved for Corning. Similarly, decisions about new products were also made at a high level in the division or the corporation.

Corning Glass Works was established in Corning, New York, in the mid-1800s. For many years all of its operations were based in Corning but, as the company grew, plants and sales offices were located throughout the country. In 1968 most of its 40 plants were located east of the Mississippi River. Headquarters for all but two of its divisions were located in Corning, New York. Therefore, in the case of most of the divisions, business problems could be discussed on a face-to-face basis. People from the several divisions saw each other frequently on Corning's premises, on the streets of Corning, and on social occasions. In a sense, the corporation operated like a relatively close-knit family. People at all levels and from diverse parts of the corporation interacted informally. Even top officers were addressed on a first-name basis. It would not be uncommon for top-level corporate officers to meet divisional personnel in the main office building and to engage them in informal discussions about the state of their business—asking about orders, shipments, sales and profits for the period.

HISTORY OF EPD

The business

The Electronic Products Division (EPD) manufactured passive components[2] for several markets. More than half of EPD's sales in 1968 were OEMs who bought resistors and capacitors in large volume for use in a variety of their products. The remainder of the division's sales were to distributors who resold the components in smaller quantities.

Much like other Corning businesses, the components business grew, based upon Corning's unique capabilities in glass, which when used as a substrate[3] gave the components desirable electrical qualities. Corning's knowledge base allowed them to develop and manufacture highly reliable components for the military market. The growth of the space program and the growing reliance in defense on missiles in the late 1950s and

---

[2] A device used in electrical circuitry which does not perform an electrical function by itself but does act upon or modify an external electrical signal.

[3] A substrate is the material (carbon, glass, etc.) on which various coatings are deposited to make a resistor or capacitor of given electrical quality.

early 1960s demanded components that had a low probability of failure in order to ensure the integrity of very sophisticated and expensive systems. The government customer, however, was willing to pay premium prices for components that met its very strict specifications. In response to market demands EPD expanded its plant operations in Bradford, Pennsylvania, and in the early 1960s build a new plant in Raleigh, North Carolina. Bradford manufactured resistors and Raleigh produced capacitors.

In the early 1960s the nature of EPD's business began to shift. As the military market leveled off, new commercial markets were developing and growing and EPD concentrated more of its efforts in these. For example, color television was emerging as a significant market and color sets required a larger number of components with more stringent specifications than those for black-and-white televisions. The growth of the data processing industry also provided a new market for EPD components. EPD, using its unique technological capabilities in product development and manufacturing, was able to enter these new markets and quickly establish a major position in them. In 1965 EPD built a plant in Wilmington, North Carolina, to supply high volume demands in the consumer electronics and data processing markets. By 1968, 60 percent of EPD's sales were to the data processing, consumer electronics (primarily TV), and telecommunication (telephones) markets.

Between 1966 and 1968 the needs of commercial customers for low-cost components resulted in increased and often fierce competition among a number of firms. As companies competed for large volume contracts from major OEMs, prices fell severely with resultant pressure on costs. Often it appeared that EPD was in a commodity business.

In addition, there was continual pressure on component manufacturers for extensions of existing product lines as OEMs developed new end-use products for their growing markets. Thus, added to the price competition for large contracts was a need to respond to customers with new products which met their unique specifications. A component manufacturer could not bid on a contract until his product had passed tests conducted in his and in the customer's laboratory. Often it was also necessary to meet military specifications since commercial customers sometimes ordered against these specifications.

EPD's response to customer needs with new products was necessary because new products commanded higher prices in their early stages of development and thereby offered an opportunity for growth. As the technology of integrated circuits was introduced in the early 1960s, top management in EPD feared that the total volume of components sold would decline, making an increase in market share mandatory for survival. EPD's poor performance in 1967 and 1968 was a reflection of a major shakeout in the electronic components industry compounded by a weakening of demand. A large number of component manufacturers were competing for what they perceived to be a declining total market in the future. Competition was on price, but quality and service were also important. Customers were giving special consideration to manufacturers which could assure short delivery lead times (usually no more than four weeks) while manufacturing operations depended on long lead times. Stricter quality standards were also being demanded because poor quality often could shut down an OEM production operation.

The intense competitive pressures within a declining economy came at the time the Wilmington plant was completed in 1965. The future looked bleak indeed and some managers in EPD wondered whether the division would survive and, if so, whether it could meet Corning's high expectations for profitability and growth.

Management history

Prior to 1966 EPD was headed by Joe Bennett. Bennett had been in charge of the division in its infancy and nurtured it into a significant business for Corning. He was an entrepreneur who was always seeking to get EPD into new businesses. Recognizing the importance of the new integrated circuit technology in the early 1960s and its threat to the passive components business, Bennett prevailed on Corning to purchase Signetics Corporation, a small company which at that time was on the forefront of the new integrated circuits technology. Similarly, EPD had started a major effort to develop a new product and markets using microcircuit technology—a technology that bridged both passive components and integrated circuits, and offered opportunities for further growth.

Scott Allen, the division's controller until 1966, described the division's strengths by pointing at Bennett.

We always try new things. We always experiment. We set a fast pace. There is a feeling of urgency and commitment and dissatisfaction with the status quo. As an example, we are 1½ steps ahead in computer applications. This stems from Bennett and the dynamic industry we are in.

The entrepreneurial spirit, the desire to grow, and the spirit of experimentation fostered by Bennett created an air of excitement and anticipation about the future. People talked about growth and opportunity being "around the corner." These expectations were not always met. Signetics had been acquired but was operating as a separate organizational entity, resulting in relatively few promotional opportunities for EPD personnel. An even greater disappointment was the microcircuit project. It had been dropped as a failure after large sums of money were spent in development.

Joe Bennett

Joe Bennett was 48 years old in 1966. He was a big man with a quick and creative mind who ran the division almost single-handedly. Many of the key decisions were made by him and none were made without consulting him and gaining his approval. People respected yet also feared him.

Tom Reed, Product Development Manager for capacitors and the new microcircuit project described Bennett and his style:

Joe is very authoritarian with me and others. As a result those working for Bennett who are most successful are political and manipulative.

People around here do not extend themselves very much to disagree with Bennett. The way to disagree with him is in a manipulative way. If he wants something done, tell him you'll do it and carry it out immediately. Then after a period of time go back to him and tell him that following through on his suggestion is going to cost us X number of dollars and we could make more the other way; but if he still wants to do it his way, it will be done.

Bennett has a significant impact on our organization with all of us reflecting him in our managerial styles. We are all more authoritarian than before. I am less willing to let my people make mistakes even though I think it is important that people learn from their mistakes. The pressure and unrealistic standards are transmitted down to people throughout the organization. This results in our commitments often being unrealistic.

There is little group activity and decision making by the top team except where there is a specific problem. It is not a natural group. We are never together. I don't think we have been together, except at formal managers' meetings once in the last three months or so. There is no cohesiveness in the group reporting to Bennett.

Joe Bennett was a man of paradoxes. Although he was widely recognized as being extremely directive in his management style, he also had an intense interest in the behavioral sciences and their applications to management. He was widely read in the field. Mark Bell, Corning's industrial psychologist, claimed that Joe Bennett was better read in the field than he was. In addition to reading, Joe Bennett also attended a number of sensitivity training sessions where participants spent a week in a unstructured group learning about themselves through the eyes of others.

Participation in the managerial grid program

Bennett's interest in the behavioral sciences stimulated a number of attempts to apply behavioral sciences to management within the Division. In 1965 EPD undertook a division-wide management and organization development program called the Managerial Grid.[4] The program was to include an examination of individual management styles, group effectiveness, intergroup relations, and organization-wide problems. In all phases, action plans for improvements were to be developed.

The Grid program was to span a three-year period. It was discontinued following Joe Bennett's untimely death due to cancer. Dr. Don Rogers, a Director in Corning's Technical Staff Division took over as Vice President and Division Manager. Upon taking over the Division he asked for and received a report on the current state of the Managerial Grid in EPD. The report indicated that the Grid had had a positive impact on the division but that Phase III, dealing with the improvement of intergroup relations, which was yet to come, was particularly needed.

In light of business difficulties and his relative newness to the division, Rogers decided to discontinue the program.

EPD IN 1968

The division manager

Don Rogers' promotion to VP was considered unusual, given his lack of line experience, but his knowledge and background were relevant to EPD's business and he had a number of qualities which indicated his potential for a top management position.

As Director of Physical Research, Don Rogers had responsibility for all research and development work going on in Technical Staffs in support of EPD's business. He was therefore knowledgeable about EPD's technology. He often sat in on many of EPD's meetings and had a general knowledge of their business. He had even served as a member of the board of Signetics, which manufactured integrated circuits and which Joe Bennett had urged Corning to purchase.

Don Rogers also had considerable personal assets. He was very bright and quick thinking. EPD managers were impressed with his capacity to grasp a wide variety of complex problems ranging from technical to managerial. He was always very pleasant and friendly and was able to get people to be open with him. This openness was stimulated by his readiness to share information and his own thoughts. In fact, he often surprised people with the things he was willing to reveal and discuss. He also involved people in problems and consulted them on decisions.

Despite these very positive attributes and managers' genuine liking

---

[4] For more information on the Managerial Grid see R. R. Blake and J. S. Mouton, *The Managerial Grid* (Houston, Tex.: Gulf Publishing, 1964) and *Corporate Excellence Through Grid Organization Development* (Houston, Tex.: Gulf Publishing, 1968).

and respect for Rogers, people did have some criticisms of Rogers. His personality and his superior intellectual capabilities almost always assured that he was a dominant force in meetings. There were also some questions about how much confronting Don did or tolerated or how much leadership he took in difficult situations. Managers' comments about Rogers included:

> He does not listen too well. His interruptions of others prevent him from sharing others' opinions and make it seem as if he really does not want criticism. What's more he has been too soft on me. He should be holding me to my goals. I have not met some of these goals and he should be climbing all over me.

> He is not involved enough in the problems that arise from differences in the goals of functional departments. This may be because he spends too much time away at Ion Physics and Signetics. But it doesn't change the fact that he is not involved enough.

> You get the same record back from him regardless of what you say. It is safe to be open with him and tell him what's on your mind but he does not listen.

> Rogers is too gentlemanly, is not tough enough, has not demonstrated risk-taking, and is encumbered by Corning Glass Works philosophy and standards. I am not sure how well he fences with others in the company.

> Wave makers are not wanted in the division and are being pushed out. People at the top do not create and confront conflict.

EPD's organization

In June of 1968 EPD employed 1,200 people, 250 of whom were salaried managerial and professional employees. It had three plants and four sales districts, and with the exception of some R&D support from Corning's laboratory, was a self-contained multifunctional organization. Reporting to Don Rogers were a controller, a manufacturing manager, a marketing manager, a sales manager, and a product development manager. (See Exhibit 4 for organization of EPD.)

EPD's organization was representative of a typical division with two exceptions. First, the marketing and sales functions were separated by Rogers shortly after he became division manager. As he said later:

> It seemed to me that Marketing and Sales had sufficiently different responsibilities to justify their separation. Sales, I felt, should be concerned with knocking on doors and getting the order while marketing should be concerned with strategies for pricing, new products, and the identification of new opportunities for the future. Marketing is a strategic function, as opposed to a day-to-day function.

A second difference was the existence of a Product Development group. Most other divisions relied totally on the Technical Staffs division for

Exhibit 4
Electronic products division organization chart

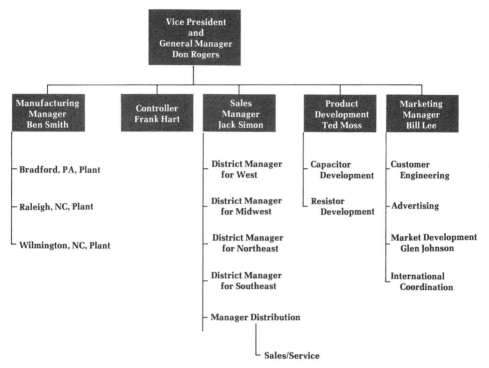

technical product development support and only had engineering groups for manufacturing staff support. EPD's Product Development Department was responsible for developing new products although they also relied on Technical Staffs for research and development support. In addition to product development, the Product Development Department often became involved in manufacturing process development.

Don Rogers made a number of additional organizational changes shortly after his takeover.

1. EPD headquarters had been in Raleigh, North Carolina. Joe Bennett had prided himself in EPD's difference from the rest of Corning—EPD being one of only two divisions not headquartered in Corning, New York. At the urging of top management Don Rogers moved the headquarters to Corning, New York. He believed that EPD had to learn to relate more closely to the corporation.

2. Prior to 1966 the division had been geographically decentralized. The Raleigh, North Carolina plant, which manufactured capacitors, not

only housed the plant, but also had located on site a Market Development group and a Product Development group for capacitors. Similarly, the Bradford plant had on site a market development group and a product development group for resistors. The Product Development managers had reported to Bennett, the Market Development managers to the General Sales and Marketing manager. In 1968 product development was consolidated under Ted Moss, who was located in Corning, New York, though the groups themselves remained at the plants. The Market Development groups were brought back to Corning, New York.

3. Rogers also replaced all of his key managers with the exception of Ted Moss, the Product Development Manager. Ben Smith, the new Manufacturing Manager, had held a similar job in Corning's Laboratory Products Department. Bill Lee, the new Marketing Manager, had held positions in manufacturing in Corning's other divisions and had recently been in charge of Corporate Market Planning. Frank Hart, the new Controller, had worked in plants in Corning's Lighting Products Division. Of the new division staff only Jack Simon, the new Sales Manager, came from within EPD. he had been a District Sales Manager. (See Exhibit 5 for a listing of key managers and their backgrounds.)

4. Prior to 1966 a Market Planning function had reported to Joe Bennett. As part of the cost-cutting efforts in 1967 and 1968 this function had been eliminated and its responsibilities given to the new Marketing function.

5. One of EPD's major problems in 1966 and 1967 had been service to customers. The number of missed commitments was very high; EPD's reputation for delivery and service was slipping. Under Rogers' direction EPD undertook a successful program to improve service. The Manufacturing Manager held plant managers responsible for meeting delivery commitments and shortening delivery lead times based upon specific goals that were developed. In addition, an information system was developed by the sales service function in an effort to improve service.

EPD and the corporation

Don Rogers reported to the President of Corning (see Exhibit 2) and was responsible for managing all aspects of the division's operations. He was held responsible for achieving profitability and growth goals. These goals were established at the end of each year (September–October) for the following year, through a process of negotiation. The division would generate its sales budget through a bottoms up process in the Sales Department, using price guidelines from Marketing. The plants would then generate their gross margin budget based on their estimate of plant sales and costs. These would be consolidated at the top of the

Exhibit 5
Background of EPD executives

> *Don Rogers—Vice President and General Manager—Electronic Products Division,*
> 40 years old: He received a Ph.D. in Chemistry from the University of Cincinnati, a
> Masters in Chemistry from St. John's University, and a BS from Queens College in New
> York City. He joined Corning in 1957 as a chemist in its Technical Staffs Division (R&D).
> In 1961 he became Manager of Electronic Research and in 1964 Director of Physical
> Research in the same division. He was appointed as EPD's division manager in June
> of 1966.
>
> *Bill Lee—Marketing Manager,* 39 years old: He received a BS in Chemical Engineering
> from Rutgers. He joined Corning Glass Works in 1950 as a staff engineer. This was
> followed by several engineering and supervisory positions in glass plants. Following
> an assignment in corporate market planning he became Manager of Marketing in EPD
> in 1967.
>
> *Ben Smith—Manufacturing Manager,* 43 years old: Received an engineering degree
> from Clarkson College. He became EPD's Manufacturing Manager in 1967 following nu-
> merous manufacturing positions in Corning's Lighting Products and Technical Products
> Division. He had worked as a plant engineer, department foreman, production superin-
> tendent, and plant manager in several glass plants in these divisions. Just prior to moving
> to EPD he had been Manufacturing Manager in the Laboratory Glassware Department.
>
> *Ted Moss—Product Development Manager,* 45 years old: After receiving a degree
> in Mechanical Engineering from City College in New York City, he joined Corning Glass
> Works as a staff engineer. After five years in other divisions he joined EPD in its early
> infancy. He served as a project engineer first and then held several managerial positions
> in product and process development. He became Manager of Product Development for
> EPD in 1968
>
> *Frank Hart—Division Controller,* 31 years old: He joined Corning Glass Works in
> 1962 after completing a BS in Industrial Administration at Yale, serving in the U.S.
> Army, and completing an MBA at the Harvard Business School. Prior to joining EPD
> as its Division Controller in 1967 he served in a variety of plant accounting positions
> in Corning's Lighting Products and Television Divisions.
>
> *Jack Simon—Sales Manager,* 34 years old: He went to St. Bonaventure University
> where he received a degree in Sociology. He joined Corning Glass Works in 1960 as a
> salesman in the Electronic Products Division. All of his experience with Corning was
> with EPD, where he became a District Sales Manager before taking over as Sales Manager
> in 1967.

division and submitted to corporate staff. Invariably, corporation staff
would return to the division and, based on its corporate forecast of sales
and profits, ask the division to modify it sales and profit plans. If corporate
sales were forecasted to be lower than desired, the division might be
asked to increase its sales goals. The same was done with profits. This
process often caused great consternation at the division level as budget
proposals, which took a lot of time and energy to generate, were modified
by corporate needs.

EPD, along with the other divisions, was expected to grow at an average
rate of 10 percent a year, the corporation's historic average growth rate.

In the area of profits the EPD was expected to approach the profitability levels the corporation had come to expect of its more traditional OEM businesses. These typically were higher than the prevailing profitability levels among electronic component manufacturers. The ability of EPD to attain these objectives was a subject of much discussion and controversy in the division. A number of key people wondered whether both growth and profit objectives could be met. Volume could always be increased by taking low-price business, but this reduced profitability. Most people within EPD looked to new products as a major source of both new volume and profits.

THE FUNCTIONAL DEPARTMENTS IN 1968

Manufacturing

Resistors and capacitors were manufactured in high volume at three plants, located in Wilmington, North Carolina (resistors), Bradford, Pennsylvania (resistors), and Raleigh, North Carolina (capacitors). Each of these plants had a plant manager and a full complement of manufacturing functions, including production, engineering, quality control, purchasing, accounting and control, and personnel. With all manufacturing operations under him, the production superintendent had the greatest power in the plant. The head of engineering was second in line of influence. The plants (as other plants in Corning) were held responsible for gross margin and thus were profit centers.

The plant managers, with one exception, had grown up in EPD. Their performance was evaluated on gross margins and assorted other manufacturing variances, including delivery lead times and missed commitments to customers. Plant accounts were closed every 28 days and the plant's performance was reviewed in meetings in Corning, New York, 13 times each year.

The plant managers' reputations and therefore their promotability were perceived by them to be dependent on plant growth and good gross margin performance. All saw their future advancement within the manufacturing hierarchy of the company leading to the possibility of promotion to general manager of a division. Since manufacturing was the dominant function, such an expectation was not unrealistic.

Because plants were profit centers their performance was well known around the corporation. There were many opportunities for exchanges at plant managers' meetings and the corporation had established an informal system for comparing plant performance. All of this heightened the individual plant manager's concerns about plant gross margin and growth.

EPD's plant managers were extremely upset with the lack of growth in the division's business. In the last two years their volume had shrunk and, through price cuts, their dollar volume had dropped substantially. This put enormous pressures on them for cost reduction in order to maintain their gross margins. While they were able to reduce some costs, gross margins still declined. With some exceptions, EPD's plants had the lowest gross margins in the company. Plant managers expressed the following statements:

We're experiencing price erosion in our product lines and I don't see a large number of new products. We need something new and unique. I don't see growth potential in our existing products.

We need direction on resistors. We cannot afford two plants. We need a process to allow us to make low-cost resistors.

There are no operational objectives. I get the feeling that everyone is concerned but no clear objectives are set.

The frustration experienced by the manufacturing people was expressed most in their attitudes toward Marketing and Sales. They viewed Sales as being concerned exclusively with volume with no concern for gross margin. They blamed Sales for getting low-gross-margin business and not fighting hard enough to get better prices. In other words, as they saw it, Sales was giving the store away at the plant's expense and Sales wasn't penalized for it.

A Production superintendent:

There is a breakdown in common agreement when it comes to pricing. Sales will sell for anything and the plant won't buy it unless 40 percent margin is involved.

The Manufacturing manager, Ben Smith:

There is a feeling of mutual distrust between Sales and Manufacturing because Manufacturing believes Sales is not putting enough of a price on the products. This is a typical problem that results when two groups have different goals.

Manufacturing's negative feelings about Sales were only exceeded by their feelings about Marketing. They felt that it was Marketing's responsibility to provide direction to the division for profitable growth and that such direction was not apparent. They particularly blamed Bill Lee, the Marketing manager, for lack of "strong leadership." They were upset by what they called the "disappearing carrot syndrome." As Manufacturing saw it, Marketing would come to the plant and project a several-million-dollar market for a new resistor or capacitor (the carrot). Manufacturing, based on the projection, would run samples and make other investments in preparation for the new product only to find out six months or a year later that Marketing was now projecting much smaller sales and profits for the product. Manufacturing's explanation of this situation was that

marketing lacked the ability to forecast marketing trends accurately and
was generally incompetent. They saw a need to replace the Marketing
manager and many others in Marketing.

A Production superintendent:

*What is slowing down EPD is weak marketing, lack of marketing direction,
and a very narrow product base. You can't sell what you do not have and if
you do not have it and you do not know where you are going to be in two years,
you probably will not sell what you have.*

A Production superintendent:

*The last five years have left people quite cold as far as strategies are concerned.
For example, Marketing does not have the same strategy as we do and they
give us no direction.*

The Manufacturing manager, Ben Smith:

*No one has confidence in Marketing people. Plant managers don't believe
them now since they have been wrong so many times.*

Manufacturing was also unhappy with Product Development. They felt
that Product Development had not always given them products that would
run well on their production lines. They looked to Product Development
to develop low-cost components and saw nothing coming. When Product
Development requested special runs on their manufacturing lines to develop new products, they wondered what the benefits were for this sacrifice in their efficiency.

Marketing

Marketing included several functions such as customer engineering
and advertising. However, its most important function was Market Development under Glen Johnson. It was Market Development's responsibility
to develop sales projections for the next year, market plans for the next
three years, analyses of market share, and plans for improving market
position. One of the primary means for increasing market share was the
development of new types of resistors and capacitors. It was Market
Development's responsibility to identify these new opportunities and to
assure the development of new products in coordination with other functions. Marketing specialists reporting to Johnson had responsibility for
scanning and analyzing different market segments and for developing
new products in them. Measures of profitability and growth by market
segment were used by them to assess their progress. Because the identification of new market opportunities was primarily Marketing's responsibility (with help from Sales), as was the development of the new-product
plan, they felt the pressure for new-product development was on them.

The marketing function had many new people as it had been established as a separate function just a year earlier. Most of the people had transferred from the Sales department where they were salesmen or in sales service. Johnson, for example, had been a district sales manager himself. The marketing specialists were generally recent technical or business graduates with one or two years of sales experience.

The Marketing people felt overwhelmed with the tough job of forecasting, planning, and strategizing in a very turbulent marketplace and felt that no one appreciated their difficulties.

The Marketing Manager, Bill Lee:

We have not defined the resistor business. When the government business dropped, we did not face up to a need to produce at lower cost.

A Marketing specialist:

You can't be stodgy in this business. You must be fast moving and quick acting. You must be decisive, adaptable, a long-range thinker and deal with a very ambiguous situation.

Some felt that Corning had such high standards for profitability on new products that it was impossible to meet them in the components business.

The Market Development Manager, Glen Johnson:

While corporate financial people will admit that we need a different set of criteria, they informally convey to us that we are doing a lousy job, and it makes us run conservatively. The corporate environment is not a risk-taking one. We tend to want to bring a proprietary advantage to our business which we cannot do. This is slowing us down.

Glass K (a new product) took seven years in product development. Technological development of unique characteristics is not an effective strategy in a dynamic environment. There were some original conceptions, but these quickly passed by the board as the development process took seven years instead of the original three years projected for it.

Marketing people were also critical of Product Development and their responsiveness to division needs. As Marketing people saw it, Product Development's priorities were wrong and their projects were always late. According to the Market Development Manager, Glen Johnson:

Moss bootlegs projects. There are no ways to establish priorities in development; no criteria have even been set up. Seventy percent of his time is in process development.

Marketing felt most resentful about Manufacturing's lack of cooperation and the continual sniping which came from them. They saw the plants as conservative and unwilling to take risks. This was particularly aggravating because many of them saw themselves spending inordinate amounts of time dealing with the plants which they felt took time away from their primary task of marketing. Glen Johnson indicated that he would not have taken the Marketing job had he known that it would involve the many frustrations of getting Manufacturing and others to do things.

Sales

The products produced by the plants were sold through a direct selling force of approximately 25 salesmen organized into four sales districts. Each district was managed by a district sales manager who reported to the national sales manager. The direct sales force visited manufacturers who used passive components in the end products they manufactured. Their job involved learning about manufacturers' needs by talking to purchasing agents and design engineers, and then obtaining contracts for resistors or capacitors.

In addition to direct sales, products were sold in small lot sizes through distributors. Distributor strategy and relations were the responsibility of the Distributor Sales Manager who reported to Jack Simon, the National Sales Manager. It was his job to coordinate the efforts of field salesmen in support of his objectives.

A sales service manager reported to the distribution manager. The sales service group was split geographically, with a sales service group located in each plant. It was their job to work with the plants to expedite order processing and keep the plant informed about customer needs for delivery and service.

The sales force consisted of college graduates interested in sales or marketing careers and older and experienced salesmen who had worked in this industry for a long time. Salesmen identified strongly with their industry. Jack Simon, the National Sales Manager had come up through sales as had all of the district sales managers.

The sales task in EPD differed from that of other Corning divisions even though they also served OEM customers. They served a much larger set of customers in several markets. They had to develop a large number of relationships with purchasing agents and engineers and relied on good relationships to obtain market intelligence and an opportunity to bid on contracts. But, salesmen also had to negotiate with these same people to obtain the best possible price. They were measured on sales volume and worked hard to beat their budgeted sales target in order to obtain recognition from top management. They were not paid on a commission basis though this had often been a point of some discussion and discontent.

Jack Simon reported mistrust, gamesmanship, maneuvering, and politicking between Sales and Marketing:

Most people (in Marketing) do not believe that sales competence is high. On the other hand we in Sales do not believe that the information Marketing gives us is the best.

Simon reported that major conflict developed in budget-setting sessions. This came in part because Sales developed their forecast from customer canvassing while Marketing developed theirs based on analytical tools. He said:

Conflicts are not resolved based on facts. Instead there are accusations. I don't trust them (Marketing) and I don't trust that they have the capability to do their jobs.

Simon's view of Manufacturing was somewhat more positive.

Relations with Manufacturing are personally good, but I have a number of concerns. I do not know and no one knows about actual cost reductions in the plant. I don't think Manufacturing gets hit as hard for lack of cost reduction as Sales takes it on the chin for price reductions. Another problem is Bradford's service. It's putrid! There is constant gamesmanship in the Bradford plant.

At lower levels of the organization, relationships between Sales and Manufacturing were viewed as even worse. There were shouting matches over the telephone between the Midwest district sales manager and the Wilmington, North Carolina, plant manager. In one instance Sales wanted quick delivery to meet a major customer's needs. They felt that EPD's position with the customer would be hurt if it were not provided. The plant said they could not provide delivery on such short notice without upsetting plant operations.

The Sales Service Manager:

The relationship with the Bradford plant is bad. Measurement for plant managers has to change. They are not really measured on service. Things have improved somewhat, however, and they are a bit more concerned about service.

Product development

Product Development was responsible for the development of extensions to the current product line. There were generally between 10 and 12 new-product development projects under way and they often required significant technological development. To handle this work, the development group was divided into two parts—a development group for resistors located in the Bradford, Pennsylvania, plant (which manufactured resistors) and a development group for capacitors, located in Raleigh, North Carolina. No product development group was located in Wilmington, North Carolina. The manager of product development was located in Corning, New York, along with the rest of the divisional staff.

The product development group was composed of technical people who had spent their careers in research and development work. While some of these people had come from the corporate R&D group, many had worked in the division for most of their careers or had held technical positions in other companies in the electronic industry.

Ted Moss, Manager of Product Development, described his relationship with other groups:

> In general my department's relations with the plants are pretty good although some problems existed at Bradford. My biggest concern is with Marketing. I do not feel that Marketing provides detailed product specification for new products. In addition, Marketing people do not understand what is involved in specification changes. I think that writing specifications jointly with Marketing would help this problem. Another problem is that Marketing people have to look ahead more and predict the future better. They always need it yesterday. We need time!

Ted Moss was also critical of Corning's Technical Staffs Division, which also did some product development work for EPD.

> It is difficult to get a time schedule from them. Their direction is independent of ours since they report elsewhere. They will not wring their hands if they are behind schedule. They will more quickly try to relax requirements for the development if it is behind schedule. I need more influence on specifications when it comes to things they are working on. I often have to go upstairs to solve the problems that occur with this group.

Moss also cited problems with the Sales group.

> We need comments from the Sales group on our new products. I wanted to get the call reports they write and asked Simon for copies. His argument for not giving them to me is that the Marketing Department has the responsibility for interpretation. I finally had to go to Rogers to resolve the problem.

The controller

It was the division controller's responsibility to maintain all accounting records for the division, provide a financial summary every 28 days, and report the performance of the division to the division staff and the corporate controller. It was also his responsibility to develop quarterly forecasts of business performance.

Frank Hart, the division's Controller:

> In most cases three-period forecasts are extremely inaccurate. It is very difficult to forecast the business this way. Our forecasts are always off. Yet it is a corporate requirement.

Not only did EPD find it difficult to forecast its business but they had difficulty explaining the reason for upturns and downturns.

The new-product development process

While there were several attempts to develop completely new components or products beyond components, such as the microcircuits effort—most of the new-product development effort concentrated on developing product extensions. These were resistors and capacitors with different technical characteristics than existing products, which were intended to meet new market needs.

Product Development was going far from smoothly in the division. In one case, the focus divider, a new product for the television market, was killed and resurrected four times with different parts of the organization having differing knowledge of its status at given points in time. Marketing clearly thought that this was an opportunity and Product Development saw it as feasible from a technical point of view. Yet as far as Sales was concerned, Manufacturing's cost quotes called into question EPD's ability to compete in the marketplace. As discussions progressed on needed product modifications to reduce costs, Marketing's estimate of the potential market changed and Product Development's estimate of technical feasibility changed. Thus each function's management made its own estimate of the viability of this product and, at different points in time, told people in their function that the project was on or off depending on their optimism at the time. At one point, salesmen were obtaining orders for samples of the product at a time when Manufacturing and Marketing had decided that the product was not feasible and had killed the idea. Similar problems occurred on other projects because it was not uncommon for Product Development to bootleg samples for Sales people for products that did not have the commitment of Manufacturing or even Marketing.

In another case severe conflict between marketing and plant personnel erupted over a new coating for resistors. Marketing had determined that a new and uniform coating was needed for competitive and efficiency reasons. They presented their views to the division's management and received what they thought was a commitment to change resistor coatings. Yet no significant progress had been made by Marketing in getting plants to convert their operations. The plants questioned whether Product Development had proved that the new coating would work and could be manufactured to meet product specifications at no additional cost. Since they also completely distrusted Marketing on the need for this change they dragged their feet on this project. In 1968, two years after this project had started, there was still no project completion in sight. The Marketing specialist in charge of this project would return from meetings at the plant angry and completely discouraged about his ability to influence plant people to do things to advance the project.

The forum for the product development process was the two-day meetings held once each accounting period (28 days) in Corning, New York. One meeting was for new capacitor developments. The other meeting was for resistor developments. In all, approximately 20 people attended each meeting, including the division manager, his immediate staff, plant managers, and a few other key people in the other functions. The purpose of the meetings was to discuss, coordinate, and make decisions about new products. In 1968 the division was working on approximately 12 of these new projects.

The meetings were chaired by Glen Johnson, the Market Development Manager. He typically sat at the head of the table. At the other end of the table sat Don Rogers. Johnson would publish an agenda ahead of time and would direct the discussion as it moved from one project to another. For each project, progress was checked against goals as they had been agreed to by each function at the previous review. Each function would describe in some detail what had been done in their area to support the project. For example, plant managers might describe what equipment changes had been made in their plant. If the goals had not been met by a function, as was often the case, new dates for the accomplishment of the goal would be extracted. While problems encountered were always described, the issue of slippage in goals and the underlying reasons for it were rarely discussed. When differences in opinion on a project did surface, there was great difficulty in resolving them. People would end them by agreeing to disagree and moving on to the next item on the agenda. While tempers flared occasionally there was rarely any open hostility or aggression expressed in the meetings. However, after meetings, people were often observed meeting in pairs or smaller groups in the hallways, over coffee, or in others offices to continue the debate.

There was a continual stream of people in and out of these meetings to obtain information from subordinates in their functional area about a project's current status. It was not uncommon for a plant manager to leave the meeting to call an engineer in his plant for details about a project's status. On one occasion Ted Young, a Marketing specialist, was continually mentioned as the person who knew the most about a project under discussion, yet he was not at the meeting. On other occasions marketing specialists would be called into the meetings (which was possible since they all were located in Corning, New York) to provide information about a project. Plant people and product development people were sometimes brought to Corning for parts of the meeting if their input was thought to be needed.

Prior to 1968, product development meetings had not been attended by the Division Manager. In 1968 Marketing asked Don Rogers to attend these meetings to help in moving decisions along. Rogers became very active in the meetings. He often became involved in the discussion of a new product, particularly its technical aspects. He could be seen explaining a technical point to others who did not understand it. His viewpoints were clearly heard and felt by others and people thought that meetings had improved since he had decided to sit in. Despite these improvements in June of 1968, Glen Johnson still dreaded the product development meetings.

I never sleep well on the night before the meetings. I start thinking about the various projects and the problems I have in getting everyone to agree and be committed to a direction. We spend long hours in these meetings but people just don't seem to stick to their commitments to accomplish their objectives by a given date. Projects are slipping badly and we just can't seem to get them moving. In my opinion, we also have some projects that should be killed but we can't seem to be able to do that either. Frankly, if I had it to do over again, I would not take this job. After all, how much marketing am I really doing? I seem to spend most of my time in meetings getting others to do things.

The outlook for 1969

As 1968 was drawing to a close Don Rogers and the top management group were preparing for their second GLF meeting (Great Leap Forward). This meeting had been instituted the year before to discuss major problem areas and to develop commitment to division objectives for 1968. Now it was time to look ahead to 1969. In a memo to the key managers Rogers summarized what he viewed as the problems which needed to be addressed in the coming year:

It is obvious that division growth is our major problem and that we need to develop new products to get growth. Achievement of budgeted operating margin is a close second. Morale has become a more acute problem and the need for communication, coordination, and the proper balance of long- and short-range efforts continue to require our attention.

As the top managers in EPD prepared for a two-day offsite meeting in Ithaca, it was clear that they had survived the shakeout in the industry. But it was also clear to them that many major problems remained. They all wanted growth and saw it as their major problem, but they were not developing new products fast enough to meet this objective nor were they in agreement about strategies, priorities, or what constituted acceptable criteria for profitability.

To complicate matters, morale was low, risk taking was down, and significant problems in communication and coordination existed. All of this was occurring in an environment where the price/cost squeezes were continuing and competition was as fierce as ever.

As key managers prepared for their GLF meeting the Corning Organization Development Staff was preparing to present the findings of their study of EPD to Don Rogers.